COMPOSITION OF FOODS

- raw
- processed
- prepared

By
BERNICE K. WATT *and* ANNABEL L. MERRILL

with the assistance of
REBECCA K. PECOT, CATHERINE F. ADAMS,
MARTHA LOUISE ORR, *and* DONALD F. MILLER

Agriculture Handbook No. 8

Consumer and Food Economics Institute
Agricultural Research Service
UNITED STATES DEPARTMENT OF AGRICULTURE

Washington, D.C.

Revised December 1963
Approved for reprinting October 1975

For sale by the Superintendent of Documents, U.S. Government Printing Office, Washington, D.C. 20402
Stock No. 001-000-00768-8 / Catalog No. A 1.76 8/963

CONTENTS

LIST OF TABLES

NOTE: Punched cards or magnetic tape of the data in tables 1, 2, and 3 can be made available upon request.

COMPOSITION OF FOODS

. . . raw, processed, prepared

INTRODUCTION

Nutritive values of foods in this edition of Agriculture Handbook No. 8 are based on extensive review of information available both before and since the first issue in 1950. Data previously published have been reexamined and values for some nutrients in nearly every food item have been revised to take into account more recent findings. The major changes have been in data for fruits, vegetables, and meats. Many new foods have been added to the tables, bringing the total to nearly 2,500 items.

New food products added to the tables include numerous kinds of nut, fish, and poultry items; various foods in prepared or partially prepared forms; a number of foods of tropical or semitropical origin for which there has been steadily increasing consumer demand; and many new miscellaneous items.

As in the original Handbook No. 8, values are presented in table 1 in terms of amount of nutrient for 100 grams of edible portion of food and in table 2 in terms of amount of nutrient in the edible portion of one pound of food "as purchased."

Tables 1 and 2 include data not only for energy, proximate composition, five vitamins—vitamin A, thiamine, riboflavin, niacin, and ascorbic acid—and the minerals—calcium, phosphorus, and iron—as in the 1950 publication, but also for sodium and potassium. Data for water, ash, and fiber have been included in table 1 but not in table 2. These data are useful for identifying some items.

Information on selected fatty acids, cholesterol, and magnesium is provided in tables 3, 4, and 5, respectively. Data in these three tables have been added because of widespread interest in these nutrients. They were not included in tables 1 and 2 because the data generally have a less firm experimental basis than those in the main tables.

Information about the nutrients covered in this publication is presented in Appendix A, "Notes on Energy Values and Nutrients." Supplementary information about some of the foods or groups of foods is in Appendix B, "Notes on Foods," and technical names in Appendix C, "Identification of Foods."

Table 3 in the earlier publication of this Handbook contained the nutritive values of foods in common household units for most of the items listed in table 1. To meet the growing needs for revised data of this type, Home and Garden Bulletin No. 72, "Nutritive Value of Foods," was issued in 1960 (*32*).[1] It has been revised to reflect the new values in Handbook No. 8 that were not available in 1960.

[1] Italic numbers in parentheses refer to Literature Cited, p. 190.

HISTORICAL BACKGROUND OF TABLES AND DEVELOPMENT OF VALUES

This revision of Handbook No. 8 is the current link in a long chain of tables on the composition of food that have been issued by the U.S. Department of Agriculture over the past 70 years.

Compilation and evaluation of data on the composition and nutritive value of foods was initiated in the Department by W. O. Atwater toward the end of the 19th century. A preliminary table on the composition of numerous foods was published in 1892. The first major publication in this field, the now classic Bulletin No. 28, "The Chemical Composition of American Food Materials," prepared by Doctor Atwater and his coworkers, was published in 1896 (*6*) and revised in 1899 (*3*) and 1906 (*5*).

Three other major publications in the series have been Circular 549, "Proximate Composition of American Food Materials," 1940 (*7*); Miscellaneous Publication 572, "Tables of Food Composition in Terms of Eleven Nutrients," 1945 (*26*); and Handbook No. 8, "Composition of Foods—raw, processed, prepared," 1950 (*34*). Several other publications with tables of nutritive value of foods, also based on compilation and evaluation of data in the literature, have been issued for special uses (*9, 17, 22, 25*).

In the continuing program of research, the scientific literature and much unpublished work have been studied and the findings added to the Department's files on the composition of food. Successive publications have reflected the ever-increasing information on nutrients and on food products. In the course of reviewing the data on file prior to preparing each new publication, some analyses accepted for a previous publication were eliminated from later consideration. For example, new methods of processing some foods have often resulted in nutritive values different from those that were applicable at an earlier period. Also, methods of analyses used at one time may have been replaced by procedures having greater specificity or by methods found to be better tailored to the particular type of food.

The data shown in this publication are the values currently considered most representative for each product described (*33*). The single figures in each line are not necessarily arithmetic averages of all acceptable analyses available for each nutrient. They may be weighted figures arrived at after pertinent factors have been taken into account. These include variety, breed, stage of maturity, and seasonal and geographic differences. Also considered are production, storage, trimming, manufacturing, and other preparation and handling practices.

The many factors involved are of varying importance in developing representative values on a countrywide, year-round basis for nutrients in different types of food. Insofar as present knowledge permits, the factors of most significance for each food were given primary consideration in developing the values in these tables. However, the data and information available were not sufficient for deriving equally satisfactory values for all nutrients in all foods.

The question of listing a range in compositional data along with the single values was considered early in the planning of this edition. Also considered was the inclusion of the number of cases (or samples) on which each figure listed in the tables was based, as well as the number of separate investigations or laboratories represented in the figure. These statistical expressions of data are important to the investigator planning or conducting research on the composition of foods and to a few others who apply the values to particular problems. Most users, however, including research workers, dietitians, teachers, and other professional workers, find single representative values more serviceable.

Where feasible, separate representative values have been developed for the different classifications of foods that show distinctly different nutritive values. For example, the content of fat in avocados varies widely. One factor among others is variety; varieties grown in California have more fat than the average of the varieties grown in Florida. Thus, in addition to the single general figure based on the total crop for the nation as a whole, data have been provided for avocados from California and from Florida as separate items in the tables. This procedure, in effect, provides a basis for estimating a reasonable range of values for nutrients in those foods for which greater detail is possible.

To include in the tables the extreme ranges of data used in an average (either a weighted average or a simple arithmetic mean) might even be a disservice, inasmuch as maximum and minimum values, although they indicate the variation found in the samples analyzed, do not insure representativeness of the sampling. If the range is wide and the number of samples is small, the average may or may not be representative, and the situation clearly points to the need for further studies. If the range is small and the number of samples also is small, the sampling may have been too limited to indicate the range that actually exists. The number of samples, whether large or small, is not necessarily a satisfactory criterion of the representativeness of either a range or an average. Sheer numbers, if small, may cast doubt; if large, they may lend an unfounded, spurious aura of confidence.

SOURCE OF DATA

The data shown in this publication have been compiled chiefly from analyses of samples reported by chemists or other scientists who conducted the experiments. Research from colleges, universities, and agricultural experiment stations as well as from other Government laboratories and from industry has contributed the major portion of the analyses used for deriving the figures in the tables. More than 100 scientific and technical periodicals have been consulted regularly for information relating to food composition; also, numerous special bulletins, reports, and other documents having data or relevant material have been reviewed. In addition to the vast amount of published work, much unpublished material has been drawn upon for the values shown in this publication. Another valuable source of information was the advice of experts who were consulted about specific knotty problems related to data in their field. As new data on any food item became available, they were, if suitable, added to the data cards on file.

Calculated values have been used in a few cases in preference to those determined by chemical analyses. For example, calculated values were used if there was reason to believe that the samples analyzed were not typical and that a more representative value could be calculated. Again, calculated values have been used for a few important prepared items although analyses were available. In some instances the calculated value was selected when, practically speaking, there was no important difference between it and the value determined by analysis. The calculated values provided the basis for estimating proportionate amounts of nutrients supplied by specific ingredients in the formula and for estimating the probable effects of proposed changes in formulas—kinds of information requested at times for administrative or other planning purposes. In addition, calculated values have been used for those prepared dishes for which no analyses were available. The formulas upon which the calculations were based are available upon request.

EXPLANATION OF TABLES

Organization

An alphabetical arrangement of foods has been followed in the tables, with such exceptions and deviations as were considered desirable either for the convenience of the users of the tables or for permitting comparisons of closely related forms of one kind of food. Commercially prepared foods for infants and small children, listed in tables 1 and 2, for example, have *not* been distributed throughout the table according to alphabetical order, but kept together and entered as a group under the heading, Baby Foods. The various forms of commercial soups have been entered under Soups. Again, soft drinks and alcoholic beverages are listed under the heading, Beverages.

Brand-name cereals of the so-called breakfast type composed of several ingredients, especially those made from mixed cereals, pose special problems of nomenclature. Since no brand names are used in this publication, these mixed cereals have been entered under the first kind of grain listed on the package and will be found under Corn, Oats, Rice, or Wheat. For example, a product that lists sugar, wheat, corn sirup, and honey as ingredients will be found under Wheat; a product that lists degerminated yellow cornmeal, oat flour, sugar, and wheat starch will be found under Corn.

Items have been numbered uniformly in tables 1, 2, and 3 to identify corresponding items when data from the different tables are needed. That is, the items in table 1 are numbered consecutively, and if they are included in table 2 or table 3 they have the same numbers as in table 1. Letters are used with the numbers in tables 2 and 3 if data for the item are included in those tables on more than one basis. For example, Almonds, item 8 in table 1, may be purchased either shelled or in the shell. This item is included in tables 2 and 3 and carries the same numbers in those tables, but to differentiate the two forms, Shelled and In shell, the letters a and b are used.

The lists of foods in table 4, "Cholesterol Content of Foods," and in table 5, "Magnesium Content of Foods," are less extensive than those in the first three tables. In each of these two shorter tables the items are arranged alphabetically and numbered consecutively.

Use of Terms "Edible Portion" and "As Purchased"

The terms "edible portion" and "as purchased" have been used in these tables in the same sense as in all preceding publications of this series.

Data in table 1 and the data in terms of "100 grams, edible portion" in tables 3, 4, and 5 may be applied to foods when the entire weight is edible.

The data for the "edible portion" of foods are based on chemical analyses of the parts of food ordinarily considered edible in this country. They apply to such foods as bread, milk, and boneless meat, which are totally edible, and to fruits, vegetables, and any other foods from which inedible parts have been removed before the food is weighed.

Questions sometimes arise on the meaning of the term "edible portion" as applied to foods having parts that are eaten by some individuals but are considered inedible and discarded by others. For example, apple skins may be eaten along with the flesh of the apples, or the apples may be pared to remove the skins. The skins on boiled or baked potatoes are sometimes eaten, but more often the skins are removed before the potatoes are boiled, and many individuals eat only the inner portion of a baked potato.

To lessen confusion concerning edible portion for foods consisting of different parts, any of which may be eaten by some individuals and not by others, an effort has been made to describe the foods in these tables as specifically as possible. Also for some foods, values have been listed both with and without the part that is not always eaten. For example, data have been entered for 100 grams of apple, including skin, and for 100 grams of apple without skin. Unfortunately, data on composition were not available for all desired forms of foods, as, for example, the composition of cooked potato including skin.

As information on separate parts is often needed, this also has been shown for many foods. For example, in addition to the data for yolk and white combined in the proportion found in eggs, data are shown for yolk only and for white only. For many meat items, values are included for the total edible portion (muscle and adhering fat), also for the separable lean meat and separable fat.

If items on which the data are expressed in terms of "100 grams, edible portion" have no specific description, it may be assumed that the edible portion includes only the part or parts that most individuals in this country would eat.

Data in table 2 and the data in terms of "1 pound as purchased" in tables 3, 4, and 5 are the amounts of nutrients present in the edible part of 1 pound of food as obtained from the retail market including delicatessen, or from the home garden. In a few cases, the figures refer to foods from wholesale sources for institutional or other large-quantity use. Additional data are provided for several meat items in tables 2 and 3, so that composition may be calculated for cuts having proportions of lean and separable fat that differ from the averages specified for the cuts listed.

The data on the "1 pound" basis are suitable for many different purposes. They may be used directly in dietary planning and in evaluating family, institutional, or national food supplies. They provide a basis for comparing different foods as sources of nutrients and for determining their suitability for various food distribution programs both in this country and abroad, for stockpiling, and for other programs related to food.

Values in table 2 and for 1 pound of items listed in tables 3, 4, and 5 were calculated by applying data on yield of edible portion per pound to data on the composition of the edible portion of the item. Amounts of nutrients in the parts of the product ordinarily considered inedible are not included in the values listed. For example, any nutrients that might be present in the peel of banana, bone and gristle of meat, shell of eggs, or tough outside leaves of cabbage would not be included.

Bananas may be used to illustrate the procedure for obtaining figures such as those in table 2 for amounts of nutrients in the edible part of a pound as ordinarily purchased. If the peel comprises 32 percent of the total weight of the banana with peel, then a pound of bananas as purchased would have only 68 percent (308.4 grams, or 0.68×453.6) of a pound as the edible portion. The amounts of nutrients in the edible part of 1 pound of bananas as purchased would be calculated by applying the factor 3.084 to the data in table 1 or to the data in terms of "100 grams of edible portion" in the other tables.

Average amounts of material removed and discarded in the preparation of food have been shown under the column headed "Refuse" in table 2. These averages are expressed as percentage of the total weight of the item as purchased—including the part to be discarded. The material to be removed is specified in the preceding column, along with the description of the food. Usually any losses of edible material that occur when the inedible parts are removed, as grapefruit juice lost while removing seeds and core, are included in the figures for refuse. For some foods, such losses may be fairly sizable.

Data listed under the column headed "Refuse" in table 2 were used in computing the values for 1 pound in tables 3, 4, and 5. Most of these data for refuse were the average losses reported in a summary published in 1956 (*23*).

The figures listed for refuse in table 2 are considered reasonably applicable to foods as ordinarily obtained from the market. Inasmuch as most foods, especially items of fresh produce, vary in quality, the average figures listed for refuse may not apply to a particular purchase lot, and for some purposes they may have to be adjusted.

If the percentage of refuse for any given food is known and differs from the figure shown in the column, adjustment may be made in either of two ways, as follows:

1. A new set of nutritive values may be calculated from data such as in table 1 for edible portion, by using the known percentage of edible portion that applies and changing the base from 100 grams to 1 pound. In this case the steps would be the same as those used in the illustration with bananas.
2. Adjustment may be made on the weight of product to compensate for the difference in yield. This adjusted weight could then be used with the present figures in table 2 and those figures for 1 pound of items in tables 3, 4, and 5. For example, if a vegetable has only 30 percent refuse instead of 50 percent, as listed in table 2, then 1 pound having the 30 percent refuse could be counted as 70/50ths, or 1.4 pounds having 50 percent refuse. See formula below.

$$\frac{\text{100 minus percent of refuse considered more suitable}}{\text{100 minus percent of refuse shown in table}} \times \text{weight of food purchased} = \text{adjusted weight.}$$

TABLE 1.—COMPOSITION OF FOODS, 100 GRAMS, EDIBLE PORTION

[Numbers in parentheses denote values imputed—usually from another form of the food or from a similar food. Zero in parentheses indicates that the amount of a constituent probably is none or is too small to measure. Dashes denote lack of reliable data for a constituent believed to be present in measurable amount. Calculated values, as those based on a recipe, are not in parentheses]

Item No.	Food and description	Water	Food energy	Protein	Fat	Carbohydrate		Ash	Calcium	Phosphorus	Iron	Sodium	Potassium	Vitamin A value	Thiamin	Riboflavin	Niacin	Ascorbic acid
						Total	Fiber											
(A)	(B)	(C)	(D)	(E)	(F)	(G)	(H)	(I)	(J)	(K)	(L)	(M)	(N)	(O)	(P)	(Q)	(R)	(S)
		Percent	Calories	Grams	Grams	Grams	Grams	Grams	Milligrams	Milligrams	Milligrams	Milligrams	Milligrams	International units	Milligrams	Milligrams	Milligrams	Milligrams
	Abalone:																	
1	Raw	75.8	98	18.7	0.5	3.4	0	1.6	37	191	2.4	—	—	—	0.18	0.14	—	—
2	Canned	80.2	80	16.0	.3	2.3	0	1.2	14	128	—	—	—	—	.12	—	—	—
3	**Acerola** (Barbados-cherry or West Indian cherry), raw, pulp and skin	92.3	28	.4	.3	6.8	.4	.2	12	11	.2	8	83	—	.02	.06	0.4	[2] 1,300
4	**Acerola juice,** raw	94.3	23	.4	.3	4.8	.3	.2	10	9	.5	3	—	—	.02	.06	.4	[2] 1,600
5	**Albacore,** raw [3]	66.2	177	25.3	7.6	0	0	1.3	26	—	—	40	293	—	—	—	—	5
	Ale. See Beverages: Beer, item 394																	
	Alewife:																	
6	Raw	74.4	127	19.4	4.9	0	0	1.5	—	218	—	—	—	—	—	—	—	—
7	Canned, solids and liquid	73.0	141	18.2	8.0	0	0	3.4	—	—	—	—	—	—	—	—	—	—
	Algae. See Seaweeds, items 2027–2031.																	
	Alimentary pastes. See Macaroni, Noodles, Pastinas, Spaghetti.																	
	Almonds:																	
8	Dried	4.7	598	18.6	54.2	19.5	2.6	3.0	234	504	4.7	4	773	0	.24	.92	3.5	Trace
9	Roasted and salted	.7	627	18.6	57.7	19.5	2.6	3.5	235	504	4.7	198	773	0	.05	.92	3.5	0
	Sugar-coated. See Candy, item 613.																	
10	**Almond meal,** partially defatted	7.2	408	39.5	18.3	28.9	2.3	6.1	424	914	8.5	7	1,400	0	.32	1.68	6.3	Trace
11	**Amaranth,** raw	86.9	36	3.5	.5	6.5	1.3	2.6	267	67	3.9	—	411	6,100	.08	.16	1.4	80
12	**Anchovy,** pickled, with and without added oil, not heavily salted	58.6	176	19.2	10.3	.3	0	11.6	168	210	—	—	—	—	—	—	—	—
	Apples:																	
	Raw, commercial varieties: [4]																	
	Freshly harvested and stored:																	
13	Not pared	84.4	58	.2	.6	14.5	1.0	.3	7	10	.3	1	110	90	.03	.02	.1	4
14	Pared	85.1	54	.2	.3	14.1	.6	.3	6	10	.3	1	110	40	.03	.02	.1	2
	Freshly harvested:																	
15	Not pared	84.8	56	.2	.6	14.1	1.0	.3	7	10	.3	1	110	90	.03	.02	.1	7
16	Pared	85.3	53	.2	.3	13.9	.6	.3	6	10	.3	1	110	40	.03	.02	.1	4
	Stored:																	
17	Not pared	83.9	60	.2	.7	14.8	1.0	.4	7	10	.3	1	110	90	.03	.02	.1	3
18	Pared	84.8	55	.2	.3	14.4	.6	.3	6	10	.3	1	110	40	.03	.02	.1	2
	Canned. See Applesauce, items 28–29.																	
	Dehydrated, sulfured:																	
19	Uncooked	2.5	353	1.4	2.0	92.1	3.8	2.0	40	66	2.0	7	730	—	Trace	.06	.5	10
20	Cooked, with added sugar	79.6	76	.2	.3	19.6	.5	.3	6	10	.3	1	106	—	Trace	.01	.1	1
	Dried, sulfured:																	
21	Uncooked	24.0	275	1.0	1.6	71.8	3.1	1.6	31	52	1.6	5	569	—	.06	.12	.5	10
	Cooked:																	
22	Without added sugar	78.4	78	.3	.5	20.3	.9	.5	9	15	.5	1	162	—	.01	.03	.1	Trace
23	With added sugar	69.7	112	.3	.4	29.2	.8	.4	8	13	.4	1	144	—	.01	.03	.1	Trace
24	Frozen, sliced, sweetened, not thawed	75.1	93	.2	.1	24.3	.7	.3	5	6	.5	*14	68	20	.01	.03	.2	7
25	**Apple brown betty**	64.5	151	1.6	3.5	29.7	.5	.7	18	22	.6	153	100	100	.06	.04	.4	1
26	**Apple butter**	51.6	186	.4	.8	46.8	1.1	.4	14	36	.7	2	252	0	.01	.02	.2	2
27	**Apple juice,** canned or bottled	87.8	47	.1	Trace	11.9	.1	.2	6	9	.6	1	101	—	.01	.02	.1	1
	Applesauce, canned:																	
28	Unsweetened or artificially sweetened	88.5	41	.2	.2	10.8	.6	.3	4	5	.5	2	78	40	.02	.01	Trace	1
29	Sweetened	75.7	91	.2	.1	23.8	.5	.2	4	5	.5	2	65	40	.02	.01	Trace	1
	Apricots:																	
30	Raw	85.3	51	1.0	.2	12.8	.6	.7	17	23	.5	1	281	2,700	.03	.04	.6	10
31	Candied	12.0	338	.6	.2	86.5	.6	.7	—	—	—	—	—	—	—	—	—	—
	Canned, solids and liquid:																	
32	Water pack, with or without artificial sweetener	89.1	38	.7	.1	9.6	.4	.5	12	16	.3	1	246	1,830	.02	.02	.4	4
33	Juice pack	84.5	54	1.0	.2	13.8	.4	.7	17	23	.5	1	362	2,700	.03	.03	.5	6
	Sirup pack:																	
34	Light	81.9	66	.7	.1	16.8	.4	.5	11	15	.3	1	239	1,780	.02	.02	.4	4
35	Heavy	76.9	86	.6	.1	22.0	.4	.4	11	15	.3	1	234	1,740	.02	.02	.4	4
36	Extra heavy	72.9	101	.6	.1	26.0	.4	.4	11	15	.3	1	230	1,720	.02	.02	.3	4
	Dehydrated, sulfured, nugget-type and pieces:																	
37	Uncooked	3.5	332	5.6	1.0	84.6	3.6	5.3	86	139	5.3	33	1,260	14,100	Trace	.08	3.6	15
38	Cooked, fruit and liquid, sugar added	66.7	119	1.3	.2	30.5	.9	1.3	20	33	1.3	8	299	2,800	Trace	.02	.8	2
	Dried, sulfured:																	
39	Uncooked	25.0	260	5.0	.5	66.5	3.0	3.0	67	108	5.5	26	979	10,900	.01	.16	3.3	12

	Cooked, fruit and liquid:																	
40	Without added sugar	75.6	85	1.6	.2	21.6	1.0	1.0	22	35	1.8	8	318	3,000	Trace	.05	1.0	3
41	With added sugar	66.2	122	1.4	.1	31.4	.9	.9	19	31	1.6	7	278	2,600	Trace	.04	.9	2
42	Frozen, sweetened, not thawed	73.3	98	.7	.1	25.1	.6	.8	10	19	.9	4	229	1,680	.02	.04	.8	[5] 28
43	**Apricot nectar**, canned (approx. 40% fruit) [4]	84.6	57	.3	.1	14.6	.2	.4	9	12	.2	Trace	151	950	.01	.01	.2	3
	Artichokes, globe or French:																	
44	Raw	85.5	(7)	2.9	.2	[8] 10.6	2.4	.8	51	88	1.3	43	430	160	.08	.05	1.0	12
45	Cooked, boiled, drained	86.5	(7)	2.8	.2	[8] 9.9	2.4	.6	51	69	1.1	30	301	150	.07	.04	.7	8
	Artichokes, Jerusalem. See Jerusalem-artichokes, item 1150.																	
	Asparagus:																	
46	Raw spears	91.7	26	2.5	.2	5.0	.7	.6	22	62	1.0	2	278	900	.18	.20	1.5	33
47	Cooked spears, boiled, drained	93.6	20	2.2	.2	3.6	.7	.4	21	50	.6	1	183	900	.16	.18	1.4	26
	Canned spears																	
	Green:																	
	Regular pack:																	
48	Solids and liquid	93.6	18	1.9	.3	2.9	.5	1.3	18	43	1.7	[9] 236	166	510	.06	.09	.8	15
49	Drained solids	92.5	21	2.4	.4	3.4	.8	1.3	19	53	1.9	[9] 236	166	800	.06	.10	.8	15
50	Drained liquid	95.6	11	.8	Trace	2.4	Trace	1.2	15	24	1.4	[9] 236	166	Trace	.06	.07	.8	15
	Special dietary pack (low-sodium):																	
51	Solids and liquid	94.7	16	2.0	.2	2.7	.5	.4	18	43	1.7	3	166	510	.06	.09	.8	15
52	Drained solids	93.6	20	2.6	.3	3.1	.7	.4	19	53	1.9	3	166	800	.06	.10	.8	15
53	Drained liquid	96.8	9	.8	Trace	2.0	Trace	.4	15	24	1.4	3	166	Trace	.06	.07	.8	15
	White (bleached):																	
	Regular pack:																	
54	Solids and liquid	93.3	18	1.6	.3	3.3	.5	1.5	15	33	.9	[9] 236	140	50	.05	.06	.7	15
55	Drained solids	92.3	22	2.1	.5	3.6	.8	1.5	16	41	1.0	[9] 236	140	80	.05	.06	.7	15
56	Drained liquid	95.4	11	.7	Trace	2.5	Trace	1.4	13	18	.7	[9] 236	140	Trace	.05	.04	.7	15
	Special dietary pack (low-sodium):																	
57	Solids and liquid	95.0	16	1.4	.2	3.0	.5	.4	15	33	.9	4	140	50	.05	.06	.7	15
58	Drained solids	94.0	19	1.9	.2	3.5	.7	4	16	41	1.0	4	140	80	.05	.06	.7	15
59	Drained liquid	97.2	8	.6	Trace	1.8	Trace	.4	13	18	.7	4	140	Trace	.05	.04	.7	15
	Frozen:																	
	Cuts and tips:																	
60	Not thawed	92.3	23	3.3	.2	3.6	.8	.6	23	66	1.3	2	239	850	.16	.14	1.2	25
61	Cooked, boiled, drained	92.5	22	3.2	.2	3.5	.8	.6	22	64	1.2	1	220	850	.14	.13	1.0	23
	Spears:																	
62	Not thawed	92.0	24	3.3	2	3.9	.8	.6	23	69	1.2	2	259	780	.18	.15	1.3	29
63	Cooked, boiled, drained	92.2	23	3.2	.2	3.8	.8	.6	22	67	1.1	1	238	780	.16	.14	1.1	26
	Avocados, raw:																	
64	All commercial varieties [10]	74.0	167	2.1	16.4	6.3	1.6	1.2	10	42	.6	4	604	290	.11	.20	1.6	14
65	California, mainly Fuerte	73.6	171	2.2	17.0	6.0	1.5	1.2	10	42	.6	4	604	290	.11	.20	1.6	14
66	Florida	78.0	128	1.3	11.0	8.8	(1.5)	.9	10	42	.6	4	604	290	.11	.20	1.6	14
	Baby foods: [11]																	
	Cereals, precooked, dry, and other cereal products:																	
67	Barley, added nutrients	6.6	348	13.4	1.2	73.6	1.2	5.2	736	821	53.2	452	413	(0)	3.71	1.20	32.2	(0)
68	High protein, added nutrients	5.9	357	35.2	3.7	48.1	2.2	7.1	815	904	63.1	653	1,078	—	3.67	1.15	24.0	(0)
69	Mixed, added nutrients	6.5	368	15.2	2.9	70.6	1.1	4.8	820	741	56.4	470	345	—	3.15	1.35	22.3	(0)
70	Oatmeal, added nutrients	7.0	375	16.5	5.5	66.0	1.5	5.0	757	734	48.2	437	374	(0)	2.58	1.05	21.3	(0)
71	Rice, added nutrients	7.2	371	6.6	1.6	80.0	.5	4.6	858	646	50.2	530	208	(0)	2.56	1.24	19.7	(0)
72	Teething biscuit	5.6	378	11.1	2.3	78.0	.7	3.0	322	347	4.6	421	250	—	.47	.57	3.0	(0)
	Wheat. See Farina, instant-cooking: items 995-996.																	
	Desserts, canned:																	
73	Custard pudding, all flavors	76.5	100	2.3	1.8	18.6	.2	.8	64	62	.3	150	94	100	.02	.12	.1	1
74	Fruit pudding with starch base, milk and/or egg (banana, orange, or pineapple).	75.7	96	1.2	.9	21.6	.3	.6	27	34	.3	128	75	100	.03	.05	.1	3
	Dinners, canned:																	
	Cereal, vegetable, meat mixtures (approx. 2%-4% protein):																	
75	Beef noodle dinner	88.2	48	2.8	1.1	6.8	.3	1.1	12	29	.5	269	159	620	.02	.05	.5	2
76	Cereal, egg yolk, and bacon	84.7	82	2.9	4.9	6.6	.1	.9	29	60	.8	301	36	520	.05	.06	.4	—
77	Chicken noodle dinner	88.5	49	2.1	1.3	7.2	.1	.9	27	30	.3	297	42	800	.03	.06	.4	1
78	Macaroni, tomatoes, meat, and cereal	84.5	67	2.6	2.0	9.6	.3	1.3	21	35	.5	381	77	500	.14	.12	1.0	1
79	Split peas, vegetables, and ham or bacon	81.5	80	4.0	2.1	11.2	.2	1.2	29	79	.7	295	112	600	.08	.05	.5	1
80	Vegetables and bacon, with cereal	85.7	68	1.7	2.9	8.7	.4	1.0	17	28	.6	282	130	2,200	.07	.05	.6	1
81	Vegetables and beef, with cereal	87.0	56	2.7	1.6	7.6	.4	1.1	17	39	.8	307	143	2,800	.03	.04	.9	1
82	Vegetables and chicken, with cereal	87.8	52	2.1	1.4	7.7	.2	1.0	33	33	.4	307	55	1,000	.03	.04	.5	Trace
83	Vegetables and ham, with cereal	85.6	64	2.8	2.2	8.3	.3	1.1	25	42	.3	360	90	1,000	.08	.05	.5	3

[1] Average for fully ripened fruit grown in Florida, Puerto Rico, Hawaii; range is from 1,000 to 2,000 mg per 100 grams. At firm-ripe stage, average is 1,900 mg.; range, 1,200 to 2,700 mg. At partially ripe stage, average is 2,500 mg.; range, 1,200 to 4,500 mg. See also Notes on Foods, p. 178.

[2] Average for juice from ripe fruit, range is from 1,000 to 2,200 mg. per 100 grams.

[3] Almost all of catch is canned as tuna.

[4] See Notes on Foods p. 174 for Apples; p. 177 for item 43.

[5] Average weighted in accordance with commercial freezing practices. See also Notes on Foods, p. 177.

[6] Average weighted in accordance with commercial freezing practices For products without added ascorbic acid, average is about 9 mg. per 100 grams; for those with added ascorbic acid, about 65 mg.

[7] Values may range from 9 Calories per 100 grams for freshly harvested raw artichokes to as many as 47 for stored product, the corresponding range for boiled artichokes is 8 to 44 Calories.

[8] A large proportion of the carbohydrate in the unstored product may be inulin, which is of doubtful availability. During storage, inulin is converted to sugars.

[9] Estimated average based on addition of salt in the amount of 0.6 percent of the finished product.

[10] Values weighted according to production, estimated as 90 percent from California, 10 percent from Florida.

[11] Values for items in this group apply to both strained and chopped (or junior) foods, unless otherwise specified.

TABLE 1.—COMPOSITION OF FOODS, 100 GRAMS, EDIBLE PORTION—Continued

[Numbers in parentheses denote values imputed—usually from another form of the food or from a similar food. Zero in parentheses indicates that the amount of a constituent probably is none or is too small to measure. Dashes denote lack of reliable data for a constituent believed to be present in measurable amount. Calculated values, as those based on a recipe, are not in parentheses]

Item No.	Food and description	Water	Food energy	Protein	Fat	Carbohydrate Total	Carbohydrate Fiber	Ash	Calcium	Phosphorus	Iron	Sodium	Potassium	Vitamin A value	Thiamine	Riboflavin	Niacin	Ascorbic acid
(A)	(B)	(C)	(D)	(E)	(F)	(G)	(H)	(I)	(J)	(K)	(L)	(M)	(N)	(O)	(P)	(Q)	(R)	(S)
		Percent	Calories	Grams	Grams	Grams	Grams	Grams	Milligrams	Milligrams	Milligrams	Milligrams	Milligrams	International units	Milligrams	Milligrams	Milligrams	Milligrams
	Baby foods [11]—Continued																	
	Dinners, canned—Continued																	
	Cereal, vegetable, meat mixtures (approx. 2%-4% protein)—Continued																	
84	Vegetables and lamb, with cereal	87.0	58	2.2	2.0	7.7	0.3	1.1	23	37	0.7	260	148	2,200	0.03	0.05	0.7	1
85	Vegetables and liver, with cereal	87.8	47	3.1	.4	7.8	.3	.9	17	57	2.7	226	162	4,700	.05	.37	1.6	3
86	Vegetables and liver, with bacon and cereal	87.2	52	2.4	1.9	7.5	.3	1.0	11	42	2.6	284	121	4,500	.03	.35	[illegible]	2
87	Vegetables and turkey, with cereal	88.9	44	2.1	.8	7.2	.2	1.0	22	26	.3	307	36	400	.01	.03	.4	1
	Meat or poultry (approx. 6%-8% protein):																	
88	Beef with vegetables	81.6	87	7.4	3.7	6.0	.2	1.3	13	84	1.2	304	115	1,100	.07	.17	1.6	2
89	Chicken with vegetables	79.5	100	7.3	4.6	7.2	.2	1.2	22	85	.9	265	71	1,000	.09	.15	1.6	3
90	Turkey with vegetables	81.3	86	6.7	3.2	7.6	.3	1.2	38	62	.6	348	122	1,000	.13	.13	1.8	2
91	Veal with vegetables	85.0	63	7.1	1.6	5.1	.2	1.2	11	71	.8	323	95	800	.08	.15	2.0	2
	Fruits and fruit products, with or without thickening, canned:																	
92	Applesauce	80.8	72	.2	.2	18.8	.5	.2	4	7	.4	6	64	40	.01	.02	.1	Trace
93	Applesauce and apricots	76.7	86	.3	.1	22.6	.5	.3	4	14	.3	(6)	105	600	.01	.02	.1	2
94	Bananas (with tapioca or cornstarch, added ascorbic acid), strained	77.5	84	.4	.2	21.6	.1	.3	13	10	.2	23	118	70	.02	.02	.2	35
95	Bananas and pineapple (with tapioca or cornstarch)	78.6	80	.4	.1	20.7	.1	.2	20	12	.2	59	72	30	.01	.01	.1	2
96	Fruit dessert with tapioca (apricot, pineapple, and/or orange)	77.6	84	.3	.3	21.5	.2	.3	15	9	.4	38	73	150	.02	.01	.2	4
97	Peaches	78.1	81	.6	.2	20.7	.5	.4	6	14	.3	(4)	90	500	.01	.02	.7	3
98	Pears	82.2	66	.3	.1	*17.1	1.0	.3	7	8	.2	4	62	30	.02	.02	.2	2
99	Pears and pineapple	81.5	69	.4	.2	17.6	.9	.3	7	12	.2	(4)	72	25	.03	.02	.2	2
100	Plums with tapioca, strained	74.8	94	.4	.2	24.3	.5	.3	5	12	.4	15	44	250	.01	.02	.2	3
101	Prunes with tapioca	76.7	86	.3	.2	22.4	.8	.4	7	21	.9	15	120	400	.02	.06	.4	4
	Meats, poultry, and eggs, canned:																	
	Beef:																	
102	Strained	80.3	99	14.7	4.0	(0)	(0)	1.0	8	127	2.0	225	182	—	.01	.16	3.5	0
103	Junior	75.6	118	19.3	3.9	(0)	(0)	1.1	8	163	2.5	253	212	—	.02	.23	4.3	0
104	Beef heart	81.1	93	13.5	3.8	.4	(0)	1.2	5	115	4.7	208	—	—	.06	.62	4.0	0
105	Chicken	77.2	127	13.7	7.6	(0)	(0)	1.5	—	123	1.9	263	95	—	.02	.16	3.5	0
106	Egg yolks, strained	70.0	210	10.0	18.4	.2	(0)	1.4	81	256	3.0	273	59	1,900	.12	.22	Trace	Trace
107	Egg yolks with ham or bacon	70.3	208	10.0	18.1	.3	(0)	1.3	71	183	2.8	313	82	1,500	.10	.23	.5	—
	Lamb:																	
108	Strained	79.3	107	14.6	4.9	(0)	(0)	1.2	9	124	2.1	241	181	—	.02	.17	3.3	—
109	Junior	76.9	121	17.5	5.1	(0)	(0)	1.4	13	156	2.7	294	228	—	.02	.21	4.1	—
110	Liver, strained	79.7	97	14.1	3.4	1.5	(0)	1.3	6	182	5.6	254	202	24,000	.05	2.00	7.6	10
111	Liver and bacon, strained	77.0	123	13.7	6.6	1.3	(0)	1.4	6	157	4.2	302	192	22,000	.05	1.99	7.8	7
	Pork:																	
112	Strained	77.7	118	15.4	5.8	(0)	(0)	1.1	8	136	1.5	223	178	—	.19	.20	2.7	—
113	Junior	74.3	134	18.6	6.0	(0)	(0)	1.3	9	144	1.2	257	210	—	.23	.23	2.8	—
	Veal:																	
114	Strained	80.7	91	15.5	2.7	(0)	(0)	1.1	10	145	1.7	226	214	—	.03	.20	4.3	—
115	Junior	76.9	107	18.8	3.0	(0)	(0)	1.4	8	157	1.6	275	206	—	.03	.22	6.0	—
	Vegetables, canned:																	
116	Beans, green	92.5	22	1.4	.1	5.1	.8	.9	33	25	1.1	213	93	400	.03	.08	.3	3
117	Beets, strained	89.2	37	1.4	.1	8.3	.6	1.0	18	27	.7	212	228	20	.02	.03	.1	3
118	Carrots	91.5	29	.7	.1	6.8	.6	.9	23	21	.5	169	181	13,000	.02	.03	.4	3
119	Mixed vegetables, including vegetable soup	88.5	37	1.6	.3	8.5	.5	1.1	22	36	.5	272	170	4,700	.05	.04	.6	2
120	Peas, strained	85.5	54	4.2	.2	9.3	.8	.8	11	53	1.2	194	100	500	.08	.09	1.2	10
121	Spinach, creamed	88.1	43	2.3	.7	7.5	.4	1.4	64	53	.6	272	142	5,600	.02	.13	.3	6
122	Squash	92.1	25	.7	.1	6.2	.8	.9	24	17	.3	262	138	2,400	.02	.04	.3	8
123	Sweetpotatoes	82.5	67	1.0	.2	15.5	.5	1.0	16	34	.4	187	180	4,900	.04	.03	.3	8
124	Tomato soup, strained	83.4	54	1.9	.1	13.5	.2	1.1	24	32	.4	294	300	1,000	.05	.12	.7	3
	Bacon, cured:																	
125	Raw, slab or sliced	19.3	665	8.4	69.3	1.0	0	2.0	13	108	1.2	680	130	(0)	.36	.11	1.8	
126	Cooked, broiled or fried, drained	8.1	611	30.4	52.0	3.2	0	6.3	14	224	3.3	1,021	236	(0)	.51	.34	5.2	—
127	Canned	16.7	685	8.5	71.5	1.0	0	2.3	15	92	1.4	—	—	(0)	.23	.10	1.8	—
	Bacon, Canadian:																	
128	Unheated	61.7	216	20.0	14.4	.3	0	3.6	12	180	3.0	1,891	392	(0)	.83	.22	4.7	—
129	Cooked, broiled or fried, drained	49.9	277	27.6	17.5	.3	0	4.7	19	218	4.1	2,555	432	(0)	.92	.17	5.0	—

	Baking powders: [13]																	
	Home use: [14]																	
	Sodium aluminum sulfate:																	
130	With monocalcium phosphate monohydrate	1.6	129	.1	Trace	31.2	Trace	—	1,932	2,904	—	10,953	150	(0)	(0)	(0)	(0)	(0)
131	With monocalcium phosphate monohydrate and calcium carbonate.	1.0	78	.1	Trace	18.9	Trace	—	5,778	1,452	—	11,618	—	(0)	(0)	(0)	(0)	(0)
132	With monocalcium phosphate monohydrate and calcium sulfate.	1.3	104	.1	Trace	25.1	Trace	—	6,320	1,560	—	10,000	—	(0)	(0)	(0)	(0)	(0)
133	Straight phosphate	1.6	121	.1	Trace	29.3	Trace	—	6,279	9,438	—	8,220	170	(0)	(0)	(0)	(0)	(0)
	Tartrate:																	
134	Cream of tartar, with tartaric acid	1.0	78	.1	Trace	18.9	Trace	—	0	0	0	7,300	3,800	(0)	(0)	(0)	(0)	(0)
	Special low-sodium preparations:																	
135	Commercial powder	2.2	172	.1	Trace	41.6	Trace	—	4,816	7,308	—	[14] 6	10,948	(0)	(0)	(0)	(0)	(0)
136	Noncommercial formula [15]	1.1	83	.1	Trace	20.1	Trace	—	—	—	—	—	20,729	(0)	(0)	(0)	(0)	(0)
	Commercial use:																	
	Pyrophosphate:																	
137	No additional leavening acid	1.4	109	.1	Trace	26.5	Trace	—	0	11,954	—	16,804	—	(0)	(0)	(0)	(0)	(0)
138	With monocalcium phosphate monohydrate	1.4	105	.1	Trace	25.5	Trace	—	900	12,245	—	16,210	—	(0)	(0)	(0)	(0)	(0)
139	With monocalcium phosphate monohydrate and calcium lactate.	1.3	103	.1	Trace	25.0	Trace	—	[16] 993	11,580	—	15,947	—	(0)	(0)	(0)	(0)	(0)
140	**Bamboo shoots, raw**	91.0	27	2.6	.3	5.2	.7	.9	13	59	.5	—	533	20	.15	.07	.6	4
	Bananas:																	
	Raw:																	
141	Common	75.7	85	1.1	.2	22.2	.5	.8	8	26	.7	1	370	190	.05	.06	.7	10
142	Red	74.4	90	1.2	.2	23.4	.4	.8	10	18	.8	1	370	400	.05	.04	.6	(10)
143	Dehydrated, or banana powder	3.	340	4.4	.8	88.6	2.0	3.2	32	104	2.8	4	1,477	760	.18	.24	2.8	7
	Bananas, baking type. See Plantain, item 1634.																	
	Barbados-cherry. See Acerola, item 3.																	
144	**Barbecue sauce**	80.9	91	1.5	6.9	8.0	.6	2.7	21	20	.8	815	174	360	.01	.01	.3	5
	Barley, pearled:																	
145	Light	11.1	349	8.2	1.0	78.8	.5	.9	16	189	2.0	3	160	(0)	.12	.05	3.1	(0)
146	Pot or Scotch	10.8	348	9.6	1.1	77.2	.9	1.3	34	290	2.7	—	296	(0)	.21	.07	3.7	(0)
147	**Barracuda, Pacific, raw**	75.4	113	21.0	2.6	0	0	1.3	—	—	—	—	—	—	—	—	—	—
	Basella. See Vinespinach, item 2408.																	
	Bass, black sea:																	
148	Raw	79.3	93	19.2	1.2	0	0	1.2	—	—	—	68	256	—	—	—	—	—
149	Cooked, baked, stuffed [17]	52.9	259	16.2	15.8	11.4	—	3.7	—	—	—	—	—	—	—	—	—	—
150	**Bass, smallmouth and largemouth, raw**	77.3	104	18.9	2.6	0	0	1.2	—	192	—	—	—	—	.10	.03	2.1	—
	Bass, striped:																	
151	Raw	77.7	105	18.9	2.7	0	0	1.2	—	212	—	—	—	—	—	—	—	—
152	Cooked, oven-fried [18]	60.8	196	21.5	8.5	6.7	—	2.5	—	—	—	—	—	—	—	—	—	—
153	**Bass, white, raw**	78.8	98	18.0	2.3	0	0	1.0	—	—	—	—	—	—	—	—	—	—
	Beans, broad. See Broadbeans, items 481–482.																	
	Beans, common, mature seeds, dry:																	
	White:																	
154	Raw	10.9	340	22.3	1.6	61.3	4.3	3.9	144	425	7.8	19	1,196	0	.65	.22	2.4	—
155	Cooked	69.0	118	7.8	.6	21.2	1.5	1.4	50	148	2.7	[4] 7	416	0	.14	.07	.7	0
	Canned, solids and liquid.																	
156	With pork and tomato sauce	70.7	122	6.1	2.6	19.0	1.4	1.6	54	92	1.8	463	210	130	.08	.03	.6	2
157	With pork and sweet sauce	66.4	150	6.2	4.7	21.1	1.7	1.6	63	114	2.3	380	—	—	.06	.04	.5	—
158	Without pork	68.5	120	6.3	.5	23.0	1.4	1.7	68	121	2.0	338	268	60	.07	.04	.6	2
	Red:																	
159	Raw	10.4	343	22.5	1.5	61.9	4.2	3.7	110	406	6.9	10	984	20	.51	.20	2.3	—
160	Cooked	69.0	118	7.8	.5	21.4	1.5	1.3	38	140	2.4	[4] 3	340	Trace	.11	.06	.7	—
161	Canned, solids and liquid	76.0	90	5.7	.4	16.4	.9	1.5	29	109	1.8	3	264	Trace	.05	.04	.6	—
162	Pinto, calico, and red Mexican, raw	8.3	349	22.9	1.2	63.7	4.3	3.9	135	457	6.4	10	984	—	.84	.21	2.2	—
163	Other, including black, brown, and Bayo, raw	11.2	339	22.3	1.5	61.2	4.4	3.8	135	420	7.9	25	1,038	30	.55	.20	2.2	—
	Beans, hyacinth. See Hyacinth-beans, items 1137–1138.																	
	Beans, lima																	
	Immature seeds																	
164	Raw	67.5	123	8.4	.5	22.1	1.8	1.5	52	142	2.8	2	650	290	.24	.12	1.4	29
165	Cooked, boiled, drained	71.1	111	7.6	.5	19.8	1.8	1.0	47	121	2.5	1	422	280	.18	.10	1.3	17
	Canned																	
	Regular pack:																	
166	Solids and liquid	80.8	71	4.1	.3	13.4	1.3	1.4	26	67	2.4	[9] 236	222	130	.04	.04	.5	7
167	Drained solids	74.7	96	5.4	.3	18.3	1.8	1.3	28	70	2.4	[9] 236	222	190	.03	.05	.5	6
168	Drained liquid	93.3	20	1.3	Trace	3.9	Trace	1.5	22	60	2.3	[9] 236	222	Trace	.04	.03	.6	10
	Special dietary pack (low-sodium):																	
169	Solids and liquid	81.7	70	4.4	.3	12.9	1.2	.7	26	67	2.4	4	222	130	.04	.04	.5	7
170	Drained solids	75.6	95	5.8	.3	17.7	1.8	.6	28	70	2.4	4	222	190	.03	.05	.5	6
171	Drained liquid	94.4	19	1.4	Trace	3.5	Trace	.7	22	60	2.3	4	222	Trace	.04	.03	.6	10

[4] See Notes on Foods: p. 176 for items 155 and 160; p. 177 for items 93, 97, and 99

[9] Estimated average based on addition of salt in the amount of 0.6 percent of the finished product.

[13] Values for energy and proximate constituents are based on starch content.

[13] List of ingredients on label indicates type of baking powder.

[14] Value based on single brand.

[15] Values are based on formula in "Planning Low-Sodium Meals," Newton Health Dept, Newton, Mass, 1951, as cited in National Academy of Sciences–National Research Council Publication No. 325 "Sodium-Restricted Diets," p 20, 1954, Washington, D C.

[16] Calcium content depends largely on amount of monocalcium phosphate in the product. Values range from 200 to 1,600 mg. per 100 grams.

[17] Prepared with bacon, butter, onion, celery, and bread cubes

[18] Prepared with milk, bread crumbs, butter, and salt.

TABLE 1.—COMPOSITION OF FOODS, 100 GRAMS, EDIBLE PORTION—Continued

[Numbers in parentheses denote values imputed—usually from another form of the food or from a similar food. Zero in parentheses indicates that the amount of a constituent probably is none or is too small to measure. Dashes denote lack of reliable data for a constituent believed to be present in measurable amount. Calculated values, as those based on a recipe, are not in parentheses]

Item No.	Food and description	Water	Food energy	Protein	Fat	Carbohydrate		Ash	Calcium	Phosphorus	Iron	Sodium	Potassium	Vitamin A value	Thiamine	Riboflavin	Niacin	Ascorbic acid
						Total	Fiber											
(A)	(B)	(C)	(D)	(E)	(F)	(G)	(H)	(I)	(J)	(K)	(L)	(M)	(N)	(O)	(P)	(Q)	(R)	(S)
		Percent	Calories	Grams	Grams	Grams	Grams	Grams	Milligrams	Milligrams	Milligrams	Milligrams	Milligrams	International units	Milligrams	Milligrams	Milligrams	Milligrams
	Beans, lima—Continued																	
	Immature seeds—Continued																	
	Frozen:																	
	Thick-seeded types, commonly called Fordhooks:																	
172	Not thawed	72.7	102	6.2	0.1	19.5	1.7	1.5	23	96	1.9	[28] 129	490	230	0.10	0.06	1.2	22
173	Cooked, boiled, drained	73.5	99	6.0	.1	19.1	1.6	1.3	20	90	1.7	101	426	230	.07	.05	1.0	17
	Thin-seeded types, commonly called baby limas:																	
174	Not thawed	67.8	122	7.6	.2	23.0	1.9	1.4	38	131	2.8	[28] 147	435	220	.10	.06	1.2	19
175	Cooked, boiled, drained	68.8	118	7.4	.2	22.3	1.9	1.3	35	126	2.6	129	394	220	.09	.05	1.2	12
	Mature seeds, dry:																	
176	Raw	10.3	345	20.4	1.6	64.0	4.3	3.7	72	385	7.8	4	1,529	Trace	.48	.17	1.9	----
177	Cooked	64.1	138	8.2	.6	25.6	1.7	1.5	29	154	3.1	[1] 2	612	----	.13	.06	.7	----
178	Bean flour, lima	10.5	343	21.5	1.4	63.0	2.	3.6	----	----	----	----	----	(0)	----	----	----	(0)
	Beans, mung:																	
179	Mature seeds, dry, raw	10.7	340	24.2	1.3	60.3	4.4	3.5	118	340	7.7	6	1,028	80	.38	.21	2.6	----
	Sprouted seeds:																	
180	Uncooked	88.8	35	3.8	.2	6.6	.7	.6	19	64	1.3	5	223	20	.13	.13	.8	19
181	Cooked, boiled, drained	91.0	28	3.2	.2	5.2	.7	.4	17	48	.9	4	156	20	.09	.10	.7	6
	Beans, snap:																	
	Green:																	
182	Raw	90.1	32	1.9	.2	7.1	1.0	.7	56	44	.8	7	243	600	.08	.11	.5	19
	Cooked, boiled, drained, cooked in—																	
183	Small amount of water, short time	92.4	25	1.6	.2	5.4	1.0	.4	50	37	.6	4	151	540	.07	.09	.5	12
184	Large amount of water, long time	92.4	25	1.6	.2	5.4	1.0	.4	50	37	.6	4	151	540	.06	.08	.3	10
	Canned:																	
	Regular pack:																	
185	Solids and liquid	93.5	18	1.0	.1	4.2	.6	1.2	34	21	1.2	[9] 236	95	290	.03	.04	.3	4
186	Drained solids	91.9	24	1.4	.2	5.2	1.0	1.3	45	25	1.5	[9] 236	95	470	.03	.05	.3	4
187	Drained liquid	95.9	10	.4	.1	2.4	Trace	1.2	15	14	.9	[9] 236	95	Trace	.03	.03	.3	4
	Special dietary pack (low-sodium):																	
188	Solids and liquid	94.8	16	1.1	.1	3.6	.6	.4	34	21	1.2	2	95	290	.03	.04	.3	4
189	Drained solids	93.2	22	1.5	.1	4.8	.9	.4	45	25	1.5	2	95	470	.03	.05	.3	4
190	Drained liquid	97.3	8	.4	.1	1.8	Trace	.4	15	14	.9	2	95	Trace	.03	.03	.3	4
	Frozen:																	
	Cut:																	
191	Not thawed	91.7	26	1.7	.1	6.0	1.0	.5	42	33	.8	1	167	580	.07	.10	.4	9
192	Cooked, boiled, drained	92.1	25	1.6	.1	5.7	1.0	.5	40	32	.7	1	152	580	.07	.09	.4	5
	French style:																	
193	Not thawed	91.6	27	1.7	.1	6.1	1.1	.5	40	32	.9	2	153	530	.07	.09	.4	10
194	Cooked, boiled, drained	91.9	26	1.6	.1	6.0	1.1	.4	38	30	.9	2	136	530	.06	.08	.3	7
	Yellow or wax:																	
195	Raw	91.4	27	1.7	.2	6.0	1.0	.7	56	43	.8	7	243	250	.08	.11	.5	20
196	Cooked, boiled, drained	93.4	22	1.4	.2	4.6	1.0	.4	50	37	.6	3	151	230	.07	.09	.5	13
	Canned:																	
	Regular pack:																	
197	Solids and liquid	93.7	19	1.0	.2	4.2	.6	.9	34	21	1.2	[9] 236	95	60	.03	.04	.3	5
198	Drained solids	92.2	24	1.4	.3	5.2	.9	.9	45	25	1.5	[9] 236	95	100	.03	.05	.3	5
199	Drained liquid	96.1	11	.4	.1	2.5	Trace	.9	15	14	.9	[9] 236	95	Trace	.03	.03	.3	5
	Special dietary pack (low-sodium):																	
200	Solids and liquid	95.2	15	.9	.1	3.4	.6	.4	(34)	(21)	(1.2)	2	95	(60)	(.03)	(.04)	(.3)	(5)
201	Drained solids	93.6	21	1.2	.1	4.7	.9	.4	(45)	(25)	(1.5)	2	95	(100)	(.03)	(.05)	(.3)	(5)
202	Drained liquid	97.7	7	.4	.1	1.4	Trace	.4	(15)	(14)	(.9)	2	95	Trace	(.03)	(.03)	(.3)	(5)
	Frozen, cut:																	
203	Not thawed	91.1	28	1.8	.1	6.5	1.1	.5	36	32	.8	1	180	100	.08	.09	.5	12
204	Cooked, boiled, drained	91.5	27	1.7	.1	6.2	1.1	.5	35	31	.7	1	164	100	.07	.08	.4	6
	Bean sprouts. See Beans, mung: items 180–181; and Soybeans: items 2143–2144.																	
205	Beans and frankfurters, canned	70.7	144	7.6	7.1	12.6	1.0	2.0	37	119	1.9	539	262	130	.07	.06	1.3	Trace
206	Beaver, cooked, roasted	56.2	248	29.2	13.7	0	0	.9	----	----	----	----	----	----	.08	.38	----	----
207	Beechnuts	6.6	568	19.4	50.0	20.3	3.7	2.7	----	----	----	----	----	----	----	----	----	----

No.	Food																
	Beef: [4]																
	Carcass:																
	Total edible, including kidney and kidney fat, raw:																
208	Prime grade (54% lean, 46% fat)	44.8	428	13.6	41.	0	0	.6	8	124	2.0			80	.06	.12	3.3	—
209	Choice grade (60% lean, 40% fat)	49.4	379	14.9	35.	0	0	.7	9	136	2.2			70	.06	.13	3.6	—
210	Good grade (66% lean, 34% fat)	54.7	323	16.5	28.	0	0	.8	10	152	2.5			60	.07	.15	4.0	—
211	Standard grade (73% lean, 27% fat)	60.1	266	18.0	21.	0	0	.9	10	166	2.7			40	.08	.16	4.3	—
212	Commercial grade (64% lean, 36% fat)	52.4	347	15.8	31.	0	0	.8	9	145	2.4			60	.07	.14	3.8	—
213	Utility grade (76% lean, 24% fat)	62.5	242	18.6	18.	0	0	.9	11	172	2.8			40	.08	.17	4.5	—
	Total edible, trimmed to retail level, raw:																
214	Choice grade (75% lean, 25% fat)	56.7	301	17.4	25.1	0	0	.8	10	161	2.6			50	.07	.15	4.2	—
215	Good grade (78% lean, 22% fat)	60.3	263	18.5	20.4	0	0	.8	11	171	2.8			40	.08	.16	4.4	—
216	Standard grade (82% lean, 18% fat)	63.9	225	19.4	15.8	0	0	.9	11	180	2.9			30	.08	.17	4.7	—
	Separable fat:																
	Raw. See individual cuts.																
217	Cooked	15.7	729	5.7	78.1	0	0	.5	—	—	—			—	—	—	—	—
	Retail cuts, trimmed to retail level:																
	Chuck cuts:																
	Entire chuck, 1st–5th ribs, arm, and neck:																
	Choice grade:																
	Total edible:																
218	Raw (82% lean, 18% fat)	60.8	257	18.7	19.6	0	0	.9	11	188	2.8			40	.08	.17	4.5	—
219	Cooked, braised or pot-roasted (81% lean, 19% fat).	49.4	327	26.0	23.9	0	0	.7	11	140	3.3			40	.05	.20	4.0	—
	Separable lean:																
220	Raw	70.3	158	21.3	7.4	0	0	1.0	12	214	3.2			10	.09	.19	5.1	—
221	Cooked, braised or pot-roasted	59.7	214	30.0	9.5	0	0	.8	13	160	3.8			20	.05	.23	4.6	—
	Separable fat.																
222	Raw	16.9	716	6.6	76.3	0	0	.2	4	72	1.0			150	.03	.06	1.6	—
	Chuck rib, 5th:																
	Choice grade:																
	Total edible:																
223	Raw (70% lean, 30% fat)	51.7	352	16.2	31.4	0	0	.7	9	148	2.4			60	.07	.14	3.9	—
224	Cooked, braised (69% lean, 31% fat)	40.3	427	22.4	36.7	0	0	.6	10	110	2.9			70	.04	.17	3.5	—
	Separable lean:																
225	Raw	67.4	188	20.7	11.0	0	0	.9	12	192	3.1			20	.09	.18	5.0	—
226	Cooked, braised	56.5	249	28.9	13.9	0	0	.7	13	143	3.7	(19)	(20)	20	.05	.22	4.5	—
	Separable fat:																
227	Raw	14.3	745	5.5	80.0	0	0	.2	3	45	.8			160	.02	.05	1.3	—
	Good grade:																
	Total edible:																
228	Raw (74% lean, 26% fat)	56.3	303	17.5	25.3	0	0	.8	10	162	2.6			50	.08	.16	4.2	—
229	Cooked, braised (73% lean, 27% fat)	44.8	377	24.2	30.3	0	0	.7	10	121	3.1			60	.04	.19	3.8	—
	Separable lean:																
230	Raw	69.8	163	21.2	8.0	0	0	1.0	12	197	3.2			20	.09	.19	5.1	—
231	Cooked, braised	59.2	219	29.8	10.2	0	0	.8	13	147	3.8			20	.05	.23	4.6	—
	Separable fat:																
232	Raw	17.8	705	7.0	74.9	0	0	.3	4	60	1.0			150	.03	.06	1.7	—
	Arm:																
	Choice grade:																
	Total edible:																
233	Raw (86% lean, 14% fat)	64.2	223	19.4	15.5	0	0	.9	12	180	2.9			30	.08	.17	4.7	—
234	Cooked, braised or pot-roasted (85% lean, 15% fat).	63.0	289	27.1	19.2	0	0	.7	12	134	3.4			30	.05	.21	4.2	—
	Separable lean:																
235	Raw	72.0	141	21.6	5.4	0	0	1.0	13	201	3.2			10	.09	.19	5.2	—
236	Cooked, braised or pot-roasted	61.7	193	30.5	7.0	0	0	.8	14	150	3.8			10	.06	.23	4.6	—
	Separable fat:																
237	Raw	15.2	736	5.8	78.8	0	0	.2	3	48	.9			160	.02	.05	1.4	—
	Good grade:																
	Total edible:																
238	Raw (89% lean, 11% fat)	67.3	191	20.3	11.6	0	0	.9	12	188	3.1			20	.09	.18	4.8	—
239	Cooked, braised or pot-roasted (88% lean, 12% fat).	56.3	253	28.4	14.6	0	0	.7	13	140	3.7			30	.05	.21	4.3	—
	Separable lean:																
240	Raw	73.2	129	21.8	4.0	0	0	1.0	13	203	3.3			10	.09	.19	5.2	—
241	Cooked, braised or pot-roasted	63.1	179	30.9	5.2	0	0	.8	14	151	3.9			10	.06	.23	4.7	—
	Separable fat:																
242	Raw	17.9	704	7.1	74.7	0	0	.3	4	61	1.1			150	.03	.06	1.7	—

[4] See Notes on Foods, p. 176 for item 177, p. 179 for Beef.

[9] Estimated average based on addition of salt in the amount of 0.6 percent of the finished product.

[19] Average weighted in accordance with commercial practices in freezing vegetables. See also Notes on Foods, p. 177.

[20] Average value for 100 grams, all cuts, is 65 mg. for raw beef and 60 mg. for cooked beef. See also Notes on Foods, p. 179

[21] Average value per 100 grams of beef of all cuts is 355 mg for raw meat and 370 mg. for cooked meat.

TABLE 1.—COMPOSITION OF FOODS, 100 GRAMS, EDIBLE PORTION—Continued

[Numbers in parentheses denote values imputed—usually from another form of the food or from a similar food. Zero in parentheses indicates that the amount of a constituent probably is none or is too small to measure. Dashes denote lack of reliable data for a constituent believed to be present in measurable amount. Calculated values, as those based on a recipe, are not in parentheses]

Item No.	Food and description	Water	Food energy	Protein	Fat	Carbohydrate		Ash	Calcium	Phosphorus	Iron	Sodium	Potassium	Vitamin A value	Thiamine	Riboflavin	Niacin	Ascorbic acid
						Total	Fiber											
(A)	(B)	(C)	(D)	(E)	(F)	(G)	(H)	(I)	(J)	(K)	(L)	(M)	(N)	(O)	(P)	(Q)	(R)	(S)
	Beef[1]—Continued	Percent	Calories	Grams	Grams	Grams	Grams	Grams	Milligrams	Milligrams	Milligrams	Milligrams	Milligrams	International units	Milligrams	Milligrams	Milligrams	Milligrams
	Retail cuts, trimmed to retail level—Continued																	
	Flank steak:																	
	Choice grade:																	
	Total edible:																	
243	Raw (100% lean)	71.7	144	21.6	5.7	0	0	1.0	13	201	3.2			10	0.09	0.19	5.2	----
244	Cooked, braised (100% lean)	61.4	196	30.5	7.3	0	0	.8	11	150	3.8			10	.06	.22	4.6	----
	Good grade:																	
	Total edible:																	
245	Raw (100% lean)	72.1	139	21.8	5.1	0	0	1.0	13	203	3.3			10	.09	.19	5.2	----
246	Cooked, braised (100% lean)	61.8	191	30.8	6.6	0	0	.8	14	151	3.9			10	.06	.23	4.7	----
	Hindshank:																	
	Choice grade:																	
	Total edible:																	
247	Raw (67% lean, 33% fat)	57.6	289	18.2	23.4	0	0	.8	11	168	2.8			50	.08	.16	4.4	----
248	Cooked, simmered (66% lean, 34% fat)	46.1	361	25.1	28.1	0	0	.7	11	125	3.3			50	.05	.19	3.9	----
	Separable lean:																	
249	Raw	72.7	134	21.7	4.6	0	0	1.0	13	202	3.3			10	.09	.19	5.2	----
250	Cooked, simmered	62.5	184	30.7	5.9	0	0	.8	14	151	3.9			10	.06	.23	4.7	----
	Separable fat:																	
251	Raw	27.0	602	11.1	61.5	0	0	.4	6	100	1.7			120	.05	.10	2.7	
	Good grade:																	
	Total edible:																	
252	Raw (71% lean, 29% fat)	62.5	239	19.7	17.2	0	0	.8	12	182	3.0			30	.08	.17	4.7	----
253	Cooked, simmered (70% lean, 30% fat)	51.0	307	27.2	21.1	0	0	.7	12	136	3.6			40	.05	.21	4.2	----
	Separable lean:																	
254	Raw	73.5	126	21.8	3.7	0	0	1.0	13	203	3.3			10	.09	.19	5.2	----
255	Cooked, simmered	63.4	176	31.0	4.8	0	0	.8	14	151	3.9			10	.06	.23	4.7	----
	Separable fat:																	
256	Raw	34.6	517	14.5	50.4	0	0	.5	8	132	2.2			100	.06	.13	3.5	----
	Loin or short loin:																	
	Porterhouse steak:																	
	Choice grade:												([illegible])	([illegible])					
	Total edible:																	
257	Raw (63% lean, 37% fat)	48.3	390	14.8	36.2	0	0	.7	8	136	2.2			70	.06	.13	3.6	----
258	Cooked, broiled (57% lean, 43% fat)	37.2	465	19.7	42.2	0	0	.9	9	168	2.6			70	.08	.16	4.2	----
	Separable lean:																	
259	Raw	69.7	164	21.1	8.2	0	0	1.0	12	196	3.2			20	.09	.19	5.1	----
260	Cooked, broiled	57.9	224	30.2	10.5	0	0	1.4	12	242	3.7			20	.08	.23	5.6	----
	Separable fat:																	
261	Raw	11.5	777	4.2	84.1	0	0	.2	2	33	.6			170	.02	.04	1.0	----
	Good grade:																	
	Total edible:																	
262	Raw (64% lean, 36% fat)	50.2	370	15.3	33.8	0	0	.7	8	140	2.3			70	.06	.14	3.7	----
263	Cooked, broiled (58% lean, 42% fat)	38.9	446	20.5	39.7	0	0	1.0	9	173	2.6			70	.06	.17	4.5	----
	Separable lean:																	
264	Raw	72.0	141	21.5	5.5	0	0	1.0	12	200	3.2			10	.09	.19	5.2	----
265	Cooked, broiled	60.3	197	31.1	7.1	0	0	1.4	13	247	3.7			10	.08	.24	6.0	----
	Separable fat:																	
266	Raw	11.6	775	4.3	83.9	0	0	.2	2	34	.6			170	.02	.04	1.0	----
	T-bone steak:																	
	Choice grade:																	
	Total edible:																	
267	Raw (62% lean, 38% fat)	47.5	397	14.7	37.1	0	0	.7	8	135	2.2			70	.06	.13	3.5	----
268	Cooked, broiled (56% lean, 44% fat)	36.4	473	19.5	43.2	0	0	.9	8	166	2.6			80	.06	.16	4.1	----
	Separable lean:																	
269	Raw	69.7	164	21.2	8.1	0	0	1.0	12	197	3.2			20	.09	.19	5.1	----
270	Cooked, broiled	57.9	223	30.4	10.3	0	0	1.4	12	243	3.7			20	.08	.23	5.9	----
	Separable fat:																	
271	Raw	11.7	774	4.3	83.8	0	0	.2	2	34	.6			170	.02	.04	1.0	----
	Good grade:																	
	Total edible:																	
272	Raw (64% lean, 36% fat)	50.6	368	15.4	33.3	0	0	.7	9	142	2.3			70	.07	.14	3.7	----
273	Cooked, broiled (58% lean, 42% fat)	39.2	442	20.6	39.2	0	0	1.0	9	175	2.7			70	.06	.17	4.3	----

	Separable lean:																	
274	Raw	71.9	142	21.5	5.6	0	0	1.0	12	200	3.2			10	.09	.19	5.2	—
275	Cooked, broiled	60.2	199	31.1	7.3	0	0	1.4	12	247	3.7			10	.08	.24	6.0	—
	Separable fat:																	
276	Raw	12.9	761	4.8	82.1	0	0	.2	3	39	.7			160	.02	.04	1.2	—
	Club steak:																	
	Choice grade:																	
	Total edible:																	
277	Raw (64% lean, 36% fat)	49.1	380	15.5	34.8	0	0	.7	9	142	2.3			70	.07	.14	3.7	—
278	Cooked, broiled (58% lean, 42% fat)	37.9	454	20.6	40.6	0	0	.9	9	175	2.7			70	.06	.17	4.3	—
	Separable lean:																	
279	Raw	67.9	182	20.8	10.3	0	0	1.0	12	193	3.1			20	.09	.19	5.0	—
280	Cooked, broiled	56.0	244	29.6	13.0	0	0	1.4	12	238	3.6			20	.08	.23	5.8	—
	Separable fat:																	
281	Raw	15.6	731	6.0	78.2	0	0	.2	3	50	.9			160	.03	.05	1.4	—
	Good grade:																	
	Total edible:																	
282	Raw (70% lean, 30% fat)	54.5	324	16.9	27.9	0	0	.8	10	156	2.6			60	.07	.15	4.0	—
283	Cooked, broiled (64% lean, 36% fat)	42.8	398	22.9	33.3	0	0	1.0	10	192	3.0			60	.06	.18	4.7	—
	Separable lean:																	
284	Raw	70.3	158	21.2	7.5	0	0	1.0	12	197	3.2			20	.09	.19	5.1	—
285	Cooked, broiled	58.5	217	30.5	9.6	0	0	1.4	12	243	3.7			20	.08	.23	5.9	—
	Separable fat:																	
286	Raw	17.0	716	6.6	76.2	0	0	.2	4	56	1.0			150	.03	.06	1.6	—
	Loin end or sirloin:																	
	Wedge and round-bone sirloin steak:																	
	Choice grade:																	
	Total edible:																	
287	Raw (73% lean, 27% fat)	55.7	313	16.9	26.7	0	0	.8	10	155	2.5			50	.07	.15	4.1	—
288	Cooked, broiled (66% lean, 34% fat)	43.9	387	23.0	32.0	0	0	1.1	10	191	2.9			50	.06	.18	4.7	—
	Separable lean:																	
289	Raw	71.8	143	21.5	5.7	0	0	1.0	12	200	3.2			10	.09	.19	5.2	—
290	Cooked, broiled	58.7	207	32.2	7.7	0	0	1.5	13	261	3.9			10	.09	.25	6.4	—
	Separable fat:																	
291	Raw	11.8	773	4.4	83.6	0	.0	.2	3	35	.7			170	.02	.04	1.1	—
	Good grade:																	
	Total edible:																	
292	Raw (75% lean, 25% fat)	58.7	281	17.8	22.7	0	0	.8	10	164	2.7			50	.08	.16	4.3	—
293	Cooked, broiled (68% lean, 32% fat)	46.9	353	24.5	27.5	0	0	1.1	11	202	3.1	(30)	(31)	50	.07	.19	5.0	—
	Separable lean:																	
294	Raw	73.2	129	21.8	4.0	0	0	1.0	13	203	3.3			10	.09	.19	5.2	—
295	Cooked, broiled	61.6	183	31.7	5.3	0	0	1.4	13	250	3.8			10	.08	.24	6.1	—
	Separable fat:																	
296	Raw	14.4	744	5.5	79.9	0	0	.2	3	45	.8			160	.02	.05	1.3	—
	Double-bone sirloin steak:																	
	Choice grade:																	
	Total edible:																	
297	Raw (72% lean, 28% fat)	53.7	333	16.4	29.1	0	0	.8	9	151	2.5			60	.07	.15	3.9	—
298	Cooked, broiled (66% lean, 34% fat)	42.1	408	22.2	34.7	0	0	1.0	10	186	2.9			60	.06	.18	4.6	—
	Separable lean:																	
299	Raw	70.3	158	21.3	7.4	0	0	1.0	12	198	3.2			20	.09	.19	5.1	—
300	Cooked, broiled	58.5	216	30.6	9.5	0	0	1.4	12	244	3.7			20	.08	.23	6.0	—
	Separable fat:																	
301	Raw	10.1	793	3.6	86.2	0	0	.1	2	27	.5			170	.02	.03	9	—
	Good grade:																	
	Total edible:																	
302	Raw (75% lean, 25% fat)	57.6	293	17.6	24.1	0	0	.8	10	161	2.7			50	.08	.16	4.2	—
303	Cooked, broiled (67% lean, 33% fat)	45.7	365	24.1	29.1	0	0	1.1	11	198	3.1			50	.07	.19	4.9	—
	Separable lean:																	
304	Raw	72.6	135	21.7	4.7	0	0	1.0	13	202	3.3			10	.09	.19	5.2	—
305	Cooked, broiled	61.0	190	31.5	6.1	0	0	1.4	13	249	3.8			10	.08	.24	6.1	—
	Separable fat:																	
306	Raw	13.8	751	5.3	80.7	0	0	.2	3	43	.8			160	.02	.05	1.3	—
	Hipbone sirloin steak:																	
	Choice grade:																	
	Total edible:																	
307	Raw (61% lean, 39% fat)	46.0	412	14.5	38.8	0	0	.7	8	132	2.2			80	.06	.13	3.5	—
308	Cooked, broiled (55% lean, 45% fat)	35.1	487	19.1	44.9	0	0	.9	9	163	2.5			80	.06	.16	4.0	—
	Separable lean:																	
309	Raw	68.2	179	20.9	9.9	0	0	1.0	12	194	3.1			20	.09	.19	5.0	—
310	Cooked, broiled	56.3	240	29.8	12.5	0	0	1.4	12	239	3.6			20	.08	.23	5.8	—
	Separable fat:																	
311	Raw	12.0	771	4.5	83.3	0	0	.2	3	36	.7			170	.02	.04	1.1	—
	Good grade:																	
	Total edible:																	
312	Raw (64% lean, 36% fat)	50.4	367	15.7	33.2	0	0	.7	9	143	2.3			70	.07	.14	3.8	—
313	Cooked, broiled (58% lean, 42% fat)	39.0	441	21.0	39.0	0	0	1.0	9	176	2.7			70	.06	.17	4.4	—

[30] Average value for 100 grams, all cuts, is 65 mg. for raw beef and 60 mg. for cooked beef. See also Notes on Foods, p. 179.

[31] Average value per 100 grams of beef of all cuts is 355 mg. for raw meat and 370 mg. for cooked meat.

TABLE 1.—COMPOSITION OF FOODS, 100 GRAMS, EDIBLE PORTION—Continued

[Numbers in parentheses denote values imputed—usually from another form of the food or from a similar food. Zero in parentheses indicates that the amount of a constituent probably is none or is too small to measure. Dashes denote lack of reliable data for a constituent believed to be present in measurable amount. Calculated values, as those based on a recipe, are not in parentheses]

Item No.	Food and description	Water	Food energy	Protein	Fat	Carbohydrate: Total	Carbohydrate: Fiber	Ash	Calcium	Phosphorus	Iron	Sodium	Potassium	Vitamin A value	Thiamine	Riboflavin	Niacin	Ascorbic acid
(A)	(B)	(C)	(D)	(E)	(F)	(G)	(H)	(I)	(J)	(K)	(L)	(M)	(N)	(O)	(P)	(Q)	(R)	(S)
		Percent	*Calories*	*Grams*	*Grams*	*Grams*	*Grams*	*Grams*	*Milligrams*	*Milligrams*	*Milligrams*	*Milligrams*	*Milligrams*	*International units*	*Milligrams*	*Milligrams*	*Milligrams*	*Milligrams*
	Beef—Continued																	
	Retail cuts, trimmed to retail level—Continued																	
	Loin end or sirloin—Continued																	
	Hipbone sirloin steak—Continued																	
	Good grade—Continued																	
	Separable lean:																	
314	Raw	70.9	152	21.4	6.7	0	0	1.0	12	199	3.2			10	0.09	0.19	5.1	—
315	Cooked, broiled	59.2	209	30.8	8.6	0	0	1.4	12	245	3.7			10	.08	.23	6.0	—
	Separable fat:																	
316	Raw	14.4	744	5.5	79.9	0	0	.2	3	46	.8			160	.03	.05	1.5	—
	Short plate:																	
	Choice grade:																	
	Total edible:																	
317	Raw (59% lean, 41% fat)	47.2	400	14.8	37.3	0	0	.7	8	135	2.2			70	.06	.13	3.6	—
318	Cooked, simmered (58% lean, 42% fat)	36.0	474	20.6	42.8	0	0	.6	9	101	2.7			80	.04	.16	3.2	—
	Separable lean:																	
319	Raw	69.7	164	21.1	8.2	0	0	1.0	12	196	3.2			20	.09	.19	5.1	—
320	Cooked, simmered	59.1	222	29.7	10.5	0	0	.8	13	146	3.8			20	.05	.22	4.5	—
	Separable fat:																	
321	Raw	15.3	734	5.9	78.6	0	0	.2	3	45	.9			180	.03	.05	1.4	—
	Good grade:																	
	Total edible:																	
322	Raw (62% lean, 38% fat)	51.3	356	16.1	31.9	0	0	.7	9	147	2.4			60	.07	.14	3.8	—
323	Cooked, simmered (61% lean, 39% fat)	39.9	432	22.3	37.3	0	0	.6	9	110	2.9			70	.04	.17	3.4	—
	Separable lean:																	
324	Raw	71.5	146	21.5	6.0	0	0	1.0	12	200	3.2			10	.09	.19	5.2	—
325	Cooked, simmered	61.1	199	30.3	7.7	0	0	.8	13	149	3.8			10	.05	.23	4.6	—
	Separable fat:																	
326	Raw	18.2	701	7.2	74.3	0	0	.3	4	62	1.1			150	.03	.06	1.7	—
	Rib:																	
	Entire rib, (6th–12th ribs):																	
	Choice grade:																	
	Total edible:																	
327	Raw (64% lean, 36% fat)	47.2	401	14.8	37.4	0	0	.6	9	151	2.2			70	.06	.13	3.6	—
328	Cooked, roasted (64% lean, 36% fat)	40.0	440	19.9	39.4	0	0	.7	9	186	2.6	(8)	(8)	80	.05	.15	3.6	—
	Separable lean:																	
329	Raw	66.8	193	20.7	11.6	0	0	.9	12	208	3.1			20	.09	.18	5.0	—
330	Cooked, roasted	57.2	241	28.2	13.4	0	0	1.1	12	256	3.6			20	.07	.21	5.1	—
	Separable fat:																	
331	Raw	12.8	762	4.8	82.2	0	0	.2	3	54	.7			160	.02	.04	1.2	—
	Ribs, 11th–12th:																	
	Choice grade:																	
	Total edible:																	
332	Raw (55% lean, 45% fat)	43.0	444	13.7	42.7	0	0	.6	8	124	2.1			90	.06	.12	3.3	—
333	Cooked, roasted (55% lean, 45% fat)	36.3	481	18.3	44.7	0	0	.7	8	153	2.4			90	.05	.14	3.4	—
	Separable lean:																	
334	Raw	66.9	192	20.7	11.5	0	0	.9	12	192	3.1			20	.09	.18	5.0	—
335	Cooked, roasted	57.3	240	28.2	13.3	0	0	1.1	12	237	3.6			20	.07	.21	5.1	—
	Separable fat:																	
336	Raw	13.3	756	5.0	81.5	0	0	.2	3	41	.8			160	.02	.04	1.2	—
	Good grade:																	
	Total edible:																	
337	Raw (63% lean, 37% fat)	49.5	376	15.5	34.3	0	0	.7	9	142	2.3			70	.07	.14	3.7	—
338	Cooked, roasted (63% lean, 37% fat)	41.9	417	20.9	36.3	0	0	.9	9	175	2.7			70	.06	.16	3.8	—
	Separable lean:																	
339	Raw	69.5	166	21.1	8.4	0	0	1.0	12	196	3.2			20	.09	.19	5.1	—
340	Cooked, roasted	59.7	215	28.9	10.2	0	0	1.3	12	242	3.7			20	.07	.22	5.2	—
	Separable fat:																	
341	Raw	16.0	720	6.2	77.6	0	0	.2	4	52	.9			160	.03	.06	1.5	—
	Rib, 6th or blade:																	
	Choice grade:																	
	Total edible:																	
342	Raw (71% lean, 29% fat)	50.7	363	16.0	32.7	0	0	.7	9	146	2.4			70	.07	.14	3.8	—
343	Cooked, braised (70% lean, 30% fat)	39.3	437	22.1	38.0	0	0	.6	10	109	2.9			70	.04	.17	3.4	—

	Separable lean:																	
344	Raw	66.1	200	20.5	12.5	0	0	.9	12	190	3.1			20	.09	.18	4.9	—
345	Cooked, braised	55.1	263	28.5	15.7	0	0	.7	13	142	3.7			30	.05	.22	4.4	—
	Separable fat:																	
346	Raw	12.6	764	4.7	82.5	0	0	.2	3	38	.7			160	.02	.04	1.1	—
	Good grade:																	
	Total edible:																	
347	Raw (77% lean, 23% fat)	56.6	300	17.5	25.0	0	0	.8	10	162	2.6			50	.08	.16	4.2	—
348	Cooked, braised (76% lean, 24% fat)	45.1	373	24.3	29.9	0	0	.7	10	121	3.2			60	.05	.19	3.8	—
	Separable lean:																	
349	Raw	69.3	168	21.1	8.6	0	0	1.0	12	196	3.2			20	.09	.19	5.1	—
350	Cooked, braised	58.6	225	29.6	10.9	0	0	.8	13	146	3.8			20	.05	.22	4.5	—
	Separable fat:																	
351	Raw	14.7	741	5.6	79.5	0	0	2	3	46	.8			160	.02	.05	1.3	—
	Round, entire (round and heel of round):																	
	Choice grade:																	
	Total edible:																	
352	Raw (89% lean, 11% fat)	66.6	197	20.2	12.3	0	0	.9	12	203	3.0			20	.09	.18	4.8	—
353	Cooked, broiled (81% lean, 19% fat)	54.7	261	28.6	15.4	0	0	1.3	12	250	3.5			30	.08	.22	5.6	—
	Separable lean:																	
354	Raw	72.7	135	21.6	4.7	0	0	1.0	13	217	3.2			10	.09	.19	5.2	—
355	Cooked, broiled	61.2	189	31.3	6.1	0	0	1.4	13	268	3.7	(30)	(31)	10	.08	.24	6.0	—
	Separable fat:																	
356	Raw	18.7	696	7.5	73.6	0	0	.2	4	80	1.1			150	.03	.07	1.8	—
	Rump:																	
	Choice grade:																	
	Total edible:																	
357	Raw (75% lean, 25% fat)	56.5	303	17.4	25.3	0	0	.8	10	160	2.6			50	.08	.16	4.2	—
358	Cooked, roasted (75% lean, 25% fat)	48.1	347	23.6	27.3	0	0	1.0	10	197	3.1			50	.06	.18	4.3	—
	Separable lean:																	
359	Raw	70.3	158	21.2	7.5	0	0	1.0	12	197	3.2			20	.09	.19	5.1	—
360	Cooked, roasted	60.4	208	29.1	9.3	0	0	1.3	12	243	3.7			20	.07	.22	5.2	—
	Separable fat:																	
361	Raw	16.0	726	6.2	77.6	0	0	.2	4	52	.9			160	.03	.06	1.5	—
	Good grade:																	
	Total edible:																	
362	Raw (76% lean, 24% fat)	59.4	271	18.3	21.4	0	0	.8	11	168	2.7			40	.08	.16	4.4	—
363	Cooked, roasted (76% lean, 24% fat)	50.7	317	24.9	23.4	0	0	1.0	11	207	3.1			40	.06	.19	4.5	—
	Separable lean:																	
364	Raw	72.0	141	21.6	5.4	0	0	1.0	13	201	3.2			10	.09	.19	5.2	—
365	Cooked, roasted	62.0	190	29.6	7.1	0	0	1.3	13	248	3.7			10	.08	.22	5.3	—
	Separable fat:																	
366	Raw	19.0	692	7.5	73.2	0	0	.3	4	65	1.1			150	.03	.07	1.8	—
	Hamburger (ground beef):																	
	Lean:																	
367	Raw	68.3	179	20.7	10.0	0	0	1.0	12	192	3.1	—	—	20	.09	.18	5.0	—
368	Cooked	60.0	219	27.4	11.3	0	0	1.3	12	230	3.5	48	558	20	.09	.23	6.0	—
	Regular ground:																	
369	Raw	60.2	268	17.9	21.2	0	0	.7	10	156	2.7	—	236	40	.08	.16	4.3	—
370	Cooked	54.2	286	24.2	20.3	0	0	1.3	11	194	3.2	47	450	40	.09	.21	5.4	—
	Beef and vegetable stew:																	
371	Cooked (home recipe, with lean beef chuck)	82.4	89	6.4	4.3	6.2	.4	.7	12	75	1.2	37	250	980	.06	.07	1.9	7
372	Canned	82.5	79	5.8	3.1	7.1	.3	1.5	12	45	.9	411	174	970	.03	.05	1.0	3
373	**Beef, canned, roast beef**	60	224	25.	13.	0	0	2.	16	116	2.4	—	259	—	.02	.23	4.2	0
	Beef, corned, boneless																	
374	Uncooked, medium-fat	54.2	293	15.8	25	0	0	5.0	9	125	2.4	1,300	60	—	.03	.15	1.7	0
375	Cooked, medium-fat	43.9	372	22.9	30.4	0	0	2.9	9	93	2.9	1,740	150	—	.02	.18	1.5	0
	Canned:																	
376	Fat	55.3	263	23.5	18.	0	0	3.2	19	98	4.0	—	—	—	.01	.22	3.2	0
377	Medium-fat	59.3	216	25.3	12.	0	0	3.4	20	106	4.3	—	—	—	.02	.24	3.4	0
378	Lean	62.0	185	26.4	8.	0	0	3.6	21	110	4.5	—	—	—	.02	.25	3.5	0
379	Canned corned-beef hash (with potato)	67.4	181	8.8	11.3	10.7	.5	1.8	13	67	2.0	540	200	—	.01	.09	2.1	—
	Beef, dried, chipped:																	
380	Uncooked	47.7	203	34.3	6.3	0	0	11.6	20	404	5.1	4,300	200	—	(.07)	(.32)	(3.8)	0
381	Cooked, creamed	72.0	154	8.2	10.3	7.1	Trace	2.4	105	140	.8	716	153	360	.06	.19	.6	Trace
	Beef, potted. See Sausage, cold cuts, and luncheon meats: item 2008.																	
	Beef potpie:																	
382	Home-prepared, baked	55.1	246	10.1	14.5	18.8	.4	1.5	14	71	1.8	284	159	820	.11	.12	2.0	3
383	Commercial, frozen, unheated	63.3	192	7.3	9.9	18.0	.1	1.5	10	48	1.0	366	93	410	.03	.06	1.2	Trace
	Beer. See Beverages, item 394.																	
	Beets, common, red:																	
384	Raw	87.3	43	1.6	.1	9.9	.8	1.1	16	33	.7	60	335	20	.03	.05	.4	10
385	Cooked, boiled, drained	90.9	32	1.1	.1	7.2	.8	.7	14	23	.5	43	208	20	.03	.04	.3	6

[30] Average value for 100 grams, all cuts, is 65 mg. for raw beef and 60 mg. for cooked beef. See also Notes on Foods, p. 179.

[31] Average value per 100 grams of beef of all cuts is 355 mg. for raw meat and 370 mg. for cooked meat.

284-853 O - 79 - 2

TABLE 1.—COMPOSITION OF FOODS, 100 GRAMS, EDIBLE PORTION—Continued

[Numbers in parentheses denote values imputed—usually from another form of the food or from a similar food. Zero in parentheses indicates that the amount of a constituent probably is none or is too small to measure. Dashes denote lack of reliable data for a constituent believed to be present in measurable amount. Calculated values, as those based on a recipe, are not in parentheses]

Item No.	Food and description	Water	Food energy	Protein	Fat	Carbohydrate Total	Carbohydrate Fiber	Ash	Calcium	Phosphorus	Iron	Sodium	Potassium	Vitamin A value	Thiamine	Riboflavin	Niacin	Ascorbic acid
(A)	(B)	(C)	(D)	(E)	(F)	(G)	(H)	(I)	(J)	(K)	(L)	(M)	(N)	(O)	(P)	(Q)	(R)	(S)
		Percent	Calories	Grams	Grams	Grams	Grams	Grams	Milligrams	Milligrams	Milligrams	Milligrams	Milligrams	International units	Milligrams	Milligrams	Milligrams	Milligrams
	Beets, common, red—Continued																	
	Canned:																	
	Regular pack:																	
386	Solids and liquid	90.5	34	0.9	0.1	7.9	0.5	0.8	14	17	0.6	[9] 236	167	10	0.01	0.02	0.1	3
387	Drained solids	89.2	37	1.0	.1	8.8	.8	.8	15	18	.7	[9] 236	167	20	.01	.03	.1	2
388	Drained liquid	92.2	26	.8	Trace	6.2	Trace	.8	5	15	.4	[9] 236	167	Trace	.01	.02	.1	3
	Special dietary pack (low-sodium):																	
389	Solids and liquid	90.8	32	.9	Trace	7.8	.5	.5	14	17	.6	46	167	10	.01	.02	.1	3
390	Drained solids	89.8	37	.9	.1	8.7	.8	.5	15	18	.7	46	167	20	.01	.03	.1	3
391	Drained liquid	92.8	25	.8	Trace	5.9	Trace	.5	5	15	.4	46	167	Trace	.01	.02	.1	2
	Beet greens, common:																	
392	Raw	90.9	24	2.2	.3	4.6	1.3	2.0	119	40	3.3	130	570	6,100	.10	.22	.4	30
393	Cooked, boiled, drained	93.6	18	1.7	.2	3.3	1.1	1.2	99	25	1.9	76	332	5,100	.07	.15	.3	15
	Beverages, alcoholic and carbonated nonalcoholic:																	
	Alcoholic:																	
394	Beer, alcohol 4.5% by volume (3.6% by weight)	92.1	[22] 42	.3	0	3.8	—	.2	5	30	Trace	7	25	—	Trace	.03	.6	—
	Gin, rum, vodka, whisky:																	
395	80-proof (33.4% alcohol by weight)	66.6	[22] 231	—	—	Trace	—	—	—	—	—	1	2	—	—	—	—	—
396	86-proof (36.0% alcohol by weight)	64.0	[22] 249	—	—	Trace	—	—	—	—	—	1	2	—	—	—	—	—
397	90-proof (37.9% alcohol by weight)	62.1	[22] 263	—	—	Trace	—	—	—	—	—	1	2	—	—	—	—	—
398	94-proof (39.7% alcohol by weight)	60.3	[22] 275	—	—	Trace	—	—	—	—	—	1	2	—	—	—	—	—
399	100-proof (42.5% alcohol by weight)	57.5	[22] 295	—	—	Trace	—	—	—	—	—	1	2	—	—	—	—	—
	Wines:[4]																	
400	Dessert, alcohol 18.8% by volume (15.3% by weight).	76.7	[22] 137	.1	0	7.7	—	.2	8	—	—	4	75	—	.01	.02	.2	—
401	Table, alcohol 12.2% by volume (9.9% by weight)	85.6	[22] 85	.1	0	4.2	—	.2	9	10	.4	5	92	—	Trace	.01	.1	—
	Carbonated, nonalcoholic:																	
	Carbonated waters:																	
402	Sweetened (quinine sodas)	92.	31	(0)	(0)	8.	(0)	—	—	—	—	—	—	(0)	(0)	(0)	(0)	(0)
403	Unsweetened (club sodas)	100.	0	(0)	(0)	0.	(0)	—	—	—	—	—	—	(0)	(0)	(0)	(0)	(0)
404	Cola type	90.	39	(0)	(0)	10.	(0)	—	—	—	—	—	—	(0)	(0)	(0)	(0)	(0)
405	Cream sodas	89.	43	(0)	(0)	11.	(0)	—	—	—	—	—	—	(0)	(0)	(0)	(0)	(0)
406	Fruit-flavored sodas (citrus, cherry, grape, strawberry, Tom Collins mixer, other) (10%–13% sugar).	88.	46	(0)	(0)	12.	(0)	—	—	—	—	—	—	(0)	(0)	(0)	(0)	(0)
407	Ginger ale, pale dry and golden	92.	31	(0)	(0)	8.	(0)	—	—	—	—	—	—	(0)	(0)	(0)	(0)	(0)
408	Root beer	89.5	41	(0)	(0)	10.5	(0)	—	—	—	—	—	—	(0)	(0)	(0)	(0)	(0)
409	Special dietary drinks with artificial sweetener (less than 1 Calorie per ounce).	100.	—	(0)	(0)	—	(0)	—	—	—	—	—	—	(0)	(0)	(0)	(0)	(0)
	Biscuits, baking powder, baked from home recipe, made with—																	
410	Enriched flour[25]	27.4	369	7.4	17.0	45.8	.2	2.4	121	175	1.6	626	117	Trace	.21	.21	1.8	Trace
411	Unenriched flour[26]	27.4	369	7.4	17.0	45.8	.2	2.4	121	175	.5	626	117	Trace	.04	.10	.5	Trace
412	Self-rising flour, enriched	26.8	372	7.1	17.4	46.0	.2	2.7	[28] 209	[28] 317	1.7	[28] 660	64	Trace	.22	.22	2.1	Trace
	Biscuit dough, commercial, with enriched flour:																	
413	Chilled in cans	37.5	277	7.3	6.4	46.4	.2	2.4	53	497	1.7	868	65	Trace	.26	.17	2.1	0
414	Frozen	30.9	327	8.7	11.9	48.9	.1	2.6	71	466	1.4	910	86	Trace	.22	.17	1.7	Trace
	Biscuit mix, with enriched flour, and biscuits baked from mix:																	
415	Mix, dry form	7.5	424	7.7	12.6	68.7	.3	3.5	27	285	[29] 3.1	1,300	80	Trace	[29] .44	[29] .26	[29] 3.6	Trace
416	Biscuits, made with milk	28.5	325	7.1	9.3	52.3	.2	2.8	68	232	[29] 2.5	973	116	Trace	[29] .27	[29] .23	[29] 2.0	Trace
417	**Blackberries,** including dewberries, boysenberries and youngberries, raw.	84.5	58	1.2	.9	12.9	4.1	.5	32	19	.9	1	170	200	.03	.04	.4	21
	Blackberries, canned, solids and liquid:																	
418	Water pack, with or without artificial sweetener	89.3	40	.8	.6	9.0	2.8	.3	22	13	.6	1	115	140	.02	.02	.2	7
419	Juice pack	85.8	54	.8	.8	12.1	2.7	.5	25	17	.9	1	170	150	.02	.03	.3	10
	Sirup pack:																	
420	Light	81.0	72	.8	.6	17.3	2.7	.3	21	12	.6	1	111	130	.01	.02	.2	7
421	Heavy	76.1	91	.8	.6	22.2	2.6	.3	21	12	.6	1	109	130	.01	.02	.2	7
422	Extra heavy	71.2	110	.8	.6	27.1	2.6	.3	20	12	.6	1	107	130	.01	.02	.2	7
	Blackberries, frozen. See Boysenberries, items 436–437.																	
423	**Blackberry juice,** canned, unsweetened	90.9	37	.3	.6	7.8	Trace	.4	12	12	(.9)	(1)	(170)	—	(.02)	(.03)	(.3)	(10)
	Blackeye peas. See Cowpeas, items 896–904.																	

	Blackfish. See Tautog, item 2275.																	
	Blanc mange. See Puddings, item 1824.																	
	Blueberries:																	
424	Raw	83.2	62	.7	.5	15.3	1.5	.3	15	13	1.0	1	81	100	(.03)	(.06)	(.5)	14
	Canned, solids and liquid:																	
425	Water pack, with or without artificial sweetener	89.3	39	.5	.2	9.8	1.0	.2	10	9	.7	1	60	40	.01	.01	.2	7
426	Sirup pack, extra heavy	73.2	101	.4	.2	26.0	.9	.2	9	8	.6	1	55	40	.01	.01	.2	6
	Frozen, not thawed:																	
427	Unsweetened	85.0	55	.7	.5	13.6	1.5	.2	10	13	.8	1	81	70	.03	.06	.5	7
428	Sweetened	72.3	105	.6	.3	26.5	.9	.3	6	11	.4	1	66	30	.04	.05	.4	8
	Bluefish:																	
429	Raw	75.4	117	20.5	3.3	0	0	1.2	23	243	.6	74	—	—	.12	.09	1.9	—
	Cooked:																	
430	Baked or broiled [27]	68.0	159	26.2	5.2	0	0	1.4	29	287	.7	104	—	50	.11	.10	1.9	—
431	Fried [28]	60.8	205	22.7	9.8	4.7	—	2.0	35	257	.9	146	—	—	.11	.11	1.8	—
	Bockwurst. See Sausage, cold cuts, and luncheon meats: item 1981.																	
	Bologna. See Sausage, cold cuts, and luncheon meats: items 1982–1985.																	
432	**Bonito,** including Atlantic, Pacific, and striped; raw	67.6	168	24.0	7.3	0	0	1.4	—	—	—	—	—	—	—	—	—	—
433	**Boston brown bread**	45.0	211	5.5	1.3	45.6	.7	2.6	90	160	1.9	251	292	[29] 0	.11	.06	1.2	0
434	**Bouillon cubes or powder**	4.	120	20.	3.	5.	—	68	—	—	—	24,000	100	—	—	—	—	—
	Boysenberries:																	
435	Canned, water pack, solids and liquid, with or without artificial sweetener.	89.8	36	.7	.1	9.1	1.9	.3	(19)	(19)	(1.2)	1	85	130	(.01)	(.10)	(.7)	7
	Frozen, not thawed:																	
436	Unsweetened	86.8	48	1.2	.3	11.4	2.7	.3	25	24	1.6	1	153	(170)	.02	.13	1.0	13
437	Sweetened	74.3	96	.8	.3	24.4	1.8	.2	17	17	.6	1	105	(140)	.02	.10	.6	8
438	**Brains,** all kinds (beef, calf, hog, sheep), raw	78.9	125	10.4	8.6	.8	0	1.4	10	312	2.4	125	219	0	.23	.26	4.4	18
	Bran:																	
439	Added sugar and malt extract	3.6	240	12.6	3.0	74.3	7.8	6.5	70	1,176	([30])	1,060	1,070	(0)	[31] .10	.29	17.8	Trace
440	Added sugar and defatted wheat germ	3.0	238	10.8	1.8	78.8	6.5	5.6	73	977	8.8	490	—	(0)	.28	.21	14.0	(0)
441	**Bran flakes** (40% bran), added thiamine	3.0	303	10.2	1.8	80.6	3.6	4.4	71	495	4.4	925	—	(0)	.40	.17	6.2	(0)
442	**Bran flakes with raisins,** added thiamine	7.3	287	8.3	1.4	79.3	3.0	3.7	56	396	4.0	800	—	Trace	.32	.13	5.3	(0)
	Braunschweiger. See Sausage, cold cuts, and luncheon meats: item 1986																	
443	**Brazilnuts**	4.6	654	14.3	66.9	10.9	3.1	3.3	186	693	3.4	1	715	Trace	.96	.12	1.6	—
	Breads: [32]																	
444	Cracked-wheat	34.9	263	8.7	2.2	52.1	.5	2.1	88	128	1.1	529	134	Trace	.12	.09	1.3	Trace
445	Toasted	22.5	313	10.4	2.6	62.0	.6	2.5	105	152	1.3	630	160	Trace	.11	.11	1.5	Trace
	French or vienna:																	
446	Enriched	30.6	290	9.1	3.0	55.4	.2	1.9	43	85	2.2	580	90	Trace	.28	.22	2.5	Trace
447	Toasted	19.3	338	10.6	3.5	64.4	.2	2.2	50	99	2.6	674	105	Trace	.26	.25	2.9	Trace
448	Unenriched	30.6	290	9.1	3.0	55.4	.2	1.9	43	85	.7	580	90	Trace	.08	.08	.8	Trace
449	Toasted	19.3	338	10.6	3.5	64.4	.2	2.2	50	99	.8	674	105	Trace	.08	.10	.9	Trace
	Italian:																	
450	Enriched	31.8	276	9.1	.8	56.4	.2	1.9	17	77	2.2	585	74	(0)	.29	.20	2.6	(0)
451	Unenriched	31.8	276	9.1	.8	56.4	.2	1.9	17	77	.7	585	74	(0)	.09	.06	.8	(0)
452	Raisin	35.3	262	6.6	2.8	53.6	.9	1.7	71	87	1.3	365	233	Trace	.05	.09	.7	Trace
453	Toasted	22.0	316	8.0	3.4	64.6	1.1	2.0	86	105	1.6	440	281	Trace	.05	.11	.8	Trace
	Rye:																	
454	American (⅓ rye, ⅔ clear flour)	35.5	243	9.1	1.1	52.1	.4	2.2	75	147	1.6	557	145	(0)	.18	.07	1.4	(0)
455	Toasted	25.0	282	10.6	1.3	60.5	.5	2.6	87	171	1.9	648	169	(0)	.17	.08	1.6	(0)
456	Pumpernickel	34.0	246	9.1	1.2	53.1	1.1	2.6	84	229	2.4	569	454	(0)	.23	.14	1.2	(0)
457	Salt-rising	36.5	267	7.9	2.4	52.2	.2	1.0	23	69	.6	265	67	10	.04	.05	.6	Trace
458	Toasted	29.4	297	8.8	2.7	58.0	.2	1.1	26	77	.7	294	74	10	.04	.05	.6	Trace
	White:																	
	Enriched, made with—																	
459	1%–2% nonfat dry milk	35.8	269	8.7	3.2	50.4	.2	1.9	70	87	2.4	507	85	Trace	.25	.17	2.3	Trace
460	Toasted	25.3	314	10.1	3.7	58.7	.2	2.2	81	101	2.8	590	99	Trace	.23	.20	2.7	Trace
461	3%–4% nonfat dry milk [33]	35.6	270	8.7	3.2	50.5	.2	2.0	84	97	2.5	507	105	Trace	.25	.21	2.4	Trace
462	Toasted	25.1	314	10.1	3.7	58.8	.2	2.3	98	113	2.9	590	122	Trace	.23	.24	2.8	Trace
463	5%–6% nonfat dry milk	35.0	275	9.0	3.8	50.2	.2	2.0	96	102	2.5	495	121	Trace	.27	.20	2.4	Trace
464	Toasted	24.4	320	10.5	4.4	58.4	.2	2.3	112	119	2.9	576	141	Trace	.25	.23	2.8	Trace

[4] See Notes on Foods, p. 181.

[9] Estimated average based on addition of salt in the amount of 0.6 percent of the finished product.

[22] See Notes on Foods, p. 181, concerning calculation of energy values.

[23] Values are based on biscuits made with baking powder, item 130, and cooking fats, item 999.

[24] Based on use of self-rising flour, item 2445, containing anhydrous monocalcium phosphate. With flour containing leavening ingredients noted in footnote 169, approximate values per 100 grams are: Calcium, 124 mg., phosphorus, 363 mg.; sodium, 826 mg.

[25] With unenriched flour, approximate values per 100 grams are: Iron, 0.6 mg.; thiamine, 0.05 mg., riboflavin, 0.05 mg.; niacin, 0.7 mg.

[26] With unenriched flour, approximate values per 100 grams are. Iron, 0.5 mg., thiamine, 0.04 mg.; riboflavin, 0.10 mg., niacin, 0.5 mg.

[27] Prepared with butter or margarine.

[28] Prepared with egg, milk or water, and bread crumbs.

[29] Applies to product made with white cornmeal. With yellow degermed cornmeal, value is 70 I.U. per 100 grams.

[30] Values range from 4 to 12 mg. per 100 grams.

[31] For product containing added thiamine, value is 0.4 mg. per 100 grams.

[32] For additional data and information, see discussion of bread and rolls in Notes on Foods, p. 172.

[33] When amount of nonfat dry milk in commercial bread is unknown, values for bread with 3 to 4 percent nonfat dry milk, item 461 or item 467, are suggested. See also Notes on Foods, p. 172.

TABLE 1.—COMPOSITION OF FOODS, 100 GRAMS, EDIBLE PORTION—Continued

[Numbers in parentheses denote values imputed—usually from another form of the food or from a similar food. Zero in parentheses indicates that the amount of a constituent probably is none or is too small to measure. Dashes denote lack of reliable data for a constituent believed to be present in measurable amount. Calculated values, as those based on a recipe, are not in parentheses]

Item No.	Food and description	Water	Food energy	Protein	Fat	Carbohydrate Total	Carbohydrate Fiber	Ash	Calcium	Phosphorus	Iron	Sodium	Potassium	Vitamin A value	Thiamine	Riboflavin	Niacin	Ascorbic acid
(A)	(B)	(C)	(D)	(E)	(F)	(G)	(H)	(I)	(J)	(K)	(L)	(M)	(N)	(O)	(P)	(Q)	(R)	(S)
		Percent	Calories	Grams	Grams	Grams	Grams	Grams	Milligrams	Milligrams	Milligrams	Milligrams	Milligrams	International units	Milligrams	Milligrams	Milligrams	Milligrams
	Breads [30]—Continued																	
	White—Continued																	
	Unenriched, made with—																	
465	1%–2% nonfat dry milk	35.8	269	8.7	3.2	50.4	0.2	1.9	70	87	0.7	507	85	Trace	0.09	0.08	1.2	Trace
466	Toasted	25.3	314	10.1	3.7	58.7	.2	2.2	81	101	.8	590	89	Trace	.08	.09	1.4	Trace
467	3%–4% nonfat dry milk [32]	35.6	270	8.7	3.2	50.5	.2	2.0	84	97	.7	507	105	Trace	.07	.09	1.1	Trace
468	Toasted	25.1	314	10.1	3.7	58.8	.2	2.3	98	113	.8	590	122	Trace	.08	.10	1.3	Trace
469	5%–6% nonfat dry milk	35.0	275	9.0	3.8	50.2	.2	2.0	96	102	.7	495	121	Trace	.07	.13	.9	Trace
470	Toasted	24.3	320	10.5	4.4	58.4	.2	2.3	112	119	.8	576	141	Trace	.07	.15	1.0	Trace
	Whole-wheat, made with—																	
471	2% nonfat dry milk	36.4	243	10.5	3.0	47.7	1.6	2.4	99	228	2.3	527	273	Trace	.26	.12	2.8	Trace
472	Toasted	24.3	289	12.5	3.6	56.7	1.9	2.9	118	271	2.7	627	325	Trace	.25	.15	3.4	Trace
473	Water	36.4	241	9.1	2.6	49.3	1.5	2.6	84	254	2.3	530	256	Trace	.30	.10	2.8	Trace
474	Toasted	24.3	287	10.8	3.1	58.7	1.8	3.1	100	302	2.7	631	305	Trace	.29	.12	3.3	Trace
	See also Biscuits; Boston brown bread; Cornbread; Muffins; Rolls; Salt sticks.																	
475	**Breadcrumbs**, dry, grated	6.5	392	12.6	4.6	73.4	.3	2.9	122	141	3.6	736	152	Trace	.22	.30	3.5	Trace
476	**Bread pudding** with raisins	58.6	187	5.6	6.1	28.4	.1	1.3	109	114	1.1	201	215	300	.06	.19	1	1
	Bread sticks (vienna). See Salt sticks, item 1966.																	
	Bread stuffing mix and stuffings prepared from mix:																	
477	Mix, dry form	6.3	371	12.9	3.8	72.4	.8	4.6	124	189	3.2	1,331	172	Trace	.22	.26	3.2	Trace
	Stuffing:																	
478	Dry, crumbly; prepared with water, table fat	33.2	358	6.5	21.8	35.6	.4	2.9	66	97	1.6	896	90	650	.09	.12	1.5	Trace
479	Moist; prepared with water, egg, table fat	61.4	208	4.4	12.8	19.7	.2	1.7	40	66	1.0	504	58	420	.05	.09	.8	Trace
480	**Breadfruit**, raw	70.8	103	1.7	.3	26.2	1.2	1.0	33	32	1.2	15	439	40	.11	.03	.9	29
	Breakfast cereals. See Corn, Oats, Rice, Wheat, also Bran, Farina.																	
	Broadbeans, raw:																	
481	Immature seeds	72.3	105	8.4	.4	17.8	2.2	1.1	27	157	2.2	4	471	220	.28	.17	1.6	30
482	Mature seeds, dry	11.9	338	25.1	1.7	58.2	6.7	4.1	102	391	7.1	—	—	70	.50	.30	2.5	—
	Broccoli:																	
483	Raw spears	89.1	32	3.6	.3	5.9	1.5	1.1	103	78	1.1	15	382	[32]2,500	.10	.23	.9	113
484	Cooked spears, boiled, drained	91.3	26	3.1	.3	4.5	1.5	.8	88	62	.8	10	267	2,500	.09	.20	.8	90
	Frozen:																	
	Chopped:																	
485	Not thawed	90.6	29	3.2	.3	5.2	1.1	.7	58	59	.7	17	241	2,600	.07	.13	.6	70
486	Cooked, boiled, drained	91.6	26	2.9	.3	4.6	1.1	.6	54	56	.7	15	212	2,600	.06	.12	.5	57
	Spears:																	
487	Not thawed	90.7	28	3.3	.2	5.1	1.1	.7	43	60	.7	13	244	1,900	.07	.13	.6	78
488	Cooked, boiled, drained	91.4	26	3.1	.2	4.7	1.1	.6	41	58	.7	12	220	1,900	.06	.11	.5	73
	Brown betty. See Apple brown betty, item 25.																	
	Brownies. See Cookies, items 813–814.																	
	Brussels sprouts:																	
489	Raw	85.2	45	4.9	.4	8.3	1.6	1.2	36	80	1.5	14	390	550	.10	.16	.9	102
490	Cooked, boiled, drained	88.2	36	4.2	.4	6.4	1.6	.8	32	72	1.1	10	273	520	.08	.14	.8	87
	Frozen:																	
491	Not thawed	88.4	36	3.3	.2	7.3	1.2	.8	22	62	.9	16	328	570	.10	.11	.6	87
492	Cooked, boiled, drained	89.3	33	3.2	.2	6.5	1.2	.8	21	61	.8	14	295	570	.08	.10	.6	81
	Buckwheat:																	
493	Whole-grain	11.0	335	11.7	2.4	72.9	9.9	2.0	114	282	3.1	—	448	(0)	.60	—	4.4	(0)
	Flour:																	
494	Dark	12.	333	11.7	2.5	72.0	1.6	1.8	33	347	2.8	—	—	(0)	.58	.15	2.9	(0)
495	Light	12.	347	6.4	1.2	79.5	.5	.9	11	88	1.0	—	320	(0)	.08	(.04)	(.4)	(0)
	Buckwheat pancake mix. See Pancake mix, item 1461.																	
496	**Buffalofish**, raw	77.4	113	17.5	4.2	0	0	1.1	—	—	—	52	293	—	—	—	—	—
	Bulgur (parboiled wheat):																	
	Dry, commercial, made from—																	
497	Club wheat	9.	359	8.7	1.4	79.5	1.7	1.4	36	319	4.7	—	262	(0)	.30	.10	4.2	(0)
498	Hard red winter wheat	10.	354	11.2	1.5	75.7	1.7	1.6	29	338	3.7	—	229	(0)	.28	.14	4.5	(0)
499	White wheat	(9.)	357	10.3	1.2	78.1	1.3	1.4	36	300	(4.7)	—	310	(0)	(.30)	(.10)	(4.2)	(0)
	Canned, made from hard red winter wheat:																	
500	Unseasoned [34]	56.0	168	6.2	.7	35.0	.8	2.1	20	200	1.3	599	87	(0)	.05	.03	2.4	(0)
501	Seasoned [35]	56.0	182	6.2	3.3	32.8	.8	1.7	20	195	1.4	460	112	(0)	.06	.04	3.0	(0)
502	**Bullhead, black**, raw	81.3	84	16.3	1.6	0	0	1.0	—	—	—	—	—	—	—	—	—	—

No.	Food																	
	Bullocksheart. See Custardapple, item 949.																	
	Burbot:																	
503	Raw	81.1	82	17.4	.9	0	0	1.0	—	190	—	—	—	—	.39	.14	1.5	—
504	Cooked, fried	60.5	—	37.0	—	0	0	—	—	—	—	—	—	—	.54	.23	3.7	—
	Burghul. See Bulgur, items 497–501.																	
505	**Butter** [37]	15.5	716	.6	81.	.4	0	2.5	20	16	0	987	23	3,300	—	—	—	0
506	**Butter oil or dehydrated butter**	.2	876	.3	99.5	0	0	0	—	—	—	—	—	4,080	—	—	—	0
	Butterfish, raw:																	
507	From northern waters	71.4	169	18.1	10.2	0	0	1.4	—	—	—	—	—	—	—	—	—	—
508	From gulf waters	78.2	95	16.2	2.9	0	0	2.9	—	—	—	—	—	—	—	—	—	—
	Buttermilk:																	
509	Fluid, cultured (made from skim milk)	90.5	36	3.6	.1	5.1	0	.7	121	95	Trace	130	140	Trace	.04	.18	.1	1
510	Dried	2.8	387	34.3	5.3	50.0	0	7.6	1,248	970	6	507	1,606	220	.26	1.72	.9	—
511	**Butternuts**	3.8	629	23.7	61.2	8.4	—	2.9	—	—	6.8	—	—	—	—	—	—	—
	Cabbage:																	
	Common varieties (Danish, domestic, and pointed types):																	
512	Raw	92.4	24	1.3	.2	5.4	.8	.7	49	29	.4	20	233	130	.05	.05	.3	[38] 47
	Cooked, boiled until tender, drained																	
513	Shredded, cooked in small amount of water	93.9	20	1.1	.2	4.3	.8	.5	44	20	.3	14	163	130	.04	.04	.3	33
514	Wedges, cooked in large amount of water	94.3	18	1.0	.2	4.0	.8	.5	42	17	.3	13	151	120	.02	.02	.1	24
515	Dehydrated	4.	308	12.4	1.7	73.7	10.3	8.2	405	287	3.9	190	2,207	1,300	[39] .45	.40	3.0	[39] 211
516	Red, raw	90.2	31	2.0	.2	6.9	1.0	.7	42	35	.8	26	268	40	.09	.06	.4	61
517	Savoy, raw	92.0	24	2.4	.2	4.6	.8	.8	67	54	.9	22	269	200	.05	.08	.3	55
518	**Cabbage, Chinese** (also called celery cabbage or petsai), compact heading type, raw.	95.0	14	1.2	.1	3.0	.6	.7	43	40	.6	23	253	150	.05	.04	6	25
	Cabbage, spoon (also called white mustard cabbage or pakchoy), nonheading green leaf type:																	
519	Raw	94.3	16	1.6	.2	2.9	.6	1.0	165	44	.8	26	306	3,100	.05	.10	.8	25
520	Cooked, boiled, drained	95.2	14	1.4	.2	2.4	.6	.8	148	33	6	18	214	3,100	.04	.08	.7	15
	Cabbage salad. See Coleslaw, items 801–804.																	
	Cakes:																	
	Baked from home recipes: [40]																	
521	Angelfood	31.5	269	7.1	.2	60.2	0	1.0	9	22	.2	283	88	0	.01	.14	2	0
522	Boston cream pie	34.5	302	5.0	9.4	49.9	0	1.2	67	101	.5	186	89	210	.03	.11	.2	Trace
	Caramel																	
523	Without icing	23.0	385	4.5	17.3	53.7	.1	1.5	78	106	1.3	305	68	180	.02	.08	.2	Trace
524	With caramel icing	20.9	379	3.7	14.8	59.1	0	1.5	84	95	1.5	252	64	200	.02	.07	.1	Trace
	Chocolate (devil's food):																	
525	Without icing	24.6	366	4.8	17.2	52.0	.3	1.4	74	137	9	294	140	150	.02	.10	.2	Trace
526	With chocolate icing	22.0	369	4.5	16.4	55.8	.3	1.3	70	131	1.0	235	154	160	.02	.10	.2	Trace
527	With uncooked white icing	21.3	369	3.8	14.6	59.2	.2	1.1	59	106	7	234	110	180	.02	.08	.2	Trace
	Cottage pudding, made with enriched flour																	
528	Without sauce	26.6	344	6.4	11.3	54.3	.1	1.4	90	115	1.4	299	88	140	.15	.17	1.2	Trace
529	With chocolate sauce	27.9	318	5.3	8.8	56.7	.3	1.3	71	109	1.4	233	140	100	.12	.14	1.0	Trace
530	With fruit sauce (strawberry)	36.6	292	5.1	8.8	48.4	.3	1.1	73	93	1.2	233	93	120	.12	.15	1.1	12
	Fruitcake, made with enriched flour:																	
531	Dark	18.1	379	4.8	15.3	59.7	.6	2.1	72	113	2.6	158	496	120	.13	.14	.8	Trace
532	Light	18.7	389	6.0	16.5	57.4	.7	1.4	68	115	1.6	193	233	70	.10	.11	.7	Trace
533	Gingerbread, made with enriched flour	30.8	317	3.8	10.7	52.0	.1	2.7	68	65	2.3	237	454	90	.12	.11	9	0
	Plain cake or cupcake																	
534	Without icing	24.5	364	4.5	13.9	55.9	.1	1.2	64	102	.4	300	79	170	.02	.09	.2	Trace
535	With chocolate icing	21.4	368	4.2	13.9	59.4	.2	1.1	63	104	.6	229	114	180	.02	.09	.2	Trace
536	With boiled white icing	22.9	352	3.8	10.5	61.8	Trace	1.0	49	77	.3	262	64	130	.02	.07	.2	Trace
537	With uncooked white icing	20.6	367	3.4	11.8	63.3	Trace	.9	50	75	.3	227	61	200	.02	.07	.1	Trace
	Pound:																	
538	Old-fashioned (equal weights flour, sugar, table fat, eggs).	17.2	473	5.7	29.5	47.0	.1	.6	21	79	.8	110	60	280	.03	.09	.2	0
539	Modified	19.4	411	6.4	18.7	54.7	.1	.9	40	104	.8	178	78	290	.04	.11	.2	Trace
540	Sponge	31.8	297	7.6	5.7	54.1	0	.8	30	112	1.2	167	87	450	.05	.14	2	Trace
	White:																	
541	Without icing	24.2	375	4.6	16.0	54.0	.1	1.2	63	91	.2	323	76	30	.01	.08	2	Trace
542	With coconut icing	21.3	371	3.7	13.3	60.7	.3	1.0	45	72	.3	257	106	20	.01	.07	.2	Trace
543	With uncooked white icing	20.0	375	3.3	12.9	62.9	0	.9	48	65	.1	234	58	110	.01	.06	.1	Trace
	Yellow																	
544	Without icing	23.5	363	4.5	12.7	58.2	.1	1.1	71	112	.4	258	78	150	.02	.08	.2	Trace
545	With caramel icing	21.8	362	4.0	11.7	61.3	.1	1.2	77	103	7	226	73	170	.02	.08	.2	Trace
546	With chocolate icing	21.2	365	4.2	13.0	60.4	.2	1.1	68	112	.6	208	108	160	.02	.08	.2	Trace
	Frozen, commercial, devil's food:																	
547	With chocolate icing	21.0	380	4.3	17.6	55.6	.3	1.5	54	92	.8	420	119	430	.02	.08	.2	Trace
548	With whipped-cream filling, chocolate icing	29.7	371	3.5	21.9	43.8	.2	1.1	80	122	.6	190	113	270	.02	.08	2	Trace

[33] When amount of nonfat dry milk in commercial bread is unknown, values for bread with 3 to 4 percent nonfat dry milk, item 461 or item 467, are suggested. See also Notes on Foods, p. 172

[34] Value for leaves is 16,000 I U. per 100 grams; flower clusters, 3,000 I U.; stalks, 400 I U.

[35] Processed, partially debranned, whole-kernel wheat with salt added.

[36] Processed, partially debranned, whole-kernel wheat with chicken fat, chicken stock base, dehydrated onion flakes, salt, monosodium glutamate, and herbs.

[37] Values apply to salted butter. Unsalted butter contains less than 10 mg of either sodium or potassium per 100 grams. Value for vitamin A is the year-round average.

[38] For freshly harvested cabbage, average value is 51 mg. per 100 grams; for stored cabbage, 42 mg. per 100 grams.

[39] Applies to unsulfited product For sulfited product, values per 100 grams are Thiamine, 0.10 mg , ascorbic acid, 300 mg.

[40] Unenriched cake flour used unless otherwise specified Values for cakes that contain baking powder and/or fat are based on use of baking powder, item 130, and cooking fats, item 999 See also Notes on Foods, p. 173.

TABLE 1.—COMPOSITION OF FOODS, 100 GRAMS, EDIBLE PORTION—Continued

[Numbers in parentheses denote values imputed—usually from another form of the food or from a similar food. Zero in parentheses indicates that the amount of a constituent probably is none or is too small to measure. Dashes denote lack of reliable data for a constituent believed to be present in measurable amount. Calculated values, as those based on a recipe, are not in parentheses]

Item No.	Food and description	Water	Food energy	Protein	Fat	Carbohydrate Total	Carbohydrate Fiber	Ash	Calcium	Phosphorus	Iron	Sodium	Potassium	Vitamin A value	Thiamine	Riboflavin	Niacin	Ascorbic acid
(A)	(B)	(C)	(D)	(E)	(F)	(G)	(H)	(I)	(J)	(K)	(L)	(M)	(N)	(O)	(P)	(Q)	(R)	(S)
		Percent	Calories	Grams	Grams	Grams	Grams	Grams	Milligrams	Milligrams	Milligrams	Milligrams	Milligrams	International units	Milligrams	Milligrams	Milligrams	Milligrams
	Cake mixes and cakes baked from mixes:																	
	Angelfood:																	
549	Mix, dry form	1.8	385	8.4	0.2	88.5	Trace	1.1	108	125	0.4	150	112	0	0.01	0.17	0.2	0
550	Cake, made with water, flavorings	34.0	259	5.7	.2	59.4	Trace	.7	95	119	.2	146	88	0	Trace	.11	.1	0
	Chocolate malt:																	
551	Mix, dry form	3.8	412	4.0	10.7	79.0	0.2	2.5	160	270	1.0	531	119	70	.04	.08	.1	0
552	Cake, made with eggs, water, uncooked white icing	19.8	346	3.4	8.7	66.6	.1	1.5	93	160	.7	318	80	100	.03	.07	.2	Trace
	Coffeecake, with enriched flour:																	
553	Mix, dry form	3.8	431	5.9	11.0	77.2	.2	2.1	56	191	[9]2.0	613	87	Trace	[9].30	[9].11	[9]2.4	Trace
554	Cake, made with egg, milk	30.6	322	6.3	9.6	52.4	.1	1.7	61	174	[9]1.6	434	109	140	[9].18	[9].16	[9]1.4	Trace
	Cupcake:																	
555	Mix, dry form	4.9	438	3.7	13.6	75.8	.2	2.0	173	262	.4	506	46	0	.05	.06	.3	0
556	Cake, made with eggs, milk, without icing	25.6	350	4.0	12.0	55.8	.2	1.7	161	235	.5	452	84	150	.04	.11	.2	Trace
557	Cake, made with eggs, milk, chocolate icing	22.2	358	4.5	12.6	59.2	.3	1.5	130	197	.8	340	117	170	.04	.11	.2	Trace
	Devil's food:																	
558	Mix, dry form	3.5	406	4.8	11.7	77.0	.3	2.6	89	120	1.2	457	121	Trace	.05	.08	.5	Trace
559	Cake, made with eggs, water, chocolate icing	23.5	349	4.4	12.3	58.3	.3	1.4	53	105	.8	262	120	140	.03	.08	.3	Trace
	Gingerbread:																	
560	Mix, dry form	4.0	425	5.4	10.4	78.2	.1	2.0	180	200	1.4	603	418	Trace	.04	.14	.4	Trace
561	Cake, made with water	37.0	276	3.1	6.8	51.1	Trace	2.0	90	100	1.6	304	274	Trace	.03	.09	.8	Trace
	Honey spice:																	
562	Mix, dry form	3.5	443	4.3	14.0	76.3	.4	1.9	74	274	.2	573	98	Trace	.02	.08	.3	Trace
563	Cake, made with eggs, water, caramel icing	22.7	352	4.1	10.8	60.9	.2	1.5	71	163	.8	243	87	160	.02	.09	.2	Trace
	Marble:																	
564	Mix, dry form	4.0	425	4.9	13.5	75.6	.1	2.0	130	270	1.0	581	188	Trace	.03	.09	.4	Trace
565	Cake, made with eggs, water, boiled white icing	23.5	331	4.4	8.7	62.0	.1	1.3	78	171	.8	259	122	60	.02	.08	.2	Trace
	White:																	
566	Mix, dry form	3.4	434	4.1	11.9	78.4	.2	2.2	150	270	.2	573	58	Trace	.02	.07	.3	Trace
567	Cake, made with egg whites, water, chocolate icing	21.1	351	3.9	10.7	62.8	.2	1.5	90	179	.3	227	118	90	.02	.08	.2	Trace
	Yellow:																	
568	Mix, dry form	3.3	438	4.0	12.9	77.6	.1	2.2	140	270	.2	407	86	Trace	.02	.07	.3	Trace
569	Cake, made with eggs, water, chocolate icing	25.5	337	4.1	11.3	57.6	.2	1.4	93	182	.6	227	106	140	.02	.08	.2	Trace
	Cake icings:																	
570	Caramel	14.1	360	1.3	6.7	76.5	0	1.4	102	62	2.0	83	52	280	.01	.06	Trace	Trace
571	Chocolate	14.3	376	3.2	13.9	67.4	.4	.9	66	111	1.2	61	195	210	.02	.10	.2	Trace
572	Coconut	15.0	364	1.9	7.7	74.9	.8	.5	8	30	.5	118	167	0	.01	.04	.2	0
	White:																	
573	Uncooked	11.4	376	.5	6.6	81.6	0	.2	15	12	Trace	49	18	270	Trace	.02	Trace	Trace
574	Boiled	17.9	316	1.4	0	80.3	0	.4	2	2	Trace	142	18	0	Trace	.03	Trace	0
	Cake icing mixes and icings made from mixes:																	
	Chocolate fudge:																	
575	Mix, dry form	.8	409	2.5	9.8	86.4	.6	.5	18	92	1.3	95	78	Trace	.01	.06	.3	0
576	Icing, made with water, table fat	15.3	378	2.2	14.4	67.0	.5	1.1	16	66	1.0	156	65	270	.01	.04	.2	0
	Creamy fudge (contains nonfat dry milk):																	
577	Mix, dry form	3.1	386	3.2	7.9	85.1	.6	1.2	45	102	1.3	265	111	Trace	.02	.09	.2	Trace
	Icing:																	
578	Made with water	15.1	339	2.8	6.5	74.6	.5	1.0	39	89	1.1	232	97	Trace	.02	.08	.3	Trace
579	Made with water, table fat	15.1	383	2.6	15.2	65.9	.5	1.2	37	81	1.0	224	88	390	.02	.07	.3	Trace
	Candied fruits. See Apricots, Cherries, Citron, Figs, Ginger root, Grapefruit peel, Lemon peel, Orange peel, Pear, Pineapple.																	
	Candy:																	
580	Butterscotch	1.5	397	Trace	3.4	94.8	0	.3	17	6	1.4	66	2	140	0	Trace	Trace	0
	Candy corn. See Fondant, item 602.																	
	Caramels:																	
581	Plain or chocolate	7.6	399	4.0	10.2	76.6	.2	1.6	148	122	1.4	226	192	10	.03	.17	.2	Trace
582	Plain or chocolate, with nuts	7.1	428	4.5	16.3	70.5	.4	1.6	140	139	1.5	200	232	20	.11	.17	.3	Trace
583	Chocolate-flavored roll	5.6	396	2.2	8.2	82.7	.2	1.2	68	119	1.8	197	123	Trace	.02	.07	.1	Trace
	Chocolate:																	
584	Bittersweet	1.8	477	7.9	39.7	46.8	1.8	2.3	58	284	5.0	3	615	40	.03	.17	1.0	0
585	Semisweet	1.1	507	4.2	35.7	57.0	1.0	1.2	30	150	2.6	2	325	20	.01	.08	.5	0
586	Sweet	.9	528	4.4	35.1	57.9	.5	1.2	94	142	1.4	33	269	10	.02	.14	.3	Trace

	Chocolate, milk:																	
587	Plain	.9	520	7.7	32.3	56.9	.4	1.9	228	231	1.1	94	384	270	.06	.34	.3	Trace
588	With almonds	1.5	532	9.3	35.6	51.3	.7	2.0	229	272	1.6	80	442	230	.08	.41	.8	Trace
589	With peanuts	1.0	543	14.1	38.1	44.6	.9	2.0	174	294	1.4	66	487	180	.25	.26	5.0	Trace
	Chocolate-coated:																	
590	Almonds	2.0	569	12.3	43.7	39.6	1.5	2.3	203	343	2.8	59	546	Trace	.12	.53	1.7	Trace
591	Chocolate fudge	6.2	430	3.8	16.0	73.1	.2	.9	101	110	1.3	228	193	Trace	.04	.13	.2	0
592	Chocolate fudge, with nuts	6.0	452	4.9	20.8	67.3	.4	1.0	101	137	1.5	205	219	Trace	.06	.13	.2	Trace
593	Coconut center	6.6	438	2.8	17.6	72.0	.6	1.0	48	77	1.1	197	165	0	.02	.07	.2	0
594	Fondant	5.8	410	1.7	10.5	81.0	.1	.9	57	54	1.1	185	91	Trace	.03	.06	.1	Trace
595	Fudge, caramel, and peanuts	8.3	433	7.7	18.1	64.1	.4	1.7	179	186	1.4	204	301	Trace	.16	.22	1.9	Trace
596	Fudge, peanuts, and caramel	7.0	459	9.4	23.1	58.7	.7	1.7	127	192	1.1	128	222	Trace	.26	.15	3.7	Trace
597	Honeycombed hard candy, with peanut butter	1.7	463	6.6	19.5	70.6	.4	1.5	80	135	1.8	163	225	Trace	.05	.09	2.9	Trace
598	Nougat and caramel	7.7	416	4.0	13.9	72.8	.2	1.4	127	123	1.6	173	211	40	.06	.17	.2	Trace
599	Peanuts	1.0	561	16.4	41.3	39.1	1.2	2.0	116	298	1.5	60	504	Trace	.37	.18	7.4	Trace
600	Raisins	4.8	425	5.4	17.1	70.5	.6	2.1	152	174	2.5	64	603	150	.08	.21	.4	Trace
601	Vanilla creams	7.5	435	3.8	17.1	70.3	.1	1.2	128	110	.6	182	178	Trace	.05	.07	.1	Trace
602	Fondant	7.6	364	.1	2.0	89.6	Trace	.7	14	6	1.1	212	5	0	Trace	Trace	Trace	0
	Fudge:																	
603	Chocolate	8.2	400	2.7	12.2	75.0	.2	1.8	77	84	1.0	190	147	Trace	.02	.09	.2	Trace
604	Chocolate, with nuts	7.8	426	3.9	17.4	69.0	.4	1.8	79	114	1.2	171	177	Trace	.04	.09	.3	Trace
605	Vanilla	10.0	398	3.0	11.1	74.8	0	1.1	112	83	.5	208	127	Trace	.02	.13	.1	Trace
606	Vanilla, with nuts	9.4	424	4.2	16.4	68.8	.2	1.2	111	113	.8	187	114	Trace	.05	.13	.1	Trace
607	Gum drops, starch jelly pieces	11.7	347	.1	.7	87.4	0	.1	6	Trace	.5	35	5	0	0	Trace	Trace	0
608	Hard	1.4	386	0	1.1	97.2	0	.3	21	7	1.9	32	4	0	0	0	0	0
609	Jelly beans	6.3	367	Trace	.5	93.1	Trace	.1	12	4	1.1	12	1	0	0	Trace	Trace	0
610	Marshmallows	17.3	319	2.0	Trace	80.4	0	.3	18	6	1.6	39	6	0	0	Trace	Trace	0
	Mints, uncoated. See Fondant, item 602.																	
611	Peanut bars	1.5	515	17.5	32.2	47.2	1.2	1.6	44	273	1.8	10	448	0	.43	.08	9.4	0
612	Peanut brittle (no added salt or soda)	2.0	421	5.7	10.4	81.0	.5	.9	35	95	2.3	31	151	0	.16	.03	3.4	0
	Sugar-coated:																	
613	Almonds	2.3	456	7.8	18.6	70.2	.9	1.1	100	166	1.9	20	255	0	.05	.27	1.0	0
614	Chocolate discs	1.2	466	5.2	19.7	72.7	.3	1.2	135	140	1.3	72	250	100	.06	.20	.3	Trace
	Cantaloups. See Muskmelons, item 1358.																	
	Cape-gooseberries. See Groundcherries, item 1092.																	
	Capicola. See Sausage, cold cuts, and luncheon meats: item 1989.																	
615	**Carambola,** raw	90.4	35	.7	.5	8.0	.9	.4	4	17	1.5	2	192	1,200	.04	.02	.3	35
	Caribou. See Reindeer, items 1855–1858.																	
616	**Carissa** (natalplum) raw	80.8	70	.5	1.3	16.0	.9	.4	—	—	—	—	—	40	.04	.06	.2	38
617	**Carob flour** (St Johnsbread)	11.2	180	4.5	1.4	80.7	7.7	2.2	352	81	—	—	—	—	—	—	—	—
618	**Carp,** raw	77.8	115	18.0	4.2	0	0	1.1	50	253	.9	50	286	170	.01	.04	1.5	1
	Carrots:																	
619	Raw	88.2	42	1.1	.2	9.7	1.0	.8	37	36	.7	47	341	[43]11,000	.06	.05	.6	8
620	Cooked, boiled, drained	91.2	31	.9	.2	7.1	1.0	.6	33	31	.6	33	222	10,500	.05	.05	.5	6
	Canned																	
	Regular pack:																	
621	Solids and liquid	91.8	28	.6	.2	6.5	.6	.9	25	20	.7	[*] 236	120	10,000	.02	.02	.4	2
622	Drained solids	91.2	30	.8	.3	6.7	.8	1.0	30	22	.7	[*] 236	120	15,000	.02	.03	.4	2
623	Drained liquid	93.3	22	.4	0	5.5	Trace	.8	14	15	.8	[*] 236	120	Trace	.02	.02	.4	2
	Special dietary pack (low-sodium):																	
624	Solids and liquid	93.7	22	.7	.1	5.0	.6	.5	25	20	.7	39	120	10,000	.02	.02	.4	2
625	Drained solids	93.0	25	.8	.1	5.6	.8	.5	30	22	.7	39	120	15,000	.02	.03	.4	2
626	Drained liquid	95.2	16	.4	0	4.0	Trace	.4	14	15	.8	39	120	Trace	.02	.02	.4	2
627	Dehydrated	4.	341	6.6	1.3	81.1	9.3	7.0	256	234	6.0	268	1,944	100,000	.31	.30	3.0	15
	Casaba melon. See Muskmelons, item 1359.																	
628	**Cashew nuts**	5.2	561	17.2	45.7	29.3	1.4	2.6	38	373	3.8	[44]15	464	100	.43	.25	1.8	—
629	**Catfish,** freshwater, raw	78.0	103	17.6	3.1	0	0	1.3	—	—	.4	60	330	—	.04	.03	1.7	—
	Catsup. See Tomato catsup, item 2286.																	
	Cauliflower:																	
630	Raw	91.0	27	2.7	.2	5.2	1.0	.9	25	56	1.1	13	295	60	.11	.10	.7	78
631	Cooked, boiled, drained	92.8	22	2.3	.2	4.1	1.0	.6	21	42	.7	9	206	60	.09	.08	.6	55
	Frozen:																	
632	Not thawed	92.9	22	2.0	.2	4.3	.8	.6	19	42	.6	11	225	30	.06	.06	.5	56
633	Cooked, boiled, drained	94.0	18	1.9	.2	3.3	.8	.6	17	38	.5	10	207	30	.04	.05	.4	41
	Caviar, sturgeon:																	
634	Granular	46.0	262	26.9	15.0	3.3	—	8.8	276	355	11.8	2,200	180	—	—	—	—	—
635	Pressed	36.0	316	34.4	16.7	4.9	—	8.0	—	—	—	—	—	—	—	—	—	—
636	**Celeriac,** root, raw	88.4	40	1.8	.3	8.5	1.3	1.0	43	115	.6	100	300	—	.05	.06	.7	8
	Celery, all, including green and yellow varieties:																	
637	Raw	94.1	17	.9	.1	3.9	.6	1.0	39	28	.3	126	341	[45]240	.03	.03	.3	9
638	Cooked, boiled, drained	95.3	14	.8	.1	3.1	.6	.7	31	22	.2	88	239	230	.02	.03	.3	6
	Cereals, breakfast. See Corn, Oats, Rice, Wheat, also Bran, Farina																	

[*] Estimated average based on addition of salt in the amount of 0.6 percent of the finished product

[41] With unenriched flour, approximate values per 100 grams are Iron, 0.5 mg, thiamine, 0.07 mg, riboflavin, 0.06 mg; niacin, 1.0 mg.

[42] With unenriched flour, approximate values per 100 grams are Iron, 0.6 mg, thiamine, 0.05 mg, riboflavin, 0.11 mg, niacin, 0.6 mg

[43] Average for carrots marketed as fresh vegetable See also Notes on Foods, p. 175

[44] Applies to unsalted nuts For salted nuts, value is approximately 200 mg per 100 grams

[45] Average for all varieties For green varieties, value is 270 I U per 100 grams, for yellow varieties, 140 I U

TABLE 1.—COMPOSITION OF FOODS, 100 GRAMS, EDIBLE PORTION—Continued

[Numbers in parentheses denote values imputed—usually from another form of the food or from a similar food. Zero in parentheses indicates that the amount of a constituent probably is none or is too small to measure. Dashes denote lack of reliable data for a constituent believed to be present in measurable amount. Calculated values, as those based on a recipe, are not in parentheses]

Item No.	Food and description	Water	Food energy	Protein	Fat	Carbohydrate		Ash	Calcium	Phosphorus	Iron	Sodium	Potassium	Vitamin A value	Thiamine	Riboflavin	Niacin	Ascorbic acid
						Total	Fiber											
(A)	(B)	(C)	(D)	(E)	(F)	(G)	(H)	(I)	(J)	(K)	(L)	(M)	(N)	(O)	(P)	(Q)	(R)	(S)
	Cervelat. See Sausage, cold cuts, and luncheon meats: items 1980–1991.	Percent	Calories	Grams	Grams	Grams	Grams	Grams	Milligrams	Milligrams	Milligrams	Milligrams	Milligrams	International units	Milligrams	Milligrams	Milligrams	Milligrams
	Chard, Swiss:																	
639	Raw	91.1	25	2.4	0.3	4.6	0.8	1.6	88	39	3.2	147	550	6,500	0.06	0.17	0.5	32
640	Cooked, boiled, drained	93.7	18	1.8	.2	3.3	.7	1.0	73	24	1.8	86	321	5,400	.04	.11	.4	16
641	**Charlotte russe,** with ladyfingers, whipped-cream filling.	45.5	286	5.9	14.6	33.5	Trace	.5	46	91	.7	43	64	740	.05	.10	.1	Trace
642	**Chayote,** raw	91.8	28	.6	.1	7.1	.7	.4	13	26	.5	5	102	20	.03	.03	.4	19
	Cheeses, natural and processed; cheese foods; cheese spreads:																	
	Natural cheeses:																	
643	Blue or Roquefort type	40.0	368	21.5	30.5	2.0	0	6.0	315	339	(.5)	----	----	(1,240)	.03	.61	1.2	(0)
644	Brick	41.0	370	22.2	30.5	1.9	0	4.4	730	455	(.9)	----	----	(1,240)	----	.45	.1	(0)
645	Camembert (domestic)	52.2	299	17.5	24.7	1.8	0	3.8	105	184	.5	----	111	(1,010)	.04	.75	.8	(0)
646	Cheddar (domestic type, commonly called American)	37.0	398	25.0	32.2	2.1	0	3.7	750	478	1.0	700	82	(1,310)	.03	.46	.1	(0)
	Cottage (large or small curd):																	
647	Creamed	78.3	106	13.6	4.2	2.9	0	1.0	94	152	.3	229	85	(170)	.03	.25	.1	(0)
648	Uncreamed	79.0	86	17.0	.3	2.7	0	1.0	90	175	.4	290	72	(10)	.03	.28	(.1)	(0)
649	Cream	51.0	374	8.0	37.7	2.1	0	1.2	62	95	.2	250	74	(1,540)	(.02)	.24	.1	(0)
650	Limburger	45.0	345	21.2	28.0	2.2	0	3.6	590	393	.6	----	----	(1,140)	.08	.50	.2	(0)
651	Parmesan	30.0	393	36.0	26.0	2.9	0	5.1	1,140	781	.4	734	149	(1,060)	.02	.73	.2	(0)
652	Swiss (domestic)	39.0	370	27.5	28.0	1.7	0	3.8	925	563	.9	710	104	(1,140)	.01	(.40)	(.1)	(0)
	Pasteurized process cheese:																	
653	American	40.0	370	23.2	30.0	1.9	0	4.9	697	[6]771	.9	[6]1,136	80	(1,220)	.02	.41	Trace	(0)
654	Pimiento (American)	40.0	371	23.0	30.2	1.8	Trace	5.0	----	----	----	----	----	----	----	----	----	----
655	Swiss	40.0	355	26.4	26.9	1.6	0	5.1	887	[6]867	(.9)	[6]1,167	100	(1,100)	(.01)	.40	.1	(0)
656	Pasteurized process cheese food, American	43.2	323	19.8	24.0	7.1	0	5.9	570	[6]754	(.8)	----	----	(980)	(.02)	.58	.2	(0)
657	Pasteurized process cheese spread, American	48.6	288	16.0	21.4	8.2	0	5.8	565	[6]875	(.6)	[6]1,625	240	(870)	.01	.54	.1	(0)
658	**Cheese fondue,** from home recipe	54.2	265	14.8	18.3	10.0	Trace	2.7	317	294	1.2	542	155	880	.06	.34	.2	Trace
659	**Cheese souffle,** from home recipe	65.0	218	9.9	17.1	6.2	Trace	1.8	201	195	1.0	364	121	800	.05	.24	.2	Trace
660	**Cheese straws**	21.7	453	11.2	29.9	34.5	.1	2.7	239	206	.6	721	63	390	.02	.16	.3	0
661	**Cherimoya,** raw	73.5	94	1.3	.4	24.0	2.2	.8	23	40	.5	----	----	10	.10	.11	1.3	9
	Cherries:																	
	Raw:																	
662	Sour, red	83.7	58	1.2	.3	14.3	.2	.5	22	19	.4	2	191	1,000	.05	.06	.4	10
663	Sweet	80.4	70	1.3	.3	17.4	.4	.6	22	19	.4	2	191	110	.05	.06	.4	10
664	Candied	12.0	339	.5	.2	86.7	.5	.6	----	----	----	----	----	----	----	----	----	----
	Canned:																	
	Sour, red, solids and liquid:																	
665	Water pack	88.0	43	.8	.2	10.7	.1	.3	15	13	.3	2	130	680	.03	.02	.2	5
	Sirup pack:																	
666	Light	80.0	74	.8	.2	18.7	.1	.3	14	13	.3	1	126	660	.03	.02	.2	5
667	Heavy	76.0	89	.8	.2	22.7	.1	.3	14	12	.3	1	124	650	.03	.02	.2	5
668	Extra heavy	70.1	112	.8	.2	28.6	.1	.3	14	12	.3	1	121	630	.03	.02	.2	5
	Sweet, solids and liquid:																	
669	Water pack, with or without artificial sweetener	86.6	48	.9	.2	11.9	.3	.4	15	13	.3	1	130	60	.02	.02	.2	3
	Sirup pack:																	
670	Light	82.0	65	.9	.2	16.5	.3	.4	15	13	.3	1	128	60	.02	.02	.2	3
671	Heavy	78.0	81	.9	.2	20.5	.3	.4	15	13	.3	1	126	60	.02	.02	.2	3
672	Extra heavy	73.6	100	.8	.2	25.0	.3	.4	14	12	.3	1	123	50	.02	.02	.2	3
	Frozen, not thawed:																	
	Sour, red:																	
673	Unsweetened	84.9	55	1.0	.4	13.4	.3	.3	13	22	.7	2	188	1,000	.04	.07	.3	5
674	Sweetened	70.6	112	1.0	.4	27.8	.2	.2	12	15	.3	2	130	480	.03	.06	.3	6
675	**Cherries, maraschino,** bottled, solids and liquid	70.0	116	.2	.2	29.4	.3	.2	----	----	----	----	----	----	----	----	----	----
676	**Chervil,** raw	80.7	57	3.4	.9	11.5	----	3.5	----	----	----	----	----	----	----	----	----	9
	Chestnuts:																	
677	Fresh	52.5	194	2.9	1.5	42.1	1.1	1.0	27	88	1.7	6	454	----	.22	.22	.6	----
678	Dried	8.4	377	6.7	4.1	78.6	2.5	2.2	52	162	3.3	12	875	----	.32	.38	1.2	----
679	**Chestnut flour**	11.4	362	6.1	3.7	76.2	2.0	2.6	50	164	3.2	11	847	----	.23	.37	1.0	----
680	**Chewing gum**	3.5	317	----	----	95.2	----	1.3	----	----	----	----	----	(0)	(0)	(0)	(0)	(0)

	Chicken:																	
	All classes:																	
	Light meat without skin:																	
681	Raw	73.7	117	23.4	1.9	0	0	1.0	11	218	1.1	50	320	60	.05	.09	10.7	—
682	Cooked, roasted	63.8	166	31.6	3.4	0	0	1.2	11	265	1.3	64	411	60	.01	.10	11.6	—
	Dark meat without skin.																	
683	Raw	73.7	130	20.6	4.7	0	0	1.0	13	188	1.5	67	250	150	.08	.20	5.2	—
684	Cooked, roasted	64.4	176	28.0	6.3	0	0	1.2	13	229	1.7	86	321	150	.07	.23	5.6	—
685	**Broilers,** flesh only, cooked, broiled	71.0	136	23.8	3.8	0	0	1.1	9	201	1.7	66	274	90	.05	.19	8.8	—
	Fryers (weight, ready to cook, with giblets, more than 1¾ lbs.)																	
	Flesh, skin, and giblets:																	
686	Raw	75.7	124	18.6	4.9	0	0	.8	12	201	1.9	—	—	730	.07	.38	5.6	—
687	Cooked, fried	53.3	249	30.7	11.8	2.9	—	1.3	13	254	2.3	—	—	820	.07	.57	9.1	—
	Flesh and skin.																	
688	Raw	75.4	126	18.8	5.1	0	0	.7	11	198	1.5	—	—	170	.05	.23	5.6	—
689	Cooked, fried	53.5	250	30.6	11.9	2.8	—	1.2	12	243	1.8	—	—	170	.06	.36	9.2	—
	Flesh only																	
690	Raw	77.2	107	19.3	2.7	0	0	.8	12	203	1.3	58	285	90	.06	.25	6.4	—
691	Cooked, fried	58.6	209	31.2	7.8	1.2	—	1.2	13	257	1.6	78	381	90	.06	.35	9.7	—
	Skin only:																	
692	Raw	66.3	223	16.1	17.1	0	0	.5	9	174	2.4	—	—	550	.03	.13	2.0	—
693	Cooked, fried	32.5	419	28.3	28.9	9.1	—	1.2	8	186	2.4	—	—	490	.07	.41	7.0	—
	Giblets:																	
694	Raw	78.4	103	17.5	3.1	.1	0	.9	14	220	4.5	—	—	4,530	.16	1.36	4.9	—
695	Cooked, fried	51.7	252	30.8	11.2	4.7	—	1.6	18	336	6.5	—	—	5,760	.17	2.18	8.0	—
	Light meat with skin:																	
696	Raw	75.4	120	19.9	3.9	0	0	.8	11	211	1.3	—	—	130	.05	.16	6.7	—
697	Cooked, fried	55.0	234	31.5	9.9	2.4	—	1.2	11	260	1.5	—	—	130	.05	.27	11.9	—
	Dark meat with skin:																	
698	Raw	75.3	132	17.7	6.3	0	0	.7	12	185	1.7	—	—	200	.06	.30	4.7	—
699	Cooked, fried	52.1	263	29.9	13.6	3.1	—	1.3	12	228	2.0	—	—	210	.07	.45	6.7	—
	Light meat without skin:																	
700	Raw	77.2	101	20.5	1.5	0	0	.8	11	218	1.1	50	320	50	.05	.17	7.6	—
701	Cooked, fried	59.5	197	32.1	6.1	1.1	—	1.2	12	280	1.3	68	434	50	.05	.25	12.9	—
	Dark meat without skin:																	
702	Raw	77.3	112	18.1	3.8	0	0	.8	13	188	1.5	67	250	120	.06	.34	5.3	—
703	Cooked, fried	57.5	220	30.4	9.3	1.5	—	1.3	14	235	1.8	88	330	130	.07	.45	6.8	—
	Cut-up parts:																	
	Back:																	
704	Raw	73.3	157	16.5	9.6	0	0	.6	12	185	1.7	—	—	310	.05	.23	4.3	—
705	Cooked, fried	40.5	347	30.0	21.2	6.8	0	1.5	15	262	2.7	—	—	390	.07	.50	6.8	—
	Breast:																	
706	Raw	76.0	110	20.8	2.4	0	0	.8	11	214	1.2	—	—	80	.05	.16	7.9	—
707	Cooked, fried	58.4	203	32.5	6.4	1.5	—	1.2	12	276	1.7	—	—	90	.05	.22	14.7	—
	Drumstick:																	
708	Raw	76.5	115	18.8	3.9	0	0	.8	13	186	1.6	—	—	120	.06	.32	4.3	—
709	Cooked, fried	55.0	235	32.6	10.2	1.0	—	1.2	15	236	2.3	—	—	140	.07	.40	7.1	—
	Neck:																	
710	Raw	74.5	151	15.5	9.4	0	0	.6	11	182	1.9	—	—	310	.05	.25	3.0	—
711	Cooked, fried	50.2	289	26.7	17.4	4.5	—	1.2	12	234	2.7	—	—	350	.09	.41	5.7	—
	Rib:																	
712	Raw	76.2	124	17.7	5.4	0	0	.7	11	212	1.3	—	—	170	.04	.18	5.1	—
713	Cooked, fried	45.7	298	31.5	15.4	5.9	—	1.5	13	291	2.0	—	—	210	.05	.47	9.4	—
	Thigh:																	
714	Raw	75.5	128	18.1	5.6	0	0	.8	12	186	1.6	—	—	180	.06	.33	5.7	—
715	Cooked, fried	55.8	237	29.1	11.4	2.5	—	1.2	13	236	2.3	—	—	200	.06	.48	6.8	—
	Wing:																	
716	Raw	73.5	146	18.5	7.4	0	0	.6	10	203	1.5	—	—	240	.04	.14	4.1	—
717	Cooked, fried	52.6	268	29.0	14.8	2.7	—	.9	10	236	2.0	—	—	250	.05	.26	6.8	—
	Roasters:																	
	Total edible:																	
718	Raw	63.0	239	18.2	17.9	0	0	.9	10	176	1.6	—	—	920	.08	.19	6.7	—
719	Cooked, roasted	53.5	290	25.2	20.2	0	0	1.1	10	220	1.9	—	—	960	.07	.22	7.4	—
	Flesh, skin, and giblets:																	
720	Raw	67.5	191	19.6	11.9	0	0	1.0	12	194	1.7	—	—	760	.08	.21	7.3	—
721	Cooked, roasted	57.5	242	27.2	14.0	0	0	1.3	12	242	2.0	—	—	790	.08	.25	8.1	—
	Flesh and skin:																	
722	Raw	66.9	197	19.5	12.6	0	0	1.0	11	191	1.5	—	—	410	.08	.12	7.4	—
723	Cooked, roasted	57.0	248	27.1	14.7	0	0	1.3	11	239	1.8	—	—	420	.08	.14	8.2	—
	Flesh only:																	
724	Raw	73.3	131	21.1	4.5	0	0	1.1	12	203	1.3	58	285	150	.10	.12	7.7	—
725	Cooked, roasted	62.8	183	29.5	6.3	0	0	1.4	12	254	1.5	77	376	150	.10	.15	8.5	—

[a] Values for phosphorus and sodium are based on use of 1.5 percent anhydrous disodium phosphate as the emulsifying agent. If emulsifying agent does not contain either phosphorus or sodium, the content of these two nutrients in milligrams per 100 grams is as follows

	P	Na
Item 653, American process cheese	444	650
Item 655, Swiss process cheese	540	681
Item 656, American cheese food	427	—
Item 657, American cheese spread	548	1,139

TABLE 1.—COMPOSITION OF FOODS, 100 GRAMS, EDIBLE PORTION—Continued

[Numbers in parentheses denote values imputed—usually from another form of the food or from a similar food. Zero in parentheses indicates that the amount of a constituent probably is none or is too small to measure. Dashes denote lack of reliable data for a constituent believed to be present in measurable amount. Calculated values, as those based on a recipe, are not in parentheses]

Item No.	Food and description	Water	Food energy	Protein	Fat	Carbohydrate: Total	Carbohydrate: Fiber	Ash	Calcium	Phosphorus	Iron	Sodium	Potassium	Vitamin A value	Thiamine	Riboflavin	Niacin	Ascorbic acid
(A)	(B)	(C)	(D)	(E)	(F)	(G)	(H)	(I)	(J)	(K)	(L)	(M)	(N)	(O)	(P)	(Q)	(R)	(S)
		Percent	Calories	Grams	Grams	Grams	Grams	Grams	Milligrams	Milligrams	Milligrams	Milligrams	Milligrams	International units	Milligrams	Milligrams	Milligrams	Milligrams
	Chicken—Continued																	
	Roasters—Continued																	
	Giblets:																	
726	Raw	72.4	125	18.8	4.8	1.7	0	1.3	15	218	4.4	—	—	4,290	0.09	1.07	6.7	6
	Light meat without skin:																	
727	Raw	72.3	128	23.3	3.9	0	0	1.2	11	218	1.1	60	330	100	.08	.08	10.6	—
728	Cooked, roasted	61.3	182	32.3	4.9	0	0	1.5	11	272	1.3	66	411	110	.08	.10	11.8	—
	Dark meat without skin:																	
729	Raw	73.2	132	21.0	4.7	0	0	1.1	13	188	1.5	67	250	150	.13	.16	4.7	—
730	Cooked, roasted	62.7	184	29.3	6.5	0	0	1.4	14	235	1.8	86	330	160	.12	.19	5.3	—
	Hens and cocks:																	
	Total edible:																	
731	Raw	56.0	298	17.4	24.8	0	0	.9	10	167	1.4	—	—	1,080	.06	.10	8.2	—
732	Cooked, stewed	45.9	369	24.0	29.5	0	0	.7	10	123	1.6	—	—	1,150	.04	.21	7.8	—
	Flesh, skin, and giblets:																	
733	Raw	61.7	246	19.0	18.3	0	0	1.0	11	185	1.5	—	—	990	.07	.20	9.1	—
734	Cooked, stewed	50.6	312	26.2	22.2	0	0	.8	11	156	1.8	—	—	990	.04	.23	8.6	—
	Flesh and skin:																	
735	Raw	61.3	251	19.0	18.8	0	0	.9	11	187	1.3	—	—	610	.06	.13	9.2	—
736	Cooked, stewed	50.4	317	26.1	22.8	0	0	.7	11	134	1.5	—	—	670	.04	.14	8.8	—
	Flesh only:																	
737	Raw	70.5	155	21.6	7.0	0	0	1.0	12	203	1.3	58	285	230	.08	.14	10.1	—
738	Cooked, stewed	60.4	208	30.0	8.9	0	0	.8	12	149	1.5	55	272	250	.04	.15	8.6	—
	Giblets:																	
739	Raw	66.8	191	18.6	11.6	1.6	0	1.2	15	214	4.4	—	—	4,300	.09	1.09	6.7	6
	Light meat without skin:																	
740	Raw	71.7	133	23.4	3.7	0	0	1.2	11	218	1.1	50	320	120	.05	.09	11.5	—
741	Cooked, stewed	62.1	180	32.2	4.7	0	0	.9	11	160	1.3	48	306	130	.03	.09	11.0	—
	Dark meat without skin:																	
742	Raw	71.2	154	20.2	7.5	0	0	1.1	13	188	1.5	67	250	240	.10	.18	8.2	—
743	Cooked, stewed	61.1	207	28.3	9.5	0	0	.9	13	188	1.8	64	250	270	.06	.20	8.5	—
	Capons:																	
	Total edible:																	
744	Raw	56.2	284	21.4	21.2	0	0	1.2	—	—	—	—	—	—	—	—	—	—
	Flesh and skin:																	
745	Raw	55.2	291	21.6	22.0	0	0	1.2	—	—	—	—	—	—	—	—	—	—
	Giblets:																	
746	Raw	63.3	220	20.4	14.6	.4	0	1.3	—	—	—	—	—	—	—	—	—	—
747	**Chicken, canned,** meat only, boned	65.2	198	21.7	11.7	0	0	1.4	21	247	1.5	—	138	230	.04	.12	4.4	4
	Chicken, potted. See Sausage, cold cuts, and luncheon meats: item 2008.																	
748	**Chicken a la king,** cooked, from home recipe	68.2	191	11.2	14.0	5.0	Trace	1.6	52	146	1.0	310	164	460	.04	.17	2.2	5
749	**Chicken fricassee,** cooked, from home recipe	71.3	161	15.3	9.3	3.2	Trace	.9	6	113	.9	154	140	70	.02	.07	3.4	0
	Chicken potpie:																	
750	Home-prepared, baked	56.6	235	10.1	13.5	18.3	.4	1.5	30	100	1.3	256	148	1,530	.11	.11	1.8	2
751	Commercial, frozen, unheated	57.8	219	6.7	11.5	22.2	.4	1.8	11	50	1.0	411	153	910	.10	.14	1.4	4
752	**Chicken and noodles,** cooked, from home recipe	71.1	153	9.3	7.7	10.7	Trace	1.2	11	103	.9	250	62	180	.02	.07	1.8	Trace
753	**Chickpeas** or garbanzos, mature seeds, dry, raw	10.7	360	20.5	4.8	61.0	5.0	3.0	150	331	6.9	26	797	50	.31	.15	2.0	—
754	**Chicory, Witloof** (also called French or Belgian endive), bleached head (forced), raw.[a]	95.1	15	1.0	.1	3.2	—	.6	18	21	.5	7	182	Trace	—	—	—	—
755	**Chicory greens,** raw	92.8	20	1.8	.3	3.8	.8	1.3	86	40	.9	—	420	4,000	.06	.10	.5	22
	Chili con carne, canned:																	
756	With beans	72.4	133	7.5	6.1	12.2	.6	1.8	32	126	1.7	531	233	60	.03	.07	1.3	—
757	Without beans [a]	66.9	200	10.3	14.8	5.8	.2	2.2	38	152	1.4	—	—	150	.02	.12	2.2	—
	Chili powder. See Peppers, item 1544.																	
	Chili sauce. See Peppers, items 1539, 1542, and Tomatoes, item 2287.																	
758	**Chives,** raw	91.3	28	1.8	.3	5.8	1.1	.8	69	44	1.7	—	250	5,800	.08	.13	.5	56
	Chocolate:																	
759	Bitter or baking [a]	2.3	505	10.7	53.0	28.9	2.5	3.1	78	384	6.7	4	830	60	.05	.24	1.5	0
	Bittersweet. See Candy, item 584.																	
	Chocolate sirup:																	
760	Thin type	31.6	245	2.3	2.0	62.7	.6	1.0	17	92	1.6	52	282	Trace	.02	.07	.4	0
761	Fudge type	25.4	330	5.1	13.7	54.0	.4	1.4	127	159	1.3	89	284	150	.04	.22	.4	Trace

	Chop suey, with meat:																	
762	Cooked, from home recipe	75.4	120	10.4	6.8	5.1	.5	2.3	24	99	1.9	421	170	240	.11	.15	2.0	13
763	Canned	85.5	62	4.4	3.2	4.2	.8	2.7	35	116	1.9	551	138	30	.05	.05	.7	2
	Chow mein, chicken (without noodles):																	
764	Cooked, from home recipe	78.0	102	12.4	4.0	4.0	.3	1.6	23	117	1.0	287	189	110	.03	.09	1.7	4
765	Canned	88.8	38	2.6	.1	7.1	.3	1.4	18	34	.5	290	167	60	.02	.04	.4	5
766	**Chub, raw**	74.9	145	15.3	8.8	0	0	1.0	—	—	—	—	—	—	—	—	—	—
	Cider. See Apple juice, item 27.																	
	Cisco. See Lake herring, item 1168.																	
767	**Citron, candied**	18.0	314	.2	.3	80.2	1.4	1.3	83	24	.8	290	120	—	—	—	—	—
	Clams, raw:																	
	Soft:																	
768	Meat and liquid	85.8	54	8.6	1.0	2.0	—	2.6	—	208	—	—	—	—	—	—	—	—
769	Meat only	80.8	82	14.0	1.9	1.3	—	2.0	—	183	3.4	36	235	—	—	—	—	—
	Hard or round:																	
770	Meat and liquid	86.2	49	6.5	.4	4.2	—	2.7	—	175	—	—	—	—	—	.13	—	—
771	Meat only	79.8	80	11.1	.9	5.9	—	2.3	69	151	7.5	205	311	—	—	—	—	—
	Hard, soft, and unspecified:																	
772	Meat and liquid	85.9	53	8.1	.9	2.5	—	2.6	—	197	—	—	—	—	—	—	—	—
773	Meat only	81.7	76	12.6	1.6	2.0	—	2.1	69	162	6.1	120	181	100	.10	.18	1.3	10
	Clams, canned, including hard, soft, razor, and unspecified:																	
774	Solids and liquid	86.3	52	7.9	.7	2.8	—	2.3	55	137	4.1	—	140	—	.01	.11	1.0	—
775	Drained solids	77.0	98	15.8	2.5	1.9	—	2.8	—	—	—	—	—	—	—	—	—	—
776	Liquor, bouillon, or nectar	93.6	19	2.3	.1	2.1	0	1.9	—	—	—	—	—	—	—	—	—	—
777	**Clam fritters** [50]	40.3	311	11.4	15.0	30.9	—	2.4	76	195	3.5	—	147	—	.03	.12	.9	—
	Cocoa and chocolate-flavored beverage powders:																	
778	Cocoa powder with nonfat dry milk	1.9	359	18.6	2.9	70.8	.5	5.4	589	545	1.8	525	800	20	.13	.73	.7	3
779	Cocoa powder without milk	1.3	347	4.0	2.0	89.4	1.0	2.5	30	171	2.1	268	500	—	.02	.09	.5	0
780	Mix for hot chocolate [51]	3.1	392	9.4	10.6	73.9	.8	2.6	275	290	1.4	382	605	10	.08	.41	.5	1
	Cocoa, dry powder: [49]																	
	High-fat or breakfast:																	
781	Plain	3.0	299	16.8	23.7	48.3	4.3	5.0	133	648	10.7	6	1,522	30	.11	.46	2.4	0
782	Processed with alkali	3.0	295	16.8	23.7	45.4	4.3	8.2	133	648	10.7	717	651	30	.11	.46	2.4	0
	Medium-fat:																	
	High-medium fat:																	
783	Plain	4.1	265	17.3	19.0	51.5	4.3	4.9	123	649	10.7	6	1,522	20	.11	.46	2.4	0
784	Processed with alkali	4.1	261	17.3	19.0	48.5	4.3	7.9	123	649	10.7	717	651	20	.11	.46	2.4	0
	Low-medium fat:																	
785	Plain	5.2	220	19.2	12.7	53.8	5.2	5.5	152	686	10.7	6	1,522	20	.11	.46	2.4	0
786	Processed with alkali	5.2	215	19.2	12.7	50.2	5.2	9.1	152	686	10.7	717	651	20	.11	.46	2.4	0
787	Low-fat	4.4	187	20.2	7.3	58.0	5.8	5.7	153	752	10.7	6	1,522	10	.11	.46	2.4	0
788	**Coconut cream** (liquid expressed from grated coconut meat).	54.1	334	4.4	32.2	8.3	—	1.0	15	126	1.8	4	324	0	.02	.01	.5	1
	Coconut meat:																	
789	Fresh	50.9	346	3.5	35.3	9.4	4.0	.9	13	95	1.7	23	256	0	.05	.02	.5	3
	Dried:																	
790	Unsweetened	3.5	662	7.2	64.9	23.0	3.9	1.4	26	187	3.3	—	588	0	.06	.04	.6	0
791	Sweetened, shredded	3.3	548	3.6	39.1	53.2	4.1	.8	16	112	2.0	—	353	0	.04	.03	.4	0
792	**Coconut milk** (liquid expressed from mixture of grated coconut meat and water).	65.7	252	3.2	24.9	5.2	—	1.0	16	100	1.6	—	—	0	.03	Trace	.8	2
793	**Coconut water** (liquid from coconuts)	94.2	22	.3	.2	4.7	Trace	.6	20	13	.3	25	147	0	Trace	Trace	.1	2
	Cod:																	
794	Raw	81.2	78	17.6	.3	0	0	1.2	10	194	.4	[52] 70	382	0	.06	.07	2.2	2
795	Cooked, broiled	64.6	170	28.5	5.3	0	0	—	31	274	1.0	110	407	180	.08	.11	3.0	—
796	Canned	78.6	85	19.2	.3	0	0	1.0	—	—	—	—	—	—	—	.08	—	—
797	Dehydrated, lightly salted	12.3	375	81.8	2.8	0	0	7.0	—	891	3.6	8,100	160	0	.08	.45	10.9	—
798	Dried, salted	52.4	130	29.0	.7	0	0	19.7	225	—	—	—	—	—	—	—	—	—
	Codfish cakes. See Fishcakes, items 1010–1011.																	
	Coffee, instant, water-soluble solids. [49] [53]																	
799	Dry powder	2.6	129	Trace	Trace	(35)	Trace	9.7	179	383	5.6	72	3,256	0	0	.21	30.6	0
800	Beverage	98.1	1	Trace	Trace	Trace	Trace	.1	2	4	.1	1	36	0	0	Trace	.3	0
	Cola or coke. See Beverages, item 404.																	
	Coleslaw, [54] made with—																	
801	French dressing (homemade)	80.6	129	1.1	12.3	5.1	.7	.9	42	25	.4	131	197	110	.04	.04	.3	29
802	French dressing (commercial)	82.6	95	1.2	7.3	7.6	.7	1.3	42	26	.4	268	205	110	.04	.04	.3	29
803	Mayonnaise	79.0	144	1.3	14.0	4.8	.7	.9	44	29	.4	120	199	160	.05	.05	.3	29
804	Salad dressing (mayonnaise type)	82.9	99	1.2	7.9	7.1	.7	.9	43	28	.4	124	192	150	.05	.05	.3	29

[47] For further description of product, see Notes on Foods, p. 178

[48] Contains not less than 60 percent meat, not more than 8 percent cereals, seasonings.

[49] See Appendix A, section on Protein, p. 162, and see Appendix B, section on Foods containing considerable nonprotein nitrogen, p. 182.

[50] Prepared with flour, baking powder, butter, egg.

[51] Values apply to products without added vitamins and minerals

[52] Value is about 255 mg per 100 grams if cod has been dipped or rinsed in brine.

[53] Contains 3,000 to 4,000 mg caffeine per 100 grams of powder and 35 to 45 mg per 100 grams of beverage made with 2.5 grams, or 1 rounded teaspoon of instant coffee per 8 fluid oz of beverage.

[54] Values are for product immediately after preparation. Values for energy and fat are reduced if dressing drains from slaw and is not served

TABLE 1.—COMPOSITION OF FOODS, 100 GRAMS, EDIBLE PORTION—Continued

[Numbers in parentheses denote values imputed—usually from another form of the food or from a similar food. Zero in parentheses indicates that the amount of a constituent probably is none or is too small to measure. Dashes denote lack of reliable data for a constituent believed to be present in measurable amount. Calculated values, as those based on a recipe, are not in parentheses]

Item No.	Food and description	Water	Food energy	Protein	Fat	Carbohydrate: Total	Carbohydrate: Fiber	Ash	Calcium	Phosphorus	Iron	Sodium	Potassium	Vitamin A value	Thiamine	Riboflavin	Niacin	Ascorbic acid
(A)	(B)	(C)	(D)	(E)	(F)	(G)	(H)	(I)	(J)	(K)	(L)	(M)	(N)	(O)	(P)	(Q)	(R)	(S)
		Percent	Calories	Grams	Grams	Grams	Grams	Grams	Milligrams	Milligrams	Milligrams	Milligrams	Milligrams	International units	Milligrams	Milligrams	Milligrams	Milligrams
	Collards:																	
	Raw:																	
805	Leaves, without stems	85.3	45	4.8	0.8	7.5	1.2	1.6	250	82	1.5	—	450	9,300	0.16	0.31	1.7	152
806	Leaves, including stems	86.9	40	3.6	.7	7.2	.9	1.6	203	63	1.0	43	401	6,500	.20	(.31)	(1.7)	92
	Cooked, boiled, drained:																	
	Leaves without stems, cooked in—																	
807	Small amount of water	89.6	33	3.6	.7	5.1	1.0	1.0	188	52	.8	—	262	7,800	.11	.20	1.2	76
808	Large amount of water	90.2	31	3.4	.7	4.8	1.0	.9	177	48	.8	—	243	7,800	.07	.14	1.1	51
	Leaves, including stems, cooked in—																	
809	Small amount of water	90.8	29	2.7	.6	4.9	.8	1.0	152	39	.6	25	234	5,400	.14	.20	1.2	46
	Frozen:																	
810	Not thawed	89.7	32	3.1	.4	5.8	1.0	1.0	191	53	1.1	18	259	6,800	.07	.16	.7	68
811	Cooked, boiled, drained	90.2	30	2.9	.4	5.6	1.0	.9	176	51	1.0	16	236	6,800	.06	.14	.6	33
	Cookies:[illegible]																	
812	Assorted, packaged, commercial	2.6	480	5.1	20.2	71.0	.1	1.1	37	163	.7	365	67	80	.03	.05	.4	Trace
	Brownies with nuts:																	
813	Baked from home recipe, enriched flour	9.8	485	6.5	31.3	50.9	.7	1.5	41	148	1.9	251	190	200	.19	.12	.7	Trace
814	Frozen, with chocolate icing, commercial	12.5	419	4.9	20.6	60.7	.6	1.3	40	125	[8]1.6	200	179	220	[8].09	[8].08	[8].3	Trace
815	Butter, thin, rich	4.5	457	6.1	16.9	70.9	.1	1.6	126	94	.5	418	60	650	.03	.06	.4	0
816	Chocolate	4.0	445	7.1	15.7	71.5	.3	1.7	32	127	1.1	137	128	160	.04	.08	.5	Trace
	Chocolate chip:																	
817	Baked from home recipe, enriched flour	3.0	516	5.4	30.1	60.1	.4	1.4	34	99	2.1	348	117	110	.11	.11	.9	Trace
818	Commercial type	2.7	471	5.4	21.0	69.7	.4	1.2	39	111	1.8	401	134	120	.04	.07	.4	Trace
819	Coconut bars	3.8	494	6.2	24.5	63.9	.6	1.6	72	120	1.4	148	228	160	.04	.06	.4	0
820	Fig bars	13.6	358	3.9	5.6	75.4	1.7	1.5	78	60	1.0	252	198	110	.04	.07	.3	Trace
821	Gingersnaps	3.1	420	5.5	8.9	79.8	.1	2.7	73	47	2.3	571	462	70	.04	.06	.4	Trace
822	Ladyfingers	19.2	360	7.8	7.8	64.5	.1	.7	41	164	1.5	71	71	630	.06	.14	.2	0
823	Macaroons	4.4	475	5.3	23.2	66.1	2.1	1.0	27	84	.6	34	463	0	.04	.15	.6	0
824	Marshmallow	9.8	409	4.0	13.2	72.3	.3	.7	21	57	.5	209	91	260	.02	.06	.2	Trace
825	Molasses	4.0	422	6.4	10.6	76.0	.1	3.0	51	83	2.1	386	138	80	.04	.06	.7	0
826	Oatmeal with raisins	2.8	451	6.2	15.4	73.5	.4	2.1	21	102	2.3	162	370	50	.11	.08	.5	Trace
827	Peanut	2.3	473	10.0	19.1	67.0	.8	1.6	42	118	1.0	173	175	260	.07	.09	2.8	Trace
828	Raisin	8.2	379	4.4	5.3	80.8	.9	1.3	71	157	2.1	52	272	210	.04	.08	.6	Trace
829	Sandwich type	2.2	495	4.8	22.5	69.3	.1	1.2	26	241	.7	483	38	0	.03	.04	.5	0
830	Shortbread	3.0	498	7.2	23.1	65.1	.2	1.6	70	150	.5	60	66	80	.04	.05	.5	0
831	Sugar, soft, thick, with enriched flour, home recipe	7.9	444	6.0	16.8	68.0	.1	1.3	78	103	1.4	318	76	110	.16	.16	1.3	Trace
832	Sugar wafers	1.4	485	4.9	19.4	73.4	.1	.6	35	89	.3	189	60	130	.01	.04	.5	0
833	Vanilla wafers	2.8	462	5.4	16.1	74.4	.1	1.2	41	63	.4	252	72	130	.02	.07	.3	0
	Cooky mixes and cookies baked from mixes:																	
	Brownie, with enriched flour:																	
	Complete mix:																	
834	Dry form	3.9	419	4.8	12.0	78.7	.5	1.5	21	105	1.2	290	163	90	.10	.11	.9	0
835	Brownies, made with water, nuts	15.3	403	4.9	18.7	59.8	.7	1.3	26	117	1.2	218	180	80	.16	.09	.7	Trace
	Incomplete mix:																	
836	Dry form	2.5	442	4.0	16.4	76.0	.5	1.1	42	118	1.8	194	149	Trace	.09	.09	.5	0
837	Brownies, made with egg, water, nuts	10.7	428	5.0	20.1	63.1	.6	1.1	45	137	1.9	166	168	100	.13	.10	.7	Trace
	Plain, with unenriched flour:																	
838	Mix, dry form	4.2	494	3.5	24.2	66.8	.1	1.3	86	147	.3	352	29	0	.02	.02	.3	0
839	Cookies, made with egg, water	4.5	493	4.8	24.3	65.0	.1	1.4	88	163	.5	347	42	120	.02	.05	.3	0
840	Cookies, made with milk	4.4	490	3.7	23.8	66.7	.1	1.4	95	151	.3	345	42	10	.02	.03	.3	Trace
	Cooky dough, plain, chilled in roll:																	
841	Unbaked	13.6	449	3.5	22.6	58.8	.1	1.5	33	66	.3	490	44	70	.02	.03	.2	0
842	Baked	4.5	496	3.9	25.0	64.9	.1	1.7	36	73	.3	548	48	70	.02	.03	.2	0
	Cooking oil. See Oils, item 1401.																	
843	**Corn, field,** whole-grain, raw	13.8	348	8.9	3.9	72.2	2.0	1.2	22	268	2.1	1	284	[illegible]490	.37	.12	2.2	(0)
	Corn, sweet:																	
844	Raw, white and yellow	72.7	96	3.5	1.0	22.1	.7	.7	3	111	.7	Trace	280	[illegible]400	.15	.12	1.7	12
	Cooked, boiled, drained, white and yellow:																	
845	Kernels, cut off cob before cooking	76.5	83	3.2	1.0	18.8	.7	.5	3	89	.6	Trace	165	[illegible]400	.11	.10	1.3	7

No.	Food																	
846	Kernels, cooked on cob	74.1	91	3.3	1.0	21.0	.7	.6	3	89	.6	Trace	196	[57] 400	.12	.10	1.4	9
	Canned:																	
	Regular pack:																	
	Cream style, white and yellow:																	
847	Solids and liquid	76.3	82	2.1	.6	20.0	.5	1.0	3	56	.6	[*] 236	(97)	[57] 330	.03	.05	1.0	5
	Whole kernel:																	
	Vacuum pack, yellow:																	
848	Solids and liquid	75.5	83	2.5	.5	20.5	.8	1.0	3	73	.5	[*] 236	(97)	350	(.03)	(.06)	(1.1)	5
	Wet pack, white and yellow:																	
849	Solids and liquid	80.9	66	1.9	.6	15.7	.6	.9	4	48	.4	[*] 236	97	[57] 270	.03	.05	.9	5
850	Drained solids	75.9	84	2.6	.8	19.8	.8	.9	5	49	.5	[*] 236	97	[57] 350	.03	.05	.9	4
851	Drained liquid	91.7	26	.5	Trace	6.9	Trace	.9	3	45	.3	[*] 236	97	Trace	.03	.04	.9	7
	Special dietary pack (low-sodium):																	
	Cream style, white and yellow:																	
852	Solids and liquid	77.3	82	2.6	1.1	18.5	.3	.5	3	56	.6	2	(97)	[57] 270	.03	.05	1.0	5
	Whole kernel, wet pack, white and yellow:																	
853	Solids and liquid	83.6	57	1.9	.5	13.6	.5	.4	4	48	.4	2	97	[57] 270	.03	.05	.9	5
854	Drained solids	78.4	76	2.5	.7	18.0	.7	.4	5	49	.5	2	97	[57] 350	.03	.05	.9	4
855	Drained liquid	94.8	17	.5	Trace	4.3	Trace	.4	3	45	.3	2	97	Trace	.03	.04	.9	7
	Frozen:																	
	Kernels, cut off cob:																	
856	Not thawed	76.2	82	3.1	.5	19.7	.5	.5	3	78	.8	1	202	[57](350)	.11	.07	1.6	8
857	Cooked, boiled, drained	77.2	79	3.0	.5	18.8	.5	.5	3	73	.8	1	184	[57](350)	.09	.06	1.5	5
	Kernels, on cob:																	
858	Not thawed	72.1	98	3.6	1.0	22.6	.7	.7	3	102	.8	1	254	[57](350)	.17	.09	1.9	10
859	Cooked, boiled, drained	73.2	94	3.5	1.0	21.6	.7	.7	3	96	.8	1	231	[57](350)	.14	.08	1.7	7
860	**Corn flour**	12.	368	7.8	2.6	76.8	.7	.8	6	(164)	1.8	(1)	—	[57] 340	.20	.06	1.4	(0)
861	**Corn fritters**	29.1	377	7.8	21.5	39.7	.5	1.9	64	155	1.7	477	133	[58] 400	.16	.20	1.6	2
	Corn grits, degermed:																	
	Enriched:																	
862	Dry form	12.	362	8.7	.8	78.1	.4	.4	4	73	[59] 2.9	1	80	[57] 440	[59] .44	[59] .26	[59] 3.5	(0)
863	Cooked	87.1	51	1.2	.1	11.0	.1	.6	1	10	[59] .3	205	11	[57] 60	[59] .04	[59] .03	[59] .4	(0)
	Unenriched:																	
864	Dry form	12.	362	8.7	.8	78.1	.4	.4	4	73	1.0	1	80	[57] 440	.13	.04	1.2	(0)
865	Cooked	87.1	51	1.2	.1	11.0	.1	.6	1	10	.1	205	11	[57] 60	.02	.01	.2	(0)
	Corn muffins. See Muffins, corn: items 1347–1348.																	
	Corn oil. See Oils, item 1401.																	
	Corn products used mainly as ready-to-eat breakfast cereals:																	
	Corn flakes:																	
866	Added nutrients	3.8	386	7.9	.4	85.3	.7	2.6	17	45	1.4	1,005	120	(0)	.43	.08	2.1	(0)
867	Added nutrients, sugar-covered	2.2	386	4.4	.2	91.3	.4	1.9	12	24	1.0	775	—	(0)	.41	.04	1.9	(0)
	Corn, puffed:																	
868	Added nutrients	3.6	399	8.1	4.2	80.8	.4	3.3	20	90	5.8	1,060	—	(0)	.88	.18	2.7	(0)
	Presweetened:																	
869	Added nutrients	5.0	379	4.0	.2	89.8	.3	1.0	11	28	1.8	300	—	(0)	.42	.17	2.1	(0)
870	Cocoa-flavored, added nutrients	2.1	390	6.2	2.2	86.7	.5	2.8	20	90	6.0	850	—	(0)	.79	.18	2.5	(0)
871	Fruit-flavored, added nutrients	2.1	395	5.6	2.7	87.4	.3	2.2	30	70	5.0	600	—	(0)	.99	.17	2.5	106
872	Corn, shredded, added nutrients	3.0	389	7.0	.4	86.9	.6	2.7	5	39	2.4	988	—	(0)	.42	.18	2.1	(0)
873	Corn, rice, and wheat flakes, mixed, added nutrients	2.8	389	7.4	.7	86.1	1.2	3.0	39	120	1.8	950	—	(0)	.39	—	3.2	(0)
874	Corn, flaked, with protein concentrate (casein) and other added nutrients.	3.6	378	23.0	1.6	67.0	.2	4.8	310	330	17.9	1,100	—	(0)	1.65	1.96	14.2	35
875	**Corn pudding**	76.7	104	4.0	4.7	13.0	.5	1.6	66	84	.5	436	169	260	.03	.13	.4	2
	Corn sirup. See Sirup, table blends: item 2051.																	
	Cornbread, baked from home recipes:																	
	Cornbread, southern style, made with—																	
876	Whole-ground cornmeal	53.9	207	7.4	7.2	29.1	.5	2.4	120	211	1.1	628	157	[60] 150	.13	.19	.6	1
877	Degermed cornmeal, enriched	50.2	224	7.1	6.0	34.7	.2	2.0	109	156	[61] 1.4	591	157	[60] 150	[61] .17	[61] .24	[61] 1.1	1
878	Johnnycake (northern style cornbread), made with enriched, yellow degermed cornmeal.	37.9	267	8.7	5.2	45.5	.3	2.7	111	155	1.8	690	188	340	.20	.30	1.5	1
879	Corn pone, made with white, whole-ground cornmeal	51.8	204	4.5	5.3	36.2	.8	2.2	62	163	1.2	396	61	Trace	.15	.05	.9	0
880	Spoonbread, made with white whole-ground cornmeal.	63.0	195	6.7	11.4	16.9	.3	2.0	96	164	1.0	482	132	290	.09	.18	.4	Trace
	See also Muffins, corn: items 1347–1348.																	

[*] Estimated average based on addition of salt in the amount of 0.6 percent of the finished product.

[55] Products are commercial unless otherwise specified.

[56] Based on product made with unenriched flour. With enriched flour, approximate values per 100 grams are: Iron, 1.6 mg.; thiamine, 0.12 mg.; riboflavin, 0.10 mg.; niacin, 0.5 mg.

[57] Based on yellow varieties; white varieties contain only a trace of cryptoxanthin and carotenes, the pigments in corn that have biological activity.

[58] Based on fritters made with yellow sweet corn; with white corn, value is 230 I.U. per 100 grams.

[59] Based on product with minimum level of enrichment. See Notes on Foods, p. 171.

[60] Based on cornbread made with white cornmeal; with yellow cornmeal, value is about 310 I.U. per 100 grams.

[61] For cornbread made with unenriched degermed cornmeal, values per 100 grams are: Iron, 0.7 mg.; thiamine, 0.07 mg.; riboflavin, 0.17 mg.; niacin, 0.4 mg.

TABLE 1.—COMPOSITION OF FOODS, 100 GRAMS, EDIBLE PORTION—Continued

[Numbers in parentheses denote values imputed—usually from another form of the food or from a similar food. Zero in parentheses indicates that the amount of a constituent probably is none or is too small to measure. Dashes denote lack of reliable data for a constituent believed to be present in measurable amount. Calculated values, as those based on a recipe, are not in parentheses]

Item No.	Food and description	Water	Food energy	Protein	Fat	Carbohydrate		Ash	Calcium	Phosphorus	Iron	Sodium	Potassium	Vitamin A value	Thiamine	Riboflavin	Niacin	Ascorbic acid
						Total	Fiber											
(A)	(B)	(C)	(D)	(E)	(F)	(G)	(H)	(I)	(J)	(K)	(L)	(M)	(N)	(O)	(P)	(Q)	(R)	(S)
		Percent	Calories	Grams	Grams	Grams	Grams	Grams	Milligrams	Milligrams	Milligrams	Milligrams	Milligrams	International units	Milligrams	Milligrams	Milligrams	Milligrams
	Cornbread mix and cornbread baked from mix:																	
881	Mix, dry form	6.7	432	7.0	12.8	71.0	0.3	2.0	28	474	2.5	1,156	81	220	0.35	0.21	2.6	0
882	Cornbread, made with egg, milk	50.8	233	6.1	8.4	32.9	.2	1.8	[illegible]	268	1.2	744	127	270	.15	.20	1.2	Trace
	Cornmeal, white or yellow:																	
883	Whole-ground, unbolted	12.	355	9.2	3.9	73.7	1.6	1.2	20	256	2.4	(1)	(284)	510	.38	.11	2.0	(0)
884	Bolted (nearly whole-grain)	12.	362	9.0	3.4	74.5	1.0	1.1	(17)	(223)	1.8	(1)	(248)	480	.30	.08	1.9	(0)
	Degermed, enriched:																	
885	Dry form	12.	364	7.9	1.2	78.4	.6	.5	6	99	2.9	1	120	440	.44	.26	3.5	(0)
886	Cooked	87.7	50	1.1	.2	10.7	.1	.3	1	14	.4	110	16	60	.06	.04	.5	(0)
	Degermed, unenriched:																	
887	Dry form	12.	364	7.9	1.2	78.4	.6	.5	6	99	1.1	1	120	440	.14	.05	1.0	(0)
888	Cooked	87.7	50	1.1	.2	10.7	.1	.3	1	14	.2	110	16	60	.02	.01	.1	(0)
	Self-rising:																	
	Whole-ground:																	
889	With soft wheat flour added	12.3	347	8.6	2.9	71.9	.8	5.3	301	624	1.6	1,380	212	380	.25	.07	1.7	(0)
890	Without wheat flour added	11.3	347	8.5	3.2	71.6	.9	5.4	309	641	1.7	1,380	274	450	.28	.08	1.8	(0)
	Degermed:																	
891	With soft wheat flour added	11.3	348	7.7	1.1	75.1	.5	4.8	292	524	1.0	1,380	109	330	.12	.05	1.0	(0)
892	Without wheat flour added	11.3	348	7.5	1.1	75.3	.6	4.5	290	524	1.0	1,380	113	420	.13	.05	.9	(0)
893	**Cornsalad, raw**	92.8	21	2.0	.4	3.6	.6	1.2	—	—	—	—	—	—	—	—	—	—
894	**Cornstarch**	12.	362	.3	Trace	87.6	.1	.1	(0)	(0)	(0)	Trace	Trace	(0)	(0)	(0)	(0)	(0)
	Cottage pudding. See Cakes, items 528–530.																	
895	**Cottonseed flour**	6.1	356	48.1	6.6	33.0	2.0	6.2	289	1,112	12.6	—	—	60	1.21	.84	6.5	—
	Cottonseed oil. See Oils, item 1401.																	
	Cowpeas, including blackeye peas:																	
	Immature seeds:																	
896	Raw	66.8	127	9.0	.8	21.8	1.8	1.6	27	172	2.3	2	541	370	.43	.13	1.6	29
897	Cooked, boiled, drained	71.8	108	8.1	.8	18.1	1.8	1.2	24	146	2.1	1	379	350	.30	.11	1.4	17
898	Canned, solids and liquid	81.0	70	5.0	.3	12.4	.7	1.3	18	112	1.5	236	352	60	.09	.05	.5	3
	Frozen (blackeye peas only):																	
899	Not thawed	65.8	131	9.0	.4	23.6	1.5	1.2	28	179	3.1	40	387	170	.45	.12	1.4	12
900	Cooked, boiled, drained	66.1	130	8.9	.4	23.5	1.5	1.1	25	168	2.8	39	357	170	.40	.11	1.4	9
	Young pods, with seeds:																	
901	Raw	86.0	44	3.3	.3	9.5	1.7	.9	65	65	1.0	4	215	1,600	.15	.14	1.2	33
902	Cooked, boiled, drained	89.5	34	2.6	.3	7.0	1.7	.6	55	49	.7	3	196	1,400	.09	.09	.8	17
	Mature seeds, dry:																	
903	Raw	10.5	343	22.8	1.5	61.7	4.4	3.5	74	426	5.8	35	1,024	30	1.05	.21	2.2	—
904	Cooked	80.0	76	5.1	.3	13.8	1.0	.8	17	95	1.3	8	229	10	.16	.04	.4	—
	Crab, including blue, Dungeness, rock and king:																	
905	Cooked, steamed	78.5	93	17.3	1.9	.5	—	1.8	43	175	.8	—	—	2,170	.16	.08	2.8	2
906	**Crab, canned**	77.2	101	17.4	2.5	1.1	—	1.8	45	182	.8	1,000	110	—	.08	.08	1.9	—
907	**Crab, deviled**	63.3	188	11.4	9.4	13.3	—	2.6	47	127	1.2	867	166	—	.08	.11	1.5	6
908	**Crab imperial**	71.9	147	14.6	7.6	3.9	—	2.0	60	166	.9	728	131	—	.06	.12	1.1	5
909	**Crabapples, raw**	81.1	68	.4	.3	17.8	.6	.4	(6)	13	(.3)	(1)	(110)	(40)	(.03)	(.02)	(.1)	8
	Crackers:																	
910	Animal	3.0	429	6.6	9.4	79.9	.1	1.1	52	114	.5	303	95	130	.04	.40	.3	Trace
911	Butter	4.6	458	7.0	17.8	67.3	.3	3.3	148	260	.6	1,092	113	220	.01	.04	1.0	(0)
912	Cheese	3.9	479	11.2	21.3	60.4	.2	3.2	336	300	.9	1,039	109	360	.01	.10	.8	(0)
	Graham:																	
913	Chocolate-coated	1.9	475	5.1	23.5	67.9	.8	1.6	113	204	2.6	407	320	60	.07	.28	1.2	(0)
914	Plain	6.4	384	8.0	9.4	73.3	1.1	2.9	40	149	1.5	670	384	(0)	.04	.21	1.5	(0)
915	Sugar-honey coated	3.3	411	6.7	11.4	76.4	.8	2.2	68	329	1.6	564	270	—	.03	.02	1.0	(0)
916	Saltines	4.3	433	9.0	12.0	71.5	.4	3.2	21	90	1.2	(1,100)	(120)	(0)	.01	.04	1.0	(0)
917	Sandwich type, peanut-cheese	2.4	491	15.2	23.9	56.1	.5	2.4	56	179	.9	992	226	40	.03	.07	3.5	(0)
918	Soda	4.0	439	9.2	13.1	70.6	.2	3.1	22	89	1.5	1,100	120	(0)	.01	.05	1.0	(0)
919	Whole-wheat	6.9	403	8.4	13.8	68.2	2.4	2.7	23	190	.3	547	—	(0)	.06	.04	.9	(0)
	Cracker meal. See Crackers, soda: item 918.																	
	Cranberries:																	
920	Raw	87.9	46	.4	.7	10.8	1.4	.2	14	10	.5	2	82	40	.03	.02	.1	11
921	Dehydrated, uncooked	4.9	368	2.8	6.6	84.5	8.7	1.4	62	22	3.4	16	644	300	.17	.12	.8	32
922	**Cranberry juice cocktail,** bottled (approx. 33% cranberry juice).	83.2	65	.1	.1	16.5	Trace	.1	5	3	.3	1	10	Trace	.01	.01	Trace	([89])
	Cranberry sauce, sweetened:																	
923	Canned, strained	62.1	146	.1	.2	37.5	.2	.1	6	4	.2	1	30	20	.01	.01	Trace	2

924	Home-prepared, unstrained	53.9	178	.2	.3	45.5	.7	.1	7	5	.2	1	38	20	.01	.01	.1	2
925	**Cranberry-orange relish,** uncooked	53.6	178	.4	.4	45.4	—	.2	19	8	.4	1	72	70	.03	.02	.1	18
926	**Crappie, white,** raw	81.8	79	16.8	.8	0	0	1.0	—	—	—	—	—	—	Trace	.03	1.4	—
927	**Crayfish, freshwater; and spiny lobster;** raw	82.5	72	14.6	.5	1.2	—	1.2	77	201	1.5	—	—	—	.01	.04	1.9	—
	Cream, fluid:																	
928	Half-and-half (cream and milk)	79.7	134	3.2	11.7	4.6	0	.6	108	85	Trace	46	129	480	.03	.16	.1	1
929	Light, coffee, or table	71.5	211	3.0	20.6	4.3	0	.6	102	80	Trace	43	122	840	.03	.15	.1	1
930	Light whipping	62.1	300	2.5	31.3	3.6	0	.5	85	67	Trace	36	102	1,280	.02	.12	.1	1
931	Heavy whipping	56.6	352	2.2	37.6	3.1	0	.4	75	59	Trace	32	89	1,540	.02	.11	Trace	1
	Cream substitutes, dried, containing—																	
932	Cream, skim milk (calcium reduced) and lactose	1.4	508	8.5	26.7	61.3	0	2.1	82	—	.2	575	—	960	.05	1.17	.1	—
933	Cream, skim milk, lactose, and sodium hexametaphosphate.	.9	509	13.9	27.7	53.2	0	4.3	495	—	.3	—	—	520	.14	.71	.3	—
934	**Cream puffs** with custard filling	58.3	233	6.5	13.9	20.5	Trace	.8	81	114	.7	83	121	350	.04	.17	.1	Trace
	Cress, garden: [47]																	
935	Raw	89.4	32	2.6	.7	5.5	1.1	1.8	81	76	1.3	14	606	9,300	.08	.26	1.0	69
	Cooked, boiled, drained, cooked in—																	
936	Small amount of water, short time	92.5	23	1.9	.6	3.8	.9	1.2	61	48	.8	8	353	7,700	.06	.16	.8	34
937	Large amount of water, long time	92.9	22	1.8	.6	3.6	.9	1.1	58	44	.7	8	328	7,000	.04	.15	.7	23
	Croaker, Atlantic:																	
938	Raw	79.2	96	17.8	2.2	0	0	1.3	—	—	—	87	234	60	.12	.08	5.5	—
939	Cooked, baked	71.3	133	24.3	3.2	0	0	1.2	—	—	—	120	323	70	.13	.10	6.5	—
940	**Croaker, white,** raw	79.7	84	18.0	.8	0	0	1.3	—	—	—	—	—	—	—	—	—	—
941	**Croaker, yellowfin,** raw	79.0	89	19.2	.8	0	0	1.2	—	—	—	—	—	—	—	—	—	—
	Cucumbers, raw: [4]																	
942	Not pared	95.1	15	.9	.1	3.4	.6	.5	25	27	1.1	6	160	250	.03	.04	.2	11
943	Pared	95.7	14	.6	.1	3.2	.3	.4	17	18	.3	6	160	Trace	.03	.04	.2	11
	Cucumber pickles. See Pickles, items 1558–1561.																	
	Currants, raw: [69]																	
944	Black, European	84.2	54	1.7	.1	13.1	2.4	.9	60	40	1.1	3	372	230	.05	.05	.3	200
945	Red and white	85.7	50	1.4	.2	12.1	3.4	.6	32	23	1.0	2	257	[70] 120	.04	(.05)	.1	41
	Cusk:																	
946	Raw	81.3	75	17.2	.2	0	0	.9	—	—	—	—	—	—	.03	.08	2.3	—
947	Cooked, steamed	74.3	106	23.4	.7	0	0	—	27	283	1.0	74	386	—	.03	.10	2.7	—
948	**Custard, baked**	77.2	115	5.4	5.5	11.1	0	.8	112	117	.4	79	146	350	.04	.19	.1	Trace
	Custard, frozen. See Ice cream, items 1139–1141.																	
	Custard dessert mix. See Pudding mixes, item 1829.																	
949	**Custardapple, bullocksheart,** raw	71.5	101	1.7	.6	25.2	3.4	1.0	27	20	.8	—	—	Trace	.08	.10	.5	22
	Daikon. See Radishes, oriental: item 1845.																	
	Dandelion greens:																	
950	Raw	85.6	45	2.7	.7	9.2	1.6	1.8	187	66	3.1	76	397	14,000	.19	.26	—	35
951	Cooked, boiled, drained	89.8	33	2.0	.6	6.4	1.3	1.2	140	42	1.8	44	232	11,700	.13	.16	—	18
	Danish pastry. See Rolls and buns, item 1899.																	
	Dasheens. See Taros, items 2271–2272.																	
952	**Dates,** domestic, natural and dry	22.5	274	2.2	.5	72.9	2.3	1.9	59	63	3.0	1	648	50	.09	.10	2.2	0
	Deviled ham. See Sausage, cold cuts, and luncheon meats: item 1993.																	
	Dewberries. See Blackberries, item 417.																	
	Dock (curly or narrowleaf dock, broadleaf dock, and sheep sorrel):																	
953	Raw	90.9	28	2.1	.3	5.6	.8	1.1	66	41	1.6	5	338	12,900	.09	.22	.5	119
954	Cooked, boiled, drained	93.6	19	1.6	.2	3.9	.7	.7	55	26	.9	3	198	10,800	.06	.13	.4	54
955	**Dogfish, spiny (grayfish),** raw	72.3	156	17.6	9.0	0	0	1.0	—	—	—	—	—	—	.05	—	—	—
956	**Dolly Varden,** raw	73.1	144	19.9	6.5	0	0	1.2	—	—	—	—	—	—	.06	.06	—	—
	Doughnuts:																	
957	Cake type	23.7	391	4.6	18.6	51.4	.1	1.7	40	190	[71] 1.4	501	90	80	[71] .16	[71] .16	[71] 1.2	Trace
958	Yeast-leavened	28.3	414	6.3	26.7	37.7	.2	1.0	38	76	[72] 1.5	234	80	60	[72] .16	[72] .17	[72] 1.3	0
959	**Drum, freshwater,** raw	77.0	121	17.3	5.2	0	0	1.0	—	—	—	70	286	—	—	—	—	—
960	**Drum, red (redfish),** raw	80.2	80	18.0	.4	0	0	1.3	—	—	—	55	273	—	.15	.05	3.5	—

[4] See Notes on Foods, p. 176.

[9] Estimated average based on addition of salt in the amount of 0.6 percent of the finished product.

[19] Average weighted in accordance with commercial practices in freezing vegetables. See also Notes on Foods, p. 177.

[47] For further description of product, see Notes on Foods, p. 178.

[57] Based on yellow varieties; white varieties contain only a trace of cryptoxanthin and carotenes, the pigments in corn that have biological activity.

[58] Based on product with minimum level of enrichment. See Notes on Foods, p. 171.

[62] Based on mix made with enriched yellow degermed cornmeal. With unenriched cornmeal, approximate values per 100 grams are: Iron, 1.0 mg.; thiamine, 0.08 mg.; riboflavin, 0.06 mg.; niacin, 0.7 mg. If white cornmeal is used, vitamin A value is 160 I.U. per 100 grams.

[63] Based on mix made with enriched yellow degermed cornmeal. With unenriched cornmeal, approximate values per 100 grams are: Iron, 0.6 mg., thiamine, 0.05 mg.; riboflavin, 0.14 mg.; niacin, 0.3 mg. If white cornmeal is used, vitamin A value is 210 I.U. per 100 grams.

[64] Value applies to unenriched product. Much of the self-rising cornmeal on the market is enriched. For enriched products, minimum values per 100 grams are: Iron, 2.9 mg.; thiamine, 0.44 mg.; riboflavin, 0.26 mg.; niacin, 3.5 mg. For further information on self-rising cornmeal, especially on calcium, see Notes on Foods, p. 171.

[65] Amount of potassium contributed by cornmeal and flour. Small quantities of additional potassium may be provided by other ingredients.

[66] Prepared with bread cubes, butter, parsley, eggs, lemon juice, and catsup.

[67] Prepared with butter, flour, milk, onion, green pepper, eggs, and lemon juice.

[68] About 2 mg. per 100 grams is from cranberries. Ascorbic acid is usually added to approximately 40 mg. per 100 grams.

[69] Production of the European black currant in particular, and, to less extent, of other currants and of gooseberries, is restricted by Federal or State regulations that prohibit shipments of the plants to certain designated States and areas within some States. The regulations have been enacted to prevent further spread of the whitepine blister rust inasmuch as these plants are alternate hosts of this disease.

[70] Based on red currants only.

[71] Based on product made with enriched flour. With unenriched flour, approximate values per 100 grams are: Iron, 0.5 mg.; thiamine, 0.03 mg.; riboflavin, 0.06 mg.; niacin, 0.3 mg.

[72] Based on product made with enriched flour. With unenriched flour, approximate values per 100 grams are: Iron, 0.6 mg.; thiamine, 0.04 mg.; riboflavin, 0.08 mg.; niacin, 0.5 mg.

TABLE 1.—COMPOSITION OF FOODS, 100 GRAMS, EDIBLE PORTION—Continued

[Numbers in parentheses denote values imputed—usually from another form of the food or from a similar food. Zero in parentheses indicates that the amount of a constituent probably is none or is too small to measure. Dashes denote lack of reliable data for a constituent believed to be present in measurable amount. Calculated values, as those based on a recipe, are not in parentheses]

Item No.	Food and description	Water	Food energy	Protein	Fat	Carbohydrate Total	Carbohydrate Fiber	Ash	Calcium	Phosphorus	Iron	Sodium	Potassium	Vitamin A value	Thiamine	Riboflavin	Niacin	Ascorbic acid
(A)	(B)	(C)	(D)	(E)	(F)	(G)	(H)	(I)	(J)	(K)	(L)	(M)	(N)	(O)	(P)	(Q)	(R)	(S)
		Percent	*Calories*	*Grams*	*Grams*	*Grams*	*Grams*	*Grams*	*Milligrams*	*Milligrams*	*Milligrams*	*Milligrams*	*Milligrams*	*International units*	*Milligrams*	*Milligrams*	*Milligrams*	*Milligrams*
	Duck, domesticated, raw:																	
961	Total edible	54.3	326	16.0	28.6	0	0	1.0	(10)	(176)	(1.6)	—	—	—	(0.08)	(0.19)	(8.7)	—
962	Flesh only	68.8	165	21.4	8.2	0	0	1.2	(12)	(203)	(1.3)	74	285	—	(.10)	(.12)	(7.7)	—
	Duck, wild, raw:																	
963	Total edible	61.1	233	21.1	15.8	0	0	1.1	—	—	—	—	—	—	—	—	—	—
964	Flesh only	70.8	138	21.3	5.2	0	0	1.3	—	—	—	—	—	—	—	—	—	—
965	**Eclairs** with custard filling and chocolate icing	56.2	239	6.2	13.6	23.2	Trace	.8	80	112	.7	82	122	340	.04	.16	.1	Trace
966	**Eel,** American, raw	64.6	233	15.9	18.3	0	0	1.0	18	202	.7	—	—	1,610	.22	.36	1.4	—
967	**Eel, smoked**	50.2	330	18.6	27.8	0	0	2.4	—	—	—	—	—	—	—	—	—	—
	Eggs:																	
	Chicken:																	
	Raw:																	
968	Whole, fresh, and frozen	73.7	163	12.9	11.5	.9	0	1.0	54	205	2.3	122	129	1,180	.11	.30	.1	0
969	Whites, fresh, and frozen	87.6	51	10.9	Trace	.8	0	.7	9	15	.1	146	139	0	Trace	.27	.1	0
970	Yolks, fresh [23]	51.1	348	16.0	30.6	.6	0	1.7	141	569	5.5	52	98	3,400	.22	.44	.1	0
971	Yolks, frozen [23]	55.5	312	15.4	26.9	.6	0	1.6	125	502	4.9	63	100	2,980	.20	.42	.1	0
972	Yolks, frozen, sugared	50.7	315	14.3	24.9	9.0	0	1.1	113	455	4.4	57	91	2,710	.18	.38	.1	0
	Cooked:																	
973	Fried	67.7	216	13.8	17.2	.3	0	1.0	60	222	2.4	338	140	1,420	.10	.30	.1	0
974	Hard-cooked	73.7	163	12.9	11.5	.9	0	1.0	54	205	2.3	122	129	1,180	.09	.28	.1	0
975	Omelet	72.1	173	11.2	12.9	2.4	0	1.4	80	189	1.7	257	146	1,080	.08	.28	.1	0
976	Poached	73.3	163	12.7	11.6	.8	0	1.4	55	204	2.2	271	128	1,170	.08	.25	.1	0
977	Scrambled	72.1	173	11.2	12.9	2.4	0	1.4	80	189	1.7	257	146	1,080	.08	.28	.1	0
	Dried:																	
978	Whole	4.1	592	47.0	41.2	4.1	0	3.6	187	800	8.7	427	463	4,290	.35	1.20	.2	0
979	Whole, stabilized (glucose reduced)	2.0	615	48.9	42.9	2.5	0	3.7	194	832	9.0	444	482	4,460	.34	1.25	.2	0
980	White, flakes	14.6	349	75.1	.2	5.3	0	4.8	62	103	1.0	1,033	937	0	.04	1.87	.7	0
981	White, powder	8.8	377	80.2	.2	5.7	0	5.1	66	110	1.0	1,103	1,000	0	.04	1.99	.7	0
982	Yolk	4.8	664	33.2	56.6	2.5	0	3.2	273	1,109	10.8	109	186	5,080	.41	.86	.1	0
983	Duck, whole, fresh, raw	70.4	191	13.3	14.5	.7	0	1.1	56	195	2.8	(122)	(129)	1,230	.18	(.30)	.1	0
984	Goose, whole, fresh, raw	70.4	185	13.9	13.3	1.3	0	1.1	—	—	—	—	—	—	—	—	—	—
985	Turkey, whole, fresh, raw	72.6	170	13.1	11.8	1.7	0	.8	—	—	—	—	—	—	—		Trace	—
	Eggplant:																	
986	Raw	92.4	25	1.2	.2	5.6	.9	.6	12	26	.7	2	214	10	.05	.05	.6	5
987	Cooked, boiled, drained	94.3	19	1.0	.2	4.1	.9	.4	11	21	.6	1	150	10	.05	.04	.5	3
988	**Elderberries,** raw	79.8	72	2.6	(.5)	16.4	7.0	.7	38	28	1.6	—	300	600	.07	.06	.5	36
989	**Endive** (curly endive and escarole), raw [6]	93.1	20	1.7	.1	4.1	.9	1.0	81	54	1.7	14	294	3,300	.07	.14	.5	10
	Escarole, raw. See Endive, item 989.																	
990	**Eulachon** (smelt), raw	79.6	118	14.6	6.2	0	0	1.2	—	—	—	—	—	—	.04	.04	—	—
	Farina:																	
	Enriched:																	
	Regular:																	
991	Dry form	10.3	371	11.4	.9	77.0	.4	.4	25	107	[25] 2.9	2	83	(0)	[25] .44	[25] .26	[25] 3.5	(0)
992	Cooked	89.5	42	1.3	.1	8.7	Trace	.4	4	12	[25] .3	144	9	(0)	[25] .04	[25] .03	[25] .4	(0)
	Quick-cooking:																	
993	Dry form	10.3	362	11.4	.9	74.9	.4	2.5	500	561	([25])	250	83	(0)	[25] .44	[25] .26	[25] 3.5	(0)
994	Cooked	89.0	43	1.2	.1	8.9	Trace	.7	60	66	([25])	190	10	(0)	[25] .05	[25] .03	[25] .4	(0)
	Instant-cooking:																	
995	Dry form	10.3	362	11.4	.9	74.9	.4	2.5	500	396	([25])	7	83	(0)	[25] .44	[25] .26	[25] 3.5	(0)
996	Cooked	85.9	55	1.7	.1	11.4	.1	.9	77	60	([25])	188	13	(0)	[25] .07	[25] .04	[25] .5	(0)
	Unenriched, regular:																	
997	Dry form	10.3	371	11.4	.9	77.0	.4	.4	25	107	1.5	2	83	(0)	.06	.10	.7	(0)
998	Cooked	89.5	42	1.3	.1	8.7	Trace	.4	4	12	.2	144	9	(0)	.01	.01	.1	(0)
999	**Fats, cooking** (vegetable fat)	0	884	0	100	0	0	0	0	0	0	0	0	—	0	0	0	0
1000	**Fennel,** common, leaves, raw	90.0	28	2.8	.4	5.1	.5	1.7	100	51	2.7	—	397	3,500	—	—	—	31
	Figs:																	
1001	Raw	77.5	80	1.2	.3	20.3	1.2	.7	35	22	.6	2	194	80	.06	.05	.4	2
1002	Candied	21.0	299	3.5	.2	73.7	—	1.6	—	—	—	—	—	—	—	—	—	—
	Canned, solids and liquid:																	
1003	Water pack, with or without artificial sweetener	86.6	48	.5	.2	12.4	.7	.3	14	14	.4	2	155	30	.03	.03	.2	1
	Sirup pack:																	
1004	Light	82.2	65	.5	.2	16.8	.7	.3	13	13	.4	2	152	30	.03	.03	.2	1
1005	Heavy	77.2	84	.5	.2	21.8	.7	.3	13	13	.4	2	149	30	.03	.03	.2	1
1006	Extra heavy	72.3	103	.5	.2	26.7	.6	.3	13	13	.4	2	146	30	.03	.03	.2	1
1007	Dried, uncooked	23.0	274	4.3	1.3	69.1	5.6	2.3	126	77	3.0	34	640	80	.10	.10	.7	(0)

1008	**Filberts** (hazelnuts)	5.8	634	12.6	62.4	16.7	3.0	2.5	209	337	3.4	2	704	—	.46	—	.9	Trace
1009	**Finnan haddie** (smoked haddock)	72.6	103	23.2	.4	0	0	3.1	—	—	—	—	—	—	.06	.05	2.1	—
	Fish. See individual kinds; Cod, etc. Also see table 13, page 183.																	
	Fish cakes, cooked:																	
1010	Fried [77]	66.0	172	14.7	8.0	9.3	—	2.0	—	—	—	—	—	—	—	—	—	—
1011	Frozen, fried, reheated	52.9	270	9.2	17.9	17.2	—	2.8	—	—	—	—	—	—	—	—	—	—
1012	**Fish flakes,** canned	72.1	111	24.7	.6	0	0	2.6	49	232	.8	—	—	—	—	—	—	—
	Fish flour:																	
1013	From whole fish	2.0	336	78.0	.3	0	—	19.7	4,610	3,100	41.0	170	430	—	.07	62	2.2	—
1014	From fillets	3.0	398	93.0	.1	0	0	3.9	920	610	8.0	40	80	—	—	—	—	—
1015	From fillet waste	3.0	305	71.0	.2	0	0	25.8	6,040	4,060	54.0	220	540	—	—	—	—	—
1016	**Fish loaf,** cooked [78]	72.2	124	14.1	3.7	7.3	—	2.7	—	—	—	—	—	—	—	—	—	—
1017	**Fish sticks,** frozen, cooked	65.8	176	16.6	8.9	6.5	—	2.2	11	167	.4	—	—	0	.04	.07	1.6	—
1018	**Flatfishes** (flounders, soles, and sanddabs), raw	81.3	79	16.7	.8	0	0	1.2	12	195	.8	78	342	—	.05	.05	1.7	—
1019	**Flounder,** cooked, baked	58.1	202	30.0	8.2	0	0	2.2	23	344	1.4	237	587	—	.07	.08	2.5	2
	Flour. See Corn, Rice, Rye, Soya, Wheat.																	
	Frankfurters. See Sausage, cold cuts, and luncheon meats: items 1994–2000.																	
1020	**Frog legs,** raw	81.9	73	16.4	.3	0	0	1.1	18	147	1.5	—	—	0	.14	.25	1.2	—
	Frostings. See Cake icings, items 570–579.																	
	Frozen custard. See Ice cream, items 1139–1141.																	
	Fruit cocktail, canned, solids and liquid:																	
1021	Water pack, with or without artificial sweetener	89.6	37	.4	.1	9.7	.4	.2	9	13	.4	5	168	150	.02	.01	.5	2
	Sirup pack:																	
1022	Light	83.6	60	.4	.1	15.7	.4	.2	9	12	.4	5	164	140	.02	.01	.5	2
1023	Heavy	79.6	76	.4	.1	19.7	.4	.2	9	12	.4	5	161	140	.02	.01	.4	2
1024	Extra heavy	75.6	92	.4	.1	23.7	.4	.2	9	12	.4	5	159	140	.01	.01	.4	2
	Fruit salad, canned, solids and liquid:																	
1025	Water pack, with or without artificial sweetener	90.1	35	.4	.1	9.1	.5	.3	8	11	.3	1	139	470	.01	.03	.6	3
	Sirup pack:																	
1026	Light	83.9	59	.3	.1	15.5	.4	.2	8	11	.3	1	136	460	.01	.03	.6	2
1027	Heavy	80.0	75	.3	.1	19.4	.4	.2	8	11	.3	1	134	450	.01	.03	.6	2
1028	Extra heavy	76.0	90	.3	.1	23.4	.4	.2	8	11	.3	1	131	450	.01	.03	.6	2
	Garbanzos. See Chickpeas, item 753.																	
1029	**Garlic,** cloves, raw	61.3	137	6.2	.2	30.8	1.5	1.5	29	202	1.5	19	529	Trace	.25	.08	.5	15
1030	**Gelatin,** dry	13.0	335	85.6	.1	0	0	1.3	—	—	—	—	—	—	—	—	—	—
	Gelatin dessert powder and desserts made from dessert powder:																	
1031	Dessert powder	1.6	371	9.4	0	88.0	0	1.0	—	—	—	318	—	—	—	—	—	—
	Desserts, made with water:																	
1032	Plain	84.2	59	1.5	0	14.1	0	.2	—	—	—	51	—	—	—	—	—	—
1033	With fruit added	81.8	67	1.3	.1	16.4	.2	.4	—	—	—	34	—	—	—	—	—	3
	Gin. See Beverages, items 395–399																	
	Ginger ale. See Beverages, item 407.																	
	Gingerbread. See Cakes, item 533, Cake mixes, items 560–561.																	
1034	**Ginger root, crystallized** (candied)	12.0	340	.3	.2	87.1	.7	.4	—	—	—	—	—	—	—	—	—	—
1035	**Ginger root, fresh**	87.0	49	1.4	1.0	9.5	1.1	1.1	23	36	2.1	6	264	10	.02	.04	.7	4
	Gizzard:																	
	Chicken, all classes:																	
1036	Raw	75.0	113	20.1	2.7	.7	0	1.5	10	105	2.9	65	240	—	.03	.20	4.5	—
1037	Cooked, simmered	68.0	148	27.0	3.3	.7	0	1.0	9	71	3.1	57	211	—	.02	.21	5.1	—
1038	Goose, raw	73.0	139	21.4	5.3	0	0	1.0	—	—	—	—	—	—	—	—	—	—
	Turkey, all classes:																	
1039	Raw	70.3	157	20.3	7.3	1.1	0	1.0	—	—	—	58	170	—	.05	.13	5.0	—
1040	Cooked, simmered	62.7	196	26.8	8.6	1.1	0	.7	—	—	—	51	149	—	.03	.14	5.8	—
	Gizzard shad. See Shad, gizzard: item 2038.																	
	Gluten flour. See Wheat flours, item 2444.																	
	Goat milk. See Milk, goat: item 1335																	
	Goose, domesticated:																	
	Total edible:																	
1041	Raw	51.1	354	16.4	31.5	0	0	.9	(10)	(176)	(1.6)	—	—	—	(.08)	(.19)	(6.7)	—
1042	Cooked, roasted	39.1	426	23.7	36.0	0	0	1.2	(11)	(240)	(2.1)	—	—	—	(.08)	(.24)	(8.1)	—
	Flesh and skin:																	
1043	Raw	49.7	371	15.9	33.6	0	0	.9	(11)	(191)	(1.5)	—	—	—	(.08)	(.12)	(7.4)	—
1044	Cooked, roasted	37.9	441	22.9	38.1	0	0	1.2	(13)	(260)	(1.9)	—	—	—	(.09)	(.16)	(8.9)	—
	Flesh only:																	
1045	Raw	68.3	159	22.3	7.1	0	0	1.1	(12)	(203)	(1.3)	86	420	—	(.10)	(.12)	(7.7)	—
1046	Cooked, roasted	54.8	233	33.9	9.8	0	0	1.5	(14)	(277)	(1.7)	124	605	—	(.11)	(.16)	(9.3)	—
1047	Giblets, raw	69.9	156	21.1	7.0	.6	0	1.4	—	—	—	—	—	—	—	—	—	—

[47] For further description of product, see Notes on Foods, p. 178.

[72] Fresh yolks include a small proportion of white; frozen yolks, a considerable amount.

[74] Based on products with minimum level of enrichment. See Notes on Foods, p. 171. In several brands, however, values for iron range from 2.8 to 7.1 mg. per 100 grams, corresponding to 0.3 to 0.8 mg. per 100 grams cooked form.

[75] Value of 42.4 mg. per 100 grams reported for one brand, corresponding values per 100 grams cooked form are 5.0 mg. for quick-cooking and 6.4 mg. for instant farina.

[76] Based on product with minimum level of enrichment. See Notes on Foods, p. 171.

[77] Prepared with canned flaked fish, potato, and egg.

[78] Prepared with canned flaked fish, bread cubes, eggs, tomatoes, onion, and fat.

TABLE 1.—COMPOSITION OF FOODS, 100 GRAMS, EDIBLE PORTION—Continued

[Numbers in parentheses denote values imputed—usually from another form of the food or from a similar food. Zero in parentheses indicates that the amount of a constituent probably is none or is too small to measure. Dashes denote lack of reliable data for a constituent believed to be present in measurable amount. Calculated values, as those based on a recipe, are not in parentheses]

Item No.	Food and description	Water	Food energy	Protein	Fat	Carbohydrate Total	Carbohydrate Fiber	Ash	Calcium	Phosphorus	Iron	Sodium	Potassium	Vitamin A value	Thiamine	Riboflavin	Niacin	Ascorbic acid
(A)	(B)	(C)	(D)	(E)	(F)	(G)	(H)	(I)	(J)	(K)	(L)	(M)	(N)	(O)	(P)	(Q)	(R)	(S)
		Percent	Calories	Grams	Grams	Grams	Grams	Grams	Milligrams	Milligrams	Milligrams	Milligrams	Milligrams	International units	Milligrams	Milligrams	Milligrams	Milligrams
	Gooseberries: [38]																	
1048	Raw	88.9	39	0.8	0.2	9.7	1.9	0.4	18	15	0.5	1	155	290	—	—	—	33
	Canned, solids and liquid:																	
1049	Water pack, with or without artificial sweetener	92.5	26	.5	.1	6.6	1.3	.3	12	10	.3	1	105	200	—	—	—	11
	Sirup pack:																	
1050	Heavy	76.1	90	.5	.1	23.0	1.2	.3	11	9	.3	1	98	190	—	—	—	10
1051	Extra heavy	69.2	117	.5	.1	30.0	1.2	.2	11	9	.3	1	95	180	—	—	—	10
	Gourd, dishcloth. See Towelgourd, item 2315.																	
1052	Granadilla, purple (passionfruit) pulp and seeds, raw	75.1	90	2.2	.7	21.2	—	.8	13	64	1.6	28	348	700	Trace	0.13	1.5	30
	Grapefruit:																	
	Raw.																	
	Pulp:																	
	Pink, red, white.																	
1053	All varieties	88.4	41	.5	.1	10.6	.2	.4	16	16	.4	1	135	80	0.04	.02	.2	[39] 38
1054	California and Arizona (Marsh Seedless)	87.5	44	.5	.1	11.5	.2	.4	32	20	.4	1	135	10	.04	.02	.2	[39] 40
1055	Florida, all varieties	89.1	38	.5	.1	9.9	.2	.4	15	15	.4	1	135	80	.04	.02	.2	[39] 37
1056	Texas, all varieties	87.7	43	.5	.1	11.3	.2	.4	15	15	.4	1	135	([40])	.04	.02	.2	38
	Pink and red:																	
1057	Seeded (Foster Pink)	88.6	40	.5	.1	10.4	.2	.4	16	16	.4	1	135	440	.04	.02	.2	[39] 39
1058	Seedless (including Pink Marsh, Redblush)	88.6	40	.5	.1	10.4	.2	.4	16	16	.4	1	135	440	.04	.02	.2	[39] 36
	White:																	
1059	Seeded (Duncan, other varieties)	88.2	41	.5	.1	10.8	.2	.4	16	16	.4	1	135	10	.04	.02	.2	[39] 38
1060	Seedless (Marsh Seedless)	88.9	39	.5	.1	10.1	.2	.4	16	16	.4	1	135	10	.04	.02	.2	[39] 37
	Juice:																	
	Pink, red, and white:																	
1061	All varieties	90.0	39	.5	.1	9.2	Trace	.2	9	15	.2	1	162	80	.04	.02	.2	[39] 38
1062	California and Arizona (Marsh Seedless)	89.0	42	.4	.1	10.2	Trace	.3	9	15	.2	1	162	10	.04	.02	.2	[39] 40
1063	Florida, all varieties	90.4	37	.5	.1	8.8	Trace	.2	9	15	.2	1	162	80	.04	.02	.2	[39] 37
1064	Texas, all varieties	89.2	42	.5	.1	10.0	Trace	.2	9	15	.2	1	162	([40])	.04	.02	.2	38
	Pink and red:																	
1065	Seeded (Foster Pink)	90.0	38	.5	.1	9.1	Trace	.3	9	15	.2	1	162	440	.04	.02	.2	[39] 39
1066	Seedless (including Pink Marsh, Redblush)	90.0	39	.4	.1	9.3	Trace	.2	9	15	.2	1	162	440	.04	.02	.2	[39] 38
	White:																	
1067	Seeded (Duncan, other varieties)	89.6	40	.5	.1	9.5	Trace	.3	9	15	.2	1	162	10	.04	.02	.2	[39] 38
1068	Seedless (Marsh Seedless)	90.2	38	.5	.1	9.0	Trace	.2	9	15	.2	1	162	10	.04	.02	.2	[39] 37
	Canned:																	
	Segments, solids and liquid.																	
1069	Water pack, with or without artificial sweetener.	91.3	30	.6	.1	7.6	.2	.4	13	14	.3	4	144	10	.03	.02	.2	30
1070	Sirup pack	81.1	70	.6	.1	17.8	.2	.4	13	14	.3	1	135	10	.03	.02	.2	30
	Juice:																	
1071	Unsweetened	89.2	41	.5	.1	9.8	Trace	.4	8	14	.4	1	162	10	.03	.02	.2	34
1072	Sweetened	86.2	53	.5	.1	12.8	Trace	.4	8	14	.4	1	162	10	.03	.02	.2	31
	Frozen concentrated juice:																	
	Unsweetened:																	
1073	Undiluted	62	145	1.9	.4	34.6	.1	1.1	34	60	.4	4	604	30	.14	.06	.7	138
1074	Diluted with 3 parts water, by volume	89.3	41	.5	.1	9.8	Trace	.3	10	17	.1	1	170	10	.04	.02	.2	39
	Sweetened:																	
1075	Undiluted	57	165	1.6	.3	40.2	.1	.9	28	50	.3	3	508	20	.12	.05	.6	116
1076	Diluted with 3 parts water, by volume	87.8	47	.4	.1	11.4	Trace	.3	8	14	.1	1	144	10	.03	.01	.2	33
	Dehydrated juice (crystals):																	
1077	Dry form	1.0	378	4.8	1.0	90.3	.4	2.9	87	155	1.0	10	1,572	80	.38	.16	1.7	350
1078	Prepared with water (1 lb. yields approx. 1 gal.)	89.5	40	.5	.1	9.6	Trace	.3	9	16	.1	1	167	10	.04	.02	.2	37
	Grapefruit juice and orange juice blended:																	
	Canned:																	
1079	Unsweetened	88.7	43	.6	.2	10.1	.1	.4	10	15	.3	1	184	100	.05	.02	.2	34
1080	Sweetened	86.9	50	.5	.1	12.2	.1	.4	10	15	.3	1	184	100	.05	.02	.2	34
	Frozen concentrate, unsweetened:																	
1081	Undiluted	59.1	157	2.1	.5	37.1	.1	1.2	29	47	.4	2	623	360	.23	.03	1.1	144
1082	Diluted with 3 parts water, by volume	88.4	44	.6	.1	10.5	Trace	.4	8	13	.1	Trace	177	110	.06	.01	.3	41
1083	Grapefruit peel, candied	17.4	316	.4	.3	80.6	2.3	1.3	—	—	—	—	—	—	—	—	—	—
	Grapes:																	
	Raw:																	
1084	American type (slip skin) as Concord, Delaware, Niagara, Catawba, and Scuppernong.	81.6	69	1.3	1.0	15.7	.6	.4	16	12	.4	3	158	100	(.05)	(.03)	(.3)	4

1085	European type (adherent skin) as Malaga, Muscat, Thompson Seedless, Emperor, and Flame Tokay.	81.4	67	.6	.3	17.3	.5	.4	12	20	.4	3	173	(100)	.05	.03	.3	4
	Canned:																	
	Thompson Seedless, solids and liquid:																	
1086	Water pack, with or without artificial sweetener.	85.5	51	.5	.1	13.6	.2	.3	8	13	.3	4	110	70	.04	.01	.2	2
1087	Sirup pack, heavy	79.1	77	.5	.1	20.0	.2	.3	8	13	.3	4	105	70	.04	.01	.2	2
	Grapejuice:																	
1088	Canned or bottled	82.9	66	.2	Trace	16.6	Trace	.3	11	12	.3	2	116	—	.04	.02	.2	Trace
	Frozen concentrate, sweetened:																	
1089	Undiluted	52.8	183	.6	Trace	46.3	.1	.3	10	15	.4	3	118	20	.06	.10	.7	15
1090	Diluted with 3 parts water, by volume	86.4	53	.2	Trace	13.3	Trace	.1	3	4	.1	1	34	Trace	.02	.03	.2	4
1091	**Grapejuice drink,** canned (approx. 30% grapejuice) [61]	86.0	54	.1	Trace	13.8	Trace	.1	3	4	.1	1	35	—	.01	.01	.1	16
	Griddlecakes. See Pancakes, items 1453–1462.																	
	Grits. See Corn grits, items 862–865.																	
1092	**Groundcherries** (poha or cape-gooseberries), raw	85.4	53	1.9	.7	11.2	2.8	.8	9	40	1.0	—	—	720	.11	.04	2.8	11
1093	**Grouper,** including red, black, and speckled hind; raw	79.2	87	19.3	.5	0	0	1.2	—	—	—	—	—	—	.17	—	—	—
	Guavas, whole, raw:																	
1094	Common	83.0	62	.8	.6	15.0	5.6	.6	23	42	.9	4	289	280	.05	.05	1.2	[62] 242
1095	Strawberry	81.8	65	1.0	.6	15.8	6.4	.8	(23)	(42)	(.9)	(4)	(289)	90	.03	.03	.6	37
	Guinea hen, raw:																	
1096	Total edible	69.0	156	23.1	6.4	0	0	1.2	—	—	—	—	—	—	—	—	—	—
1097	Flesh and skin	68.9	158	23.4	6.4	0	0	1.2	—	—	—	—	—	—	—	—	—	—
1098	Giblets	69.8	157	20.8	7.0	1.2	0	1.2	—	—	—	—	—	—	—	—	—	—
	Haddock:																	
1099	Raw	80.5	79	18.3	.1	0	0	1.4	23	197	.7	61	304	—	.04	.07	3.0	—
1100	Cooked, fried [63]	66.3	165	19.6	6.4	5.8	—	1.9	40	247	1.2	177	348	—	.04	.07	3.2	2
1101	Smoked, canned or not canned	72.6	103	23.2	.4	0	0	3.1	—	—	—	—	—	—	.06	.05	4.2	—
1102	**Hake,** including Pacific hake, squirrel hake, and silver hake or whiting; raw.	81.8	74	16.5	.4	0	0	1.3	41	142	—	74	363	—	.10	.20	—	—
	Halibut, Atlantic and Pacific:																	
1103	Raw	76.5	100	20.9	1.2	0	0	1.4	13	211	.7	[64] 54	449	440	.07	.07	8.3	—
1104	Cooked, broiled	66.6	171	25.2	7.0	0	0	1.7	16	248	.8	134	525	680	.05	.07	8.3	—
1105	Smoked	49.4	224	20.8	15.0	0	0	15.0	—	—	—	—	—	—	—	—	—	—
1106	**Halibut, California,** raw	77.8	97	19.8	1.4	0	0	1.3	—	—	—	—	—	—	—	—	—	—
1107	**Halibut, Greenland,** raw	74.5	146	16.4	8.4	0	0	1.0	—	210	—	—	—	—	.01	—	—	—
	Ham. See Pork, items 1693–1707, 1765–1772, 1783.																	
1108	**Ham croquette**	54.0	251	16.3	15.1	11.7	.1	2.9	69	160	2.1	342	83	260	.28	.22	2.5	Trace
	Hamburger. See Beef, items 367–370.																	
1109	**Haws, scarlet,** flesh and skin, raw	75.8	87	2.0	.7	20.8	2.1	.8	—	—	—	—	—	—	—	—	—	—
	Hazelnuts. See Filberts, item 1008.																	
	Headcheese. See Sausage, cold cuts, and luncheon meats: item 2001.																	
	Heart:																	
	Beef, lean:																	
1110	Raw	77.5	108	17.1	3.6	.7	0	1.1	5	195	4.0	86	193	20	.53	.88	7.5	2
1111	Cooked, braised	61.3	188	31.3	5.7	.7	0	1.1	6	181	5.9	104	232	30	.25	1.22	7.6	1
	Beef, lean with visible fat:																	
1112	Raw	63.0	253	15.4	20.7	.1	0	.8	—	182	—	—	—	—	—	—	—	—
1113	Cooked, braised	44.4	372	25.8	29.0	.1	0	.8	—	169	—	—	—	—	—	—	—	—
	Calf																	
1114	Raw	76.2	124	15.0	5.9	1.8	0	1.1	3	160	3.0	94	208	30	.63	1.05	8.1	1
1115	Cooked, braised	60.3	208	27.8	9.1	1.8	0	1.0	4	148	4.4	113	250	40	.29	1.44	8.1	Trace
	Chicken, all classes:																	
1116	Raw	74.3	134	18.6	6.0	.1	0	1.0	4	158	3.3	79	159	(30)	.06	.80	4.6	4
1117	Cooked, simmered	66.7	173	25.3	7.2	.1	0	.8	4	107	3.6	69	140	(30)	.06	.92	5.3	4
	Hog.																	
1118	Raw	77.4	113	16.8	4.4	.4	0	1.0	3	131	3.3	54	106	30	.43	1.24	6.6	3
1119	Cooked, braised	61.0	195	30.8	6.9	.3	0	1.0	4	121	4.9	65	128	40	.20	1.72	6.7	1
	Lamb:																	
1120	Raw	71.6	162	16.8	9.6	1.0	0	1.0	11	249	—	—	—	70	.45	.74	6.3	1
1121	Cooked, braised	54.1	260	29.5	14.4	1.0	0	.9	14	231	—	—	—	100	.21	1.03	6.4	Trace
	Turkey, all classes:																	
1122	Raw	71.3	171	16.2	11.2	.2	0	1.1	—	—	—	69	240	(30)	.23	.86	5.0	(4)
1123	Cooked, simmered	63.2	216	22.6	13.2	.2	0	.8	—	—	—	61	211	(30)	.25	.98	5.7	(4)

[58] Production of the European black currant in particular, and, to less extent, of other currants and of gooseberries, is restricted by Federal or State regulations that prohibit shipments of the plants to certain designated States and areas within some States. The regulations have been enacted to prevent further spread of the whitepine blister rust inasmuch as these plants are alternate hosts of this disease.

[59] Value weighted by monthly and total season shipments for marketing as fresh fruit.

[60] For white-fleshed varieties, value is about 10 I.U. per 100 grams; for red-fleshed, about 440 I.U.

[61] Fruit juice content ranges from 10 to 50 percent. Ascorbic acid may be added as a preservative or as a nutrient. Value listed is based on product with label stating 30 mg. per 6 fl. oz. serving. If label claim is 30 mg. per 8 fl. oz. serving, values would be 12 mg. per 100 grams. If thiamine and riboflavin have been added, the values expected would be 0.20 mg. and 0.24 mg. per 100 grams.

[62] Average for varieties grown in the United States; range is wide, from 23 to 1,160 mg. per 100 grams.

[63] Dipped in egg, milk, and breadcrumbs.

[64] Two frozen samples dipped in brine contained 360 mg. sodium per 100 grams.

TABLE 1.—COMPOSITION OF FOODS, 100 GRAMS, EDIBLE PORTION—Continued

[Numbers in parentheses denote values imputed—usually from another form of the food or from a similar food. Zero in parentheses indicates that the amount of a constituent probably is none or is too small to measure. Dashes denote lack of reliable data for a constituent believed to be present in measurable amount. Calculated values, as those based on a recipe, are not in parentheses.]

Item No.	Food and description	Water	Food energy	Protein	Fat	Carbohydrate: Total	Carbohydrate: Fiber	Ash	Calcium	Phosphorus	Iron	Sodium	Potassium	Vitamin A value	Thiamine	Riboflavin	Niacin	Ascorbic acid
(A)	(B)	(C)	(D)	(E)	(F)	(G)	(H)	(I)	(J)	(K)	(L)	(M)	(N)	(O)	(P)	(Q)	(R)	(S)
		Percent	Calories	Grams	Grams	Grams	Grams	Grams	Milligrams	Milligrams	Milligrams	Milligrams	Milligrams	International units	Milligrams	Milligrams	Milligrams	Milligrams
	Herring. (See also Lake herring, item 1168.)																	
	Raw:																	
1124	Atlantic	69.0	176	17.3	11.3	0	0	2.1	---	256	1.1	---	---	110	0.02	0.15	3.6	---
1125	Pacific	79.4	98	17.5	2.6	0	0	1.2	---	225	1.3	74	420	100	.02	.16	3.5	3
	Canned, solids and liquid:																	
1126	Plain	62.9	208	19.9	13.6	0	0	3.7	147	297	1.8	---	---	---	---	.18	---	---
1127	In tomato sauce	66.7	176	15.8	10.5	3.7	---	3.3	---	243	---	---	---	---	---	.11	3.5	---
1128	Pickled, Bismarck type	59.4	223	20.4	15.1	0	0	4.0	---	---	---	---	---	---	---	---	---	---
1129	Salted or brined	53.8	218	19.0	15.2	0	0	12.0	---	---	---	---	---	---	---	.19	---	---
	Smoked:																	
1130	Bloaters	64.0	196	19.6	12.4	0	0	3.2	---	---	---	---	---	---	---	---	---	---
1131	Hard	34.6	300	36.9	15.8	0	0	13.2	---	---	---	6,231	157	---	---	---	---	---
1132	Kippered	61.0	211	22.2	12.9	0	0	4.0	66	254	1.4	---	---	30	---	.28	3.3	---
1133	**Hickorynuts**	3.3	673	13.2	68.7	12.8	1.9	2.0	Trace	360	2.4	---	---	---	---	---	---	---
	Hominy grits, dry. See Corn grits, items 862-865.																	
1134	**Honey,** strained or extracted	17.2	304	.3	0	82.3	---	.2	5	6	.5	5	51	0	Trace	.04	.3	1
	Honeydew melon. See Muskmelons, item 1360.																	
	Horseradish:																	
1135	Raw	74.6	87	3.2	.3	19.7	2.4	2.2	140	64	1.4	8	564	---	.07	---	---	81
1136	Prepared	87.1	38	1.3	.2	9.6	.9	1.8	61	32	.9	96	290	---	---	---	---	
	Hyacinth-beans, raw:																	
1137	Young pods	88.8	35	2.8	.3	7.3	1.8	.8	57	53	1.0	2	285	580	.08	.11	.9	20
1138	Mature seeds, dry	11.8	338	22.2	1.5	61.0	6.9	3.5	73	418	5.1	---	---	---	.62	.18	2.1	---
	Ice cream and frozen custard: [illegible]																	
	Regular:																	
1139	Approximately 10% fat	63.2	193	4.5	10.6	20.8	0	.9	146	115	.1	[illegible] 63	181	440	.04	.21	.1	1
1140	Approximately 12% fat	62.1	207	4.0	12.5	20.6	0	.8	123	99	.1	[illegible] 40	112	520	.04	.19	.1	1
1141	Rich, approximately 16% fat	62.8	222	2.6	16.1	18.0	0	.5	78	61	Trace	[illegible] 33	95	660	.02	.11	.1	1
1142	**Ice cream cones**	8.9	377	10.0	2.4	77.9	.2	.8	156	198	.4	232	244	Trace	.05	.21	.5	Trace
1143	**Ice milk**	66.7	152	4.8	5.1	22.4	0	1.0	156	124	.1	[illegible] 68	195	210	.05	.22	.1	1
1144	**Ices, water, lime**	66.9	78	.4	Trace	32.6	Trace	Trace	Trace	Trace	Trace	Trace	3	0	Trace	Trace	Trace	1
	Icings and icing mixes. See Cake icings and Cake icing mixes, items 570-579.																	
1145	**Inconnu** (sheefish), raw	72.6	146	19.9	6.8	0	0	1.3	---	---	---	---	---	---	---	---	---	---
1146	**Jack mackerel,** raw	71.4	143	21.6	5.6	0	0	1.2	---	---	---	---	---	---	---	---	---	---
1147	**Jackfruit,** raw	72.0	98	1.3	.3	25.4	1.0	1.0	22	38	---	2	407	---	.03	---	.4	8
1148	**Jams and preserves**	29.	272	.6	.1	70.0	1.0	.3	20	9	1.0	12	88	10	.01	.03	.2	[illegible] 2
1149	**Jellies**	29.	273	.1	.1	70.6	0	.2	21	7	1.5	17	75	10	.01	.03	.2	[illegible] 4
1150	**Jerusalem-artichoke,** raw	79.8	([illegible])	2.3	.1	[illegible] 16.7	.8	1.1	14	78	3.4	---	---	20	.20	.06	1.3	4
	Jujube, common (Chinese date):																	
1151	Raw	79.2	105	1.2	.2	27.6	1.4	.8	29	37	.7	3	269	40	.02	.04	.9	69
1152	Dried	19.7	287	3.7	1.1	73.6	3.0	1.9	79	100	1.8	---	531	---	---	---	---	13
	Kale:																	
	Raw:																	
1153	Leaves, without stems, midribs	82.7	53	(6.0)	(.8)	9.0	---	(1.5)	249	93	2.7	(75)	(378)	10,000	.16	.26	2.1	186
1154	Leaves, including stems	87.5	38	4.2	.8	6.0	1.3	1.5	179	73	2.2	75	378	8,900	---	---	---	125
	Cooked, boiled, drained:																	
1155	Leaves, without stems, midribs	87.8	39	(4.5)	(.7)	6.1	---	(.9)	187	58	1.6	(43)	(221)	8,300	.10	.18	1.6	93
1156	Leaves, including stems	91.2	28	3.2	.7	4.0	1.1	.9	134	46	1.2	43	221	7,400	---	---	---	62
	Frozen:																	
1157	Not thawed	90.0	32	3.2	.5	5.5	.9	.8	134	50	1.1	28	241	8,200	.08	.18	.8	64
1158	Cooked, boiled, drained	90.5	31	3.0	.5	5.4	.9	.6	121	48	1.0	21	193	8,200	.06	.15	.7	38
	Kidneys:																	
	Beef:																	
1159	Raw	75.9	130	15.4	6.7	.9	0	1.1	11	219	7.4	176	225	690	.36	2.55	6.4	(15)
1160	Cooked, braised	53.0	252	33.0	12.0	.8	0	1.2	18	244	13.1	253	324	1,150	.51	4.82	10.7	---
1161	Calf, raw	77.4	113	16.6	4.6	.1	0	1.3	---	---	4.0	---	---	---	---	---	---	6
1162	Hog, raw	77.8	106	16.3	3.6	1.1	0	1.2	11	218	6.7	115	178	130	.58	1.73	9.8	12
1163	Lamb, raw	77.7	105	16.8	3.3	.9	0	1.3	13	218	7.6	200	230	690	.51	2.42	7.4	15
1164	**Kingfish;** southern, gulf, and northern (whiting); raw	77.3	105	18.3	3.0	0	0	1.3	---	---	---	83	250	---	---	---	---	---
	Knockwurst. See Sausage, cold cuts, and luncheon meats, item 2002.																	
	Kohlrabi, thickened bulb-like stems:																	
1165	Raw	90.3	29	2.0	.1	6.6	1.0	1.0	41	51	.5	8	372	20	.06	.04	.3	66

1166	Cooked, boiled, drained	92.2	24	1.7	.1	5.3	1.0	.7	33	41	.3	6	260	20	.06	.03	.2	43
1167	**Kumquats, raw**	81.3	65	.9	.1	17.1	3.7	.6	63	23	.4	7	236	600	.08	.10	—	36
	Ladyfingers. See Cookies, item 822.																	
1168	**Lake herring (cisco), raw**	79.7	96	17.7	2.3	0	0	1.1	12	206	.5	47	319	—	.09	.10	3.3	—
1169	**Lake trout, raw**	70.6	168	18.3	10.0	0	0	1.1	—	238	.8	—	—	—	.09	.12	2.7	—
	Lake trout (siscowet), raw:																	
1170	Less than 6.5 lbs., round weight	64.9	241	14.3	19.9	0	0	.9	—	—	—	—	—	—	—	—	—	—
1171	6.5 lbs. and over, round weight	36.8	524	7.9	54.4	0	0	.6	—	—	—	—	—	—	—	—	—	—
	Lamb: [4]																	
	Carcass, raw:																	
	Total edible, including kidney and kidney fat:																	
1172	Prime grade (60% lean, 40% fat)	—	—	—	—	—	—	—	—	—	—	—	—	—	—	—	—	—
1173	Choice grade (67% lean, 33% fat)	—	—	—	—	—	—	—	—	—	—	—	—	—	—	—	—	—
1174	Good grade (70% lean, 30% fat)	—	—	—	—	—	—	—	—	—	—	—	—	—	—	—	—	—
	Composite of cuts (leg, loin, rib, and shoulder) trimmed to retail level:																	
1175	Prime grade (72% lean, 28% fat)	56.3	310	15.4	27.1	0	0	1.2	9	135	1.1			—	.14	.19	4.5	—
1176	Choice grade (77% lean, 23% fat)	61.0	263	16.5	21.3	0	0	1.2	10	147	1.2			—	.15	.20	4.8	—
1177	Good grade (79% lean, 21% fat)	62.5	247	16.8	19.4	0	0	1.3	10	151	1.3			—	.15	.21	4.9	—
	Separable fat:																	
	Raw. See individual cuts.																	
1178	Cooked	17.7	709	6.3	75.6	0	0	.4	—	—	—			—	—	—	—	—
	Retail cuts, trimmed to retail level:																	
	Leg:																	
	Prime grade:																	
	Total edible:																	
1179	Raw (79% lean, 21% fat)	60.8	262	16.9	21.0	0	0	1.3	10	152	1.3			—	.15	.21	4.9	—
1180	Cooked, roasted (79% lean, 21% fat)	50.4	319	23.9	24.0	0	0	1.7	10	195	1.6			—	.14	.25	5.2	—
	Separable lean:																	
1181	Raw	73.0	135	19.8	5.6	0	0	1.6	11	184	1.8			—	.18	.25	5.7	—
1182	Cooked, roasted	61.6	192	28.6	7.7	0	0	2.1	12	237	2.2			—	.16	.30	6.1	—
	Separable fat:																	
1183	Raw	15.8	730	5.9	78.1	0	0	.2	3	29	0			—	.05	.07	1.7	—
	Choice grade:																	
	Total edible:																	
1184	Raw (83% lean, 17% fat)	64.8	222	17.8	16.2	0	0	1.3	10	162	1.4			—	.16	.22	5.1	—
1185	Cooked, roasted (83% lean, 17% fat)	54.0	279	25.3	18.9	0	0	1.7	11	208	1.7			—	.15	.27	5.5	—
	Separable lean:																	
1186	Raw	73.6	130	19.9	5.0	0	0	1.5	12	185	1.8	(89)	(90)	—	.18	.25	5.8	—
1187	Cooked, roasted	62.2	186	28.7	7.0	0	0	2.0	13	238	2.2			—	.16	.30	6.2	—
1188	Separable fat:																	
	Raw	20.3	682	7.3	72.2	0	0	.2	4	44	0			—	.06	.09	2.1	—
	Good grade:																	
	Total edible:																	
1189	Raw (85% lean, 15% fat)	65.9	209	18.1	14.6	0	0	1.4	10	165	1.5			—	.16	.22	5.2	—
1190	Cooked, roasted (85% lean, 15% fat)	55.1	266	25.8	17.3	0	0	1.8	11	212	1.8			—	.15	.27	5.6	—
	Separable lean:																	
1191	Raw	73.8	127	19.9	4.7	0	0	1.6	12	185	1.8			—	.18	.25	5.8	—
1192	Cooked, roasted	62.4	183	28.7	6.7	0	0	2.1	12	238	2.2			—	.16	.30	6.2	—
1193	Separable fat:																	
	Raw	22.3	661	7.9	69.5	0	0	.3	5	51	0			—	.07	.10	2.3	—
	Loin:																	
	Prime grade:																	
	Total edible:																	
1194	Raw (67% lean, 33% fat)	52.0	351	14.7	32.0	0	0	1.1	9	127	1.0			—	.13	.18	4.3	—
1195	Cooked, broiled chops (61% lean, 39% fat)	41.7	420	19.5	37.3	0	0	1.4	8	150	1.1			—	.11	.21	4.5	—
	Separable lean:																	
1196	Raw	71.8	146	19.8	6.8	0	0	1.6	11	184	1.8			—	.18	.25	5.7	—
1197	Cooked, broiled	61.3	197	28.0	8.6	0	0	2.2	11	218	2.0			—	.15	.28	6.0	—
	Separable fat:																	
1198	Raw	12.2	770	4.6	83.2	0	0	0	3	14	0			—	.04	.06	1.3	—
	Choice grade:																	
	Total edible:																	
1199	Raw (72% lean, 28% fat)	57.7	293	16.3	24.8	0	0	1.3	9	145	1.2			—	.14	.20	4.7	—
1200	Cooked, broiled chops (66% lean, 34% fat)	47.0	359	22.0	29.4	0	0	1.7	9	172	1.3			—	.12	.23	5.0	—
	Separable lean:																	
1201	Raw	72.6	138	19.9	5.9	0	0	1.6	12	185	1.8			—	.18	.25	5.8	—
1202	Cooked, broiled	62.1	188	28.2	7.5	0	0	2.2	12	219	2.0			—	.15	.28	6.1	—
	Separable fat:																	
1203	Raw	18.4	699	7.0	74.2	0	0	.4	4	41	0			—	.06	.09	2.0	—

[4] See Notes on Foods, p. 180

[8] A large proportion of the carbohydrate in the unstored product may be inulin, which is of doubtful availability. During storage, inulin is converted to sugars

[85] Commercial products. Frozen custard must contain egg yolk which contributes somewhat more vitamin A value than is present in ice creams made with milk products only

[86] Value for product without added salt

[87] Higher values were found for the following jams or jellies: Gooseberry, 10 mg; red cherry or strawberry, 15 mg; guava, 40 mg; black currant, 45 mg; rose hip or acerola, 330 mg per 100 grams.

[88] Values range from 7 Calories per 100 grams for freshly harvested Jerusalem-artichokes to 75 Calories for those stored for a long period

[89] Average value per 100 grams of lamb of all cuts is 75 mg for raw meat and 70 mg for cooked meat. See also Notes on Foods, p 180

[90] Average value per 100 grams of lamb of all cuts is 295 mg for raw meat and 290 mg for cooked meat. See also Notes on Foods, p 180

TABLE 1.—COMPOSITION OF FOODS, 100 GRAMS, EDIBLE PORTION—Continued

[Numbers in parentheses denote values imputed—usually from another form of the food or from a similar food. Zero in parentheses indicates that the amount of a constituent probably is none or is too small to measure. Dashes denote lack of reliable data for a constituent believed to be present in measurable amount. Calculated values, as those based on a recipe, are not in parentheses]

Item No.	Food and description	Water	Food energy	Protein	Fat	Carbohydrate		Ash	Calcium	Phosphorus	Iron	Sodium	Potassium	Vitamin A value	Thiamine	Riboflavin	Niacin	Ascorbic acid
						Total	Fiber											
(A)	(B)	(C)	(D)	(E)	(F)	(G)	(H)	(I)	(J)	(K)	(L)	(M)	(N)	(O)	(P)	(Q)	(R)	(S)
		Percent	Calories	Grams	Grams	Grams	Grams	Grams	Milligrams	Milligrams	Milligrams	Milligrams	Milligrams	International units	Milligrams	Milligrams	Milligrams	Milligrams
	Lamb—Continued																	
	Retail cuts, trimmed to retail level—Continued																	
	Loin—Continued																	
	Good grade:																	
	Total edible:																	
1204	Raw (74% lean, 26% fat)	59.3	276	16.8	22.6	0	0	1.3	10	151	1.3			—	0.15	0.21	4.9	—
1205	Cooked, broiled chops (67% lean, 33% fat).	48.6	341	22.8	27.0	0	0	1.7	10	179	1.5			—	.13	.23	5.1	—
	Separable lean:																	
1206	Raw	72.9	135	19.9	5.6	0	0	1.6	12	185	1.8			—	.18	.25	5.8	—
1207	Cooked, broiled	62.5	184	28.2	7.1	0	0	2.2	11	219	2.0			—	.15	.28	6.1	—
	Separable fat:																	
1208	Raw	21.2	668	8.1	70.2	0	0	.5	5	53	0			—	.07	.10	2.3	—
	Rib:																	
	Prime grade:																	
	Total edible:																	
1209	Raw (58% lean, 42% fat)	45.3	424	13.0	40.8	0	0	.8	8	108	.7			—	.12	.16	3.8	—
1210	Cooked, broiled chops (53% lean, 47% fat).	35.5	492	16.9	46.5	0	0	1.0	7	128	.8			—	.10	.18	4.0	—
	Separable lean:																	
1211	Raw	69.7	169	19.2	9.7	0	0	1.4	11	178	1.7			—	.17	.24	5.5	—
1212	Cooked, broiled	59.1	224	26.9	12.1	0	0	1.9	11	211	1.9			—	.15	.27	5.8	—
	Separable fat:																	
1213	Raw	11.2	779	4.4	84.3	0	0	.1	3	12	0			—	.04	.05	1.3	—
	Choice grade:																	
	Total edible:																	
1214	Raw (68% lean, 32% fat)	53.4	339	15.1	30.4	0	0	1.1	9	132	1.0			—	.14	.19	4.4	—
1215	Cooked, broiled chops (62% lean, 38% fat).	42.9	407	20.1	35.6	0	0	1.4	9	156	1.1			—	.12	.21	4.6	—
	Separable lean:																	
1216	Raw	70.8	158	19.3	8.4	0	0	1.5	11	179	1.7			—	.17	.24	5.6	—
1217	Cooked, broiled	60.3	211	27.2	10.5	0	0	2.0	11	212	1.9			—	.15	.27	5.9	—
	Separable fat:																	
1218	Raw	16.5	722	6.2	77.1	0	0	.2	4	32	0	([illegible])	([illegible])	—	.06	.08	1.8	—
	Good grade:																	
	Total edible:																	
1219	Raw (71% lean, 29% fat)	56.1	312	15.8	27.1	0	0	1.2	9	139	1.1			—	.14	.20	4.6	—
1220	Cooked, broiled chops (64% lean, 36% fat).	45.4	378	21.2	31.9	0	0	1.6	9	165	1.2			—	.12	.22	4.8	—
	Separable lean:																	
1221	Raw	71.2	154	19.4	7.9	0	0	1.5	11	180	1.7			—	.17	.24	5.6	—
1222	Cooked, broiled	60.7	206	27.4	9.9	0	0	2.0	11	213	1.9			—	.15	.27	5.9	—
	Separable fat:																	
1223	Raw	18.8	697	7.0	74.0	0	0	.2	4	41	0			—	.06	.09	2.0	—
	Shoulder:																	
	Prime grade:																	
	Total edible:																	
1224	Raw (71% lean, 29% fat)	55.9	318	14.7	28.3	0	0	1.1	9	127	1.0			—	.13	.18	4.3	—
1225	Cooked, roasted (71% lean, 29% fat)	46.2	374	20.7	31.7	0	0	1.4	9	163	1.2			—	.12	.22	4.6	—
	Separable lean:																	
1226	Raw	71.4	158	18.4	8.8	0	0	1.4	11	169	1.5			—	.16	.25	5.3	—
1227	Cooked, roasted	60.4	215	26.6	11.2	0	0	1.9	11	217	1.8			—	.15	.28	5.7	—
	Separable fat:																	
1228	Raw	17.2	718	5.5	77.0	0	0	.3	3	24	0			—	.05	.07	1.6	—
	Choice grade:																	
	Total edible:																	
1229	Raw (74% lean, 26% fat)	59.6	281	15.3	23.9	0	0	1.1	9	134	1.0			—	.14	.19	4.4	—
1230	Cooked, roasted (74% lean, 26% fat)	49.6	338	21.7	27.2	0	0	1.4	10	172	1.2			—	.13	.23	4.7	—
	Separable lean:																	
1231	Raw	72.4	148	18.5	7.7	0	0	1.4	11	170	1.6			—	.16	.23	5.3	—
1232	Cooked, roasted	61.4	205	26.8	10.0	0	0	1.9	12	219	1.9			—	.15	.28	5.7	—
	Separable fat:																	
1233	Raw	23.1	659	6.3	70.1	0	0	.5	4	33	0			—	.06	.08	1.8	—

	Good grade:																	
	Total edible:																	
1234	Raw (75% lean, 25% fat)	61.2	265	15.5	22.0	0	0	1.2	9	136	1.1	([89])	([90])	—	.14	.19	4.5	—
1235	Cooked, roasted (75% lean, 25% fat)	51.1	322	22.1	25.2	0	0	1.6	10	175	1.3			—	.13	.23	4.9	—
	Separable lean:																	
1236	Raw	72.8	145	18.5	7.3	0	0	1.4	11	170	1.6			—	.16	.23	5.3	—
1237	Cooked, roasted	61.8	201	26.8	9.6	0	0	1.9	11	219	1.9			—	.15	.28	5.7	—
	Separable fat:																	
1238	Raw	25.8	633	6.7	67.0	0	0	.5	4	38	0			—	.06	.08	1.9	—
	Lambsquarters:																	
1239	Raw	84.3	43	4.2	.8	7.3	2.1	3.4	309	72	1.2	—	—	11,600	.16	.44	1.2	80
1240	Cooked, boiled, drained	88.9	32	3.2	.7	5.0	1.8	2.2	258	45	.7	—	—	9,700	.10	.26	.9	37
1241	**Lard**	0	902	0	100	0	0	0	0	0	0	0	0	0	0	0	0	0
1242	**Leeks, bulb and lower leaf portion,** raw	85.4	52	2.2	.3	11.2	1.3	.9	52	50	1.1	5	347	40	.11	.06	.5	17
	Lemons, raw:																	
1243	Peeled fruit	90.1	27	1.1	.3	8.2	.4	.3	26	16	.6	2	138	20	.04	.02	.1	[91] 53
1244	Fruit, including peel	87.4	[92] 20	1.2	.3	10.7	—	.4	61	15	.7	3	145	30	.05	.04	.2	77
	Lemon juice:																	
1245	Raw	91.0	25	.5	.2	8.0	Trace	.3	7	10	.2	1	141	20	.03	.01	.1	46
1246	Canned or bottled, unsweetened	91.6	23	.4	.1	7.6	Trace	.3	7	10	.2	1	141	20	.03	.01	.1	42
	Frozen, unsweetened:																	
1247	Single-strength juice	92.0	22	.4	.2	7.2	Trace	.2	7	9	.3	1	141	20	.03	.01	.1	44
1248	Concentrate	58.0	116	2.3	.9	37.4	Trace	1.4	33	47	.9	5	658	80	.14	.06	.3	230
	Lemon peel:																	
1249	Raw	81.6	([93])	1.5	.3	16.0	—	.6	134	12	.8	6	160	50	.06	.08	.4	129
1250	Candied	17.4	316	.4	.3	80.6	2.3	1.3	—	—	—	—	—	—	—	—	—	—
	Lemonade concentrate, frozen:																	
1251	Undiluted	48.5	195	.2	.1	51.1	.1	.1	4	6	.2	2	70	20	.02	.03	.3	30
1252	Diluted with 4⅓ parts water, by volume	88.5	44	.1	Trace	11.4	Trace	Trace	1	1	Trace	Trace	16	Trace	Trace	.01	.1	7
	Lentils, mature seeds, dry:																	
	Whole:																	
1253	Raw	11.1	340	24.7	1.1	60.1	3.9	3.0	79	377	6.8	30	790	60	.37	.22	2.0	—
1254	Cooked	72.0	106	7.8	Trace	19.3	1.2	.9	25	119	2.1	—	249	20	.07	.06	.6	0
1255	Split, without seed coat, raw	10.4	345	24.7	.9	61.8	1.7	2.2	46	260	6.8	—	—	60	.37	.22	2.0	—
	Lettuce, raw:																	
1256	Butterhead varieties such as Boston types and Bibb	95.1	14	1.2	.2	2.5	.5	1.0	35	26	2.0	9	264	970	.06	.06	.3	8
1257	Cos, or romaine, such as Dark Green and White Paris.	94.0	18	1.3	.3	3.5	.7	.9	68	25	1.4	9	264	1,900	.05	.08	.4	18
1258	Crisphead varieties such as Iceberg, New York, and Great Lakes strains.	95.5	13	.9	.1	2.9	.5	.6	20	22	.5	9	175	330	.06	.06	.3	6
1259	Looseleaf, or bunching varieties, such as Grand Rapids, Salad Bowl, Simpson.	94.0	18	1.3	.3	3.5	.7	.9	68	25	1.4	9	264	1,900	.05	.08	.4	18
	Lima beans. See Beans, lima: items 164–177.																	
1260	**Limes, acid type, raw**	89.3	28	.7	.2	9.5	.5	.3	33	18	.6	2	102	10	.03	.02	2	37
	Lime juice:																	
1261	Raw	90.3	26	.3	.1	9.0	Trace	.3	9	11	.2	1	104	10	.02	.01	.1	32
1262	Canned or bottled, unsweetened	90.3	26	.3	.1	9.0	Trace	.3	9	11	.2	1	104	10	.02	.01	.1	21
	Limeade concentrate, frozen:																	
1263	Undiluted	50.0	187	.2	.1	49.5	Trace	.2	5	6	.1	Trace	59	Trace	.01	.01	.1	12
1264	Diluted with 4⅓ parts water, by volume	88.9	41	Trace	Trace	11.0	Trace	Trace	1	1	Trace	Trace	13	Trace	Trace	Trace	Trace	2
1265	**Lingcod, raw**	80.0	84	17.9	.8	0	0	1.2	—	—	—	59	433	0	.05	.04	—	—
	Liver:																	
	Beef:																	
1266	Raw	69.7	140	19.9	3.8	5.3	0	1.3	8	352	6.5	136	281	[94] 43,900	.25	3.26	13.6	31
1267	Cooked, fried	56.0	229	26.4	10.6	5.3	0	1.7	11	476	8.8	184	380	[94] 53,400	.26	4.19	16.5	27
	Calf:																	
1268	Raw	70.7	140	19.2	4.7	4.1	0	1.3	8	333	8.8	73	281	[94] 22,500	.20	2.72	11.4	36
1269	Cooked, fried	51.4	261	29.5	13.2	4.0	0	1.9	13	537	14.2	118	453	[94] 32,700	.24	4.17	16.5	37
	Chicken, all classes:																	
1270	Raw	72.2	129	19.7	3.7	2.9	0	1.5	12	236	7.9	70	172	[94] 12,100	.19	2.49	10.8	17
1271	Cooked, simmered	65.0	165	26.5	4.4	3.1	0	1.0	11	159	8.5	61	151	[94] 12,300	.17	2.69	11.7	16
1272	Goose, raw	66.9	182	16.5	10.0	5.4	0	1.2	—	—	—	140	230	—	—	—	—	—
	Hog:																	
1273	Raw	71.6	131	20.6	3.7	2.6	0	1.5	10	356	19.2	73	261	[94] 10,900	.30	3.03	16.4	23
1274	Cooked, fried	54.0	241	29.9	11.5	2.5	0	2.1	15	539	29.1	111	395	[94] 14,900	.34	4.36	22.3	22
	Lamb:																	
1275	Raw	70.8	136	21.0	3.9	2.9	0	1.4	10	349	10.9	52	202	[94] 50,500	.40	3.28	16.9	33
1276	Cooked, broiled	50.4	261	32.3	12.4	2.8	0	2.1	16	572	17.9	85	331	[94] 74,500	.49	5.11	24.9	36
	Turkey, all classes:																	
1277	Raw	70.4	138	21.2	4.0	2.9	0	1.5	—	—	—	63	160	[94] 17,700	.18	1.93	13.2	—
1278	Cooked, simmered	63.3	174	27.9	4.8	3.1	0	1.0	—	—	—	55	141	[94] 17,500	.16	2.09	14.3	—

[89] Average value per 100 grams of lamb of all cuts is 75 mg. for raw meat and 70 mg. for cooked meat. See also Notes on Foods, p. 180.

[90] Average value per 100 grams of lamb of all cuts is 295 mg. for raw meat and 290 mg. for cooked meat. See also Notes on Foods, p. 180.

[91] Applies to lemons marketed in summer.

[92] Based on the pulp. There is no basis for assessing the calorie value of the peel or the effect that inclusion of the peel may have on the digestibility of the product.

[93] Value cannot be calculated inasmuch as digestibility of peel is not known.

[94] Values vary widely in all kinds of liver, ranging from about 100 I U. to more than 100,000 I U. per 100 grams.

TABLE 1.—COMPOSITION OF FOODS, 100 GRAMS, EDIBLE PORTION—Continued

[Numbers in parentheses denote values imputed—usually from another form of the food or from a similar food. Zero in parentheses indicates that the amount of a constituent probably is none or is too small to measure. Dashes denote lack of reliable data for a constituent believed to be present in measurable amount. Calculated values, as those based on a recipe, are not in parentheses]

Item No.	Food and description	Water	Food energy	Protein	Fat	Carbohydrate		Ash	Calcium	Phosphorus	Iron	Sodium	Potassium	Vitamin A value	Thiamine	Riboflavin	Niacin	Ascorbic acid
						Total	Fiber											
(A)	(B)	(C)	(D)	(E)	(F)	(G)	(H)	(I)	(J)	(K)	(L)	(M)	(N)	(O)	(P)	(Q)	(R)	(S)
		Percent	Calories	Grams	Grams	Grams	Grams	Grams	Milligrams	Milligrams	Milligrams	Milligrams	Milligrams	International units	Milligrams	Milligrams	Milligrams	Milligrams
	Liver paste. See Pâté de foie gras, item 1478.																	
	Liver sausage or liverwurst. See Sausage, cold cuts, and luncheon meats: items 2003–2004.																	
	Lobster, northern:																	
1279	Raw, whole	78.5	91	16.9	1.9	0.5	—	2.2	29	183	0.6	—	—	—	0.40	0.05	1.5	—
1280	Canned or cooked	76.8	95	18.7	1.5	.3	—	2.7	65	192	.8	210	180	—	.10	.07	—	—
1281	**Lobster Newburg** [95]	64.0	194	18.5	10.6	5.1	—	1.8	87	192	.9	229	171	—	.07	.11	—	—
1282	**Lobster salad** [96]	80.3	110	10.1	6.4	2.3	—	.9	36	95	.9	124	264	—	.09	.08	—	18
	Lobster paste. See Shrimp or lobster paste, canned: item 2047.																	
	Lobster, spiny. See Crayfish, item 927.																	
	Loganberries:																	
1283	Raw	83.0	62	1.0	.6	14.9	3.0	.5	35	17	1.2	(1)	170	(200)	(.03)	(.04)	(.4)	24
	Canned, solids and liquid:																	
1284	Water pack, with or without artificial sweetener	89.2	40	.7	.4	9.4	2.0	.3	24	11	.8	1	115	140	.01	.02	.2	8
1285	Juice pack	85.7	54	.7	.5	12.7	2.1	.4	27	15	1.2	1	170	150	.02	.03	.3	12
	Sirup pack:																	
1286	Light	81.4	70	.7	.4	17.2	2.0	.3	23	11	.8	1	111	130	.01	.02	.2	8
1287	Heavy	76.5	89	.6	.4	22.2	1.9	.3	22	11	.8	1	109	130	.01	.02	.2	8
1288	Extra heavy	71.5	108	.6	.4	27.2	1.9	.3	22	11	.8	1	107	130	.01	.02	.2	7
	Longans:																	
1289	Raw	82.4	61	1.0	.1	15.8	.4	.7	10	42	1.2	—	—	—	—	—	—	(6)
1290	Dried	17.6	286	4.9	.4	74.0	2.0	3.1	45	196	5.4	—	—	—	.04	—	—	28
1291	**Loquats, raw**	86.5	48	.4	.2	12.4	.5	.5	20	36	.4	—	348	670	—	—	—	1
	Luncheon meat. See Sausage, cold cuts, and luncheon meats: items 2005–2006.																	
	Lungs, raw:																	
1292	Beef	78.8	96	17.6	2.3	0	0	1.0	—	216	—	—	—	—	—	—	6.2	—
1293	Calf	77.4	106	16.8	3.8	0	0	1.2	—	—	—	—	—	—	—	—	—	—
1294	Lamb	76.7	103	19.3	2.3	0	0	1.2	—	180	—	—	—	—	—	—	—	—
	Lychees:																	
1295	Raw	81.9	64	.9	.3	16.4	.3	.5	8	42	.4	3	170	—	—	.05	—	42
1296	Dried	22.3	277	3.8	1.2	70.7	1.4	2.0	33	181	1.7	3	1,100	—	—	—	—	—
1297	**Macadamia nuts**	3.0	691	7.8	71.6	15.9	2.5	1.7	48	161	2.0	—	264	0	.34	.11	1.3	0
	Macaroni:																	
	Enriched:																	
1298	Dry form	10.4	369	12.5	1.2	75.2	.3	.7	27	162	[59] 2.9	2	197	(0)	[59] .88	[59] .37	[59] 6.0	(0)
1299	Cooked, firm stage (8–10 min.)	63.6	148	5.0	.5	30.1	.1	1.3	11	65	[59] 1.1	1	79	(0)	[59] .18	[59] .10	[59] 1.4	(0)
1300	Cooked, tender stage (14–20 min.)	72.0	111	3.4	.4	23.0	.1	1.2	8	50	.9	1	61	(0)	.14	.08	1.1	(0)
	Unenriched:																	
1301	Dry form	10.4	369	12.5	1.2	75.2	.3	.7	27	162	1.3	2	197	(0)	.09	.06	1.7	(0)
1302	Cooked, firm stage (8–10 min.)	63.6	148	5.0	.5	30.1	.1	1.3	11	65	.5	1	79	(0)	.02	.02	.4	(0)
1303	Cooked, tender stage (14–20 min.)	72.0	111	3.4	.4	23.0	.1	1.2	8	50	.4	1	61	(0)	.01	.01	.3	(0)
	Macaroni and cheese:																	
1304	Baked, made from home recipe [97]	58.2	215	8.4	11.1	20.1	.1	2.2	181	161	.9	543	120	430	.10	.20	.9	Trace
1305	Canned	80.2	95	3.9	4.0	10.7	.1	1.2	83	76	.4	304	58	110	.05	.10	.4	Trace
	Mackerel, Atlantic:																	
1306	Raw	67.2	191	19.0	12.2	0	0	1.6	5	239	1.0	—	—	(450)	.15	.33	8.2	—
1307	Canned, solids and liquid [98]	66.0	183	19.3	11.1	0	0	3.2	185	274	2.1	—	—	430	.06	.21	5.8	—
1308	Cooked, broiled with butter or margarine	61.6	236	21.8	15.8	0	0	1.6	6	280	1.2	—	—	(530)	.15	.27	7.6	—
	Mackerel, Pacific:																	
1309	Raw	69.8	159	21.9	7.3	0	0	1.4	8	274	2.1	—	—	120	—	—	—	—
1310	Canned, solids and liquid [98]	66.4	180	21.1	10.0	0	0	2.5	260	288	2.2	—	—	30	.03	.33	8.8	—
	Mackerel:																	
1311	Salted	43.0	305	18.5	25.1	0	0	13.0	—	—	—	—	—	—	—	—	—	—
1312	Smoked	59.4	219	23.8	13.0	0	0	2.0	—	—	—	—	—	—	—	—	—	—
1313	**Malt, dry**	5.2	368	13.1	1.9	77.4	5.7	2.4	—	—	4.0	—	—	—	.49	.31	9.0	—
1314	**Malt extract, dried**	3.2	367	6.0	Trace	89.2	Trace	1.6	48	294	8.7	80	230	—	.36	.45	9.8	—
1315	**Mamey (mammeeapple), raw**	86.2	51	.5	.5	12.5	1.0	.3	11	11	.7	15	47	230	.02	.04	.4	14
	Mandarin oranges. See Tangerines, item 2262.																	
1316	**Mangos, raw**	81.7	66	.7	.4	16.8	.9	.4	10	13	.4	7	189	4,800	.05	.05	1.1	35
1317	**Margarine** [99]	15.5	720	.6	81.	.4	0	2.5	20	16	0	987	23	3,300	—	—	—	0
1318	**Marmalade, citrus**	29.0	257	.5	.1	70.1	.4	.3	35	9	.6	14	33	—	.02	.02	.1	6
	Marmalade plums. See Sapotes, item 1970.																	

	Matai. See Waterchestnut, Chinese, item 2422																	
	Mayonnaise. See Salad dressings, item 1938.																	
	Meat loaf. See Sausage, cold cuts, and luncheon meats: item 2007.																	
	Meat. See Beef, Lamb, Pork, Veal																	
	Meilorine. See Notes on Foods, page 182																	
	Melons. See Muskmelons, items 1358-1361; and Watermelons, item 2424.																	
1319	**Menhaden,** Atlantic, canned, solids and liquid	67.9	172	18.7	10.2	0	0	3.8	—	—	1.3	—	—	—	—	—	—	—
	Milk, cow:																	
	Fluid (pasteurized and raw):																	
	Whole:																	
1320	3.5% fat [100]	87.4	65	3.5	3.5	4.9	0	.7	118	93	Trace	50	144	140	.03	.17	.1	1
1321	3.7% fat [100]	87.2	66	3.5	3.7	4.9	0	.7	117	92	Trace	50	140	150	.03	.17	.1	1
1322	Skim	90.5	36	3.6	.1	5.1	0	.7	121	95	Trace	52	145	Trace	.04	.18	.1	1
1323	Partially skimmed with 2% nonfat milk solids added.	87.0	59	4.2	2.0	6.0	0	.8	143	112	.1	61	175	80	.04	.21	.1	1
	Half-and-half (cream and milk). See Cream, item 928.																	
	Canned:																	
1324	Evaporated (unsweetened)	73.8	137	7.0	7.9	9.7	0	1.6	252	205	.1	118	303	320	.04	.34	.2	1
1325	Condensed (sweetened)	27.1	321	8.1	8.7	54.3	0	1.8	262	206	.1	112	314	360	.08	.38	.2	1
	Dry:																	
1326	Whole	2.0	502	26.4	27.5	38.2	0	5.9	909	708	.5	405	1,330	1,130	.29	1.46	.7	6
1327	Skim (nonfat solids), regular	3.0	363	35.9	.8	52.3	0	8.0	1,308	1,016	.6	532	1,745	30	.35	(1.80)	.9	7
1328	Skim (nonfat solids), instant	4.0	359	35.8	.7	51.6	0	7.9	1,293	1,005	.6	526	1,725	30	.35	1.78	.9	7
	Malted:																	
1329	Dry powder [101]	2.6	410	14.7	8.3	70.8	.3	3.6	288	380	2.1	440	720	1,020	.33	.54	.3	(0)
1330	Beverage [102]	78.2	104	4.7	4.4	11.7	Trace	1.0	135	122	.3	91	200	250	.06	.21	.1	1
	Chocolate drink, fluid, commercial.																	
1331	Made with skim milk	82.8	76	3.3	2.3	10.9	Trace	.7	108	91	.2	46	142	80	.04	.16	.1	1
1332	Made with whole (3.5% fat) milk	81.5	85	3.4	3.4	11.0	Trace	.7	111	94	.2	47	146	130	.03	.16	.1	1
	Chocolate beverages, homemade.																	
1333	Hot chocolate	80.5	95	3.3	5.0	10.4	.1	.7	104	94	.2	48	148	140	.03	.16	.1	1
1334	Hot cocoa	79.0	97	3.8	4.6	10.9	.1	.9	118	113	.4	51	145	160	.04	.18	.2	1
	Buttermilk. See Buttermilk, items 509-510.																	
1335	**Milk, goat,** fluid	87.5	67	3.2	4.0	4.6	0	.7	129	106	.1	34	180	(160)	.04	.11	.3	1
1336	**Milk, human,** U.S. samples	85.2	77	1.1	4.0	9.5	0	.2	33	14	.1	16	51	240	.01	.04	.2	5
1337	**Milk, reindeer**	64.1	234	10.8	19.6	4.1	0	1.4	254	198	.1	157	159	—	—	—	—	—
1338	**Millet,** proso (broomcorn, hogmillet), whole-grain	11.8	327	9.9	2.9	72.9	3.2	2.5	20	311	6.8	—	430	(0)	.73	.38	2.3	(0)
	Mixed vegetables, frozen. See Vegetables, mixed, frozen: items 2403-2404.																	
	Molasses, cane:																	
1339	First extraction or light	24.	252	—	—	[103] 65.	—	[104] 6.3	165	45	4.3	15	917	—	.07	.06	.2	—
1340	Second extraction or medium	24.	232	—	—	[103] 60	—	[104] 8.5	290	69	6.0	37	1,063	—	—	.12	1.2	—
1341	Third extraction or blackstrap	24.	213	—	—	[103] 55.	—	[104] 10.5	684	84	16.1	96	2,927	—	.11	.19	2.0	—
1342	Barbados	24.	271	—	—	[103] 70.	—	[104] 1.6	245	50	—	—	—	—	.06	.20	—	—
	Mortadella. See Sausage, cold cuts, and luncheon meats: item 2010.																	
	Muffins, baked from home recipes.																	
	Plain, made with—																	
1343	Enriched flour	38.0	294	7.8	10.1	42.3	.1	1.8	104	151	1.6	441	125	100	.17	.23	1.4	Trace
1344	Unenriched flour	38.0	294	7.8	10.1	42.3	.1	1.8	104	151	.6	441	125	100	.04	.14	.4	Trace
	Other, made with enriched flour.																	
1345	Blueberry	39.0	281	7.3	9.3	41.9	.3	2.5	84	132	1.6	632	115	220	.16	.20	1.2	1
1346	Bran	35.1	261	7.7	9.8	43.1	1.8	4.3	142	405	3.7	448	431	230	.14	.24	4.0	Trace
	Corn, made with—																	
1347	Enriched degermed cornmeal	32.7	314	7.1	10.1	48.1	.2	2.0	105	169	1.7	481	135	300	.20	.23	1.6	Trace
1348	Whole-ground cornmeal	37.8	288	7.2	10.3	42.5	.5	2.2	112	216	1.4	495	132	310	.17	.17	1.0	Trace
	Muffin mixes, corn, and muffins baked from mixes: [105]																	
1349	Mix, dry form, with enriched flour	7.8	417	6.2	11.5	71.8	.5	2.7	300	473	1.8	660	76	150	.24	.16	2.1	0
1350	Muffins, made with egg, milk	30.4	324	6.9	10.6	50.0	.2	2.1	241	380	1.5	479	110	240	.18	.19	1.4	Trace
1351	Mix, dry form, with cake flour, nonfat dry milk	7.8	409	6.2	10.7	71.6	.2	3.7	222	328	.9	811	133	100	.13	.15	1.1	Trace
1352	Muffins, made with egg, water	33.1	297	4.5	7.8	51.9	.1	2.7	148	228	1.1	346	104	150	.12	.12	1.3	Trace

[93] Based on product with minimum level of enrichment. See Notes on Foods, p. 171.

[94] Prepared with butter, egg yolks, sherry, and cream.

[95] Prepared with onion, sweet pickle, celery, eggs, mayonnaise, and tomatoes.

[97] Prepared with enriched macaroni.

[98] Vitamin values based on drained solids.

[99] Values apply to salted margarine. Unsalted margarine contains less than 10 mg. per 100 grams of either sodium or potassium. Vitamin A value based on the minimum required to meet Federal specifications for margarine with vitamin A added; namely 15,000 I.U. of vitamin A per pound.

[100] Minimum standards for fat in different States vary considerably, and commercial milks may range somewhat above the required minimums. Selection of values to be used in dietary calculations may need to be based on information at the local level. The value, 3.7 percent, is considered valid as a national average for milk on the farm production basis.

[101] Values are based on unfortified products.

[102] Prepared with malted milk powder and whole milk.

[103] Value for total sugars.

[104] Value is for sulfated ash and overestimates ash by approximately 8 to 20 percent.

[105] Contain yellow degermed cornmeal.

TABLE 1.—COMPOSITION OF FOODS, 100 GRAMS, EDIBLE PORTION—Continued

[Numbers in parentheses denote values imputed—usually from another form of the food or from a similar food. Zero in parentheses indicates that the amount of a constituent probably is none or is too small to measure. Dashes denote lack of reliable data for a constituent believed to be present in measurable amount. Calculated values, as those based on a recipe, are not in parentheses]

Item No.	Food and description	Water	Food energy	Protein	Fat	Carbohydrate: Total	Carbohydrate: Fiber	Ash	Calcium	Phosphorus	Iron	Sodium	Potassium	Vitamin A value	Thiamine	Riboflavin	Niacin	Ascorbic acid
(A)	(B)	(C)	(D)	(E)	(F)	(G)	(H)	(I)	(J)	(K)	(L)	(M)	(N)	(O)	(P)	(Q)	(R)	(S)
		Percent	Calories	Grams	Grams	Grams	Grams	Grams	Milligrams	Milligrams	Milligrams	Milligrams	Milligrams	International units	Milligrams	Milligrams	Milligrams	Milligrams
1353	Mullet, striped, raw	72.6	146	19.6	6.9	0	0	1.3	26	220	1.8	81	292	—	0.07	0.08	5.2	—
	Mushrooms: [48]																	
	Agaricus campestris, cultivated commercially:																	
1354	Raw	90.4	28	2.7	.3	4.4	.8	.9	6	116	.8	15	414	Trace	.10	.46	4.2	3
1355	Canned, solids and liquid	93.1	17	1.9	.1	2.4	.6	1.6	6	68	.5	400	197	Trace	.02	.25	2.0	2
1356	Other edible species, raw	89.1	35	1.9	.6	6.5	1.1	1.0	13	97	1.4	10	375	Trace	.10	.43	6.8	3
1357	**Muskellunge, raw**	76.3	109	20.2	2.5	0	0	1.6	—	227	.6	—	—	—	—	—	—	—
	Muskmelons:																	
	Raw:																	
1358	Cantaloups, other netted varieties	91.2	30	.7	.1	7.5	.3	.5	14	16	.4	12	251	[30] 3,400	.04	.03	.6	33
1359	Casaba (Golden Beauty)	91.5	27	1.2	Trace	6.5	.5	.8	(14)	(16)	(.4)	(12)	(251)	30	(.04)	(.03)	(.6)	13
1360	Honeydew	90.6	33	.8	.3	7.7	.6	.6	14	16	.4	12	251	40	.04	.03	.6	23
	Frozen:																	
1361	Melon balls (cantaloup and Honeydew) in sirup, not thawed	83.2	62	.6	.1	15.7	.3	.4	10	12	.3	9	188	1,540	.03	.02	.5	16
1362	**Muskrat,** cooked, roasted	67.3	153	27.2	4.1	0	0	1.4	—	—	—	—	—	—	.16	.21	—	—
	Mussels, Atlantic and Pacific, raw:																	
1363	Meat and liquid	83.8	66	9.6	1.4	3.1	—	2.1	—	—	—	—	—	—	—	—	—	—
1364	Meat only	78.6	95	14.4	2.2	3.3	—	1.5	88	236	3.4	289	315	—	.16	.21	—	—
1365	**Mussels, Pacific,** canned, drained solids	74.6	114	18.2	3.3	1.5	—	2.4	—	—	—	—	—	—	—	.13	—	—
	Mustard greens:																	
1366	Raw	89.5	31	3.0	.5	5.6	1.1	1.4	183	50	3.0	32	377	7,000	.11	.22	.8	97
1367	Cooked, boiled, drained	92.6	23	2.2	.4	4.0	.9	.8	138	32	1.8	18	220	5,800	.08	.14	.6	48
	Frozen:																	
1368	Not thawed	93.5	20	2.3	.4	3.2	1.0	.6	115	46	1.6	12	196	6,000	.04	.12	.4	34
1369	Cooked, boiled, drained	93.8	20	2.2	.4	3.1	1.0	.5	104	43	1.5	10	157	6,000	.03	.10	.4	29
	Mustard spinach (tendergreen):																	
1370	Raw	92.2	22	2.2	.3	3.9	1.0	1.4	210	28	1.5	—	—	9,900	—	—	—	130
1371	Cooked, boiled, drained	94.5	16	1.7	.2	2.8	.8	.8	158	18	.8	—	—	8,200	—	—	—	65
	Mustard, prepared:																	
1372	Brown	78.1	91	5.9	6.3	5.3	1.3	4.4	124	134	1.8	1,307	130	—	—	—	—	—
1373	Yellow	80.2	75	4.7	4.4	6.4	1.0	4.3	84	73	2.0	1,252	130	—	—	—	—	—
1374	**Nectarines,** raw	81.8	64	.6	Trace	17.1	.4	.5	4	24	.5	6	294	1,650	—	—	—	13
	New Zealand spinach:																	
1375	Raw	92.6	19	2.2	.3	3.1	.7	1.8	58	46	2.6	159	795	4,300	.04	.17	.6	30
1376	Cooked, boiled, drained	94.8	13	1.7	.2	2.1	.6	1.2	48	28	1.5	92	463	3,600	.03	.10	.5	14
	Noodles, egg noodles:																	
	Enriched:																	
1377	Dry form	9.8	388	12.8	4.6	72.0	.4	.8	31	183	[38] 2.9	5	136	220	[38] .88	[38] .38	[38] 6.0	(0)
1378	Cooked	70.4	125	4.1	1.5	23.3	.1	.7	10	59	[38] .9	2	44	70	[38] .14	[38] .08	[38] 1.2	(0)
	Unenriched:																	
1379	Dry form	9.8	388	12.8	4.6	72.0	.4	.8	31	183	1.9	5	136	220	.17	.09	2.1	(0)
1380	Cooked	70.4	125	4.1	1.5	23.3	.1	.7	10	59	.6	2	44	70	.03	.02	.4	(0)
1381	**Noodles, chow mein,** canned	1.1	489	13.2	23.5	58.0	—	4.2	—	—	—	—	—	—	—	—	—	—
	Nuts. See individual kinds.																	
	Oat products used mainly as hot breakfast cereals:																	
	Oat cereal with toasted wheat germ and soy grits:																	
1382	Dry form	8.7	382	20.5	9.0	58.6	3.5	3.2	70	590	7.1	8	—	(0)	1.06	.17	1.4	(0)
1383	Cooked	84.4	62	3.3	1.5	9.5	.6	1.3	13	96	1.1	292	Trace	(0)	.16	.02	.2	(0)
	Oat flakes, maple-flavored, instant-cooking:																	
1384	Dry form	7.4	384	14.6	4.2	72.3	.7	1.5	50	360	3.5	1	—	(0)	.35	—	—	(0)
1385	Cooked	83.0	69	2.6	.8	13.0	.1	.6	10	65	.6	107	—	(0)	.06	—	—	(0)
	Oat granules, maple-flavored, quick-cooking:																	
1386	Dry form	7.0	383	14.8	4.0	72.5	1.1	1.7	60	400	3.8	1	—	(0)	.40	—	—	(0)
1387	Cooked	85.2	60	2.3	.6	11.4	.2	.5	10	63	.6	72	—	(0)	.06	—	—	(0)
	Oat and wheat cereal:																	
1388	Dry form	10.0	364	14.7	5.0	68.3	1.5	2.0	53	423	3.9	2	—	(0)	.49	.18	2.6	(0)
1389	Cooked	83.6	65	2.6	.9	12.1	.3	.8	11	75	.7	168	—	(0)	.09	.03	.5	(0)
	Oatmeal or rolled oats:																	
1390	Dry form	8.3	390	14.2	7.4	68.2	1.2	1.9	53	405	4.5	2	352	(0)	.60	.14	1.0	(0)
1391	Cooked	86.5	55	2.0	1.0	9.7	.2	.8	9	57	.6	218	61	(0)	.08	.02	.1	(0)

	Oat products used mainly as ready-to-eat breakfast cereals:																	
1392	Oats, shredded, with protein and other added nutrients	3.9	379	18.8	2.1	72.0	1.8	3.2	265	317	5.3	610	—	(0)	3.53	4.23	35.3	(0)
1393	Oats (with or without corn), puffed, added nutrients	3.4	397	11.9	5.5	75.2	1.1	4.0	177	408	4.7	1,267	—	(0)	.98	.18	1.9	(0)
1394	Oats (with or without corn, wheat), puffed, added nutrients, sugar-covered	1.9	396	6.7	3.4	85.6	.7	2.4	72	202	4.4	588	—	(0)	1.03	.12	1.7	(0)
1395	Oats (with soy flour and rice), flaked, added nutrients	3.5	397	14.9	5.7	70.7	.9	5.2	150	350	8.5	1,200	—	(0)	.71	.33	8.5	(0)
	Ocean perch, Atlantic (redfish):																	
1396	Raw	79.7	88	18.0	1.2	0	0	1.1	20	207	1.0	79	269	—	.10	.08	1.9	—
1397	Cooked, fried [82]	59.0	227	19.0	13.3	6.8	0	1.9	33	226	1.3	153	284	—	.10	.11	1.8	—
1398	Frozen, breaded, fried, reheated	43.2	319	18.9	18.9	16.5	—	2.5	—	—	—	—	—	—	—	—	—	—
1399	Ocean perch, Pacific, raw	79.0	95	19.0	1.5	0	0	1.1	—	—	—	63	390	—	—	—	—	—
1400	Octopus, raw	82.2	73	15.3	.8	0	0	1.5	29	173	—	—	—	—	.02	.06	1.8	—
1401	Oils, salad or cooking	0	884	0	100.	0	0	0	0	0	0	0	0	—	0	0	0	0
	Okra:																	
1402	Raw	88.9	36	2.4	.3	7.6	1.0	.8	92	51	.6	3	249	520	(.17)	(.21)	(1.0)	31
1403	Cooked, boiled, drained	91.1	29	2.0	.3	6.0	1.0	.6	92	41	.5	2	174	490	(.13)	(.18)	(.9)	20
	Frozen, cuts and pods:																	
1404	Not thawed	87.9	39	2.3	.1	9.0	1.0	.7	94	51	.6	2	219	480	.17	.21	1.0	16
1405	Cooked, boiled, drained	88.3	38	2.2	.1	8.8	1.0	.6	94	43	.5	2	164	480	.14	.17	1.0	12
	Oleomargarine. See Margarine, item 1317.																	
	Olives, pickled; canned or bottled:																	
1406	Green	78.2	116	1.4	12.7	1.3	1.3	6.4	61	17	1.6	2,400	55	300	—	—	—	—
	Ripe:																	
1407	Ascolano (extra large, mammoth, giant, jumbo)	80.0	129	1.1	13.8	2.6	1.4	2.5	84	16	1.6	813	34	60	Trace	Trace	—	—
1408	Manzanilla (small, medium, large, extra large)	80.0	129	1.1	13.8	2.6	1.4	2.5	84	16	1.6	813	34	60	Trace	Trace	—	—
1409	Mission (small, medium, large, extra large)	73.0	184	1.2	20.1	3.2	1.5	2.5	106	17	1.7	750	27	70	Trace	Trace	—	—
1410	Sevillano (giant, jumbo, colossal, supercolossal)	84.4	93	1.1	9.5	2.7	1.2	2.3	74	20	1.6	828	44	60	Trace	Trace	—	—
1411	Ripe, salt-cured, oil-coated, Greek style	43.8	338	2.2	35.8	8.7	3.8	(9.5)	—	29	—	3,288	—	—	—	—	—	—
	Omelet. See Eggs, omelet: item 975.																	
	Onions, mature (dry):																	
1412	Raw	89.1	38	1.5	.1	8.7	.6	.6	27	36	.5	10	157	[107] 40	.03	.04	.2	10
1413	Cooked, boiled, drained	91.8	29	1.2	.1	6.5	.6	.4	24	29	.4	7	110	[107] 40	.03	.03	.2	7
1414	Dehydrated, flaked	4.	350	8.7	1.3	82.1	4.4	3.9	166	273	2.9	88	1,383	[107] 200	.25	.18	1.4	35
	Onions, young green (bunching varieties), raw:																	
1415	Bulb and entire top	89.4	36	1.5	.2	8.2	(1.2)	.7	51	39	1.0	5	231	(2,000)	.05	.05	.4	32
1416	Bulb and white portion of top	87.6	45	1.1	.2	10.5	1.0	.6	40	39	.6	5	231	Trace	.05	.04	.4	25
1417	Tops only (green portion)	91.8	27	1.6	.4	5.5	1.3	.7	56	39	2.2	5	231	4,000	.07	.10	.6	51
1418	Onions, Welsh, raw	90.5	34	1.9	.4	6.5	1.0	.7	18	49	—	—	—	—	.05	.09	.4	27
1419	Opossum, cooked, roasted	57.3	221	30.2	10.2	0	0	2.3	—	—	—	—	—	—	.12	.38	—	—
	Oranges, raw:																	
	Peeled fruit:																	
1420	All commercial varieties	86.0	49	1.0	.2	12.2	.5	.6	41	20	.4	1	200	200	.10	.04	.4	[79] (50)
	California:																	
1421	Navels (winter oranges)	85.4	51	1.3	.1	12.7	.5	.5	40	22	.4	1	194	(200)	.10	.04	.4	[79] (61)
1422	Valencias (summer oranges)	85.6	51	1.2	.3	12.4	(.5)	.5	40	22	.8	1	190	(200)	.10	.04	.4	[79] (49)
	Florida:																	
1423	All commercial varieties	86.4	47	.7	(.2)	12.0	(.5)	.7	43	17	.2	1	(206)	(200)	10	.04	4	[79] (45)
1424	Fruit, including peel (California Valencias)	82.3	[83] 40	1.3	.3	15.5	—	.6	70	22	.8	2	196	250	.10	05	.5	71
	Orange juice:																	
	Raw:																	
1425	All commercial varieties	88.3	45	.7	.2	10.4	.1	.4	11	17	.2	1	200	200	.09	.03	.4	[79] 50
	California:																	
1426	Navels (winter oranges)	87.2	48	1.0	.1	11.3	(.1)	.4	11	18	.2	1	194	200	.09	.03	.4	[79] 61
1427	Valencias (summer oranges)	87.8	47	1.0	.3	10.5	(.1)	.4	11	19	.3	1	190	200	.09	.03	.4	[79] 49
	Florida:																	
1428	All commercial varieties	88.8	43	.6	.2	10.0	(.1)	.4	10	16	.2	1	206	200	09	.03	.4	[79] 45
1429	Early and midseason oranges (Hamlin, Parson Brown, Pineapple)	89.6	40	.5	.2	9.3	(.1)	.4	10	15	.2	1	208	200	.09	.03	.4	[79] 51
1430	Late season (Valencias)	88.3	45	.6	.2	10.5	(.1)	.4	10	18	.2	1	203	200	.09	.03	4	[79] 37
1431	Temple [47]	88.0	54	(.5)	(.2)	12.9	(.1)	.4	(10)	17	.2	1	—	(200)	.09	.03	.4	[79] 50
	Canned:																	
1432	Unsweetened	87.4	48	.8	.2	11.2	.1	.4	10	18	.4	1	199	200	.07	.02	.3	40
1433	Sweetened	86.5	52	.7	.2	12.2	.1	.4	(10)	18	.4	1	(199)	200	.07	.02	.3	40
	Canned concentrate, unsweetened:																	
1434	Undiluted	42.0	223	4.1	1.3	50.7	.5	1.9	51	86	1.3	5	942	960	.39	.12	1.7	229
1435	Diluted with 5 parts water, by volume	88.2	46	.8	.3	10.3	.1	.4	10	18	.3	1	192	200	.08	.02	.3	47
	Frozen concentrate, unsweetened:																	
1436	Undiluted	58.2	158	2.3	.2	38.0	.2	1.3	33	55	.4	2	657	710	.30	.05	1.2	158
1437	Diluted with 3 parts water, by volume	88.1	45	.7	.1	10.7	Trace	.4	9	16	.1	1	186	200	09	.01	.3	45

[47] For further description see Notes on Foods, pp. 175 and 178

[48] See Appendix A, section on Protein, p. 162, and see Appendix B, section on Foods containing considerable nonprotein nitrogen, p. 182

[80] Based on product with minimum level of enrichment. See Notes on Foods, p. 171.

[79] Value weighted by monthly and total season shipments for marketing as fresh fruit.

[82] Dipped in egg, milk, and breadcrumbs.

[83] Based on the pulp. There is no basis for assessing the calorie value of the peel or the effect that inclusion of the peel may have on the digestibility of the product.

[106] Value based on varieties with orange-colored flesh; for green-fleshed varieties, value is about 280 I.U. per 100 grams.

[107] Value based on yellow-fleshed varieties; white-fleshed varieties contain only a trace.

TABLE 1.—COMPOSITION OF FOODS, 100 GRAMS, EDIBLE PORTION—Continued

[Numbers in parentheses denote values imputed—usually from another form of the food or from a similar food. Zero in parentheses indicates that the amount of a constituent probably is none or is too small to measure. Dashes denote lack of reliable data for a constituent believed to be present in measurable amount. Calculated values, as those based on a recipe, are not in parentheses]

Item No.	Food and description	Water	Food energy	Protein	Fat	Carbohydrate Total	Carbohydrate Fiber	Ash	Calcium	Phosphorus	Iron	Sodium	Potassium	Vitamin A value	Thiamine	Riboflavin	Niacin	Ascorbic acid
(A)	(B)	(C)	(D)	(E)	(F)	(G)	(H)	(I)	(J)	(K)	(L)	(M)	(N)	(O)	(P)	(Q)	(R)	(S)
		Percent	Calories	Grams	Grams	Grams	Grams	Grams	Milligrams	Milligrams	Milligrams	Milligrams	Milligrams	International units	Milligrams	Milligrams	Milligrams	Milligrams
	Orange juice—Continued																	
	Dehydrated (crystals):																	
1438	Dry form	1.0	380	5.0	1.7	88.9	0.8	3.4	84	134	1.7	8	1,728	1,680	0.67	0.21	2.9	359
1439	Prepared with water (1 lb. yields approx. 1 gal.)	88.0	46	.6	.2	10.8	.1	.4	10	16	.2	1	200	200	.08	.03	.4	44
	Orange peel:																	
1440	Raw	72.5	(55)	1.5	.2	25.0	—	.8	161	21	.8	3	212	420	.12	.09	.9	136
1441	Candied	17.4	316	.4	.3	80.6	—	1.3	—	—	—	—	—	—	—	—	—	—
	Orange-cranberry relish. See Cranberry-orange relish, item 925.																	
1442	**Orange juice and apricot juice drink,** canned (approx. 40% fruit juices).	86.7	50	.3	.1	12.7	.2	.2	5	8	.1	Trace	94	580	.02	.01	.2	[58] 16
	Oysterplant. See Salsify, items 1961–1962.																	
	Oysters:																	
	Raw, meat only:																	
1443	Eastern	84.6	66	8.4	1.8	3.4	—	1.8	94	143	5.5	73	121	310	.14	.18	2.5	—
1444	Pacific and Western (Olympia)	79.1	91	10.6	2.2	6.4	—	1.7	85	153	7.2	—	—	—	12	—	1.3	30
1445	Cooked, fried [9]	54.7	239	8.6	13.9	18.6	Trace	1.5	152	241	8.1	206	203	440	.17	.29	3.2	—
1446	Canned, solids and liquid	82.2	76	8.5	2.2	4.9	.1	2.2	28	124	5.6	—	70	—	.02	.20	.8	—
1447	Frozen, solids and liquid	87.4	—	6.1	—	—	—	.8	—	—	—	380	210	310	.14	.18	2.5	—
	Oyster stew:																	
	Commercial, frozen:																	
1448	Condensed	79.8	102	4.6	6.3	6.9	.1	2.4	131	116	1.1	680	205	190	.06	.16	.3	—
1449	Prepared with equal volume of water	89.9	51	2.3	3.2	3.4	Trace	1.2	66	58	.6	340	102	100	.03	.08	.2	—
1450	Prepared with equal volume of milk	83.4	84	4.2	4.9	5.9	Trace	1.6	127	106	.6	366	176	170	.05	.17	.2	Trace
	Home-prepared:																	
1451	1 part oysters to 2 parts milk by volume [19]	82.0	97	5.2	6.4	4.5	—	1.8	114	111	1.9	339	133	340	.06	.18	.9	—
1452	1 part oysters to 3 parts milk by volume [19]	83.7	86	4.9	5.3	4.7	—	1.4	117	109	1.4	203	138	280	.06	.18	.7	—
	Pancakes, baked from home recipe, made with—																	
1453	Enriched flour	50.1	231	7.1	7.0	34.1	.1	1.7	101	139	1.3	425	123	120	.17	.22	1.3	Trace
1454	Unenriched flour	50.1	231	7.1	7.0	34.1	.1	1.7	101	139	.6	425	123	120	.05	.14	.4	Trace
	Pancake and waffle mixes and pancakes baked from mixes:																	
	Plain and buttermilk:																	
1455	Mix (pancake and waffle), with enriched flour, dry form.	8.3	356	8.6	1.8	75.7	.4	5.6	450	590	3.1	1,433	162	0	.44	.34	2.9	0
	Pancakes:																	
1456	Made with milk	53.9	202	6.1	5.6	31.9	.1	2.5	221	242	.9	451	156	120	.14	.23	.8	Trace
1457	Made with egg, milk	50.6	225	7.2	7.3	32.4	.1	2.5	215	260	1.2	564	154	250	.15	.24	.8	Trace
1458	Mix (pancake and waffle), with unenriched flour, dry form.	8.3	356	8.6	1.8	75.7	.4	5.6	450	590	1.4	1,433	162	0	.12	.08	1.1	0
	Pancakes:																	
1459	Made with milk	53.9	202	6.1	5.6	31.9	.1	2.5	221	242	.4	451	156	120	.06	.15	.4	Trace
1460	Made with egg, milk	50.6	225	7.2	7.3	32.4	.1	2.5	215	260	.7	564	154	250	.06	.17	.4	Trace
	Buckwheat and other cereal flours:																	
1461	Mix, dry form	11.2	328	10.5	1.9	70.3	1.4	6.1	466	826	3.1	1,334	476	Trace	.36	.12	2.2	0
1462	Pancakes, made with egg, milk	57.9	200	6.8	9.1	23.8	.4	2.4	220	337	1.3	464	245	230	.12	16	.7	Trace
	Pancreas, raw:																	
	Beef:																	
1463	Very fat	53.	357	11.8	34.	0	0	1.1	—	222	—	—	—	—	—	—	—	—
1464	Fat	57.	316	12.8	29.	0	0	1.1	—	267	—	—	—	—	—	—	—	—
1465	Medium-fat	60.	283	13.5	25.	0	0	1.2	—	270	—	—	—	—	—	—	—	—
1466	Thin	67.	217	14.9	17.	0	0	1.3	—	307	—	—	—	—	—	.55	5.8	—
1467	Lean only, adhering fat removed	73.	141	17.6	7.3	0	0	1.8	8	330	2.8	67	276	—	—	—	—	—
1468	Calf	69.7	161	19.2	8.8	0	0	1.4	—	326	—	—	—	—	—	—	—	—
1469	Hog (hog sweetbread)	63.4	242	14.7	19.9	0	0	1.1	11	282	1.0	44	217	—	—	—	—	—
1470	**Papaws,** common, North American type, raw	76.6	85	5.2	.9	16.8	—	.5	—	—	—	—	—	—	—	—	—	—
1471	**Papayas,** raw	88.7	39	.6	.1	10.0	.9	.6	20	16	.3	3	234	1,750	.04	.04	.3	56
1472	**Parsley,** common garden (plain) and curled-leaf varieties, raw.	85.1	44	3.6	.6	8.5	1.5	2.2	203	63	6.2	45	727	8,500	12	.26	1.2	172
	Parsnips:																	
1473	Raw	79.1	76	1.7	.5	17.5	2.0	1.2	50	77	.7	12	541	30	.08	.09	.2	[19] 16
1474	Cooked, boiled, drained	82.2	66	1.5	.5	14.9	2.0	.9	45	62	.6	8	379	30	.07	.08	.1	10
	Passionfruit. See Granadilla, item 1052.																	
	Pastinas, enriched, dry form:																	
1475	Egg	10.4	383	12.9	4.1	71.8	.3	.8	35	194	[28] 2.9	5	—	220	[28] .88	[28] .38	[28] 6.0	(0)

	Vegetable:																	
1476	Carrot	10.0	371	11.9	1.6	75.7	.6	.8	38	160	[79] 2.9	—	—	730	[79] .88	[79] .38	[79] 6.0	(0)
1477	Spinach	10.1	368	12.4	1.6	74.8	.5	1.1	63	173	[79] 2.9	—	—	640	[79] .88	[79] .38	[79] 6.0	(0)
	Pastry shell, plain. See Piecrust, items 1598, 1600.																	
1478	**Pâté de foie gras, canned**	37.0	462	11.4	43.8	4.8	0	3.0	—	—	—	—	—	—	.09	.30	2.5	—
	Peaches:																	
1479	Raw	89.1	38	.6	.1	9.7	.6	.5	9	19	.5	1	202	[111] 1,330	.02	.05	1.0	7
	Canned, solids and liquid:																	
1480	Water pack, with or without artificial sweetener	91.1	31	.4	.1	8.1	.4	.3	4	13	.3	2	137	450	.01	.03	.6	3
1481	Juice pack	87.2	45	.6	.1	11.6	.4	.5	6	19	.5	2	205	670	.01	.04	.9	4
	Sirup pack:																	
1482	Light	84.1	58	.4	.1	15.1	.4	.3	4	13	.3	2	133	440	.01	.03	.6	3
1483	Heavy	79.1	78	.4	.1	20.1	.4	.3	4	12	.3	2	130	430	.01	.02	.6	3
1484	Extra heavy	74.1	97	.4	.1	25.1	.4	.3	4	12	.3	2	128	420	.01	.02	.5	3
	Dehydrated, sulfured, nugget-type and pieces:																	
1485	Uncooked	3.0	340	4.8	(.9)	88.0	(4.0)	3.3	(62)	(151)	3.5	(21)	(1,229)	(5,000)	Trace	.10	7.8	14
1486	Cooked, fruit and liquid, with added sugar	66.6	121	1.1	(.2)	31.3	(.9)	.8	(15)	(36)	.8	(5)	(292)	(890)	Trace	.02	1.7	2
	Dried, sulfured:																	
1487	Uncooked	25.0	262	3.1	.7	68.3	3.1	2.9	48	117	6.0	16	950	3,900	.01	.19	5.3	18
	Cooked, fruit and liquid:																	
1488	Without added sugar	76.5	82	1.0	.2	21.4	1.0	.9	15	37	1.9	5	297	1,220	Trace	.06	1.5	2
1489	With added sugar	67.3	119	.9	.2	30.8	.9	.8	13	32	1.6	4	261	1,070	Trace	.05	1.4	2
1490	Frozen, sliced, sweetened, not thawed	76.5	88	.4	.1	22.6	.4	.4	4	13	.5	2	124	650	.01	.04	.7	[112] 40
1491	**Peach nectar,** canned (approx 40% fruit) [4]	87.2	48	.2	Trace	12.4	.1	.2	4	11	.2	1	78	430	.01	.02	.4	Trace
	Peanuts:																	
1492	Raw, with skins	5.6	564	26.0	47.5	18.6	2.4	2.3	69	401	2.1	5	674	—	1.14	.13	17.2	0
1493	Raw, without skins	5.4	568	26.3	48.4	17.6	1.9	2.3	59	409	2.0	5	674	0	.99	.13	15.8	0
1494	Boiled	36.4	376	15.5	31.5	14.5	1.8	2.1	43	181	1.3	4	462	—	.48	.08	10.0	0
1495	Roasted, with skins	1.8	582	26.2	48.7	20.6	2.7	2.7	72	407	2.2	5	701	—	.32	.13	17.1	0
1496	Roasted and salted	1.6	585	26.0	49.8	18.8	2.4	3.8	74	401	2.1	418	674	—	.32	.13	17.2	0
	Peanut butters made with—																	
1497	Small amounts of added fat, salt	1.8	581	27.8	49.4	17.2	1.9	3.8	63	407	2.0	607	670	—	.13	.13	15.7	0
1498	Small amounts of added fat, sweetener, salt	1.7	582	25.5	49.5	19.5	1.9	3.8	61	395	2.0	606	652	—	.12	.12	15.3	0
1499	Moderate amounts of added fat, sweetener, salt	1.7	589	25.2	50.6	18.8	1.8	3.7	59	380	1.9	605	627	—	.12	.12	14.7	0
1500	**Peanut spread**	2.2	601	20.3	52.1	22.0	1.5	3.4	50	322	1.5	597	530	—	.10	.10	12.4	0
1501	**Peanut flour,** defatted	7.3	371	47.9	9.2	31.5	2.7	4.1	104	720	3.5	9	1,186	—	.75	.22	27.8	0
	Pears:																	
1502	Raw, including skin	83.2	61	.7	.4	15.3	1.4	.4	8	11	.3	2	130	20	.02	.04	.1	4
1503	Candied	21.0	303	1.3	.6	75.9	—	1.2	—	—	—	—	—	—	—	—	—	—
	Canned, solids and liquid:																	
1504	Water pack, with or without artificial sweetener	91.1	32	.2	.2	8.3	.7	.2	5	7	.2	1	88	Trace	.01	.02	.1	1
1505	Juice pack	87.3	46	.3	.3	11.8	.8	.3	8	11	.3	1	130	Trace	.02	.03	.1	2
	Sirup pack:																	
1506	Light	83.8	61	.2	.2	15.6	.7	.2	5	7	.2	1	85	Trace	.01	.02	.1	1
1507	Heavy	79.8	76	.2	.2	19.6	.6	.2	5	7	.2	1	84	Trace	.01	.02	.1	1
1508	Extra heavy	75.8	92	.2	.2	23.6	.6	.2	5	7	.2	1	83	Trace	.01	.02	.1	1
	Dried, sulfured:																	
1509	Uncooked	26.0	268	3.1	1.8	67.3	6.2	1.8	35	48	1.3	7	573	70	.01	.18	.6	7
	Cooked, fruit and liquid:																	
1510	Without added sugar	65.2	126	1.5	.8	31.7	2.9	.8	16	23	.6	3	269	30	Trace	.08	.3	2
1511	With added sugar	59.1	151	1.3	.8	38.0	2.6	.8	15	20	.6	3	244	30	Trace	.07	.2	2
1512	**Pear nectar,** canned (approx. 40% fruit) [4]	86.2	52	.3	.2	13.2	.3	.1	3	5	.1	1	39	Trace	Trace	.02	Trace	Trace
	Peas, edible-podded:																	
1513	Raw	83.3	53	3.4	.2	12.0	1.2	1.1	62	90	.7	—	170	(680)	.28	.12	—	21
1514	Cooked, boiled, drained	86.6	43	2.9	.2	9.5	1.2	.8	56	76	.5	—	119	(610)	.22	.11	—	14
	Peas, green, immature:																	
1515	Raw	78.0	84	6.3	.4	14.4	2.0	.9	26	116	1.9	2	316	640	.35	.14	2.9	27
1516	Cooked, boiled, drained	81.5	71	5.4	.4	12.1	2.0	.6	23	99	1.8	1	196	540	.28	.11	2.3	20
	Canned:																	
	Alaska (Early or June peas):																	
	Regular pack:																	
1517	Solids and liquid	82.6	66	3.5	.3	12.5	1.5	1.1	20	66	1.7	[9] 236	96	450	.09	.05	.9	9
1518	Drained solids	77.0	88	4.7	.4	16.8	2.3	1.1	26	76	1.9	[9] 236	96	690	.09	.06	.8	8
1519	Drained liquid	92.3	26	1.3	Trace	5.2	Trace	1.2	10	48	1.3	[9] 236	96	Trace	.10	.04	1.0	10
	Special dietary pack (low-sodium):																	
1520	Solids and liquid	85.9	55	3.6	.3	9.8	1.3	.4	20	66	1.7	3	96	450	.09	.05	.9	9
1521	Drained solids	80.1	78	4.8	.4	14.3	2.0	.4	26	76	1.9	3	96	690	.09	.06	.8	8
1522	Drained liquid	94.1	22	1.4	Trace	4.1	Trace	.4	10	48	1.3	3	96	Trace	.10	.04	1.0	10

[4] See Notes on Foods, p. 177.

[9] Estimated average based on addition of salt in the amount of 0.6 percent of the finished product.

[79] Based on product with minimum level of enrichment. See notes on Foods, p. 171.

[80] Dipped in egg, milk, and breadcrumbs.

[81] Value cannot be calculated inasmuch as digestibility of peel is not known.

[108] Ascorbic acid may be added as a preservative or as a nutrient. Value listed is based on product with label stating 30 mg. per 6 fl. oz. serving. If label claim is 30 mg. per 8 fl. oz. serving, value would be 12 mg. per 100 grams.

[109] Contains added salt and butter.

[110] Year-round average. Value for parsnips in the fall within 3 months of harvest is about 24 mg. per 100 grams, and drops to less than half this value if storage exceeds 6 months.

[111] Based on yellow-fleshed varieties, for white-fleshed varieties, value is about 50 I.U. per 100 grams.

[112] Average weighted in accordance with commercial freezing practices. For products without added ascorbic acid, average is about 11 mg. per 100 grams, for those with added ascorbic acid, around 41 mg.

TABLE 1.—COMPOSITION OF FOODS, 100 GRAMS, EDIBLE PORTION—Continued

[Numbers in parentheses denote values imputed—usually from another form of the food or from a similar food. Zero in parentheses indicates that the amount of a constituent probably is none or is too small to measure. Dashes denote lack of reliable data for a constituent believed to be present in measurable amount. Calculated values, as those based on a recipe, are not in parentheses]

Item No.	Food and description	Water	Food energy	Protein	Fat	Carbohydrate Total	Carbohydrate Fiber	Ash	Calcium	Phosphorus	Iron	Sodium	Potassium	Vitamin A value	Thiamine	Riboflavin	Niacin	Ascorbic acid
(A)	(B)	(C)	(D)	(E)	(F)	(G)	(H)	(I)	(J)	(K)	(L)	(M)	(N)	(O)	(P)	(Q)	(R)	(S)
		Percent	Calories	Grams	Grams	Grams	Grams	Grams	Milligrams	Milligrams	Milligrams	Milligrams	Milligrams	International units	Milligrams	Milligrams	Milligrams	Milligrams
	Peas, green, immature—Continued																	
	Canned—Continued																	
	Sweet (sweet wrinkled peas, sugar peas):																	
	Regular pack:																	
1523	Solids and liquid	84.8	57	3.4	0.3	10.4	1.4	1.1	19	58	1.5	[6] 236	96	450	0.11	0.06	1.0	9
1524	Drained solids	79.0	80	4.6	.4	15.0	2.2	1.0	25	67	1.7	[6] 236	96	690	.11	.06	1.0	8
1525	Drained liquid	93.3	22	1.3	Trace	4.3	Trace	1.1	9	42	1.1	[6] 236	96	Trace	.12	.05	1.1	10
	Special dietary pack (low-sodium):																	
1526	Solids and liquid	87.8	47	3.3	.3	8.2	1.3	.4	19	58	1.5	3	96	450	.11	.06	1.0	9
1527	Drained solids	81.8	72	4.4	.4	13.0	2.0	.4	25	67	1.7	3	96	690	.11	.06	1.0	8
1528	Drained liquid	94.9	18	1.3	Trace	3.4	Trace	.4	9	42	1.1	3	96	Trace	.12	.05	1.1	10
	Frozen:																	
1529	Not thawed	80.7	73	5.4	.3	12.8	1.9	.8	20	90	2.0	[10] 129	150	680	.32	.10	2.0	19
1530	Cooked, boiled, drained	82.1	68	5.1	.3	11.8	1.9	.7	19	86	1.9	115	135	600	.27	.09	1.7	13
	Peas, mature seeds, dry:																	
	Whole:																	
1531	Raw	11.7	340	24.1	1.3	60.3	4.9	2.6	64	340	5.1	35	1,005	120	.74	.29	3.0	----
	Split, without seed coat:																	
1532	Raw	9.3	348	24.2	1.0	62.7	1.2	2.8	33	268	5.1	40	895	120	.74	.29	3.0	----
1533	Cooked	70.0	115	8.0	.3	20.8	.4	.9	11	89	1.7	[6] 13	296	40	.15	.09	.9	----
	Peas and carrots, frozen:																	
1534	Not thawed	85.4	55	3.3	.3	10.4	1.5	.6	26	59	1.2	[10] 92	171	9,300	.20	.07	1.3	10
1535	Cooked, boiled, drained	85.8	53	3.2	.3	10.1	1.5	.6	25	57	1.1	84	157	9,300	.19	.07	1.3	8
1536	**Pecans**	3.4	687	9.2	71.2	14.6	2.3	1.6	73	289	2.4	Trace	603	130	.86	.13	.9	2
	Peppers, hot, chili:																	
	Immature, green:																	
1537	Raw pods, excluding seeds	88.8	37	1.3	.2	9.1	1.8	.6	10	25	.7	----	----	770	.09	.06	1.7	235
	Canned:																	
1538	Pods, excluding seeds; solids and liquid	92.5	25	.9	.1	6.1	1.2	.4	7	17	.5	----	----	610	.03	.05	.8	68
1539	Chili sauce	93.9	20	.7	.1	5.0	1.0	.3	5	14	.4	----	----	610	.03	.03	.7	68
	Mature, red:																	
	Raw:																	
1540	Pods, including seeds	74.3	93	3.7	2.3	18.1	9.0	1.6	29	78	1.2	----	----	21,600	.22	.36	4.4	369
1541	Pods, excluding seeds	80.3	65	2.3	.4	15.8	2.3	1.2	16	49	1.4	25	564	21,600	.1	.2	2.9	369
1542	Canned, chili sauce	94.1	21	.9	.6	3.9	1.7	.5	9	16	.5	----	----	9,500	.01	.09	.6	30
	Dried:																	
1543	Pods	12.6	321	12.9	9.1	59.8	26.2	7.4	130	240	7.8	373	1,201	77,000	.23	1.33	10.5	[11] 12
1544	Chili powder with added seasoning	8.5	340	14.3	12.4	56.5	22.2	8.3	265	204	15.2	1,574	1,000	65,000	.19	1.13	8.9	10
	Peppers, sweet, garden varieties:																	
	Immature, green:																	
1545	Raw	93.4	22	1.2	.2	4.8	1.4	.4	9	22	.7	13	213	420	.08	.08	.5	128
	Cooked:																	
1546	Boiled, drained	94.7	18	1.0	.2	3.8	1.4	.3	9	16	.5	9	149	420	.06	.07	.5	96
1547	Stuffed with beef and crumbs	65.1	170	13.0	5.5	16.8	.7	1.6	42	121	2.1	314	258	280	.09	.17	2.5	40
1548	Mature, red, raw	90.7	31	1.4	.3	7.1	1.7	.5	13	30	.6	----	----	4,450	(.08)	(.08)	(.5)	204
1549	**Perch, white, raw**	75.7	118	19.3	4.0	0	0	1.2	----	192	----	----	----	----	----	----	----	----
1550	**Perch, yellow, raw**	79.2	91	19.5	.9	0	0	1.3	----	180	.6	68	230	----	.06	.17	1.7	----
	Persimmons, raw:																	
1551	Japanese or kaki	78.6	77	.7	.4	19.7	1.6	.6	6	26	.3	6	174	2,710	.03	.02	.1	11
1552	Native	64.4	127	.8	.4	33.5	1.5	.9	27	26	2.5	1	310	----	----	----	----	66
	Pheasant, raw:																	
1553	Total edible	69.2	151	24.3	5.2	0	0	1.2	----	----	----	----	----	----	----	----	----	----
1554	Flesh and skin	68.9	152	24.7	5.2	0	0	1.2	----	----	----	----	----	----	----	----	----	----
1555	Flesh only	67.3	162	23.6	6.8	0	0	1.3	----	----	----	----	----	----	----	----	----	----
1556	Giblets	71.4	139	20.8	4.9	1.6	0	1.3	----	----	----	----	----	----	----	----	----	----
1557	**Pickerel, chain, raw**	79.7	84	18.7	.5	0	0	1.2	----	----	.7	----	----	----	----	----	----	----
	Pickles:																	
	Cucumber:																	
1558	Dill	93.3	11	.7	.2	2.2	.5	3.6	26	21	1.0	1,428	200	100	Trace	.02	Trace	6
1559	Fresh (as bread-and-butter pickles)	78.7	73	.9	.2	17.9	.5	2.3	32	27	1.8	673	----	140	Trace	.03	Trace	9
1560	Sour	94.8	10	.5	.2	2.0	.5	2.5	17	15	3.2	1,353	----	100	Trace	.02	Trace	7

1561	Sweet	60.7	146	.7	.4	36.5	—	1.7	12	16	1.2	—	—	90	Trace	.02	Trace	6
	Chowchow (Cucumber with added cauliflower, onion, mustard):																	
1562	Sour	87.6	29	1.4	1.3	4.1	.6	5.6	32	53	2.6	1,338	—	—	—	—	—	—
1563	Sweet	68.9	116	1.5	.9	27.0	.9	1.7	23	22	1.5	527	—	—	—	—	—	—
	Relish, finely cut or chopped:																	
1564	Sour	(93.0)	19	(.7)	(.9)	(2.7)	(1.1)	(2.7)	(29)	(20)	(1.1)	—	—	—	—	—	—	—
1565	Sweet	63.0	138	.5	.6	34.0	.8	1.9	20	14	.8	712	—	—	—	—	—	—
	Pies:																	
	Baked, piecrust made with unenriched flour: [114]																	
1566	Apple	47.6	256	2.2	11.1	38.1	.4	1.0	8	22	.3	301	80	30	.02	.02	.4	1
1567	Banana custard	54.4	221	4.5	9.3	30.7	.2	1.1	66	82	.5	194	203	250	.04	.13	.3	1
1568	Blackberry	51.0	243	2.6	11.0	34.4	1.9	1.0	19	26	.5	268	100	90	.02	.02	.3	4
1569	Blueberry	51.0	242	2.4	10.8	34.9	.7	.9	11	23	.6	268	65	30	.02	.02	.3	3
	Boston cream. See Cakes, item 522.																	
1570	Butterscotch	45.1	267	4.4	11.0	38.3	Trace	1.2	75	81	.9	214	95	260	.03	.10	.2	Trace
1571	Cherry	46.6	261	2.6	11.3	38.4	.1	1.1	14	25	.3	304	105	440	.02	.02	.5	Trace
1572	Chocolate chiffon	33.0	328	6.8	15.3	43.7	.2	1.1	24	97	1.2	252	110	310	.03	.10	.2	0
1573	Chocolate meringue	48.4	252	4.8	12.0	33.5	.2	1.2	69	98	.7	256	139	190	.03	.12	.2	Trace
1574	Coconut custard	55.4	235	6.0	12.5	24.9	.2	1.2	94	116	.7	247	163	230	.06	.19	.3	0
1575	Custard	58.1	218	6.1	11.1	23.4	Trace	1.3	96	113	.6	287	137	230	.05	.16	.3	0
1576	Lemon chiffon	35.6	313	7.0	12.6	43.8	Trace	1.0	23	83	.9	261	81	170	.03	.08	.2	3
1577	Lemon meringue	47.4	255	3.7	10.2	37.7	Trace	1.0	14	49	.5	282	50	170	.03	.08	.2	3
1578	Mince	43.0	271	2.5	11.5	41.2	.4	1.8	28	38	1.0	448	178	Trace	.07	.04	.4	1
1579	Peach	47.5	255	2.5	10.7	38.2	.4	1.1	10	29	.5	268	149	730	.02	.04	.7	3
1580	Pecan	19.5	418	5.1	22.9	51.3	.5	1.2	47	103	2.8	221	123	160	.16	.07	.3	Trace
1581	Pineapple	48.0	253	2.2	10.7	38.1	.2	1.0	13	21	.5	271	72	20	.04	.02	.4	1
1582	Pineapple chiffon	41.1	288	6.6	12.1	39.1	.1	1.1	24	76	.9	256	98	350	.04	.09	.4	1
1583	Pineapple custard	54.3	220	4.0	8.7	32.1	.1	.9	50	65	.4	186	97	180	.04	.09	.4	1
1584	Pumpkin	59.2	211	4.0	11.2	24.5	.5	1.1	51	69	.5	214	160	2,470	.03	.10	.5	Trace
1585	Raisin	42.5	270	2.6	10.7	43.0	.3	1.2	18	40	.9	285	192	Trace	.03	.03	.3	1
1586	Rhubarb	47.4	253	2.5	10.7	38.2	.6	1.2	64	26	.7	270	159	50	.02	.04	.3	3
1587	Strawberry	58.4	198	1.9	7.9	30.9	.8	.9	16	25	.7	194	120	40	.02	.04	.4	25
1588	Sweetpotato	59.3	213	4.5	11.3	23.7	.2	1.2	69	84	.5	218	163	2,400	.05	.12	.3	4
	Frozen in unbaked form:																	
	Apple:																	
1589	Unbaked	56.3	210	1.6	8.3	33.2	.2	.6	7	17	.2	177	60	10	.02	.01	.2	1
1590	Baked	47.3	254	1.9	10.1	40.0	.3	.7	8	21	.3	213	72	10	.02	.02	.2	Trace
	Cherry:																	
1591	Unbaked	47.8	256	1.9	10.6	39.0	.1	.7	11	21	.2	202	72	280	.02	.02	.2	2
1592	Baked	40.6	291	2.2	12.0	44.4	.1	.8	12	23	.3	229	82	290	.02	.02	.2	2
	Coconut custard:																	
1593	Unbaked	58.0	205	5.2	8.5	27.1	.2	1.2	86	104	.6	238	157	190	.04	.15	.2	Trace
1594	Baked	51.2	249	6.0	12.0	29.5	.2	1.3	95	115	.6	252	172	160	.04	.16	.2	Trace
	Pie mix, coconut custard, and pie baked from mix:																	
1595	Mix, filling and piecrust, dry form	4.2	470	3.3	20.0	70.6	.7	1.9	13	46	.5	628	142	0	.02	.02	.4	0
1596	Pie prepared with egg yolk and milk, baked	57.6	203	4.3	7.9	29.1	.3	1.1	93	103	.4	235	154	210	.03	.14	.2	Trace
	Piecrust or plain pastry, made with—																	
	Enriched flour:																	
1597	Unbaked	20.9	464	5.7	31.0	40.7	.1	1.7	13	47	1.6	568	46	0	.24	.14	1.9	0
1598	Baked	14.9	500	6.1	33.4	43.8	.2	1.8	14	50	1.7	611	50	0	.20	.14	1.8	0
	Unenriched flour:																	
1599	Unbaked	20.9	464	5.7	31.0	40.7	.1	1.7	13	47	.4	568	46	0	.03	.03	.5	0
1600	Baked	14.9	500	6.1	33.4	43.8	.2	1.8	14	50	.5	611	50	0	.03	.03	.5	0
	Piecrust mix (including stick form) and piecrust baked from mix:																	
1601	Mix, dry form	8.6	522	7.2	32.7	49.5	.2	2.0	46	96	.5	693	63	0	.04	.04	.7	0
1602	Piecrust, prepared with water, baked	18.7	464	6.4	29.1	44.0	.2	1.8	41	85	.4	813	56	0	.03	.03	.5	0
	Pigeonpeas, raw:																	
1603	Immature seeds	69.5	117	7.2	.6	21.3	3.3	1.4	42	127	1.6	5	552	140	.40	.17	2.2	39
1604	Mature seeds, dry	10.8	342	20.4	1.4	63.7	7.0	3.7	107	316	8.0	26	981	80	.32	.16	3.0	—
1605	**Pigs' feet,** pickled	66.9	199	16.7	14.8	0	0	1.7	—	—	—	—	—	—	—	—	—	—
1606	**Pike, blue,** raw	78.8	90	19.1	.9	0	0	1.2	—	—	—	—	—	—	—	—	—	—
1607	**Pike, northern,** raw	80.0	88	18.3	1.1	0	0	1.1	—	—	—	—	—	—	—	—	—	—
1608	**Pike, walleye,** raw	78.3	93	19.3	1.2	0	0	1.2	—	214	.4	51	319	—	.25	.16	2.3	—
1609	**Pilinuts**	6.3	669	11.4	71.1	8.4	2.7	2.8	140	554	3.4	3	489	40	.88	.09	.5	Trace
1610	**Pimientos,** canned, solids and liquid	92.4	27	.9	.5	5.8	.6	.4	[115] 7	17	1.5	—	—	2,300	.02	.06	.4	95

[4] See Notes on Foods, p. 176.

[9] Estimated average based on addition of salt in the amount of 0.6 percent of the finished product.

[19] Average weighted in accordance with commercial practices in freezing vegetables. See also Notes on Foods, p. 177.

[113] Based on 1 sample described as ground powder, stored; for freshly processed product, value is 154 mg. per 100 grams.

[114] If piecrust is made with enriched flour, increase values for nutrients in milligrams per 100 grams of pie by the following amounts:

	Iron	Thiamine	Riboflavin	Niacin
One-crust pie	0.3	0.03	0.03	0.3
Two-crust pie	.4	.06	.04	.5

[115] Federal standards provide for addition of certain calcium salts as firming agents; if used, these salts may add calcium not to exceed 26 mg. per 100 grams of finished product.

TABLE 1.—COMPOSITION OF FOODS, 100 GRAMS, EDIBLE PORTION—Continued

[Numbers in parentheses denote values imputed—usually from another form of the food or from a similar food. Zero in parentheses indicates that the amount of a constituent probably is none or is too small to measure. Dashes denote lack of reliable data for a constituent believed to be present in measurable amount. Calculated values, as those based on a recipe, are not in parentheses]

Item No.	Food and description	Water	Food energy	Protein	Fat	Carbohydrate: Total	Carbohydrate: Fiber	Ash	Calcium	Phosphorus	Iron	Sodium	Potassium	Vitamin A value	Thiamine	Riboflavin	Niacin	Ascorbic acid
(A)	(B)	(C)	(D)	(E)	(F)	(G)	(H)	(I)	(J)	(K)	(L)	(M)	(N)	(O)	(P)	(Q)	(R)	(S)
		Percent	Calories	Grams	Grams	Grams	Grams	Grams	Milligrams	Milligrams	Milligrams	Milligrams	Milligrams	International units	Milligrams	Milligrams	Milligrams	Milligrams
	Pineapple:																	
1611	Raw	85.3	52	0.4	0.2	13.7	0.4	0.4	17	8	0.5	1	146	70	0.09	0.03	0.2	17
1612	Candied	18.0	316	.8	.4	80.0	.8	.8	—	—	—	—	—	—	—	—	—	—
	Canned, solids and liquid:																	
1613	Water pack, all styles except crushed, with or without artificial sweetener.	89.1	39	.3	.1	10.2	.3	.3	12	5	.3	1	99	50	.08	.02	.2	7
1614	Juice pack, all styles	84.0	58	.4	.1	15.1	.3	.4	16	8	.4	1	147	60	.10	.03	.3	10
	Sirup pack, all styles:																	
1615	Light	83.9	59	.3	.1	15.4	.3	.3	11	5	.3	1	97	50	.08	.02	.2	7
1616	Heavy	79.9	74	.3	.1	19.4	.3	.3	11	5	.3	1	96	50	.08	.02	.2	7
1617	Extra heavy	75.9	90	.3	.1	23.4	.3	.3	11	5	.3	1	94	40	.08	.02	.2	6
1618	Frozen chunks, sweetened, not thawed	77.1	85	.4	.1	22.2	.3	.2	9	4	.4	2	100	30	.10	.03	.3	8
	Pineapple juice:																	
1619	Canned, unsweetened	85.6	55	.4	.1	13.5	.1	.4	15	9	.3	1	149	50	.05	.02	.2	9
	Frozen concentrate, unsweetened:																	
1620	Undiluted	53.1	179	1.3	.1	44.3	.3	1.2	39	28	.9	3	472	40	.23	.06	.9	42
1621	Diluted with 3 parts water, by volume	86.5	52	.4	Trace	12.8	.1	.3	11	8	.3	1	136	10	.07	.02	.2	12
1622	**Pineapple juice and grapefruit juice drink,** canned (approx. 40% fruit juices).[118]	86.0	54	.2	Trace	13.6	Trace	.2	5	5	.2	Trace	62	10	.02	.01	.1	16
1623	**Pineapple juice and orange juice drink,** canned (approx. 40% fruit juices).[118]	86.0	54	.2	.1	13.5	Trace	.2	5	6	.2	Trace	70	50	.02	.01	.1	16
	Pinenuts:																	
1624	Pignolias	5.6	552	31.1	47.4	11.6	.9	4.3	—	—	—	—	—	—	.62	—	—	—
1625	Piñon	3.1	635	13.0	60.5	20.5	1.1	2.9	12	604	5.2	—	—	30	1.28	.23	4.5	Trace
1626	**Pistachionuts**	5.3	594	19.3	53.7	19.0	1.9	2.7	131	500	7.3	—	972	230	.67	—	1.4	0
1627	**Pitanga** (Surinam-cherry), raw	85.8	51	.8	.4	12.5	.6	.5	9	11	.2	—	—	1,500	.03	.04	.3	30
	Pizza, with cheese:																	
	From home recipe, baked:[117]																	
1628	With cheese topping	48.3	236	12.0	8.3	28.3	.3	3.1	221	195	1.0	702	130	630	.06	.20	1.0	8
1629	With sausage topping	50.6	234	7.8	9.3	29.6	.3	2.7	17	93	1.2	729	168	560	.09	.12	1.5	9
	Chilled:																	
1630	Partially baked	53.3	208	7.8	5.8	30.9	.3	2.2	121	126	.7	538	94	420	.06	.11	.9	6
1631	Baked	45.1	245	9.2	6.8	36.3	.3	2.6	143	148	.9	633	111	390	.06	.16	1.0	6
	Frozen:																	
1632	Partially baked	48.9	229	8.9	6.6	33.1	.3	2.5	146	146	.9	605	107	450	.08	.16	.9	5
1633	Baked	45.3	245	9.5	7.1	35.4	.3	2.7	156	156	.9	647	114	440	.06	.17	1.0	6
1634	**Plantain** (baking banana), raw	66.4	119	1.1	.4	31.2	.4	.9	7	30	.7	5	385	(90)	.06	.04	.6	14
	Plate dinners, frozen, commercial, unheated:																	
1635	Beef pot roast, whole oven-browned potatoes, peas, and corn.	76.3	106	13.1	3.2	6.1	.3	1.3	10	76	1.6	259	244	110	.06	.10	2.1	5
1636	Chicken, fried; mashed potatoes; mixed vegetables (carrots, peas, corn, beans).	66.1	173	12.8	8.5	11.3	.4	1.3	41	145	1.2	344	112	500	.07	.18	5.2	4
1637	Meat loaf with tomato sauce, mashed potatoes, and peas.	73.7	131	8.0	6.7	9.8	.3	1.8	19	117	1.2	393	115	430	.10	.14	1.7	4
1638	Turkey, sliced; mashed potatoes; peas	74.7	112	8.4	3.0	12.7	.3	1.2	26	87	1.1	400	176	150	.07	.09	2.3	4
	Plums:																	
	Raw:																	
1639	Damson	81.1	66	.5	Trace	17.8	.4	.6	18	17	.5	2	299	(300)	.08	.03	.5	—
1640	Japanese and hybrid	86.6	48	.5	.2	12.3	.6	.4	12	18	.5	1	170	250	.03	.03	.5	6
1641	Prune-type	78.7	75	.8	.2	19.7	.4	.6	12	18	.5	1	170	[119]300	.03	.03	.5	4
	Canned, solids and liquid:																	
1642	Greengage, water pack, with or without artificial sweetener.	90.6	33	.4	.1	8.6	.2	.3	(9)	(13)	(.2)	1	82	(160)	(.01)	(.02)	(.3)	2
	Purple (Italian prunes):																	
1643	Water pack, with or without artificial sweetener.	86.8	46	.4	.2	11.9	.3	.7	9	10	1.0	2	148	1,250	.02	.02	.4	2
	Sirup pack:																	
1644	Light	82.4	63	.4	.1	16.6	.3	.5	9	10	.9	1	145	1,230	.02	.02	.4	2
1645	Heavy	77.4	83	.4	.1	21.6	.3	.5	9	10	.9	1	142	1,210	.02	.02	.4	2
1646	Extra heavy	72.4	102	.4	.1	26.7	.3	.4	8	9	.9	1	139	1,180	.02	.02	.4	2
	Poha. See Groundcherries, item 1092																	
	Pokeberry (poke) shoots:																	
1647	Raw	91.6	23	2.6	.4	3.7	—	1.7	53	44	1.7	—	—	8,700	.08	.33	1.2	136
1648	Cooked, boiled, drained	92.9	20	2.3	.4	3.1	—	1.3	53	33	1.2	—	—	8,700	.07	.25	1.1	82

No.	Food																	
	Pollock:																	
1649	Raw	77.4	95	20.4	.9	0	0	1.3	—	—	—	48	350	—	05	.10	1.6	—
1650	Cooked, creamed [120]	74.7	128	13.9	5.9	4.0	—	1.5	—	—	—	111	238	—	.03	.13	.7	Trace
1651	**Pomegranate pulp, raw**	82.3	63	.5	.3	16.4	.2	.5	3	8	.3	3	259	Trace	.03	.03	.3	4
1652	**Pompano, raw**	70.9	166	18.8	9.5	0	0	1.1	—	—	—	47	191	—	.41	.22	—	—
	Popcorn:																	
1653	Unpopped	9.8	362	11.9	4.7	72.1	2.1	1.5	(10)	(264)	(2.5)	(3)	—	—	(.39)	(.11)	(2.1)	(0)
	Popped:																	
1654	Plain	4.0	386	12.7	5.0	76.7	2.2	1.6	(11)	(281)	(2.7)	(3)	—	—	—	(.12)	(2.2)	(0)
1655	Oil and salt added	3.1	456	9.8	21.8	59.1	1.7	6.2	8	216	2.1	1,940	—	—	—	.09	1.7	0
1656	Sugar-coated	4.0	383	6.1	3.5	85.4	1.1	1.0	5	135	1.3	[86] 1	—	—	—	.06	1.1	0
1657	**Popovers,** baked (from home recipe with enriched flour).	54.9	224	8.8	9.2	25.8	.1	1.3	96	140	[121] 1.5	220	150	330	[121] .14	[121] 25	[121] 1.0	Trace
1658	**Porgy and scup, raw**	76.2	112	19.0	3.4	0	0	1.3	54	250	—	63	287	—	—	—	—	—
	Pork, fresh: [4]																	
	Carcass, raw:																	
	Fat class:																	
1659	Total edible (41% lean, 59% fat)	33.4	553	9.1	57.0	0	0	.5	5	88	1.4			(0)	.44	.10	2.4	—
1660	Separable lean	68.0	185	17.3	12.3	0	0	2.4	10	197	2.6			(0)	.84	.20	4.5	—
1661	Separable fat	11.1	784	3.2	85.4	0	0	.3	2	10	.5			(0)	.16	.04	.8	—
	Medium-fat class:																	
1662	Total edible (47% lean, 53% fat)	37.3	513	10.2	52.0	0	0	.5	6	103	1.5			(0)	.50	.12	2.7	—
1663	Separable lean	69.3	171	17.8	10.5	0	0	2.4	10	204	2.7			(0)	.87	.21	4.6	—
1664	Separable fat	12.4	770	3.5	83.7	0	0	.4	2	14	.5			(0)	.17	.04	.9	—
	Thin class:																	
1665	Total edible (53% lean, 47% fat)	41.1	472	11.2	47.0	0	0	.6	6	116	1.7			(0)	.54	.13	2.9	—
1666	Separable lean	70.7	156	18.3	8.6	0	0	2.4	11	210	2.7			(0)	.89	.21	4.8	—
1667	Separable fat	13.8	755	3.7	81.9	0	0	.6	2	16	.6			(0)	.18	.04	1.0	—
	Wholesale cuts, raw:																	
	Bacon or belly:																	
1668	Fat class (25% lean, 75% fat)	26.4	631	7.1	66.6	0	0	.3	4	62	1.1			(0)	.35	.08	1.8	—
1669	Medium-fat class (33% lean, 67% fat)	30.3	588	8.2	61.3	0	0	.4	5	76	1.2			(0)	.40	.10	2.1	—
1670	Thin class (40% lean, 60% fat)	34.3	545	9.4	56.0	0	0	.5	5	92	1.4			(0)	.46	.11	2.4	—
	Backfat:																	
	Total edible:																	
1671	Fat class (100% fat)	6.4	841	1.7	92.4	0	0	.1	1	0	.3			(0)	.08	.02	.4	—
1672	Medium-fat class (100% fat)	7.5	827	2.1	90.7	0	0	.1	1	0	.3			(0)	.10	.02	.5	—
1673	Thin class (100% fat)	8.6	814	2.4	89.1	0	0	.1	1	0	.4			(0)	.12	.03	.6	—
	Shoulder:																	
	Total edible																	
1674	Fat class (58% lean, 42% fat)	45.4	435	11.8	42.6	0	0	.6	7	124	1.8			(0)	.57	.14	3.1	—
1675	Medium-fat class (67% lean, 33% fat)	48.5	401	12.7	38.5	0	0	.6	7	136	1.9			(0)	.62	.15	3.3	—
1676	Thin class (75% lean, 25% fat)	51.7	368	13.6	34.4	0	0	.7	8	148	2.0			(0)	.66	.16	3.5	—
	Composite of trimmed lean cuts, ham, loin, shoulder, and spareribs:											(122)	(123)					
	Fat class.																	
	Total edible																	
1677	Raw (72% lean, 28% fat)	52.6	346	14.6	31.4	0	0	1.0	8	161	2.2			(0)	.71	.17	3.8	—
1678	Cooked, roasted (72% lean, 28% fat)	42.1	410	20.9	35.6	0	0	1.3	9	213	2.7			(0)	.47	.21	4.2	—
	Separable lean:																	
1679	Raw	68.0	182	18.8	11.3	0	0	1.4	11	217	2.8			(0)	.91	.22	4.9	—
1680	Cooked, roasted	56.4	245	27.6	14.1	0	0	1.9	12	287	3.5			(0)	.60	.28	5.4	—
	Separable fat:																	
1681	Raw	13.2	764	3.9	82.8	0	0	.1	2	19	.6			(0)	.19	.05	1.0	—
	Medium-fat class:																	
	Total edible:																	
1682	Raw (77% lean, 23% fat)	56.3	308	15.7	26.7	0	0	1.2	9	175	2.3			(0)	.76	.18	4.1	—
1683	Cooked, roasted (77% lean, 23% fat)	45.2	373	22.6	30.6	0	0	1.6	10	232	2.9			(0)	.50	.23	4.9	—
	Separable lean:																	
1684	Raw	69.0	174	19.1	10.2	0	0	1.4	11	221	2.9			(0)	.93	.22	5.0	—
1685	Cooked, roasted	57.2	236	28.0	12.9	0	0	1.9	12	292	3.6			(0)	61	.28	5.5	—
	Separable fat																	
1686	Raw	14.3	751	4.1	81.3	0	0	.4	2	22	.6			(0)	.20	.05	1.1	—
	Thin class																	
	Total edible																	
1687	Raw (81% lean, 19% fat)	59.5	276	16.7	22.7	0	0	1.2	10	188	2.5			(0)	.81	.19	4.3	—
1688	Cooked, roasted (81% lean, 19% fat)	48.0	341	24.0	26.4	0	0	1.6	11	249	3.1			(0)	.53	24	4.8	—
	Separable lean:																	
1689	Raw	69.9	165	19.5	9.1	0	0	1.4	11	226	2.9			(0)	.95	23	5.1	—
1690	Cooked, roasted	57.9	228	28.6	11.7	0	0	1.9	12	299	3.6			(0)	.63	28	5.6	—

[4] See Notes on Foods, p. 180.

[86] Value for product without added salt.

[116] Fruit juice content ranges from 10 to 50 percent. Ascorbic acid may be added as a preservative or as a nutrient. Value listed is based on product with label stating 30 mg. per 6 fl. oz. serving If label claim is 30 mg. per 8 fl. oz. serving, value would be 12 mg. per 100 grams.

[117] Values are based on products made with unenriched flour. With enriched flour, values per 100 grams are increased approximately as follows: Iron, 0.8 mg.; thiamine, 0 12 mg.; riboflavin, 0 08 mg.; niacin, 0 9 mg.

[118] Values per 100 grams range from 10 I.U. for white-fleshed varieties to as much as 1,200 I.U. for those with deep-yellow flesh.

[119] Value applies to all prune-type plums except Italian prunes and Imperial prunes, which average 1,340 I.U. per 100 grams.

[120] Prepared with flour, butter, and milk

[121] With unenriched flour, values per 100 grams are: Iron, 0.9 mg.; thiamine, 0 05 mg.; riboflavin, 0.20 mg.; niacin, 0 3 mg

[122] Average value per 100 grams of pork of all cuts is 70 mg for raw meat and 65 mg. for cooked meat. See also Notes on Foods, p. 180.

[123] Average value per 100 grams of pork of all cuts is 285 mg. for raw meat and 390 mg. for cooked meat. See also Notes on Foods, p. 180.

TABLE 1.—COMPOSITION OF FOODS, 100 GRAMS, EDIBLE PORTION—Continued

[Numbers in parentheses denote values imputed—usually from another form of the food or from a similar food. Zero in parentheses indicates that the amount of a constituent probably is none or is too small to measure. Dashes denote lack of reliable data for a constituent believed to be present in measurable amount. Calculated values, as those based on a recipe, are not in parentheses]

Item No.	Food and description	Water	Food energy	Protein	Fat	Carbohydrate: Total	Carbohydrate: Fiber	Ash	Calcium	Phosphorus	Iron	Sodium	Potassium	Vitamin A value	Thiamine	Riboflavin	Niacin	Ascorbic acid
(A)	(B)	(C)	(D)	(E)	(F)	(G)	(H)	(I)	(J)	(K)	(L)	(M)	(N)	(O)	(P)	(Q)	(R)	(S)
		Percent	Calories	Grams	Grams	Grams	Grams	Grams	Milligrams	Milligrams	Milligrams	Milligrams	Milligrams	International units	Milligrams	Milligrams	Milligrams	Milligrams
	Pork, fresh [1]—Continued																	
	Composite of trimmed lean cuts, ham, loin, shoulder, and spareribs—Continued																	
	Thin class—Continued																	
	Separable fat:																	
1691	Raw	15.4	737	4.5	79.6	0	0	0.5	3	27	0.7			(0)	0.22	0.05	1.2	—
	Separable fat, from lean cuts:																	
	Raw. See individual cuts.																	
1692	Cooked	11.1	773	4.8	83.4	0	0	.7	—	—	—			—	—	—	—	—
	Retail cuts, trimmed to retail level:																	
	Ham:																	
	Fat class:																	
	Total edible:																	
1693	Raw (72% lean, 28% fat)	54.3	327	15.2	29.1	0	0	.8	9	170	2.3			(0)	.74	.18	4.0	—
1694	Cooked, roasted (72% lean, 28% fat)	43.7	394	21.9	33.5	0	0	1.0	10	225	2.9			(0)	.49	.22	4.4	—
	Separable lean:																	
1695	Raw	70.2	160	19.7	8.4	0	0	1.1	11	229	3.0			(0)	.96	.23	5.1	—
1696	Cooked, roasted	58.2	225	29.3	11.1	0	0	1.5	13	303	3.7			(0)	.63	.29	5.6	—
	Separable fat:																	
1697	Raw	14.2	755	4.0	81.8	0	0	0	2	20	.6			(0)	.19	.05	1.0	—
	Medium-fat class:																	
	Total edible:																	
1698	Raw (74% lean, 26% fat)	56.5	308	15.9	26.6	0	0	.7	9	178	2.4			(0)	.77	.19	4.1	—
1699	Cooked, roasted (74% lean, 26% fat)	45.5	374	23.0	30.6	0	0	.9	10	236	3.0			(0)	.51	.23	4.6	—
	Separable lean:																	
1700	Raw	71.1	153	20.0	7.5	0	0	1.0	12	233	3.0			(0)	.97	.23	5.2	—
1701	Cooked, roasted	58.9	217	29.7	10.0	0	0	1.4	13	308	3.8			(0)	.64	.29	5.7	—
	Separable fat:																	
1702	Raw	15.0	746	4.3	80.7	0	0	0	2	21	.6			(0)	.21	.05	1.1	—
	Thin class:																	
	Total edible:																	
1703	Raw (77% lean, 23% fat)	59.2	281	16.7	23.2	0	0	.8	10	190	2.5			(0)	.82	.20	4.4	—
1704	Cooked, roasted (77% lean, 23% fat)	47.8	346	24.2	26.9	0	0	1.0	11	252	3.2	(35)	(35)	(0)	.54	.25	4.8	—
	Separable lean:																	
1705	Raw	72.0	147	20.4	6.6	0	0	1.1	12	238	3.1			(0)	.99	.24	5.3	—
1706	Cooked, roasted	59.3	210	30.2	9.0	0	0	1.5	13	315	3.8			(0)	.66	.30	5.8	—
	Separable fat:																	
1707	Raw	15.9	737	4.6	79.5	0	0	0	3	28	.7			(0)	.22	.05	1.2	—
	Loin:																	
	Fat class:																	
	Total edible:																	
1708	Raw (76% lean, 24% fat)	54.8	323	16.4	28.0	0	0	.8	9	185	2.5			(0)	.80	.19	4.2	—
1709	Cooked, roasted (76% lean, 24% fat)	43.7	387	23.5	31.8	0	0	1.0	10	245	3.1			(0)	.88	.25	6.3	—
1710	Cooked, broiled (68% lean, 32% fat)	40.2	418	23.5	35.2	0	0	1.1	10	256	3.2			(0)	.92	.27	5.6	—
	Separable lean:																	
1711	Raw	67.5	189	20.1	11.4	0	0	1.0	12	234	3.0			(0)	.98	.24	5.2	—
1712	Cooked, roasted	55.0	254	29.4	14.2	0	0	1.3	13	310	3.8			(0)	1.08	.31	6.5	—
1713	Cooked, broiled	52.6	270	30.6	15.4	0	0	1.5	13	324	3.9			(0)	1.13	.33	6.8	—
	Separable fat:																	
1714	Raw	15.5	739	4.8	79.7	0	0	0	3	31	.7			(0)	.23	.06	1.2	—
	Medium-fat class:																	
	Total edible:																	
1715	Raw (80% lean, 20% fat)	57.2	298	17.1	24.9	0	0	.9	10	193	2.6			(0)	.83	.20	4.4	—
1716	Cooked, roasted (80% lean, 20% fat)	45.8	362	24.5	28.5	0	0	1.2	11	256	3.2			(0)	.92	.26	5.6	—
1717	Cooked, broiled (72% lean, 28% fat)	42.3	391	24.7	31.7	0	0	1.3	12	268	3.4			(0)	.96	.28	5.8	—
	Separable lean:																	
1718	Raw	67.5	189	20.1	11.4	0	0	1.0	12	234	3.0			(0)	.98	.24	5.2	—
1719	Cooked, roasted	55.0	254	29.4	14.2	0	0	1.3	13	310	3.8			(0)	1.08	.31	6.5	—
1720	Cooked, broiled	52.6	270	30.6	15.4	0	0	1.5	13	324	3.9			(0)	1.13	.33	6.8	—
	Separable fat:																	
1721	Raw	16.7	723	5.2	77.7	0	0	4	3	36	.8			(0)	.25	.06	1.4	—
	Thin class:																	
	Total edible:																	
1722	Raw (85% lean, 15% fat)	60.0	268	17.9	21.2	0	0	.9	10	204	2.7			(0)	.87	.21	4.7	—
1723	Cooked, roasted (85% lean, 15% fat)	48.3	333	25.8	24.7	0	0	1.2	11	270	3.4			(0)	.96	.28	5.8	—

1724	Cooked, broiled (77% lean, 23% fat)	45.1	359	26.2	27.4	0	0	1.3	12	282	3.5			(0)	1.00	.29	6.1	—
	Separable lean:																	
1725	Raw	67.5	189	20.1	11.4	0	0	1.0	12	234	3.0			(0)	.98	.24	5.2	—
1726	Cooked, roasted	55.0	254	29.4	14.2	0	0	1.3	13	310	3.8			(0)	1.08	.31	6.5	—
1727	Cooked, broiled	52.6	270	30.6	15.4	0	0	1.5	13	324	3.9			(0)	1.13	.33	6.8	—
	Separable fat:																	
1728	Raw	18.2	706	5.6	75.6	0	0	.6	3	42	.8			(0)	.27	.07	1.5	—
	Boston butt:																	
	Fat class:																	
	Total edible:																	
1729	Raw (76% lean, 24% fat)	55.9	323	14.5	29.0	0	0	.7	8	160	2.2			(0)	.71	.17	3.8	—
1730	Cooked, roasted (76% lean, 24% fat)	45.0	389	20.9	33.2	0	0	.9	9	212	2.7			(0)	.47	.21	4.2	—
	Separable lean:																	
1731	Raw	68.1	196	17.7	13.3	0	0	.9	10	202	2.7			(0)	.86	.21	4.6	—
1732	Cooked, roasted	56.2	261	26.2	16.5	0	0	1.2	11	267	3.3			(0)	.57	.26	5.1	—
	Separable fat:																	
1733	Raw	17.6	721	4.7	77.7	0	0	.0	3	30	.7			(0)	.23	.05	1.2	—
	Medium-fat class:																	
	Total edible																	
1734	Raw (79% lean, 21% fat)	59.3	287	15.5	24.5	0	0	.7	9	173	2.3			(0)	.75	.18	4.0	—
1735	Cooked, roasted (79% lean, 21% fat)	48.1	353	22.5	28.5	0	0	.9	10	229	2.9			(0)	.50	.23	4.4	—
	Separable lean:																	
1736	Raw	69.6	180	18.2	11.3	0	0	.9	11	209	2.7			(0)	.88	.21	4.7	—
1737	Cooked, roasted	57.5	244	27.0	14.3	0	0	1.2	12	277	3.4			(0)	.59	.27	5.2	—
	Separable fat:																	
1738	Raw	20.1	696	5.3	74.6	0	0	0	3	38	.8			(0)	.26	.06	1.4	—
	Thin class:																	
	Total edible:																	
1739	Raw (83% lean, 17% fat)	62.7	251	16.5	20.0	0	0	.7	10	187	2.5			(0)	.80	.19	4.3	—
1740	Cooked, roasted (83% lean, 17% fat)	51.2	317	24.2	23.7	0	0	.9	11	248	3.1			(0)	.53	.24	4.7	—
	Separable lean:																	
1741	Raw	70.9	166	18.7	9.5	0	0	.9	11	215	2.8			(0)	.91	.22	4.9	—
1742	Cooked, roasted	58.7	230	27.8	12.3	0	0	1.2	12	285	3.5			(0)	.60	.27	5.4	—
	Separable fat.																	
1743	Raw	22.5	671	6.0	71.5	0	0	0	3	47	.9			(0)	.29	.07	1.6	—
	Picnic:																	
	Fat class:																	
	Total edible:																	
1744	Raw (69% lean, 31% fat)	54.7	334	14.9	30.0	0	0	.5	9	165	2.2	([133])	([134])	(0)	.72	.17	3.9	—
1745	Cooked, simmered (69% lean, 31% fat)	41.5	420	21.8	36.2	0	0	.5	9	129	2.8			(0)	.51	.23	4.5	—
	Separable lean:																	
1746	Raw	71.0	165	19.1	9.2	0	0	.7	11	221	2.9			(0)	.93	.22	5.0	—
1747	Cooked, simmered	58.8	231	28.5	12.1	0	0	.7	12	173	3.6			(0)	.65	.30	5.8	—
	Separable fat:																	
1748	Raw	18.1	713	5.4	76.5	0	0	0	3	39	.8			(0)	.26	.06	1.4	—
	Medium-fat class:																	
	Total edible:																	
1749	Raw (74% lean, 26% fat)	58.9	290	15.8	24.7	0	0	.7	9	178	2.4			(0)	.77	.19	4.1	—
1750	Cooked, simmered (74% lean, 26% fat)	45.7	374	23.2	30.5	0	0	.6	10	139	3.0			(0)	.54	.25	4.8	—
	Separable lean:																	
1751	Raw	72.3	150	19.4	7.4	0	0	.9	11	225	2.9			(0)	.94	.23	5.0	—
1752	Cooked, simmered	60.3	212	29.0	9.8	0	0	.8	12	176	3.6			(0)	.66	.30	5.9	—
	Separable fat:																	
1753	Raw	20.9	685	5.8	73.2	0	0	.1	3	44	.9			(0)	.28	.07	1.5	—
	Thin class:																	
	Total edible:																	
1754	Raw (78% lean, 22% fat)	62.7	249	16.9	19.6	0	0	.8	10	191	2.5			(0)	.82	.20	4.4	—
1755	Cooked, simmered (78% lean, 22% fat)	49.7	329	24.9	24.7	0	0	.7	11	149	3.2			(0)	.58	.26	5.2	—
	Separable lean:																	
1756	Raw	73.7	135	19.8	5.6	0	0	.9	11	230	3.0			(0)	.96	.23	5.1	—
1757	Cooked, simmered	62.0	194	29.7	7.5	0	0	.8	13	180	3.7			(0)	.68	.31	6.0	—
	Separable fat:																	
1758	Raw	23.3	657	6.3	69.9	0	0	.5	4	51	.9			(0)	.31	.07	1.6	—
	Spareribs:																	
	Fat class:																	
	Total edible:																	
1759	Raw	49.2	390	13.7	36.8	0	0	.7	8	149	2.1			(0)	.67	.16	3.6	—
1760	Cooked, braised	37.2	467	19.7	42.5	0	0	.6	8	113	2.5			(0)	.40	.19	3.2	—
	Medium-fat class:																	
	Total edible																	
1761	Raw	51.8	361	14.5	33.2	0	0	.7	8	160	2.2			(0)	.70	.17	3.8	—
1762	Cooked, braised	39.7	440	20.8	38.9	0	0	.6	9	121	2.6			(0)	.43	.21	3.4	—
	Thin class																	
	Total edible.																	
1763	Raw	54.5	331	15.3	29.5	0	0	.8	9	170	2.3			(0)	.74	.18	4.0	—
1764	Cooked, braised	42.4	410	21.9	35.1	0	0	.7	9	129	2.8			(0)	.45	.22	3.6	—

[133] Average value per 100 grams of pork of all cuts is 70 mg. for raw meat and 65 mg. for cooked meat. See also Notes on Foods, p. 180.

[134] Average value per 100 grams of pork of all cuts is 285 mg for raw meat and 390 mg. for cooked meat. See also Notes on Foods, p. 180.

TABLE 1.—COMPOSITION OF FOODS, 100 GRAMS, EDIBLE PORTION—Continued

[Numbers in parentheses denote values imputed—usually from another form of the food or from a similar food. Zero in parentheses indicates that the amount of a constituent probably is none or is too small to measure. Dashes denote lack of reliable data for a constituent believed to be present in measurable amount. Calculated values, as those based on a recipe, are not in parentheses]

Item No.	Food and description	Water	Food energy	Protein	Fat	Carbohydrate		Ash	Calcium	Phosphorus	Iron	Sodium	Potassium	Vitamin A value	Thiamine	Riboflavin	Niacin	Ascorbic acid
						Total	Fiber											
(A)	(B)	(C)	(D)	(E)	(F)	(G)	(H)	(I)	(J)	(K)	(L)	(M)	(N)	(O)	(P)	(Q)	(R)	(S)
		Percent	*Calories*	*Grams*	*Grams*	*Grams*	*Grams*	*Grams*	*Milligrams*	*Milligrams*	*Milligrams*	*Milligrams*	*Milligrams*	*International units*	*Milligrams*	*Milligrams*	*Milligrams*	*Milligrams*
	Pork, cured:																	
	Dry, long-cure, country-style:																	
	Ham:																	
1765	Fat	36	460	14.6	44.	0.3	0	5.1	—	—	—	—	—	(0)	—	—	—	—
1766	Medium-fat	42.	389	16.9	35.	.3	0	5.4	—	—	—	—	—	(0)	—	—	—	—
1767	Lean	49.	310	19.5	25	.3	0	5.8	—	—	—	—	—	(0)	—	—	—	—
	Light-cure, commercial																	
	Ham, medium-fat class:																	
	Total edible:																	
1768	Raw (76% lean, 24% fat)	56.5	282	17.5	23.0	0	0	3.0	10	162	2.6	—	—	(0)	0.72	0.19	4.1	—
1769	Cooked, roasted (84% lean, 16% fat)	53.6	289	20.9	22.1	0	0	3.4	9	172	2.6	—	—	(0)	.47	.18	3.6	—
	Separable lean																	
1770	Raw	66.4	168	21.5	8.5	0	0	3.6	12	188	3.2	1,100	340	(0)	.89	.24	5.0	—
1771	Cooked, roasted	61.9	187	25.3	8.8	0	0	4.0	11	200	3.2	930	326	(0)	.58	.23	4.5	—
	Separable fat																	
1772	Raw	25.7	636	5.2	68.1	0	0	1.0	3	82	.8	—	—	(0)	.21	.06	1.2	—
	Boston butt, medium-fat class:																	
	Total edible																	
1773	Raw (75% lean, 25% fat)	55.7	291	17.2	24.1	0	0	3.0	10	152	2.6	—	—	(0)	.71	.19	4.0	—
1774	Cooked, roasted (83% lean, 17% fat)	47.7	330	22.9	25.7	0	0	3.7	10	185	3.0	—	—	(0)	.53	.21	4.1	—
	Separable lean:																	
1775	Raw	63.2	200	20.9	12.3	0	0	3.6	12	179	3.1	(1,100)	(340)	(0)	.86	.23	4.9	—
1776	Cooked, roasted	53.9	243	27.8	13.8	0	0	4.5	12	218	3.6	(930)	(326)	(0)	.64	.25	5.0	—
	Separable fat																	
1777	Raw	32.8	569	6.0	60.2	0	0	1.0	3	69	.9	—	—	(0)	.25	.07	1.4	—
	Picnic, medium-fat class:																	
	Total edible:																	
1778	Raw (70% lean, 30% fat)	56.7	285	16.8	23.6	0	0	2.9	10	150	2.5	—	—	(0)	.69	.19	3.9	—
1779	Cooked, roasted (82% lean, 18% fat)	48.8	323	22.4	25.2	0	0	3.6	10	182	2.9	—	—	(0)	.52	.20	4.0	—
	Separable lean:																	
1780	Raw	66.7	167	21.3	8.4	0	0	3.6	12	181	3.2	(1,100)	(340)	(0)	.88	.24	5.0	—
1781	Cooked, roasted	57.2	211	28.4	9.9	0	0	4.5	13	220	3.7	(930)	(326)	(0)	.65	.26	5.0	—
	Separable fat:																	
1782	Raw	33.9	553	6.4	58.3	0	0	1.4	4	79	1.0	—	—	(0)	.26	.07	1.5	—
	Pork, cured, canned:																	
1783	**Ham,** contents of can	65.0	193	18.3	12.3	.9	0	3.5	11	156	2.7	(1,100)	(340)	(0)	.53	.19	3.8	—
	Pork, cured. See also Bacon, items 125–129, and Salt pork, item 1964.																	
1784	**Pork and gravy,** canned (90% pork, 10% gravy)	56.9	256	16.4	17.8	6.3	0	2.6	13	183	2.4	—	—	(0)	.49	.17	3.5	—
	Potatoes:																	
1785	Raw	79.8	76	2.1	.1	17.1	.5	.9	7	53	.6	3	407	Trace	.10	.04	1.5	[124] 20
	Cooked:																	
1786	Baked in skin	75.1	93	2.6	.1	21.1	.6	1.1	9	65	.7	[125] 4	503	Trace	.10	.04	1.7	20
1787	Boiled in skin	79.8	76	2.1	.1	17.1	.5	.9	7	53	.6	[125] 3	407	Trace	.09	.04	1.5	16
1788	Boiled, pared before cooking	82.8	65	1.9	.1	14.5	.5	.7	6	42	.5	[125] 2	285	Trace	.09	.03	1.2	16
1789	French-fried	44.7	274	4.3	13.2	36.0	1.0	1.8	15	111	1.3	[126] 6	853	Trace	.13	.08	3.1	21
1790	Fried from raw	46.9	268	4.0	14.2	32.6	1.0	2.3	15	101	1.1	223	775	Trace	.12	.07	2.8	19
1791	Hash-browned after holding overnight	54.2	229	3.1	11.7	29.1	.8	1.9	12	79	.9	288	475	Trace	.08	.05	2.1	9
1792	Mashed, milk added	82.8	65	2.1	.7	13.0	.4	1.4	24	49	.4	301	261	20	.08	.05	1.0	10
1793	Mashed, milk and table fat added	79.8	94	2.1	4.3	12.3	.4	1.5	24	48	.4	331	250	170	.08	.05	1.0	9
	Scalloped and au gratin:																	
1794	With cheese	71.1	145	5.3	7.9	13.6	.3	2.1	127	122	.5	447	306	320	.06	.12	.9	10
1795	Without cheese	76.7	104	3.0	3.9	14.7	.3	1.7	54	74	.4	355	327	160	.06	.09	1.0	11
	Canned:																	
1796	Solids and liquid	88.5	44	1.1	.2	9.8	.2	.4	[126] (4)	(30)	(.3)	[125] 1	250	Trace	.04	.02	.6	13
	Dehydrated mashed:																	
	Flakes without milk:																	
1797	Dry form	5.2	364	7.2	.6	84.0	(1.6)	3.0	35	(173)	1.7	89	(1,600)	Trace	.23	.06	5.4	[127] 32
1798	Prepared, water, milk, table fat added	79.3	93	1.9	3.2	14.5	.3	1.1	31	47	.3	231	286	130	.04	.04	.9	[127] 5
	Granules without milk:																	
1799	Dry form	7.1	352	8.3	.6	80.4	1.4	3.6	44	203	2.4	84	(1,600)	Trace	.16	.11	4.9	[127] 19
1800	Prepared, water, milk, table fat added	78.6	96	2.0	3.6	14.4	.2	1.4	32	52	.5	256	290	110	.04	.05	.7	[127] 3
	Granules with milk:																	
1801	Dry form	6.3	358	10.9	1.1	77.7	1.5	4.0	142	237	3.5	82	1,848	60	.19	.30	4.2	[127] 16

1802	Prepared, water, table fat added	81.4	79	2.0	2.2	13.1	.3	1.3	31	44	.6	234	335	90	.03	.05	.8	[137] 3
	Frozen:																	
	Diced, for hash-browning:																	
1803	Not thawed	81.0	73	1.2	Trace	17.4	.4	.4	10	30	.7	8	170	Trace	.07	.01	.6	9
1804	Cooked, hash-browned	56.1	224	2.0	11.5	29.0	.7	1.4	18	50	1.2	299	283	Trace	.07	.02	1.0	8
	French-fried:																	
1805	Not thawed	63.5	170	2.8	6.5	26.1	.6	1.1	7	67	1.4	[135] 3	506	Trace	.14	.02	2.1	20
1806	Heated	52.9	220	3.6	8.4	33.7	.7	1.4	9	86	1.8	[135] 4	652	Trace	.14	.02	2.6	21
	Mashed:																	
1807	Not thawed	80.4	75	1.7	.1	17.1	.4	.7	16	39	.7	79	229	30	.07	.03	.8	6
1808	Heated	78.3	93	1.8	2.8	15.7	.4	1.4	25	42	.6	359	215	140	.06	.04	.7	4
1809	**Potato chips**	1.8	568	5.3	39.8	50.0	(1.6)	3.1	40	139	1.8	[128] —	1,130	Trace	.21	.07	4.8	16
1810	**Potato flour**	7.6	351	8.0	.8	79.9	1.6	3.7	33	178	17.2	34	1,588	Trace	.42	.14	3.4	(19)
	Potato salad, from home recipe, made with—																	
1811	Cooked salad dressing, seasonings	76.0	99	2.7	2.8	16.3	.4	2.2	32	64	.6	528	319	140	.08	.07	1.1	11
1812	Mayonnaise and French dressing, hard-cooked eggs, seasonings.	72.4	145	3.0	9.2	13.4	.4	2.0	19	63	.8	480	296	180	.07	.06	.9	11
1813	**Potato sticks**	1.5	544	6.4	36.4	50.8	1.5	4.9	44	139	1.8	[128] —	1,130	Trace	.21	.07	4.8	40
1814	**Pretzels**	4.5	390	9.8	4.5	75.9	.3	5.3	22	131	1.5	[129] 1,680	130	(0)	.02	.03	.7	(0)
1815	**Pricklypears,** raw	88.0	42	.5	.1	10.9	1.6	.5	20	28	.3	2	166	60	.01	.03	.4	22
	Prunes:																	
	Dehydrated, nugget-type and pieces:																	
1816	Uncooked	2.5	344	3.3	.5	91.3	(2.2)	2.4	90	107	4.4	11	940	2,170	.12	.22	2.1	4
1817	Cooked, fruit and liquid, with added sugar	50.7	180	1.2	.2	47.1	(.8)	.8	31	37	1.5	4	329	760	.03	.07	.7	1
	Dried, "softenized":																	
1818	Uncooked	28.0	255	2.1	.6	67.4	1.6	1.9	51	79	3.9	8	694	1,600	.09	.17	1.6	3
	Cooked (fruit and liquid):																	
1819	Without added sugar	66.4	119	1.0	.3	31.4	.8	.9	24	37	1.8	4	327	750	.03	.07	.7	1
1820	With added sugar	53.2	172	.8	.2	45.1	.6	.7	19	30	1.5	3	262	600	.03	.06	.6	1
1821	**Prune juice,** canned or bottled	80.	77	.4	.1	19.0	Trace	.5	14	20	4.1	2	235	—	.01	.01	.4	2
1822	**Prune whip**	57.3	156	4.4	.2	36.9	.6	1.2	22	33	1.3	164	290	460	.02	.14	.5	2
	Puddings with starch base, prepared from home recipe:																	
1823	Chocolate	65.8	148	3.1	4.7	25.7	.2	.7	96	98	.5	56	171	150	.02	.14	.1	Trace
1824	Vanilla (blanc mange)	76.0	111	3.5	3.9	15.9	Trace	.7	117	91	Trace	65	138	160	.03	.16	.1	1
	See also Bread, Rennin products, Rice; Tapioca; Baby foods.																	
	Pudding mixes and puddings made from mixes:																	
	With starch base.																	
1825	Mix, chocolate, regular, dry form	1.7	361	3.0	2.1	91.5	.6	1.7	20	94	1.6	447	95	Trace	.02	.07	.4	0
1826	Pudding made with milk, cooked	70.0	124	3.4	3.0	22.8	.1	.8	102	95	.3	129	136	130	.02	.15	.1	Trace
1827	Mix, chocolate, instant, dry form	.7	357	3.1	1.6	90.8	.6	3.8	245	88	2.0	404	85	Trace	.01	.06	.3	0
1828	Pudding made with milk, without cooking	68.7	125	3.0	2.5	24.4	.1	1.4	144	91	.5	124	129	130	.03	.15	.1	Trace
	With vegetable gum base:																	
1829	Mix, custard-dessert, dry form	.1	384	(0)	.1	98.9	Trace	.9	9	2	.1	297	25	0	0	0	0	0
1830	Pudding made with milk, cooked	70.0	131	3.1	3.5	22.6	Trace	.8	106	82	Trace	99	129	140	.02	.14	.1	Trace
	Pumpkin:																	
1831	Raw	91.6	26	1.0	.1	6.5	1.1	.8	21	44	.8	1	340	1,600	.05	.11	.6	9
1832	Canned [130]	90.2	33	1.0	.3	7.9	1.3	.6	25	26	.4	[133] 2	240	6,400	.03	.05	.6	5
1833	**Pumpkin and squash seed kernels,** dry	4.4	553	29.0	46.7	15.0	1.9	4.9	51	1,144	11.2	—	—	70	.24	.19	2.4	—
	Purslane leaves, including stems:																	
1834	Raw	92.5	21	1.7	.4	3.8	.9	1.6	103	39	3.5	—	—	2,500	.03	.10	.5	25
1835	Cooked, boiled, drained	94.7	15	1.2	.3	2.8	.8	1.0	86	24	1.2	—	—	2,100	.02	.06	.4	12
	Quail, raw:																	
1836	Total edible	65.9	168	25.0	6.8	0	0	1.6	—	—	—	—	—	—	—	—	—	—
1837	Flesh and skin	66.3	172	25.4	7.0	0	0	1.4	—	—	—	40	175	—	—	—	—	—
1838	Giblets	63.0	176	21.8	6.2	6.7	0	2.3	—	—	—	—	—	—	—	—	—	—
1839	**Quinces,** raw	83.8	57	.4	.1	15.3	1.7	.4	11	17	.7	4	197	40	.02	.03	.2	15
	Rabbit, domesticated:																	
	Flesh only:																	
1840	Raw	70.	162	21.	8.	0	0	1.	20	352	1.3	43	385	—	.08	.06	12.8	—
1841	Cooked, stewed	59.8	216	29.3	10.1	0	0	.8	21	259	1.5	41	368	—	.05	.07	11.3	—
	Rabbit, wild:																	
1842	Flesh only, raw	73.	135	21	5	0	0	1.	—	—	—	—	—	—	—	—	—	—
1843	**Raccoon,** cooked, roasted	54.8	255	29.2	14.5	0	0	1.5	—	—	—	—	—	—	.59	.52	—	—
	Radishes, raw:																	
1844	Common	94.5	17	1.0	.1	3.6	.7	.8	30	31	1.0	18	322	10	.03	.03	.3	26
1845	Oriental, including daikon (Japanese) and Chinese	94.1	19	.9	.1	4.2	.7	.7	35	26	.6	—	180	10	.03	.02	.4	32
	Raisins, natural (unbleached):																	
1846	Uncooked	18.0	289	2.5	.2	77.4	.9	1.9	62	101	3.5	27	763	20	.11	.08	.5	1
1847	Cooked, fruit and liquid, added sugar	41.4	213	1.2	.1	56.4	.4	.9	29	47	1.6	13	355	10	.04	.03	.2	Trace

[124] Year-round average. Recently dug potatoes contain about 26 mg. ascorbic acid per 100 grams. After 3 months' storage the value is only half as high; after 6 months', about one-third as high.

[125] Applies to product without added salt. If salt is added, an estimated average value for sodium is 236 mg. per 100 grams

[126] Federal standards provide for addition of certain calcium salts as firming agents; if used, these salts may add calcium not to exceed 200 mg. per 100 grams of finished product.

[127] Value varies widely. It is dependent on content of ascorbic acid in raw potatoes, method of processing, and length of storage of dehydrated product. Present values for dehydrated forms range from 10 to 35 mg. per 100 grams.

[128] Sodium content is variable and may be as high as 1,000 mg. per 100 grams.

[129] Sodium content is variable For example, very thin pretzel sticks contain about twice the average amount listed.

[130] May be a mixture of pumpkin and winter squash.

TABLE 1.—COMPOSITION OF FOODS, 100 GRAMS, EDIBLE PORTION—Continued

[Numbers in parentheses denote values imputed—usually from another form of the food or from a similar food. Zero in parentheses indicates that the amount of a constituent probably is none or is too small to measure. Dashes denote lack of reliable data for a constituent believed to be present in measurable amount. Calculated values, as those based on a recipe, are not in parentheses]

Item No.	Food and description	Water	Food energy	Protein	Fat	Carbohydrate: Total	Carbohydrate: Fiber	Ash	Calcium	Phosphorus	Iron	Sodium	Potassium	Vitamin A value	Thiamine	Riboflavin	Niacin	Ascorbic acid
(A)	(B)	(C)	(D)	(E)	(F)	(G)	(H)	(I)	(J)	(K)	(L)	(M)	(N)	(O)	(P)	(Q)	(R)	(S)
		Percent	Calories	Grams	Grams	Grams	Grams	Grams	Milligrams	Milligrams	Milligrams	Milligrams	Milligrams	International units	Milligrams	Milligrams	Milligrams	Milligrams
	Raja fish. See Skate, item 2053.																	
	Raspberries:																	
	Raw:																	
1848	Black	80.8	73	1.5	1.4	15.7	5.1	0.6	30	22	0.9	1	199	Trace	(0.03)	(0.09)	(0.9)	18
1849	Red	84.2	57	1.2	.5	13.6	3.0	.5	22	22	.9	1	168	130	.03	.09	.9	25
	Canned, solids and liquid, water pack, with or without artificial sweetener:																	
1850	Black	86.7	51	1.1	1.1	10.7	3.3	.4	20	14	.6	1	135	Trace	.01	.04	.5	6
1851	Red	90.1	35	.7	.1	8.8	2.6	.3	15	15	.6	1	114	90	.01	.04	.5	9
1852	Frozen, red, sweetened, not thawed	74.3	98	.7	.2	24.6	2.2	.2	13	17	.6	1	100	(70)	.02	.06	.6	21
1853	**Red and gray snapper,** raw	78.5	93	19.8	.9	0	0	1.3	16	214	.8	67	323	—	.17	.02	—	—
	Redfish. See Drum, red, item 960; and Ocean perch, Atlantic, items 1396–1398.																	
1854	**Redhorse,** silver, raw	78.6	98	18.0	2.3	0	0	1.2	—	—	—	—	—	—	—	—	—	—
	Reindeer, raw:																	
1855	Lean only	73.3	127	21.8	3.8	0	0	1.1	—	—	5.3	—	—	—	.33	.68	5.5	—
	Total edible:																	
1856	Side (84% lean, 16% fat)	63.3	217	20.5	14.4	0	0	1.0	—	—	—	—	—	—	—	—	—	—
1857	Forequarter (91% lean, 9% fat)	67.4	178	21.8	9.4	0	0	1.1	—	—	—	—	—	—	—	—	—	—
1858	Hindquarter (78% lean, 22% fat)	59.6	256	19.4	19.2	0	0	.9	—	—	—	—	—	—	—	—	—	—
	Rennin products:																	
1859	Tablet (salts, starch, rennin enzyme)	9.0	107	.1	1.6	24.3	0	65.6	3,510	200	—	22,300	—	0	0	0	0	0
1860	Dessert, home-prepared with tablet	81.1	89	3.1	3.5	11.6	0	.7	111	83	Trace	82	126	140	.03	.15	.1	1
	Dessert mixes and desserts prepared from mixes:																	
	Chocolate:																	
1861	Mix, dry form	1.0	387	2.8	5.3	91.5	.9	1.4	186	129	—	70	—	—	—	—	—	—
1862	Dessert made with milk	77.9	102	3.4	3.8	14.1	.1	.8	122	96	Trace	52	125	140	.03	.15	.1	1
	Other flavors (vanilla, caramel, fruit flavorings):																	
1863	Mix, dry form	.4	353	Trace	Trace	99.0	—	.6	[9] 117	[9] 61	—	6	—	—	—	—	—	—
1864	Dessert made with milk	79.7	95	3.2	3.6	12.8	0	.7	[8] 117	[8] 92	Trace	46	128	150	.03	.16	.1	1
	Rhubarb:																	
1865	Raw	94.8	16	.6	.1	3.7	.7	.8	96	18	.8	2	251	100	(.03)	(.07)	(.3)	9
1866	Cooked, added sugar	62.8	141	.5	.1	36.0	.6	.6	78	15	.6	2	203	80	(.02)	(.05)	(.3)	6
	Frozen, sweetened:																	
1867	Not thawed	80.1	75	.6	.2	18.5	.9	.6	93	14	.8	4	211	80	.02	.05	.2	8
1868	Cooked, added sugar	62.6	143	.5	.2	36.2	.8	.5	78	12	.7	3	176	70	.02	.04	.2	6
	Rice:																	
	Brown:																	
1869	Raw	12.0	360	7.5	1.9	77.4	.9	1.2	32	221	1.6	9	214	(0)	.34	.05	4.7	(0)
1870	Cooked	70.3	119	2.5	.6	25.5	.3	1.1	12	73	.5	282	70	(0)	.09	.02	1.4	(0)
	White (fully milled or polished):																	
	Enriched:																	
	Common commercial varieties, all types:																	
1871	Raw	12.0	363	6.7	.4	80.4	.3	.5	24	94	[32] 2.9	5	92	(0)	[32] .44	([32])	[32] 3.5	(0)
1872	Cooked	72.6	109	2.0	.1	24.2	.1	1.1	10	28	[32] .9	374	28	(0)	[32] .11	([32])	[32] 1.0	(0)
	Long-grain:																	
	Parboiled:																	
1873	Dry form	10.3	369	7.4	.3	81.3	.2	.7	60	200	[32] 2.9	9	150	(0)	[32] .44	([32])	[32] 3.5	(0)
1874	Cooked	73.4	106	2.1	.1	23.3	.1	1.1	19	57	[32] .8	358	43	(0)	[32] .11	([32])	[32] 1.2	(0)
	Precooked (instant):																	
1875	Dry form	9.6	374	7.5	.2	82.5	.4	.2	5	65	[32] 2.9	1	—	(0)	[32] .44	([32])	[32] 3.5	(0)
1876	Ready-to-serve	72.9	109	2.2	Trace	24.2	.1	.7	3	19	[32] .8	273	Trace	(0)	[32] .13	([32])	[32] 1.0	(0)
	Unenriched:																	
	Common commercial varieties, all types:																	
1877	Raw	12.0	363	6.7	.4	80.4	.3	.5	24	94	.8	5	92	(0)	.07	.03	1.6	(0)
1878	Cooked	72.6	109	2.0	.1	24.2	.1	1.1	10	28	.2	374	28	(0)	.02	.01	.4	(0)
1879	Glutinous (Mochi Gomi), raw	13.2	361	5.6	.9	79.8	.3	.5	36	100	2.0	10	130	(0)	.07	.04	2.0	(0)
1880	**Rice bran**	9.7	276	13.3	15.8	50.8	11.5	10.4	76	1,386	19.4	Trace	1,495	(0)	2.26	.25	29.8	(0)
1881	**Rice polish**	9.8	265	12.1	12.8	57.7	2.4	7.6	69	1,106	16.1	Trace	714	(0)	1.84	.18	28.2	(0)
	Rice products used mainly as hot breakfast cereals:																	
	Rice, granulated, added nutrients:																	
1882	Dry form	7.4	383	6.0	.3	85.9	.2	.4	9	96	5.4	—	—	(0)	.42	.11	5.8	(0)
1883	Cooked	87.5	50	.8	Trace	11.2	Trace	.5	2	13	.7	176	Trace	(0)	.06	.01	.8	(0)

	Rice products used mainly as ready-to-eat breakfast cereals:																		
1884	Rice flakes, added nutrients	3.2	390	5.9	.3	87.7	.6	2.9	29	132	1.6	987	180	(0)	.35	.05	5.4	(0)
1885	Rice, puffed, added nutrients, without salt	3.7	399	6.0	.4	89.5	.6	.4	20	92	1.8	2	100	(0)	.44	.04	4.4	(0)
	Rice, puffed or oven-popped, presweetened:																	
1886	Honey and added nutrients	1.8	388	4.2	.7	90.6	.2	2.7	46	74	.9	706	—	(0)	.33	—	4.6	(0)
1887	Honey or cocoa and added nutrients, including fat.	3.4	401	4.5	4.0	86.7	.4	1.4	51	82	3.3	358	61	(0)	.42	.06	6.3	(0)
1888	Rice, shredded; added nutrients	3.0	392	5.2	.3	88.8	.3	2.7	14	95	1.8	846	—	(0)	.39	—	7.0	(0)
	Rice, with protein concentrate, mainly—																	
1889	Casein, other added nutrients	3.0	382	40.0	.2	54.8	.5	2.0	159	318	17.6	600	—	(0)	1.70	2.10	17.6	53
1890	Wheat gluten, other added nutrients	2.5	386	20.0	.3	74.4	.5	2.8	53	187	12.4	800	—	(0)	1.40	1.70	17.0	35
1891	**Rice pudding** with raisins	65.8	146	3.6	3.1	26.7	.1	.8	98	94	.4	71	177	110	.03	.14	.2	Trace
	Rockfish, including black, canary, yellowtail, rasphead, and bocaccio:																	
1892	Raw	78.9	97	18.9	1.8	0	0	1.2	—	—	—	60	388	—	.06	.12	—	—
1893	Cooked, oven-steamed [133]	75.4	107	18.1	2.5	1.9	—	2.1	—	—	—	68	446	—	.05	.12	—	1
	Roe:																	
	Raw:																	
1894	Including carp, cod, haddock, herring, pike, and shad	70.1	130	24.4	2.3	1.5	—	1.7	—	—	.6	—	—	—	.10	.76	1.4	14
1895	Including salmon, sturgeon, and turbot	61.3	207	25.2	10.4	1.4	—	1.7	—	—	—	—	—	—	.38	.72	2.3	18
1896	Cooked, baked or broiled, cod and shad [134]	71.3	126	22.0	2.8	1.9	—	2.0	13	402	2.3	73	132	—	—	—	—	—
1897	Canned, including cod, haddock, and herring, solids and liquid.	72.4	118	21.5	2.8	.3	—	2.0	15	346	1.2	—	—	—	—	—	—	2
	Rolls and buns:																	
1898	Baked from home recipe, with milk and enriched flour.	26.1	339	8.2	8.7	56.1	.2	.9	47	102	[135] 2.1	279	117	80	[135] .25	[135] .26	[135] 2.3	Trace
	Commercial. [32]																	
	Ready-to-serve:																	
1899	Danish pastry	22.0	422	7.4	23.5	45.6	.1	1.5	50	109	.9	366	112	310	.07	.15	.8	Trace
	Hard rolls:																	
1900	Enriched	25.4	312	9.8	3.2	59.5	.2	2.1	47	92	2.3	625	97	Trace	.26	.23	2.7	Trace
1901	Unenriched	25.4	312	9.8	3.2	59.5	.2	2.1	47	92	.8	625	97	Trace	.05	.09	.8	Trace
	Plain (pan rolls):																	
1902	Enriched	31.4	298	8.2	5.6	53.0	.2	1.8	74	85	1.9	506	95	Trace	.28	.18	2.2	Trace
1903	Unenriched	31.4	298	8.2	5.6	53.0	.2	1.8	74	85	.7	506	95	Trace	.06	.09	.8	Trace
1904	Raisin rolls or buns	32.0	275	6.9	2.9	56.4	.9	1.8	75	91	1.4	384	245	Trace	.06	.10	.7	Trace
1905	Sweet rolls	31.5	316	8.5	9.1	49.3	.2	1.6	85	107	.8	389	124	70	.07	.15	.8	Trace
1906	Whole-wheat rolls	32.0	257	10.0	2.8	52.3	1.6	2.9	106	281	2.4	564	292	Trace	.34	.13	3.0	Trace
	Partially baked (brown-and-serve):																	
	Enriched																	
1907	Unbrowned	33.0	299	7.9	6.8	50.6	.2	1.7	47	82	1.8	513	91	Trace	.24	.20	2.1	Trace
1908	Browned	26.9	328	8.7	7.8	54.8	.2	1.8	51	89	2.0	562	100	Trace	.26	.22	2.3	Trace
	Unenriched																	
1909	Unbrowned	33.0	299	7.9	6.8	50.6	.2	1.7	47	82	.7	513	91	Trace	.06	.09	.8	Trace
1910	Browned	26.9	328	8.7	7.8	54.8	.2	1.8	51	89	.7	562	100	Trace	.06	.10	.8	Trace
	Roll dough and rolls baked from dough:																	
	Enriched																	
1911	Dough, unraised, frozen	38.5	268	7.5	5.0	47.4	.2	1.6	33	76	1.7	482	82	Trace	.27	.20	2.2	Trace
1912	Rolls, baked	28.3	311	8.5	5.4	56.0	.3	1.8	39	88	2.0	560	96	Trace	.27	.22	2.3	Trace
	Unenriched:																	
1913	Dough, unraised, frozen	38.5	268	7.5	5.0	47.4	.2	1.6	33	76	.9	482	82	Trace	.08	.09	1.0	Trace
1914	Rolls, baked	28.3	311	8.5	5.4	56.0	.3	1.8	39	88	1.0	560	96	Trace	.08	.10	1.0	Trace
	Roll mix and rolls baked from mix:																	
1915	Mix, dry form	8.6	393	11.2	5.9	72.3	.2	2.0	74	128	[136] .8	412	162	Trace	[136] .08	[136] .16	[136] 1.1	Trace
1916	Rolls, made with water	30.6	299	9.0	4.5	54.5	.2	1.4	56	97	[136] .6	313	123	Trace	[136] .05	[136] .12	[136] .7	Trace
	Root beer. See Beverages, item 408.																	
1917	**Roseapples**, raw	84.5	56	.6	.3	14.2	1.1	.4	29	16	1.2	—	—	130	.02	.03	.8	22
	Rum. See Beverages, items 395–399.																	
1918	**Rusk**	4.8	419	13.8	8.7	71.0	.2	1.7	20	119	1.3	246	161	230	.08	.22	1.1	Trace
	Rutabagas:																	
1919	Raw	87.0	46	1.1	.1	11.0	1.1	.8	66	39	.4	5	239	580	.07	.07	1.1	43
1920	Cooked, boiled, drained	90.2	35	.9	.1	8.2	1.1	.6	59	31	.3	4	167	550	.06	.06	.8	26
	Rye:																	
1921	Whole-grain	11.	334	12.1	1.7	73.4	2.0	1.8	(38)	376	3.7	(1)	467	(0)	.43	.22	1.6	(0)
	Flours																	
1922	Light	11.	357	9.4	1.0	77.9	.4	.7	22	185	1.1	(1)	156	(0)	.15	.07	.6	(0)
1923	Medium	11.	350	11.4	1.7	74.8	1.0	1.1	(27)	262	2.6	(1)	203	(0)	.30	.12	2.5	(0)
1924	Dark	11.	327	16.3	2.6	68.1	2.4	2.0	54	(536)	4.5	1	860	(0)	.61	.22	2.7	(0)

[32] For additional data and information, see discussion of bread and rolls in Notes on Foods, p. 172.

[131] Raspberry- and strawberry-flavored mixes contain about 170 mg. calcium and a trace of phosphorus per 100 grams. Values per 100 grams of prepared dessert are: Calcium, 121 mg.; phosphorus, 84 mg.

[132] Values for iron, thiamine, and niacin are based on the minimum levels of enrichment specified in standards of identity. See Notes on Foods, p. 171, for appropriate value for riboflavin.

[133] Prepared with onion.

[134] Prepared with butter or margarine and lemon juice or vinegar.

[135] With unenriched flour, values per 100 grams are: Iron, 0.8 mg.; thiamine, 0.06 mg.; riboflavin, 0.14 mg.; niacin, 0.8 mg.

[136] Based on mix containing unenriched flour. If mix is made with enriched flour, approximate values in milligrams per 100 grams are as follows:

	Iron	Thiamine	Riboflavin	Niacin
Dry mix	2.6	0.40	0.34	3.3
Rolls	2.0	.25	.25	2.2

TABLE 1.—COMPOSITION OF FOODS, 100 GRAMS, EDIBLE PORTION—Continued

[Numbers in parentheses denote values imputed—usually from another form of the food or from a similar food. Zero in parentheses indicates that the amount of a constituent probably is none or is too small to measure. Dashes denote lack of reliable data for a constituent believed to be present in measurable amount. Calculated values, as those based on a recipe, are not in parentheses]

Item No.	Food and description	Water	Food energy	Protein	Fat	Carbohydrate Total	Carbohydrate Fiber	Ash	Calcium	Phosphorus	Iron	Sodium	Potassium	Vitamin A value	Thiamine	Riboflavin	Niacin	Ascorbic acid
(A)	(B)	(C)	(D)	(E)	(F)	(G)	(H)	(I)	(J)	(K)	(L)	(M)	(N)	(O)	(P)	(Q)	(R)	(S)
		Percent	Calories	Grams	Grams	Grams	Grams	Grams	Milligrams	Milligrams	Milligrams	Milligrams	Milligrams	International units	Milligrams	Milligrams	Milligrams	Milligrams
1925	**Rye wafers,** whole-grain	6.0	344	13.0	1.2	76.3	2.2	3.5	53	388	3.9	882	600	(0)	0.32	0.25	1.2	(0)
1926	**Sablefish,** raw	71.6	190	13.0	14.9	0	0	1.0	—	—	—	56	358	—	.11	.09	—	—
1927	**Safflower seed kernels,** dry	5.0	615	19.1	59.5	12.4	—	4.0	—	—	—	—	—	—	—	—	—	—
1928	**Safflower seed meal,** partially defatted	9.1	355	39.6	8.2	36.5	7.4	6.6	75	620	—	—	—	—	1.12	.40	2.2	0
	Salad dressings, commercial: [137]																	
	Blue and Roquefort cheese:																	
1929	Regular	32.3	504	4.8	52.3	7.4	.1	3.2	81	74	.2	1,094	37	210	.01	.10	.1	2
	Special dietary (low-calorie):																	
1930	Low-fat (approx. 5 Cal. per tsp.)	83.7	76	3.0	5.9	4.1	.1	3.3	64	47	.1	1,108	34	176	Trace	.07	.1	2
1931	Low-fat (approx. 1 Cal. per tsp.)	93.1	19	1.4	1.1	1.4	.1	3.0	35	24	.1	1,134	29	80	Trace	.04	Trace	2
	French:																	
1932	Regular	38.8	410	.6	38.9	17.5	.3	4.2	11	14	.4	1,370	79	—	—	—	—	—
	Special dietary (low-calorie):																	
1933	Low-fat (approx. 5 Cal. per tsp.)	77.3	96	.4	4.3	15.6	.3	2.4	11	14	.4	787	79	—	—	—	—	—
1934	Low-fat with artificial sweetener (approx. 1 Cal. per tsp.).	95.2	10	.4	.2	1.8	.3	2.4	11	14	.4	787	79	—	—	—	—	—
1935	Medium-fat with artificial sweetener (approx. 10 Cal. per tsp.).	78.8	156	.7	16.9	1.2	.3	2.4	11	14	.4	787	79	—	—	—	—	—
	Italian:																	
1936	Regular	27.5	552	.2	60.0	6.9	Trace	5.4	10	4	.2	2,092	15	Trace	Trace	Trace	Trace	—
1937	Special dietary (low-calorie, approx. 2 Cal. per tsp.).	90.1	50	.2	4.7	2.6	Trace	2.4	2	5	.2	787	15	Trace	Trace	Trace	Trace	—
1938	Mayonnaise	15.1	718	1.1	79.9	2.2	Trace	1.7	18	28	.5	597	34	280	.02	.04	Trace	—
1939	Russian	34.5	494	1.6	50.8	10.4	.3	2.7	19	37	.6	868	157	690	.05	.05	.6	6
	Salad dressing (mayonnaise type):																	
1940	Regular	40.6	435	1.0	42.3	14.4	—	1.7	14	26	.2	586	9	220	.01	.03	Trace	—
1941	Special dietary (low-calorie, approx. 8 Cal. per tsp.).	80.7	136	1.1	12.7	4.8	.5	.7	18	28	.2	118	9	220	.01	.03	Trace	—
	Thousand island:																	
1942	Regular	32.0	502	.8	50.2	15.4	.3	1.6	11	17	.6	700	113	320	.02	.03	.2	3
1943	Special dietary (low-calorie, approx. 10 Cal. per tsp.).	68.2	180	.9	13.7	15.6	.3	(1.6)	11	17	.6	700	113	320	.02	.03	.2	3
	Salad dressings, made from home recipe:																	
1944	French	24.2	632	.3	70.1	3.6	.1	1.8	6	3	.1	659	26	—	—	—	—	—
1945	Cooked	68.0	164	4.4	9.9	15.2	0	2.5	89	93	.6	728	116	490	.05	.16	.2	Trace
	Salad oil. See Oils, item 1401.																	
	Salami. See Sausage, cold cuts, and luncheon meats items 2017–2018.																	
	Salmon:																	
	Atlantic:																	
1946	Raw	63.6	217	22.5	13.4	0	0	1.4	79	186	.9	—	—	—	—	.08	7.2	9
1947	Canned, solids and liquid	64.2	203	21.7	12.2	0	0	1.6	—	—	—	—	—	—	—	—	—	—
	Chinook (king):																	
1948	Raw	64.2	222	19.1	15.6	0	0	1.1	—	301	—	45	399	310	.10	.23	—	—
1949	Canned, solids and liquid	64.4	210	19.6	14.0	0	0	2.0	[138] 154	289	.9	[139] —	366	230	.03	.14	7.3	—
	Chum:																	
1950	Raw	—	—	—	—	—	—	—	—	—	—	53	429	—	.10	.08	—	—
1951	Canned, solids and liquid	70.8	139	21.5	5.2	0	0	2.6	[138] 249	352	.7	[139] —	336	60	.02	.16	7.1	—
	Coho (silver):																	
1952	Raw	—	—	—	—	—	—	—	175	231	—	[139] 48	421	—	.09	.11	—	1
1953	Canned, solids and liquid	69.3	153	20.8	7.1	0	0	2.4	[138] 244	288	.9	[139] 351	339	80	.03	.18	7.4	—
	Pink (humpback):																	
1954	Raw	76.0	119	20.0	3.7	0	0	1.2	—	—	—	[140] 64	[140] 306	—	.14	.05	—	—
1955	Canned, solids and liquid	70.8	141	20.5	5.9	0	0	2.3	[138] 196	286	.8	[139] 387	361	70	.03	.18	8.0	—
	Sockeye (red):																	
1956	Raw	—	—	—	—	—	—	—	—	—	—	48	391	150	.14	.07	—	—
1957	Canned, solids and liquid	67.2	171	20.3	9.3	0	0	2.7	[138] 259	344	1.2	[139] 522	344	230	.04	.16	7.3	—
1958	**Salmon, cooked,** broiled or baked	63.4	182	27.0	7.4	0	0	1.6	—	414	1.2	116	443	160	.16	.06	9.8	—
1959	**Salmon rice loaf**	74.4	122	12.0	4.5	7.3	—	1.8	—	—	—	—	—	—	—	—	—	—
1960	**Salmon, smoked**	58.9	176	21.6	9.3	0	0	9.4	14	245	—	—	—	—	—	—	—	—
	Salsify:																	
1961	Raw	77.6	([141])	2.9	.6	*18.0	1.8	.9	47	66	1.5	—	380	10	.04	.04	.3	11
1962	Cooked, boiled, drained	81.0	([141])	2.6	.6	*15.1	1.8	.7	42	53	1.3	—	266	10	.03	.04	.2	7

1963	Salt, table	.2	0	0	0	0	0	99.8	253	—	.1	38,758	4	0	0	0	0	0
1964	Salt pork, raw	8	783	3.9	85.	0	0	3.5	Trace	Trace	.6	1,212	42	(0)	(.18)	(.04)	(.[illegible])	—
	Salt sticks:																	
1965	Regular type	5.	384	12.0	2.9	75.3	.3	4.8	28	99	.9	1,674	92	Trace	.06	.07	1.[illegible]	Trace
1966	Vienna bread type	25.	304	9.5	3.1	58.0	.2	4.4	45	89	.8	1,565	94	Trace	.05	.08	[illegible]	Trace
	Sanddab. See Flatfishes, item 1018.																	
	Sandwich spread (with chopped pickle):																	
1967	Regular	45.4	379	.7	36.2	15.9	.4	1.8	15	20	.7	626	92	280	.01	.03	Trace	6
1968	Special dietary (low-calorie, approx. 5 Cal. per tsp.)	80.2	112	1.0	9.0	8.0	.4	1.8	15	20	.7	626	92	280	.01	.03	Trace	6
1969	**Sapodilla, raw**	76.1	89	.5	1.1	21.8	1.4	.5	21	12	.8	12	193	60	Trace	.02	.[illegible]	14
1970	**Sapotes** (marmalade plums), raw	64.9	125	1.8	.6	31.6	1.9	1.1	39	28	1.0	—	—	410	.01	.02	1.[illegible]	20
	Sardines, Atlantic, canned in oil.																	
1971	Solids and liquid	50.6	311	20.6	24.4	.6	—	3.8	354	434	3.5	510	560	180	.02	.16	4.[illegible]	—
1972	Drained solids	61.8	203	24.0	11.1	—	—	3.1	[143] 437	[143] 499	2.9	823	590	220	.03	.20	5.[illegible]	—
	Sardines, Pacific:																	
1973	Raw	70.7	160	19.2	8.6	0	0	2.4	33	215	1.8	—	—	—	—	—	—	—
	Canned:																	
1974	In brine or mustard, solids and liquid	64.1	196	18.8	12.0	1.7	—	3.4	303	354	5.2	760	260	50	—	—	—	—
1975	In oil, drained solids	—	—	—	—	—	—	—	—	—	—	—	—	—	.01	.30	7.[illegible]	—
1976	In tomato sauce, solids and liquid	64.3	197	18.7	12.2	1.7	—	3.1	449	478	4.1	400	320	30	.01	.27	5.[illegible]	—
1977	**Sauerkraut,** canned, solids and liquid	92.8	18	1.0	.2	4.0	.7	2.0	36	18	.5	[144] 747	140	50	.03	.04	.[illegible]	14
1978	**Sauerkraut juice,** canned	94.6	10	.7	Trace	2.3	Trace	2.4	37	14	1.1	[144] 787	—	—	.03	.04	.[illegible]	18
1979	**Sauger, raw**	80.8	84	17.9	.8	0	0	1.1	—	—	—	—	—	—	—	—	—	—
	Sausage, cold cuts, and luncheon meats:																	
1980	Blood sausage or blood pudding	46.4	394	14.1	36.9	.3	0	2.3	—	—	—	—	—	—	—	—	—	—
1981	Bockwurst	61.9	264	11.3	23.7	.6	0	2.5	—	—	—	—	—	—	—	—	—	—
	Bologna																	
1982	All samples	56.2	304	12.1	27.5	1.1	—	3.1	7	128	1.8	1,300	230	—	.16	.22	2.[illegible]	—
1983	All meat	57.4	277	13.3	22.8	3.7	0	2.8	—	—	—	—	—	—	—	—	—	—
1984	With nonfat dry milk	57.1	—	13.4	—	—	—	—	—	—	—	—	—	—	—	—	—	—
1985	With cereal	57.9	262	14.2	20.6	3.9	—	3.4	—	—	—	—	—	—	—	—	—	—
1986	Braunschweiger	52.6	319	14.8	27.4	2.3	—	2.9	10	245	5.9	—	—	6,530	.17	1.44	8.[illegible]	—
	Brown-and-serve sausage:																	
1987	Before browning	45.3	393	13.5	36.0	2.7	0	2.5	—	—	—	—	—	—	—	—	—	—
1988	Browned	39.9	422	16.5	37.8	2.8	0	3.0	—	—	—	—	—	—	—	—	—	—
1989	Capicola or Capacola	26.2	499	20.2	45.8	0	0	7.9	—	—	—	—	—	—	—	—	—	—
	Cervelat																	
1990	Dry	29.4	451	24.6	37.6	1.7	0	6.7	14	294	2.7	—	—	(0)	.27	.23	5.[illegible]	—
1991	Soft	48.5	307	18.6	24.5	1.6	0	6.8	11	214	2.8	—	—	—	.11	.26	4.[illegible]	—
1992	Country-style sausage	49.9	345	15.1	31.1	0	0	3.9	9	168	2.3	—	—	—	.22	.19	3.[illegible]	—
1993	Deviled ham, canned	50.5	351	13.9	32.3	0	0	3.3	8	92	2.1	—	—	(0)	.14	.10	1.[illegible]	—
	Frankfurters																	
	Raw																	
1994	All samples	55.6	309	12.5	27.6	1.8	—	2.5	7	133	1.9	1,100	220	—	.16	.20	2.[illegible]	—
1995	All meat	56.5	296	13.1	25.5	2.5	0	2.4	—	—	—	—	—	—	—	—	—	—
1996	With nonfat dry milk	54.2	300	13.1	25.6	3.4	—	3.7	—	—	—	—	—	—	—	—	—	—
1997	With cereal	61.7	248	14.4	20.6	.2	—	3.1	—	—	—	—	—	—	—	—	—	—
1998	With nonfat dry milk and cereal	50.5	—	14.2	21.7	—	—	—	—	—	—	—	—	—	—	—	—	—
1999	Cooked	57.3	304	12.4	27.2	1.6	—	1.5	5	102	1.5	—	—	—	.15	.20	2.[illegible]	—
2000	Canned	66.0	221	13.4	18.1	.2	0	2.3	9	145	2.2	—	—	—	.03	.12	2.[illegible]	—
2001	Headcheese	58.8	268	15.5	22.0	1.0	0	2.7	9	173	2.3	—	—	(0)	.04	.10	[illegible]	—
2002	Knockwurst	57.6	278	14.1	23.2	2.2	0	(2.9)	8	154	2.1	—	—	—	(.17)	(.21)	(2.[illegible])	—
	Liverwurst																	
2003	Fresh	53.9	307	16.2	25.6	1.8	0	2.5	9	238	5.4	—	—	6,350	.20	1.30	5.[illegible]	—
2004	Smoked	52.6	319	14.8	27.4	2.3	0	2.9	10	245	5.9	—	—	6,530	.17	1.44	8.[illegible]	—
	Luncheon meat																	
2005	Boiled ham	59.1	234	19.0	17.0	0	0	4.9	11	166	2.8	—	—	(0)	.44	.15	2.[illegible]	—
2006	Pork, cured ham or shoulder, chopped, spiced or unspiced, canned.	54.9	294	15.0	24.9	1.3	0	3.9	9	108	2.2	1,234	222	(0)	.31	.21	3.[illegible]	—
2007	Meat loaf	64.1	200	15.9	13.2	3.3	0	3.5	9	178	1.8	—	—	—	.13	.22	2.[illegible]	—
2008	Meat, potted (includes potted beef, chicken, and turkey).	60.7	248	17.5	19.2	0	0	2.8	—	—	—	—	—	—	.03	.22	1.[illegible]	—
2009	Minced ham	61.7	228	13.7	16.9	4.4	0	3.3	8	89	2.1	—	—	(0)	.37	.22	3.[illegible]	—
2010	Mortadella	48.9	315	20.4	25.0	.6	0	5.1	12	238	3.1	—	—	—	—	—	—	—
2011	Polish-style sausage	53.7	304	15.7	25.8	1.2	0	3.6	9	176	2.4	—	—	(0)	.34	.19	3.[illegible]	—
2012	Pork and beef (chopped together)	53.5	336	15.6	29.9	0	0	1.0	9	174	2.3	—	—	—	—	—	—	—
	Pork sausage, links or bulk																	
2013	Raw	38.1	498	9.4	50.8	Trace	0	1.7	5	92	1.4	740	140	(0)	.43	.17	2.[illegible]	—
2014	Cooked	34.8	476	18.1	44.2	Trace	0	2.9	7	162	2.4	958	269	(0)	.79	.34	3.[illegible]	—

[a] A large proportion of the carbohydrate in the unstored product may be inulin, which is of doubtful availability. During storage, inulin is converted to sugars

[137] Values apply to products containing salt. For those without salt, sodium content is low, ranging from less than 10 mg to 50 mg. per 100 grams, the amount usually is indicated on the label.

[138] Based on total contents of can. If bones are discarded, value will be greatly reduced.

[139] For product canned without added salt, value is approximately the same as for raw salmon.

[140] Sample dipped in brine contained 215 mg sodium per 100 grams.

[141] Values for salmon dipped in brine averaged 473 mg. of sodium and 126 mg of potassium per 100 grams

[142] Values for raw salsify range from 13 Calories per 100 grams for the freshly harvested vegetable to 82 Calories for the product after storage, corresponding range for boiled salsify is from 12 to 70 Calories

[143] Values for sardines without skin and bones canned in oil are. Calcium, 54 mg per 100 grams, phosphorus, 319 mg

[144] Values for sauerkraut and sauerkraut juice are based on salt contents of 1.9 and 2.0 percent respectively in the finished products The amounts in some samples may vary significantly from this estimate.

TABLE 1.—COMPOSITION OF FOODS, 100 GRAMS, EDIBLE PORTION—Continued

[Numbers in parentheses denote values imputed—usually from another form of the food or from a similar food. Zero in parentheses indicates that the amount of a constituent probably is none or is too small to measure. Dashes denote lack of reliable data for a constituent believed to be present in measurable amount. Calculated values, as those based on a recipe, are not in parentheses]

Item No.	Food and description	Water	Food energy	Protein	Fat	Carbohydrate: Total	Carbohydrate: Fiber	Ash	Calcium	Phosphorus	Iron	Sodium	Potassium	Vitamin A value	Thiamine	Riboflavin	Niacin	Ascorbic acid
(A)	(B)	(C)	(D)	(E)	(F)	(G)	(H)	(I)	(J)	(K)	(L)	(M)	(N)	(O)	(P)	(Q)	(R)	(S)
	Sausage, cold cuts, and luncheon meats—Continued	Percent	Calories	Grams	Grams	Grams	Grams	Grams	Milligrams	Milligrams	Milligrams	Milligrams	Milligrams	International units	Milligrams	Milligrams	Milligrams	Milligrams
	Pork sausage, canned:																	
2015	Solids and liquid	42.1	415	13.8	38.4	2.4	0	3.3	8	150	2.1	—	—	(0)	0.19	0.19	3.3	—
2016	Drained solids	43.2	381	18.3	32.8	1.9	0	3.8	11	210	2.8	—	—	—	—	—	—	—
	Pork sausage, link, smoked. See Sausage, country-style item 1992.																	
	Salami.																	
2017	Dry	29.8	450	23.8	38.1	1.2	0	7.1	14	283	3.6	—	—	—	.37	25	5.3	—
2018	Cooked	51.0	311	17.5	25.6	1.4	0	4.5	10	200	2.6	—	—	—	.25	.24	4.1	—
2019	Scrapple	61.3	215	8.8	13.6	14.6	.1	1.7	5	64	1.2	—	—	—	.19	.09	1.8	—
2020	Souse	70.3	181	13.0	13.4	1.2	0	2.1	—	—	—	—	—	(0)	—	—	—	—
2021	Thuringer	48.5	307	18.6	24.5	1.6	0	6.8	11	214	2.8	—	—	—	.11	.26	4.2	—
2022	Vienna sausage, canned	63.0	240	14.0	19.8	.3	0	2.9	8	153	2.1	—	—	—	.08	.13	2.6	—
	Scallops, bay and sea																	
2023	Raw	79.8	81	15.3	.2	3.3	—	1.4	26	208	1.8	[145] 255	[145] 396	—	—	.06	1.3	—
2024	Cooked, steamed	73.1	112	23.2	1.4	—	—	—	115	338	3.0	265	476	—	—	—	—	—
2025	Frozen, breaded, fried, reheated	60.2	194	18.0	8.4	10.5	—	2.9	—	—	—	—	—	—	—	—	—	—
	Scrapple. See Sausage, cold cuts, and luncheon meats. item 2019.																	
	Scup. See Porgy, item 1658.																	
2026	**Seabass, white, raw**	76.3	96	21.4	.5	0	0	1.4	—	—	—	—	—	—	—	—	—	—
	Seaweeds, raw:																	
2027	Agar	16.3	—	—	.3	—	.7	3.7	567	22	6.3	—	—	—	—	—	—	—
2028	Dulse	16.6	—	—	3.2	—	1.2	22.4	296	267	—	2,085	8,060	—	—	—	—	—
2029	Irishmoss	19.2	—	—	1.8	—	2.1	17.6	885	157	8.9	2,892	2,844	—	—	—	—	—
2030	Kelp	21.7	—	—	1.1	—	6.8	22.8	1,093	240	—	3,007	5,273	—	—	—	—	—
2031	Laver	17.0	—	—	.6	—	3.5	11.0	—	—	—	—	—	—	—	—	—	—
	Sesame seeds, dry:																	
2032	Whole	5.4	563	18.6	49.1	21.6	6.3	5.3	1,160	616	10.5	60	725	30	.98	.24	5.4	0
2033	Decorticated	5.5	582	18.2	53.4	17.6	2.4	5.3	110	592	2.4	—	—	—	18	.13	5.4	0
	Shad or American shad:																	
2034	Raw	70.4	170	18.6	10.0	0	0	1.3	20	260	.5	54	330	—	15	.24	8.4	—
	Cooked:																	
2035	Baked [146]	64.0	201	23.2	11.3	0	0	1.4	24	313	.6	79	377	30	.13	.26	8.6	—
2036	Creole [147]	73.3	152	15.0	8.7	1.6	—	1.4	19	190	.6	73	280	450	.09	.16	5.1	8
2037	Canned, solids and liquid	71.1	152	16.9	8.8	0	0	2.8	—	—	.7	—	—	—	—	.16	—	—
2038	**Shad, gizzard** (gizzard shad), raw	67.8	200	17.2	14.0	0	0	1.2	—	—	—	—	—	—	—	—	—	—
2039	**Shallot** bulbs, raw	79.8	72	2.5	.1	16.8	.7	.8	37	60	1.2	12	334	Trace	.06	.02	.2	8
	Sheefish. See Inconnu, item 1145.																	
2040	**Sheepshead, Atlantic, raw**	75.9	113	20.6	2.8	0	0	1.3	—	197	—	101	234	—	—	—	—	—
	Sheepshead, fresh water. See Drum, item 959.																	
2041	**Sherbet,** orange	67.0	134	.9	1.2	30.8	0	.1	16	13	Trace	10	22	60	.01	.03	Trace	2
	Shortbread. See Cookies, item 830.																	
	Shrimp:																	
2042	Raw	78.2	91	18.1	.8	1.5	—	1.4	63	166	1.6	140	220	—	.02	.03	3.2	—
2043	Cooked, french-fried [148]	56.9	225	20.3	10.8	10.0	—	2.0	72	191	2.0	186	229	—	.04	.08	2.7	—
	Canned.																	
2044	Wet pack, solids and liquid	78.2	80	16.2	.8	.8	—	4.0	59	152	1.8	—	—	50	.01	.03	1.5	—
2045	Dry pack or drained solids of wet pack	70.4	116	24.2	1.1	.7	—	3.6	115	263	3.1	—	122	60	.01	.03	1.8	—
2046	Frozen, breaded, raw; not more than 50% breading.	65.0	139	12.3	.7	19.9	.1	2.1	38	111	1.0	—	—	—	.03	.03	2.0	—
2047	**Shrimp or lobster paste, canned**	61.3	180	20.8	9.4	1.5	—	7.0	—	—	—	—	—	—	—	.26	—	—
	Sirups:																	
2048	Cane	26.	263	0	0	68.	0	1.5	60	29	3.6	—	425	0	.13	.06	.1	0
2049	Maple	33.	252	—	—	65.	—	.7	104	8	1.2	10	176	—	—	—	—	0
2050	Sorghum	23.	257	—	—	68.	—	2.4	172	25	12.5	—	—	—	—	.10	.1	—
	Table blends.																	
2051	Chiefly corn, light and dark	24.	290	0	0	75.	0	.7	46	16	4.1	68	4	0	0	0	0	0
2052	Cane and maple	33.	252	0	0	65.	0	.1	16	1	Trace	2	26	0	0	0	0	0
	Siscowet. See Lake trout, items 1170–1171.																	
2053	**Skate (raja fish), raw**	77.8	98	21.5	.7	0	0	1.2	—	—	—	—	—	—	.02	—	—	—
	Smelt, Atlantic, jack, and bay:																	
2054	Raw	79.0	98	18.6	2.1	0	0	1.1	—	272	.4	—	—	—	01	.12	1.4	—
2055	Canned, solids and liquid	62.7	200	18.4	13.5	0	—	5.4	358	370	1.7	—	—	—	—	—	—	—
	Smelt, eulachon. See Eulachon, item 990.																	

2056	**Snail, raw**	79.2	90	16.1	1.4	2.0	—	1.3	—	—	3.5	—	—	—	—	—	—	—
2057	**Snail, Giant African, raw**	82.2	73	9.9	1.4	4.4	—	2.1	—	—	—	—	—	—	—	—	—	—
	Snapper, red. See Red and gray snapper, item 1853.																	
	Soft drinks. See Beverages, items 402–409.																	
	Sole. See Flatfishes, item 1018.																	
2058	**Sorghum grain, all types**	11.	332	11 0	3.3	73.0	1.7	1 7	28	287	4 4	—	350	(0)	.38	.15	3.9	(0)
	Sorrel. See Dock, items 953–954.																	
	Soups, commercial:																	
	Canned:																	
	Asparagus, cream of:																	
2059	Condensed	85 8	54	2 0	1.4	8 4	6	2 4	22	31	.6	820	100	250	.03	.07	.6	—
2060	Prepared with equal volume of water	92.9	27	1 0	.7	4.2	.3	1.2	11	16	.3	410	50	130	.02	.04	.3	—
2061	Prepared with equal volume of milk	86.4	60	2 8	2.4	6 8	.3	1 6	72	64	.3	436	123	200	.03	12	.3	Trace
	Bean with pork.																	
2062	Condensed	68.9	134	6.4	4.6	17.3	1.3	2 8	50	101	1.8	806	316	520	.11	.06	.8	2
2063	Prepared with equal volume of water	84.4	67	3.2	2.3	8 7	.6	1.4	25	51	9	403	158	260	.05	.03	.4	1
	Beef broth, bouillon, and consomme:																	
2064	Condensed	91 6	26	4.2	0	2.2	.1	2.0	Trace	26	4	652	108	Trace	Trace	.02	1 0	—
2065	Prepared with equal volume of water	95 8	13	2.1	0	1.1	Trace	1.0	Trace	13	.2	326	54	Trace	Trace	.01	.5	—
	Beef noodle.																	
2066	Condensed	86.4	57	3.2	2.2	5.8	.1	2.4	6	40	.7	764	64	50	.04	.05	.9	1
2067	Prepared with equal volume of water	93.2	28	1.6	1.1	2.9	Trace	1 2	3	20	.4	382	32	20	.02	.03	.4	Trace
	Celery, cream of																	
2068	Condensed	84.6	72	1 4	4 2	7 4	.4	2 4	40	30	.5	796	90	170	01	.04	4	1
2069	Prepared with equal volume of water	92 3	36	.7	2.1	3.7	.2	1 2	20	15	.2	398	45	80	.01	.02	Trace	Trace
2070	Prepared with equal volume of milk	85 8	69	2.6	3.8	6.2	.2	1.6	81	63	.3	424	118	160	.02	.11	.3	1
	Chicken consomme.																	
2071	Condensed	93 7	18	2.8	.1	1.5	Trace	1.9	10	59	1.0	602	—	—	—	—	—	—
2072	Prepared with equal volume of water	96.8	9	1.4	Trace	.8	Trace	1.0	5	30	.5	301	—	—	—	—	—	—
	Chicken, cream of.																	
2073	Condensed	83.8	79	2 4	4.8	6.7	.1	2.3	19	29	.4	809	66	350	01	.04	5	Trace
2074	Prepared with equal volume of water	91.9	39	1 2	2 4	3.3	.1	1.2	10	14	2	404	33	170	.01	.02	.2	Trace
2075	Prepar. with equal volume of milk	85.4	73	3 0	4 2	5.9	.1	1.5	70	62	.2	430	106	250	.02	.11	.3	1
	Chicken gumbo																	
2076	Condensed	87.6	46	2.6	1 3	6.1	.2	2.4	16	21	.5	792	89	180	.02	.03	1 1	4
2077	Prepared with equal volume of water	93.8	23	1.3	6	3.1	.1	1.2	8	10	.2	396	45	90	01	.02	5	2
	Chicken noodle:																	
2078	Condensed	86 6	53	2 8	1 6	6.6	.1	2.4	7	30	.4	816	46	30	01	.02	7	Trace
2079	Prepared with equal volume of water	93.3	26	1.4	.8	3 3	.1	1 2	4	15	.2	408	23	20	.01	01	.3	Trace
	Chicken with rice.																	
2080	Condensed	89.6	39	2.6	1 0	4.7	1	2.1	7	21	.3	764	82	130	Trace	.02	.6	—
2081	Prepared with equal volume of water	94.8	20	1.3	.5	2 4	Trace	1.0	3	10	.1	382	41	60	Trace	.01	3	—
	Chicken vegetable																	
2082	Condensed	84.5	62	3 4	2.0	7.7	.3	2 4	15	33	.5	845	80	1,800	.02	.03	.9	—
2083	Prepared with equal volume of water	92.2	31	1.7	1 0	3 9	.1	1 2	7	16	2	422	40	880	.01	.02	.4	—
	Clam chowder, Manhattan type (with tomatoes, without milk):																	
2084	Condensed	83 7	66	1 8	2.1	10.0	.3	2 4	29	38	.9	766	150	710	02	.02	.9	—
2085	Prepared with equal volume of water	91.9	33	9	1 0	5 0	.2	1 2	14	19	.4	383	75	360	.01	.01	.4	—
	Minestrone:																	
2086	Condensed	79.0	87	4.0	2.8	11.6	.6	2 6	30	49	.7	813	255	1,900	.06	.05	.9	—
2087	Prepared with equal volume of water	89 5	43	2.0	1.4	5 8	.3	1 3	15	24	4	406	128	960	.03	02	.4	—
	Mushroom, cream of:																	
2088	Condensed	79.3	111	1 9	8 0	8.4	.2	2 4	34	43	.3	795	82	60	01	10	.6	Trace
2089	Prepared with equal volume of water	89.6	56	1.0	4 0	4 2	.1	1 2	17	21	.2	398	41	30	.01	.05	.3	Trace
2090	Prepared with equal volume of milk	83.2	88	2 8	5 8	6.6	.1	1.6	78	69	.2	424	114	100	.02	.14	.3	Trace
	Onion																	
2091	Condensed	86 9	54	4.4	2.1	4 3	.4	2.3	23	23	.4	875	86	Trace	Trace	.02	Trace	—
2092	Prepared with equal volume of water	93.4	27	2.2	1.0	2 2	.2	1.2	12	11	.2	438	43	Trace	Trace	01	Trace	—
	Pea, green:																	
2093	Condensed	72.8	106	4.6	1 8	18.4	9	2.4	36	91	.7	734	160	280	04	.05	9	6
2094	Prepared with equal volume of water	86.4	53	2 3	9	9.2	.4	1 2	18	46	.4	367	80	140	.02	.02	.4	3
2095	Prepared with equal volume of milk	79.9	85	4 2	2 6	11 7	.4	1 6	79	94	.4	393	153	210	.04	11	5	4
	Pea, split:																	
2096	Condensed	70.7	118	7 0	2 6	17 0	.4	2 7	25	122	1 1	767	220	360	20	12	1 1	1
2097	Prepared with equal volume of water	85 4	59	3.5	1.3	8 4	.2	1 4	12	61	.6	384	110	180	.10	06	6	Trace
	Tomato																	
2098	Condensed	81 0	72	1.6	2.1	12 7	4	2 6	11	27	6	792	188	810	.05	.03	.9	10
2099	Prepared with equal volume of water	90 5	36	.8	1 0	6.4	.2	1 3	6	14	.3	396	94	410	02	02	.5	5
2100	Prepared with equal volume of milk	84.0	69	2.6	2 8	9 0	.2	1 6	67	62	.3	422	167	480	04	.10	5	6
	Turkey noodle:																	
2101	Condensed	84.6	65	3 6	2 4	7 0	.1	2 4	12	36	.5	832	64	160	.04	.04	1 0	Trace
2102	Prepared with equal volume of water	92.3	33	1.8	1 2	3.5	.1	1 2	6	18	.3	416	32	80	02	02	.5	Trace

[143] Based on frozen scallops, possibly brined.

[146] Prepared with butter or margarine and bacon slices.

[147] Prepared with tomatoes, onion, green pepper, butter, and flour.

[148] Dipped in egg, breadcrumbs, and flour or in batter.

TABLE 1.—COMPOSITION OF FOODS, 100 GRAMS, EDIBLE PORTION—Continued

[Numbers in parentheses denote values imputed—usually from another form of the food or from a similar food. Zero in parentheses indicates that the amount of a constituent probably is none or is too small to measure. Dashes denote lack of reliable data for a constituent believed to be present in measurable amount. Calculated values, as those based on a recipe, are not in parentheses]

Item No.	Food and description	Water	Food energy	Protein	Fat	Carbohydrate		Ash	Calcium	Phosphorus	Iron	Sodium	Potassium	Vitamin A value	Thiamine	Riboflavin	Niacin	Ascorbic acid
						Total	Fiber											
(A)	(B)	(C)	(D)	(E)	(F)	(G)	(H)	(I)	(J)	(K)	(L)	(M)	(N)	(O)	(P)	(Q)	(R)	(S)
		Percent	Calories	Grams	Grams	Grams	Grams	Grams	Milligrams	Milligrams	Milligrams	Milligrams	Milligrams	International units	Milligrams	Milligrams	Milligrams	Milligrams
	Soups, commercial—Continued																	
	Canned—Continued																	
	Vegetable beef:																	
2103	Condensed	83.8	65	4.2	1.8	7.9	0.4	2.3	10	39	0.6	854	131	2,200	0.03	0.04	0.8	—
2104	Prepared with equal volume of water	91.9	32	2.1	.9	3.9	.2	1.2	5	20	.3	427	66	1,100	.02	.02	.4	—
	Vegetable with beef broth:																	
2105	Condensed	83.4	64	2.2	1.4	11.0	.5	2.0	16	32	.7	690	196	2,500	.03	.02	1.0	—
2106	Prepared with equal volume of water	91.7	32	1.1	.7	5.5	.3	1.0	8	16	.3	345	98	1,300	.02	.01	.5	—
	Vegetarian vegetable:																	
2107	Condensed	83.7	61	1.8	1.7	10.6	.4	2.2	16	32	.8	684	140	2,300	.03	.03	.7	—
2108	Prepared with equal volume of water	91.8	32	.9	.8	5.4	.2	1.1	8	16	.4	342	70	1,200	.02	.02	.4	—
	Dehydrated:																	
	Beef noodle:																	
2109	Mix, dry form	6.1	387	13.6	7.4	65.3	.6	7.6	48	148	2.0	2,369	230	120	.53	.28	4.1	4
2110	Prepared with 2 oz. mix in 3 cups water	93.1	28	1.0	.5	4.8	Trace	.6	4	11	.2	175	17	10	.04	.02	.3	Trace
	Chicken noodle:																	
2111	Mix, dry form	5.7	382	14.5	10.0	58.1	.4	11.7	59	143	2.4	4,278	146	330	.52	.27	4.2	5
2112	Prepared with 2 oz. mix in 4 cups water	94.7	22	.8	.6	3.2	Trace	.7	3	8	.1	241	8	20	.03	.02	.2	Trace
	Chicken rice:																	
2113	Mix, dry form	9.8	353	9.0	6.8	62.8	.2	11.6	45	69	.6	4,362	71	Trace	.04	.02	1.1	—
2114	Prepared with 1½ oz mix in 3 cups water	91.9	20	.5	.4	3.5	Trace	.7	3	4	Trace	259	4	Trace	Trace	Trace	.1	—
	Onion																	
2115	Mix, dry form	2.8	349	13.9	10.5	53.9	1.8	18.8	97	113	1.4	6,676	553	60	.11	.07	.7	15
2116	Prepared with 1½ oz. mix in 4 cups water	95.8	15	.6	.5	2.3	.1	.8	4	5	.1	287	24	Trace	Trace	Trace	Trace	1
	Pea, green:																	
2117	Mix, dry form	3.1	362	22.4	4.1	61.6	1.2	8.8	60	313	5.4	2,360	874	120	.44	.46	4.1	1
2118	Prepared with 2 oz mix in 3 cups water	86.7	50	3.4	.6	8.4	.2	1.2	8	43	.8	325	120	20	.06	.06	.6	Trace
	Tomato vegetable with noodles:																	
2119	Mix, dry form	3.7	348	8.7	8.0	62.7	1.5	16.9	46	112	2.0	6,137	173	2,400	.30	.19	2.6	26
2120	Prepared with 2½ oz. mix in 4 cups water	92.5	27	.6	.6	5.1	.1	1.2	3	8	.1	427	12	200	.02	.01	.2	2
	Frozen:																	
	Clam chowder, New England type (with milk, without tomatoes):																	
2121	Condensed	78.5	107	3.7	6.4	8.6	.2	2.8	75	68	.8	870	185	50	.03	.07	.4	—
2122	Prepared with equal volume of water	89.2	54	1.8	3.2	4.4	.1	1.4	38	34	.4	435	92	20	.02	.04	.2	—
2123	Prepared with equal volume of milk	82.8	56	3.7	5.0	6.7	.1	1.8	98	82	.4	461	166	100	.03	.12	.2	Trace
	Oyster stew. See items 1448–1450																	
	Pea, green, with ham.																	
2124	Condensed	71.8	112	7.6	2.3	16.0	1.4	2.3	25	102	1.6	750	201	180	.16	.06	1.0	—
2125	Prepared with equal volume of water	85.9	57	3.8	1.2	8.0	.7	1.2	12	51	.8	375	100	90	.08	.03	.5	—
	Potato, cream of:																	
2126	Condensed	79.8	87	2.7	4.3	10.0	.3	3.2	48	51	.7	980	185	340	.04	.05	.4	—
2127	Prepared with equal volume of water	89.9	44	1.4	2.2	4.9	.2	1.6	24	26	.4	490	92	170	.02	.02	.2	—
2128	Prepared with equal volume of milk	83.4	76	3.2	3.9	7.5	.2	2.0	85	74	.4	516	166	240	.04	.11	.2	Trace
	Shrimp, cream of:																	
2129	Condensed	76.6	134	4.0	9.9	7.2	.3	2.3	32	40	.4	860	48	90	.03	.05	.3	—
2130	Prepared with equal volume of water	88.3	66	2.0	5.0	3.5	.2	1.2	16	20	.2	430	24	50	.02	.02	.2	—
2131	Prepared with equal volume of milk	81.8	99	3.8	6.7	6.2	.2	1.5	77	68	.2	456	97	120	.03	.11	.2	Trace
	Vegetable with beef:																	
2132	Condensed	82.7	70	5.4	2.3	7.0	.5	2.6	22	63	.8	792	145	2,200	.04	.07	1.5	—
2133	Prepared with equal volume of water	91.4	35	2.7	1.2	3.4	.2	1.3	11	32	.4	396	72	1,100	.02	.04	.8	—
2134	**Soursop,** raw	81.7	65	1.0	.3	16.3	1.1	.7	14	27	.6	14	265	10	.07	.05	.9	20
	Souse. See Sausage, cold cuts, and luncheon meats: item 2020.																	
	Soybeans:																	
	Immature seeds:																	
2135	Raw	69.2	134	10.9	5.1	13.2	1.4	1.6	67	225	2.8	—	—	690	.44	.16	1.4	29
2136	Cooked, boiled, drained	73.8	118	9.8	5.1	10.1	1.4	1.2	60	191	2.5	—	—	660	.31	.13	1.2	17
	Canned:																	
2137	Solids and liquid	81.8	75	6.5	3.2	6.3	.7	2.2	55	100	2.9	[9]236	—	—	.09	.09	—	8
2138	Drained solids	76.7	103	9.0	5.0	7.4	1.4	1.9	67	114	2.8	[9]236	—	340	.06	—	—	2
	Mature seeds, dry:																	
2139	Raw	10.0	403	34.1	17.7	33.5	4.9	4.7	226	554	8.4	5	1,677	80	1.10	.31	2.2	—
2140	Cooked	71.0	130	11.0	5.7	10.8	1.6	1.5	73	179	2.7	[9]2	540	30	.21	.09	.6	0

No.	Food																	
	Fermented products:																	
2141	Natto (soybeans)	62.7	167	16.9	7.4	11.5	3.2	1.5	103	182	3.7	—	249	0	.07	.50	1.1	0
2142	Miso (cereal and soybeans)	53.0	171	10.5	4.6	23.5	2.3	8.4	68	309	1.7	2,950	334	40	.06	.10	.3	0
	Sprouted seeds:																	
2143	Raw	86.3	46	6.2	1.4	5.3	.8	.8	48	67	1.0	—	—	80	.23	.20	.8	13
2144	Cooked, boiled, drained	89.0	38	5.3	1.4	3.7	.8	.6	43	50	.7	—	—	80	.16	.15	.7	4
2145	**Soybean curd (tofu)**	84.8	72	7.8	4.2	2.4	.1	.8	128	126	1.9	7	42	0	.06	.03	.1	0
	Soybean flours:																	
2146	Full-fat	8.0	421	36.7	20.3	30.4	2.4	4.6	199	558	8.4	1	1,660	110	.85	.31	2.1	0
2147	High-fat	8.0	380	41.2	12.1	33.3	2.2	5.4	240	650	9.0	1	1,775	—	.89	.36	2.3	0
2148	Low-fat	8.0	356	43.4	6.7	36.6	2.5	5.3	263	634	9.1	1	1,859	80	.83	.36	2.6	0
2149	Defatted	8.0	326	47.0	.9	38.1	2.3	6.0	265	655	11.1	1	1,820	40	1.09	.34	2.6	0
	Soybean milk:																	
2150	Fluid	92.4	33	3.4	1.5	2.2	0	.5	21	48	.8	—	—	40	.08	.03	.2	0
2151	Powder	4.2	429	41.8	20.3	28.0	.2	5.7	275	—	—	—	—	—	—	—	—	—
	Soybean milk products, sweetened: [58]																	
2152	Liquid concentrate	74.4	126	4.8	7.3	12.3	.2	1.2	30	59	.8	43	237	Trace	.06	.03	.2	0
2153	Powder	3.7	452	20.4	23.2	48.4	.5	4.3	115	285	5.0	1	915	20	.30	.24	1.4	0
2154	**Soybean protein**	8.2	322	74.9	.1	15.1	.4	1.7	120	674	—	210	180	—	—	—	—	0
2155	**Soybean proteinate**	5.5	312	80.6	.1	7.7	.6	6.1	—	—	—	1,200	—	—	—	—	—	0
2156	**Soy sauce**	62.8	68	5.6	1.3	9.5	0	20.8	82	104	4.8	7,325	366	0	.02	.25	.4	0
	Spaghetti:																	
	Enriched																	
2157	Dry form	10.4	369	12.5	1.2	75.2	.3	.7	27	162	[59] 2.9	2	197	(0)	[59] .88	[59] .37	[59] 6.0	(0)
2158	Cooked, firm stage, "al dente" (8–10 min.)	63.6	148	5.0	.5	30.1	.1	1.3	11	65	[59] 1.1	1	79	(0)	[59] .18	[59] .10	[59] 1.4	(0)
2159	Cooked, tender stage (14–20 min.)	72.0	111	3.4	.4	23.0	.1	1.2	8	50	[59] .9	1	61	(0)	[59] .14	[59] .08	[59] 1.1	(0)
	Unenriched:																	
2160	Dry form	10.4	369	12.5	1.2	75.2	.3	.7	27	162	1.3	2	197	(0)	.09	.06	1.7	(0)
2161	Cooked, firm stage, "al dente" (8–10 min.)	63.6	148	5.0	.5	30.1	.1	1.3	11	65	.5	1	79	(0)	.02	.02	.4	(0)
2162	Cooked, tender stage (14–20 min.)	72.0	111	3.4	.4	23.0	.1	1.2	8	50	.4	1	61	(0)	.01	.01	.3	(0)
	Spaghetti in tomato sauce with cheese:																	
2163	Cooked, from home recipe	77.0	104	3.5	3.5	14.8	.2	1.2	32	54	.9	(382)	163	430	.10	.07	.9	5
2164	Canned	80.1	76	2.2	.6	15.4	.2	1.7	16	35	1.1	382	121	370	.14	.11	1.8	4
	Spaghetti with meat balls in tomato sauce:																	
2165	Cooked, from home recipe	70.0	134	7.5	4.7	15.6	.3	2.2	50	95	1.5	407	268	640	.10	.12	1.6	9
2166	Canned	78.0	103	4.9	4.1	11.4	.1	1.6	21	45	1.3	488	98	400	.06	.07	.9	2
2167	**Spanish mackerel, raw**	68.9	177	19.5	10.4	0	0	1.2	71	249	1.0	68	264	—	.13	.14	4.8	—
2168	**Spanish rice, cooked from home recipe**	78.5	87	1.8	1.7	16.6	.5	1.4	14	39	.6	316	231	660	.04	.03	.7	15
	Spinach:																	
2169	Raw	90.7	26	3.2	.3	4.3	.6	1.5	93	51	3.1	71	470	8,100	.10	.20	.6	51
2170	Cooked, boiled, drained	92.0	23	3.0	.3	3.6	.6	1.1	93	38	2.2	50	324	8,100	.07	.14	.5	28
	Canned:																	
	Regular pack:																	
2171	Solids and liquid	93.0	19	2.0	.4	3.0	.7	1.6	85	26	2.1	[8] 236	250	5,500	.02	.10	.3	14
2172	Drained solids	91.4	24	2.7	.6	3.6	.9	1.7	118	26	2.6	[8] 236	250	8,000	.02	.12	.3	14
2173	Drained liquid	96.8	6	.5	0	1.3	Trace	1.4	2	25	.9	[8] 236	250	Trace	.02	.07	.3	14
	Special dietary pack (low-sodium):																	
2174	Solids and liquid	92.8	21	2.5	.4	3.3	.7	1.0	85	26	2.1	34	250	5,500	.02	.10	.3	14
2175	Drained solids	91.3	26	3.2	.5	4.0	1.0	1.0	118	26	2.6	32	250	8,000	.02	.12	.3	14
2176	Drained liquid	96.7	8	.5	0	2.0	Trace	.8	2	25	.9	32	250	Trace	.02	.07	.3	14
	Frozen:																	
	Chopped																	
2177	Not thawed	91.6	24	3.1	.3	3.8	.8	1.2	113	45	2.1	57	354	7,900	.09	.16	.5	29
2178	Cooked, boiled, drained	91.9	23	3.0	.3	3.7	.8	1.1	113	44	2.1	52	333	7,900	.07	.15	.4	19
	Leaf:																	
2179	Not thawed	91.3	25	3.0	.3	4.2	.8	1.2	105	45	2.5	53	385	8,100	.10	.16	.5	35
2180	Cooked, boiled, drained	91.8	24	2.9	.3	3.9	.8	1.1	105	44	2.5	49	362	8,100	.08	.14	.5	28
	Spinach, New Zealand. See New Zealand spinach, items 1375–1376																	
	Spiny lobster. See Crayfish, item 927.																	
	Spleen, raw:																	
2181	Beef and calf	76.9	104	18.1	3.0	0	0	1.4	—	272	10.6	—	—	—	—	.37	8.2	—
2182	Hog	77.4	107	17.1	3.8	0	0	1.4	—	298	29.4	—	—	—	—	.40	—	—
2183	Lamb	74.4	115	18.8	3.9	0	0	1.6	—	—	—	—	—	—	—	—	—	—
	Spot:																	
2184	Raw [149]	65.3	219	17.6	15.9	0	0	1.2	—	—	—	61	—	—	.16	.22	—	—
2185	Cooked, baked	53.8	295	22.8	21.9	0	0	1.5	—	—	—	[150] 312	—	—	—	—	—	—
	Squab (pigeon), raw:																	
2186	Total edible	58.0	279	18.6	22.1	0	0	1.5	17	411	—	—	—	—	—	—	—	—
2187	Flesh and skin	56.6	294	18.5	23.8	0	0	1.4	—	—	—	—	—	—	—	—	—	—
2188	Flesh only	72.8	142	17.5	7.5	0	0	1.2	—	—	—	—	—	—	—	—	6.6	—
2189	Light meat without skin	74.0	125	20.4	4.2	0	0	1.2	—	—	—	—	—	—	—	—	7.6	—
2190	Giblets	69.8	154	19.8	7.2	1.2	0	2.0	—	—	—	—	—	—	—	—	—	—

[4] See Notes on Foods, p. 176.

[8] Estimated average based on addition of salt in the amount of 0.6 percent of the finished product.

[58] Values apply to products without added vitamins and minerals.

[59] Based on product with minimum level of enrichment. See notes on Foods, p. 171.

[149] Values are based on samples caught in October. Content of fat may vary greatly from this average at other seasons of the year.

[150] Based on fish with salt added in cooking.

TABLE 1.—COMPOSITION OF FOODS, 100 GRAMS, EDIBLE PORTION—Continued

[Numbers in parentheses denote values imputed—usually from another form of the food or from a similar food. Zero in parentheses indicates that the amount of a constituent probably is none or is too small to measure. Dashes denote lack of reliable data for a constituent believed to be present in measurable amount. Calculated values, as those based on a recipe, are not in parentheses]

Item No.	Food and description	Water	Food energy	Protein	Fat	Carbohydrate		Ash	Calcium	Phosphorus	Iron	Sodium	Potassium	Vitamin A value	Thiamine	Riboflavin	Niacin	Ascorbic acid
						Total	Fiber											
(A)	(B)	(C)	(D)	(E)	(F)	(G)	(H)	(I)	(J)	(K)	(L)	(M)	(N)	(O)	(P)	(Q)	(R)	(S)
		Percent	*Calories*	*Grams*	*Grams*	*Grams*	*Grams*	*Grams*	*Milligrams*	*Milligrams*	*Milligrams*	*Milligrams*	*Milligrams*	*International units*	*Milligrams*	*Milligrams*	*Milligrams*	*Milligrams*
	Squash:																	
	Summer:																	
	All varieties:																	
2191	Raw	94.0	19	1.1	0.1	4.2	0.6	0.6	28	29	0.4	1	202	410	0.05	0.09	1.0	22
2192	Cooked, boiled, drained	95.5	14	.9	.1	3.1	.6	.4	25	25	.4	1	141	390	.05	.08	.8	10
	Crookneck and Straightneck, Yellow:																	
2193	Raw	93.7	20	1.2	.2	4.3	.6	.6	28	29	.4	1	202	460	.05	.09	1.0	25
2194	Cooked, boiled, drained	95.3	15	1.0	.2	3.1	.6	.4	25	25	.4	1	141	440	.05	.08	.8	11
	Scallop varieties, white and pale green:																	
2195	Raw	93.3	21	.9	.1	5.1	.6	.6	28	29	.4	1	202	190	.05	.09	1.0	18
2196	Cooked, boiled, drained	95.0	16	.7	.1	3.8	.6	.4	25	25	.4	1	141	180	.05	.08	.8	8
	Zucchini and Cocozelle (Italian marrow type), green:																	
2197	Raw	94.6	17	1.2	.1	3.6	.6	.5	28	29	.4	1	202	[151] 320	.05	.09	1.0	19
2198	Cooked, boiled, drained	96.0	12	1.0	.1	2.5	.6	.4	25	25	.4	1	141	[151] 300	.05	.08	.8	9
	Winter.																	
	All varieties:																	
2199	Raw	85.1	50	1.4	.3	12.4	1.4	.8	22	38	.6	1	369	[152] 3,700	.05	.11	.6	13
	Cooked:																	
2200	Baked	81.4	63	1.8	.4	15.4	1.8	1.0	28	48	.8	1	461	[152] 4,200	.05	.13	.7	13
2201	Boiled, mashed	88.8	38	1.1	.3	9.2	1.4	.6	20	32	.5	1	258	[152] 3,500	.04	.10	.4	8
	Acorn:																	
2202	Raw	86.3	44	1.5	.1	11.2	1.4	.9	31	23	.9	1	384	[152] 1,200	.05	.11	.6	14
	Cooked:																	
2203	Baked	82.9	55	1.9	.1	14.0	1.8	1.1	39	29	1.1	1	480	[152] 1,400	.05	.13	.7	13
2204	Boiled, mashed	89.7	34	1.2	.1	8.4	1.4	.6	28	20	.8	1	269	[152] 1,100	.04	.10	.4	8
	Butternut:																	
2205	Raw	83.7	54	1.4	.1	14.0	1.4	.8	32	58	.8	1	487	[152] 5,700	.05	.11	.6	9
	Cooked:																	
2206	Baked	79.6	68	1.8	.1	17.5	1.8	1.0	40	72	1.0	1	609	[152] 6,400	.05	.13	.7	8
2207	Boiled, mashed	87.8	41	1.1	.1	10.4	1.4	.6	29	49	.7	1	341	[152] 5,400	.04	.10	.4	5
	Hubbard:																	
2208	Raw	88.1	39	1.4	.3	9.4	1.4	.8	19	31	.6	1	217	[152] 4,300	.05	.11	.6	11
	Cooked:																	
2209	Baked	85.1	50	1.8	.4	11.7	1.8	1.0	24	39	.8	1	271	[152] 4,800	.05	.13	.7	10
2210	Boiled, mashed	91.1	30	1.1	.3	6.9	1.4	.6	17	26	.5	1	152	[152] 4,100	.04	.10	.4	6
	Squash, frozen:																	
	Summer, Yellow Crookneck:																	
2211	Not thawed	93.4	21	1.4	.1	4.7	.6	.4	14	32	.7	3	167	150	.07	.04	.4	10
2212	Cooked, boiled, drained	93.4	21	1.4	.1	4.7	.6	.4	14	32	.7	3	167	140	.06	.04	.4	8
	Winter:																	
2213	Not thawed	88.8	38	1.2	.3	9.2	1.2	.5	25	32	1.0	1	207	3,900	.03	.07	.5	10
2214	Heated	88.8	38	1.2	.3	9.2	1.2	.5	25	32	1.0	1	207	3,900	.03	.07	.5	8
2215	**Squid, raw**	80.2	84	16.4	.9	1.5	—	1.0	12	119	.5	—	—	—	.02	.12	—	—
	Starch. See Cornstarch, item 894.																	
	St. Johnsbread. See Carob flour, item 617.																	
2216	**Stomach, pork, scalded**	74.0	152	16.5	9.0	0	0	.6	—	118	—	—	—	—	—	—	—	—
	Strawberries:																	
2217	Raw	89.9	37	.7	.5	8.4	1.3	.5	21	21	1.0	1	164	60	.03	.07	.6	59
	Canned, solids and liquid:																	
2218	Water pack, with or without artificial sweetener	93.7	22	.4	.1	5.6	.6	.2	14	14	.7	1	111	40	.01	.03	.4	20
	Frozen, sweetened, not thawed:																	
2219	Sliced	71.3	109	.5	.2	27.8	.8	.2	14	17	.7	1	112	30	.02	.06	.5	53
2220	Whole	75.7	92	.4	.2	23.5	.6	.2	13	16	.6	1	104	30	.02	.06	.5	55
	Sturgeon:																	
2221	Raw	78.7	94	18.1	1.9	0	0	1.4	—	—	—	—	—	—	—	—	—	—
2222	Cooked, steamed	67.5	160	25.4	5.7	0	0	—	40	263	2.0	108	235	—	—	—	—	—
2223	Smoked	63.7	149	31.2	1.8	0	0	1.9	—	—	—	—	—	—	—	—	—	—
	Succotash (corn and lima beans), frozen:																	
2224	Not thawed	73.0	97	4.3	.4	21.5	.9	.8	14	89	1.1	[19] 45	273	(300)	.11	.06	1.5	9
2225	Cooked, boiled, drained	74.1	93	4.2	.4	20.5	.9	.8	13	85	1.0	38	246	(300)	.09	.05	1.3	6
2226	**Suckers, including white and mullet suckers, raw**	76.4	104	20.6	1.8	0	0	1.2	—	220	—	56	336	—	Trace	—	1.2	—
2227	**Sucker, carp, raw**	76.2	111	19.2	3.2	0	0	1.2	—	—	—	—	—	—	—	—	—	—
2228	**Suet (beef kidney fat), raw**	4.	854	1.5	94.	0	0	.1	—	—	—	—	—	—	—	—	—	—

	Sugars:																	
	Beet or cane:																	
2229	Brown	2.1	373	0	0	96.4	0	1.5	85	19	3.4	30	344	0	.01	.03	.2	0
2230	Granulated	.5	385	0	0	99.5	0	Trace	0	0	.1	1	3	0	0	0	0	0
2231	Powdered	.5	385	0	0	99.5	0	Trace	0	0	.1	1	3	0	0	0	0	0
	Dextrose																	
2232	Anhydrous	.5	366	0	0	99.5	0	—	—	—	—	—	—	0	0	0	0	0
2233	Crystallized	9.	335	0	0	91.	0	—	—	—	Trace	—	—	0	0	0	0	0
2234	Maple	8.	348	—	—	90	—	.9	143	11	1.4	14	242	—	—	—	—	0
2235	**Sugarapples (sweetsop), raw**	73.3	94	1.8	.3	23.7	1.7	.9	22	41	.6	11	275	10	.10	.14	1.0	34
2236	**Sunflower seed kernels, dry**	4.8	560	24.0	47.3	19.9	3.8	4.0	120	837	7.1	30	920	50	1.96	.23	5.4	—
2237	**Sunflower seed flour, partially defatted**	7.3	339	45.2	3.4	37.7	4.6	6.4	348	898	13.2	56	1,080	—	3.6	.46	27.3	—
	Surinam-cherry. See Pitanga, item 1627.																	
	Swamp cabbage:																	
2238	Raw	89.7	29	3.0	.3	5.4	1.1	1.6	73	51	2.5	—	150	6,300	.07	.12	.7	32
2239	Cooked, boiled, drained	92.7	21	2.2	.2	3.9	.9	1.0	55	32	1.5	—	88	5,200	.05	.08	.5	16
	Sweetbreads (thymus):																	
	Beef (yearlings):																	
2240	Raw	67.8	207	14.6	16.0	0	0	1.6	—	393	—	96	360	—	—	—	—	—
2241	Cooked, braised	49.6	320	25.9	23.2	0	0	1.3	—	364	—	116	433	—	—	—	—	—
	Calf:																	
2242	Raw	78.4	94	17.8	2.0	0	0	1.8	—	—	—	—	—	—	.08	.17	2.6	—
2243	Cooked, braised	62.7	168	32.6	3.2	0	0	1.5	—	—	—	—	—	—	.06	.16	2.9	—
	Lamb																	
2244	Raw	79.5	94	14.1	3.8	0	0	1.3	—	220	—	—	—	—	—	—	—	—
2245	Cooked, braised	64.6	175	28.1	6.1	0	0	1.2	—	204	—	—	—	—	—	—	—	—
	Sweetbread, hog. See Pancreas, hog: item 1469.																	
	Sweetpotatoes:																	
	Raw:																	
2246	All commercial varieties	70.6	114	1.7	.4	26.3	.7	1.0	32	47	.7	10	243	8,800	.10	.06	.6	21
2247	Firm-fleshed [153] (Jersey types)	74.0	102	1.8	.7	22.5	.9	1.0	32	47	.7	10	243	[154] 9,200	.10	.06	.6	23
2248	Soft-fleshed [153] (mainly Porto Rico variety)	69.7	117	1.7	.3	27.3	.7	1.0	32	47	.7	10	243	[155] 8,700	.10	.06	.6	20
	Cooked, all																	
2249	Baked in skin	63.7	141	2.1	.5	32.5	.9	1.2	40	58	.9	12	300	8,100	.09	.07	.7	22
2250	Boiled in skin	70.6	114	1.7	.4	26.3	.7	1.0	32	47	.7	10	243	7,900	.09	.06	.6	17
2251	Candied	60.0	168	1.3	3.3	34.2	.6	1.2	37	43	.9	42	190	6,300	.06	.04	.4	10
	Canned:																	
	Liquid pack, solids and liquid:																	
2252	Regular pack in sirup	70.7	114	1.0	.2	27.5	.6	.6	13	29	.7	48	(120)	5,000	.03	.03	.6	8
2253	Special dietary pack, without added sugar and salt.	88.0	46	.7	.1	10.8	.3	.4	13	29	.7	12	120	5,000	.03	.03	.6	8
2254	Vacuum or solid pack	71.9	108	2.0	.2	24.9	1.0	1.0	25	41	.8	[156] 48	200	7,800	.05	.04	.6	14
	Dehydrated flakes																	
2255	Dry form	2.8	379	4.2	.6	90.0	3.2	2.4	60	80	2.2	181	562	[157] 47,000	.06	.13	1.3	45
2256	Prepared with water	75.7	95	1.0	.1	22.6	.8	.6	15	20	.6	45	140	[157] 12,000	.02	.03	.3	11
	Sweetsop. See Sugarapples, item 2235.																	
	Swisschard. See Chard, Swiss: items 639–640.																	
	Swordfish:																	
2257	Raw	75.9	118	19.2	4.0	0	0	1.3	19	195	.9	—	—	1,580	.05	.05	8.0	—
2258	Cooked, broiled [158]	64.6	174	28.0	6.0	0	0	1.7	27	275	1.3	—	—	2,050	.04	.05	10.9	—
2259	Canned, solids and liquid	78.0	102	17.5	3.0	0	0	1.5	—	—	—	—	—	1,580	.01	.05	11.4	—
2260	**Tamarinds, raw**	31.4	239	2.8	.6	62.5	5.1	2.7	74	113	2.8	51	781	30	.34	.14	1.2	2
2261	**Tangelo juice, raw**	89.4	41	.5	(.1)	9.7	Trace	.3	—	—	—	—	—	—	—	—	—	27
2262	**Tangerines, raw (Dancy variety)**	87.	46	.8	.2	11.6	.5	.4	40	18	.4	2	126	420	.06	.02	.1	31
	Tangerine juice:																	
2263	Raw (Dancy variety)	88.9	43	.5	.2	10.1	(.1)	.3	18	14	.2	1	178	420	.06	.02	.1	31
	Canned																	
2264	Unsweetened	88.8	43	.5	.2	10.2	(.1)	.3	18	14	.2	1	178	420	(.06)	(.02)	(.1)	22
2265	Sweetened	87.0	50	.5	.2	12.0	(.1)	.3	18	14	.2	1	178	420	(.06)	(.02)	(.1)	22
	Frozen concentrate, unsweetened:																	
2266	Undiluted	58.	162	1.7	(.7)	38.3	(.3)	1.3	62	48	.7	2	613	1,460	.20	.06	.4	96
2267	Diluted with 3 parts water, by volume	88.1	46	.5	(.2)	10.8	(.1)	.4	18	14	.2	1	174	410	.06	.02	.1	27
2268	**Tapioca, dry**	12.6	352	.6	.2	86.4	.1	.2	10	18	.4	3	18	(0)	(0)	(0)	(0)	(0)
	Tapioca desserts:																	
2269	Apple tapioca	70.1	117	.2	.1	29.4	.1	.2	3	4	.2	51	26	10	Trace	Trace	Trace	Trace
2270	Tapioca cream pudding	71.8	134	5.0	5.1	17.1	0	1.0	105	109	.4	156	135	290	.04	.18	.1	1
	Taros, raw:																	
2271	Corms and tubers	73.0	98	1.9	.2	23.7	.8	1.2	28	61	1.0	7	514	20	.13	.04	1.1	4
2272	Leaves and stems	87.2	40	3.0	.8	7.4	1.4	1.6	76	59	1.0	—	—	—	—	—	—	31

[19] Average weighted in accordance with commercial practices in freezing vegetables See also Notes on Foods, p 177.

[151] Applies to squash including skin; flesh has no appreciable vitamin A value.

[152] Value based on freshly harvested squash. The carotenoid content increases during storage, the amount of increase varying according to variety and conditions of storage. More information is needed on the relative contents of the individual carotenoids and their rates of increase under usual storage conditions before a suitable vitamin A value can be derived for the stored product.

[153] Term refers to the flesh of the cooked product.

[154] Values for commercial varieties having deep-orange flesh average about 10,000 I.U per 100 grams; light-yellow, about 600 I U.

[155] Values for commercial varieties range from 8,000 to more than 20,000 I U. per 100 grams. Porto Rico, the main variety, has a value around 8,000 I.U.

[156] Applies to regular pack. For special dietary pack (low-sodium), value is 12 mg per 100 grams.

[157] Value varies widely; it is related to variety of sweetpotato Range in dehydrated form is 21,000 to 72,000 I U. per 100 grams, and 5,000 to 18,000 I U. in product prepared for serving.

[158] Prepared with butter or margarine

TABLE 1.—COMPOSITION OF FOODS, 100 GRAMS, EDIBLE PORTION—Continued

[Numbers in parentheses denote values imputed—usually from another form of the food or from a similar food. Zero in parentheses indicates that the amount of a constituent probably is none or is too small to measure. Dashes denote lack of reliable data for a constituent believed to be present in measurable amount. Calculated values, as those based on a recipe, are not in parentheses]

Item No.	Food and description	Water	Food energy	Protein	Fat	Carbohydrate: Total	Carbohydrate: Fiber	Ash	Calcium	Phosphorus	Iron	Sodium	Potassium	Vitamin A value	Thiamine	Riboflavin	Niacin	Ascorbic acid
(A)	(B)	(C)	(D)	(E)	(F)	(G)	(H)	(I)	(J)	(K)	(L)	(M)	(N)	(O)	(P)	(Q)	(R)	(S)
		Percent	*Calories*	*Grams*	*Grams*	*Grams*	*Grams*	*Grams*	*Milligrams*	*Milligrams*	*Milligrams*	*Milligrams*	*Milligrams*	*International units*	*Milligrams*	*Milligrams*	*Milligrams*	*Milligrams*
	Tartar sauce:																	
2273	Regular	34.4	531	1.4	57.8	4.2	0.5	2.2	18	32	0.9	707	78	220	0.01	0.03	Trace	1
2274	Special dietary (low-calorie, approx. 10 Cal. per tsp.)	68.1	224	.6	22.4	6.7	.3	2.2	18	32	.9	707	78	220	.01	.03	Trace	1
2275	**Tautog** (blackfish), raw	79.3	89	18.6	1.1	0	0	1.1	—	227	—	—	—	—	—	—	—	—
	Tea, instant (water-soluble solids) carbohydrate added:																	
2276	Dry powder	3.8	294	—	Trace	80	.1	6.1	11	—	1.6	—	4,530	—	—	.95	8.9	—
2277	Beverage	99.4	2	—	Trace	.4	Trace	Trace	Trace	—	Trace	—	25	—	—	.01	Trace	—
	Tendergreen. See Mustard spinach, items 1370–1371.																	
2278	**Terrapin** (diamond back), raw	77.0	111	18.6	3.5	0	0	1.0	—	—	3.2	—	—	—	—	—	—	—
	Thuringer. See Sausage, cold cuts, and luncheon meats: item 2021.																	
	Tilefish:																	
2279	Raw	80.3	79	17.5	.5	0	0	1.4	—	—	—	—	—	—	—	—	—	—
2280	Cooked, baked	71.6	138	24.5	3.7	0	0	1.1	—	—	—	—	—	—	—	—	—	—
2281	**Tomatoes, green,** raw	93.0	24	1.2	.2	5.1	.5	.5	13	27	.5	3	244	270	.06	.04	.5	20
	Tomatoes, ripe:																	
2282	Raw	93.5	22	1.1	.2	4.7	.5	.5	13	27	.5	3	244	900	.06	.04	.7	[154] 23
2283	Cooked, boiled	92.4	26	1.3	.2	5.5	.6	.6	15	32	.6	4	287	1,000	.07	.05	.8	24
	Canned, solids and liquid:																	
2284	Regular pack	93.7	21	1.0	.2	4.3	.4	.8	[155] 6	19	.5	130	217	900	.05	.03	.7	17
2285	Special dietary pack (low-sodium)	94.1	20	1.0	.2	4.2	.4	.5	[155] 6	19	.5	3	217	900	.05	.03	.7	17
2286	**Tomato catsup,** bottled	68.6	106	2.0	.4	25.4	.5	3.6	22	50	.8	[156] 1,042	363	1,400	.09	.07	1.6	15
2287	**Tomato chili sauce,** bottled	68.0	104	2.5	.3	24.8	.7	4.4	20	52	(.8)	[156] 1,338	(370)	(1,400)	(.09)	(.07)	(1.6)	(16)
	Tomato juice:																	
	Canned or bottled:																	
2288	Regular pack	93.6	19	.9	.1	4.3	.2	1.1	7	18	.9	200	227	800	.05	.03	.8	16
2289	Special dietary pack (low-sodium)	94.2	19	.8	.1	4.3	.2	.6	7	18	.9	3	227	800	.05	.03	.7	16
	Canned concentrate:																	
2290	Undiluted	75.0	76	3.4	.4	17.1	.9	4.1	27	70	3.5	790	888	3,300	.20	.12	3.1	49
2291	Diluted with 3 parts water, by volume	93.4	20	.9	.1	4.5	.2	1.1	7	19	.9	209	235	900	.05	.03	.8	13
	Dehydrated (crystals):																	
2292	Dry form	1.0	303	11.6	2.2	68.2	3.1	17.0	85	279	7.8	(3,334)	3,518	13,100	.52	.40	13.5	239
2293	Prepared with water (1 lb. yields approx. 1½ gals.)	93.5	20	.8	.1	4.5	.2	1.1	6	18	.5	(258)	231	860	.03	.03	.9	16
2294	**Tomato juice cocktail,** canned or bottled	93.0	21	.7	.1	5.0	.2	1.2	10	18	.9	200	221	800	.05	.02	.6	16
2295	**Tomato paste,** canned	75.0	82	3.4	.4	18.6	.9	2.6	27	70	3.5	[161] 38	888	3,300	.20	.12	3.1	49
	Tomato puree, canned:																	
2296	Regular pack	87.0	39	1.7	.2	8.9	.4	2.2	13	34	1.7	399	426	1,600	.09	.05	1.4	33
2297	Special dietary pack (low-sodium)	88.0	39	1.7	.2	8.9	.4	1.2	13	34	1.7	6	426	1,600	.09	.05	1.4	33
2298	**Tomcod,** Atlantic, raw	81.5	77	17.2	.4	0	0	1.0	—	—	—	—	—	—	—	.17	—	—
	Tongue:																	
	Beef:																	
2299	Very fat, raw	62.	271	14.4	23.	.4	0	.7	—	—	—	—	—	—	—	—	—	—
2300	Fat, raw	65	231	15.7	18.	.4	0	.8	—	—	—	—	—	—	—	—	—	—
	Medium-fat:																	
2301	Raw	68	207	16.4	15.	.4	0	.9	8	182	2.1	73	197	—	.12	.29	5.0	—
2302	Cooked, braised	60.8	244	21.5	16.7	.4	0	.6	7	117	2.2	61	164	—	.05	.29	3.5	—
2303	Thin (very thin), raw	70	175	17.4	11.	.4	0	.9	—	—	—	—	—	—	—	—	—	—
2304	Smoked	48.9	—	17.2	28.8	—	0	—	—	—	—	—	—	—	.04	.21	3.6	—
	Calf:																	
2305	Raw	74.3	130	18.5	5.3	.9	0	1.0	—	—	—	—	—	—	—	—	—	—
2306	Cooked, braised	68.5	160	23.9	6.0	1.0	0	.7	—	—	—	—	—	—	—	—	—	—
	Hog:																	
2307	Raw	66.1	215	16.8	15.6	.5	0	1.0	29	186	1.4	—	—	—	.17	(.29)	(5.0)	—
2308	Cooked, braised	59.4	253	22.0	17.4	.5	0	.7	26	119	1.4	—	—	—	.07	(.29)	(3.5)	—
	Lamb:																	
2309	Raw	69.5	199	13.9	15.3	.5	0	.8	—	147	—	—	—	—	—	—	—	—
2310	Cooked, braised	60.2	254	20.5	18.2	.5	0	.7	—	102	—	—	—	—	—	—	—	—
	Sheep:																	
2311	Raw	61.0	265	13.7	21.8	2.4	0	1.1	—	—	—	—	—	—	—	—	—	—
2312	Cooked, braised	51.6	323	19.8	25.3	2.4	0	.8	—	—	3.4	—	—	—	—	—	—	—

	Tongue, canned or cured (beef, lamb, etc.):																	
2313	Whole, canned or pickled	56.6	267	19.3	20.3	.3	0	3.5	—	—	—	—	—	—	—	—	—	—
2314	Potted or deviled	52.8	290	18.6	23.0	.7	0	4.9	—	—	—	—	—	—	.04	.11	1.3	—
2315	**Towelgourd, raw**	94.5	18	.8	.2	4.1	.5	.4	19	33	.9	—	—	380	.03	.04	.4	8
	Tripe, beef:																	
2316	Commercial	79.1	100	19.1	2.0	0	0	.4	127	86	1.6	72	9	—	—	.15	1.6	—
2317	Pickled	86.5	62	11.8	1.3	0	0	.3	—	—	—	46	19	—	—	—	—	—
	Trout. See Lake trout, items 1170–1171.																	
2318	**Trout, brook, raw**	77.7	101	19.2	2.1	0	0	1.2	—	266	—	—	—	—	—	.07	—	—
	Trout, rainbow or steelhead:																	
2319	Raw	66.3	195	21.5	11.4	0	0	1.3	—	—	—	—	—	—	.08	.20	8.4	—
2320	Canned	63.2	209	20.6	13.4	0	0	2.4	—	—	—	—	—	—	—	—	—	—
	Tuna:																	
	Raw:																	
2321	Bluefin	70.5	145	25.2	4.1	0	0	1.3	—	—	1.3	—	—	—	—	—	—	—
2322	Yellowfin	71.5	133	24.7	3.0	0	0	1.4	—	—	—	[162] 37	—	—	—	—	—	—
	Canned:																	
	In oil:																	
2323	Solids and liquid	52.6	288	24.2	20.5	0	0	2.4	6	294	1.1	800	301	90	.04	.09	10.1	—
2324	Drained solids	60.6	197	28.8	8.2	0	0	2.0	(8)	234	1.9	—	—	80	.05	.12	11.9	—
	In water:																	
2325	Solids and liquid	70.0	127	28.0	.8	0	0	1.2	16	190	1.6	[161] 41	[163] 279	—	—	.10	13.3	—
2326	**Tuna salad** [164]	69.8	170	14.6	10.5	3.5	—	1.6	20	142	1.3	—	—	290	.04	.11	5.0	1
	Turkey:																	
	All classes:																	
	Total edible:																	
2327	Raw	64.2	218	20.1	14.7	0	0	1.0	—	—	—	—	—	—	—	—		—
2328	Cooked, roasted	55.4	263	27.0	16.4	0	0	1.2	—	—	—	—	—	—	—	—	—	—
	Flesh and skin:																	
2329	Cooked, roasted	57.3	223	31.9	9.6	0	0	1.2	—	—	—	—	—	—	.07	.16	8.1	—
	Flesh only:																	
2330	Raw	68.3	162	24.0	6.6	0	0	1.1	8	212	1.5	66	315	—	.08	.14	8.0	—
2331	Cooked, roasted	61.2	190	31.5	6.1	0	0	1.2	8	251	1.8	130	367	—	.05	.18	7.7	—
	Skin only:																	
2332	Raw	48.2	405	12.1	39.2	0	0	.5	—	—	—	—	—	—	.03	.04	4.6	—
2333	Cooked, roasted	40.0	451	17.0	42.0	0	0	1.0	—	—	—	—	—	—	—	—	—	—
	Light meat:																	
2334	Raw	73.0	116	24.6	1.2	0	0	1.2	—	—	1.0	51	320	—	.06	.11	11.3	—
2335	Cooked, roasted	62.1	176	32.9	3.9	0	0	1.2	—	—	1.2	82	411	—	.05	.14	11.1	—
	Dark meat:																	
2336	Raw	73.6	128	20.9	4.3	0	0	1.1	—	—	2.0	81	310	—	.09	.18	4.7	—
2337	Cooked, roasted	60.5	203	30.0	8.3	0	0	1.2	—	—	2.3	99	398	—	.04	.23	4.2	—
	Giblets:																	
2338	Raw	71.0	150	20.1	6.6	1.2	0	1.1	—	—	—	—	—	—	—	—	—	—
2339	Cooked (some gizzard fat), simmered	61.0	233	20.6	15.4	1.6	0	1.4	—	—	—	—	—	—	—	2.72	—	—
	Young birds (24 weeks and under), raw:																	
2340	Total edible	71.5	145	21.4	6.0	0	0	1.1	—	—	—	—	—	—	—	—	—	—
2341	Flesh and skin	72.0	151	19.8	7.4	0	0	.8	—	—	—	—	—	—	—	—	—	—
2342	Light meat	73.8	108	24.5	.4	0	0	1.3	—	—	—	—	—	—	—	—	—	—
2343	Dark meat	75.7	111	20.6	2.6	0	0	1.1	—	—	—	—	—	—	—	—	—	—
	Medium-fat birds (26–32 weeks), raw:																	
2344	Total edible	63.3	227	19.9	15.8	0	0	1.0	—	—	—	—	—	—	—	—	—	—
2345	Flesh and skin	65.7	197	21.6	11.6	0	0	1.1	—	—	—	—	—	—	—	—	—	—
2346	Light meat	73.0	115	24.7	1.1	0	0	1.2	—	—	—	—	—	—	—	—	—	—
2347	Dark meat	73.9	127	20.8	4.2	0	0	1.1	—	—	—	—	—	—	—	—	—	—
	Fat mature birds (more than 32 weeks), raw:																	
2348	Total edible	51.3	343	18.4	29.3	0	0	.9	—	—	—	—	—	—	—	—	—	—
2349	**Turkey, canned,** meat only	64.9	202	20.9	12.5	0	0	1.7	10	—	1.4	—	—	130	.02	.14	4.7	—
	Turkey, potted. See Sausage, cold cuts, and luncheon meats: item 2008.																	
	Turkey potpie:																	
2350	Home-prepared, baked	56.2	237	10.4	13.5	18.5	.4	1.4	27	101	1.4	273	198	1,330	.11	.13	2.5	2
2351	Commercial, frozen, unheated	62.3	197	5.8	10.4	20.1	.3	1.4	12	56	.9	369	114	890	.09	.08	1.6	2
	Turnips:																	
2352	Raw	91.5	30	1.0	.2	6.6	.9	.7	39	30	.5	49	268	Trace	.04	.07	.6	36
2353	Cooked, boiled, drained	93.6	23	.8	.2	4.9	.9	.5	35	24	.4	34	188	Trace	.04	.05	.3	22
	Turnip greens, leaves, including stems:																	
2354	Raw	90.3	28	3.0	.3	5.0	.8	1.4	246	58	1.8	—	—	7,600	(.21)	(.39)	(.8)	139
	Cooked, boiled, drained, cooked in—																	
2355	Small amount of water, short time	93.2	20	2.2	.2	3.6	.7	.8	184	37	1.1	—	—	6,300	.15	.24	.6	69
2356	Large amount of water, long time	93.5	19	2.2	.2	3.3	.7	.8	174	34	1.0	—	—	5,700	.10	.23	.5	47

[158] Federal standards provide for addition of certain calcium salts as firming agents; if used, these salts may add calcium not to exceed 26 mg. per 100 grams of finished product.

[159] Year-round average. Samples marketed from November through May average around 10 mg. per 100 grams; from June through October, around 26 mg.

[160] Applies to regular pack. For special dietary pack (low-sodium), values range from 5 to 35 mg. per 100 grams.

[161] Applies to the more usual product with no salt added. If salt is added, the sodium content is about 790 mg. per 100 grams.

[162] Brined sample contained 439 mg. of sodium per 100 grams.

[163] One sample with salt added contained 875 mg. of sodium per 100 grams and 275 mg. of potassium.

[164] Prepared with tuna, celery, mayonnaise, pickle, onion, and egg.

TABLE 1.—COMPOSITION OF FOODS, 100 GRAMS, EDIBLE PORTION—Continued

[Numbers in parentheses denote values imputed—usually from another form of the food or from a similar food. Zero in parentheses indicates that the amount of a constituent probably is none or is too small to measure. Dashes denote lack of reliable data for a constituent believed to be present in measurable amount. Calculated values, as those based on a recipe, are not in parentheses]

Item No.	Food and description	Water	Food energy	Protein	Fat	Carbohydrate Total	Carbohydrate Fiber	Ash	Calcium	Phosphorus	Iron	Sodium	Potassium	Vitamin A value	Thiamine	Riboflavin	Niacin	Ascorbic acid
(A)	(B)	(C)	(D)	(E)	(F)	(G)	(H)	(I)	(J)	(K)	(L)	(M)	(N)	(O)	(P)	(Q)	(R)	(S)
		Percent	Calories	Grams	Grams	Grams	Grams	Grams	Milligrams	Milligrams	Milligrams	Milligrams	Milligrams	International units	Milligrams	Milligrams	Milligrams	Milligrams
	Turnip greens, leaves, including stems—Continued																	
2357	Canned, solids and liquid	93.7	18	1.5	0.3	3.2	0.7	1.3	100	30	1.6	[9] 236	243	4,700	0.02	0.09	0.6	19
	Frozen:																	
2358	Not thawed	92.3	23	2.6	.3	4.0	1.0	.8	131	41	1.7	12	188	6,900	.05	.11	.5	34
2359	Cooked, boiled, drained	92.7	23	2.5	.3	3.9	1.0	.6	118	39	1.6	17	149	5,900	.05	.09	.4	19
	Turtle, green:																	
2360	Raw	78.5	89	19.8	.5	0	0	1.2	—	—	—	—	—	—	—	—	—	—
2361	Canned	76.0	106	23.4	.7	0	0	.9	—	—	—	—	—	—	—	—	—	—
	Veal:[1]																	
	Carcass, raw:																	
	Including kidney and kidney fat:																	
2362	Fat class (76% lean, 24% fat)	62.	248	18.0	19.	0	0	.9	10	178	2.7			—	.13	.24	6.0	—
2363	Medium-fat class (81% lean, 19% fat)	66.	207	18.8	14	0	0	1.0	11	190	2.8			—	.14	.25	6.3	—
2364	Thin class (86% lean, 14% fat)	70.	173	19.4	10	0	0	1.0	11	199	2.9			—	.14	.26	6.5	—
	Excluding kidney and kidney fat:																	
2365	Fat class (79% lean, 21% fat)	65.	223	18.5	16	0	0	.9	11	185	2.8			—	.13	.25	6.2	—
2366	Medium-fat class (84% lean, 16% fat)	68.	190	19.1	12	0	0	1.0	11	193	2.9			—	.14	.25	6.4	—
2367	Thin class (88% lean, 12% fat)	71.	156	19.7	8	0	0	1.0	11	201	3.0			—	.14	.26	6.6	—
	Retail cuts, untrimmed:																	
	Chuck:																	
	Fat class:																	
2368	Total edible, raw (83% lean, 17% fat)	67.	198	19.0	13	0	0	1.0	11	193	2.8			—	.14	.25	6.4	—
	Medium-fat class:																	
	Total edible:																	
2369	Raw (86% lean, 14% fat)	70.	173	19.4	10	0	0	1.0	11	199	2.9			—	.14	.26	6.5	—
2370	Cooked, braised (85% lean, 15% fat)	58.5	236	27.9	12.8	0	0	.8	12	151	3.5			—	.06	.29	6.4	—
	Thin class:																	
2371	Total edible, raw (90% lean, 10% fat)	73.	139	19.9	6	0	0	1.1	12	206	3.0			—	.15	.26	6.7	—
	Flank:																	
	Fat class:																	
2372	Total edible, raw (49% lean, 51% fat)	48.	387	14.5	36	0	0	.7	8	126	2.2			—	.11	.19	4.9	—
	Medium-fat class:																	
	Total edible:																	
2373	Raw (61% lean, 39% fat)	56.	314	16.5	27	0	0	.8	10	155	2.5			—	.12	.22	5.5	—
2374	Cooked, stewed (60% lean, 40% fat)	42.8	390	23.2	32.3	0	0	.7	11	117	3.0			—	.05	.22	4.2	—
	Thin class:																	
2375	Total edible, raw (73% lean, 27% fat)	63.	240	18.1	18	0	0	.9	10	179	2.7	(90)	(320)	—	.13	.24	6.1	—
	Foreshank:																	
	Fat class:																	
2376	Total edible, raw (84% lean, 16% fat)	70.	173	19.4	10	0	0	1.0	11	199	2.9			—	.14	.26	6.5	—
	Medium-fat class:																	
	Total edible:																	
2377	Raw (87% lean, 13% fat)	71.	156	19.7	8	0	0	1.0	11	203	3.0			—	.14	.26	5.6	—
2378	Cooked, stewed (86% lean, 14% fat)	60.1	216	28.7	10.4	0	0	.8	12	154	3.6			—	.05	.26	5.9	—
	Thin class:																	
2379	Total edible, raw (91% lean, 9% fat)	74.	131	20.1	5	0	0	1.1	12	209	3.0			—	.15	.27	6.7	—
	Loin:																	
	Fat class:																	
2380	Total edible, raw (80% lean, 20% fat)	64.	215	18.6	15	0	0	1.0	11	187	2.8			—	.14	.25	6.2	—
	Medium-fat class:																	
	Total edible:																	
2381	Raw (85% lean, 15% fat)	69.	181	19.2	11	0	0	1.0	11	195	2.9			—	.14	.26	6.4	—
2382	Cooked, broiled (77% lean, 23% fat)	55.9	234	26.4	13.4	0	0	1.3	11	324	3.2			—	.07	.25	5.4	—
	Thin class:																	
2383	Total edible, raw (89% lean, 11% fat)	71.	156	19.7	8	0	0	1.0	11	203	3.0			—	.14	.26	6.6	—
	Plate:																	
	Fat class:																	
2384	Total edible, raw (66% lean, 34% fat)	59.	281	17.3	23	0	0	.9	10	168	2.6			—	.13	.23	5.8	—
	Medium-fat class:																	
	Total edible:																	
2385	Raw (74% lean, 26% fat)	64.	231	18.3	17.	0	0	.9	11	182	2.7			—	.13	.24	6.1	—
2386	Cooked, stewed (73% lean, 27% fat)	52.1	303	26.1	21.2	0	0	.7	12	138	3.3			—	.05	.21	4.5	—
	Thin class:																	
2387	Total edible, raw (82% lean, 18% fat)	68.	190	19.1	12	0	0	1.0	11	193	2.9			—	.14	.25	6.4	—

	Rib:																	
	Fat class:																	
2388	Total edible, raw (76% lean, 24% fat)	62.	248	18. 0	19	0	0	. 9	10	178	2. 7			—	. 13	24	6 0	—
	Medium-fat class:																	
	Total edible.																	
2389	Raw (82% lean, 18% fat)	66.	207	18 8	14.	0	0	1. 0	11	190	2. 8			—	. 14	. 25	6 3	—
2390	Cooked, roasted (82% lean, 18% fat)	54. 6	269	27. 2	16. 9	0	0	1 3	12	248	3 4			—	. 13	. 31	7 8	—
	Thin class:																	
2391	Total edible, raw (87% lean, 13% fat)	70.	164	19 5	9	0	0	1. 0	11	200	2. 9	([165])	([166])	—	. 14	. 26	6 5	—
	Round with rump:																	
	Fat class																	
2392	Total edible, raw (84% lean, 16% fat)	68	190	19 1	12	0	0	1 0	11	193	2 9			—	. 14	. 25	6. 4	—
	Medium-fat class:																	
	Total edible:																	
2393	Raw (87% lean, 13% fat)	70.	164	19. 5	9	0	0	1 0	11	200	2 9			—	. 14	. 26	6 5	—
2394	Cooked, broiled (79% lean, 21% fat)	60. 4	216	27. 1	11. 1	0	0	1. 4	11	231	3. 2			—	07	. 25	5. 4	—
	Thin class																	
2395	Total edible, raw (91% lean, 9% fat)	73.	139	19 9	6.	0	0	1. 1	12	206	3 0			—	15	. 26	6. 7	—
2396	**Vegetable juice cocktail, canned**	94. 1	17	. 9	. 1	3 6	. 3	1. 3	12	22	. 5	(200)	(221)	700	. 05	. 03	. 8	9
	Vegetable main dishes, canned.																	
	Principal ingredients:																	
2397	Peanuts and soya	55. 3	237	11. 7	16. 9	13. 4	. 9	2 7	—	—	—	—	—	—	—	—	—	—
2398	Wheat protein	72. 9	109	16. 3	. 8	8. 8	. 1	1 2	—	—	—	—	—	—	—	—	—	—
2399	Wheat protein, nuts or peanuts	52. 4	212	20. 3	7. 1	17. 7	. 4	2 5	—	—	—	—	—	—	—	—	—	—
2400	Wheat protein, vegetable oil	63. 5	189	19. 1	10. 4	5 2	—	1. 8	—	—	—	—	—	—	—	—	—	—
2401	Wheat and soy protein	73. 4	104	16 1	1. 2	7. 6	. 3	1 7	—	—	—	—	—	—	—	—	—	—
2402	Wheat and soy protein, soy or other vegetable oil	66 6	150	16 1	5. 6	9 5	. 6	2 2	—	—	—	—	—	—	—	—	—	—
	Vegetables, mixed (carrots, corn, peas, green snap beans, lima beans), frozen:																	
2403	Not thawed	82. 1	65	3 3	3	13 7	1 2	6	26	66	1. 4	[19] 59	208	5, 000	. 13	. 07	1 2	9
2404	Cooked, boiled, drained	82 6	64	3. 2	. 3	13 4	1. 2	. 5	25	63	1. 3	33	191	4, 950	. 12	. 07	1. 1	8
	Vegetable-oyster. See Salsify, items 1961–1962.																	
2405	**Venison, lean meat only, raw**	74.	126	21	4	0	0	1.	10	249	—	—	—	—	. 23	. 48	6. 3	—
	Vienna sausage. See Sausage, cold cuts, and luncheon meats: item 2022.																	
	Vinegar:																	
2406	Cider	93 8	14	Trace	(0)	5 9	—	. 3	(6)	(9)	(. 6)	1	100	—	—	—	—	—
2407	Distilled	95	12	—	—	5.	—	Trace	—	—	—	1	15	—	—	—	—	—
2408	**Vinespinach** (basella), raw	93. 1	19	1 8	. 3	3. 4	. 7	1. 4	109	52	1. 2	—	—	8, 000	. 05	—	. 5	102
	Vodka. See Beverages, items 395–399.																	
	Waffles:																	
	Baked from home recipe, made with—																	
2409	Enriched flour	41. 4	279	9. 3	9 8	37 5	. 1	2 0	113	173	1. 7	475	145	330	. 17	. 25	1 3	Trace
2410	Unenriched flour	41. 4	279	9. 3	9 8	37. 5	. 1	2 0	113	173	. 9	475	145	330	. 05	. 18	4	Trace
2411	Frozen, made with enriched flour	42. 1	253	7 1	6. 2	42. 0	. 2	2 6	122	208	[167] 1. 8	644	158	130	[167] 17	[167] . 16	[167] 1 2	Trace
	Waffle mixes and waffles baked from mixes:																	
2412	Mix, with enriched flour, dry form	5. 6	458	6. 4	19 2	65 4	. 2	3 4	118	196	1 6	1, 027	85	120	. 22	18	1 7	Trace
2413	Waffles, made with water	38. 6	305	4. 8	14 0	40. 2	. 1	2 4	76	127	1 0	560	55	80	. 12	. 11	1. 0	Trace
2414	Mix, with unenriched flour, dry form	5. 6	458	6 4	19. 2	65. 4	. 2	3 4	118	196	. 6	1, 027	85	120	. 04	. 08	. 4	Trace
2415	Waffles, made with water	38 6	305	4. 8	14. 0	40. 2	. 1	2. 4	76	127	. 4	560	55	80	. 02	05	. 3	Trace
2416	Mix (pancake and waffle), with enriched flour, dry form.	8 3	356	8 6	1. 8	75 7	. 4	5. 6	450	590	3 1	1, 433	162	0	. 44	. 34	2. 9	0
2417	Waffles, made with egg, milk	41. 7	275	8 8	10 6	36 2	. 2	2 7	239	343	1. 3	686	195	230	. 14	. 23	. 9	Trace
2418	Mix (pancake and waffle), with unenriched flour, dry form	8 3	356	8. 6	1. 8	75 7	. 4	5. 6	450	590	1 4	1, 433	162	0	. 12	. 08	1 1	0
2419	Waffles, made with egg, milk	41 7	275	8. 8	10 6	36 2	. 2	2 7	239	343	. 9	686	195	230	. 08	. 19	. 4	Trace
	Walnuts:																	
2420	Black	3 1	628	20. 5	59 3	14 8	1. 7	2. 3	Trace	570	6 0	3	460	300	. 22	. 11	. 7	—
2421	Persian or English	3. 5	651	14. 8	64 0	15. 8	2. 1	1 9	99	380	3. 1	2	450	30	. 33	. 13	. 9	2
2422	**Waterchestnut,** Chinese (matai, waternut), raw	78. 3	79	1 4	2	19 0	. 8	1 1	4	65	. 6	20	500	0	. 14	. 20	1 0	4
2423	**Watercress** leaves including stems, raw	93. 3	19	2 2	. 3	3. 0	. 7	1 2	151	54	1 7	52	282	4, 900	. 08	. 16	. 9	79
	Water ice. See Ices, water item 1144																	
2424	**Watermelon,** raw	92 6	26	. 5	. 2	6. 4	. 3	. 3	7	10	. 5	1	100	590	. 03	. 03	. 2	7
2425	**Waxgourd** (Chinese preserving melon), raw	96 1	13	. 4	. 2	3 0	. 5	. 3	19	19	. 4	6	111	0	. 04	. 11	. 4	13
	Weakfish:																	
2426	Raw	76 7	121	16 5	5 6	0	0	1 2	—	—	—	75	317	—	09	. 06	2 7	—
2427	Cooked, broiled	61 4	208	24. 6	11 4	0	0	2 6	—	—	—	[168] 560	465	—	. 10	. 08	3 5	—
2428	**Welsh rarebit**	70. 2	179	8. 1	13 6	6 3	0	1. 8	251	186	. 3	332	138	530	. 04	23	. 1	Trace
	West Indian Cherry. See Acerola, item 3.																	
2429	**Whale meat,** raw	70 9	156	20 6	7. 5	0	0	1 0	12	144	—	78	22	1, 860	. 09	. 08	—	6

[4] See Notes on Foods, p. 180.

[6] Estimated average based on addition of salt in the amount of 0 6 percent of the finished product.

[19] Average weighted in accordance with commercial practices in freezing vegetables See also Notes on Foods, p. 177.

[168] Based on fish with salt added in cooking

[165] Average value per 100 grams of veal of all cuts is 90 mg. for raw meat and 80 mg for cooked meat. See also Notes on Foods, p. 180.

[166] Average value per 100 grams of veal of all cuts is 320 mg for raw meat and 500 mg. for cooked meat. See also Notes on Foods, p 180.

[167] With unenriched flour, approximate values per 100 grams are: Iron, 1 1 mg.; thiamine, 0 06 mg , riboflavin, 0 09 mg , niacin, 0 4 mg

TABLE 1.—COMPOSITION OF FOODS, 100 GRAMS, EDIBLE PORTION—Continued

[Numbers in parentheses denote values imputed—usually from another form of the food or from a similar food. Zero in parentheses indicates that the amount of a constituent probably is none or is too small to measure. Dashes denote lack of reliable data for a constituent believed to be present in measurable amount. Calculated values, as those based on a recipe, are not in parentheses]

Item No.	Food and description	Water	Food energy	Protein	Fat	Carbohydrate: Total	Carbohydrate: Fiber	Ash	Calcium	Phosphorus	Iron	Sodium	Potassium	Vitamin A value	Thiamine	Riboflavin	Niacin	Ascorbic acid
(A)	(B)	(C)	(D)	(E)	(F)	(G)	(H)	(I)	(J)	(K)	(L)	(M)	(N)	(O)	(P)	(Q)	(R)	(S)
		Percent	*Calories*	*Grams*	*Grams*	*Grams*	*Grams*	*Grams*	*Milligrams*	*Milligrams*	*Milligrams*	*Milligrams*	*Milligrams*	*International units*	*Milligrams*	*Milligrams*	*Milligrams*	*Milligrams*
	Wheat, whole-grain: [168]																	
2430	Hard red spring	13.0	330	14.0	2.2	69.1	2.3	1.7	36	383	3.1	(3)	370	(0)	0.57	0.12	4.3	(0)
2431	Hard red winter	12.5	330	12.3	1.8	71.7	2.3	1.7	46	354	3.4	(3)	370	(0)	.52	.12	4.3	(0)
2432	Soft red winter	14.0	326	10.2	2.0	72.1	2.3	1.7	42	400	3.5	(3)	376	(0)	.43	.11	(3.6)	(0)
2433	White	11.5	335	9.4	2.0	75.4	1.9	1.7	36	394	3.0	(3)	390	(0)	.53	.12	5.3	(0)
2434	Durum	13.0	332	12.7	2.5	70.1	1.8	1.7	37	386	4.3	(3)	435	(0)	.66	.12	(4.4)	(0)
	Wheat flours:																	
2435	Whole (from hard wheats)	12.	333	13.3	2.0	71.0	2.3	1.7	41	372	3.3	3	370	(0)	.55	.12	4.3	(0)
2436	80% extraction (from hard wheats)	12.	365	12	1.3	74.1	.5	.65	24	191	1.3	2	95	(0)	.26	.07	2.0	(0)
2437	Straight, hard wheat	12	365	11.8	1.2	74.5	.4	.46	20	97	1.4	2	95	(0)	.12	.07	1.4	(0)
2438	Straight, soft wheat	12.	364	9.7	1.0	76.9	.4	.42	20	97	1.1	2	95	(0)	.08	.05	1.2	(0)
	Patent:																	
	All-purpose or family flour.																	
2439	Enriched	12.	364	10.5	1.0	76.1	.3	.43	16	87	[59] 2.9	2	95	(0)	[59] .44	[59] .26	[59] 3.5	(0)
2440	Unenriched	12.	364	10.5	1.0	76.1	.3	.43	16	87	.8	2	95	(0)	.06	.05	.9	(0)
	Bread flour:																	
2441	Enriched	12.	365	11.8	1.1	74.7	.3	.44	16	95	[59] 2.9	2	95	(0)	[59] .44	[59] .26	[59] 3.5	(0)
2442	Unenriched	12.	365	11.8	1.1	74.7	.3	.44	16	95	.9	2	95	(0)	.08	.06	1.0	(0)
2443	Cake or pastry flour	12.	364	7.5	.8	79.4	.2	.31	17	73	.5	2	95	(0)	.03	.03	.7	(0)
2444	Gluten flour (45% gluten, 55% patent flour)	8.5	378	41.4	1.9	47.2	.4	1.0	40	140	—	2	60	(0)	—	—	—	(0)
2445	Self-rising flour, enriched (anhydrous monocalcium phosphate used as a baking acid). [169]	11.5	352	9.3	1.0	74.2	.4	4.0	265	466	[59] 2.9	1,079	[170] —	(0)	[59] .44	[59] .26	[59] 3.5	(0)
2446	**Wheat bran, crude, commercially milled**	11.5	213	16.0	4.6	61.9	9.1	6.0	119	1,276	14.9	9	1,121	(0)	.72	.35	21.0	(0)
2447	**Wheat germ, crude, commercially milled**	11.5	363	26.6	10.9	46.7	2.5	4.3	72	1,118	9.4	3	827	(0)	2.01	.68	4.2	(0)
	Wheat, parboiled. See Bulgur, items 497–501.																	
	Wheat products used mainly as hot breakfast cereals:																	
	Wheat, rolled																	
2448	Dry form	10.1	340	9.9	2.0	76.2	2.2	1.8	36	342	3.2	2	380	(0)	.36	.12	4.1	(0)
2449	Cooked	79.7	75	2.2	.4	16.9	.5	.8	8	76	.7	295	84	(0)	.07	.03	.9	(0)
	Wheat, whole-meal:																	
2450	Dry form	10.4	338	13.5	2.0	72.3	2.2	1.8	45	398	3.7	2	370	(0)	.51	.13	4.7	(0)
2451	Cooked	87.7	45	1.8	.3	9.4	.3	.8	7	52	.5	212	48	(0)	.06	.02	.6	(0)
	Wheat and malted barley cereal, toasted:																	
	Quick-cooking																	
2452	Dry form	6.4	383	12.0	1.6	78.5	1.5	1.5	50	350	2.6	1	—	(0)	.34	.06	—	(0)
2453	Cooked	84.1	65	2.0	.3	13.2	.2	.4	9	59	.4	72	Trace	(0)	.05	.01	—	(0)
	Instant-cooking:																	
2454	Dry form	6.6	382	14.0	1.6	76.2	1.6	1.6	40	390	4.1	1	—	(0)	.34	.09	—	(0)
2455	Cooked	80.0	80	3.0	.3	16.1	.3	.6	9	82	.9	102	Trace	(0)	.07	.02	—	(0)
	Also see Farina, items 991–998.																	
	Wheat products used mainly as ready-to-eat breakfast cereals:																	
	Wheat bran. See Bran, items 439–442.																	
2456	Wheat flakes, added nutrients	3.5	354	10.2	1.6	80.5	1.6	4.2	41	309	4.4	1,032	—	(0)	.64	.14	4.9	(0)
2457	Wheat-germ, toasted	4.2	391	30.0	11.5	49.5	1.7	4.8	47	1,084	8.9	2	947	110	1.65	.98	5.3	10
	Wheat, puffed:																	
2458	Added nutrients, without salt	3.4	363	15.0	1.5	78.5	2.0	1.6	28	322	4.2	4	340	(0)	.55	.23	7.8	(0)
2459	Added nutrients, [171] with sugar and honey	2.8	376	6.0	2.1	88.3	.9	.8	26	150	3.3	161	99	(0)	.48	.18	6.4	(0)
	Wheat, shredded:																	
2460	Without salt or other added ingredients	6.6	354	9.9	2.0	79.9	2.3	1.6	43	388	3.5	3	348	(0)	.22	.11	4.4	(0)
2461	With malt, salt, and sugar added	3.2	366	9.1	2.9	81.7	2.2	3.1	39	370	3.4	697	—	(0)	.09	.15	4.8	(0)
2462	Wheat and malted barley flakes, nutrients added	3.1	392	8.8	1.3	84.3	1.8	2.5	49	250	2.6	780	—	(0)	.46	.11	3.9	(0)
2463	Wheat and malted barley granules, nutrients added	2.9	391	10.0	.6	84.4	1.5	2.1	53	176	2.8	710	230	(0)	.46	.07	5.3	(0)
	Whey:																	
2464	Fluid	93.1	26	.9	.3	5.1	0	.6	51	53	.1	—	—	10	.03	.14	.1	—
2465	Dried	4.5	349	12.9	1.1	73.5	0	8.0	646	589	1.4	—	—	50	.50	2.51	.8	—
	Whisky. See Beverages, items 395–399.																	
	Whitefish, lake:																	
2466	Raw	71.7	155	18.9	8.2	0	0	1.2	—	270	.4	52	299	2,260	.14	.12	3.0	—
2467	Cooked, baked, stuffed [172]	63.2	215	15.2	14.0	5.8	—	1.8	—	246	.5	195	291	2,000	.11	.11	2.3	Trace
2468	Smoked	68.2	155	20.9	7.3	0	0	3.7	22	274	—	—	—	—	—	—	—	—

	White sauce:																	
2469	Thin	78.7	121	3.9	8.7	7.2	Trace	1.5	122	97	.1	351	146	320	.04	.17	.2	Trace
2470	Medium	73.3	162	3.9	12.5	8.8	Trace	1.5	115	93	.2	379	139	460	.04	.17	.2	Trace
2471	Thick	67.9	198	4.0	15.6	11.0	Trace	1.5	107	90	.3	399	133	570	.05	.16	.3	Trace
	Whiting. See Kingfish, item 1164.																	
2472	Wildrice, raw	8.5	353	14.1	.7	75.3	1.0	1.4	19	339	4.2	7	220	(0)	.45	.63	6.2	(0)
	Wine. See Beverages, items 400-401.																	
2473	Wreckfish, raw	76.5	114	18.4	3.9	0	0	1.2	47	171	3.2	----	282	----	----	----	----	----
2474	Yam, tuber, raw	73.5	101	2.1	.2	23.2	.9	1.0	20	69	.6	----	600	Trace	.10	.04	.5	9
2475	Yambean, tuber, raw	85.1	55	1.4	.2	12.8	.7	.5	15	18	.6	----	----	Trace	.04	.03	.3	20
	Yeast: [48]																	
	Baker's:																	
2476	Compressed [173]	71.0	86	(12.1)	.4	11.0	----	2.4	13	394	4.9	16	610	Trace	.71	1.65	11.2	Trace
2477	Dry (active)	5.0	282	(36.9)	1.6	38.9	----	8.3	(44)	(1,291)	(16.1)	(52)	(1,998)	Trace	2.33	5.41	36.7	Trace
2478	Brewer's, debittered	5.0	283	(38.8)	1.0	38.4	1.7	7.1	[174]210	1,753	17.3	121	1,894	Trace	15.61	4.28	37.9	Trace
2479	Torula	6.0	277	(38.6)	1.0	37.0	3.3	7.7	[175]424	1,713	19.3	15	2,046	Trace	14.01	5.06	44.4	Trace
2480	Yellowtail (Pacific coast), raw	72.7	138	21.0	5.4	0	0	1.3	----	----	----	----	----	----	----	----	----	----
	Yoghurt:																	
2481	Made from partially skimmed milk	89.0	50	3.4	1.7	5.2	0	.7	120	94	Trace	51	143	70	.04	.18	.1	1
2482	Made from whole milk	88.0	62	3.0	3.4	4.9	0	.7	111	87	Trace	47	132	140	.03	.16	.1	1
	Youngberries. See Blackberries, item 417.																	
2483	Zwieback	5.0	423	10.7	8.8	74.3	.3	1.2	13	69	.6	250	150	40	.05	.07	.9	(0)

[48] See Appendix A, section on Protein, p. 162, and see Appendix B, section on Foods containing considerable nonprotein nitrogen, p. 182.

[52] Based on product with minimum level of enrichment. See Notes on Foods, p. 171.

[145] Values for moisture are based on product as it reaches the mill prior to tempering; data for other proximate constituents are adjusted to this basis.

[169] The acid ingredient most commonly used in self-rising flour. When sodium acid pyrophosphate in combination with either anhydrous monocalcium phosphate or calcium carbonate is used, the value for calcium is approximately 120 mg. per 100 grams; for phosphorus, 540 mg.; for sodium, 1,360 mg.

[170] 90 mg. of potassium per 100 grams contributed by flour. Small quantities of additional potassium may be provided by other ingredients.

[171] Values are based on the addition of iron, sodium (as salt), thiamine, riboflavin, and niacin; however, not all of these nutrients are added in every brand. If the label does not indicate the addition of a specified nutrient, values per 100 grams are: Iron, 2.2 mg.; sodium, 10 mg.; thiamine, 0.03 mg.; riboflavin, 0.04 mg.; niacin, 3.5 mg.

[172] Prepared with bacon, butter, onion, celery, and breadcrumbs.

[173] Product is sometimes fortified. For fortified compressed yeast, value for thiamine ranges from 2.6 to 25.1 mg. per 100 grams; for niacin, from 111 to 176 mg.

[174] Values range from 70 mg. to 760 mg. per 100 grams.

[175] Values range from 60 mg. to 1,000 mg. per 100 grams.

TABLE 2.—NUTRIENTS IN THE EDIBLE PORTION OF 1 POUND OF FOOD AS PURCHASED

[Numbers in parentheses denote values imputed—usually from another form of the food or from a similar food. Zero in parentheses indicates that the amount of a constituent probably is none or is too small to measure. Dashes denote lack of reliable data for a constituent believed to be present in measurable amount. Calculated values, as those based on a recipe, are not in parentheses]

Item No.		Food and description	Refuse	Food energy	Protein	Fat	Carbohydrate total	Calcium	Phosphorus	Iron	Sodium	Potassium	Vitamin A value	Thiamine	Riboflavin	Niacin	Ascorbic acid
(A)		(B)	(C)	(D)	(E)	(F)	(G)	(H)	(I)	(J)	(K)	(L)	(M)	(N)	(O)	(P)	(Q)
		Abalone:															
1		Raw:	Percent	Calories	Grams	Grams	Grams	Milligrams	Milligrams	Milligrams	Milligrams	Milligrams	International units	Milligrams	Milligrams	Milligrams	Milligrams
	a	In shell (refuse: shell and viscera)	59	187	35.0	1.0	6.5	70	344	4.6	—	—	—	0.35	0.29	—	—
	b	Flesh only	0	445	84.8	2.3	15.4	168	866	10.9	—	—	—	.84	.67	—	—
2		Canned	0	363	72.6	1.4	10.4	64	581	—	—	—	—	.54	—	—	—
3		Acerola (Barbados-cherry or West Indian cherry), raw (refuse: stones)	18	104	1.6	1.1	26.3	45	41	.7	30	309	—	.09	.23	1.6	4,830
4		Acerola juice, raw, and acerola, raw, used for juice:															
	a	Juice	0	104	1.8	1.4	21.8	45	41	2.3	14	—	—	.11	.29	1.9	7,258
	b	Acerola used for juice (refuse: stones, skins, residue)	37	71	1.2	.9	14.8	31	28	1.3	9	—	—	.07	.20	1.3	4,934
5		Albacore, flesh only, raw[1]	0	803	114.8	34.5	0	118	—	—	181	1,329	—	—	—	—	23
		Ale. See Beverages: Beer, item 394															
		Alewife:															
6		Raw:															
	a	Whole (refuse: head, tail, fins, entrails, scales, bones, and skin)	51	282	43.1	10.6	0	—	485	—	—	—	—	—	—	—	—
	b	Flesh only	0	576	88.0	22.2	0	—	989	—	—	—	—	—	—	—	—
7		Canned, solids and liquid	0	640	73.5	36.3	0	—	—	—	—	—	—	—	—	—	—
		Algae. See Seaweeds, items 2027–2031.															
		Alimentary Pastes. See Macaroni; Noodles; Pastinas; Spaghetti.															
		Almonds:															
8		Dried:															
	a	In shell (refuse: shells)	49	1,381	43.0	125.4	45.1	541	1,166	10.9	9	1,788	0	.55	2.14	8.1	Trace
	b	Shelled	0	2,713	84.4	246.0	88.5	1,061	2,286	21.3	18	3,509	0	1.08	4.18	15.9	Trace
9		Roasted and salted	0	2,844	84.4	261.7	88.5	1,066	2,288	21.3	894	3,506	0	.23	4.20	15.9	0
		Sugar-coated. See Candy, item 613.															
10		Almond meal, partially defatted	0	1,851	179.2	83.6	131.1	1,923	4,146	38.6	32	6,350	0	1.42	7.03	28.8	Trace
11		Amaranth, raw (refuse: tough stems, rootlets)	37	103	10.0	1.4	18.6	765	191	11.1	—	1,175	17,130	.23	.44	4.0	229
12		Anchovy, pickled, with and without added oil, not heavily salted.	0	798	87.1	46.7	1.4	762	953	—	—	—	—	—	—	—	—
		Apples:															
		Raw, commercial varieties:[2]															
		Freshly harvested and stored, portion used—															
13		Fruit with skin:															
	a	Good quality (refuse: core, stem)	8	242	.8	2.5	60.5	29	42	1.3	4	459	380	.12	.08	.3	16
	b	Fair quality (refuse: core, stem, defects)	18	216	.7	2.2	53.9	26	37	1.1	4	405	340	.10	.07	.3	14
14		Pared fruit:															
	a	Good quality (refuse: core, stem, thin parings)	14	211	.8	1.2	55.0	23	39	1.2	4	429	160	.11	.07	.3	9
	b	Fair quality (refuse: core, stem, thin parings, defects)	24	186	.7	1.0	48.6	21	34	1.0	3	379	140	.10	.07	.2	8
		Freshly harvested, portion used—															
15		Fruit with skin (refuse: core, stem)	8	224	.8	2.5	58.8	29	42	1.3	4	459	380	.12	.08	.3	29
16		Pared fruit (refuse: core, stem, thin parings)	14	207	.8	1.2	54.2	23	39	1.2	4	429	160	.11	.07	.3	15
		Stored, portion used—															
17		Fruit with skin (refuse: core, stem)	8	250	.8	2.9	61.8	29	42	1.3	4	459	380	.12	.08	.3	14
18		Pared fruit (refuse: core, stem, thin parings)	14	216	.8	1.2	56.3	23	39	1.2	4	429	160	.11	.07	.3	8
		Canned. See Applesauce, items 28–29.															
19		Dehydrated, sulfured (2.5% moisture)	0	1,601	6.4	9.1	417.8	181	299	9.1	32	3,311	—	.23	.28	2.6	47
21		Dried, sulfured (24.0% moisture)	0	1,247	4.5	7.3	325.7	141	236	7.3	23	2,581	—	.26	.53	2.3	48
24		Frozen, sliced, sweetened	0	422	.9	.5	110.2	23	27	2.3	[4]64	308	80	.05	.14	1.0	31
26		Apple butter	0	844	1.8	3.6	212.3	64	163	3.2	9	1,143	0	.05	.09	.7	9
27		Apple juice, canned or bottled	0	213	.5	.1	54.0	27	41	2.7	5	458	—	.03	.07	.4	4
		Applesauce, canned:															
28		Unsweetened or artificially sweetened	0	186	.9	.9	49.0	18	23	2.3	9	354	180	.08	.05	.2	5
29		Sweetened	0	413	.9	.5	108.0	18	23	2.3	9	295	180	.05	.05	.2	5
		Apricots:															
30		Raw (12 per lb.) (refuse: pits)	6	217	4.3	.9	54.8	72	98	2.1	4	1,198	11,510	.14	.16	2.6	42
31		Candied	0	1,533	2.7	.9	392.4	—	—	—	—	—	—	—	—	—	—
		Canned, solids and liquid:															
32		Water pack, with or without artificial sweetener	0	172	3.2	.5	43.5	64	73	1.4	5	1,116	8,310	.09	.10	1.7	18
33		Juice pack	0	245	4.5	.9	61.7	77	104	2.3	5	1,642	12,250	.12	.13	2.5	27

	Sirup pack:															
34	Light	0	299	3.2	.5	76.2	50	68	1.4	5	1,084	8,080	.08	.10	1.6	18
35	Heavy	0	390	2.7	.5	99.8	50	68	1.4	5	1,061	7,920	.08	.10	1.6	17
36	Extra heavy	0	458	2.7	.5	117.9	50	68	1.4	5	1,043	7,780	.08	.10	1.6	17
37	Dehydrated, sulfured, nugget-type and pieces (3.5% moisture).	0	1,506	25.4	4.5	383.7	390	631	24.0	150	5,715	63,960	Trace	.36	16.2	69
39	Dried, sulfured (25.0% moisture)	0	1,179	22.7	2.3	301.6	304	490	24.9	118	4,441	49,440	.06	.71	14.9	57
42	Frozen, sweetened	0	445	3.2	.5	113.9	45	86	4.1	18	1,039	7,620	.09	.18	3.5	[7] 125
43	**Apricot nectar**, canned (approx. 40% fruit)[5]	0	259	1.4	.5	66.2	41	54	.9	Trace	685	4,310	.05	.03	.9	12
44	**Artichokes, globe or French**, raw (refuse: stem and inedible part of bracts and flower).	60	(8)	5.3	.4	[9] 19.2	93	160	2.4	78	780	290	.14	.09	1.7	22
	Artichokes, Jerusalem. See Jerusalem-artichokes, item 1150															
	Asparagus:															
46	Raw spears (refuse: butt ends)	44	66	6.4	.5	12.7	56	157	2.5	5	706	2,290	.46	.51	3.9	84
	Canned spears:															
	Green, solids and liquid:															
48	Regular pack	0	82	8.6	1.4	13.2	82	195	7.7	[10] 1,070	753	2,310	.29	.42	3.7	68
51	Special dietary pack (low-sodium)	0	73	9.1	.9	12.2	82	195	7.7	14	753	2,310	.29	.42	3.7	68
	White (bleached) solids and liquid:															
54	Regular pack	0	82	7.3	1.4	15.0	68	150	4.1	[10] 1,070	635	230	.23	.26	3.2	68
57	Special dietary pack (low-sodium)	0	73	6.4	.9	13.6	68	150	4.1	18	635	230	.23	.26	3.2	68
	Frozen:															
60	Cuts and tips	0	104	15.0	.9	16.3	104	299	5.9	9	1,084	3,860	.73	.64	5.3	114
62	Spears	0	109	15.0	.9	17.7	104	313	5.4	9	1,175	3,540	.82	.68	5.7	132
	Avocados, raw:															
64	All commercial varieties[11] (refuse: seed, skin)	25	568	7.1	55.8	21.4	34	143	2.0	14	2,055	990	.37	.67	5.4	48
65	California, mainly Fuerte (refuse: seed, skin)	24	589	7.6	58.6	20.7	34	145	2.1	14	2,082	1,000	.37	.68	5.5	49
66	Florida (refuse: seed, skin)	33	389	4.0	33.4	26.7	30	128	1.8	12	1,836	880	.33	.60	4.9	43
	Baby foods:[12]															
	Cereals, precooked, dry, and other cereal products:															
67	Barley, added nutrients	0	1,579	60.8	5.4	333.8	3,338	3,724	241.3	2,050	1,873	(0)	16.83	5.46	146.1	(0)
68	High protein, added nutrients	0	1,619	159.7	16.8	218.2	3,697	4,101	286.2	2,962	4,890	—	16.65	5.22	108.9	(0)
69	Mixed, added nutrients	0	1,669	68.9	13.2	320.2	3,720	3,361	255.8	2,132	1,565	—	14.27	6.11	101.1	(0)
70	Oatmeal, added nutrients	0	1,701	74.8	24.9	299.4	3,434	3,329	218.6	1,982	1,696	(0)	11.68	4.77	96.8	(0)
71	Rice, added nutrients	0	1,683	29.9	7.3	362.9	3,892	2,930	227.7	2,404	943	(0)	11.63	5.60	89.5	(0)
72	Teething biscuit	0	1,715	50.3	10.4	353.8	1,461	1,574	20.9	1,910	1,134	—	2.15	2.60	13.8	(0)
	Wheat. See Farina, instant-cooking: item 995.															
	Desserts, canned:															
73	Custard pudding, all flavors	0	454	10.4	8.2	84.4	290	281	1.4	680	426	450	.09	.54	.6	3
74	Fruit pudding with starch base, milk, and/or egg (banana, orange, or pineapple).	0	435	5.4	4.1	98.0	122	154	1.4	581	340	450	.14	.20	.7	12
	Dinners, canned:															
	Cereal, vegetable, meat mixtures (approx. 2%–4% protein):															
75	Beef noodle dinner	0	218	12.7	5.0	30.8	54	132	2.3	1,220	721	2,810	.10	.21	2.3	9
76	Cereal, egg yolk, and bacon	0	372	13.2	22.2	29.9	132	272	3.6	1,365	163	2,360	.23	.27	1.6	—
77	Chicken noodle dinner	0	222	9.5	5.9	32.7	122	136	1.4	1,347	191	3,630	.16	.26	2.0	5
78	Macaroni, tomatoes, meat, and cereal	0	304	11.8	9.1	43.5	95	159	2.3	1,728	349	2,270	.64	.54	4.4	5
79	Split peas, vegetables, and ham or bacon	0	363	18.1	9.5	50.8	132	358	3.2	1,338	508	2,720	.39	.22	2.4	5
80	Vegetables and bacon, with cereal	0	308	7.7	13.2	39.5	77	127	2.7	1,279	590	9,980	.30	.22	2.9	5
81	Vegetables and beef, with cereal	0	254	12.2	7.3	34.5	77	177	3.6	1,393	649	12,700	.14	.20	3.9	5
82	Vegetables and chicken, with cereal	0	236	9.5	6.4	34.9	150	150	1.8	1,393	249	4,540	.12	.18	2.3	2
83	Vegetables and ham, with cereal	0	290	12.7	10.0	37.6	113	191	1.4	1,633	408	4,540	.34	.22	2.1	14
84	Vegetables and lamb, with cereal	0	263	10.0	9.1	34.9	104	168	3.2	1,220	671	9,980	.14	.24	3.2	5
85	Vegetables and liver, with cereal	0	213	14.1	1.8	35.4	77	259	12.2	1,070	735	21,320	.17	1.70	7.4	14
86	Vegetables and liver, with bacon and cereal	0	259	10.9	8.6	34.0	50	191	11.8	1,288	594	20,870	.15	1.48	6.0	9
87	Vegetables and turkey, with cereal	0	200	9.5	3.6	32.7	100	118	1.4	1,393	209	1,810	.05	.14	1.7	5
	Meat or poultry (approx. 6%–8% protein).															
88	Beef with vegetables	0	395	33.6	16.8	27.2	59	381	5.4	1,379	513	4,990	.33	.77	7.1	9
89	Chicken with vegetables	0	454	33.6	20.9	32.7	100	386	4.1	1,202	322	4,540	.39	.69	7.3	9
90	Turkey with vegetables	0	390	30.4	14.5	34.5	172	286	2.7	1,579	553	4,540	.57	.57	8.2	9
91	Veal with vegetables	0	286	32.2	7.3	23.1	50	322	3.6	1,465	431	3,630	.39	.68	9.2	9
	Fruits and fruit products, with or without thickening, canned															
92	Applesauce	0	327	.9	.9	84.4	18	32	1.8	27	290	180	.06	.08	.2	2
93	Applesauce and apricots[6]	0	390	1.4	.5	102.5	18	64	1.4	(3)	476	2,720	.05	.08	.6	9

[1] Average for fully ripened fruit grown in Florida, Puerto Rico, Hawaii, range is from 3,700 to 7,400 mg. per pound. At firm-ripe stage, average is 7,100 mg., range, 4,500 to 10,000 mg. At partially ripe stage, average is 9,300 mg., range, 4,500 to 16,700. See also Notes on Foods, p. 178.

[2] Average for juice from ripe fruit, range is from 4,500 to 10,000 mg. per pound.

[3] Average for juice from ripe fruit, range is from 3,100 to 6,800 mg. per pound.

[4] Almost all of catch is canned as tuna.

[5] See Notes on Foods, p. 174 for Apples; p. 177 for items 43 and 93.

[6] Average weighted in accordance with commercial freezing practices. See also Notes on Foods, p. 177.

[7] Average weighted in accordance with commercial freezing practices. For products without added ascorbic acid, average is about 41 mg. per pound; for those with added ascorbic acid, about 295 mg.

[8] Values may range from 16 Calories per pound for freshly harvested raw artichokes to as many as 85 for stored.

[9] A large proportion of the carbohydrate in the unstored product may be inulin, which is of doubtful availability. During storage, inulin is converted to sugars.

[10] Estimated average based on addition of salt in the amount of 0.6 percent of the finished product.

[11] Values weighted according to production, estimated as 90 percent from California, 10 percent from Florida.

[12] Values for items in this group apply to both strained and chopped (or junior) foods, unless otherwise specified.

TABLE 2.—NUTRIENTS IN THE EDIBLE PORTION OF 1 POUND OF FOOD AS PURCHASED—Continued

[Numbers in parentheses denote values imputed—usually from another form of the food or from a similar food. Zero in parentheses indicates that the amount of a constituent probably is none or is too small to measure. Dashes denote lack of reliable data for a constituent believed to be present in measurable amount. Calculated values, as those based on a recipe, are not in parentheses]

Item No.	Food and description	Refuse	Food energy	Protein	Fat	Carbohydrate total	Calcium	Phosphorus	Iron	Sodium	Potassium	Vitamin A value	Thiamine	Riboflavin	Niacin	Ascorbic Acid
(A)	(B)	(C)	(D)	(E)	(F)	(G)	(H)	(I)	(J)	(K)	(L)	(M)	(N)	(O)	(P)	(Q)
	Baby foods[12]—Continued	Percent	Calories	Grams	Grams	Grams	Milligrams	Milligrams	Milligrams	Milligrams	Milligrams	International units	Milligrams	Milligrams	Milligrams	Milligrams
	Fruits and fruit products, with or without thickening, canned—Continued															
94	Bananas (with tapioca or cornstarch, added ascorbic acid), strained	0	281	1.8	0.9	96.6	59	45	0.9	132	535	320	0.07	0.08	0.8	157
95	Bananas and pineapple (with tapioca or cornstarch)	0	365	1.8	.5	93.9	91	54	.9	265	327	140	.06	.05	.5	9
96	Fruit dessert with tapioca (apricot, pineapple, and/or orange)	0	391	1.4	1.4	97.5	68	41	1.8	240	331	2,040	.08	.05	.8	18
97	Peaches	0	367	2.7	.9	93.9	27	63	1.4	(9)	363	2,270	.07	.10	3.4	14
98	Pears	0	299	1.4	.5	77.6	32	36	.9	18	281	140	.07	.10	.8	9
99	Pears and pineapple	0	313	1.8	.9	78.8	32	41	.9	(9)	327	90	.11	.09	.9	9
100	Plums with tapioca, strained	0	429	1.8	.9	110.2	23	54	1.8	172	290	1,130	.06	.11	1.0	9
101	Prunes with tapioca	0	390	1.4	.9	101.6	32	95	4.1	150	544	1,810	.08	.25	2.0	18
	Meats, poultry, and eggs, canned:															
	Beef:															
102	Strained	0	449	64.7	18.1	(0)	36	576	9.1	1,644	830	—	.07	.73	15.8	0
103	Junior	0	545	87.5	17.7	(0)	36	739	11.3	1,284	1,068	—	.07	.92	19.4	0
104	Beef heart	0	422	61.2	17.2	1.8	23	703	16.8	944	—	—	.22	2.81	16.4	0
105	Chicken	0	576	67.1	34.5	(0)	—	585	8.6	1,193	435	—	.07	.72	15.7	0
106	Egg yolks, strained	0	955	45.4	81.6	.5	367	1,161	18.6	1,248	268	8,620	.53	1.00	.2	Trace
107	Egg yolks with ham or bacon	0	943	45.4	82.1	1.4	322	839	12.7	1,450	372	5,620	.46	1.04	2.5	—
	Lamb:															
108	Strained	0	485	66.2	22.2	(0)	41	582	9.5	1,093	821	—	.09	.78	14.8	—
109	Junior	0	549	79.4	23.1	(0)	36	708	12.2	1,334	1,034	—	.11	.98	18.4	—
110	Liver, strained	0	440	64.6	15.4	6.8	27	826	25.4	1,148	916	108,840	.21	9.09	34.5	45
111	Liver and bacon, strained	0	558	62.1	29.9	5.9	27	712	19.1	1,370	871	95,790	.24	9.01	35.6	32
	Pork:															
112	Strained	0	535	69.6	26.3	(0)	36	590	6.8	1,017	807	—	.87	.89	12.3	—
113	Junior	0	608	84.4	27.2	(0)	36	653	5.4	1,075	953	—	1.04	1.08	12.7	—
	Veal:															
114	Strained	0	413	70.3	12.2	(0)	45	658	7.7	1,025	971	—	.15	.92	19.5	—
115	Junior	0	455	85.5	13.6	(0)	56	712	7.3	1,252	934	—	.12	1.02	27.4	—
	Vegetables, canned:															
116	Beans, green	0	100	6.4	.5	23.1	150	113	5.9	966	421	1,810	.11	.29	1.6	11
117	Beets, strained	0	168	6.4	.5	37.6	82	122	3.2	952	1,034	90	.07	.15	.6	14
118	Carrots	0	132	3.2	.5	30.8	104	95	2.3	767	821	58,970	.09	.15	2.0	12
119	Mixed vegetables, including vegetable soup	0	168	7.3	1.4	38.6	100	163	4.1	1,234	771	21,320	.23	.20	2.7	9
120	Peas, strained	0	245	19.1	.9	42.2	50	286	5.4	880	454	2,270	.37	.40	5.7	45
121	Spinach, creamed	0	195	10.4	3.2	34.0	290	286	2.7	1,251	644	22,680	.11	.59	1.2	29
122	Squash	0	113	3.2	.5	28.1	109	77	1.8	1,325	626	16,880	.09	.20	1.3	36
123	Sweetpotatoes	0	304	4.5	.9	70.3	75	154	1.8	848	816	22,230	.17	.14	1.6	36
124	Tomato soup, strained	0	245	8.6	.5	61.2	109	236	1.8	1,334	1,361	4,540	.23	.05	3.1	14
	Bacon, cured:															
125	Raw:															
a	Sliced	0	2,016	38.1	314.3	4.5	59	490	5.4	3,084	590	(0)	1.64	.52	8.2	—
b	Slab (refuse: rind)	6	2,836	35.8	295.5	4.3	55	461	5.1	2,990	554	(0)	1.54	.49	7.8	—
127	Canned	0	3,167	38.6	324.3	4.5	68	417	6.4	—	—	(0)	1.06	.44	6.8	—
128	**Bacon, Canadian,** unheated	0	980	90.7	65.3	1.4	54	816	13.6	8,578	1,778	(0)	3.75	1.01	21.2	—
	Baking powders:[13]															
	Home use:[14]															
	Sodium aluminum sulfate:															
130	With monocalcium phosphate monohydrate	0	585	.5	Trace	141.5	8,764	13,175	—	49,083	680	(0)	(0)	(0)	(0)	(0)
131	With monocalcium phosphate monohydrate and calcium carbonate	0	354	.5	Trace	85.7	26,209	6,586	—	52,689	—	(0)	(0)	(0)	(0)	(0)
132	With monocalcium phosphate monohydrate and calcium sulfate	0	472	.5	Trace	113.9	28,668	7,076	—	45,360	—	(0)	(0)	(0)	(0)	(0)
133	Straight phosphate	0	549	.5	Trace	132.9	28,482	42,811	—	37,286	771	(0)	(0)	(0)	(0)	(0)
	Tartrate:															
134	Cream of tartar, with tartaric acid	0	354	.5	Trace	85.7	0	0	0	33,113	17,237	(0)	(0)	(0)	(0)	(0)
135	Special low-sodium preparation, commercial powder	0	780	.5	Trace	188.7	21,845	33,149	—	[15] 27	49,669	(0)	(0)	(0)	(0)	(0)

No.		Food															
		Commercial use:															
		Pyrophosphate:															
137		No additional leavening acid	0	494	.5	Trace	120.2	0	54,223	—	76,223	—	(0)	(0)	(0)	(0)	(0)
138		With monocalcium phosphate monohydrate	0	476	.5	Trace	115.7	4,082	55,543	—	73,529	—	(0)	(0)	(0)	(0)	(0)
139		With monocalcium phosphate monohydrate and calcium lactate.	0	467	.5	Trace	113.4	[15] 4,504	52,527	—	72,336	—	(0)	(0)	(0)	(0)	(0)
140		**Bamboo shoots, raw** (refuse: sheaths)	71	36	3.4	.4	6.8	17	78	.7	—	701	30	.19	.09	.8	5
		Bananas:															
		Raw:															
141		Common:															
	a	Good quality (refuse: skin)	32	262	3.4	.6	68.5	25	80	2.2	3	1,141	590	.14	.18	2.2	31
	b	Fair quality (refuse: skin, defects)	45	212	2.7	.5	55.4	20	65	1.7	2	923	470	.12	.15	1.7	25
142		Red (refuse: skin)	(32)	278	3.7	.6	72.2	31	56	2.5	3	1,141	1,230	.15	.12	1.8	(31)
143		Dehydrated, or banana powder (3.0% moisture)	0	1,542	20.0	3.6	401.9	145	472	12.7	18	6,700	3,450	.82	1.07	12.7	29
		Bananas, baking type. See Plantain, item 1634.															
		Barbados-cherry. See Acerola, item 3.															
144		**Barbecue sauce**	0	413	6.8	31.3	36.3	95	91	3.6	3,697	789	1,630	.03	.05	1.5	23
		Barley, pearled															
145		Light	0	1,583	37.2	4.5	357.4	73	857	9.1	14	726	(0)	.55	.23	14.1	(0)
146		Pot or Scotch	0	1,579	43.5	5.0	350.2	154	1,315	12.2	—	1,343	(0)	.93	.32	16.8	(0)
147		**Barracuda, Pacific,** flesh only, raw	0	513	95.3	11.8	0	—	—	—	—	—	—	—	—	—	—
		Basella. See Vinespinach, item 2408.															
148		**Bass, black sea, raw:**															
	a	Whole (refuse: head, tail, fins, entrails, scales, bones, and skin).	61	165	34.0	2.1	0	—	—	—	120	453	—	—	—	—	—
	b	Flesh only	0	422	87.1	5.4	0	—	—	—	308	1,161	—	—	—	—	—
150		**Bass, smallmouth and largemouth, raw**															
	a	Whole (refuse: head, fins, entrails, skin, and bones)	69	146	26.6	3.7	0	—	270	—	—	—	—	.14	.04	3.0	—
	b	Flesh only	0	472	85.7	11.8	0	—	871	—	—	—	—	.46	.13	9.6	—
151		**Bass, striped, raw:**															
	a	Whole (refuse: head, tail, entrails, scales, bones, and skin).	57	205	36.9	5.3	0	—	413	—	—	—	—	—	—	—	—
	b	Flesh only	0	476	85.7	12.2	0	—	962	—	—	—	—	—	—	—	—
153		**Bass, white, raw:**															
	a	Whole (refuse: head, tail, entrails, fins, scales, bones, and skin).	61	173	31.8	4.1	0	—	—	—	—	—	—	—	—	—	—
	b	Flesh only	0	445	81.6	10.4	0	—	—	—	—	—	—	—	—	—	—
		Beans, broad. See Broadbeans, items 481–482.															
		Beans, common, mature seeds, dry:															
		White.															
154		Raw	0	1,542	101.2	7.3	278.1	653	1,928	35.4	86	5,425	0	2.96	1.02	10.8	—
		Canned, solids and liquid:															
156		With pork and tomato sauce	0	553	27.7	11.8	86.2	245	417	8.2	2,100	953	590	.34	.14	2.6	9
157		With pork and sweet sauce	0	680	28.1	21.3	95.7	286	517	10.4	1,724	—	—	.26	.20	2.3	—
158		Without pork	0	544	28.6	2.3	104.3	308	549	9.1	1,533	1,216	270	.32	.16	2.5	9
		Red.															
159		Raw	0	1,556	102.1	6.8	280.8	499	1,842	31.3	45	4,463	90	2.33	.92	10.6	—
161		Canned, solids and liquid	0	408	25.9	1.8	74.4	132	494	8.2	14	1,198	Trace	.23	.18	2.7	—
162		Pinto, calico, and red Mexican, raw	0	1,583	103.9	5.4	288.9	612	2,073	29.0	45	4,463	—	3.80	.95	10.0	—
163		Other, including black, brown, and Bayo, raw	0	1,538	101.2	6.8	277.6	612	1,905	35.8	113	4,708	140	2.51	.91	9.8	—
		Beans, hyacinth. See Hyacinth-beans, items 1137–1138.															
		Beans, lima:															
		Immature seeds															
164		Raw:															
	a	In pod (refuse: pods)	60	223	15.2	.9	40.1	94	258	5.1	4	1,179	530	.43	.22	2.5	52
	b	Shelled	0	558	38.1	2.3	100.2	236	644	12.7	9	2,948	1,320	1.08	.55	6.4	130
		Canned, solids and liquid:															
166		Regular pack	0	322	18.6	1.4	60.8	118	304	10.9	[10] 1,070	1,007	590	.16	.20	2.4	32
169		Special dietary pack (low-sodium)	0	318	20.0	1.4	58.5	118	304	10.9	18	1,007	590	.16	.20	2.4	32
		Frozen:															
172		Thick-seeded types, commonly called Fordhooks.	0	463	28.1	.5	88.5	104	435	8.6	[17] 585	2,223	1,040	.45	.27	5.4	101
174		Thin-seeded types, commonly called baby limas.	0	553	34.5	.9	104.3	172	594	12.7	[17] 667	1,987	1,000	.45	.27	5.6	85
176		Mature seeds, dry, raw	0	1,565	92.5	7.3	290.3	327	1,746	35.4	18	6,936	Trace	2.17	.75	8.6	—
178		**Bean flour, lima**	0	1,556	97.5	6.4	285.8	—	—	—	—	—	(0)	—	—	—	(0)
		Beans, mung, raw															
179		Mature seeds, dry	0	1,542	109.8	5.9	273.5	535	1,542	34.9	27	4,663	360	1.71	.96	11.7	—
180		Sprouted seeds	0	159	17.2	.9	29.9	86	290	5.9	23	1,012	90	.60	.61	3.4	86

[8] See Notes on Foods, p. 177.

[10] Estimated average based on addition of salt in the amount of 0.6 percent of the finished product.

[13] Values for energy and proximate constituents are based on starch content.

[14] List of ingredients on label indicates type of baking powder.

[15] Values based on single brand.

[16] Calcium content depends largely on amount of monocalcium phosphate in the product. Values range from 900 to 7,300 mg. per pound.

[17] Average weighted in accordance with commercial practices in freezing vegetables. See also Notes on Foods, p. 177.

TABLE 2.—NUTRIENTS IN THE EDIBLE PORTION OF 1 POUND OF FOOD AS PURCHASED—Continued

[Numbers in parentheses denote values imputed—usually from another form of the food or from a similar food. Zero in parentheses indicates that the amount of a constituent probably is none or is too small to measure. Dashes denote lack of reliable data for a constituent believed to be present in measurable amount. Calculated values, as those based on a recipe, are not in parentheses]

Item No. (A)		Food and description (B)	Refuse (C)	Food energy (D)	Protein (E)	Fat (F)	Carbohydrate total (G)	Calcium (H)	Phosphorus (I)	Iron (J)	Sodium (K)	Potassium (L)	Vitamin A value (M)	Thiamine (N)	Riboflavin (O)	Niacin (P)	Ascorbic Acid (Q)
			Percent	Calories	Grams	Grams	Grams	Milligrams	Milligrams	Milligrams	Milligrams	Milligrams	International units	Milligrams	Milligrams	Milligrams	Milligrams
		Beans, snap:															
		Green:															
182		Raw (refuse: ends, strings, trimmings)	12	128	7.6	0.8	28.3	225	178	3.2	28	970	2,390	0.33	0.43	2.0	76
		Canned, solids and liquid:															
184		Regular pack	0	82	4.5	.5	19.1	154	95	6.4	[7] 1,070	431	1,430	.14	.19	1.4	18
186		Special dietary pack (low-sodium)	0	77	5.0	.5	18.3	154	95	9.4	9	431	1,320	.14	.19	1.4	18
		Frozen:															
191		Cut	0	118	7.7	.5	27.2	163	150	3.6	5	758	2,630	.32	.45	2.3	43
193		French style	0	122	7.3	.5	27.7	181	145	4.1	9	694	2,490	.32	.41	1.7	45
		Yellow or wax:															
195		Raw (refuse: ends, strings, trimmings)	12	108	6.8	.8	24.0	204	172	3.2	28	970	1,000	.32	.42	2.0	80
		Canned, solids and liquid:															
197		Regular pack	0	86	4.5	.9	19.1	154	95	5.4	[7] 1,070	431	270	.14	.18	1.4	23
200		Special dietary pack (low-sodium)	0	68	4.1	.5	15.4	(154)	(95)	(5.4)	9	431	(270)	(.14)	(.18)	(1.4)	(23)
203		Frozen, cut	0	127	8.2	.5	29.5	163	145	3.6	5	816	490	.28	.41	2.1	54
		Bean sprouts. See Beans, mung, item 180; and Soybeans, item 2143.															
205		Beans and frankfurters, canned	0	653	34.5	32.2	57.2	168	540	8.6	2,442	1,188	590	.30	.26	5.7	Trace
207		Beechnuts:															
	a	In shell (refuse: shells)	39	1,572	52.7	138.4	56.2	---	---	---	---	---	---	---	---	---	—
	b	Shelled	0	2,576	88.0	226.8	92.1	---	---	---	---	---	---	---	---	---	—
		Beef: [8]															
		Carcass, with bone, raw:															
		Total edible, including kidney and kidney fat:															
208		Prime grade, 47% lean, 39% fat	14	1,673	55.2	161	0	24	485	7.8			320	.21	.47	12.8	—
209		Choice grade, 51% lean, 34% fat	15	1,466	57.6	135	0	33	526	8.5			270	.25	.51	13.8	—
210		Good grade, 56% lean, 28% fat	15	1,228	62.7	106	0	28	578	9.5			210	.27	.56	15.1	—
211		Standard grade, 60% lean, 22% fat	18	965	67.4	79	0	37	621	10.1			150	.29	.60	16.2	—
212		Commercial grade, 54% lean, 31% fat	16	1,228	60.5	119	0	34	555	9.2			240	.26	.54	14.5	—
213		Utility grade, 62% lean, 20% fat	18	869	69.1	67	0	41	650	10.4			130	.30	.62	16.6	—
		Total edible, trimmed to retail level:															
214		Choice grade, 64% lean, 21% fat	15	1,165	67.3	97.1	0	39	623	10.1			200	.29	.60	16.2	—
215		Good grade, 66% lean, 19% fat	15	1,060	71.0	78.3	0	42	656	10.7			160	.30	.63	17.0	—
216		Standard grade, 68% lean, 15% fat	17	847	73.0	59.5	0	41	678	10.9			120	.32	.65	17.6	—
		Separable fat. See individual cuts.															
		Retail cuts, trimmed to retail level, raw:															
		Chuck cuts:															
		Entire chuck, 1st–5th ribs, arm, and neck:															
		Choice grade:															
218		Total edible:															
	a	With bone, 69% lean, 15% fat	16	984	71.6	75.0	0	42	726	10.7			150	.31	.64	17.2	—
	b	Without bone, 82% lean, 18% fat	0	1,166	84.8	88.9	0	50	853	12.7			180	.36	.75	20.4	—
220		Separable lean	0	717	96.6	33.6	0	54	971	14.5			70	.42	.86	23.2	—
222		Separable fat	0	3,248	23.5	346.1	0	16	327	4.5	(8)	(8)	560	.10	.27	7.2	—
		Chuck rib, 5th:															
		Choice grade:															
223		Total edible:															
	a	With bone, 59% lean, 25% fat	16	1,349	62.1	120.4	0	34	567	9.2			240	.27	.56	14.8	—
	b	Without bone, 70% lean, 30% fat	0	1,597	73.5	142.4	0	41	671	10.9			280	.32	.66	17.6	—
225		Separable lean	0	853	92.9	49.9	0	54	871	14.1			100	.41	.85	22.3	—
227		Separable fat	0	3,379	24.9	362.9	0	14	294	3.6			750	.11	.22	6.0	—
		Good grade:															
228		Total edible:															
	a	With bone, 62% lean, 22% fat	18	1,154	64.6	96.8	0	38	617	9.9			190	.29	.59	16.0	—
	b	Without bone, 74% lean, 26% fat	0	1,374	79.4	114.8	0	45	735	11.8			230	.34	.71	19.1	—
230		Separable lean	0	759	96.2	38.5	0	54	894	14.5			70	.41	.86	23.1	—
232		Separable fat	0	3,108	31.8	330.7	0	18	272	4.5			680	.14	.28	7.6	—
		Arm:															
		Choice grade:															
233		Total edible:															
	a	With bone, 77% lean, 12% fat	11	905	78.8	62.9	0	49	731	11.8			130	.34	.70	18.9	—
	b	Without bone, 86% lean, 14% fat	0	1,012	88.0	70.3	0	54	816	13.2			140	.38	.78	21.1	—
235		Separable lean	0	640	98.0	24.5	0	59	912	14.5			50	.42	.87	23.5	—

237		Separable fat	0	3,338	26.3	357.4	0	14	218	4.1			720	.11	.24	6.3	—
		Good grade:															
238		Total edible:															
	a	With bone, 79% lean, 10% fat	11	768	81.7	46.7	0	48	756	12.5			90	.35	.72	19.5	—
	b	Without bone, 89% lean, 11% fat	0	866	92.1	52.6	0	54	853	14.1			100	.39	.82	22.0	—
240		Separable lean	0	585	98.9	18.1	0	59	921	15.0			40	.43	.88	23.7	—
242		Separable fat	0	3,193	32.2	338.8	0	18	277	5.0			680	.14	.29	7.7	—
		Flank steak:															
		Choice grade:															
243		Total edible, 100% lean	0	653	98.0	25.9	0	59	912	14.5			50	.42	.87	23.5	—
		Good grade															
245		Total edible, 100% lean	0	631	98.9	23.1	0	59	921	15.0			50	.43	.88	23.7	—
		Hindshank:															
		Choice grade:															
247		Total edible															
	a	With bone, 31% lean, 15% fat	54	604	38.1	48.9	0	23	351	5.9			100	.16	.34	9.1	—
	b	Without bone, 67% lean, 33% fat	0	1,311	82.6	106.1	0	50	762	12.7			210	.35	.73	19.8	—
249		Separable lean	0	608	98.4	20.9	0	59	916	15.0			40	.42	.88	23.6	—
251		Separable fat	0	2,731	50.3	279.0	0	27	454	7.7			560	.22	.45	12.1	—
		Good grade															
252		Total edible:															
	a	With bone, 31% lean, 13% fat	56	478	39.4	34.4	0	24	364	6.0			70	.17	.35	9.5	—
	b	Without bone, 71% lean, 29% fat	0	1,084	89.4	78.0	0	54	826	13.6			150	.39	.79	21.5	—
254		Separable lean	0	572	98.9	16.8	0	59	921	15.0			30	.43	.88	23.7	—
256		Separable fat	0	2,345	65.8	228.6	0	36	590	10.0			460	.28	.59	15.8	—
		Loin or short loin:															
		Porterhouse steak:															
		Choice grade															
257		Total edible, with bone, 57% lean, 33% fat	9	1,603	60.8	148.8	0	33	559	9.0			300	.26	.55	14.6	—
259		Separable lean	0	744	95.7	37.2	0	54	889	14.5			70	.41	.85	23.0	—
261		Separable fat	0	3,524	19.1	381.5	0	9	150	2.7			760	.08	.17	4.6	—
		Good grade															
262		Total edible, with bone, 58% lean, 33% fat.	9	1,521	62.9	138.9	0	33	575	9.5			280	.27	.56	15.1	—
264		Separable lean	0	640	97.5	24.9	0	54	907	14.5			50	.42	.87	23.4	—
266		Separable fat	0	3,515	19.5	380.6	0	9	154	2.7			760	.08	.17	4.7	—
		T-bone steak															
		Choice grade															
267		Total edible, with bone, 55% lean, 34% fat	11	1,596	59.1	149.1	0	32	543	8.8			300	.25	.53	14.2	—
269		Separable lean	0	744	96.2	36.7	0	54	894	14.5			70	.41	.86	23.1	—
271		Separable fat	0	3,511	19.5	380.1	0	9	154	2.7	(18)	(19)	760	.08	.17	4.7	—
		Good grade															
272		Total edible, with bone, 56% lean, 32% fat	12	1,466	61.7	133.4	0	36	569	9.2			260	.27	.55	14.9	—
274		Separable lean	0	644	97.5	25.4	0	54	907	14.5			50	.42	.87	23.4	—
276		Separable fat	0	3,452	21.8	372.4	0	14	177	3.2			740	.10	.20	5.2	—
		Club steak:															
		Choice grade:															
277		Total edible, with bone, 54% lean, 30% fat.	16	1,443	58.9	132.1	0	34	539	8.7			260	.25	.52	14.1	—
279		Separable lean	0	826	94.3	46.7	0	54	875	14.1			100	.40	.84	22.6	—
281		Separable fat	0	3,316	27.2	354.7	0	14	227	4.1			710	.12	.24	6.5	—
		Good grade:															
282		Total edible, with bone, 58% lean, 24% fat.	18	1,210	63.1	104.2	0	37	582	9.7			210	.27	.56	15.1	—
284		Separable lean	0	717	96.2	34.0	0	54	894	14.5			70	.41	.86	23.1	—
286		Separable fat	0	3,248	29.9	345.6	0	18	254	4.5			690	.13	.27	7.2	—
		Loin end or sirloin:															
		Wedge and round-bone sirloin steak:															
		Choice grade															
287		Total edible:															
	a	With bone, 68% lean, 25% fat	7	1,316	71.1	112.3	0	42	652	10.5			220	.30	.63	17.1	—
	b	Without bone, 73% lean, 27% fat	0	1,420	76.7	121.1	0	45	703	11.3			240	.33	.68	18.4	—
289		Separable lean	0	649	97.5	25.9	0	54	907	14.5			50	.42	.87	23.4	—
291		Separable fat	0	3,506	20.0	379.2	0	14	159	3.2			760	.09	.18	4.8	—
		Good grade:															
292		Total edible.															
	a	With bone, 69% lean, 23% fat	8	1,175	74.4	94.9	0	42	686	11.3			190	.32	.66	17.9	—
	b	Without bone, 75% lean, 25% fat	0	1,275	80.7	103.0	0	45	744	12.2			210	.35	.72	19.4	—
294		Separable lean	0	585	98.9	18.1	0	59	921	15.0			40	.43	.88	23.7	—
296		Separable fat	0	3,375	24.9	362.4	0	14	204	3.6			730	.11	.22	6.0	—

[a] See Notes on Foods, p. 179.

[16] Estimated average based on addition of salt in the amount of 0.6 percent of the finished product.

[18] Average value for 1 pound, all cuts without bone or with a small proportion of bone, is 295 mg. For cuts with average bone content (15 percent), the value is 250 mg, for those with high bone content (as hindshanks), 135 mg. See also Notes on Foods, p. 179.

[19] Average value for 1 pound, all cuts without bone or with a small proportion of bone, is 1,610 mg For cuts with average bone content (15 percent), the value is 1,370 mg, for those with high bone content (as hindshanks), 740 mg. See also Notes on Foods, p. 179

TABLE 2.—NUTRIENTS IN THE EDIBLE PORTION OF 1 POUND OF FOOD AS PURCHASED—Continued

[Numbers in parentheses denote values imputed—usually from another form of the food or from a similar food. Zero in parentheses indicates that the amount of a constituent probably is none or is too small to measure. Dashes denote lack of reliable data for a constituent believed to be present in measurable amount. Calculated values, as those based on a recipe, are not in parentheses]

Item No.	Food and description	Refuse	Food energy	Protein	Fat	Carbo-hydrate total	Calcium	Phosphorus	Iron	Sodium	Potassium	Vitamin A value	Thiamine	Ribo-flavin	Niacin	Ascorbic Acid
(A)	(B)	(C)	(D)	(E)	(F)	(G)	(H)	(I)	(J)	(K)	(L)	(M)	(N)	(O)	(P)	(Q)
	Beef—Continued	Percent	Calories	Grams	Grams	Grams	Milligrams	Milligrams	Milligrams	Milligrams	Milligrams	International units	Milligrams	Milligrams	Milligrams	Milligrams
	Retail cuts, trimmed to retail level, raw—Con.															
	Loin end or sirloin—Continued															
	Double-bone sirloin steak:															
	Choice grade:															
297	Total edible:															
a	With bone, 59% lean, 23% fat	18	1,240	61.1	108.4	0	34	562	9.3			220	0.26	0.54	14.7	----
b	Without bone, 72% lean, 28% fat	0	1,510	74.4	132.0	0	41	685	11.3			260	.32	.66	17.9	----
299	Separable lean	0	717	96.6	33.6	0	54	898	14.5			70	.42	.86	23.2	----
301	Separable fat	0	4,397	16.3	391.0	0	9	122	2.3			780	.07	.15	3.9	----
	Good grade:															
302	Total edible:															
a	With bone, 60% lean, 21% fat	19	1,075	64.0	88.4	0	37	591	9.9			180	.28	.57	15.4	----
b	Without bone, 75% lean, 25% fat	0	1,329	79.5	109.3	0	45	730	12.2			220	.34	.71	19.1	----
304	Separable lean	0	612	98.4	21.3	0	59	916	15.0			40	.42	.88	23.6	----
306	Separable fat	0	3,407	24.0	366.1	0	14	195	3.6			730	.10	.21	5.8	----
	Hipbone sirloin steak:															
	Choice grade:															
307	Total edible:															
a	With bone, 51% lean, 33% fat	15	1,585	53.8	149.3	0	31	508	8.5			300	.21	.50	13.3	----
b	Without bone, 61% lean, 39% fat	0	1,869	63.8	176.0	0	36	599	10.0			350	.28	.59	15.7	----
309	Separable lean	0	812	91.8	44.9	0	54	880	14.1			90	.41	.84	22.8	----
311	Separable fat	0	3,497	20.4	377.8	0	14	163	3.2			760	.09	.18	4.9	----
	Good grade:															
312	Total edible:															
a	With bone, 54% lean, 31% fat	16	1,402	60.0	126.8	0	34	546	8.8			250	.26	.53	14.4	----
b	Without bone, 64% lean, 36% fat	0	1,665	71.2	150.6	0	41	649	10.4			300	.31	.63	17.1	----
314	Separable lean	0	689	97.1	30.4	0	54	905	14.5			60	.42	.86	23.3	----
316	Separable fat	0	3,375	24.9	362.4	0	14	201	3.6			730	.11	.22	6.0	----
	Short plate:															
	Choice grade:															
317	Total edible:															
a	With bone, 62% lean, 37% fat	11	1,615	59.7	150.6	0	32	545	8.9			300	.25	.53	14.4	----
b	Without bone, 59% lean, 41% fat	0	1,811	67.1	169.2	0	36	612	10.0	[illegible]	[illegible]	340	.29	.59	16.1	----
319	Separable lean	0	744	95.7	37.2	0	54	889	14.5			70	.41	.85	23.0	----
321	Separable fat	0	3,329	26.8	356.5	0	14	222	4.1			710	.11	.24	6.4	----
	Good grade:															
322	Total edible:															
a	With bone, 54% lean, 33% fat	15	1,413	65.9	126.6	0	36	583	9.5			250	.27	.57	15.3	----
b	Without bone, 62% lean, 38% fat	0	1,615	73.0	144.7	0	41	667	10.9			290	.31	.65	17.5	----
324	Separable lean	0	662	97.5	27.2	0	54	907	14.5			50	.42	.87	23.4	----
326	Separable fat	0	3,180	32.7	337.0	0	18	281	5.0			680	.14	.29	7.8	----
	Rib:															
	Entire rib, 6th–12th ribs:															
	Choice grade:															
327	Total edible:															
a	With bone, 59% lean, 33% fat	8	1,673	61.8	156.1	0	38	630	9.2			310	.27	.55	14.8	----
b	Without bone, 64% lean, 36% fat	0	1,819	67.1	169.6	0	41	685	10.0			340	.29	.60	16.1	----
329	Separable lean	0	875	93.9	52.6	0	54	943	14.1			100	.40	.83	22.5	----
331	Separable fat	0	3,458	21.8	372.9	0	14	245	3.2			740	.10	.19	5.2	----
	Ribs, 11th–12th:															
	Choice grade:															
332	Total edible:															
a	With bone, 51% lean, 41% fat	8	1,843	56.9	177.2	0	33	515	8.7			360	.24	.51	13.7	----
b	Without bone, 55% lean, 45% fat	0	2,014	62.1	193.7	0	36	562	9.5			390	.27	.55	14.9	----
334	Separable lean	0	871	93.9	52.2	0	54	871	14.1			100	.40	.83	22.5	----
336	Separable fat	0	3,429	22.7	368.7	0	11	186	2.6			740	.10	.20	5.4	----
	Good grade:															
337	Total edible:															
a	With bone, 56% lean, 34% fat	10	1,535	63.3	140.0	0	37	580	9.4			280	.27	.57	15.2	----
b	Without bone, 63% lean, 37% fat	0	1,706	70.3	155.6	0	41	644	10.4			310	.30	.63	16.9	----
339	Separable lean	0	753	95.7	38.1	0	54	889	14.5			80	.41	.85	23.0	----
341	Separable fat	0	3,293	28.1	352.0	0	18	236	4.1			700	.12	.25	6.8	----

		Rib, 6th or blade:															
		Choice grade:															
342		Total edible.															
	a	With bone, 66% lean, 27% fat	7	1,523	67.1	137.2	0	38	613	10.1			280	.29	.60	16.1	—
	b	Without bone, 71% lean, 29% fat	0	1,647	72.6	148.3	0	41	662	10.9			300	.31	.64	17.4	—
344		Separable lean	0	907	93.0	56.7	0	54	862	14.1			110	.40	.83	22.3	—
346		Separable fat	0	3,466	21.3	374.2	0	14	172	3.2			750	.09	.19	5.1	—
		Good grade:															
347		Total edible:															
	a	With bone, 71% lean, 21% fat	8	1,256	73.3	104.7	0	42	678	10.9			210	.32	.65	17.6	—
	b	Without bone, 77% lean, 23% fat	0	1,361	79.4	113.4	0	45	735	11.8			230	.34	.71	19.1	—
349		Separable lean	0	762	95.7	39.0	0	54	889	14.5			80	.41	.85	23.0	—
351		Separable fat	0	3,361	25.4	360.6	0	14	209	3.6			720	.11	.23	6.1	—
		Round, entire (round and heel of round):															
		Choice grade															
352		Total edible:															
	a	With bone, 86% lean, 11% fat	3	863	88.5	53.9	0	53	890	13.1			110	.38	.79	21.3	—
	b	Without bone, 89% lean, 11% fat	0	894	91.6	55.8	0	54	921	13.6			110	.39	.82	22.0	—
354		Separable lean	0	612	98.0	21.3	0	59	984	14.5	[18]	[19]	40	.42	.87	23.5	—
356		Separable fat	0	3,157	34.0	333.8	0	18	363	5.0			670	.15	.30	8.2	—
		Rump:															
		Choice grade:															
357		Total edible:															
	a	With bone, 63% lean, 22% fat	15	1,167	67.0	97.4	0	39	616	10.0			190	.29	.60	16.1	—
	b	Without bone, 75% lean, 25% fat	0	1,374	78.9	114.8	0	45	726	11.8			230	.34	.70	19.0	—
359		Separable lean	0	717	96.2	34.0	0	54	894	14.5			70	.41	.86	23.1	—
361		Separable fat	0	3,293	28.1	352.0	0	18	236	4.1			700	.12	.25	6.8	—
		Good grade.															
362		Total edible:															
	a	With bone, 64% lean, 20% fat	16	1,037	70.1	81.9	0	42	643	10.3			160	.30	.62	16.8	—
	b	Without bone, 76% lean, 24% fat	0	1,229	83.0	97.1	0	50	762	12.2			200	.36	.73	19.9	—
364		Separable lean	0	640	98.0	24.5	0	59	912	14.5			50	.42	.87	23.5	—
366		Separable fat	0	3,139	34.0	332.0	0	18	295	5.0			660	.15	.30	8.2	—
		Hamburger (ground beef), raw:															
367		Lean	0	812	93.9	45.4	0	54	871	14.1	—	—	90	.40	.83	22.5	—
369		Regular ground	0	1,216	81.2	96.2	0	45	708	12.2	—	1,070	160	.35	.72	19.5	—
372		**Beef and vegetable stew, canned**	0	358	26.3	14.1	32.2	54	204	4.1	1,864	789	4,400	.13	.23	4.4	15
373		**Beef, canned, roast beef**	0	1,016	113.	59	0	73	526	10.9	—	1,175	—	.09	1.04	19.1	0
		Beef, corned, boneless															
374		Uncooked, medium-fat	0	1,329	71.7	113.	0	41	567	10.9	5,897	272	—	.14	.68	7.7	0
		Canned:															
376		Fat	0	1,193	106.6	82.	0	86	445	18.1	—	—	—	.05	1.00	14.5	0
377		Medium-fat	0	980	114.8	54.	0	91	481	19.5	—	—	—	.09	1.09	15.4	0
378		Lean	0	839	119.8	36.	0	95	499	20.4	—	—	—	.09	1.13	15.9	0
379		Canned corned-beef hash (with potato)	0	821	39.9	51.3	48.5	59	304	9.1	2,449	907	—	.05	.42	9.6	—
380		**Beef, dried, chipped**	0	921	155.6	28.6	0	91	1,833	23.1	19,505	907	—	(.32)	(1.45)	(17.2)	0
		Beef, potted. See Sausage, cold cuts, and luncheon meats: item 2008.															
383		**Beef potpie, frozen**	0	871	33.1	44.9	81.6	45	218	4.5	1,660	422	1,860	.15	.28	5.2	Trace
		Beer. See Beverages, item 394.															
		Beets, common, red															
384		Raw															
	a	With tops (refuse: tops, parings)	60	78	2.9	.2	18.0	29	60	1.3	109	608	40	.05	.09	.7	18
	b	With part tops (refuse: part tops, parings)	51	96	3.6	.2	22.0	36	73	1.6	133	745	50	.07	.10	.8	22
	c	Without tops (refuse: parings)	30	137	5.1	.3	31.4	51	105	2.2	190	1,064	80	.10	.15	1.2	32
		Canned, solids and liquid.															
386		Regular pack	0	154	4.1	.5	35.8	64	77	2.7	[16]1,070	758	50	.04	.11	.6	14
389		Special dietary pack (low-sodium)	0	145	4.1	Trace	35.4	64	77	2.7	209	758	50	.04	.11	.6	14
392		**Beet greens,** common, raw (refuse: stems, bruised and tough leaves).	44	61	5.6	.8	11.7	302	102	8.4	330	1,448	15,490	.24	.55	1.0	76
		Beverages, alcoholic and carbonated nonalcoholic:															
		Alcoholic															
394		Beer, alcohol 4.5% by volume (3.6% by weight)	0	[20]191	1.4	0	17.2	23	136	Trace	32	113	—	.01	.13	2.9	—
		Gin, rum; vodka; whisky:															
395		80-proof (33.4% alcohol by weight)	0	[20]1,048	—	—	Trace	—	—	—	5	9	—	—	—	—	—
396		86-proof (36.0% alcohol by weight)	0	[20]1,129	—	—	Trace	—	—	—	5	9	—	—	—	—	—
397		90-proof (37.9% alcohol by weight)	0	[20]1,193	—	—	Trace	—	—	—	5	9	—	—	—	—	—
398		94-proof (39.7% alcohol by weight)	0	[20]1,247	—	—	Trace	—	—	—	5	9	—	—	—	—	—
399		100-proof (42.5% alcohol by weight)	0	[20]1,338	—	—	Trace	—	—	—	5	9	—	—	—	—	—

[16] Estimated average based on addition of salt in the amount of 0.6 percent of the finished product.

[18] Average value for 1 pound, all cuts without bone or with a small proportion of bone, is 295 mg For cuts with average bone content (15 percent), the value is 250 mg.; for those with high bone content (as hindshanks), 135 mg. See also Notes on Foods, p. 179.

[19] Average value for 1 pound, all cuts without bone or with a small proportion of bone, is 1,610 mg. For cuts with average bone content (15 percent), the value is 1,370 mg ; for those with high bone content (as hindshanks), 740 mg. See also Notes on Foods, p 179

[20] See Notes on Foods, p. 181 concerning calculation of energy values.

TABLE 2.—NUTRIENTS IN THE EDIBLE PORTION OF 1 POUND OF FOOD AS PURCHASED—Continued

[Numbers in parentheses denote values imputed—usually from another form of the food or from a similar food. Zero in parentheses indicates that the amount of a constituent probably is none or is too small to measure. Dashes denote lack of reliable data for a constituent believed to be present in measurable amount. Calculated values, as those based on a recipe, are not in parentheses]

Item No.	Food and description	Refuse	Food energy	Protein	Fat	Carbohydrate total	Calcium	Phosphorus	Iron	Sodium	Potassium	Vitamin A value	Thiamine	Riboflavin	Niacin	Ascorbic acid
(A)	(B)	(C)	(D)	(E)	(F)	(G)	(H)	(I)	(J)	(K)	(L)	(M)	(N)	(O)	(P)	(Q)
	Beverages, alcoholic and carbonated nonalcoholic—Continued	Percent	Calories	Grams	Grams	Grams	Milligrams	Milligrams	Milligrams	Milligrams	Milligrams	International units	Milligrams	Milligrams	Milligrams	Milligrams
	Alcoholic—Continued															
	Wines:															
400	Dessert, alcohol 18.8% by volume (15.3% by weight)	0	621	0.5	0	34.5	36	—	—	18	340	—	0.05	0.09	0.9	—
401	Table, alcohol 12.2% by volume (9.9% by weight)	0	386	.5	0	19.1	41	45	1.8	23	417	—	Trace	.05	.5	—
	Carbonated, nonalcoholic:															
	Carbonated waters:															
402	Sweetened (quinine sodas)	0	141	(0)	(0)	36.3	—	—	—	—	—	(0)	(0)	(0)	(0)	(0)
403	Unsweetened (club sodas)	0	0	(0)	(0)	0	—	—	—	—	—	(0)	(0)	(0)	(0)	(0)
404	Cola type	0	177	(0)	(0)	45.4	—	—	—	—	—	(0)	(0)	(0)	(0)	(0)
405	Cream sodas	0	195	(0)	(0)	49.9	—	—	—	—	—	(0)	(0)	(0)	(0)	(0)
406	Fruit-flavored sodas (citrus, cherry, grape, strawberry, Tom Collins mixer, other) (10%–13% sugar)	0	209	(0)	(0)	54.4	—	—	—	—	—	(0)	(0)	(0)	(0)	(0)
407	Ginger ale, pale dry and golden	0	141	(0)	(0)	36.3	—	—	—	—	—	(0)	(0)	(0)	(0)	(0)
408	Root beer	0	186	(0)	(0)	47.6	—	—	—	—	—	(0)	(0)	(0)	(0)	(0)
409	Special dietary drinks with artificial sweetener (less than 1 Calorie per ounce)	0	—	(0)	(0)	—	—	—	—	—	—	(0)	(0)	(0)	(0)	(0)
	Biscuits, baking powder, baked from home-type recipe, made with—															
410	Enriched flour	0	1,674	33.6	77.1	207.7	549	794	7.3	2,840	531	Trace	.54	.86	8.1	Trace
411	Unenriched flour	0	1,674	33.6	77.1	207.7	549	794	2.3	2,840	531	Trace	.10	.47	2.1	Trace
412	Self-rising flour, enriched	0	1,687	32.2	78.9	208.7	848	1,438	7.7	2,994	259	Trace	1.01	1.09	9.7	Trace
	Biscuit dough, with enriched flour:															
413	Chilled in cans	0	1,256	22.1	25.0	210.5	240	2,234	7.7	3,937	245	Trace	1.30	.77	9.5	0
414	Frozen	0	1,480	25.9	54.0	221.8	322	1,811	8.4	4,128	360	Trace	.95	.78	7.6	Trace
	Biscuit mix with enriched flour and biscuits baked from mix:															
415	Mix, dry form	0	1,928	34.9	67.2	311.6	422	1,252	13.1	5,307	365	Trace	2.00	1.10	15.4	Trace
416	Biscuits, made with milk	0	1,474	32.2	42.2	237.2	358	1,057	10.4	4,115	526	Trace	1.23	1.18	8.9	Trace
417	Blackberries, including dewberries, boysenberries, and youngberries, raw (refuse: caps, damaged berries)	5	250	5.2	3.9	55.6	138	82	3.9	4	735	840	.13	.18	1.6	90
	Blackberries, canned, solids and liquid:															
418	Water pack, with or without artificial sweetener	0	181	3.6	2.7	40.8	100	59	2.7	5	522	640	.07	.09	1.0	32
419	Juice pack	0	245	3.6	3.6	54.9	114	77	4.1	5	771	680	.10	.14	1.5	18
	Sirup pack:															
420	Light	0	327	3.6	2.7	78.0	95	54	2.7	5	508	590	.08	.09	1.0	31
421	Heavy	0	413	3.6	2.7	100.7	95	54	2.7	5	494	580	.08	.09	1.0	30
422	Extra heavy	0	494	3.6	2.7	122.9	91	54	2.7	5	485	570	.05	.09	.9	29
	Blackberries, frozen. See Boysenberries, items 439–442.															
423	Blackberry juice, canned, unsweetened	0	168	1.4	2.7	35.4	54	54	(4.1)	(5)	(771)	—	(.10)	(.14)	(1.5)	(18)
	Blackeye peas. See Cowpeas, items 896–903.															
	Blackfish. See Tautog, item 2275.															
	Blueberries:															
424	Raw (refuse: stems, soft or withered berries)	8	259	2.9	2.1	63.8	63	54	4.2	4	338	420	(.13)	(.25)	(1.9)	58
	Canned, solids and liquid:															
425	Water pack, with or without artificial sweetener	0	177	2.3	.9	44.5	45	41	3.2	5	272	180	.06	.07	.9	30
426	Sirup pack, extra heavy	0	458	1.8	.9	117.5	41	36	2.7	5	249	170	.05	.05	.8	28
	Frozen:															
427	Unsweetened	0	249	3.2	2.3	61.7	45	59	3.6	5	367	320	.14	.27	2.3	33
428	Sweetened	0	476	2.7	1.4	120.2	27	50	1.8	5	299	180	.14	.23	1.7	33
429	Bluefish, raw:															
a	Whole (refuse: head, tail, entrails, fins, bones, and skin)	48	271	47.4	7.6	0	55	562	1.4	171	—	—	.27	.22	4.5	—
b	Flesh only	0	531	93.0	15.0	0	104	1,102	2.7	336	—	—	.52	.43	8.8	—
	Bockwurst. See Sausage, cold cuts, and luncheon meats; item 1981.															
	Bologna. See Sausage, cold cuts, and luncheon meats; items 1982–1985.															

432		**Bonito**, including Atlantic, Pacific, and striped, raw															
	a	Whole (refuse head, tail, entrails, fins, bones, and skin)	42	442	63. 1	19. 2	0	—	—	—	—	—	—	—	—	—	—
	b	Flesh only	0	762	108. 9	33 1	0	—	—	—	—	—	—	—	—	—	—
433		**Boston brown bread**	0	957	24 9	5. 9	206. 8	408	726	8 6	1, 139	1, 325	[25] 0	. 50	. 28	5. 3	0
434		**Bouillon** cubes or powder	0	544	91.	14.	23.	—	—	—	108, 864	454	—	—	—	—	—
		Boysenberries:															
435		Canned, water pack, solids and liquid, with or without artificial sweetener.	0	163	3 2	. 5	41. 3	(86)	(86)	(5 4)	5	386	590	(. 06)	(. 45)	(3. 4)	29
		Frozen															
436		Unsweetened	0	218	5. 4	1 4	51 7	113	109	7 3	5	694	(770)	. 09	. 59	4. 4	57
437		Sweetened	0	435	3. 6	1. 4	110. 7	77	77	2 7	5	476	(640)	. 09	. 45	2 9	35
438		**Brains**, all kinds (beef, calf, hog, sheep), raw	0	567	47. 2	39. 0	3. 6	45	1, 415	10 9	567	993	0	1. 05	1. 18	20. 1	82
		Bran:															
439		Added sugar and malt extract	0	1, 089	57 2	13. 6	337. 0	318	5, 334	([26])	4, 808	4, 854	(0)	[27] . 45	1. 32	81 0	Trace
440		Added sugar and defatted wheat germ	0	1, 080	49 0	8. 2	357. 4	331	4, 432	39 9	2, 223	—	(0)	1. 27	. 95	63 5	(0)
441		**Bran flakes** (40% bran), added thiamine	0	1, 374	46 3	8 2	365 6	322	2, 245	20 0	4, 196	—	(0)	1. 84	. 77	27. 9	(0)
442		**Bran flakes with raisins**, added thiamine	0	1, 302	37. 6	6 4	359. 7	254	1, 796	18 1	3, 629	—	Trace	1. 43	. 58	24. 0	(0)
		Braunschweiger. See Sausage, cold cuts, and luncheon meats item 1986															
443		**Brazilnuts:**															
	a	In shell (refuse shells)	52	1, 424	31 1	145. 6	23 7	405	1, 509	7 4	2	1, 557	Trace	2 09	26	3 5	—
	b	Shelled	0	2, 967	64 9	303. 5	49. 4	844	3, 143	15 4	5	3, 243	Trace	4 35	. 54	7. 3	—
		Breads: [28]															
444		Cracked-wheat	0	1, 193	39 5	10. 0	236 3	399	581	5. 0	2, 400	608	Trace	53	. 42	5 8	Trace
		French or vienna															
446		Enriched	0	1, 315	41. 3	13. 6	251. 3	195	386	10 0	2, 631	408	Trace	1. 26	. 98	11 3	Trace
448		Unenriched	0	1, 315	41. 3	13 6	251. 3	195	386	3. 2	2, 631	408	Trace	. 39	. 39	3 6	Trace
		Italian															
450		Enriched	0	1, 252	41 3	3. 6	255 8	77	349	10 0	2, 654	336	(0)	1 31	. 93	11 7	(0)
451		Unenriched	0	1, 252	41 3	3. 6	255 8	77	349	3 2	2, 654	336	(0)	. 39	27	3 6	(0)
452		Raisin	0	1, 188	29. 9	12. 7	243. 1	322	395	5 9	1, 656	1, 057	Trace	. 24	42	3. 0	Trace
		Rye															
454		American (⅓ rye, ⅔ clear flour)	0	1, 102	41. 3	5. 0	236. 3	340	667	7. 3	2, 527	658	(0)	. 81	. 33	6 4	(0)
456		Pumpernickel	0	1, 116	41. 3	5 4	240. 9	381	1, 039	10 9	2, 581	2, 059	(0)	1 05	. 63	5 4	(0)
457		Salt-rising	0	1, 211	35 8	10 9	236. 8	104	313	2 7	1, 202	304	50	. 20	. 22	2 5	Trace
		White															
		Enriched, made with:															
459		1%-2% nonfat dry milk	0	1, 220	39 5	14. 5	228. 6	318	395	10 9	2, 300	386	Trace	1 13	77	10 4	Trace
461		3%-4% nonfat dry milk [29]	0	1, 225	39. 5	14 5	229 1	381	440	11 3	2, 300	476	Trace	1 13	. 95	10 8	Trace
463		5%-6% nonfat dry milk	0	1, 247	40 8	17. 2	227 7	435	463	11 3	2, 245	549	Trace	1 22	. 91	11. 0	Trace
		Unenriched, made with															
465		1%-2% nonfat dry milk	0	1, 220	39 5	14. 5	228. 6	318	395	3 2	2, 300	386	Trace	40	36	5 6	Trace
467		3%-4% nonfat dry milk [29]	0	1, 225	39 5	14 5	229. 1	381	440	3 2	2, 300	476	Trace	31	39	5 0	Trace
469		5%-6% nonfat dry milk	0	1, 247	40. 8	17. 2	227. 7	435	463	3 2	2, 245	549	Trace	32	59	4 1	Trace
		Whole-wheat, made with.															
471		2% nonfat dry milk	0	1, 102	47 6	13 6	216 4	449	1, 034	10 4	2, 390	1, 238	Trace	1 17	56	12 9	Trace
473		Water	0	1, 093	41 3	11. 8	223. 6	381	1, 152	10 4	2, 404	1, 161	Trace	1 37	47	12 7	Trace
		See also Biscuits, Boston brown bread, Cornbread, Muffins, Rolls, Salt sticks.															
475		**Breadcrumbs**, dry, grated	0	1, 778	57 2	20 9	332 9	553	640	16 3	3, 338	689	Trace	1 00	1 36	15 9	Trace
		Bread sticks (vienna) See Salt sticks item 1966															
		Bread stuffing mix and stuffings prepared from mix:															
477		Mix, dry form	0	1, 683	58 5	17. 2	328 4	562	857	14 5	6, 037	780	Trace	. 99	1. 17	14 7	Trace
		Stuffing															
478		Dry, crumbly, prepared with water, table fat	0	1, 624	29. 5	98 9	161. 5	299	440	7 3	4, 064	408	2, 950	. 39	56	6 6	Trace
479		Moist, prepared with water, egg, table fat	0	943	20 0	58 1	89. 4	181	299	4 5	2, 286	263	1, 910	. 24	39	3 7	Trace
480		**Breadfruit**, raw (refuse skin, stem, core)	23	360	5. 9	1 0	91. 5	115	112	4. 2	52	1, 533	150	39	. 12	3 1	101
		Breakfast cereals. See Corn, Oats, Rice, Wheat; also Bran, Farina															
		Broadbeans, raw															
481		Immature seeds in pods (refuse: pods)	66	162	13 0	. 6	27. 4	42	242	3 4	6	726	340	42	26	2 5	47
482		Mature seeds, dry	0	1, 533	113. 9	7. 7	264 0	463	1, 774	32 2	—	—	320	2 29	1 36	11 3	—
		Broccoli:															
483		Raw spears															
	a	Partially trimmed (refuse tough stalks, trimmings)	22	113	12. 7	1. 1	20 9	364	276	3 9	53	1, 352	8, 840	35	81	3 2	400
	b	Untrimmed (refuse. large leaves, tough stalks, trimmings)	39	89	10. 0	8	16 3	285	216	3 0	42	1, 057	6, 920	28	64	2 5	313

[5] See Notes on Foods, p. 181.

[20] See Notes on Foods, p. 181 concerning calculations of energy values.

[21] Values are based on biscuits made with baking powder, item 130, and cooking fat, item 999

[22] Based on use of self-rising flour, item 2445, containing anhydrous monocalcium phosphate. With flour containing leavening ingredients noted in footnote 141, approximate values per pound are: Calcium, 562 mg. phosphorus, 1,647 mg, sodium, 3,747 mg

[23] With unenriched flour, approximate values per pound are: Iron, 2 7 mg., thiamine, 0 23 mg ; riboflavin, 0 23 mg ; niacin, 3 2 mg

[24] With unenriched flour, approximate values per pound are: Iron, 2 3 mg ; thiamine, 0 18 mg.; riboflavin, 0 45 mg.; niacin, 2.3 mg

[25] Applies to product made with white cornmeal. With yellow degermed cornmeal, value is 320 I.U. per pound

[26] Values range from 18 to 54 mg. per pound

[27] For product containing added thiamine, value is 1 8 mg. per pound.

[28] For additional data and information, see discussion of bread and rolls in Notes on Foods, p. 172

[29] When amount of nonfat dry milk in commercial bread is unknown, values for bread with 3-4 percent nonfat dry milk, item 461 or item 467, are suggested. See also Notes on Foods, p 172

TABLE 2.—NUTRIENTS IN THE EDIBLE PORTION OF 1 POUND OF FOOD AS PURCHASED—Continued

[Numbers in parentheses denote values imputed—usually from another form of the food or from a similar food. Zero in parentheses indicates that the amount of a constituent probably is none or is too small to measure. Dashes denote lack of reliable data for a constituent believed to be present in measurable amount. Calculated values, as those based on a recipe, are not in parentheses]

Item No. (A)	Food and description (B)	Refuse (C)	Food energy (D)	Protein (E)	Fat (F)	Carbohydrate total (G)	Calcium (H)	Phosphorus (I)	Iron (J)	Sodium (K)	Potassium (L)	Vitamin A value (M)	Thiamine (N)	Riboflavin (O)	Niacin (P)	Ascorbic Acid (Q)
		Percent	Calories	Grams	Grams	Grams	Milligrams	Milligrams	Milligrams	Milligrams	Milligrams	International units	Milligrams	Milligrams	Milligrams	Milligrams
	Broccoli—Continued															
	Frozen:															
485	Chopped	0	132	14.5	1.4	23.6	263	268	3.2	77	1,093	11,790	0.32	0.59	2.5	318
487	Spears	0	127	15.0	.9	23.1	195	272	3.2	59	1,167	8,520	.32	.59	2.5	354
	Brownies. See Cookies, items 813-814.															
	Brussels sprouts:															
489	Raw:															
a	Good quality (refuse: trimmings)	8	188	20.4	1.7	34.6	150	334	6.2	58	1,627	2,300	.41	.68	3.9	426
b	Fair quality (refuse: outer leaves, trimmings)	25	151	16.4	1.3	27.9	121	269	5.0	47	1,309	1,850	.33	.55	3.2	342
491	Frozen	0	163	15.0	.9	33.1	100	281	4.1	73	1,188	2,590	.35	.50	2.7	395
	Buckwheat:															
493	Whole-grain	0	1,520	53.1	10.9	330.7	517	1,279	14.1	—	2,032	(0)	2.71	—	20.0	(0)
	Flour:															
494	Dark	0	1,510	53.1	11.3	326.6	150	1,574	12.7	—	—	(0)	2.61	.68	13.2	(0)
495	Light	0	1,574	29.0	5.4	360.6	50	399	4.5	—	1,452	(0)	.35	(.19)	(1.8)	(0)
	Buckwheat pancake mix. See Pancake mix, item 1461.															
496	**Buffalofish**, raw:															
a	Whole (refuse: head, fins, entrails, skin, and bones)	68	164	25.4	6.1	0	—	—	—	76	425	—	—	—	—	—
b	Flesh only	0	513	79.4	19.1	0	—	—	—	236	1,329	—	—	—	—	—
	Bulgur (parboiled wheat):															
	Dry, made from—															
497	Club wheat	0	1,627	39.5	6.4	360.6	136	1,447	21.3	—	1,188	(0)	1.36	.45	19.2	(0)
498	Hard red winter wheat	0	1,615	50.8	6.8	343.4	132	1,538	16.8	—	1,039	(0)	1.27	.64	20.5	(0)
499	White wheat	0	1,621	46.7	5.4	354.3	163	1,361	(21.3)	—	1,406	(0)	(1.36)	(.45)	(19.2)	(0)
	Canned, made from hard red winter wheat:															
500	Unseasoned [30]	0	762	28.1	3.2	158.8	91	607	5.9	2,717	395	(0)	.23	.14	10.9	(0)
501	Seasoned [31]	0	826	28.1	15.0	148.8	91	585	6.4	2,687	508	(0)	.27	.18	13.7	(0)
502	**Bullhead**, black, raw:															
a	Whole (refuse: head, fins, entrails, and bones)	81	72	14.1	1.4	0	—	—	—	—	—	—	—	—	—	—
b	Fillets	0	381	73.9	7.3	0	—	—	—	—	—	—	—	—	—	—
	Bullocksheart. See Custardapple, item 949.															
503	**Burbot**, raw:															
a	Whole (refuse: head, tail, fins, entrails, bones, and skin)	85	56	11.8	.6	0	—	129	—	—	—	—	.27	.06	1.0	—
b	Flesh only	0	372	78.9	4.1	0	—	892	—	—	—	—	1.77	.62	6.7	—
	Burghul. See Bulgur, items 497-501.															
505	**Butter** [32]	0	3,248	2.7	367.	1.8	91	73	0	4,477	104	15,000	—	—	—	0
506	**Butter oil** or dehydrated butter	0	3,974	1.4	451.3	0	—	—	—	—	—	18,510	—	—	—	0
	Butterfish, raw:															
507	From northern waters:															
a	Whole (refuse: head, tail, fins, entrails, bones, and skin)	49	331	41.9	23.6	0	—	—	—	—	—	—	—	—	—	—
b	Flesh only	0	757	92.1	46.3	0	—	—	—	—	—	—	—	—	—	—
508	From gulf waters:															
a	Whole (refuse: head, tail, fins, entrails, bones, and skin)	49	220	37.5	6.7	0	—	—	—	—	—	—	—	—	—	—
b	Flesh only	0	431	73.5	13.2	0	—	—	—	—	—	—	—	—	—	—
	Buttermilk:															
509	Fluid, cultured (made from skim milk)	0	163	16.3	.5	23.1	549	431	.2	590	635	20	.18	.80	.3	5
510	Dried	0	1,755	155.6	24.0	226.8	5,661	4,400	2.6	2,300	7,285	1,000	1.18	7.80	4.1	—
511	**Butternuts:**															
a	In shell (refuse: shells)	86	399	15.1	38.9	5.3	—	—	4.3	—	—	—	—	—	—	—
b	Shelled	0	2,853	107.5	277.6	38.1	—	—	30.8	—	—	—	—	—	—	—
	Cabbage:															
	Common varieties (Danish, domestic, and pointed types).															
512	Raw:															
a	Head, trimmed of outer leaves (refuse: core)	10	98	5.3	.8	22.0	200	118	1.6	82	951	530	.22	.20	1.3	[34] 192
b	Head, untrimmed (refuse: outer leaves, core)	21	86	4.7	.7	19.3	176	104	1.4	72	835	470	.19	.18	1.1	[34] 169
515	Dehydrated	0	1,397	56.2	7.7	334.3	1,837	1,302	17.7	862	10,011	5,900	[34] 2.94	1.80	13.6	[34] 957
516	Red, raw:															
a	Head, trimmed of outer leaves (refuse: core)	(10)	127	8.2	.8	28.2	171	143	3.3	106	1,094	180	.38	.23	1.7	249
b	Head, untrimmed (refuse: outer leaves, core)	(21)	111	7.2	.7	24.7	150	125	2.9	93	960	160	.34	.20	1.5	219

517		Savoy, raw:															
	a	Head, trimmed of outer leaves (refuse: core)	(10)	98	9.8	.8	18.8	273	220	3 7	90	1,098	820	.22	.34	1.2	225
	b	Head, untrimmed (refuse: outer leaves, core)	(21)	86	8.6	.7	16.5	240	193	3 2	79	964	720	.19	.30	1.1	197
518		**Cabbage, Chinese** (also called celery cabbage or petsai), compact heading type, raw:															
	a	Good quality (refuse: root base)	3	62	5.3	.4	13.2	189	176	2.6	101	1,113	660	.20	.18	2.5	110
	b	Fair quality (refuse: root base, tough or wilted outer leaves).	12	56	4.8	.4	12.0	172	160	2.4	92	1,010	600	.18	.16	2.3	99
519		**Cabbage, spoon** (also called white mustard cabbage or pakchoy), nonheading green leaf type, raw.															
	a	Good quality (refuse root base)	5	69	6.9	.9	12.5	711	190	3 4	112	1,319	13,360	.22	.45	3.4	108
	b	Fair quality (refuse: root base, damaged leaves)	20	58	5.8	.7	10.5	599	160	2 9	94	1,110	11,250	.19	.38	2.9	91
		Cakes:															
		From home-type recipes [35]															
521		Angelfood	0	1,220	32 2	9	273.1	41	100	.9	1,284	399	0	.03	.63	.8	0
522		Boston cream pie	0	1,370	22.7	42.6	226.3	304	458	2 3	844	404	950	.15	.50	1 0	Trace
524		Caramel, with caramel icing	0	1,719	16.8	67.1	268.1	381	431	6.8	1,143	290	910	.09	.33	.6	Trace
		Chocolate (devil's food):															
526		With chocolate icing	0	1,674	20 4	74 4	253.1	318	594	4.5	1,066	699	730	.10	.44	1.0	Trace
527		With uncooked white icing	0	1,674	17 2	66 2	268.5	268	481	3 2	1,061	499	820	.09	.35	.8	Trace
		Fruitcake, made with enriched flour															
531		Dark	0	1,719	21.8	69.4	270.8	327	513	11 8	717	2,250	540	.61	.64	3.8	Trace
532		Light	0	1,765	27.2	74 8	260.4	308	522	7.3	875	1,057	320	.44	.49	3.0	Trace
		Plain cake or cupcake:															
534		Without icing	0	1,651	20 4	63 1	253 6	290	463	1.8	1,361	358	770	.11	.39	.9	Trace
535		With chocolate icing	0	1,669	19 1	63.1	269 4	286	472	2 7	1,039	517	820	.10	.41	.9	Trace
536		With boiled white icing	0	1,597	17.2	47.6	280 3	222	349	1.4	1,188	290	590	.08	.33	.7	Trace
537		With uncooked white icing	0	1,665	15.4	53.5	287 1	227	340	1.4	1,030	277	910	.08	.30	.6	Trace
		Pound.															
538		Old-fashioned (equal weights flour, sugar, table fat, eggs)	0	2,146	25.9	133.8	213 2	95	358	3.6	499	272	1,270	.14	.41	.8	0
539		Modified	0	1,864	29 0	84.8	248 1	181	472	3 6	807	354	1,320	.16	.49	1 0	Trace
540		Sponge	0	1,347	34 5	25.9	245 4	136	508	5 4	758	395	2,040	.21	.64	.7	Trace
		White:															
542		With coconut icing	0	1,683	16 8	60.3	275 3	204	327	1.4	1,166	481	80	.05	.31	.8	Trace
543		With uncooked white icing	0	1,701	15.0	58.5	285 3	218	295	.5	1,061	263	500	.04	29	.6	Trace
		Yellow:															
545		With caramel icing	0	1,642	18 1	53.1	278 1	349	467	3 2	1,025	331	770	.10	.34	.8	Trace
546		With chocolate icing	0	1,656	19 1	59 0	274 0	308	508	2 7	943	490	730	.10	.38	1 0	Trace
		Frozen, devil's food:															
547		With chocolate icing	0	1,724	19 5	79.8	252 2	245	417	3 6	1,905	540	1,950	.07	38	.9	Trace
548		With whipped-cream filling, chocolate icing	0	1,683	15.9	99 3	198 7	363	553	2.7	862	513	1,220	.09	.36	8	Trace
		Cake mixes and cakes baked from mixes:															
		Angelfood:															
549		Mix, dry form	0	1,746	38 1	9	401 4	490	567	1 8	862	508	0	04	79	.9	0
550		Cake, made with water, flavorings	0	1,175	25 9	.9	269.4	431	540	1 4	662	272	0	.02	.50	.5	0
		Chocolate malt:															
551		Mix, dry form	0	1,869	18 1	48 5	358 3	454	1,225	4 5	2,499	540	320	.17	34	1 7	0
552		Cake, made with eggs, water, uncooked white icing	0	1,569	15.4	39.5	302.1	286	753	3.2	1,442	363	860	.11	.31	.9	Trace
		Coffeecake, with enriched flour:															
553		Mix, dry form	0	1,955	26 8	49 9	350 2	163	866	[37] 9.1	2,781	395	Trace	[37] 1.36	[37] 64	[37] 10 9	Trace
554		Cake, made with egg, milk	0	1,461	28.6	43 5	237.7	277	789	[38] 7 3	1,955	494	730	[38] .79	[38] .74	[38] 6 6	Trace
		Cupcake:															
555		Mix, dry form	0	1,987	16 8	61.7	343 8	785	1,193	1 8	2,703	209	0	.23	.27	1 4	0
556		Cake made with eggs, milk, without icing	0	1,588	22.2	54.4	253.1	730	1,066	2.3	2,055	381	680	.20	.52	1.0	Trace
557		Cake, made with eggs, milk, chocolate icing	0	1,624	20 4	57.2	268.5	590	894	3.6	1,520	531	770	.16	49	1 0	Trace
		Devil's food:															
558		Mix, dry form	0	1,842	21 8	53 1	349 3	363	544	5 4	2,073	549	Trace	.12	.39	2 1	Trace
559		Cake, made with eggs, water, chocolate icing	0	1,538	20 0	55 8	264.4	268	476	3.6	1,188	590	680	.14	.38	1 4	Trace
		Gingerbread.															
560		Mix, dry form	0	1,928	24 5	47 2	354.7	816	907	6.4	2,100	1,896	Trace	.16	.62	1 6	Trace
561		Cake, made with water	0	1,252	14 1	30 8	231.8	408	454	7 3	1,379	1,243	Trace	.12	.39	3 9	Trace
		Honey spice:															
562		Mix, dry form	0	2,009	19 5	63 5	346.1	336	1,243	.9	1,692	449	Trace	11	38	1 3	Trace
563		Cake, made with eggs, water, caramel icing	0	1,597	18 6	49 0	276.2	322	875	3.6	1,111	372	730	10	40	.7	Trace

[30] Processed, partially debranned, whole-kernel wheat with salt added.

[31] Processed, partially debranned, whole-kernel wheat with chicken fat, chicken stock base, dehydrated onion flakes, salt, monosodium glutamate, and herbs

[32] Values apply to salted butter. Unsalted butter contains less than 45 mg of either sodium or potassium per pound. Value for vitamin A is the year-round average.

[33] For freshly harvested cabbage, average value is 208 mg per pound, for stored cabbage, 171 mg.

[34] For freshly harvested cabbage, average value is 183 mg per pound, for stored cabbage, 150 mg.

[35] Applies to unsulfited product For sulfited product, values per pound are Thiamine, 0 45 mg, ascorbic acid, 1,361 mg

[36] Unenriched cake flour used unless otherwise specified. Values for cakes that contain baking powder and/or fat are based on use of baking powder, item 130, and cooking fats, item 999 See also Notes on Foods, p 173

[37] With unenriched flour, approximate values per pound are Iron, 2 3 mg, thiamine, 0 32 mg; riboflavin, 0 27 mg, niacin, 4 5 mg.

[38] With unenriched flour, approximate values per pound are Iron, 2.7 mg, thiamine, 0 23 mg., riboflavin, 0 50 mg, niacin, 2 7 mg

TABLE 2.—NUTRIENTS IN THE EDIBLE PORTION OF 1 POUND OF FOOD AS PURCHASED—Continued

[Numbers in parentheses denote values imputed—usually from another form of the food or from a similar food. Zero in parentheses indicates that the amount of a constituent probably is none or is too small to measure. Dashes denote lack of reliable data for a constituent believed to be present in measurable amount. Calculated values, as those based on a recipe, are not in parentheses]

Item No.	Food and description	Refuse	Food energy	Protein	Fat	Carbohydrate total	Calcium	Phosphorus	Iron	Sodium	Potassium	Vitamin A value	Thiamine	Riboflavin	Niacin	Ascorbic acid
(A)	(B)	(C)	(D)	(E)	(F)	(G)	(H)	(I)	(J)	(K)	(L)	(M)	(N)	(O)	(P)	(Q)
	Cake mixes and cakes baked from mixes—Continued	Percent	Calories	Grams	Grams	Grams	Milligrams	Milligrams	Milligrams	Milligrams	Milligrams	International units	Milligrams	Milligrams	Milligrams	Milligrams
	Marble:															
564	Mix, dry form	0	1,928	22.2	61.2	342.9	390	1,225	4.5	1,728	835	Trace	0.15	0.41	2.0	Trace
565	Cake, made with eggs, water, boiled white icing	0	1,501	20.0	49.5	281.2	354	776	3.6	1,175	323	410	.09	.38	1.0	Trace
	White:															
566	Mix, dry form	0	1,969	18.6	54.0	355.6	680	1,225	.9	1,592	360	Trace	.14	.36	1.4	Trace
567	Cake, made with egg whites, water, chocolate icing	0	1,592	17.7	48.5	281.9	440	812	2.3	1,050	526	270	.07	.36	1.0	Trace
	Yellow:															
568	Mix, dry form	0	1,987	18.1	56.5	352.0	635	1,225	.9	1,846	590	Trace	.14	.41	1.1	Trace
569	Cake, made with eggs, water, chocolate icing	0	1,529	18.6	51.3	261.3	413	826	2.7	1,030	404	640	.10	.39	.9	Trace
	Cake icing mixes:															
576	Chocolate fudge	0	1,845	11.3	44.5	391.9	82	372	3.9	431	354	Trace	.06	.25	1.3	0
577	Creamy fudge (contains nonfat dry milk)	0	1,751	14.5	33.6	386.0	204	463	3.9	1,292	502	Trace	.10	.31	1.4	Trace
	Candied fruits. See Apricots, Cherries, Citron, Figs, Ginger root, Grapefruit peel, Lemon peel, Orange peel, Pear, Pineapple															
	Candy:															
580	Butterscotch	0	1,801	Trace	15.4	430.0	77	27	6.4	299	9	640	0	Trace	Trace	0
	Candy corn. See Fondant, item 602															
	Caramels:															
581	Plain or chocolate	0	1,809	18.1	46.3	347.5	671	553	6.4	1,025	871	90	.14	.78	.7	Trace
582	Plain or chocolate, with nuts	0	1,941	20.4	73.0	319.8	645	621	6.8	921	1,057	90	.31	.75	1.0	Trace
583	Chocolate-flavored roll	0	1,796	10.0	37.2	375.1	308	540	8.2	894	558	Trace	.07	.30	.9	Trace
	Chocolate:															
584	Bittersweet	0	2,164	35.8	180.1	212.3	263	1,258	22.7	14	2,790	180	.13	.77	4.5	0
585	Semisweet	0	2,300	19.1	161.9	258.6	136	680	11.8	9	1,474	90	.06	.39	2.4	0
586	Sweet	0	2,395	20.0	159.2	262.4	426	644	6.4	150	1,220	60	.11	.64	1.5	Trace
	Chocolate, milk:															
587	Plain	0	2,359	34.5	146.5	258.1	1,034	1,048	5.0	426	1,742	1,220	.27	1.62	1.3	Trace
588	With almonds	0	2,413	42.2	161.5	232.7	1,039	1,234	2.3	363	2,005	1,040	.36	1.58	3.4	Trace
589	With peanuts	0	2,463	64.0	172.8	202.3	786	1,354	6.4	299	2,269	820	1.13	1.29	22.8	Trace
	Chocolate-coated:															
590	Almonds	0	2,581	58.8	198.2	179.6	621	1,256	12.7	268	2,477	Trace	.50	2.42	7.8	Trace
591	Chocolate fudge	0	1,954	17.2	72.6	331.9	458	409	5.9	1,034	875	Trace	.17	.58	.9	0
592	Chocolate fudge, with nuts	0	2,060	22.2	94.3	295.3	458	621	6.6	953	993	Trace	.27	.59	.9	Trace
593	Coconut center	0	1,987	12.7	79.8	326.6	218	249	5.0	844	748	0	.09	.32	.9	0
594	Fondant	0	1,860	7.7	47.6	367.4	259	245	5.0	834	413	Trace	.14	.29	.3	Trace
595	Fudge, caramel, and peanuts	0	1,964	34.9	82.1	299.8	812	844	4.4	925	1,362	Trace	.71	.59	8.7	Trace
596	Fudge, peanuts, and caramel	0	2,162	42.6	104.8	266.5	576	871	5.0	581	1,497	Trace	1.16	.67	16.2	Trace
597	Honeycombed hard candy, with peanut butter	0	2,150	29.0	88.5	329.2	363	612	8.2	739	1,021	Trace	.24	.41	15.5	Trace
598	Nougat and caramel	0	1,887	18.1	61.1	330.2	576	558	7.3	785	957	180	.27	.78	.9	Trace
599	Peanuts	0	2,545	74.4	187.3	177.4	526	1,352	6.8	272	2,286	Trace	1.09	.73	33.6	Trace
600	Raisins	0	1,928	21.8	77.6	311.8	689	789	11.3	290	2,735	680	.45	.97	1.9	Trace
601	Vanilla creams	0	1,974	17.2	77.6	318.9	581	499	2.7	826	807	Trace	.21	.54	.6	Trace
602	Fondant	0	1,651	.5	9.1	406.4	64	27	5.0	962	23	0	Trace	Trace	Trace	0
	Fudge:															
603	Chocolate	0	1,814	12.2	55.3	340.2	319	381	4.5	862	667	Trace	.09	.41	1.0	Trace
604	Chocolate, with nuts	0	1,932	17.7	78.9	310.6	358	517	5.4	726	803	Trace	.18	.29	1.2	Trace
605	Vanilla	0	1,805	13.6	50.3	339.1	508	376	2.3	913	576	Trace	.10	.60	.3	Trace
606	Vanilla, with nuts	0	1,921	18.1	74.4	317.1	503	513	3.6	848	517	Trace	.21	.59	.6	Trace
607	Gum drops, starch jelly pieces	0	1,578	.5	3.2	396.4	27	Trace	2.3	159	23	0	0	Trace	Trace	0
608	Hard	0	1,751	0	5.0	440.9	95	32	8.6	145	18	0	0	0	0	0
609	Jelly beans	0	1,665	Trace	2.3	422.8	54	18	5.0	54	5	0	0	Trace	Trace	0
610	Marshmallows	0	1,447	9.1	Trace	364.7	82	27	7.3	177	27	0	0	Trace	Trace	0
	Mints, uncoated. See Fondant, item 602															
611	Peanut bars	0	2,350	79.4	146.1	214.1	209	1,258	8.2	45	2,032	0	1.94	.35	42.8	0
612	Peanut brittle (no added salt or soda)	0	1,909	25.9	47.2	367.4	159	431	10.4	141	685	0	.74	.14	15.6	0
	Sugar-coated:															
613	Almonds	0	2,068	35.4	84.4	318.4	454	753	8.6	91	1,157	0	.23	1.24	4.7	0
614	Chocolate discs	0	2,113	23.6	89.4	329.8	612	635	5.9	327	1,134	450	.28	.93	1.3	Trace
	Cantaloups. See Muskmelons, item 1358															
	Cape-gooseberries. See Groundcherries, item 1092															
	Capicola. See Sausage, cold cuts, and luncheon meats, item 1989															

615		Carambola, raw (refuse: stem, ribs, seeds)	6	149	3.0	2.1	34.1	17	72	6.4	9	819	5,120	.16	.09	1.4	151
		Caribou. See Reindeer, items 1856–1858.															
616		Carissa (natalplum), raw (refuse, skin, seeds)	14	273	2.0	5.1	62.4	—	—	—	—	—	150	.14	.24	.9	148
617		Carob flour (St. Johnsbread)	0	816	20.4	6.4	366.1	1,597	367	—	—	—	—	—	—	—	—
618		Carp, raw:															
	a	Whole (refuse, head, fins, entrails, skin, and bones)	70	156	24.5	5.7	0	68	344	1.2	68	389	230	.01	.05	2.0	2
	b	Flesh only	0	522	81.6	19.1	0	227	1,148	4.1	227	1,297	770	.04	.18	6.7	5
		Carrots:															
619		Raw:															
	a	With full tops (refuse: tops, scrapings)	41	112	2.9	.5	26.0	99	96	1.9	126	913	[39] 29,440	.16	.14	1.6	21
	b	With part tops (refuse: part tops, scrapings)	22	149	3.9	.7	34.3	131	127	2.5	166	1,206	[39] 38,920	.21	.19	2.1	28
	c	Without tops (refuse: scrapings)	18	156	4.1	.7	36.1	138	134	2.6	175	1,269	[39] 40,920	.22	.20	2.2	29
		Canned, solids and liquid:															
621		Regular pack	0	127	2.7	.9	29.5	113	91	3.2	[38] 1,070	544	45,360	.11	.11	1.6	9
624		Special dietary pack (low-sodium)	0	100	3.2	.5	22.7	113	91	3.2	177	544	45,360	.11	.11	1.6	9
627		Dehydrated	0	1,547	29.9	5.9	367.9	1,161	1,061	27.2	1,216	8,818	453,600	1.39	1.36	13.7	68
		Casaba melon. See Muskmelons, item 1359.															
628		Cashew nuts	0	2,545	78.0	207.3	132.9	172	1,692	17.2	[40] 68	2,105	450	1.93	1.12	8.0	—
629		Catfish, freshwater, fillets, raw	0	467	79.8	14.1	0	—	—	1.8	272	1,497	—	.18	.13	7.7	—
		Catsup. See Tomato catsup, item 2286.															
		Cauliflower:															
630		Raw															
	a	Head, fully trimmed, or flower buds	0	122	12.2	.9	23.6	113	254	5.0	59	1,338	270	.50	.44	3.0	354
	b	Head, untrimmed (refuse: jacket leaves, inner leaves, main stalk, base, and core).	61	48	4.8	.4	9.2	44	99	1.9	23	522	110	.19	.17	1.2	138
632		Frozen	0	100	9.1	.9	19.5	86	191	2.7	50	1,021	140	.27	.27	2.2	254
		Caviar, sturgeon															
634		Granular	0	1,188	122.0	68.0	15.0	1,252	1,610	53.5	9,979	816	—	—	—	—	—
635		Pressed	0	1,433	156.0	75.8	22.2	—	—	—	—	—	—	—	—	—	—
636		Celeriac, root, raw (refuse: parings)	14	156	7.0	1.2	33.2	168	449	2.3	390	1,170	—	.20	.23	2.7	31
637		Celery, all, including green and yellow varieties, raw (refuse: leaves, root ends, trimmings)	25	58	3.1	.3	13.3	133	95	1.0	429	1,160	[41] 820	.09	.11	1.2	30
		Cereals, breakfast. See Corn, Oats, Rice, Wheat; also Bran, Farina															
		Cervelat. See Sausage, cold cuts, and luncheon meats: items 1990–1991.															
639		Chard, Swiss, raw:															
	a	Good quality (refuse: tough stem ends, damaged leaves)	8	104	10.0	1.3	19.2	367	163	13.4	613	2,295	27,120	.25	.72	2.2	132
	b	Fair quality (refuse: tough stem ends, wilted leaves)	23	87	8.4	1.0	16.1	307	136	11.2	513	1,921	22,700	.21	.60	1.9	110
641		Charlotte russe, with ladyfingers, whipped-cream filling	0	1,297	26.8	66.2	152.0	209	413	3.2	195	290	3,360	.15	.44	.5	Trace
642		Chayote, raw (refuse: parings)	15	108	2.3	.4	27.4	50	100	1.9	19	393	90	.10	.13	1.7	74
		Cheeses, natural and processed; cheese foods; cheese spreads:															
		Natural cheeses															
643		Blue or Roquefort type	0	1,669	97.5	138.3	9.1	1,429	1,538	(2.3)	—	—	(5,620)	.12	2.77	5.4	(0)
644		Brick	0	1,678	100.7	138.3	8.6	3,311	2,064	(4.1)	—	—	(5,620)	—	2.06	.5	(0)
645		Camembert (domestic)	0	1,356	79.4	112.0	8.2	476	835	2.3	—	503	(4,580)	.19	3.42	3.6	(0)
646		Cheddar (domestic type, commonly called American).	0	1,805	113.4	146.1	9.5	3,402	2,168	4.5	3,175	372	(5,940)	.12	2.07	.3	(0)
		Cottage (large or small curd):															
647		Creamed	0	481	61.7	19.1	13.2	426	689	1.4	1,039	366	(770)	.13	1.12	.5	(0)
648		Uncreamed	0	390	77.1	1.4	12.2	408	794	1.8	1,315	327	(50)	.14	1.27	(.5)	(0)
649		Cream	0	1,696	36.3	171.0	9.5	281	431	.9	1,134	336	(6,990)	(.07)	1.10	.5	(0)
650		Limburger	0	1,565	96.2	127.0	10.0	2,676	1,783	2.7	—	—	(5,170)	.36	2.27	.7	(0)
651		Parmesan	0	1,783	163.3	117.9	13.2	5,171	3,543	1.8	3,329	676	(4,810)	.09	3.31	1.0	(0)
652		Swiss (domestic)	0	1,678	124.7	127.0	7.7	4,196	2,554	4.1	3,221	472	(5,170)	.03	(1.81)	(.2)	(0)
		Pasteurized process cheese:															
653		American	0	1,678	105.2	136.1	8.6	3,162	[42] 3,497	4.1	[42] 5,153	363	(5,530)	.07	1.85	.1	(0)
654		Pimiento (American)	0	1,683	104.3	137.0	8.2	—	—	—	—	—	—	—	—	—	—
655		Swiss	0	1,610	119.8	122.0	7.3	4,023	[42] 3,933	(4.1)	[42] 5,294	454	(4,990)	(.03)	1.81	.2	(0)
656		Pasteurized process cheese food, American	0	1,465	89.8	108.9	32.2	2,586	[42] 3,420	(3.6)	—	—	(4,450)	(.11)	2.62	.7	(0)
657		Pasteurized process cheese spread, American	0	1,306	72.6	97.1	37.2	2,563	[42] 3,969	(2.7)	[42] 7,371	1,089	(3,950)	.05	2.47	.6	(0)
660		Cheese straws	0	2,055	50.8	135.6	156.5	1,175	934	2.7	3,270	286	1,770	.08	.70	1.3	0
661		Cherimoya, raw (refuse: skin, seeds)	42	247	3.4	1.1	63.1	61	105	1.3	—	—	30	.27	.29	3.3	24

[38] Estimated average based on addition of salt in the amount of 0.6 percent of the finished product.

[39] Average for carrots marketed as fresh vegetable. See also Notes on Foods, p. 175.

[40] Applies to unsalted nuts. For salted nuts, value is approximately 900 mg. per pound.

[41] Average for all varieties. For green varieties, value is 920 I.U. per pound; for yellow varieties, 480 I.U.

[42] Values for phosphorus and sodium are based on use of 1.5 percent anhydrous disodium phosphate as the emulsifying agent. If emulsifying agent does not contain either phosphorus or sodium, the content of these two nutrients in milligrams per pound is as follows:

	P	Na
Item 653, American process cheese	2,014	2,948
Item 655, Swiss process cheese	2,449	3,089
Item 656, American cheese food	1,937	—
Item 657, American cheese spread	2,186	5,167

TABLE 2.—NUTRIENTS IN THE EDIBLE PORTION OF 1 POUND OF FOOD AS PURCHASED—Continued

[Numbers in parentheses denote values imputed—usually from another form of the food or from a similar food. Zero in parentheses indicates that the amount of a constituent probably is none or is too small to measure. Dashes denote lack of reliable data for a constituent believed to be present in measurable amount. Calculated values, as those based on a recipe, are not in parentheses]

Item No.	Food and description	Refuse	Food energy	Protein	Fat	Carbohydrate total	Calcium	Phosphorus	Iron	Sodium	Potassium	Vitamin A value	Thiamine	Riboflavin	Niacin	Ascorbic Acid
(A)	(B)	(C)	(D)	(E)	(F)	(G)	(H)	(I)	(J)	(K)	(L)	(M)	(N)	(O)	(P)	(Q)
		Percent	*Calories*	*Grams*	*Grams*	*Grams*	*Milligrams*	*Milligrams*	*Milligrams*	*Milligrams*	*Milligrams*	*International units*	*Milligrams*	*Milligrams*	*Milligrams*	*Milligrams*
	Cherries:															
	Raw:															
662	Sour red:															
a	Fruit (refuse: pits)	8	242	5.0	1.3	59.7	92	79	1.7	8	797	4,170	0.21	0.25	1.7	42
b	Fruit (refuse: pits, pitting loss, stems, defects)	19	214	4.4	1.1	52.5	81	70	1.5	7	702	3,670	.18	.22	1.5	37
663	Sweet (refuse: pits and stems)	10	286	5.3	1.2	71.0	90	78	1.6	8	780	450	.20	.24	1.7	41
664	Candied	0	1,538	2.3	.9	393.3	—	—	—	—	—	—	—	—	—	—
	Canned:															
	Sour, red (without pits), solids and liquid:															
665	Water pack	0	195	3.6	.9	48.5	68	59	1.4	9	590	3,090	.13	.11	.8	23
	Sirup pack:															
666	Light	0	336	3.6	.9	84.8	64	59	1.4	5	572	2,990	.13	.11	.8	23
667	Heavy	0	404	3.6	.9	103.0	64	54	1.4	5	562	2,940	.13	.10	.7	22
668	Extra heavy	0	508	3.6	.9	129.7	64	54	.9	5	549	2,870	.12	.10	.7	21
	Sweet, solids and liquid:															
669	Water pack, with or without artificial sweetener:															
a	With pits (refuse: pits)	5	207	3.9	.9	51.5	65	56	1.3	4	569	250	.09	.11	.7	16
b	Without pits	0	218	4.1	.9	54.0	68	59	1.4	5	590	260	.09	.11	.8	15
	Sirup pack:															
670	Light:															
a	With pits (refuse: pits)	5	280	3.9	.9	71.1	65	56	1.3	4	552	250	.09	.10	.7	14
b	Without pits	0	295	4.1	.9	74.8	68	59	1.4	5	581	260	.09	.11	.7	15
671	Heavy:															
a	With pits (refuse: pits)	5	349	4.0	.9	88.3	65	56	1.3	4	543	240	.09	.10	.7	14
b	Without pits	0	367	4.1	.9	93.0	68	59	1.4	5	572	250	.09	.11	.7	15
672	Extra heavy:															
a	With pits (refuse: pits)	5	431	3.4	.9	110.3	60	52	1.3	4	530	230	.08	.10	.7	14
b	Without pits	0	454	3.6	.9	116.1	64	54	1.4	5	558	240	.09	.10	.7	15
	Frozen, sour, red:															
673	Unsweetened	0	249	4.5	1.8	60.8	59	100	3.2	9	853	4,540	.18	.32	1.4	22
674	Sweetened	0	508	4.5	1.8	126.1	64	68	2.3	9	590	2,180	.14	.27	1.4	28
675	**Cherries, maraschino,** bottled, solids and liquid	0	526	.6	.9	133.4	—	—	—	—	—	—	—	—	—	—
676	**Chervil,** raw	0	259	15.4	4.1	52.2	—	—	—	—	—	—	—	—	—	41
	Chestnuts:															
677	Fresh:															
a	In shell (refuse: shells)	16	713	10.7	5.5	154.7	99	323	6.2	23	1,668	—	.82	.84	2.2	—
b	Shelled	0	880	13.2	6.8	191.0	122	399	7.7	27	2,059	—	1.01	1.00	2.7	—
678	Dried:															
a	In shell (refuse: shells)	18	1,402	24.9	15.2	292.4	193	603	12.3	45	3,255	—	1.20	1.42	4.4	—
b	Shelled	0	1,710	30.4	18.6	356.5	236	735	15.0	54	3,969	—	1.46	1.73	5.3	—
679	**Chestnut flour**	0	1,642	27.7	16.8	345.6	227	744	14.5	50	3,842	—	1.04	1.67	4.5	—
680	**Chewing gum**	0	1,438	—	—	431.8	—	—	—	—	—	(0)	(0)	(0)	(0)	(0)
	Chicken, raw:															
	Fryers (live weight over 2½ lbs., or weight, ready-to-cook, with giblets, over 1¾ lbs.):															
686	Flesh, skin, and giblets:															
a	Live (refuse: blood, feathers, head, feet, inedible viscera, and bones)	52	270	40.5	10.7	0	26	438	4.1	—	—	1,690	.14	.82	12.1	—
b	Ready-to-cook (refuse: bones)	32	382	57.4	15.1	0	37	620	5.9	—	—	2,390	.20	1.17	17.1	—
	Cut-up parts:															
704	Back (refuse: bones)	46	485	40.4	24.5	0	29	453	4.2	—	—	760	.13	.53	10.5	—
706	Breast (refuse: bones)	21	394	71.5	8.6	0	39	767	4.3	—	—	270	.18	.37	28.5	—
708	Drumstick (refuse: bones)	40	313	51.2	10.6	0	35	506	4.4	—	—	310	.18	.87	11.7	—
710	Neck (refuse: bones)	52	329	33.7	20.5	0	24	396	4.1	—	—	860	.10	.53	8.5	—
712	Rib (refuse: bones)	49	287	40.5	12.5	0	25	490	3.6	—	—	490	.10	.41	11.8	—
714	Thigh (refuse: bones)	25	435	61.6	19.1	0	41	633	5.4	—	—	620	.20	1.10	19.5	—
716	Wing (refuse: bones)	51	325	41.1	16.5	0	22	451	3.3	—	—	550	.09	.32	9.1	—
	Roasters:															
718	Total edible:															
a	Live (refuse: blood, feathers, head, feet, inedible viscera, and bones)	48	563	42.0	42.2	0	24	415	3.8	—	—	2,170	.18	.45	16.7	—
b	Dressed (refuse: head, feet, inedible viscera, and bones)	42	629	47.0	47.1	0	26	463	4.2	—	—	2,430	.20	.50	17.6	—
c	Ready-to-cook (refuse: bones)	27	791	60.3	59.3	0	33	583	5.3	—	—	3,050	.25	.63	22.1	—

		Hens and cocks:															
731		Total edible:															
	a	Live (refuse: blood, feathers, head, feet, inedible viscera, and bones).	48	703	41.0	58.5	0	24	394	3.3	—	—	2,540	.14	.44	19.3	—
	b	Dressed (refuse: head, feet, inedible viscera, and bones).	42	784	45.8	65.2	0	26	439	3.7	—	—	2,840	.16	.49	21.5	—
	c	Ready-to-cook (refuse: bones)	27	987	57.6	82.1	0	33	553	4.6	—	—	3,570	.20	.62	27.1	—
		Capons:															
744		Total edible:															
	a	Live (refuse: blood, feathers, head, feet, inedible viscera, and bones).	48	668	50.5	50.0	0	—	—	—	—	—	—	—	—	—	—
	b	Dressed (refuse: head, feet, inedible viscera, and bones).	42	745	56.3	55.8	0	—	—	—	—	—	—	—	—	—	—
	c	Ready-to-cook (refuse: bones)	27	937	70.9	70.2	0	—	—	—	—	—	—	—	—	—	—
747		**Chicken, canned,** meat only, boned	0	898	98.4	53.1	0	95	1,120	6.8	—	626	1,060	.17	.56	19.7	17
		Chicken, potted. See Sausage, cold cuts, and luncheon meats: item 2008.															
751		**Chicken potpie, frozen**	0	993	30.4	52.2	100.7	50	227	4.5	1,864	694	4,130	.44	.62	6.3	20
753		**Chickpeas** or garbanzos, mature seeds, dry, raw	0	1,633	93.0	21.8	276.7	680	1,501	31.3	118	3,615	230	1.42	.68	9.3	—
754		**Chicory, Witloof** (also called French or Belgian endive) bleached head (forced), raw [43] (refuse: root base, core)	11	61	4.0	.4	12.9	73	85	2.0	28	735	Trace	—	—	—	—
755		**Chicory greens,** raw (refuse: stems)	18	74	6.7	1.1	14.1	320	149	3.3	—	1,562	14,880	.22	.37	1.9	82
		Chili con carne, canned:															
756		With beans	0	603	34.0	27.7	55.3	145	572	7.7	2,409	1,057	270	.14	.32	5.7	—
757		Without beans [44]	0	907	46.7	67.1	26.3	172	689	6.4	—	—	680	.08	.54	10.2	—
		Chili powder. See Peppers, item 1544.															
		Chili sauce. See Peppers, items 1539, 1542, and Tomatoes, item 2287															
758		**Chives,** raw	0	127	8.2	1.4	26.3	313	200	7.7	—	1,134	26,310	.39	.58	2.3	254
		Chocolate:															
759		Bitter or baking [45]	0	2,291	48.5	240.4	131.1	354	1,742	30.4	18	3,765	270	.21	1.09	6.8	0
		Bittersweet. See Candy, item 584.															
		Chocolate sirup:															
760		Thin type	0	1,111	10.4	9.1	284.4	77	417	7.3	236	1,279	Trace	.08	.31	1.6	0
761		Fudge type	0	1,497	23.1	62.1	244.9	576	721	5.9	404	1,288	680	.20	.99	1.6	Trace
763		**Chop suey** with meat, canned	0	281	20.0	14.5	19.1	159	526	8.6	2,499	626	140	.23	.24	3.4	11
765		**Chow mein,** chicken (without noodles), canned	0	172	11.8	.5	32.2	82	154	2.3	1,315	758	270	.09	.18	1.9	20
766		**Chub, raw:**															
	a	Whole (refuse: head, tail, fins, entrails, scales, bones, and skin)	67	217	22.9	13.2	0	—	—	—	—	—	—	—	—	—	—
	b	Flesh only	0	658	69.4	39.9	0	—	—	—	—	—	—	—	—	—	—
		Cider. See Apple juice, item 27.															
		Cisco. See Lake herring, item 1168.															
767		**Citron,** candied	0	1,424	9	1.4	363.8	376	109	3.6	1,315	544	—	—	—	—	—
		Clams, raw:															
		Soft:															
768		Meat and liquid in shell (refuse: shell)	42	142	22.6	2.6	5.3	—	547	—	—	—	—	—	—	—	—
769		Clam meat, obtained—															
	a	In shell (refuse: shell and liquid)	65	130	22.2	3.0	2.1	—	291	5.4	57	373	—	—	—	—	—
	b	As meat only	0	372	63.5	8.6	5.9	—	830	15.4	163	1,066	—	—	—	—	—
		Hard or round:															
770		Meat and liquid in shell (refuse: shell)	68	71	9.4	.6	6.1	—	254	—	—	—	—	—	.19	—	—
771		Clam meat, obtained—															
	a	In shell (refuse: shell and liquid)	83	62	8.6	.7	4.5	53	116	5.8	158	240	—	—	—	—	—
	b	As meat only	0	363	50.3	4.1	26.8	313	685	34.0	930	1,411	—	—	—	—	—
		Hard, soft, and unspecified:															
772		Meat and liquid	0	240	36.7	4.1	11.3	—	894	—	—	—	—	—	—	—	—
773		Meat only	0	345	57.2	7.3	9.1	313	735	27.7	544	821	450	.44	.82	5.7	45
		Clams, canned, including hard, soft, razor, and unspecified															
774		Solids and liquid	0	236	35.8	3.2	12.7	249	621	18.6	—	635	—	.04	.48	4.6	—
775		Solids and liquid (refuse: drained liquid)	48	231	37.3	5.9	4.5	—	—	—	—	—	—	—	—	—	—
776		Liquor, bouillon, or nectar	0	86	10.4	.5	9.5	—	—	—	—	—	—	—	—	—	—
		Cocoa and chocolate-flavored beverage powders:															
778		Cocoa powder with nonfat dry milk	0	1,628	84.4	13.2	321.1	2,672	2,472	8.2	2,381	3,629	90	.60	3.29	3.3	14
779		Cocoa powder without milk	0	1,574	18.1	9.1	405.5	136	776	9.5	1,216	2,268	—	.10	.42	2.2	0
780		Mix for hot chocolate [46]	0	1,778	42.6	48.1	335.2	1,247	1,315	6.4	1,733	2,744	50	.36	1.85	2.2	5
		Cocoa, dry powder: [45]															
		High-fat or breakfast:															
781		Plain	0	1,356	76.2	107.5	219.1	603	2,939	48.5	27	6,904	140	.51	2.09	10.9	0
782		Processed with alkali	0	1,338	76.2	107.5	204.6	603	2,939	48.5	3,252	2,953	140	.51	2.09	10.9	0

[43] For further description of product, see Notes on Foods, p. 178.

[44] Contains not less than 60 percent meat, not more than 8 percent cereals, seasonings.

[45] See Appendix A, section on Protein, p. 162, and see Appendix B, section on foods containing considerable nonprotein nitrogen, p. 182.

[46] Values apply to products without added vitamins and minerals.

TABLE 2.—NUTRIENTS IN THE EDIBLE PORTION OF 1 POUND OF FOOD AS PURCHASED—Continued

[Numbers in parentheses denote values imputed—usually from another form of the food or from a similar food. Zero in parentheses indicates that the amount of a constituent probably is none or is too small to measure. Dashes denote lack of reliable data for a constituent believed to be present in measurable amount. Calculated values, as those based on a recipe, are not in parentheses]

Item No.	Food and description	Refuse	Food energy	Protein	Fat	Carbohydrate total	Calcium	Phosphorus	Iron	Sodium	Potassium	Vitamin A value	Thiamine	Riboflavin	Niacin	Ascorbic acid
(A)	(B)	(C)	(D)	(E)	(F)	(G)	(H)	(I)	(J)	(K)	(L)	(M)	(N)	(O)	(P)	(Q)
	Cocoa, dry powder—Continued	Percent	Calories	Grams	Grams	Grams	Milligrams	Milligrams	Milligrams	Milligrams	Milligrams	International units	Milligrams	Milligrams	Milligrams	Milligrams
	Medium-fat:															
	High-medium fat:															
783	Plain	0	1,202	78.5	86.2	231.6	558	2,944	48.5	27	6,904	90	0.51	2.09	10.9	0
784	Processed with alkali	0	1,184	78.5	86.2	220.0	558	2,944	48.5	3,252	2,953	90	.51	2.09	10.9	0
	Low-medium fat:															
785	Plain	0	958	87.1	57.6	244.0	608	3,112	48.5	27	6,904	70	.51	2.09	10.9	0
786	Processed with alkali	0	973	87.1	57.6	227.7	608	3,112	48.5	3,252	2,953	70	.51	2.09	10.9	0
787	Low-fat	0	848	91.6	25.8	261.7	608	3,311	48.5	27	6,904	30	.51	2.09	10.9	0
	Coconut:															
788	Fresh:															
a	In shell (refuse: shell, brown skin, water)	48	816	8.2	83.3	22.2	31	224	4.0	54	590	0	.12	.05	1.1	7
b	Meat only	0	1,569	15.9	160.1	42.6	59	431	7.7	104	1,161	0	.23	.09	2.4	14
	Dried:															
790	Unsweetened	0	3,003	32.7	294.4	104.5	118	848	15.0	—	2,667	0	.27	.20	2.7	0
791	Sweetened, shredded	0	2,486	16.3	177.4	242.3	73	508	9.1	—	1,601	0	.16	.12	1.6	0
	Cod:															
794	Raw:															
a	Whole (refuse: head, tail, fins, entrails, scales, bones, and skin)	65	119	27.7	.4	0	16	273	.6	109	597	0	.09	.10	3.5	3
b	Flesh only	0	354	79.8	1.4	0	45	880	1.8	318	1,733	0	.27	.30	10.0	9
796	Canned	0	386	87.1	1.4	0	—	—	—	—	—	—	—	.34	—	—
797	Dehydrated, lightly salted	0	1,701	371.0	12.7	0	—	4,046	16.3	36,740	726	0	.38	2.44	49.1	—
798	Dried, salted	0	590	131.5	3.2	0	1,021	—	—	—	—	—	—	—	—	—
799	Coffee, instant (water-soluble solids), dry powder	0	585	Trace	Trace	(158.8)	812	1,737	25.4	327	14,764	0	0	.94	128.8	0
	Cola or coke. See Beverages, item 401.															
	Collards:															
	Raw, portion used—															
808	Leaves, without stems (refuse: stems)	32	139	14.8	2.5	23.1	771	255	4.6	—	1,388	28,680	.48	.97	5.1	309
809	Leaves, including stems:															
a	Good quality	0	181	16.3	3.2	32.7	921	286	4.5	195	1,819	29,480	.91	(1.42)	(7.5)	417
b	Fair quality (refuse: tough stems)	26	134	12.1	2.3	24.2	681	211	3.4	144	1,346	21,820	.67	(1.05)	(5.6)	309
810	Frozen	0	145	14.1	1.8	25.3	549	240	3.6	82	1,070	30,480	.32	.73	3.1	208
	Cookies:															
812	Assorted, packaged	0	2,177	23.1	91.6	322.1	168	730	3.2	1,656	304	300	.15	.22	2.9	Trace
	Brownies with nuts:															
813	Baked from home-type recipe, enriched flour	0	2,200	29.9	142.0	230.9	186	671	8.6	1,139	867	910	.88	.57	4.2	Trace
814	Frozen, with chocolate icing	0	1,901	22.2	93.4	275.3	181	767	6.8	567	812	1,080	.39	.37	1.2	Trace
815	Butter, thin, rich	0	2,073	27.7	75.7	321.6	572	429	2.3	1,896	272	2,990	.14	.25	1.8	0
816	Chocolate	0	2,019	32.2	71.2	321.3	236	576	5.5	621	591	730	.18	.36	2.3	Trace
	Chocolate chip:															
817	Baked from home-type recipe, enriched flour	0	2,341	24.5	136.8	272.6	164	449	9.5	1,579	531	680	.54	.50	4.1	Trace
818	Commercial type	0	2,136	24.5	95.3	318.2	177	517	8.2	1,819	608	510	.29	.32	1.8	Trace
819	Coconut bars	0	2,241	28.1	111.1	280.6	327	544	8.4	671	1,034	730	.17	.29	1.5	0
820	Fig bars	0	1,624	17.7	25.4	342.0	354	272	4.5	1,134	898	500	.16	.30	1.6	Trace
821	Gingersnaps	0	1,905	24.9	40.4	362.0	331	218	10.4	2,590	2,096	320	.20	.28	2.0	Trace
822	Ladyfingers	0	1,633	35.4	35.4	292.6	186	744	6.8	322	332	2,360	.20	.61	1.1	0
823	Macaroons	0	2,150	24.0	105.2	299.8	122	376	4.1	154	2,100	0	.19	.68	2.8	0
824	Marshmallow	0	1,855	18.1	59.9	328.0	95	222	2.3	948	413	1,180	.07	.27	.9	Trace
825	Molasses	0	1,914	29.0	48.1	344.7	231	576	9.5	1,751	626	500	.23	.25	5.4	0
826	Oatmeal with raisins	0	2,046	28.1	69.9	333.4	95	463	13.2	735	1,678	230	.31	.33	2.1	Trace
827	Peanut	0	2,146	45.4	86.6	303.9	191	935	4.1	785	794	910	.36	.35	12.5	Trace
828	Raisin	0	1,719	20.0	24.0	366.5	322	712	6.5	236	1,134	450	.19	.34	2.8	Trace
829	Sandwich type	0	2,245	21.8	102.1	314.3	118	1,093	3.2	2,191	172	0	.15	.38	2.2	0
830	Shortbread	0	2,259	32.7	104.8	295.3	318	708	2.5	272	250	350	.11	.23	2.4	0
831	Sugar, soft, thick, with enriched flour, home-type recipe	0	2,014	27.2	76.2	308.4	354	467	6.4	1,442	345	590	.72	.77	6.0	Trace
832	Sugar wafers	0	2,200	22.2	88.0	332.9	163	367	1.4	857	272	540	.06	.19	2.3	0
833	Vanilla wafers	0	2,096	24.5	73.0	337.5	186	286	1.8	1,143	327	590	.10	.31	1.4	0
	Cooky mixes and cookies baked from mixes:															
	Brownie, with enriched flour:															
	Complete mix:															
834	Dry form	0	1,901	21.8	64.4	337.0	95	476	5.4	1,356	739	410	.45	.50	3.9	0
835	Brownies, made with water, nuts	0	1,828	22.2	84.8	271.3	118	531	5.1	989	816	360	.72	.43	3.1	Trace
	Incomplete mix:															

836	Dry form	0	2,005	18.1	74.4	344.7	191	535	8.2	880	676	Trace	.42	.41	3.9	0
837	Brownies, made with egg, water, nuts	0	1,941	22.7	91.2	286.2	204	621	8.6	753	762	450	.58	.47	3.2	Trace
	Plain, with unenriched flour:															
838	Mix, dry form	0	2,236	15.9	109.8	303.0	390	667	1.4	1,597	132	0	.09	.08	1.4	0
839	Cookies, made with egg, water	0	2,236	21.8	110.2	294.8	399	739	2.3	1,574	191	540	.11	.22	1.2	0
840	Cookies, made with milk	0	2,223	16.8	108.0	302.6	431	685	1.4	1,565	191	50	.08	.15	1.2	Trace
	Cooky dough, plain, chilled in roll.															
841	Unbaked	0	2,037	15.9	102.5	266.7	150	299	1.4	2,250	200	310	.08	.15	1.1	0
842	Baked	0	2,250	17.7	113.4	294.4	163	331	1.4	2,486	218	330	.07	.15	1.1	0
	Cooking oil. See Oils, item 1401.															
843	**Corn, field**, whole-grain, raw	0	1,579	40.4	17.7	327.5	100	1,216	9.5	5	1,288	[52] 2,220	1.67	.54	9.8	(0)
	Corn, sweet:															
844	Raw, white and yellow.															
a	With husk (refuse: husk, silk, cob, trimmings)	64	157	5.7	1.6	36.1	5	181	1.1	Trace	457	[52] 650	.24	.19	2.8	20
b	Without husk (refuse: cob)	45	240	8.7	2.5	55.1	7	277	1.7	Trace	699	[52] 1,000	.37	.29	4.2	31
	Canned															
	Regular pack:															
847	Cream style, white and yellow, solids and liquid.	0	372	9.5	2.7	90.7	14	254	2.7	[10] 1,070	(440)	[52] 1,520	.13	.23	4.5	23
	Whole kernel.															
848	Vacuum pack, yellow, solids and liquid	0	376	11.3	2.3	93.0	14	331	2.3	[10] 1,070	(440)	1,570	(.15)	(.29)	(4.9)	23
849	Wet pack, white and yellow, solids and liquid.	0	299	8.6	2.7	71.2	18	218	1.8	[10] 1,070	440	[52] 1,220	.12	.22	4.1	23
	Special dietary pack (low-sodium):															
852	Cream style, white and yellow, solids and liquid	0	372	11.8	5.0	83.9	14	254	2.7	9	(440)	[52] 1,220	.13	.23	4.5	23
853	Whole kernel, wet pack, white and yellow, solids and liquid.	0	259	8.6	2.3	61.7	18	218	1.8	9	440	[52] 1,220	.12	.22	4.1	23
	Frozen															
856	Kernels, cut off cob	0	372	14.1	2.3	89.4	14	354	3.6	5	916	[52] (1,590)	.50	.32	7.3	38
858	Kernels, on cob (refuse: cob)	(45)	244	9.0	2.5	58.4	7	254	2.0	2	634	[52] (870)	.42	.22	4.7	25
860	**Corn flour**	0	1,669	35.4	11.8	348.4	27	(744)	8.2	(5)	—	[52] 1,540	.91	.27	6.4	(0)
	Corn grits, degermed.															
862	Enriched	0	1,642	39.5	3.6	354.3	18	331	[53] 13.0	5	363	[52] 2,000	[53] 2.0	[53] 1.2	[53] 16.0	(0)
864	Unenriched	0	1,642	39.5	3.6	354.3	18	331	4.5	5	363	[52] 2,000	.59	.18	5.4	(0)
	Corn muffins. See Muffins, corn: items 1347–1348															
	Corn oil. See Oils, item 1401.															
	Corn products used mainly as ready-to-eat breakfast cereals:															
	Corn flakes															
866	Added nutrients	0	1,751	35.8	1.8	386.9	77	204	6.4	4,559	544	(0)	1.94	.36	9.3	(0)
867	Added nutrients, sugar-covered	0	1,751	20.0	.9	414.1	54	109	4.5	3,515	—	(0)	1.85	.16	8.6	(0)
	Corn, puffed															
868	Added nutrients	0	1,810	36.7	19.1	366.5	91	408	26.3	4,808	—	(0)	4.00	.83	12.1	(0)
	Presweetened															
869	Added nutrients	0	1,719	18.1	.9	407.3	50	127	8.2	1,361	—	(0)	1.92	.77	9.6	(0)
870	Cocoa-flavored, added nutrients	0	1,769	28.1	10.0	393.3	91	408	27.2	3,856	—	(0)	3.60	.83	11.5	(0)
871	Fruit-flavored, added nutrients	0	1,792	25.4	12.2	396.4	136	318	22.7	2,722	—	(0)	4.50	.76	11.3	481
872	Corn, shredded, added nutrients	0	1,765	31.8	1.8	394.2	23	177	10.9	4,482	—	(0)	1.92	.80	9.6	(0)
873	Corn, rice, and wheat flakes, mixed, added nutrients	0	1,765	33.6	3.2	390.5	177	544	8.2	4,309	—	(0)	1.77	—	14.5	(0)
874	Corn, flaked, with protein concentrate (casein) and other added nutrients	0	1,715	104.3	7.3	303.9	1,406	1,497	81.2	4,990	—	(0)	7.50	8.90	64.3	159
	Corn sirup. See Sirup, table blends: item 2051.															
881	**Cornbread mix**	0	1,960	34.0	58.1	322.1	127	2,150	[54] 11.3	5,244	367	[54] 1,450	[54] 1.50	[54] .96	[54] 11.6	0
	Cornmeal, white or yellow															
883	Whole-ground, unbolted	0	1,610	41.7	17.7	334.3	91	1,161	10.9	(5)	(1,288)	[52] 2,310	1.72	.50	9.1	(0)
884	Bolted (nearly whole-grain)	0	1,642	40.8	15.4	337.9	(77)	(1,012)	8.2	(5)	(1,125)	[52] 2,180	1.36	.36	8.6	(0)
	Degermed															
885	Enriched	0	1,651	35.8	5.4	355.6	27	449	[53] 13.0	5	544	[52] 2,000	[53] 2.0	[53] 1.2	[53] 16.0	(0)
887	Unenriched	0	1,651	35.8	5.4	355.6	27	449	5.0	5	544	[52] 2,000	.64	.23	4.5	(0)
	Self-rising															
	Whole-ground															
889	With soft wheat flour added	0	1,574	39.0	13.2	326.1	[55] 1,365	2,830	[55] 7.3	6,260	[56] 962	[52] 1,720	[55] 1.14	[55] .32	[55] 7.7	(0)
890	Without wheat flour added	0	1,574	38.6	14.5	324.8	[55] 1,361	2,908	[55] 7.7	6,260	[56] 1,061	[52] 2,040	[55] 1.28	[55] .34	[55] 8.1	(0)
	Degermed															
891	With soft wheat flour added	0	1,579	34.9	5.0	340.7	[55] 1,325	2,377	[55] 4.5	6,260	[56] 494	[52] 1,590	[55] .56	[55] .21	[55] 4.4	(0)
892	Without wheat flour added	0	1,579	34.0	5.0	341.6	[55] 1,315	2,377	[55] 4.5	6,260	[56] 513	[52] 1,910	[55] .60	[55] .21	[55] 4.3	(0)

[45] Estimated average based on addition of salt in the amount of 0.6 percent of the finished product.

[46] See Appendix A, section on Protein, p. 162, and see Appendix B, section on Foods containing considerable nonprotein nitrogen, p. 182.

[47] Value is about 359 mg. per pound if cod has been dipped or rinsed in brine.

[48] Value is about 1,157 mg. per pound if cod has been dipped or rinsed in brine.

[49] Contains 13,600 to 18,100 mg. caffeine per pound of powder.

[50] Products are commercial unless otherwise specified.

[51] Based on product made with unenriched flour. With enriched flour, approximate values per pound are: Iron, 7.3 mg.; thiamine, 0.54 mg.; riboflavin, 0.45 mg.; niacin, 2.3 mg.

[52] Based on yellow varieties; white varieties contain only a trace of cryptoxanthin and carotenes, the pigments in corn that have biological activity.

[53] Based on product with minimum level of enrichment. See also Notes on Foods, p. 171.

[54] Based on mix made with enriched yellow degermed cornmeal. With unenriched cornmeal, approximate values per pound are: Iron, 4.5 mg.; thiamine, 0.36 mg.; riboflavin, 0.27 mg.; niacin, 3.2 mg. If white cornmeal is used, vitamin A value is 730 I.U. per pound.

[55] Value applies to unenriched product. Much of the self-rising cornmeal on the market is enriched. For enriched products, minimum values per pound are: Iron, 13 mg.; thiamine, 2.0 mg.; riboflavin, 1.2 mg.; niacin, 16 mg. For further information on self-rising cornmeal, especially calcium, see Notes on Foods, p. 171.

[56] Amount of potassium contributed by cornmeal and flour. Small quantities of additional potassium may be provided by other ingredients.

TABLE 2.—NUTRIENTS IN THE EDIBLE PORTION OF 1 POUND OF FOOD AS PURCHASED—Continued

[Numbers in parentheses denote values imputed—usually from another form of the food or from a similar food. Zero in parentheses indicates that the amount of a constituent probably is none or is too small to measure. Dashes denote lack of reliable data for a constituent believed to be present in measurable amount. Calculated values, as those based on a recipe, are not in parentheses]

Item No. (A)	Food and description (B)	Refuse (C)	Food energy (D)	Protein (E)	Fat (F)	Carbohydrate total (G)	Calcium (H)	Phosphorus (I)	Iron (J)	Sodium (K)	Potassium (L)	Vitamin A value (M)	Thiamine (N)	Riboflavin (O)	Niacin (P)	Ascorbic acid (Q)
		Percent	Calories	Grams	Grams	Grams	Milligrams	Milligrams	Milligrams	Milligrams	Milligrams	International units	Milligrams	Milligrams	Milligrams	Milligrams
893	**Cornsalad** (refuse: roots)	4	91	8.7	1.7	15.7	—	—	—	—	—	—	—	—	—	—
894	**Cornstarch**	0	1,642	1.4	Trace	397.4	(0)	(0)	(0)	Trace	Trace	(0)	(0)	(0)	(0)	(0)
895	**Cottonseed flour**	0	1,615	218.2	29.9	149.7	1,284	5,044	57.2	—	—	270	5.49	1.80	29.5	—
	Cottonseed oil. See Oils, item 1401.															
	Cowpeas, including blackeye peas:															
	Immature seeds:															
896	Raw:															
a	In pods (refuse: pods)	45	317	22.5	2.0	54.4	67	429	5.7	5	1,350	925	1.08	.32	4.0	71
b	Shelled	0	576	40.8	3.6	98.9	122	780	10.4	9	2,454	1,680	1.95	.59	7.3	132
898	Canned, solids and liquid	0	318	22.7	1.4	56.2	82	508	6.8	[81] 1,070	1,597	216	.41	.21	2.3	13
899	Frozen (blackeye peas only)	0	594	40.8	1.8	107.0	127	812	14.1	[9] 227	1,755	770	2.04	.54	6.3	68
901	Young pods, with seeds (refuse: ends, strings)	9	182	13.6	1.2	39.2	268	268	4.1	17	888	6,600	.61	.57	4.8	137
904	Mature seeds, dry	0	1,556	103.4	6.8	279.9	336	1,932	26.3	159	4,645	140	4.74	.97	9.8	
	Crab, including blue, Dungeness, rock, and king:															
905	Cooked, steamed:															
a	In shell (refuse: shell)	52	202	37.7	4.1	1.1	94	381	1.7	—	—	4,720	.35	.18	6.1	4
b	Meat only	0	422	78.5	8.6	2.3	195	794	3.6	—	—	9,850	.72	.36	12.7	9
906	**Crab,** canned	0	458	78.9	11.3	5.0	204	826	3.6	4,536	499	—	.36	.36	8.6	—
909	**Crabapples,** raw (refuse: cores, stems)	(8)	284	1.7	1.3	74.3	(25)	54	(1.3)	(4)	(459)	(150)	(.13)	(.08)	(.4)	33
	Crackers:															
910	Animal	0	1,946	29.9	42.6	362.4	236	517	7.3	1,374	431	590	.16	.30	1.5	Trace
911	Butter	0	2,077	31.8	80.7	305.3	671	1,179	2.7	4,954	513	1,090	.05	.25	4.4	(0)
912	Cheese	0	2,173	50.8	96.6	271.6	1,524	1,302	3.1	4,713	494	1,450	.06	.44	3.8	(0)
	Graham:															
913	Chocolate-coated	0	2,155	23.1	106.6	308.0	513	925	11.8	1,846	1,452	270	.30	1.27	5.4	(0)
914	Plain	0	1,742	36.3	42.6	332.5	181	676	6.8	3,039	1,742	(0)	.20	.95	6.7	(0)
915	Sugar-honey coated	0	1,864	30.1	51.7	346.6	359	1,492	7.3	2,286	1,225	—	.14	.87	4.7	(0)
916	Saltines	0	1,964	40.8	54.4	324.3	95	408	5.4	(4,990)	(544)	(0)	.05	.23	4.6	(0)
917	Sandwich type, peanut-cheese	0	2,227	68.5	108.4	254.5	234	812	2.7	4,808	1,025	180	.14	.23	16.1	(0)
918	Soda	0	1,994	41.7	59.4	320.2	100	404	6.8	4,990	544	(0)	.05	.20	4.7	(0)
919	Whole-wheat	0	1,828	38.1	62.6	309.4	104	862	3.4	2,481		(0)	.25	.19	4.3	(0)
	Cracker meal. See Crackers, soda; item 918.															
	Cranberries:															
920	Raw (refuse: stems, damaged berries)	4	200	1.7	3.0	47.0	61	44	2.2	9	357	190	.13	.09	.4	47
921	Dehydrated (4.9% moisture)	0	1,669	12.7	29.9	392.4	372	100	15.4	73	2,921	1,360	.78	.53	3.5	145
922	**Cranberry juice cocktail,** bottled (approx. 33% cranberry juice)	0	295	.5	.5	74.8	23	14	1.4	5	45	Trace	.04	.02	.1	[illegible]
	Cranberry sauce, sweetened:															
923	Canned, strained	0	662	.5	.9	170.1	27	18	.9	5	136	70	.05	.05	.2	8
926	**Crappie,** white, flesh only, raw	0	358	76.2	3.6	0	—	—	—	—	—	—	Trace	.12	6.3	—
927	**Crayfish, freshwater; and spiny lobster;** raw:															
a	In shell (refuse: shell)	88	39	7.9	.3	.7	42	109	.8	—	—	—	.01	.02	1.0	—
b	Meat only	0	327	66.2	2.3	5.4	349	912	6.8	—	—	—	.05	.19	8.8	—
	Cream, fluid:															
928	Half-and-half (cream and milk)	0	608	14.5	53.1	20.9	490	386	.2	209	585	2,180	.14	.72	.3	4
929	Light, coffee or table	0	957	13.6	93.4	19.5	463	363	.1	195	553	3,850	.14	.67	.3	4
930	Light whipping	0	1,361	11.3	142.0	16.3	386	304	.1	163	463	5,820	.11	.54	.2	4
931	Heavy whipping	0	1,597	10.0	170.6	14.1	340	268	.1	145	404	6,990	.10	.49	.2	4
	Cream substitutes, dried, containing:															
932	Cream, skim milk (calcium reduced), and lactose	0	2,304	38.6	121.1	278.1	372	—	.9	2,608		4,340	.22	5.30	.8	—
933	Cream, skim milk, lactose, and sodium hexametaphosphate	0	2,250	62.1	125.6	241.5	2,245	—	1.4	—	—	2,340	.04	3.24	1.5	—
934	**Cream puffs** with custard filling	0	1,057	29.5	63.1	93.0	367	517	3.2	376	549	1,590	.19	.77	.5	Trace
935	**Cress, garden,** raw [42] (refuse: stems, crowns, spoiled leaves)	29	103	8.4	2.3	17.7	261	245	4.2	45	1,952	29,960	.27	.86	3.3	222
938	**Croaker, Atlantic,** raw:															
a	Whole (refuse: head, tail, fins, skin, entrails, and bones)	66	148	27.4	3.4	0	—	—	—	134	361	90	.18	.12	8.5	—
b	Flesh only	0	435	80.7	10.0	0	—	—	—	395	1,061	270	.54	.36	24.9	—
940	**Croaker, white,** flesh only, raw	0	381	81.6	3.6	0	—	—	—	—	—	—	—	—	—	—
941	**Croaker, yellowfin,** flesh only, raw	0	404	87.1	3.6	0	—	—	—	—	—	—	—	—	—	—
	Cucumbers, raw, portion used—															

942		Whole cucumber, including skin (refuse: ends, bruised spots).	5	65	3.9	4	14.7	108	116	4.7	26	689	1,080	.15	.19	.9	48
943		Pared cucumber (refuse: parings, ends, bruised spots).	27	46	2.0	.3	10.6	56	60	1.0	20	530	Trace	.11	.14	.7	37
		Cucumber pickles. See Pickles, items 1558–1561.															
		Currants, raw [58]															
944		Black, European, (refuse stems)	2	240	7.6	.4	58.2	267	178	4.9	13	1,654	1,020	.24	.22	1.3	889
945		Red and white (refuse stems)	3	220	6.2	.9	53.2	141	101	4.4	9	1,131	[59] 530	.18	(.22)	.6	182
946		**Cusk, raw:**															
	a	Drawn (refuse: head, tail, fins, skin, and bones)	42	197	45.3	.5	0	—	—	—	—	—	—	.08	.22	6.1	—
	b	Flesh only	0	340	78.0	.9	0	—	—	—	—	—	—	.15	.38	10.4	—
		Custard, frozen. See Ice cream, items 1139–1141															
		Custard dessert mix. See Pudding mixes, item 1829.															
949		**Custardapple, bullocksheart, raw** (refuse: skin, seeds).	42	266	4.5	1.6	66.3	71	53	2.1	—	—	Trace	.20	.27	1.4	57
		Daikon. See Radishes, Oriental: item 1845.															
950		**Dandelion greens, raw, fully trimmed**	0	204	12.2	3.2	41.7	848	299	14.1	345	1,801	63,500	.85	1.17	—	161
		Danish pastry. See Rolls and buns, item 1899															
		Dasheens. See Taros, items 2271–2272.															
952		**Dates, domestic, natural and dry:**															
	a	With pits (refuse: pits)	13	1,081	8.7	2.0	287.7	233	249	11.8	4	2,557	200	.35	.38	8.6	0
	b	Without pits	0	1,243	10.0	2.3	330.7	268	286	13.6	5	2,939	230	.40	.44	9.9	0
		Deviled ham. See Sausage, cold cuts, and luncheon meats: item 1993.															
		Dewberries See Blackberries, item 417.															
953		**Dock** (curly or narrowleaf dock, broadleaf dock, and sheep sorrel), raw (refuse: stems).	30	89	6.7	1.0	17.8	210	130	5.1	16	1,073	40,960	.29	.70	1.6	378
955		**Dogfish, spiny** (grayfish), flesh only, raw	0	708	79.8	40.8	0	—	—	—	—	—	—	.23	—	—	—
956		**Dolly Varden,** flesh and skin, raw	0	653	90.3	29.5	0	—	—	—	—	—	—	.28	.29	—	—
		Doughnuts:															
957		Cake type	0	1,774	20.9	84.4	233.2	181	862	[60] 6.4	2,273	408	360	[60] .72	[60] .73	[60] 5.4	Trace
958		Yeast-leavened	0	1,878	28.6	121.1	171.0	172	345	[61] 6.8	1,061	363	270	[61] .75	[61] .76	[61] 6.1	0
959		**Drum, freshwater, raw**															
	a	Whole (refuse: head, tail, fins, skin, bones, and entrails).	74	143	20.4	6.1	0	—	—	—	83	337	—	—	—	—	—
	b	Flesh only	0	549	78.5	23.6	0	—	—	—	318	1,297	—	—	—	—	—
960		**Drum, red** (redfish), **raw:**															
	a	Whole (refuse: head, tail, fins, skin, bones, and entrails)	59	149	33.5	.7	0	—	—	—	102	508	—	.28	.09	6.5	—
	b	Flesh only	0	363	81.6	1.8	0	—	—	—	249	1,238	—	.67	.22	15.9	—
		Duck, domesticated, raw:															
961		Total edible:															
	a	Live (refuse: blood, feathers, head, feet, inedible viscera, lungs, kidneys, and bones).	43	813	41.4	74.0	0	(26)	(455)	(4.1)	—	—	—	(.20)	(.49)	(17.2)	—
	b	Dressed (refuse: head, feet, inedible viscera, lungs, kidneys, and bones)	35	961	47.2	84.3	0	(29)	(519)	(4.7)	—	—	—	(.23)	(.56)	(19.7)	—
	c	Ready-to-cook (refuse: bones)	18	1,213	59.5	106.4	0	(37)	(655)	(6.0)	—	—	—	(.29)	(.71)	(24.8)	—
		Duck, wild, raw:															
963		Total edible, dressed (refuse: head, feet, inedible viscera, and bones).	42	613	55.5	41.6	0	—	—	—	—	—	—	—	—	—	—
965		**Eclairs** with custard filling and chocolate icing	0	1,081	28.1	61.7	105.2	363	508	3.2	372	553	1,540	.19	.75	.6	2
966		**Eel, American, raw:**															
	a	Head, skin, and entrails removed (refuse: bones)	24	803	54.8	63.1	0	62	696	2.4	—	—	5,550	.76	1.26	4.7	—
	b	Flesh only	0	1,057	72.1	83.0	0	82	916	3.2	—	—	7,300	1.00	1.66	6.2	—
967		**Eel, smoked,** flesh only	0	1,497	81.4	126.1	0	—	—	—	—	—	—	—	—	—	—
		Eggs:															
		Chicken.															
		Raw:															
968		Whole:															
	a	Fresh, all sizes (refuse: shell)	11	658	52.1	46.4	3.6	218	828	9.3	493	521	4,760	.42	1.20	.2	0
	b	Frozen	0	739	58.5	52.2	4.1	245	930	10.4	553	585	5,350	.48	1.35	.3	0
969		Whites, fresh and frozen	0	231	49.4	.1	3.6	41	68	.5	662	631	0	.02	1.23	.5	0
970		Yolks, fresh [62]	0	1,579	72.6	138.8	2.7	640	2,581	24.9	236	445	15,420	1.02	2.00	.2	0
971		Yolks, frozen [62]	0	1,415	69.9	122.0	2.7	567	2,277	22.2	286	454	13,560	.92	1.91	.3	0
972		Yolks, frozen, sugared	0	1,429	64.9	108.9	44.9	513	2,064	20.0	259	413	12,290	.83	1.73	.2	0
		Dried:															
978		Whole	0	2,685	213.2	186.9	18.6	818	3,629	39.5	1,937	2,100	19,460	1.50	5.45	1.1	0
979		Whole, stabilized (glucose reduced)	0	2,762	221.8	191.6	11.3	880	3,774	40.8	2,014	2,186	20,230	1.56	5.67	1.1	0

[19] Estimated average based on addition of salt in the amount of 0.6 percent of the finished product

[17] Average weighted in accordance with commercial practices in freezing vegetables. See also Notes on Foods, p. 177.

[43] For further description of product, see Notes on Foods, p. 178

[57] About 9 mg per pound is from cranberries. Ascorbic acid is usually added to approximately 181 mg per pound

[58] Production of the European black currant, in particular, and, to less extent, of other currants and of gooseberries is restricted by Federal or State regulations that prohibit shipments of the plants to certain designated States and areas within some States. The regulations have been enacted to prevent further spread of the whitepine blister rust, inasmuch as these plants are alternate hosts of this disease

[59] Based on red currants only

[60] Based on product made with enriched flour. With unenriched flour, approximate values per pound are: Iron, 2.3 mg; thiamine, 0.14 mg; riboflavin, 0.27 mg.; niacin, 1.4 mg

[61] Based on product made with enriched flour. With unenriched flour, approximate values per pound are: Iron, 2.7 mg; thiamine, 0.18 mg; riboflavin, 0.36 mg; niacin, 2.3 mg

[62] Fresh yolks include a small proportion of white, frozen yolks, a considerable amount

TABLE 2.—NUTRIENTS IN THE EDIBLE PORTION OF 1 POUND OF FOOD AS PURCHASED—Continued

[Numbers in parentheses denote values imputed—usually from another form of the food or from a similar food. Zero in parentheses indicates that the amount of a constituent probably is none or is too small to measure. Dashes denote lack of reliable data for a constituent believed to be present in measurable amount. Calculated values, as those based on a recipe, are not in parentheses]

Item No.		Food and description	Refuse	Food energy	Protein	Fat	Carbohydrate total	Calcium	Phosphorus	Iron	Sodium	Potassium	Vitamin A value	Thiamine	Riboflavin	Niacin	Ascorbic Acid
(A)		(B)	(C)	(D)	(E)	(F)	(G)	(H)	(I)	(J)	(K)	(L)	(M)	(N)	(O)	(P)	(Q)
		Eggs—Continued	Percent	Calories	Grams	Grams	Grams	Milligrams	Milligrams	Milligrams	Milligrams	Milligrams	International units	Milligrams	Milligrams	Milligrams	Milligrams
		Chicken—Continued															
		Dried—Continued															
980		White, flakes	0	1,583	349.7	.9	21.8	281	467	1.5	4,880	4,250	0	0.18	8.58	3.1	0
981		White, powder	0	1,687	362.9	.5	25.9	268	499	4.5	5,180	4,536	0	.18	9.65	3.4	0
982		Yolk	0	3,012	150.1	259.7	11.7	1,247	4,038	49.0	454	843	27,100	1.86	3.58	.1	0
983		Duck, whole, fresh, raw (refuse: shell)	12	762	51.9	57.9	2.8	222	778	15.2	(487)	(515)	4,710	.70	(1.10)	.4	0
984		Goose, whole, fresh, raw (refuse: shell)	13	730	54.8	52.5	5.1	—	—	—	—	—	—	—	—	—	—
985		Turkey, whole, fresh, raw (refuse: shell)	12	679	52.5	47.1	6.8	—	—	—	—	—	—	—	—	—	—
986		Eggplant, raw (refuse: ends, parings, trimmings)	19	92	4.4	.7	20.6	44	96	2.6	7	780	50	.39	.17	2.3	19
988		Elderberries, raw (refuse: stems)	8	307	11.1	(2.1)	69.9	162	115	6.8	—	1,279	2,500	.29	.27	2.3	151
989		Endive (curly endive and escarole), raw:															
	a	Good quality (refuse: ends)	12	80	6.8	.4	16.3	321	215	6.8	56	1,174	13,170	.27	.56	2.0	40
	b	Fair quality (refuse: ends, outer leaves, trimmings)	25	68	5.8	.3	13.9	276	184	5.8	48	1,000	11,230	.23	.48	1.7	34
		Escarole, raw. See Endive, item 989															
990		Eulachon (smelt), flesh only, raw	0	553	66.2	28.1	0	—	—	—	—	—	—	.18	.29	—	—
		Farina:															
		Enriched:															
991		Regular	0	1,683	51.7	4.1	354.3	113	485	[9] 13.0	9	376	(0)	[9] 2.00	[9] 1.2	[9] 16.0	(0)
993		Quick-cooking	0	1,642	51.7	4.1	337.7	2,268	2,518	[illegible]	1,134	376	(0)	[9] 2.00	[9] 1.2	[9] 16.0	(0)
995		Instant-cooking	0	1,642	51.7	4.1	339.7	2,268	1,756	[illegible]	32	376	(0)	[9] 2.00	[9] 1.2	[9] 16.0	(0)
997		Unenriched, regular	0	1,683	51.7	4.1	349.3	113	485	6.8	9	376	(0)	.27	.45	3.2	(0)
999		Fats, cooking (vegetable fat)	0	4,010	0	454.	0	0	0	0	0	0	—	0	0	0	0
1000		Fennel, common, leaves, raw (refuse: trimmings)	7	118	11.8	1.7	21.5	423	215	11.4	—	1,675	14,760	—	—	—	129
		Figs:															
1001		Raw	0	363	5.4	1.4	92.1	159	100	2.7	9	880	360	.27	.23	1.8	9
1002		Candied	0	1,356	15.9	.9	334.3	—	—	—	—	—	—	—	—	—	—
		Canned, solids and liquid:															
1003		Water pack, with or without artificial sweetener	0	218	2.3	.9	56.7	64	64	1.8	9	703	150	.13	.13	1.1	5
		Sirup pack:															
1004		Light	0	295	2.3	.9	76.2	59	59	1.8	9	680	150	.13	.13	1.1	2
1005		Heavy	0	381	2.3	.9	98.9	59	59	1.8	9	676	150	.13	.13	1.1	2
1006		Extra heavy	0	467	2.3	.9	121.1	59	59	1.8	9	662	150	.13	.13	1.0	2
1007		Dried (23.0% moisture)	0	1,243	19.5	5.9	313.4	572	349	13.6	154	2,903	360	.47	.47	3.2	(0)
1008		Filberts (hazelnuts):															
	a	In shell (refuse: shells)	54	1,323	26.3	130.2	34.9	436	703	7.1	4	1,469	—	.96	—	1.9	Trace
	b	Shelled	0	2,876	57.2	283.0	75.8	948	1,529	15.4	9	3,193	—	2.09	—	4.1	Trace
1009		Finnan haddie (smoked haddock), flesh only, raw	0	467	105.2	1.8	0	—	—	—	—	—	—	.28	.24	9.6	—
		Fish. See individual kinds: Cod, etc. Also see table 13, p. 183															
1012		Fish flakes, canned	0	503	112.0	2.7	0	222	1,052	3.6	—	—	—	—	—	—	—
		Fish flour:															
1013		From whole fish	0	1,524	353.8	1.1	0	20,911	14,062	186.6	771	1,959	—	.32	2.81	9.9	—
1014		From fillets	0	1,805	421.8	.5	0	4,173	2,767	38.3	181	363	—	—	—	—	—
1015		From fillet waste	0	1,583	422.1	.9	0	27,397	18,416	244.9	998	2,449	—	—	—	—	—
1018		Flatfishes (flounders, soles, and sanddabs), raw:															
	a	Whole (refuse: head, tail, fins, skin, entrails, and bones)	67	118	25.0	1.2	0	18	292	1.2	117	512	—	.08	.08	2.5	—
	b	Flesh only	0	358	75.8	3.6	0	54	885	3.6	354	1,551	—	.24	.22	7.6	—
		Flour. See Corn, Rice, Rye, Soya, Wheat.															
		Frankfurters. See Sausage, cold cuts, and luncheon meats: items 1994–2000.															
1020		Frog legs, raw (refuse: bones)	35	215	48.3	.9	0	53	433	4.4	—	—	0	.41	.74	3.4	—
		Frosting mixes. See Cake icing mixes, items 575, 577.															
		Frozen custard. See Ice cream, items 1139–1141.															
		Fruit cocktail, canned, solids and liquid:															
1021		Water pack, with or without artificial sweetener	0	168	1.8	.5	44.0	41	59	1.8	23	762	670	.07	.05	2.1	18
		Sirup pack:															
1022		Light	0	272	1.8	.5	71.2	41	54	1.8	23	744	630	.07	.05	2.0	9
1023		Heavy	0	345	1.8	.5	89.4	41	54	1.8	23	730	610	.07	.05	2.0	9
1024		Extra heavy	0	417	1.8	.5	107.5	41	54	1.8	23	721	630	.07	.05	2.0	9
		Fruit salad, canned, solids and liquid:															
1025		Water pack, with or without artificial sweetener	0	159	1.8	.5	41.3	36	50	1.4	5	631	2,140	.06	.15	2.7	11

		Sirup pack:															
1026		Light	0	268	1. 4	. 5	70. 3	36	50	1 4	5	617	2, 090	06	. 13	2 6	11
1027		Heavy	0	340	1 4	. 5	88. 0	36	50	1 4	5	608	2, 060	. 06	. 12	2 6	11
1028		Extra heavy	0	408	1. 4	. 5	106. 1	36	50	1 4	5	594	2, 020	. 06	. 12	2 6	11
		Garbanzos. See Chickpeas, item 753.															
1029		**Garlic, cloves, raw** (refuse: skins)	12	547	24. 8	. 8	123 0	116	806	6. 0	76	2, 112	Trace	1 01	. 31	1 9	59
1030		**Gelatin, dry**	0	1, 520	388. 3	. 5	0	—	—	—	—	—	—	—	—	—	—
		Gelatin dessert powder and desserts made from dessert powder:															
1031		Dessert powder	0	1, 683	42 6	0	399 2	—	—	—	1, 442	—	—	—	—	—	—
		Desserts, made with water.															
1032		Plain	0	268	6. 8	0	64. 0	—	—	—	231	—	—	—	—	—	—
1033		With fruit added	0	304	5. 9	. 5	74. 4	—	—	—	154	—	—	—	—	—	12
		Gin. See Beverages, items 395–399															
		Ginger ale. See Beverages, item 407															
		Gingerbread. See Cake mixes, items 560–561.															
1034		**Ginger root, crystallized** (candied)	0	1, 542	1. 4	9	395 1	—	—	—	—	—	—	—	—	—	—
1035		**Ginger root, fresh** (refuse scrapings)	7	207	5. 9	4. 2	40. 1	97	152	8. 9	25	1, 114	40	. 10	. 17	2 8	17
		Gizzard, raw															
1036		Chicken, all classes	0	513	91 2	12 2	3 2	45	476	13 2	295	1, 089	—	12	. 89	20 3	—
1038		Goose	0	631	97. 1	24 0	0	—	—	—	—	—	—	—	—	—	—
1039		Turkey, all classes	0	712	92 1	33. 1	5. 0	—	—	—	263	771	—	22	. 58	22 9	—
		Gizzard shad. See Shad, gizzard: item 2038.															
		Gluten flour. See Wheat flours, item 2444															
		Goat milk. See Milk, goat: item 1335.															
		Goose, domesticated, raw:															
1041		Total edible:															
	a	Live (refuse: blood, feathers, head, feet, inedible viscera, and bones).	50	803	37. 2	71. 4	0	(23)	(399)	(3. 6)	—	—	—	(17)	(. 43)	(15. 1)	—
	b	Dressed (refuse: head, feet, inedible viscera, and bones)	43	915	42 4	81. 5	0	(26)	(455)	(4. 1)	—	—	—	(20)	(49)	(17. 2)	—
	c	Ready-to-cook (refuse: bones)	27	1, 172	54 3	104. 3	0	(33)	(583)	(5. 3)	—	—	—	(. 25)	(. 63)	(22. 1)	—
		Gooseberries: [62]															
1048		Raw	0	177	3. 6	. 9	44 0	82	68	2 3	5	703	1, 320	—	—	—	149
		Canned, solids and liquid:															
1049		Water pack, with or without artificial sweetener.	0	118	2. 3	. 5	29 9	54	45	1 4	5	476	900	—	—	—	50
		Sirup pack:															
1050		Heavy	0	408	2. 3	. 5	104 3	50	41	1. 4	5	445	840	—	—	—	47
1051		Extra heavy	0	531	2. 3	. 5	136. 1	50	41	1 4	5	431	820	—	—	—	46
		Gourd, dishcloth. See Towelgourd, item 2315															
1052		**Granadilla, purple** (passionfruit), raw (refuse. shells).	48	212	5 2	1. 7	50 0	31	151	3 8	66	821	1, 650	Trace	. 31	3 5	71
		Grapefruit, raw, used for segments (refuse: rind, rag, seeds, membranes around segments, handling loss):															
		Pink, red, and white.															
1053		All varieties	51	91	1. 1	. 2	23 6	36	36	9	2	300	180	08	. 04	4	[66] 84
1054		California and Arizona (Marsh Seedless)	57	86	1. 0	. 2	22 4	62	39	. 8	2	263	20	07	. 03	. 3	[66] 78
1055		Florida, all varieties	50	86	1 1	. 2	22. 5	34	34	9	2	306	180	08	04	. 4	[66] 84
1056		Texas, all varieties	50	98	1. 1	. 2	25 6	34	34	. 9	2	306	(67)	. 08	. 04	. 4	85
		Pink and red.															
1057		Seeded (Foster Pink)	52	87	1. 1	. 2	22 6	35	35	9	2	294	960	08	03	4	[66] 85
1058		Seedless (including Pink Marsh, Redblush)	49	93	1 2	2	24 1	37	37	. 9	2	312	1, 020	09	04	4	[66] 83
		White.															
1059		Seeded (Duncan, other varieties)	55	84	1. 0	. 2	22 0	33	33	8	2	276	20	08	03	4	[66] 78
1060		Seedless (Marsh Seedless)	51	87	1. 1	. 2	22 4	36	36	9	2	300	20	. 08	. 04	4	[66] 82
		Grapefruit juice, raw; and grapefruit, raw, used for juice:															
		Pink, red, and white:															
1061		All varieties:															
	a	Chilled juice	0	177	2 3	. 5	41. 7	41	68	. 9	5	735	360	17	07	8	[66] 171
	b	Grapefruit used for juice (refuse rind, rag, seeds, membranes, handling loss)	51	87	1. 1	. 2	20 5	20	33	. 4	2	360	180	08	. 04	. 4	[66] 84
1062		California and Arizona (Marsh Seedless):															
	a	Chilled juice	0	191	1. 8	. 5	46 3	41	68	9	5	735	50	17	07	8	[66] 181
	b	Grapefruit used for juice (refuse rind, rag, seeds, membranes, handling loss).	57	82	. 8	. 2	19 9	18	29	4	2	316	20	07	03	4	[66] 78
1063		Florida, all varieties															
	a	Chilled juice	0	168	2 3	. 5	39. 9	41	68	9	5	735	360	17	07	8	[66] 169
	b	Grapefruit used for juice (refuse rind, rag, seeds, membranes, handling loss).	50	84	1. 1	. 2	20 0	20	34	5	2	367	180	08	04	4	[66] 84

[43] For further description of product, see Notes on Foods, p 178.

[62] Production of the European black currant, in particular, and, to less extent, of other currants and of gooseberries is restricted by Federal or State regulations that prohibit shipments of the plants to certain designated States and areas within some States. The regulations have been enacted to prevent further spread of the whitepine blister rust, inasmuch as these plants are alternate hosts of this disease.

[63] Based on products with minimum level of enrichment. See Notes on Foods, p. 171. In several brands, however, values for iron range from 12.7 to 32.2 mg. per pound.

[64] Value of 192 mg. per pound reported for one brand

[65] Based on product with minimum level of enrichment. See also Notes on Foods, p. 171.

[66] Value weighted by monthly and total season shipments for marketing as fresh fruit

[67] For white-fleshed varieties, value is about 20 I.U. per pound, for red-fleshed varieties, about 1,000 I.U.

TABLE 2.—NUTRIENTS IN THE EDIBLE PORTION OF 1 POUND OF FOOD AS PURCHASED—Continued

[Numbers in parentheses denote values imputed—usually from another form of the food or from a similar food. Zero in parentheses indicates that the amount of a constituent probably is none or is too small to measure. Dashes denote lack of reliable data for a constituent believed to be present in measurable amount. Calculated values, as those based on a recipe, are not in parentheses]

Item No.		Food and description	Refuse	Food energy	Protein	Fat	Carbohydrate total	Calcium	Phosphorus	Iron	Sodium	Potassium	Vitamin A value	Thiamine	Riboflavin	Niacin	Ascorbic Acid
(A)		(B)	(C)	(D)	(E)	(F)	(G)	(H)	(I)	(J)	(K)	(L)	(M)	(N)	(O)	(P)	(Q)
		Grapefruit juice, raw; and grapefruit, raw, used for juice—Continued	Percent	Calories	Grams	Grams	Grams	Milligrams	Milligrams	Milligrams	Milligrams	Milligrams	International units	Milligrams	Milligrams	Milligrams	Milligrams
		Pink, red, and white—Continued															
1064		Texas, all varieties:															
	a	Chilled juice	0	191	2.3	0.5	45.4	41	68	0.9	5	735	(?)	0.17	0.07	0.8	171
	b	Grapefruit used for juice (refuse: rind, rag, seeds, membranes, handling loss).	50	95	1.1	.2	22.7	20	34	.5	2	367	(?)	.08	.04	.4	85
		Pink and red:															
1065		Seeded (Foster Pink):															
	a	Chilled juice	0	172	2.3	.5	41.3	41	68	.9	5	735	2,000	.17	.07	.8	177
	b	Grapefruit used for juice (refuse: rind, rag, seeds, membranes, handling loss).	52	83	1.1	.2	19.8	20	33	.4	2	353	960	.08	.03	.4	85
1066		Seedless (including Pink Marsh, Redblush):															
	a	Chilled juice	0	177	1.8	.5	42.2	41	68	.9	5	735	2,080	.17	.07	.8	163
	b	Grapefruit used for juice (refuse: rind, rag, seeds, membranes, handling loss).	49	90	.9	.2	21.5	21	35	.5	2	375	1,020	.09	.04	.4	83
		White:															
1067		Seeded (Duncan, other varieties):															
	a	Chilled juice	0	181	2.3	.5	43.1	41	68	.9	5	735	50	.17	.07	.8	172
	b	Grapefruit used for juice (refuse: rind, rag, seeds, membranes, handling loss).	56	82	1.0	.2	19.4	18	31	.4	2	331	20	.08	.03	.4	78
1068		Seedless (Marsh Seedless):															
	a	Chilled juice	0	172	2.3	.5	40.8	41	68	.9	5	735	50	.17	.07	.8	169
	b	Grapefruit used for juice (refuse: rind, rag, seeds, membranes, handling loss).	51	84	1.1	.2	20.0	20	33	.4	2	360	25	.08	.04	.4	84
		Grapefruit segments, canned, solids and liquid:															
1069		Water pack, with or without artificial sweetener	0	136	2.7	.5	34.5	59	64	1.4	18	685	50	.13	.08	.9	137
1070		Sirup pack	0	318	2.7	.5	80.7	59	64	1.4	5	612	50	.13	.08	.9	137
		Grapefruit juice, canned:															
1071		Unsweetened	0	186	2.3	.5	44.5	36	64	1.8	5	735	50	.13	.07	.8	154
1072		Sweetened	0	240	2.3	.5	58.1	36	64	1.8	5	735	50	.13	.07	.8	141
		Grapefruit juice, frozen concentrate:															
1073		Unsweetened	0	658	8.6	1.8	156.9	154	272	1.8	18	2,740	140	.61	.27	3.0	626
1075		Sweetened	0	748	7.3	1.4	182.3	127	227	1.4	14	2,304	110	.53	.23	2.5	526
1077		**Grapefruit juice, dehydrated** (crystals, 1% moisture)	0	1,715	21.8	4.5	409.6	395	703	4.5	45	7,131	360	1.63	.70	7.9	1,588
		Grapefruit juice and orange juice blended:															
		Canned:															
1079		Unsweetened	0	195	2.7	.9	45.8	45	68	1.4	5	835	450	.24	.08	1.0	154
1080		Sweetened	0	227	2.3	.5	55.3	45	68	1.4	5	835	450	.23	.08	1.0	154
1081		Frozen concentrate, unsweetened	0	712	9.5	2.3	168.3	137	215	1.8	9	2,826	1,720	1.03	.14	5.0	653
1083		**Grapefruit peel, candied**	0	1,433	1.8	1.4	365.6	—	—	—	—	—	—	—	—	—	—
		Grapes:															
		Raw:															
1084		American type (slip skin) as Concord, Delaware, Niagara, Catawba, and Scuppernong:															
	a	Good quality (refuse: stems, seeds, skins)	37	197	3.7	2.9	44.9	46	34	1.1	9	452	290	(.15)	(.08)	(.7)	10
	b	Fair quality (refuse: stems, seeds, skins, defects, handling loss).	43	178	3.4	2.6	40.6	41	31	1.0	8	409	260	(.13)	(.07)	(.7)	9
1085		European type (adherent skin) as Malaga, Muscat, Thompson Seedless, Emperor, and Flame Tokay (refuse: stems, seeds, shriveled grapes).	11	270	2.4	1.2	69.8	48	81	1.6	12	698	(400)	.21	.11	1.0	18
		Canned:															
		Thompson Seedless, solids and liquid:															
1086		Water pack, with or without artificial sweetener.	0	231	2.3	.5	61.7	36	59	1.4	18	499	310	.18	.06	.7	11
1087		Sirup pack, heavy	0	349	2.3	.5	90.7	36	59	1.4	18	476	290	.17	.06	.7	10
		Grape juice:															
1088		Canned or bottled	0	299	.9	Trace	75.3	50	54	1.4	9	526	—	.18	.10	1.1	Trace
1089		Frozen concentrate, sweetened	0	830	2.7	.1	210.0	45	68	1.8	14	535	80	.29	.45	3.2	67
1091		**Grape juice drink,** canned (approx. 30% grape juice)	0	245	.5	Trace	62.6	14	18	.5	5	159	—	.05	.05	.5	73
		Grits. See Corn grits, items 862, 864.															
1092		**Groundcherries** (poha or cape-gooseberries), raw (refuse: husks, stems).	8	221	7.9	2.9	46.7	38	167	4.2	—	—	3,000	.45	.18	11.7	44

1093		**Grouper,** including red, black, and speckled hind; raw:															
	a	Whole (refuse: head, fins, tail, bones, skin, and entrails).	57	170	37. 6	1. 0	0	—	—	—	—	—	—	. 33	—	—	—
	b	Flesh only	0	395	87. 5	2. 3	0	—	—	—	—	—	—	. 77	—	—	—
		Guavas, whole, raw:															
1094		Common (refuse: stems, blossom ends)	3	273	3. 5	2. 6	66. 0	101	185	4. 0	18	1, 272	1, 230	. 23	. 21	5. 1	[70] 1, 065
1095		Strawberry (refuse: stems, blossom ends)	2	289	4. 4	2. 7	70. 2	(102)	(187)	(4. 0)	(18)	(1, 285)	400	. 15	. 12	2. 8	165
		Guinea hen, raw:															
1096		Total edible:															
	a	Live (refuse: blood, feathers, head, feet, inedible viscera, and bones).	50	355	52. 6	14. 6	0	—	—	—	—	—	—	—	—	—	—
	b	Dressed (refuse: head, feet, inedible viscera, and bones).	40	428	63 4	17. 6	0	—	—	—	—	—	—	—	—	—	—
	c	Ready-to-cook (refuse: bones)	16	594	88. 0	24. 4	0	—	—	—	—	—	—	—	—	—	—
1099		**Haddock,** raw															
	a	Whole (refuse: head, tail, fins, bones, skin, and entrails).	52	172	39. 8	. 2	0	50	429	1. 5	133	662	—	. 09	. 14	6. 5	—
	b	Flesh only	0	358	83. 0	. 5	0	104	894	3. 2	277	1, 379	—	. 19	. 29	13. 6	—
1101		**Haddock, smoked,** canned or not canned	0	467	105. 2	1. 8	0	—	—	—	—	—	—	. 28	. 24	19. 1	—
1102		**Hake,** including Pacific hake, squirrel hake, and silver hake or whiting; raw:															
	a	Whole (refuse: head, tail, fins, skin, entrails, and bones)	57	144	32 2	. 8	0	80	277	—	144	708	—	. 19	. 39	—	—
	b	Flesh only	0	336	74. 8	1 8	0	186	644	—	336	1, 647	—	. 43	. 91	—	—
1103		**Halibut, Atlantic and Pacific,** raw:															
	a	Whole (refuse: head, tail, fins, entrails, scales, bones, and skin).	41	268	55 9	3. 2	0	35	565	1. 9	145	1, 202	1, 180	. 17	. 18	22. 3	—
	b	Flesh only	0	454	94. 8	5. 4	0	59	957	3. 2	[71] 245	2, 037	2, 000	. 29	. 30	37. 8	—
1105		**Halibut, smoked**	0	1, 016	94 3	68 0	0	—	—	—	—	—	—	—	—	—	—
1106		**Halibut, California,** flesh only, raw	0	440	89. 8	6. 4	0	—	—	—	—	—	—	—	—	—	—
1107		**Halibut, Greenland,** raw:															
	a	Whole (refuse: head, tail, fins, skin, bones, and entrails).	48	344	38 7	19. 8	0	—	495	—	—	—	—	. 03	—	—	—
	b	Flesh only	0	662	74 4	38. 1	0	—	953	—	—	—	—	. 05	—	—	—
		Ham. See Pork, items 1693–1707, 1765–1783.															
		Hamburger. See Beef, items 367, 369.															
1109		**Haws, scarlet,** raw (refuse: core)	20	316	7. 3	2. 5	75. 5	—	—	—	—	—	—	—	—	—	—
		Hazelnuts. See Filberts, item 1008.															
		Headcheese. See Sausage, cold cuts, and luncheon meats item 2001.															
		Heart, raw															
1110		Beef, lean	0	490	77. 6	16. 3	3. 2	23	885	18 1	390	875	90	2. 42	3. 98	34. 1	9
1112		Beef, lean with visible fat	0	1, 148	69. 9	93. 9	. 5	—	826	—	—	—	—	—	—	—	—
1114		Calf	0	562	68. 0	26. 8	8 2	14	726	13. 6	426	943	140	2. 86	4 76	36 7	5
1116		Chicken, all classes	0	608	84. 4	27. 2	. 5	18	717	15. 0	358	721	(140)	. 26	3. 63	20 8	18
1118		Hog	0	513	76 2	20. 0	1 8	14	594	15 0	245	481	140	1. 94	5. 62	29 8	14
1120		Lamb	0	735	76. 2	43. 5	4 5	50	1, 129	—	—	—	320	2. 04	3 36	28 6	5
1122		Turkey, all classes	0	776	73. 5	50. 8	. 9	—	—	—	313	1, 089	(140)	1. 04	3. 88	22. 5	(18)
		Herring. (See also Lake herring, item 1168.)															
		Raw:															
1124		Atlantic.															
	a	Whole (refuse: head, tail, fins, entrails, skin, and bones).	49	407	40. 0	26. 1	0	—	592	2. 5	—	—	270	. 05	. 35	8. 3	—
	b	Flesh only	0	798	78. 5	51. 3	0	—	1, 161	5. 0	—	—	520	. 10	. 68	16 4	—
1125		Pacific, flesh only	0	445	79. 4	11. 8	0	—	1, 021	5 9	336	1, 905	450	. 10	. 74	16. 0	12
		Canned, solids and liquid															
1126		Plain	0	943	90. 3	61. 7	0	667	1, 347	8 2	—	—	—	—	. 84	—	—
1127		In tomato sauce	0	798	71. 7	47. 6	16. 8	—	1, 102	—	—	—	—	—	. 50	16 0	—
1128		Pickled, Bismarck type	0	1, 012	92. 5	68 5	0	—	—	—	—	—	—	—	—	—	—
1129		Salted or brined	0	989	86 2	68 9	0	—	—	—	—	—	—	—	. 86	—	—
		Smoked															
1130		Bloaters	0	889	88 9	56 2	0	—	—	—	—	—	—	—	—	—	—
1131		Hard	0	1, 361	167 4	71. 7	0	—	—	—	28, 264	712	—	—	—	—	—
1132		Kippered	0	957	100. 7	58. 5	0	299	1, 152	6 4	—	—	110	—	1 26	15 0	—
1133		**Hickorynuts:**															
	a	In shell (refuse: shells)	65	1, 068	21 0	109. 1	20. 3	Trace	572	3 8	—	—	—	—	—	—	—
	b	Shelled	0	3, 053	59 9	311. 6	58. 1	Trace	1, 633	10 9	—	—	—	—	—	—	—
		Hominy grits, dry. See Corn grits, items 862, 864															
1134		**Honey,** strained or extracted	0	1, 379	1 4	0	373. 3	23	27	2. 3	23	231	0	. 02	. 20	1 2	5
		Honeydew melon. See Muskmelons, item 1360															

[66] Value weighted by monthly and total season shipments for marketing as fresh fruit

[67] For white-fleshed varieties, value is about 20 I U. per pound; for red-fleshed varieties, about 1,000 I U.

[68] For white-fleshed varieties, value is about 40 I.U. per pound; for red-fleshed varieties, about 2,000 I.U.

[69] Fruit juice content ranges from 10 to 50 percent Ascorbic acid may be added as a preservative or as a nutrient. Value listed is based on product with label stating 30 mg. per 6 fl oz. serving. If label claim is 30 mg per 8 fl oz serving, value would be 54 mg. per pound. If thiamine and riboflavin have been added, the values expected would be 0 91 mg and 1 09 mg per pound.

[70] Average for varieties grown in the United States; range is wide, from 100 mg to 5,100 mg. per pound.

[71] Two frozen samples dipped in brine contained 1,633 mg sodium per pound.

TABLE 2.—NUTRIENTS IN THE EDIBLE PORTION OF 1 POUND OF FOOD AS PURCHASED—Continued

[Numbers in parentheses denote values imputed—usually from another form of the food or from a similar food. Zero in parentheses indicates that the amount of a constituent probably is none or is too small to measure. Dashes denote lack of reliable data for a constituent believed to be present in measurable amount. Calculated values, as those based on a recipe, are not in parentheses]

Item No. (A)		Food and description (B)	Refuse (C)	Food energy (D)	Protein (E)	Fat (F)	Carbohydrate total (G)	Calcium (H)	Phosphorus (I)	Iron (J)	Sodium (K)	Potassium (L)	Vitamin A value (M)	Thiamine (N)	Riboflavin (O)	Niacin (P)	Ascorbic acid (Q)
			Percent	Calories	Grams	Grams	Grams	Milligrams	Milligrams	Milligrams	Milligrams	Milligrams	International units	Milligrams	Milligrams	Milligrams	Milligrams
		Horseradish:															
1135		Raw (refuse: parings)	27	288	10.8	1.0	65.2	464	212	4.6	26	1,867	—	.23	—		265
1136		Prepared	0	172	5.9	.9	43.5	277	145	4.1	435	1,315	—	—			
		Hyacinth-beans, raw:															
1137		Young pods (refuse: ends, strings, trimmings)	12	140	11.2	1.2	29.1	228	212	3.0	8	1,134	2,320	.32	0.42	3.6	80
1138		Mature seeds, dry	0	1,538	100.7	6.8	278.7	341	1,608	23.1	—	—		2.79	.81	4.5	
		Ice cream and frozen custard:															
		Regular:															
1139		Approximately 10% fat	0	873	20.4	48.1	94.8	662	522	.5	286	821	1,996	.18	.94	.5	5
1140		Approximately 12% fat	0	939	18.1	56.7	93.4	558	449	.5	286	826	2,359	.18	.86	.5	5
1141		Rich, approximately 16% fat	0	1,007	11.8	73.0	81.6	304	277	.1	136	431	2,994	.10	.51	.5	5
1142		Ice cream cones	0	1,710	45.4	10.9	353.4	708	808	1.8	1,052	1,107	10	.21	.94	2.4	Trace
1143		Ice milk	0	689	21.8	23.1	101.6	708	562	.5	308	885	953	.23	1.00	.5	5
1144		Ices, water, lime	0	354	1.8	Trace	147.9	1	3	Trace	1	13	0	Trace	Trace	Trace	5
		Icing mixes. See Cake icing mixes, items 575, 577															
1145		**Inconnu** (sheefish), raw:															
	a	Whole (refuse: entrails, head, fins, skin, and bones)	37	417	56.9	19.4	0	—	—	—	—	—	—	—	—	—	—
	b	Flesh only	0	662	90.3	30.8	0	—	—	—	—	—	—	—	—	—	—
1146		**Jack mackerel,** flesh only, raw	0	649	98.0	25.4	0	—	—	—	—	—	—	—	—	—	—
1147		**Jackfruit,** raw (refuse: seeds, skin)	72	124	1.7	.4	32.3	28	48	—	3	517	—	.04	—	.5	10
1148		**Jams and preserves**	0	1,234	2.7	.5	317.5	91	41	4.5	54	399	50	.05	.12	.9	9
1149		**Jellies**	0	1,238	.5	.5	320.2	95	32	6.8	77	340	50	.05	.18	.5	18
1150		**Jerusalem-artichokes,** raw (refuse: parings)	[illegible]	[illegible]	7.2	.3	[illegible]	44	244	10.6	—	—	50	.64	.17	4.1	12
		Jujube, common (Chinese date):															
1151		Raw (refuse: seeds)	7	443	5.1	.8	116.4	122	156	3.0	13	1,139	170	.10	.16	3.7	291
1152		Dried (refuse: seeds)	11	1,150	14.9	4.4	297.1	319	404	7.3	—	2,141	—	—	—	—	52
		Kale:															
		Raw, portion used—															
1153		Leaves, without stems and midribs (refuse: stems, midribs, trimmings, damaged leaves)	36	154	(17.4)	(2.3)	26.1	723	270	7.8	(218)	(1,096)	29,000	.47	.75	6.1	539
1154		Leaves, including stems (refuse: stem ends, tough stems, tough part of midribs)	26	128	14.1	2.7	20.1	601	245	7.4	252	1,270	29,904	—	—	—	420
1157		Frozen	0	143	14.5	2.3	24.9	608	227	5.9	118	1,093	37,195	.36	.52	2.3	209
		Kidneys, raw:															
1159		Beef	0	590	69.9	30.4	4.1	50	993	33.6	798	1,021	3,130	1.63	11.57	29.2	68
1161		Calf	0	513	75.3	20.9	.5	—	—	18.1	—	—	—	—	—	—	59
1162		Hog	0	481	73.9	16.3	5.0	50	989	30.4	522	807	680	2.63	7.85	44.6	59
1163		Lamb	0	476	76.2	15.0	4.1	59	989	34.5	907	1,048	3,130	2.32	10.39	33.6	68
1164		**Kingfish;** southern, gulf, and northern (whiting); raw:															
	a	Whole (refuse: entrails, head, fins, skin, and bones)	56	210	36.5	6.0	0	—	—	—	166	499	—	—	—	—	—
	b	Flesh only	0	476	83.0	13.6	0	—	—	—	376	1,134	—	—	—	—	—
		Knockwurst. See Sausage, cold cuts, and luncheon meats, item 2002.															
1165		**Kohlrabi,** thickened bulb-like stems, raw:															
	a	With leaves (refuse: leaves with stems, parings)	54	61	4.2	.2	13.8	86	106	1.0	17	776	40	.13	.08	.7	138
	b	Without leaves (refuse: stem ends, parings)	27	96	6.6	.3	21.9	136	169	1.7	26	1,232	70	.20	.12	1.1	219
1167		**Kumquats,** raw (refuse: seeds)	7	274	3.8	.4	72.1	266	97	1.7	30	995	2,530	.33	.40	—	151
		Ladyfingers. See Cookies, item 922.															
1168		**Lake herring** (cisco), raw:															
	a	Whole (refuse: entrails, scales, head, fins, and bones)	48	226	41.8	5.4	0	28	486	1.2	111	753	—	.21	.24	7.7	—
	b	Fillets	0	435	80.3	10.4	0	54	934	2.3	213	1,447	—	.45	.45	14.8	—
1169		**Lake trout,** raw:															
	a	Drawn (refuse: head, fins, and bones)	65	282	30.7	16.8	0	—	369	1.3	—	—	—	.15	.20	4.6	—
	b	Fillets	0	762	83.0	45.4	0	—	1,080	3.6	—	—	—	.41	.54	12.4	—
		Lake trout (siscowet), raw:															
1170		Less than 6.5 lbs., round weight:															
	a	Whole (refuse: entrails, head, fins, skin, and bones)	63	404	24.0	33.4	0	—	—	—	—	—	—	—	—	—	—
	b	Flesh only	0	1,093	64.9	90.3	0	—	—	—	—	—	—	—	—	—	—

No.		Food															
1171		6.5 lbs. and over, round weight:															
	a	Whole (refuse: entrails, head, fins, skin, and bones).	64	856	12.9	88.8	0	—	—	—	—	—	—	—	—	—	—
	b	Flesh only	0	2,377	35.8	246.8	0	—	—	—	—	—	—	—	—	—	—
		Lamb:[4]															
		Carcass, including kidney and kidney fat, with bone, raw:															
1172		Prime grade, 52% lean, 34% fat	14	—	—	—	—	—	—	—	—	—	—	—	—	—	—
1173		Choice grade, 56% lean, 27% fat	17	—	—	—	—	—	—	—	—	—	—	—	—	—	—
1174		Good grade, 57% lean, 25% fat	18	—	—	—	—	—	—	—	—	—	—	—	—	—	—
		Composite of cuts (leg, loin, rib, and shoulder), trimmed to retail level															
1175		Prime grade, 62% lean, 24% fat	14	1,214	60.3	106.1	0	35	529	4.3			—	.54	.75	17.4	—
1176		Choice grade, 65% lean, 19% fat	16	1,003	62.9	81.3	0	38	561	4.6			—	.56	.78	18.2	—
1177		Good grade, 66% lean, 18% fat	17	933	63.5	73.3	0	38	570	4.9			—	.57	.79	18.4	—
		Separable fat. See individual cuts.															
		Retail cuts, trimmed to retail level, raw:															
		Leg:															
		Prime grade															
1179		Total edible.															
	a	With bone, 68% lean, 18% fat	14	1,022	65.9	81.9	0	39	593	5.1			—	.59	.82	19.0	—
	b	Without bone, 79% lean, 21% fat	0	1,188	76.7	95.3	0	45	689	5.9			—	.68	.95	22.1	—
1181		Separable lean	0	612	89.8	25.4	0	50	835	8.2			—	.80	1.12	25.9	—
1183		Separable fat	0	3,311	26.8	354.3	0	14	132	0			—	.24	.33	7.8	—
		Choice grade															
1184		Total edible:															
	a	With bone, 70% lean, 14% fat	16	845	67.7	61.7	0	38	617	5.3			—	.61	.84	19.6	—
	b	Without bone, 83% lean, 17% fat	0	1,007	80.7	73.5	0	45	735	6.4			—	.72	1.00	23.4	—
1186		Separable lean	0	590	90.3	22.7	0	54	839	8.2			—	.80	1.12	26.1	—
1188		Separable fat	0	3,094	33.1	327.5	0	18	200	0			—	.29	.41	9.6	—
		Good grade															
1189		Total edible:															
	a	With bone, 70% lean, 13% fat	17	790	68.4	55.2	0	38	623	5.7			—	.61	.85	19.7	—
	b	Without bone, 85% lean, 15% fat	0	948	82.1	66.2	0	45	748	6.8			—	.73	1.02	23.7	—
1191		Separable lean	0	576	90.3	21.3	0	54	839	8.2			—	.80	1.12	26.1	—
1193		Separable fat	0	2,998	35.8	315.3	0	23	231	0			—	.32	.44	10.3	—
		Loin:															
		Prime grade:															
1194		Total edible:															
	a	With bone, 59% lean, 29% fat	12	1,409	59.0	128.4	0	36	510	4.0			—	.53	.74	17.1	—
	b	Without bone, 67% lean, 33% fat	0	1,592	66.7	145.2	0	41	576	4.5			—	.60	.83	19.4	—
1196		Separable lean	0	662	89.8	30.8	0	50	835	8.2			—	.80	1.12	25.9	—
1198		Separable fat	0	3,493	20.9	377.4	0	14	64	0	(76)	(77)	—	.19	.26	6.0	—
		Choice grade:															
1199		Total edible:															
	a	With bone, 62% lean, 24% fat	14	1,146	63.7	97.0	0	35	567	4.7			—	.57	.79	18.5	—
	b	Without bone, 72% lean, 28% fat	0	1,329	73.9	112.5	0	41	658	5.4			—	.66	.92	21.4	—
1201		Separable lean	0	626	90.3	26.8	0	54	839	8.2			—	.80	1.12	26.1	—
1203		Separable fat	0	3,171	31.8	336.6	0	18	186	0			—	.28	.39	9.2	—
		Good grade:															
1204		Total edible:															
	a	With bone, 63% lean, 22% fat	15	1,068	65.0	87.4	0	39	584	5.0			—	.58	.80	18.8	—
	b	Without bone, 74% lean, 26% fat	0	1,252	76.2	102.5	0	45	685	5.9			—	.68	.94	22.0	—
1206		Separable lean	0	612	90.3	25.4	0	54	839	8.2			—	.80	1.12	26.1	—
1208		Separable fat	0	3,030	36.7	318.4	0	23	240	0			—	.33	.45	10.6	—
		Rib:															
		Prime grade:															
1209		Total edible:															
	a	With bone, 49% lean, 35% fat	16	1,621	49.7	156.0	0	31	413	2.7			—	.44	.62	14.4	—
	b	Without bone, 58% lean, 42% fat	0	1,923	59.0	185.1	0	36	490	3.2			—	.53	.73	17.1	—
1211		Separable lean	0	767	87.1	44.0	0	50	807	7.7			—	.78	1.08	25.2	—
1213		Separable fat	0	3,534	20.0	382.4	0	14	54	0			—	.18	.25	5.8	—
		Choice grade:															
1214		Total edible.															
	a	With bone, 54% lean, 26% fat	20	1,229	54.7	110.2	0	33	478	3.6			—	.49	.68	15.8	—
	b	Without bone, 68% lean, 32% fat	0	1,538	68.5	137.9	0	41	599	4.5			—	.61	.85	19.8	—
1216		Separable lean	0	717	87.5	38.1	0	50	812	7.7			—	.78	1.08	25.3	—
1218		Separable fat	0	3,275	28.1	349.7	0	18	145	0			—	.25	.35	8.1	—
		Good grade:															
1219		Total edible:															
	a	With bone, 56% lean, 23% fat	22	1,108	56.1	96.3	0	32	494	3.9			—	.50	.70	16.2	—
	b	Without bone, 71% lean, 29% fat	0	1,415	71.7	122.9	0	41	631	5.0			—	.64	.89	20.7	—

[4] See Notes on Foods, p 180

[8] A large proportion of the carbohydrate in the unstored product may be inulin, which is of doubtful availability During storage, inulin is converted to sugars

[72] Commercial products Frozen custard must contain egg yolk which contributes somewhat more vitamin A value than is present in ice creams made with milk products only

[73] Value for product without added salt.

[74] Higher values were found for the following jams or jellies: Gooseberry, 45 mg ; red cherry or strawberry, 68 mg , guava, 181 mg , black currant, 204 mg ; rose hip or acerola, 1,497 mg per pound

[75] Values range from 22 Calories per pound for freshly harvested Jerusalem-artichokes to 235 Calories for those stored for a long period

[76] Average value for 1 pound, all cuts without bone, is 340 mg cuts with average bone content (17 percent), the value is 280 mg also Notes on Foods, p 180

[77] Average value for 1 pound, all cuts without bone, is 1,340 mg cuts with average bone content (17 percent), the value is 1,110 mg also Notes on Foods, p 180

For See

For See

TABLE 2.—NUTRIENTS IN THE EDIBLE PORTION OF 1 POUND OF FOOD AS PURCHASED—Continued

[Numbers in parentheses denote values imputed—usually from another form of the food or from a similar food. Zero in parentheses indicates that the amount of a constituent probably is none or is too small to measure. Dashes denote lack of reliable data for a constituent believed to be present in measurable amount. Calculated values, as those based on a recipe, are not in parentheses]

Item No.	Food and description	Refuse	Food energy	Protein	Fat	Carbohydrate total	Calcium	Phosphorus	Iron	Sodium	Potassium	Vitamin A value	Thiamine	Riboflavin	Niacin	Ascorbic Acid
(A)	(B)	(C)	(D)	(E)	(F)	(G)	(H)	(I)	(J)	(K)	(L)	(M)	(N)	(O)	(P)	(Q)
	Lamb [5]—Continued	Percent	Calories	Grams	Grams	Grams	Milligrams	Milligrams	Milligrams	Milligrams	Milligrams	International units	Milligrams	Milligrams	Milligrams	Milligrams
	Retail cuts, trimmed to retail level, raw—Con.															
	Rib—Continued															
	Good grade—Continued															
1221	Separable lean	0	691	88.0	35.8	0	50	816	7.7			—	0.78	1.09	25.4	—
1223	Separable fat	0	3,162	31.8	335.7	0	18	186	0			—	.28	.30	6.2	—
	Shoulder:															
	Prime grade:															
1224	Total edible:															
a	With bone, 62% lean, 25% fat	13	1,246	57.7	111.2	0	33	469	3.9			—	.51	.71	16.7	—
b	Without bone, 71% lean, 29% fat	0	1,342	66.7	128.4	0	41	576	4.5			—	.59	.83	19.3	—
1226	Separable lean	0	717	83.5	39.9	0	50	762	6.8			—	.74	1.03	24.1	—
1228	Separable fat	0	3,257	24.9	349.3	0	14	109	0			—	.22	.31	7.2	—
	Choice grade:									[illegible]	[illegible]					
1229	Total edible:															
a	With bone, 63% lean, 22% fat	15	1,082	58.9	92.0	0	35	516	3.9			—	.54	.73	17.1	—
b	Without bone, 74% lean, 26% fat	0	1,275	69.1	108.4	0	41	608	4.5			—	.62	.86	20.1	—
1231	Separable lean	0	671	83.9	34.9	0	50	771	7.3			—	.75	1.04	24.3	—
1233	Separable fat	0	2,980	28.6	318.0	0	18	150	0			—	.25	.35	8.3	—
	Good grade:															
1234	Total edible:															
a	With bone, 63% lean, 21% fat	16	1,010	59.1	83.8	0	34	518	4.2			—	.53	.74	17.2	—
b	Without bone, 75% lean, 25% fat	0	1,202	70.3	99.8	0	41	617	5.0			—	.63	.88	20.5	—
1236	Separable lean	0	658	85.9	33.1	0	50	771	7.3			—	.75	1.01	24.3	—
1238	Separable fat	0	2,871	30.4	303.9	0	18	172	0			—	.27	.38	8.8	—
1239	Lambsquarters, raw, fully trimmed	0	195	19.1	3.6	33.1	1,402	327	5.4	—	—	52,620	.70	2.00	5.5	363
1241	Lard	0	4,091	0	454	0	0	0	0	0	0	0	0	0	0	0
1242	Leeks, bulb and lower leaf portion, raw (refuse: tops, rootlets)	48	123	5.2	.7	26.4	123	118	2.6	12	819	90	.26	.13	1.2	40
	Lemons, raw, portion used—															
1243	Peeled fruit (refuse: rind, seeds)	33	82	3.3	.9	24.9	79	49	1.8	6	419	60	.13	.06	.3	[7] 161
1244	Fruit including peel (refuse: seeds)	1	[7] 90	5.4	1.3	48.1	274	67	3.1	13	651	130	.22	.18	.9	346
1245	Juice (refuse: rind, seeds, central axis, segment membranes)	57	49	1.0	.4	15.6	14	20	.4	2	275	30	.06	.02	.1	90
	Lemon juice:															
1246	Canned or bottled, unsweetened	0	104	1.8	.5	34.5	32	45	.9	5	640	90	.14	.05	.3	189
	Frozen, unsweetened:															
1247	Single-strength juice	0	100	1.8	.9	32.7	32	41	1.4	5	640	80	.14	.05	.5	200
1248	Concentrate	0	526	10.4	4.1	169.6	150	213	4.1	23	2,985	360	.66	.23	1.5	1,043
1250	Lemon peel, candied	0	1,433	1.8	1.4	365.6	—	—	—	—	—	—	—	—	—	—
1251	Lemonade concentrate, frozen	0	885	.9	.5	231.8	18	27	.9	9	318	80	.10	.12	1.4	137
	Lentils, mature seeds, dry, raw:															
1253	Whole	0	1,542	112.0	5.0	272.6	358	1,710	30.8	136	3,583	270	1.69	.99	9.3	—
1255	Split, without seed coat	0	1,565	112.9	4.1	280.3	209	1,179	30.8	—	—	270	1.69	.99	9.3	—
	Lettuce, raw:															
1256	Butterhead varieties such as Boston types and Bibb (refuse: outer leaves and core)	26	47	4.0	.7	8.4	117	87	6.7	30	886	3,260	.21	.20	.9	28
1257	Cos, or romaine, such as Dark Green and White Paris (refuse: outer leaves, core, trimmings)	36	52	3.8	.9	10.2	167	73	4.1	26	766	5,520	.15	.21	1.1	54
1258	Crisphead varieties such as Iceberg, New York, and Great Lakes strains.															
a	Good quality (refuse: core)	5	56	3.9	.4	12.5	86	95	2.2	39	754	1,420	.27	.25	1.2	28
b	Fair quality (refuse: coarse leaves, core)	26	44	3.0	.3	9.7	67	74	1.7	30	587	1,110	.21	.20	.9	21
1259	Looseleaf, or bunching varieties, such as Grand Rapids, Salad Bowl, Simpson (refuse: outer leaves, core, trimmings)	36	52	3.8	.9	10.2	197	73	4.1	26	766	5,520	.15	.24	1.1	54
	Lima beans. See Beans, lima; items 164–176.															
	Limes, acid type, raw, portion used—															
1260	Pulp (refuse: rind, seeds)	16	107	2.7	.8	36.2	126	69	2.3	8	389	50	.10	.08	.7	141
1261	Juice (refuse: rind, seeds, membranes)	52	57	.7	.2	19.6	20	24	.4	2	226	30	.04	.02	.3	71
1262	Lime juice, canned or bottled, unsweetened	0	118	1.4	.5	40.8	41	50	.9	5	472	60	.09	.06	.6	95
1263	Limeade concentrate, frozen	0	848	.9	.5	224.5	23	27	.5	Trace	268	Trace	.05	.04	.4	54
1265	Lingcod, raw:															
a	Whole (refuse: head, tail, fins, entrails, scales, bones, and skin)	66	130	27.6	1.2	0	—	—	—	91	668	0	.08	.06	—	—

	b	Flesh only	0	381	81.2	3.6	0	—	—	—	268	1,964	0	.22	.18	—	—
		Liver, raw:															
1266		Beef	0	635	90.3	17.2	24.0	36	1,597	29.5	617	1,275	[80] 199,130	1.16	14.79	61.6	140
1268		Calf	0	635	87.1	21.3	18.6	36	1,510	39.9	331	1,275	[80] 102,060	.90	12.32	51.8	161
1270		Chicken, all classes	0	585	89.4	16.8	13.2	54	1,070	35.8	318	780	[80] 54,890	.86	11.29	49.0	79
1272		Goose	0	826	74.8	45.4	24.5	—	—	—	635	1,043	—	—	—	—	—
1273		Hog	0	594	93.4	16.8	11.8	45	1,615	87.1	331	1,184	[80] 49,440	1.36	13.73	74.2	103
1275		Lamb	0	617	95.3	17.7	13.2	45	1,583	49.4	236	916	[80] 229,070	1.81	14.89	76.5	152
1277		Turkey, all classes	0	626	96.2	18.1	13.2	—	—	—	286	726	[80] 80,290	.81	8.75	59.9	—
		Liver paste. See Pâté de foie gras, item 1478.															
		Liver sausage or liverwurst. See Sausage, cold cuts, and luncheon meats: items 2003–2004.															
		Lobster, northern:															
1279		Raw:															
	a	Whole (refuse: shell)	74	107	19.9	2.2	.6	34	216	.7	—	—	—	.48	.06	1.7	—
	b	Meat only	0	413	76.7	8.6	2.3	132	830	2.7	—	—	—	1.84	.23	6.6	—
1280		Canned or cooked	0	431	84.8	6.8	1.4	295	871	3.6	953	816	—	.46	.31	—	—
		Lobster paste. See Shrimp or lobster paste, canned: item 2047.															
		Lobster, spiny. See Crayfish, item 927.															
		Loganberries:															
1283		Raw (refuse: caps, damaged berries)	(5)	267	4.3	2.6	64.2	151	73	5.2	(4)	733	(860)	(.14)	(.18)	(1.6)	102
		Canned, solids and liquid:															
1284		Water pack, with or without artificial sweetener	0	181	3.2	1.8	42.6	109	50	3.6	5	522	610	.07	.09	1.0	36
1285		Juice pack	0	245	3.2	2.3	57.6	122	68	5.4	5	771	680	.10	.14	1.5	54
		Sirup pack:															
1286		Light	0	318	3.2	1.8	78.0	104	50	3.6	5	503	590	.06	.09	1.0	35
1287		Heavy	0	404	2.7	1.8	100.7	100	50	3.6	5	494	580	.06	.09	1.0	34
1288		Extra heavy	0	490	2.7	1.8	123.4	100	50	3.6	5	485	570	.06	.09	.9	34
		Longans:															
1289		Raw (refuse: shell, seeds)	47	147	2.4	.2	38.0	24	101	2.9	—	—	—	—	—	—	(14)
1290		Dried (refuse: shell, seeds)	64	467	8.0	.7	120.8	73	320	8.8	—	—	—	.06	—	—	46
1291		**Loquats,** raw (refuse: seeds)	23	168	1.4	.7	43.3	70	126	1.4	—	1,216	2,340	—	—	—	3
		Luncheon meat. See Sausage, cold cuts, and luncheon meats: items 2005–2006.															
		Lungs, raw:															
1292		Beef	0	435	79.8	10.4	0	—	980	—	—	—	—	—	—	28.1	—
1293		Calf	0	481	76.2	17.2	0	—	—	—	—	—	—	—	—	—	—
1294		Lamb	0	467	87.5	10.4	0	—	816	—	—	—	—	—	—	—	—
		Lychees:															
1295		Raw (refuse: thin shell, seeds)	40	174	2.4	.8	44.6	22	114	1.1	8	463	—	—	.13	—	113
1296		Dried (refuse: thin shell, seeds)	54	578	7.9	2.5	147.6	69	378	3.5	6	2,296	—	—	—	—	—
1297		**Macadamia nuts:**															
	a	In shell (refuse: shells)	69	972	11.0	100.7	22.4	67	226	2.8	—	371	0	.48	.15	1.8	0
	b	Shelled	0	3,134	35.4	324.8	72.1	218	730	9.1	—	1,198	0	1.54	.48	5.8	0
		Macaroni:															
1298		Enriched	0	1,674	56.7	5.4	341.1	122	735	[53] 13.0	9	894	(0)	[53] 4.0	[53] 1.7	[53] 27.0	(0)
1301		Unenriched	0	1,674	56.7	5.4	341.1	122	735	5.9	9	894	(0)	.42	.29	7.7	(0)
1305		**Macaroni and cheese,** canned	0	431	17.7	18.1	48.5	376	345	1.8	1,379	263	500	.23	.44	1.9	Trace
		Mackerel, Atlantic:															
1306		Raw:															
	a	Whole (refuse: head, tail, fins, bones, skin, and entrails).	46	468	46.5	29.9	0	12	585	2.4	—	—	(1,100)	.36	.80	20.0	—
	b	Flesh only	0	866	86.2	55.3	0	23	1,084	4.5	—	—	(2,040)	.66	1.49	37.1	—
1307		Canned, solids and liquid [81]	0	830	87.5	50.3	0	839	1,243	9.5	—	—	1,950	.26	.96	26.3	—
		Mackerel, Pacific:															
1309		Raw:															
	a	Dressed (refuse: bones and skin)	28	519	71.5	23.8	0	26	895	6.9	—	—	390	—	—	—	—
	b	Flesh only	0	721	99.3	33.1	0	36	1,243	9.5	—	—	540	—	—	—	—
1310		Canned, solids and liquid [81]	0	816	95.7	45.4	0	1,179	1,306	10.0	—	—	120	.12	1.50	39.7	—
		Mackerel:															
1311		Salted	0	1,383	83.9	113.9	0	—	—	—	—	—	—	—	—	—	—
1312		Smoked	0	993	108.0	59.0	0	—	—	—	—	—	—	—	—	—	—
1313		**Malt,** dry	0	1,669	59.4	8.6	351.1	—	—	18.1	—	—	—	2.24	1.41	40.8	—
1314		**Malt extract,** dried	0	1,665	27.2	Trace	404.6	218	1,334	39.5	363	1,043	—	1.62	2.04	44.6	—
1315		**Mamey** (mammeeapple), raw (refuse: skin, seeds)	38	143	1.4	1.4	35.2	31	31	2.0	42	132	650	.06	.11	1.2	40
		Mandarin oranges. See Tangerines, item 2262.															
1316		**Mangos,** raw (refuse: seeds, skin)	33	201	2.1	1.2	51.1	30	40	1.2	21	574	14,590	.16	.16	3.2	106
1317		**Margarine** [82]	0	3,266	2.7	367.	1.8	91	73	0	4,477	104	15,000	—	—	—	0
1318		**Marmalade,** citrus	0	1,166	2.3	.5	318.0	159	41	2.7	64	150	—	.07	.11	.5	27

[53] Based on product with minimum level of enrichment. See also Notes on Foods, p. 171

[76] Average value for 1 pound, all cuts without bone, is 340 mg For cuts with average bone content (17 percent), the value is 280 mg. See also Notes on Foods, p. 180.

[77] Average value for 1 pound, all cuts without bone, is 1,340 mg. For cuts with average bone content (17 percent), the value is 1,110 mg. See also Notes on Foods, p 180

[78] Applies to lemons marketed in summer.

[79] Based on the pulp. There is no basis for assessing the calorie value of the peel or the effect that inclusion of the peel may have on the digestibility of the product

[80] Values vary widely in all kinds of liver, ranging from about 450 I.U. to more than 454,000 I.U. per pound

[81] Vitamin values based on drained solids

[82] Values apply to salted margarine Unsalted margarine contains less than 45 mg per pound of either sodium or potassium. Vitamin A value based on the minimum required to meet Federal specifications for margarine with vitamin A added, namely 15,000 I. U. of vitamin A per pound.

284-853 O - 79 - 7

TABLE 2.—NUTRIENTS IN THE EDIBLE PORTION OF 1 POUND OF FOOD AS PURCHASED—Continued

[Numbers in parentheses denote values imputed—usually from another form of the food or from a similar food. Zero in parentheses indicates that the amount of a constituent probably is none or is too small to measure. Dashes denote lack of reliable data for a constituent believed to be present in measurable amount. Calculated values, as those based on a recipe, are not in parentheses]

Item No.	Food and description	Refuse	Food energy	Protein	Fat	Carbohydrate total	Calcium	Phosphorus	Iron	Sodium	Potassium	Vitamin A value	Thiamine	Riboflavin	Niacin	Ascorbic Acid
(A)	(B)	(C)	(D)	(E)	(F)	(G)	(H)	(I)	(J)	(K)	(L)	(M)	(N)	(O)	(P)	(Q)
	Marmalade plums. See Sapotes, item 1970	*Percent*	*Calories*	*Grams*	*Grams*	*Grams*	*Milligrams*	*Milligrams*	*Milligrams*	*Milligrams*	*Milligrams*	*International units*	*Milligrams*	*Milligrams*	*Milligrams*	*Milligrams*
	Matai. See Waterchestnut, Chinese: item 2422.															
	Mayonnaise. See Salad dressings, item 1948.															
	Meat loaf. See Sausage, cold cuts, and luncheon meats: item 2007															
	Meat. See Beef, Lamb, Pork, Veal															
	Mellorine. See Notes on Foods, page 187.															
	Melons. See Muskmelons, items 1358–1361; and Watermelon, item 2424.															
1319	**Menhaden,** Atlantic, canned, solids and liquid	0	780	84.8	46.8	0	----	----	5.9	----	----	----	----	----	----	----
	Milk, cow:															
	Fluid (pasteurized and raw):															
	Whole:															
1320	3.5% fat [illegible]	0	295	15.9	15.9	22.2	535	422	.2	227	654	650	0.15	0.78	0.5	5
1321	3.7% fat [illegible]	0	299	15.9	16.8	22.2	531	417	.2	227	635	690	.15	.78	.3	5
1322	Skim	0	163	16.3	.5	23.1	549	431	.2	236	658	20	.16	.80	.8	5
1323	Partially skimmed with 2% nonfat milk solids added.	0	268	19.1	9.1	27.2	619	508	.2	277	794	370	.19	.94	.4	5
	Half-and-half (cream and milk). See Cream, item 928.															
	Canned:															
1324	Evaporated (unsweetened)	0	621	31.8	35.8	44.0	1,148	930	.5	535	1,374	1,470	.18	1.52	.8	5
1325	Condensed (sweetened)	0	1,456	36.7	39.5	246.3	1,188	934	.4	508	1,424	1,620	.34	1.74	.7	5
	Dry:															
1326	Whole	0	2,277	119.8	124.7	173.3	4,123	3,221	2.2	1,837	6,053	5,129	1.32	6.62	3.2	27
1327	Skim (nonfat solids), regular	0	1,647	162.8	3.6	237.2	5,933	4,600	2.7	2,414	7,915	140	1.59	(8.16)	4.1	32
1328	Skim (nonfat solids), instant	0	1,628	162.4	3.2	234.1	5,865	4,559	2.7	2,386	7,825	150	1.59	8.07	4.1	32
	Malted:															
1329	Dry powder [illegible]	0	1,860	66.7	37.6	321.1	1,306	1,724	3.5	1,996	3,266	4,649	1.50	2.45	1.2	(0)
1330	Beverage [illegible]	0	472	21.8	20.0	53.1	612	553	1.4	413	907	1,180	.29	.94	.4	3
	Chocolate drink, fluid, commercial:															
1331	Made with skim milk	0	345	15.0	10.4	49.4	490	413	.7	209	644	380	.16	.74	.4	5
1332	Made with whole (3.5% fat) milk	0	386	15.4	15.4	49.9	503	426	.7	213	662	590	.14	.73	.4	5
	Buttermilk. See Buttermilk, items 509–510															
1335	**Milk, goat,** fluid	0	304	14.5	18.1	20.9	585	481	.4	154	816	(730)	.20	.49	1.3	5
1336	**Milk, human,** U.S. samples	0	349	5.0	18.1	43.1	150	64	.5	73	231	1,090	.06	.16	.8	23
1337	**Milk, reindeer**	0	1,061	49.0	88.9	18.6	1,152	898	.6	712	721	----	----	----	----	----
1338	**Millet,** proso (broomcorn, hogmillet), whole-grain	0	1,483	44.9	13.2	330.7	91	1,411	30.8	----	1,950	(0)	3.30	1.70	10.6	(0)
	Mixed vegetables, frozen. See Vegetables, mixed, frozen: item 2403.															
	Molasses, cane:															
1339	First extraction or light	0	1,143	----	----	[illegible] 295.	748	204	19.5	68	4,150	----	32	.27	.9	----
1340	Second extraction or medium	0	1,052	----	----	[illegible] 272.	1,315	313	27.2	168	4,822	----	----	.54	5.4	----
1341	Third extraction or blackstrap	0	966	----	----	[illegible] 249.	3,103	381	73.0	435	13,277	----	.51	.87	9.1	----
1342	Barbados	0	1,229	----	----	[illegible] 318.	1,111	227	----	----	----	----	.27	.91	----	----
	Mortadella. See Sausage, cold cuts, and luncheon meats: item 2010.															
	Muffins, baked from home-type recipe:															
	Plain, made with—															
1343	Enriched flour	0	1,334	35.4	45.8	191.9	472	685	7.3	2,000	567	450	.76	1.04	6.5	Trace
1344	Unenriched flour	0	1,334	35.4	45.8	191.9	472	685	2.7	2,000	567	450	.19	.63	1.8	Trace
	Other, made with enriched flour:															
1345	Blueberry	0	1,275	33.1	42.2	196.1	381	599	7.3	2,867	522	1,000	.71	.92	5.7	4
1346	Bran	0	1,184	34.9	44.5	195.5	644	1,847	16.8	2,032	1,955	1,040	.65	1.08	18.2	Trace
	Corn, made with—															
1347	Enriched degermed cornmeal	0	1,424	32.2	45.8	218.2	476	767	7.7	2,182	612	1,300	.89	1.02	7.4	Trace
1348	Whole-ground cornmeal	0	1,306	32.7	46.7	192.8	508	980	6.4	2,245	599	1,410	.75	.78	4.8	Trace
	Muffin mixes, corn, and muffins baked from mixes: [illegible]															
1349	Mix, with enriched flour	0	1,892	28.1	52.2	325.7	1,361	2,146	8.2	2,994	345	680	1.09	.75	9.5	0
1350	Muffins, made with egg, milk	0	1,470	31.3	48.1	226.8	1,093	1,724	6.8	2,173	499	1,090	.80	.87	6.5	Trace
1351	Mix, with cake flour, nonfat dry milk	0	1,855	28.1	48.5	324.8	1,007	1,488	4.1	3,679	603	430	.58	.66	5.0	Trace
1352	Muffins, made with egg, water	0	1,347	20.4	35.4	235.4	671	1,034	5.0	1,569	472	650	.54	.54	3.8	Trace
1353	**Mullet,** striped, raw:															
a	Whole (refuse: head, tail, fins, bones, skin, and entrails).	47	351	47.1	16.6	0	63	529	4.3	195	702	----	.16	.10	12.4	----

	b	Flesh only	0	662	88.9	31.3	0	118	998	8.2	367	1,325	—	.30	.36	23.4	—
		Mushrooms: [48]															
		Agaricus campestris, cultivated commercially:															
1354		Raw:															
	a	Good quality (refuse: trimmings, mainly stem ends).	3	123	11.9	1.3	19.4	26	510	3.5	66	1,822	Trace	.40	2.02	18.6	14
	b	Fair quality (refuse: peelings, trimmings)	19	103	9.9	1.1	16.2	22	426	2.9	55	1,521	Trace	.34	1.69	15.5	12
1355		Canned, solids and liquid	0	77	8.6	.5	10.9	27	308	2.3	1,814	894	Trace	.07	1.12	8.9	8
1356		Other edible species, good quality, raw (refuse: trimmings, mainly stem ends).	3	154	8.4	2.6	28.6	57	427	6.2	44	1,650	Trace	.45	1.43	30.1	11
1357		**Muskellunge, raw:**															
	a	Whole (refuse: head, tail, fins, skin, bones, and entrails).	51	242	44.9	5.6	0	—	505	1.3	—	—	—	—	—	—	—
	b	Flesh only	0	494	91.6	11.3	0	—	1,030	2.7	—	—	—	—	—	—	—
		Muskmelons:															
		Raw:															
1358		Cantaloups, other netted varieties (refuse: rind, cavity contents).	50	68	1.6	.2	17.0	32	36	.9	27	569	[58] 7,710	.10	.07	1.4	74
1359		Casaba (Golden Beauty) (refuse: rind, cavity contents).	50	61	2.7	Trace	14.7	(32)	(36)	(.9)	(27)	(569)	70	(.10)	(.07)	(1.4)	29
1360		Honeydew (refuse: rind, cavity contents)	37	94	2.3	.9	22.0	40	46	1.1	34	717	120	.13	.09	1.8	65
		Frozen:															
1361		Melon balls (cantaloup and Honeydew) in sirup	0	281	2.7	.5	71.2	45	54	1.4	41	853	6,990	.14	.09	2.3	73
		Mussels, Atlantic and Pacific, raw.															
1363		Meat and liquid in shell (refuse: shell and beard)	49	153	22.2	3.2	7.2	—	—	—	—	—	—	—	—	—	—
1364		Mussel meat, obtained—															
	a	In shell (refuse: shell, beard, and liquid)	71	125	18.9	2.9	4.3	116	310	4.5	380	414	—	.21	.28	—	—
	b	As meat only	0	431	65.3	10.0	15.0	399	1,070	15.4	1,311	1,429	—	.73	.96	—	—
		Mustard greens:															
1366		Raw (refuse: coarse leaves, stems)	30	98	9.5	1.6	17.8	581	159	9.5	102	1,197	22,220	.34	.70	2.7	308
1368		Frozen	0	91	10.4	1.8	14.5	522	204	7.3	54	889	27,220	.18	.54	1.9	154
1370		**Mustard spinach** (tendergreen), raw	0	100	10.0	1.4	17.7	953	127	6.8	—	—	44,910	—	—	—	590
		Mustard, prepared.															
1372		Brown	0	413	26.8	28.6	24.0	562	608	8.2	5,929	590	—	—	—	—	—
1373		Yellow	0	340	21.3	20.0	29.0	381	331	9.1	5,679	590	—	—	—	—	—
1374		**Nectarines, raw** (refuse: pits)	8	267	2.5	Trace	71.4	17	100	2.1	25	1,227	6,890	—	—	—	54
1375		**New Zealand spinach, raw**	0	86	10.0	1.4	14.1	263	209	11.8	721	3,606	19,500	.19	.79	2.8	135
		Noodles, egg noodles															
1377		Enriched	0	1,760	58.1	20.9	326.6	141	830	[52] 13.0	23	617	1,000	[52] 4.0	[52] 1.7	[52] 27.0	(0)
1379		Unenriched	0	1,760	58.1	20.9	326.6	141	830	8.6	23	617	1,000	.75	.40	9.7	(0)
1381		**Noodles, chow mein, canned**	0	2,218	59.9	106.6	263.1	—	—	—	—	—	—	—	—	—	—
		Nuts. See individual kinds.															
		Oat products used mainly as hot breakfast cereals:															
1382		Oat cereal with toasted wheat germ and soy grits	0	1,733	93.0	40.8	265.8	318	2,676	32.2	36	—	(0)	4.80	.76	6.4	(0)
1384		Oat flakes, maple-flavored, instant-cooking	0	1,742	66.2	19.1	328.0	227	1,633	15.9	5	—	(0)	1.59	—	—	(0)
1386		Oat granules, maple-flavored, quick-cooking	0	1,737	67.1	18.1	328.9	272	1,814	17.2	5	—	(0)	1.81	—	—	(0)
1388		Oat and wheat cereal	0	1,651	66.7	22.7	309.8	240	1,919	17.7	9	—	(0)	2.24	.80	12.0	(0)
1390		Oatmeal or rolled oats	0	1,769	64.4	33.6	309.4	240	1,837	20.4	9	1,597	(0)	2.72	.64	4.5	(0)
		Oat products used mainly as ready-to-eat breakfast cereals:															
1392		Oats, shredded, with protein and other added nutrients.	0	1,719	85.3	9.5	326.6	1,202	1,438	24.0	2,767	—	(0)	16.00	19.20	160.0	(0)
1393		Oats (with or without corn) puffed, added nutrients	0	1,801	54.0	24.9	341.1	803	1,851	21.3	5,747	—	(0)	4.46	.79	8.8	(0)
1394		Oats (with or without corn, wheat) puffed, added nutrients, sugar-covered.	0	1,796	30.4	15.4	388.3	327	916	20.0	2,667	—	(0)	4.69	.55	7.8	(0)
1395		Oats (with soy flour and rice) flaked, added nutrients.	0	1,801	67.6	25.9	320.7	680	1,588	38.6	5,443	—	(0)	3.22	1.50	38.6	(0)
1396		**Ocean perch, Atlantic** (redfish), raw															
	a	Whole (refuse: head, tail, fins, entrails, scales, and bones).	69	124	25.3	1.7	0	28	291	1.4	111	378	—	.14	.12	2.6	—
	b	Fillets	0	399	81.6	5.4	0	91	939	4.5	358	1,220	—	.46	.38	8.4	—
1399		**Ocean perch, Pacific, raw:**															
	a	Whole (refuse: head, tail, fins, entrails, scales, bones, and skin).	73	116	23.3	1.8	0	—	—	—	77	478	—	—	—	—	—
	b	Flesh only	0	431	86.2	6.8	0	—	—	—	286	1,769	—	—	—	—	—
1400		**Octopus, raw**	0	331	69.4	3.6	0	132	785	—	—	—	—	.11	.28	7.9	—
1401		**Oils, salad or cooking**	0	4,010	0	454.	0	0	0	0	0	0	—	0	0	0	0
		Okra:															
1402		Raw															
	a	Good quality (refuse: stem ends, tips)	14	140	9.4	1.2	29.6	359	199	2.3	12	971	2,030	(.66)	(.82)	(4.0)	122
	b	Fair quality (refuse: stem ends, tips, culls)	22	127	8.5	1.1	26.9	325	180	2.1	11	881	1,840	(.60)	(.74)	(3.6)	111
1404		Frozen, cuts and pods	0	177	10.4	.5	40.8	426	231	2.7	9	993	2,180	.77	.95	4.7	72

[48] See Appendix A, section on Protein, p. 162, and see Appendix B, section on foods containing considerable nonprotein nitrogen, p. 182.

[52] Based on product with minimum level of enrichment. See also Notes on Foods, p. 171.

[53] Minimum standards for fat in different states vary considerably and commercial milks may range somewhat above the required minimums. Selection of values to be used in dietary calculations may need to be based on information at the local level. The value, 3.7 percent, is considered valid as a national average for milk on the farm production basis.

[54] Values are based on unfortified products.

[55] Prepared with malted milk powder and whole milk.

[56] Value for total sugars.

[57] Contain yellow degermed cornmeal.

[58] Value based on varieties with orange-colored flesh, for green-fleshed varieties, value is about 640 I.U. per pound.

TABLE 2.—NUTRIENTS IN THE EDIBLE PORTION OF 1 POUND OF FOOD AS PURCHASED—Continued

[Numbers in parentheses denote values imputed—usually from another form of the food or from a similar food. Zero in parentheses indicates that the amount of a constituent probably is none or is too small to measure. Dashes denote lack of reliable data for a constituent believed to be present in measurable amount. Calculated values, as those based on a recipe, are not in parentheses]

Item No.		Food and description	Refuse	Food energy	Protein	Fat	Carbohydrate total	Calcium	Phosphorus	Iron	Sodium	Potassium	Vitamin A value	Thiamine	Riboflavin	Niacin	Ascorbic Acid
(A)		(B)	(C)	(D)	(E)	(F)	(G)	(H)	(I)	(J)	(K)	(L)	(M)	(N)	(O)	(P)	(Q)
		Oleomargarine. See Margarine, item 1517															
		Olives, pickled; canned, or bottled:	Percent	Calories	Grams	Grams	Grams	Milligrams	Milligrams	Milligrams	Milligrams	Milligrams	International units	Milligrams	Milligrams	Milligrams	Milligrams
1406		Green:															
	a	With pits (refuse: drained liquid, pits)	47	279	3.4	30.5	3.1	147	41	3.8	5,770	132	720	—	—	—	—
	b	Without pits (refuse: drained liquid)	47	279	3.4	30.5	3.1	147	41	3.8	5,770	132	720	—	—	—	—
	c	With pits, drained (refuse: pits)	(16)	442	5.3	48.4	5.0	232	65	6.1	9,144	210	1,140	—	—	—	—
		Ripe:															
1407		Ascolano (extra large, mammoth, giant, jumbo):															
	a	With pits (refuse: drained liquid, pits)	55	263	2.2	28.2	5.3	171	33	3.3	1,639	69	130	Trace	Trace	—	—
	b	Without pits (refuse: drained liquid)	53	275	2.3	29.4	5.5	179	34	3.4	1,733	72	140	Trace	Trace	—	—
1408		Manzanilla (small, medium, large, extra large):															
	a	With pits (refuse: drained liquid, pits)	55	263	2.2	28.2	5.3	171	33	3.3	1,659	69	130	Trace	Trace	—	—
	b	Without pits (refuse: drained liquid)	53	275	2.3	29.4	5.5	179	34	3.4	1,733	72	140	Trace	Trace	—	—
1409		Mission (small, medium, large, extra large):															
	a	With pits (refuse: drained liquid, pits)	55	376	2.4	41.0	6.5	216	35	3.5	1,531	55	140	Trace	Trace	—	—
	b	Without pits (refuse: drained liquid)	53	392	2.6	42.9	6.8	226	36	3.6	1,599	58	140	Trace	Trace	—	—
1410		Sevillano (giant, jumbo, colossal, supercolossal):															
	a	With pits (refuse: drained liquid, pits)	55	190	2.2	19.4	5.5	151	41	3.3	1,690	90	120	Trace	Trace	—	—
	b	Without pits (refuse: drained liquid)	53	198	2.3	20.3	5.8	158	43	3.4	1,765	94	130	Trace	Trace	—	—
1411		Ripe, salt-cured, oil-coated, Greek style, drained (refuse: pits).	20	1,227	8.0	129.9	31.6	—	105	—	11,932	—	—	—	—	—	—
		Onions, mature (dry):															
1412		Raw (refuse: skins, ends)	9	157	6.2	.4	35.9	111	149	2.1	41	648	160	0.14	0.15	0.8	42
1414		Dehydrated, flaked	0	1,588	39.5	5.9	372.4	753	1,238	13.2	399	6,273	910	1.12	.80	6.2	159
		Onions, young, green (bunching varieties), raw, portion used—															
1415		Bulb and entire top (refuse: rootlets)	4	157	6.5	.9	35.7	222	170	4.4	22	1,006	(8,710)	.22	.20	1.7	139
1416		Bulb and white portion of top (refuse: green tops, rootlets).	63	76	1.8	.3	17.6	67	65	1.0	8	388	Trace	.08	.07	.7	42
1418		**Onions, Welsh,** raw (refuse: tops of leaves, roots)	35	100	5.6	1.2	19.2	53	144	—	—	—	—	.16	.25	1.0	80
		Oranges, raw, used for peeled fruit:															
1420		All commercial varieties (refuse: rind, seeds)	27	162	3.3	.7	40.4	136	66	1.3	3	642	660	.33	.13	1.3	(166)
		California:															
1421		Navels (winter oranges) (refuse: rind, seeds)	32	157	4.0	.3	39.2	123	68	1.2	3	598	(620)	.30	.12	1.2	(188)
1422		Valencias (summer oranges) (refuse: rind, seeds)	25	174	4.1	1.0	42.2	136	75	2.7	3	646	(680)	.34	.14	1.4	(167)
		Florida:															
1423		All commercial varieties (refuse: rind, seeds)	26	158	2.3	(.7)	40.3	144	57	.7	3	(662)	(670)	.34	.13	1.3	(151)
1424		**Oranges, raw, used with peel** (California Valencias) (refuse: seeds).	1	180	5.8	1.3	69.6	314	99	3.6	9	880	1,120	.45	.22	2.2	319
		Orange juice, raw; and oranges, raw, used for juice:															
1425		All commercial varieties:															
	a	Chilled juice	0	204	3.2	.9	47.2	50	77	.9	5	907	910	.41	.11	1.6	227
	b	Oranges used for juice (refuse: rind, membranes, seeds, handling loss).	52	98	1.5	.4	22.6	24	37	.4	2	435	440	.20	.05	.8	109
		California:															
1426		Navels (winter oranges):															
	a	Chilled juice	0	218	4.5	.5	51.3	50	82	.9	5	880	910	.41	.11	1.6	277
	b	Oranges, used for juice (refuse: rind, membranes, seeds, handling loss).	59	89	1.9	.2	21.0	20	33	.4	2	361	370	.17	.05	.7	113
1427		Valencias (summer oranges):															
	a	Chilled juice	0	213	4.5	1.4	47.6	50	86	1.4	5	862	910	.41	.11	1.6	222
	b	Oranges, used for juice (refuse: rind, membranes, seeds, handling loss).	51	104	2.2	.7	23.3	24	42	.7	2	422	440	.20	.06	.8	109
		Florida:															
1428		All commercial varieties:															
	a	Chilled juice	0	195	2.7	.9	45.4	45	73	.9	5	934	910	.41	.11	1.6	204
	b	Oranges, used for juice (refuse: rind, membranes, seeds, handling loss).	50	98	1.4	.5	22.7	23	36	.5	2	467	450	.20	.06	.8	102
1429		Early and midseason (Hamlin, Parson Brown, Pineapple):															
	a	Chilled juice	0	181	2.3	.9	42.2	45	68	.9	5	943	910	.41	.11	1.6	233
	b	Oranges, used for juice (refuse: rind, membranes, seeds, handling loss).	52	87	1.1	.4	20.2	22	33	.4	2	453	440	.20	.05	.8	112
1430		Late season (Valencias):															
	a	Chilled juice	0	204	2.7	.9	47.6	45	82	.9	5	921	910	.41	.11	1.6	168

	b	Oranges, used for juice (refuse: rind, membranes, seeds, handling loss).	48	106	1.4	.5	24.8	24	42	.5	2	479	470	.21	.06	.8	[66] 87
1431		Temple:[43]															
	a	Chilled juice	0	245	(2.3)	(.9)	58.5	(45)	77	.9	5	—	(910)	.41	.11	1.6	[66] 225
	b	Oranges, used for juice (refuse: rind, membranes, seeds, handling loss).	48	127	(1.2)	(.5)	30.4	(24)	40	.5	2	—	(470)	.21	.06	.8	[66] 117
		Orange juice, canned:															
		Single strength:															
1432		Unsweetened	0	218	3.6	.9	50.8	45	82	1.8	5	903	910	.32	.09	1.2	181
1433		Sweetened	0	236	3.2	.9	55.3	(45)	82	1.8	5	(903)	910	.32	.09	1.2	181
1434		Concentrate, unsweetened	0	1,012	18.6	5.9	230.0	231	390	5.9	23	4,273	4,350	1.77	.54	7.6	1,039
1436		**Orange juice, frozen concentrate,** unsweetened	0	717	10.4	.9	172.4	150	249	1.8	9	2,980	3,220	1.36	.21	5.2	717
1438		**Orange juice, dehydrated** (crystals, 1.0% moisture)	0	1,724	22.7	7.7	403.3	381	608	7.7	36	7,838	7,620	3.04	.95	13.3	1,628
1441		**Orange peel, candied**	0	1,433	1.8	1.4	365.6	—	—	—	—	—	—	—	—	—	—
1442		**Orange juice and apricot juice drink,** canned (approx. 40% fruit juices).	0	227	1.4	.5	57.6	23	36	.5	Trace	426	2,630	.11	.05	.8	[89] 73
		Oysterplant. See Salsify, item 1961.															
		Oysters:															
		Raw:															
1443		Eastern															
	a	In shell (refuse: shell and liquor)	90	30	3.8	.8	1.5	43	65	2.5	33	55	140	.06	.08	1.1	—
	b	Meat only	0	299	38.1	8.2	15.4	426	649	24.9	331	549	1,390	.63	.82	11.2	—
1444		Pacific and Western (Olympia), meat only	0	413	48.1	10.0	29.0	386	694	32.7	—	—	—	.56	—	5.9	137
1446		Canned, solids and liquid	0	345	38.6	10.0	22.2	127	562	25.4	—	318	—	.09	.91	3.8	—
1447		Frozen, solids and liquid	0	—	27.7	—	—	—	—	—	1,724	953	1,390	.63	.82	11.2	—
1448		**Oyster stew, frozen,** condensed	0	463	20.9	28.6	31.3	594	526	5.0	3,084	930	860	.27	.73	1.4	—
		Pancake and waffle mixes:															
		Plain and buttermilk with—															
1455		Enriched flour	0	1,615	39.0	8.2	343.4	2,041	2,676	14.1	6,500	735	0	2.00	1.53	13.0	0
1458		Unenriched flour	0	1,615	39.0	8.2	343.4	2,041	2,676	6.4	6,500	735	0	.54	.36	5.0	0
1461		Buckwheat and other cereal flours	0	1,488	47.6	8.6	318.9	2,114	3,747	14.1	6,051	2,159	Trace	1.63	.54	10.0	0
		Pancreas, raw:															
		Beef															
1463		Very fat	0	1,619	53.5	154.2	0	—	1,007	—	—	—	—	—	—	—	—
1464		Fat	0	1,433	58.1	131.5	0	—	1,211	—	—	—	—	—	—	—	—
1465		Medium-fat	0	1,284	61.2	113.4	0	—	1,225	—	—	—	—	—	—	—	—
1466		Thin	0	984	67.6	77.1	0	—	1,393	—	—	—	—	—	—	—	—
1467		Lean only, adhering fat removed	0	640	79.8	33.1	0	36	1,497	12.7	304	1,252	—	—	2.49	26.3	—
1468		Calf	0	730	87.1	39.9	0	—	1,479	—	—	—	—	—	—	—	—
1469		Hog (hog sweetbread)	0	1,098	66.7	90.3	0	50	1,279	4.5	200	984	—	—	—	—	—
1470		**Papaws,** common, North American type, raw (refuse: rind, seeds)	25	289	17.7	3.1	57.2	—	—	—	—	—	—	—	—	—	—
1471		**Papayas,** raw (refuse: skin, seeds)	33	119	1.8	.3	30.4	61	49	.9	9	711	5,320	.12	.13	.9	170
1472		**Parsley,** common garden (plain) and curled-leaf varieties, raw.	0	200	16.3	2.7	38.6	921	286	28.1	204	3,298	38,560	.54	1.19	5.6	780
1473		**Parsnips,** raw.															
	a	Good quality (refuse: parings)	15	293	6.6	1.9	67.5	193	297	2.7	46	2,086	120	.30	.35	.7	[91] 62
	b	Fair quality (refuse: parings, trimmings, pithy cores).	30	241	5.4	1.6	55.6	159	244	2.2	38	1,718	90	.24	.29	.6	[91] 50
		Passionfruit. See Granadilla, item 1052.															
		Pastinas, enriched:															
1475		Egg	0	1,737	58.5	18.6	325.7	159	880	[53] 13.0	23	—	1,000	[53] 4.0	[53] 1.7	[53] 27.0	(0)
		Vegetable.															
1476		Carrot	0	1,683	54.0	7.3	343.4	172	726	[53] 13.0	—	—	3,310	[53] 4.0	[53] 1.7	[53] 27.0	(0)
1477		Spinach	0	1,669	56.2	7.3	339.3	286	785	[53] 13.0	—	—	2,900	[53] 4.0	[53] 1.7	[53] 27.0	(0)
1478		**Pâté de foie gras,** canned	0	2,096	51.7	198.7	21.8	—	—	—	—	—	—	40	1.36	11.4	—
		Peaches:															
1479		Raw, portion used—															
	a	Peeled fruit (refuse: thin skins, pits)	13	150	2.4	.4	38.3	36	75	2.0	4	797	[92] 5,250	.07	.19	3.8	29
	b	Pared fruit (refuse: parings with some adherent flesh, pits).	24	131	2.1	.3	33.4	31	65	1.7	3	696	[92] 4,580	.06	.16	3.3	26
		Canned, solids and liquid:															
1480		Water pack, with or without artificial sweetener	0	141	1.8	.5	36.7	18	59	1.4	9	621	2,040	.04	.11	2.6	14
1481		Juice pack	0	204	2.7	.5	52.6	27	86	2.3	9	930	3,020	.06	.17	3.9	20
		Sirup pack															
1482		Light	0	263	1.8	.5	68.5	18	59	1.4	9	603	1,990	.04	.11	2.6	13
1483		Heavy	0	354	1.8	.5	91.2	18	54	1.4	9	590	1,950	.04	.11	2.5	13
1484		Extra heavy	0	440	1.8	.5	113.9	18	54	1.4	9	581	1,910	.04	.11	2.5	13
1485		Dehydrated, sulfured, nugget-type and pieces (3.0% moisture).	0	1,542	21.8	(4.1)	399.2	(281)	(685)	15.9	(95)	(5,575)	(22,680)	.01	.43	35.2	63

[43] For further description of product, see Notes on Foods, pp. 175, 178

[53] Based on product with minimum level of enrichment. See also Notes on Foods, p. 171.

[66] Value weighted by monthly and total season shipments for marketing as fresh fruit.

[71] Based on the pulp. There is no basis for assessing the calorie value of the peel or the effect that inclusion of the peel may have on the digestibility of the product.

[88] Based on yellow-fleshed varieties; white-fleshed varieties contain only a trace.

[89] Ascorbic acid may be added as a preservative or as a nutrient. Value listed is based on product with label stating 30 mg. per 6 fl. oz. serving. If label claim is 30 mg. per 8 fl. oz. serving, value would be 54 mg. per pound.

[91] Year-round average. Values per pound of parsnips in the fall within 3 months of storage are 93 mg. for good quality and 76 mg. for fair quality, and drop to less than half these values if storage exceeds 6 months.

[92] Based on yellow-fleshed varieties; for white-fleshed varieties, value is about 200 I.U. per pound for peeled fruit and 170 I.U. for pared fruit.

TABLE 2.—NUTRIENTS IN THE EDIBLE PORTION OF 1 POUND OF FOOD AS PURCHASED—Continued

[Numbers in parentheses denote values imputed—usually from another form of the food or from a similar food. Zero in parentheses indicates that the amount of a constituent probably is none or is too small to measure. Dashes denote lack of reliable data for a constituent believed to be present in measurable amount. Calculated values, as those based on a recipe, are not in parentheses]

Item No.	Food and description	Refuse	Food energy	Protein	Fat	Carbo-hydrate total	Calcium	Phosphorus	Iron	Sodium	Potassium	Vitamin A value	Thiamine	Ribo-flavin	Niacin	Ascorbic Acid
(A)	(B)	(C)	(D)	(E)	(F)	(G)	(H)	(I)	(J)	(K)	(L)	(M)	(N)	(O)	(P)	(Q)
		Percent	*Calories*	*Grams*	*Grams*	*Grams*	*Milligrams*	*Milligrams*	*Milligrams*	*Milligrams*	*Milligrams*	*International units*	*Milligrams*	*Milligrams*	*Milligrams*	*Milligrams*
	Peaches—Continued															
1487	Dried, sulfured (25.0% moisture)	0	1,188	14.1	3.2	309.8	218	531	27.2	73	4,309	17,690	0.05	0.88	24.0	81
1490	Frozen, sliced, sweetened	0	399	1.8	.5	102.5	18	59	2.3	9	562	2,950	.05	.18	3.2	[illegible]181
1491	**Peach nectar**, canned (approx. 40% fruit)[5]	0	218	.9	.2	56.2	18	50	.9	5	354	1,950	.05	.09	1.8	2
	Peanuts:															
1492	Raw:															
a	In shell (refuse: shells)	27	1,868	86.1	157.3	61.6	228	1,328	7.0	17	2,232	—	3.77	.44	56.8	0
b	Shelled	0	2,558	117.9	215.5	84.4	313	1,819	9.5	23	3,057	—	5.16	.60	77.8	0
1495	Roasted:															
a	In shell (refuse: shells)	33	1,769	79.6	148.0	62.6	219	1,237	6.7	15	2,130	—	.97	.41	52.0	0
b	Shelled	0	2,640	118.8	220.9	93.4	327	1,846	10.0	23	3,180	—	1.45	.61	77.6	0
1496	Roasted and salted	0	2,654	117.9	225.9	85.3	336	1,819	9.5	1,896	3,057	—	1.45	.60	77.8	0
	Peanut butters made with—															
1497	Small amounts of added fat, salt	0	2,635	126.1	224.1	78.0	286	1,846	9.1	2,753	3,039	—	.58	.57	71.2	0
1498	Small amounts of added fat, sweetener, salt	0	2,640	115.7	224.6	88.5	277	1,792	9.1	2,740	2,957	—	.57	.56	69.3	0
1499	Moderate amounts of added fat, sweetener, salt	0	2,672	114.8	229.5	85.3	268	1,724	8.6	2,711	2,844	—	.54	.54	66.6	0
1500	**Peanut spread**	0	2,726	92.1	236.3	99.8	227	1,461	6.8	2,708	2,404	—	.46	.45	56.3	0
1501	**Peanut flour**, defatted	0	1,683	217.3	41.7	142.9	472	3,266	15.9	41	5,380	—	3.40	1.01	126.1	0
	Pears:															
1502	Raw:															
a	Good quality (refuse: stem, core)	9	252	2.9	1.7	63.2	33	45	1.2	8	537	70	.09	.17	.6	18
b	Fair quality (refuse: stem, core, bruised areas)	22	216	2.5	1.4	54.1	28	39	1.1	7	460	60	.08	.15	.5	16
1503	Candied	0	1,374	5.9	2.7	344.3	—	—	—	—	—	—	—	—	—	—
	Canned, solids and liquid:															
1504	Water pack, with or without artificial sweetener	0	145	.9	.9	37.6	23	32	.9	5	390	Trace	.05	.09	.6	7
1505	Juice pack	0	209	1.4	1.4	53.5	36	50	1.4	5	590	Trace	.07	.13	.6	10
	Sirup pack:															
1506	Light	0	277	.9	.9	70.8	23	32	.9	5	386	Trace	.05	.09	.6	6
1507	Heavy	0	345	.9	.9	88.9	23	32	.9	5	381	Trace	.05	.09	.6	6
1508	Extra heavy	0	417	.9	.9	107.0	23	32	.9	5	376	Trace	.05	.09	.6	6
1509	Dried, sulfured (26.0% moisture)	0	1,216	14.1	8.2	305.3	159	218	5.9	32	2,369	320	.05	.84	2.8	32
1512	**Pear nectar**, canned (approx. 40% fruit)[5]	0	236	1.4	.9	59.9	14	23	.5	5	177	Trace	.01	.09	Trace	2
1513	**Peas, edible-podded**, raw (refuse: tips, strings)	5	228	14.7	.9	51.7	267	388	3.0	—	733	(2,930)	1.21	.52	—	90
	Peas, green, immature:															
1515	Raw:															
a	In pod (refuse: pods)	62	145	10.9	.7	24.8	45	200	3.3	3	545	1,100	.60	.23	4.9	47
b	Shelled	0	381	26.6	1.8	65.3	118	526	8.6	9	1,433	2,900	1.58	.62	13.0	124
	Canned:															
	Alaska (Early or June peas):															
1517	Regular pack, solids and liquid	0	299	15.9	1.4	56.7	91	299	7.7	[illegible] 1,070	435	2,040	.43	.24	3.9	40
1520	Special dietary pack (low-sodium), solids and liquid.	0	249	16.3	1.4	44.5	91	299	7.7	14	435	2,040	.43	.24	3.9	40
	Sweet (sweet wrinkled peas, sugar peas):															
1523	Regular pack, solids and liquid	0	259	15.4	1.4	47.2	86	263	6.8	[illegible] 1,070	435	2,040	.52	.26	4.5	40
1526	Special dietary pack (low-sodium), solids and liquid.	0	213	15.0	1.4	37.2	86	263	6.8	14	435	2,040	.52	.26	4.5	40
1529	Frozen	0	331	24.5	1.4	58.1	91	408	9.1	[illegible] 585	680	3,080	1.45	.45	9.3	85
	Peas, mature seeds, dry, raw:															
1531	Whole	0	1,542	109.3	5.9	273.5	290	1,542	23.1	159	4,559	540	3.38	1.31	13.7	—
1532	Split, without seed coat	0	1,579	109.8	4.5	284.4	150	1,216	23.1	181	4,060	540	3.38	1.31	13.7	—
1534	**Peas and carrots, frozen**	0	249	15.0	1.4	47.2	118	268	5.4	[illegible] 417	776	42,180	.91	.32	6.1	45
1536	**Pecans:**															
a	In shell (refuse: shells)	47	1,652	22.1	171.2	35.1	175	695	5.8	Trace	1,450	310	2.08	.31	2.2	4
b	Shelled	0	3,116	41.7	323.0	66.2	331	1,311	10.9	Trace	2,735	590	3.92	.59	4.1	7
	Peppers, hot, chili:															
	Immature, green:															
1537	Raw (refuse: stem ends, seeds, core)	(27)	123	4.3	.7	30.1	33	83	2.3	—	—	2,550	.30	.20	5.6	778
	Canned:															
1538	Pods, excluding seeds; solids and liquid	0	113	4.1	.5	27.7	32	77	2.3	—	—	2,770	.08	.22	3.7	308
1539	Chili sauce	0	91	3.2	.5	22.7	23	64	1.8	—	—	2,770	.14	.14	3.2	308
	Mature, red:															
	Raw, portion used—															
1540	Pods, including seeds (refuse: stem ends)	4	405	16.1	10.0	78.9	126	340	5.2	—	—	94,070	.96	1.57	19.2	1,607

No.		Food															
1541		Pods, excluding seeds (refuse: stem ends, seeds, core).	27	215	7.6	1.3	52.3	53	162	4.6	83	1,867	71,520	.33	.66	9.6	1,222
1542		Canned, chili sauce	0	95	4.1	2.7	17.7	41	73	2.3	—	—	43,500	.05	.41	2.7	136
		Dried.															
1543		Pods	0	1,456	58.5	41.3	271.3	590	1,089	35.4	1,602	5,448	349,270	1.04	6.03	47.6	[94] 54
1544		Chili powder with added seasoning	0	1,542	64.9	56.2	256.3	1,202	925	68.9	7,140	4,536	294,840	.86	5.13	40.4	45
		Peppers, sweet, garden varieties:															
1545		Immature, green, raw (refuse: stem ends, seeds, core).	18	82	4.5	.7	17.9	33	82	2.6	48	792	1,540	.28	.30	2.0	476
1548		Mature, red, raw (refuse: stem ends, seeds, core)	20	112	5.1	1.1	25.8	47	109	2.2	—	—	16,150	(.28)	(.29)	(1.9)	740
1549		**Perch, white,** raw:															
	a	Whole, (refuse: head, tail, fins, bones, skin, and entrails).	64	193	31.5	6.5	0	—	314	—	—	—	—	—	—	—	—
	b	Flesh only	0	535	87.5	18.1	0	—	871	—	—	—	—	—	—	—	—
1550		**Perch, yellow,** raw:															
	a	Whole (refuse: head, tail, fins, bones, skin, and entrails).	61	161	34.5	1.6	0	—	318	1.1	120	407	—	.11	.30	3.1	—
	b	Flesh only	0	413	88.5	4.1	0	—	816	2.7	308	1,043	—	27	77	7.9	—
		Persimmons, raw:															
1551		Japanese or kaki:															
	a	Varieties with seeds (refuse: seeds, calyx, skin)	18	286	2.6	1.5	73.3	22	97	1.1	22	647	10,080	.11	08	.4	41
	b	Varieties without seeds (refuse: calyx, skin)	16	293	2.7	1.5	75.1	23	99	1.1	23	663	10,330	.11	.08	.4	42
1552		Native (refuse: seeds, calyx)	18	472	3.0	1.5	124.6	100	97	9.3	4	1,153	—	—	—	—	246
		Pheasant, raw:															
1553		Total edible:															
	a	Dressed (refuse: head, feet, inedible viscera, and bones).	34	452	72.8	15.6	0	—	—	—	—	—	—	—	—	—	—
	b	Ready-to-cook (refuse: bones)	13	596	95.9	20.5	0	—	—	—	—	—	—	—	—	—	—
1557		**Pickerel,** chain, raw:															
	a	Whole (refuse: head, tail, fins, skin, entrails, and bones).	49	194	43.3	1.2	0	—	—	1.6	—	—	—	—	—	—	—
	b	Flesh only	0	381	84.8	2.3	0	—	—	3.2	—	—	—	—	—	—	—
		Pickles:															
		Cucumber:															
1558		Dill	0	50	3.2	.9	10.0	118	95	4.5	6,477	907	450	Trace	09	Trace	28
1559		Fresh (as bread-and-butter pickles)	0	331	4.1	.9	81.2	145	122	8.2	3,053	—	640	Trace	14	Trace	41
1560		Sour	0	45	2.3	.9	9.1	77	68	14.5	6,137	—	450	Trace	09	Trace	30
1561		Sweet	0	662	3.2	1.8	165.6	54	73	5.4	—	—	410	Trace	09	.1	26
		Chowchow (cucumber with added cauliflower, onion, mustard):															
1562		Sour	0	132	6.4	5.9	18.6	145	240	11.8	6,069	—	—	—	—	—	—
1563		Sweet	0	526	6.8	4.1	122.5	104	100	6.8	2,390	—	—	—	—	—	—
		Relish, finely cut or chopped															
1564		Sour	0	86	(3.2)	(4.1)	(12.2)	(132)	(91)	(5.0)	—	—	—	—	—	—	—
1565		Sweet	0	626	2.3	2.7	154.2	91	64	3.6	3,230	—	—	—	—	—	—
		Pies:															
		Baked, piecrust made with unenriched flour:[95]															
1566		Apple	0	1,161	10.0	50.3	172.8	36	100	1.4	1,365	363	140	10	.08	1.8	3
1567		Banana custard	0	1,002	20.4	42.2	139.3	299	372	2.3	880	921	1,130	17	58	1.4	5
1568		Blackberry	0	1,102	11.8	49.9	156.0	86	118	2.3	1,216	454	410	.08	10	1.3	16
1569		Blueberry	0	1,098	10.9	49.0	158.3	60	104	2.7	1,216	295	120	08	09	1.2	15
		Boston cream. See Cakes, item 522															
1570		Butterscotch	0	1,211	20.0	49.9	173.7	340	367	4.1	971	431	1,180	12	.47	8	1
1571		Cherry	0	1,184	11.8	51.3	174.2	64	113	1.4	1,379	476	2,000	11	.10	2.1	2
1572		Chocolate chiffon	0	1,488	30.8	69.4	198.2	109	440	5.4	1,143	499	1,410	14	.44	1.0	0
1573		Chocolate meringue	0	1,143	21.8	54.4	152.0	313	445	3.2	1,161	631	860	.12	.56	9	Trace
1574		Coconut custard	0	1,066	27.2	56.7	112.9	426	526	3.2	1,120	739	1,040	.28	.85	1.3	0
1575		Custard	0	989	27.7	50.3	106.1	435	513	2.7	1,302	621	1,040	23	.74	1.4	0
1576		Lemon chiffon	0	1,420	31.8	57.2	198.7	104	376	4.1	1,184	367	770	15	.38	9	14
1577		Lemon meringue	0	1,157	16.8	46.3	171.0	64	222	2.3	1,279	227	770	15	.38	9	14
1578		Mince	0	1,229	11.3	52.2	186.9	127	172	4.5	2,032	807	Trace	31	.16	1.6	3
1579		Peach	0	1,157	11.3	48.5	173.3	45	132	2.3	1,216	676	3,310	.08	.17	3.1	15
1580		Pecan	0	1,896	23.1	103.9	232.7	213	467	12.7	1,002	558	730	72	.33	1.5	1
1581		Pineapple	0	1,148	10.0	48.5	172.8	59	95	2.3	1,229	327	100	.17	.09	1.8	3
1582		Pineapple chiffon	0	1,306	29.9	54.9	177.4	109	345	4.1	1,161	445	1,590	19	43	1.8	3
1583		Pineapple custard	0	998	18.1	39.5	145.6	227	295	1.8	844	440	820	.16	.42	1.8	3
1584		Pumpkin	0	957	18.1	50.8	111.1	231	313	2.3	971	726	11,200	15	46	2.3	1
1585		Raisin	0	1,225	11.8	48.5	195.0	82	181	4.1	1,293	871	20	13	.12	1.2	4
1586		Rhubarb	0	1,148	11.3	48.5	173.3	290	118	3.2	1,225	721	210	09	18	1.2	13

[5] See Notes on Foods, p. 177

[16] Estimated average based on addition of salt in the amount of 0.6 percent of the finished product

[17] Average weighted in accordance with commercial practices in freezing vegetables. See also Notes on Foods, p. 177.

[93] Average weighted in accordance with commercial freezing practices. For products without added ascorbic acid, average is about 50 mg per pound, for those with added ascorbic acid, around 186 mg

[94] Based on one sample described as ground powder, stored; for freshly processed product, value is 699 mg per pound.

[95] If piecrust is made with enriched flour, increase values for nutrients in milligrams per pound of pie by the following amounts

	Iron	Thiamine	Riboflavin	Niacin
One-crust pie	1.4	0.14	0.14	1.4
Two-crust pie	1.8	27	.18	2.3

TABLE 2.—NUTRIENTS IN THE EDIBLE PORTION OF 1 POUND OF FOOD AS PURCHASED—Continued

[Numbers in parentheses denote values imputed—usually from another form of the food or from a similar food. Zero in parentheses indicates that the amount of a constituent probably is none or is too small to measure. Dashes denote lack of reliable data for a constituent believed to be present in measurable amount. Calculated values, as those based on a recipe, are not in parentheses]

Item No.		Food and description	Refuse	Food energy	Protein	Fat	Carbohydrate total	Calcium	Phosphorus	Iron	Sodium	Potassium	Vitamin A value	Thiamine	Riboflavin	Niacin	Ascorbic Acid
(A)		(B)	(C)	(D)	(E)	(F)	(G)	(H)	(I)	(J)	(K)	(L)	(M)	(N)	(O)	(P)	(Q)
			Percent	Calories	Grams	Grams	Grams	Milligrams	Milligrams	Milligrams	Milligrams	Milligrams	International units	Milligrams	Milligrams	Milligrams	Milligrams
		Pies—Continued															
		Baked, piecrust with unenriched flour [45]—Continued															
1587		Strawberry	0	898	8.6	35.8	140.2	73	113	3.2	880	544	160	0.09	0.20	2.0	115
1588		Sweetpotato	0	960	20.4	51.3	107.5	313	381	2.3	989	739	10,890	.21	.54	1.4	19
		Frozen in unbaked form:															
1589		Apple	0	853	7.3	37.6	130.6	32	77	.9	803	272	60	.08	.06	.7	6
1591		Cherry	0	1,161	8.6	48.1	176.9	50	95	.6	916	327	1,270	.08	.07	1.0	10
1593		Coconut custard	0	930	23.6	38.6	122.9	390	472	2.7	1,089	712	860	.20	.70	.8	2
1595		**Pie mix** (filling and piecrust), coconut custard	0	2,152	15.0	90.7	320.2	59	209	2.3	2,849	644	0	.09	.07	1.6	0
1601		**Piecrust mix,** including stick form	0	2,368	32.7	148.3	224.5	209	435	2.3	3,143	286	0	.30	.17	5.0	6
		Pigeonpeas, raw:															
1603		Immature seeds in pods (refuse: pods)	61	207	12.7	1.1	37.7	74	225	2.8	9	976	250	.70	.30	2.6	69
1604		Mature seeds, dry	0	1,551	92.5	6.4	288.9	485	1,433	36.3	118	4,450	360	1.44	.71	13.8	—
1605		**Pigs' feet,** pickled	0	903	75.8	67.1	0	—	—	—	—	—	—	—	—	—	—
1606		**Pike, blue,** raw:															
	a	Whole (refuse: head, tail, fins, skin, entrails, and bones).	56	180	38.1	1.8	0	—	—	—	—	—	—	—	—	—	—
	b	Flesh only	0	408	86.6	4.1	0	—	—	—	—	—	—	—	—	—	—
1607		**Pike, northern,** raw:															
	a	Whole (refuse: head, tail, fins, skin, entrails, and bones).	74	104	21.6	1.3	0	—	—	—	—	—	—	—	—	—	—
	b	Flesh only	0	399	83.0	5.0	0	—	—	—	—	—	—	—	—	—	—
1608		**Pike, walleye,** raw:															
	a	Whole (refuse: head, tail, fins, entrails, and bones)	43	240	49.9	3.1	0	—	553	1.0	132	825	—	.65	.41	6.0	—
	b	Flesh only	0	422	87.5	5.4	0	—	971	1.8	231	1,447	—	1.13	.73	10.5	—
1609		**Pilinuts:**															
	a	In shell (refuse: shells)	82	546	9.3	58.0	6.9	114	442	2.8	2	399	30	.72	.07	.4	Trace
	b	Shelled	0	3,035	51.7	322.5	38.1	635	2,513	15.4	14	2,218	180	3.99	.40	2.2	Trace
1610		**Pimientos,** canned, solids and liquid	0	122	4.1	2.3	26.3	[86] 32	77	6.8	—	—	10,430	.11	.29	1.7	430
		Pineapple:															
1611		Raw (refuse: crown, core, parings, defects)	48	124	.9	.5	32.3	40	19	1.2	2	344	170	.21	.06	.6	40
1612		Candied	0	1,433	3.6	1.8	362.9	—	—	—	—	—	—	—	—	—	—
		Canned, solids and liquid:															
1613		Water pack, all styles except crushed, with or without artificial sweetener.	0	177	1.4	.5	46.3	54	23	1.4	5	449	210	.36	.10	1.0	31
1614		Juice pack, all styles	0	263	1.8	.5	68.5	73	36	1.8	5	667	290	.44	.13	1.2	46
		Sirup pack, all styles:															
1615		Light	0	268	1.4	.5	69.9	50	23	1.4	5	440	210	.35	.10	1.0	30
1616		Heavy	0	336	1.4	.5	88.0	50	23	1.4	5	435	200	.35	.10	.9	30
1617		Extra heavy	0	408	1.4	.5	106.1	50	23	1.4	5	426	200	.34	.10	.9	29
1618		Frozen chunks, sweetened	0	386	1.8	.5	100.7	41	18	1.8	9	454	150	.45	.14	1.3	37
		Pineapple juice:															
1619		Canned, unsweetened	0	249	1.8	.5	61.2	68	41	1.4	5	676	230	.23	.07	.9	41
1620		Frozen concentrate, unsweetened	0	812	6.9	.5	200.9	177	127	4.1	14	2,141	230	1.04	.25	3.9	191
1622		**Pineapple juice and grapefruit juice drink,** canned (approx. 40% fruit juices).[87]	0	245	.9	Trace	61.7	23	23	.9	Trace	281	50	.07	.03	.4	73
1623		**Pineapple juice and orange juice drink,** canned (approx. 40% fruit juices).[87]	0	245	.9	.5	61.2	23	27	.9	Trace	318	230	.11	.03	.4	73
		Pinenuts:															
1624		Pignolias, shelled	0	2,504	141.1	215.0	52.6	—	—	—	—	—	—	2.83	—	—	—
1625		Piñon:															
	a	In shell (refuse: shells)	42	1,571	34.2	159.2	53.9	32	1,589	13.7	—	—	80	3.37	.61	11.8	Trace
	b	Shelled	0	2,880	59.0	274.4	93.0	54	2,740	23.6	—	—	140	5.81	1.04	20.4	Trace
1626		**Pistachionuts:**															
	a	In shell (refuse: shells)	50	1,347	43.8	121.8	43.1	297	1,134	16.6	—	2,204	520	1.52	—	3.2	0
	b	Shelled	0	2,694	87.5	243.6	86.2	594	2,268	33.1	—	4,409	1,040	3.04	—	6.4	0
1627		**Pitanga** (Surinam-cherry), raw (refuse: stems, blossom end, seeds).	19	187	2.9	1.5	45.9	33	40	.7	—	—	5,510	.10	.15	1.0	110
		Pizza, with cheese:															
		From home-type recipe, baked: [88]															
1628		With cheese topping	0	1,070	54.4	37.6	128.4	1,002	885	4.5	3,184	590	2,860	.27	.91	4.5	39
1629		With sausage topping	0	1,061	35.4	42.2	134.3	77	417	5.4	3,307	762	2,540	.45	.55	7.0	42
1630		Chilled, partially baked	0	943	35.4	26.3	140.2	549	572	3.2	2,440	426	1,910	.26	.65	4.0	25
1632		Frozen, partially baked	0	1,039	40.4	29.9	150.1	662	662	4.1	2,744	485	2,040	.26	.72	4.2	24

1634		**Plantain** (baking banana), raw (refuse: skins)	28	389	3.6	1.3	101.9	23	98	2.3	16	1,257	(99)	20	.13	2.0	46
		Plate dinners, frozen, commercial.															
1635		Beef pot roast, whole oven-browned potatoes, peas and corn.	0	481	59.4	14.5	27.7	45	345	7.3	1,175	1,107	500	27	.44	9.5	24
1636		Chicken, fried; mashed potatoes; mixed vegetables (carrots, peas, corn, beans).	6	736	54.5	36.2	48.1	174	617	5.1	1,464	477	2,510	.28	.79	22.3	18
1637		Meat loaf with tomato sauce, mashed potatoes and peas.	0	594	36.3	30.4	44.5	86	531	5.9	1,783	522	1,950	.48	.64	7.8	20
1638		Turkey, sliced; mashed potatoes; peas	0	508	38.1	13.6	57.6	118	395	5.0	1,814	798	590	30	.41	10.3	18
		Plums:															
		Raw															
1639		Damson (refuse: pits and clinging pulp)	9	272	2.1	Trace	73.5	74	70	2.1	8	1,234	(1,240)	.33	13	2.2	—
1640		Japanese and hybrid (refuse: pits)	6	205	2.1	.9	52.4	51	77	2.1	4	725	1,070	.14	.14	2.3	24
1641		Prune-type (refuse: pits)	6	320	3.4	.9	84.0	51	77	2.1	4	725	[100] 1,280	14	.14	2.3	17
		Canned, solids and liquid															
1642		Greengage, water pack, with or without artificial sweetener (refuse: pits).	4	144	1.7	.4	37.5	(39)	(57)	(.9)	4	357	(720)	(.06)	(.08)	(1.3)	9
		Purple (Italian prunes):															
1643		Water pack, with or without artificial sweetener (refuse: pits).	4	200	1.7	.9	51.8	39	44	4.4	9	645	5,460	10	09	1.7	7
		Sirup pack:															
1644		Light (refuse: pits)	4	274	1.7	4	72.3	39	44	3.9	4	631	5,360	10	.09	1.7	7
1645		Heavy (refuse: pits)	4	361	1.7	.4	94.1	39	44	3.9	4	618	5,250	.10	09	1.7	7
1646		Extra heavy (refuse: pits)	4	444	1.7	.4	116.3	35	39	3.9	4	605	5,140	.10	.09	1.6	7
		Poha See Groundcherries, item 1092.															
1647		**Pokeberry** (poke) shoots, raw	0	104	11.8	1.8	16.8	240	200	7.7	—	—	39,460	.36	1.49	5.4	617
1649		**Pollock,** raw.															
	a	Drawn (refuse: head, tail, fins, and bones)	55	194	41.6	1.8	0	—	—	—	98	714	—	.10	.21	3.2	—
	b	Fillets	0	431	92.5	4.1	0	—	—	—	218	1,588	—	.23	.46	7.1	—
1651		**Pomegranate,** raw (refuse: skin, seeds)	44	160	1.3	.8	41.7	8	20	.8	8	658	Trace	.07	.07	.7	10
1652		**Pompano,** raw.															
	a	Whole (refuse: head, tail, fins, bones, skin, and entrails).	44	422	47.8	24.1	0	—	—	—	119	485	—	1.05	.56	—	—
	b	Flesh only	0	753	85.3	43.1	0	—	—	—	213	866	—	1.87	1.00	—	—
		Popcorn:															
1653		Unpopped	0	1,642	54.0	21.3	327.0	(45)	(1,198)	(11.3)	(14)	—	—	(1.77)	(.50)	(9.5)	(0)
		Popped															
1654		Plain	0	1,751	57.6	22.7	347.9	(50)	(1,275)	(12.2)	(14)	—	—	—	(.54)	(10.0)	(0)
1655		Oil and salt added	0	2,068	44.5	98.9	268.1	36	980	9.5	8,800	—	—	—	42	7.7	0
1656		Sugar-coated	0	1,737	27.7	15.9	387.4	23	612	5.9	[73] 5	—	—	—	.26	4.8	0
1658		**Porgy and scup,** raw.															
	a	Whole (refuse: head, tail, fins, bones, skin, and entrails)	59	208	35.3	6.3	0	100	465	—	117	534	—	—	—	—	—
	b	Flesh only	0	508	86.2	15.4	0	245	1,134	—	286	1,302	—	—	—	—	—
		Pork, fresh: [4]															
		Carcass, with bone, raw:															
		Fat class															
1659		Total edible, 33% lean, 46% fat	21	1,979	32.6	204.0	0	18	315	5.0			(0)	1.58	.36	8.5	—
		Medium-fat class:															
1662		Total edible, 37% lean, 42% fat	21	1,827	36.3	185.2	0	21	367	5.3			(0)	1.77	.42	9.4	—
		Thin class															
1665		Total edible, 41% lean, 37% fat	22	1,672	39.7	166.5	0	21	411	6.0			(0)	1.93	46	10.3	—
		Wholesale cuts, raw.															
		Bacon or belly:															
1668		Fat class															
	a	With skin, 24% lean, 70% fat	6	2,699	30.4	284.8	0	17	265	4.7	(101)	(102)	(0)	1.48	.35	7.9	—
	b	Without skin, 25% lean, 75% fat	0	2,862	32.2	302.1	0	18	281	5.0			(0)	1.56	38	8.4	—
1669		Medium-fat class.															
	a	With skin, 31% lean, 63% fat	7	2,486	34.7	259.2	0	21	321	5.1			(0)	1.69	41	9.0	—
	b	Without skin, 33% lean, 67% fat	0	2,667	37.2	278.1	0	23	345	5.4			(0)	1.81	.44	9.7	—
1670		Thin class															
	a	With skin, 37% lean, 55% fat	8	2,279	39.3	234.2	0	21	385	5.9			(0)	1.91	46	10.2	—
	b	Without skin, 40% lean, 60% fat	0	2,472	42.6	254.0	0	23	417	6.4			(0)	2.07	.50	11.1	—

[4] See Notes on Foods, p. 180.

[73] Value for product without added salt

[95] If piecrust is made with enriched flour, increase values for nutrients in milligrams per pound of pie by the following amounts:

	Iron	Thiamine	Riboflavin	Niacin
One-crust pie	1.4	0.14	0.14	1.4
Two-crust pie	1.8	.27	.18	2.3

[96] Federal standards provide for addition of certain calcium salts as firming agents, if used, these salts may add calcium not to exceed 118 mg per pound of finished product.

[97] Fruit juice content ranges from 10 to 50 percent Ascorbic acid may be added as a preservative or as a nutrient Value listed is based on product with label stating 30 mg per 6 fl oz serving If label claim is 30 mg per 8 fl. oz serving, value would be 54 mg per pound.

[98] Values are based on products made with unenriched flour. With enriched flour, values per pound are increased approximately as follows Iron, 3 6 mg, thiamine, 0 54 mg, riboflavin, 0.36 mg, niacin, 4 1 mg.

[99] Values per pound range from 30 I U for white-fleshed varieties to as much as 3,900 I U. for those with deep-yellow flesh.

[100] Value applies to all prune-type plums except Italian prunes and Imperial prunes, which average 5,700 I U. per pound

[101] Average value for 1 pound, all cuts without bone and skin or with a small proportion of bone and skin, is 320 mg For cuts with average bone and skin content (18 percent), the value is 260 mg; for those with high bone and skin content (as spareribs), 190 mg. See also Notes on Foods, p 180

[102] Average value for 1 pound, all cuts without bone and skin or with a small proportion of bone and skin, is 1,295 mg For cuts with average bone and skin content (18 percent), the value is 1,060 mg, for those with high bone and skin content (as spareribs), 775 mg. See also Notes on Foods, p 180.

TABLE 2.—NUTRIENTS IN THE EDIBLE PORTION OF 1 POUND OF FOOD AS PURCHASED—Continued

[Numbers in parentheses denote values imputed—usually from another form of the food or from a similar food. Zero in parentheses indicates that the amount of a constituent probably is none or is too small to measure. Dashes denote lack of reliable data for a constituent believed to be present in measurable amount. Calculated values, as those based on a recipe, are not in parentheses]

Item No.	Food and description	Refuse	Food energy	Protein	Fat	Carbo-hydrate total	Calcium	Phosphorus	Iron	Sodium	Potassium	Vitamin A value	Thiamine	Ribo-flavin	Niacin	Ascorbic Acid
(A)	(B)	(C)	(D)	(E)	(F)	(G)	(H)	(I)	(J)	(K)	(L)	(M)	(N)	(O)	(P)	(Q)
	Pork, fresh —Continued	Percent	Calories	Grams	Grams	Grams	Milligrams	Milligrams	Milligrams	Milligrams	Milligrams	International units	Milligrams	Milligrams	Milligrams	Milligrams
	Wholesale cuts, raw—Continued															
	Backfat:															
	Total edible:															
1671	Fat class:															
a	With skin, 91% fat	9	3,452	7.0	379.3	0	4	0	1.2			(0)	0.34	0.08	1.8	----
b	Without skin, 100% fat	0	3,815	7.7	419.1	0	5	0	1.4			(0)	.38	.09	2.0	----
1672	Medium-fat class:															
a	With skin, 90% fat	10	3,372	8.6	369.9	0	4	0	1.2			(0)	.42	.10	2.2	----
b	Without skin, 100% fat	0	3,751	9.5	411.4	0	5	0	1.4			(0)	.46	.11	2.5	----
1673	Thin class:															
a	With skin, 89% fat	11	3,297	9.7	360.9	0	4	0	1.6			(0)	.47	.11	2.5	----
b	Without skin, 100% fat	0	3,692	10.9	404.2	0	5	0	1.8			(0)	.53	.13	2.8	----
	Shoulder:															
	Total edible:															
1674	Fat class:															
a	With bone and skin, 50% lean, 36% fat	14	1,691	45.9	165.6	0	27	482	7.0			(0)	2.23	.54	11.9	----
b	Without bone and skin, 58% lean, 42% fat	0	1,973	53.5	193.2	0	32	562	8.2			(0)	2.60	.63	13.9	----
1675	Medium-fat class:															
a	With bone and skin, 56% lean, 28% fat	15	1,542	48.9	148.1	0	27	523	7.3			(0)	2.37	.57	12.7	----
b	Without bone and skin, 67% lean, 33% fat	0	1,819	57.6	174.6	0	32	617	8.6			(0)	2.80	.68	15.0	----
1676	Thin class:															
a	With bone and skin, 63% lean, 21% fat	16	1,400	51.8	130.5	0	30	563	7.6			(0)	2.52	.61	13.5	----
b	Without bone and skin, 75% lean, 25% fat	0	1,669	61.7	156.0	0	36	671	9.1			(0)	3.00	.72	16.1	----
	Composite of trimmed lean cuts, ham, loin, shoulder, and spareribs, raw:															
	Fat class:															
1677	Total edible:															
a	With bone and skin, 60% lean, 23% fat	17	1,300	54.8	117.9	0	30	605	8.3			(0)	2.67	.65	14.3	----
b	Without bone and skin, 72% lean, 28% fat	0	1,569	66.2	142.4	0	36	730	10.0	(98)	(98)	(0)	3.22	.78	17.2	----
1679	Separable lean	0	825	85.3	51.3	0	50	984	12.7			(0)	4.15	1.00	22.2	----
1681	Separable fat	0	3,466	17.7	375.6	0	9	86	2.7			(0)	.86	.21	4.6	----
	Medium-fat class:															
1682	Total edible:															
a	With bone and skin, 65% lean, 19% fat	18	1,151	58.7	99.8	0	34	654	8.6			(0)	2.84	.68	15.2	----
b	Without bone and skin, 77% lean, 23% fat	0	1,397	71.2	121.1	0	41	794	10.4			(0)	3.44	.83	18.5	----
1684	Separable lean	0	789	86.6	46.3	0	50	1,002	13.2			(0)	4.21	1.01	22.5	----
1686	Separable fat	0	3,407	18.6	368.8	0	9	106	2.7			(0)	.90	.22	4.9	----
	Thin class:															
1687	Total edible:															
a	With bone and skin, 66% lean, 16% fat	18	1,028	62.2	84.5	0	37	700	9.3			(0)	3.01	.72	16.1	----
b	Without bone and skin, 81% lean, 19% fat	0	1,252	75.8	103.0	0	45	853	11.3			(0)	3.67	.88	19.6	----
1689	Separable lean	0	748	88.5	41.3	0	50	1,025	13.2			(0)	4.30	1.03	22.8	----
1691	Separable fat	0	3,343	20.4	361.1	0	14	122	3.2			(0)	.99	.24	5.3	----
	Separable fat from lean cuts. See individual cuts.															
	Retail cuts, trimmed to retail level, raw:															
	Ham:															
	Fat class:															
1693	Total edible:															
a	With bone and skin, 61% lean, 24% fat	15	1,264	58.7	112.5	0	35	657	8.9			(0)	2.86	.69	15.3	----
b	Without bone and skin, 72% lean, 28% fat	0	1,483	68.9	132.0	0	41	771	10.4			(0)	3.36	.81	18.0	----
1695	Separable lean	0	726	89.4	38.1	0	50	1,039	13.6			(0)	4.34	1.04	23.2	----
1697	Separable fat	0	3,425	18.1	371.0	0	9	91	2.7			(0)	.88	.21	4.7	----
	Medium-fat class:															
1698	Total edible:															
a	With bone and skin, 63% lean, 22% fat	15	1,188	61.3	102.6	0	35	686	9.3			(0)	2.98	.72	16.0	----
b	Without bone and skin, 74% lean, 26% fat	0	1,397	72.1	120.7	0	41	807	10.9			(0)	3.51	.84	18.8	----
1700	Separable lean	0	694	90.7	34.0	0	54	1,057	13.9			(0)	4.41	1.06	23.6	----
1702	Separable fat	0	3,384	19.5	366.1	0	9	109	2.7			(0)	.95	.23	5.1	

		Thin class															
1703		Total edible:															
	a	With bone and skin, 65% lean, 19% fat	16	1,077	64.0	88.9	0	38	728	9.6			(0)	3.13	.76	16.7	—
	b	Without bone and skin, 77% lean, 23% fat	0	1,275	75.8	105.2	0	45	862	11.3			(0)	3.70	.89	19.8	—
1705		Separable lean	0	667	92.5	29.9	0	54	1,080	14.1			(0)	4.50	1.08	24.0	—
1707		Separable fat	0	3,343	20.9	360.6	0	14	127	3.2			(0)	1.02	.24	5.4	—
		Loin:															
		Fat class:															
1708		Total edible:															
	a	With bone, 60% lean, 19% fat	21	1,153	58.5	100.0	0	32	660	8.9			(0)	2.84	.69	15.2	—
	b	Without bone, 76% lean, 24% fat	0	1,465	74.4	127.0	0	41	839	11.3			(0)	3.61	.87	19.3	—
1711		Separable lean	0	857	91.2	51.7	0	54	1,061	13.6			(0)	4.43	1.07	23.7	—
1714		Separable fat	0	3,352	21.8	361.5	0	14	141	3.2			(0)	1.06	.25	5.7	—
		Medium-fat class:															
1715		Total edible:															
	a	With bone, 63% lean, 16% fat	21	1,065	61.1	89.0	0	36	690	9.3			(0)	2.97	.71	15.9	—
	b	Without bone, 80% lean, 20% fat	0	1,352	77.6	112.9	0	45	875	11.8			(0)	3.76	.90	20.1	—
1718		Separable lean	0	857	91.2	51.7	0	54	1,061	13.6			(0)	4.43	1.07	23.7	—
1721		Separable fat	0	3,280	23.6	352.4	0	14	163	3.6			(0)	1.15	.28	6.1	—
		Thin class:															
1722		Total edible:															
	a	With bone, 67% lean, 12% fat	22	953	63.7	75.4	0	36	725	9.6			(0)	3.09	.74	16.6	—
	b	Without bone, 85% lean, 15% fat	0	1,216	81.2	96.2	0	45	925	12.2			(0)	3.95	.95	21.1	—
1725		Separable lean	0	857	91.2	51.7	0	54	1,061	13.6			(0)	4.43	1.07	23.7	—
1728		Separable fat	0	3,202	25.4	342.9	0	14	191	3.6			(0)	1.23	.30	6.6	—
		Boston butt:															
		Fat class:															
1729		Total edible:															
	a	With bone and skin, 71% lean, 23% fat	6	1,373	61.6	123.2	0	34	680	9.4			(0)	3.00	.72	16.1	—
	b	Without bone and skin, 76% lean, 24% fat	0	1,465	65.8	131.5	0	36	726	10.0			(0)	3.20	.77	17.1	—
1731		Separable lean	0	889	80.3	60.3	0	45	916	12.2			(0)	3.90	.94	20.9	—
1733		Separable fat	0	3,270	21.3	352.4	0	14	136	3.2			(0)	1.03	.25	5.5	—
		Medium-fat class:															
1734		Total edible:									(101)	(102)					
	a	With bone and skin, 74% lean, 20% fat	6	1,220	65.9	104.1	0	38	735	9.8			(0)	3.20	.77	17.1	—
	b	Without bone and skin, 79% lean, 21% fat	0	1,302	70.3	111.1	0	41	785	10.4			(0)	3.42	.82	18.3	—
1736		Separable lean	0	816	82.6	51.3	0	50	948	12.2			(0)	4.01	.97	21.5	—
1738		Separable fat	0	3,157	24.0	338.4	0	14	172	3.6			(0)	1.17	.28	6.3	—
		Thin class:															
1739		Total edible:															
	a	With bone and skin, 78% lean, 16% fat	6	1,067	70.1	85.0	0	42	795	10.6			(0)	3.42	.82	18.3	—
	b	Without bone and skin, 83% lean, 17% fat	0	1,139	74.8	90.7	0	45	848	11.3			(0)	3.65	.88	19.8	—
1741		Separable lean	0	753	84.8	43.1	0	50	975	12.7			(0)	4.12	.99	22.0	—
1743		Separable fat	0	3,044	27.2	324.3	0	14	213	4.1			(0)	1.32	.32	7.1	—
		Picnic:															
		Fat class:															
1744		Total edible:															
	a	With bone and skin, 57% lean, 25% fat	18	1,248	55.7	112.1	0	34	617	8.2			(0)	2.70	.65	14.4	—
	b	Without bone and skin, 69% lean, 31% fat	0	1,515	67.6	136.1	0	41	748	10.0			(0)	3.27	.78	17.5	—
1746		Separable lean	0	748	86.6	41.7	0	50	1,002	13.2			(0)	4.21	1.01	22.5	—
1748		Separable fat	0	3,234	24.5	347.0	0	14	177	3.6			(0)	1.19	.29	6.4	—
		Medium-fat class:															
1749		Total edible:															
	a	With bone and skin, 61% lean, 22% fat	18	1,083	59.0	92.2	0	34	664	9.0			(0)	2.87	.69	15.4	—
	b	Without bone and skin, 74% lean, 26% fat.	0	1,315	71.7	112.0	0	41	807	10.9			(0)	3.49	.84	18.6	—
1751		Separable lean	0	680	88.0	33.6	0	50	1,021	13.2			(0)	4.28	1.03	22.9	—
1753		Separable fat	0	3,107	26.3	332.0	0	14	200	4.1			(0)	1.28	.31	6.8	—
		Thin class:															
1754		Total edible:															
	a	With bone and skin, 64% lean, 18% fat	18	932	63.2	73.3	0	37	715	9.4			(0)	3.06	.74	16.4	—
	b	Without bone and skin, 78% lean, 22% fat	0	1,129	76.7	88.9	0	45	866	11.3			(0)	3.71	.89	19.9	—
1756		Separable lean	0	612	89.8	25.4	0	50	1,043	13.6			(0)	4.36	1.05	23.4	—
1758		Separable fat	0	2,980	28.6	317.1	0	18	231	4.1			(0)	1.39	.34	7.4	—
		Spareribs:															
		Fat class:															
1759		Total edible:															
	a	With bone	38	1,100	38.6	103.8	0	23	420	5.9			(0)	1.88	.45	10.0	—
	b	Without bone	0	1,769	62.1	166.9	0	36	676	9.5			(0)	3.02	.73	16.1	—

[5] See Notes on Foods, p. 180

[101] Average value for 1 pound, all cuts without bone and skin or with a small proportion of bone and skin, is 320 mg. For cuts with average bone and skin content (18 percent), the value is 260 mg., for those with high bone and skin content (as spareribs), 190 mg. See also Notes on Foods, p. 180

[102] Average value for 1 pound, all cuts without bone and skin or with a small proportion of bone and skin, is 1,295 mg. For cuts with average bone and skin content (18 percent), the value is 1,060 mg., for those with high bone and skin content (as spareribs), 775 mg. See also Notes on Foods, p. 180.

TABLE 2.—NUTRIENTS IN THE EDIBLE PORTION OF 1 POUND OF FOOD AS PURCHASED—Continued

[Numbers in parentheses denote values imputed—usually from another form of the food or from a similar food. Zero in parentheses indicates that the amount of a constituent probably is none or is too small to measure. Dashes denote lack of reliable data for a constituent believed to be present in measurable amount. Calculated values, as those based on a recipe, are not in parentheses]

Item No.		Food and description	Refuse	Food energy	Protein	Fat	Carbo-hydrate total	Calcium	Phosphorus	Iron	Sodium	Potassium	Vitamin A value	Thiamine	Ribo-flavin	Niacin	Ascorbic Acid
(A)		(B)	(C)	(D)	(E)	(F)	(G)	(H)	(I)	(J)	(K)	(L)	(M)	(N)	(O)	(P)	(Q)
			Percent	*Calories*	*Grams*	*Grams*	*Grams*	*Milligrams*	*Milligrams*	*Milligrams*	*Milligrams*	*Milligrams*	*International units*	*Milligrams*	*Milligrams*	*Milligrams*	*Milligrams*
		Pork, fresh—Continued															
		Retail cuts, trimmed to retail level, raw—Con.															
		Spareribs—Continued															
		Medium-fat class:															
1761		Total edible:															
	a	With bone	40	376	39.2	89.7	0	22	432	5.9			(0)	1.91	0.46	10.2	—
	b	Without bone	0	1,657	65.8	150.6	0	36	726	10.0			(0)	3.20	.77	17.1	—
		Thin class:									([193])	([192])					
1763		Total edible:															
	a	With bone	43	857	39.6	76.4	0	23	440	6.0			(0)	1.95	.46	10.3	—
	b	Without bone	0	1,591	69.4	133.8	0	41	771	10.4			(0)	3.37	.81	18.1	—
		Pork, cured:															
		Dry, long-cure, country-style:															
		Ham:															
1765		Fat:															
	a	With bone and skin	12	1,857	58.9	178.	1.2	—	—	—	—	—	(0)	—	—	—	—
	b	Without bone and skin	0	2,087	66.2	200.	1.4	—	—	—	—	—	(0)	—	—	—	—
1766		Medium-fat:															
	a	With bone and skin	13	1,535	66.7	138.	1.2	—	—	—	—	—	(0)	—	—	—	—
	b	Without bone and skin	0	1,765	76.7	159.	1.4	—	—	—	—	—	(0)	—	—	—	—
1767		Lean:															
	a	With bone and skin	14	1,209	76.1	98.	1.2	—	—	—	—	—	(0)	—	—	—	—
	b	Without bone and skin	0	1,406	88.5	113.	1.4	—	—	—	—	—	(0)	—	—	—	—
		Light-cure, commercial:															
		Ham, medium-fat class:															
1768		Total edible:															
	a	With bone and skin, 65% lean, 21% fat	14	1,100	68.3	89.7	0	39	632	16.1	—	—	(0)	2.82	.76	16.0	—
	b	Without bone and skin, 76% lean, 24% fat	0	1,279	79.4	104.3	0	45	735	11.8	—	—	(0)	3.28	.88	18.6	—
1770		Separable lean	0	762	97.5	38.6	0	54	853	14.5	4,990	1,542	(0)	4.03	1.08	22.8	—
1772		Separable fat	0	2,855	23.6	308.9	0	14	372	3.6	—	—	(0)	.98	.26	5.5	—
		Boston butt, medium-fat class:															
1773		Total edible:															
	a	With bone and skin, 70% lean, 23% fat	7	1,227	72.5	101.7	0	42	641	11.0	—	—	(0)	2.99	.81	17.0	—
	b	Without bone and skin, 75% lean, 25% fat	0	1,320	78.0	109.3	0	45	689	11.8	—	—	(0)	3.22	.87	18.2	—
1775		Separable lean	0	907	94.8	55.8	0	54	812	14.1	(4,990)	(1,542)	(0)	3.91	1.05	22.2	—
1777		Separable fat	0	2,581	27.2	273.1	0	14	313	4.1	—	—	(0)	1.12	.30	6.4	—
		Picnic, medium-fat class:															
1778		Total edible:															
	a	With bone and skin, 57% lean, 25% fat	18	1,060	62.5	87.8	0	37	558	9.3	—	—	(0)	2.58	.69	14.6	—
	b	Without bone and skin, 70% lean, 30% fat	0	1,293	76.2	107.0	0	45	680	11.3	—	—	(0)	3.15	.84	17.8	—
1780		Separable lean	0	758	96.6	38.1	0	54	821	14.5	(4,990)	(1,542)	(0)	3.99	1.07	22.6	—
1782		Separable fat	0	2,508	29.0	264.4	0	18	358	4.5	—	—	(0)	1.20	.32	6.8	—
		Pork, cured, canned:															
1783		Ham, contents of can	0	875	83.0	55.8	4.1	60	708	12.2	(4,990)	(1,542)	(0)	2.42	.87	17.3	—
		Pork, cured. See also Bacon, items 125 and 128; and Salt pork, item 1964.															
1784		**Pork and gravy,** canned (90% pork, 10% gravy)	0	1,161	74.4	80.7	28.6	59	830	10.9	—	—	(0)	2.22	.77	15.9	—
		Potatoes:															
1785		Raw (refuse: parings, trimmings)	19	279	7.7	.4	62.8	26	195	2.2	11	1,495	Trace	.39	.14	5.4	[193] 73
1796		Canned, solids and liquid	0	200	5.0	.9	44.5	[194] (18)	(136)	(1.4)	[195] 5	1,134	Trace	.17	.10	2.9	58
		Dehydrated, mashed:															
1797		Flakes without milk	0	1,651	32.7	2.7	381.0	159	(785)	7.7	404	(7,258)	Trace	1.05	.27	24.4	[199] 144
1799		Granules without milk	0	1,597	37.6	2.7	364.7	200	921	10.9	381	(7,258)	Trace	.73	.31	22.2	[199] 88
1801		Granules with milk	0	1,624	49.4	5.0	352.4	644	1,075	15.9	372	8,383	270	.85	1.37	19.2	[199] 70
		Frozen:															
1803		Diced, for hash-browning	0	331	5.4	Trace	78.9	45	136	3.2	36	771	Trace	.32	.05	2.9	41
1805		French-fried	0	771	12.7	29.5	118.4	32	304	6.4	[196] 14	2,295	Trace	.64	.09	9.7	91
1807		Mashed	0	340	7.7	.5	77.6	73	177	3.2	358	1,039	140	.32	.11	3.7	29
1809		**Potato chips**	0	2,576	24.0	180.5	226.8	181	631	8.2	[197] —	5,126	Trace	.93	.31	21.7	73
1810		**Potato flour**	0	1,592	36.3	3.6	362.4	150	807	78.0	154	7,203	Trace	1.91	.61	15.2	(86)
1813		**Potato sticks**	0	2,468	29.0	165.1	230.4	200	631	8.2	[197] —	5,126	Trace	.93	.31	21.7	181
1814		**Pretzels**	0	1,769	44.5	20.4	344.3	100	594	6.8	[198] 7,620	590	(0)	.09	.14	3.2	(0)
1815		**Pricklypears,** raw (refuse: rind, seeds)	56	84	1.0	.2	21.8	40	56	.6	4	331	130	.02	.06	.7	45

		Prunes:															
1816		Dehydrated, nugget-type and pieces (2.5% moisture).	0	1,560	15.0	2.3	414.1	408	485	20.0	50	4,264	9,840	.54	1.01	9.7	18
1818		Dried, "softenized" (28.0% moisture):															
	a	Large—(average: not more than 53 per pound) (refuse: pits).	12	1,018	8.4	2.4	269.1	204	315	15.6	32	2,770	6,390	.35	.66	6.3	12
	b	Medium—(average: not more than 67 per pound) (refuse: pits).	15	983	8.1	2.3	259.9	197	305	15.0	31	2,676	6,170	.34	.64	6.1	12
	c	Small—(average: not more than 85 per pound) (refuse: pits).	18	948	7.8	2.2	250.7	190	294	14.5	30	2,582	5,950	.33	.61	5.8	12
1821		**Prune juice,** canned or bottled	0	349	1.8	.5	86.2	64	91	18.6	9	1,066	—	.03	.05	2.0	7
		Pudding mixes:															
		With starch base:															
1825		Chocolate, regular	0	1,637	13.6	9.5	415.0	91	426	7.3	2,028	431	Trace	.08	.30	1.6	0
1827		Chocolate, instant	0	1,619	14.1	7.3	411.9	1,111	399	9.1	1,833	386	Trace	.06	.27	1.4	0
		With vegetable gum base:															
1829		Custard-dessert	0	1,742	(0)	.5	448.6	41	9	.5	1,347	113	0	0	0	0	0
		Pumpkin:															
1831		Raw (refuse: rind, seeds)	30	83	3.2	.3	20.6	67	140	2.5	3	1,080	5,080	.14	.35	1.8	30
1832		Canned [109]	0	150	4.5	1.4	35.8	113	118	1.8	[105] 9	1,089	29,030	.15	.24	2.5	24
1833		**Pumpkin and squash seed kernels,** dry:															
	a	In hull (refuse: hulls)	26	1,856	97.4	156.8	50.4	171	3,840	37.6	—	—	230	.82	.64	8.1	—
	b	Hulled	0	2,508	131.5	211.8	68.0	231	5,189	50.8	—	—	320	1.11	.86	10.8	—
1834		**Purslane** leaves including stems, raw	0	95	7.7	1.8	17.2	467	177	15.9	—	—	11,340	.14	.45	2.3	113
		Quail, raw:															
1836		Total edible:															
	a	Live (refuse: blood, feathers, head, feet, inedible viscera, and bones).	33	511	76.0	20.7	0	—	—	—	—	—	—	—	—	—	—
	b	Ready-to-cook (refuse: bones)	10	686	102.1	27.8	0	—	—	—	—	—	—	—	—	—	—
1839		**Quinces,** raw (refuse: parings, core, seeds)	39	158	1.1	.3	42.3	30	47	1.9	11	545	110	.06	.07	.6	40
		Rabbit, domesticated, raw:															
1840		Flesh only:															
	a	Live (refuse: head, skin, feet, inedible viscera, and bones).	57	316	41.	16.	0	39	686	2.5	84	751	—	.16	.11	25.0	—
	b	Ready-to-cook (refuse: bones)	21	581	75.	29.	0	72	1,261	4.7	154	1,379	—	.29	20	45.9	—
		Rabbit, wild, raw:															
1842		Flesh only:															
	a	Drawn (refuse: head, skin, feet, and bones)	40	367	57.	14	0	—	—	—	—	—	—	—	—	—	—
	b	Ready-to-cook (refuse: bones)	20	490	76.	18.	0	—	—	—	—	—	—	—	—	—	—
		Radishes, raw:															
1844		Common:															
	a	With tops (refuse: tops, rootlets, trimmings)	37	49	2.9	.3	10.3	86	89	2.9	51	920	30	.09	.08	.9	74
	b	Without tops (refuse: stem ends, rootlets, trimmings).	10	69	4.1	.4	14.7	122	127	4.1	73	1,314	40	.13	.12	1.3	106
1845		Oriental, including daikon (Japanese) and Chinese:															
	a	With tops (refuse: tops, parings)	(34)	57	2.7	.3	12.6	105	78	1.8	—	539	30	.10	.06	1.1	96
	b	Without tops (refuse: parings)	22	67	3.2	.4	14.9	124	92	2.1	—	637	40	.11	.07	1.3	113
1846		**Raisins,** natural (unbleached, 18.0% moisture)	0	1,311	11.3	.9	351.1	281	458	15.9	122	3,461	100	.51	.37	2.4	5
		Raja fish. See Skate, item 2053.															
		Raspberries:															
		Raw:															
1848		Black (refuse: stems, caps, damaged berries)	3	321	6.6	6.2	69.1	132	97	4.0	4	876	Trace	(.13)	(.40)	(4.0)	81
1849		Red (refuse: stems, caps, damaged berries)	3	251	5.3	2.2	59.8	97	97	4.0	4	739	590	.13	.40	4.0	111
		Canned, solids and liquid, water pack, with or without artificial sweetener:															
1850		Black	0	231	5.0	5.0	48.5	91	68	2.7	5	612	Trace	.06	.20	2.4	28
1851		Red	0	159	3.2	.5	39.9	68	68	2.7	5	517	410	.06	.20	2.4	39
1852		Frozen, red, sweetened	0	445	3.2	.9	111.6	59	77	2.7	5	454	(320)	.09	.27	2.8	94
1853		**Red and gray snapper,** raw:															
	a	Whole (refuse: head, tail, fins, bones, skin, and entrails).	48	219	46.7	2.1	0	38	505	1.9	158	762	—	.41	.06	—	—
	b	Flesh only	0	422	89.8	4.1	0	73	971	3.6	304	1,465	—	.78	.11	—	—
		Redfish. See Drum, red, item 960; and Ocean perch, Atlantic, item 1396.															
1854		**Redhorse,** silver, raw:															
	a	Drawn (refuse: head, tail, fins, bones, and skin)	54	204	37.6	4.8	0	—	—	—	—	—	—	—	—	—	—
	b	Flesh only	0	445	81.6	10.4	0	—	—	—	—	—	—	—	—	—	—

[101] Average value for 1 pound, all cuts without bone and skin or with a small proportion of bone and skin, is 320 mg For cuts with average bone and skin content (18 percent), the value is 260 mg , for those with high bone and skin content (as spareribs), 190 mg. See also Notes on Foods, p. 180.

[102] Average value for 1 pound, all cuts without bone and skin or with a small proportion of bone and skin, is 1,295 mg. For cuts with average bone and skin content (18 percent), the value is 1,060 mg.; for those with high bone and skin content (as spareribs), 775 mg. See also Notes on Foods, p. 180.

[103] Year-round average. Recently dug potatoes contain about 96 mg per pound After 3 months' storage, the value is only half as high, after 6 months, about one-third as high.

[104] Federal standards provide for addition of certain calcium salts as firming agents; if used, these salts may add calcium not to exceed 907 mg. per pound of finished product.

[105] Applies to product without added salt. If salt is added, an estimated average value for sodium is 1,070 mg. per pound.

[106] Value varies widely. It is dependent on content of ascorbic acid in raw potatoes, method of processing, and length of storage of dehydrated product. Present values for dehydrated forms range from 45 to 159 mg. per pound.

[107] Sodium content is variable and may be as high as 4,500 mg. per pound

[108] Sodium content is variable. For example, very thin pretzel sticks contain about twice the average amount listed.

[109] May be a mixture of pumpkin and winter squash.

TABLE 2.—NUTRIENTS IN THE EDIBLE PORTION OF 1 POUND OF FOOD AS PURCHASED—Continued

[Numbers in parentheses denote values imputed—usually from another form of the food or from a similar food. Zero in parentheses indicates that the amount of a constituent probably is none or is too small to measure. Dashes denote lack of reliable data for a constituent believed to be present in measurable amount. Calculated values, as those based on a recipe, are not in parentheses]

Item No.	Food and description	Refuse	Food energy	Protein	Fat	Carbohydrate total	Calcium	Phosphorus	Iron	Sodium	Potassium	Vitamin A value	Thiamine	Riboflavin	Niacin	Ascorbic acid
(A)	(B)	(C)	(D)	(E)	(F)	(G)	(H)	(I)	(J)	(K)	(L)	(M)	(N)	(O)	(P)	(Q)
		Percent	Calories	Grams	Grams	Grams	Milligrams	Milligrams	Milligrams	Milligrams	Milligrams	International units	Milligrams	Milligrams	Milligrams	Milligrams
	Reindeer, raw, with bone:															
1856	Side, 68% lean, 12% fat	25	787	74.1	52.3	0	—	—	—	—	—	—	—	—	—	—
1857	Forequarter, 67% lean, 7% fat	26	597	73.2	31.6	0	—	—	—	—	—	—	—	—	—	—
1858	Hindquarter, 67% lean, 19% fat	14	909	75.7	74.9	0	—	—	—	—	—	—	—	—	—	—
	Rennin products:															
1859	Tablet (salts, starch, rennin enzyme)	0	485	.5	1.5	119.2	15,921	907	—	101,153	—	0	0	0	0	0
	Dessert mixes:															
1861	Chocolate	0	1,755	13.7	15.0	415.0	753	585	—	318	—	—	—	—	—	—
1863	Other flavors (vanilla, caramel, fruit flavorings)	0	1,737	Trace	Trace	449.1	(19) 531	(19) 413		27						
	Rhubarb:															
1865	Raw:															
a	With full tops (freshly harvested); (refuse: ends, full leaves)	55	31	1.2	.2	7.6	196	37	1.6	4	512	200	(.06)	(.14)	(.6)	18
b	With partly trimmed tops (refuse: trimmed leaves, ends, trimmings)	25	54	2.0	.3	12.6	327	61	2.7	7	854	340	(.10)	(.23)	(1.1)	30
c	Without leaves (refuse: ends, trimmings)	14	62	2.3	.4	14.4	374	70	3.1	8	979	390	(.12)	(.26)	(1.2)	34
1867	Frozen, sweetened	0	340	2.7	.9	85.9	422	64	3.6	18	957	380	.09	.23	1.8	34
	Rice:															
1869	Brown, raw	0	1,633	34.0	8.6	351.1	145	1,002	7.3	41	971	(0)	1.52	.24	21.4	(0)
	White (fully milled or polished):															
	Enriched:															
1871	Common commercial varieties, all types, raw	0	1,647	30.4	1.8	364.7	109	426	(21) 13.0	23	417	(0)	(21) 2.0	(21)	(21) 16.0	(0)
	Long-grain (dry form):															
1873	Parboiled	0	1,674	33.6	1.4	368.8	272	907	(21) 13.0	41	680	(0)	(21) 2.0	(21)	(21) 16.0	(0)
1875	Precooked (instant)	0	1,696	34.0	.9	374.2	23	295	(21) 13.0	5	—	(0)	(21) 2.0	(21)	(21) 16.0	(0)
	Unenriched, raw:															
1877	Common commercial varieties, all types	0	1,647	30.4	1.8	364.7	109	426	3.6	23	417	(0)	.32	.12	7.2	(0)
1879	Glutinous (Mochi Gome)	0	1,637	25.4	4.1	362.6	163	454	9.1	45	540	(0)	.32	.20	9.3	(0)
1880	**Rice bran**	0	1,252	60.3	71.7	230.4	345	6,287	88.9	Trace	6,781	(0)	10.25	1.14	135.4	(0)
1881	**Rice polish**	0	1,202	54.9	58.1	261.7	312	5,017	73.0	Trace	3,239	(0)	8.35	.82	127.8	(0)
	Rice products used mainly as hot breakfast cereals:															
1882	Rice, granulated, added nutrients	0	1,737	27.2	1.1	389.6	41	435	24.5	—	—	(0)	1.92	.48	29.4	(0)
	Rice products used mainly as ready-to-eat breakfast cereals:															
1884	Rice flakes, added nutrients	0	1,769	26.8	1.4	397.8	132	599	7.3	4,477	816	(0)	1.59	.23	24.4	(0)
1885	Rice, puffed, added nutrients, without salt	0	1,810	27.2	1.8	406.0	91	417	8.2	9	454	(0)	2.00	.18	20.0	(0)
	Rice, puffed or oven-popped, presweetened:															
1886	Honey and added nutrients	0	1,760	19.1	3.2	411.0	209	336	4.1	3,202	—	(0)	1.50	—	20.9	(0)
1887	Honey or cocoa and added nutrients including fat	0	1,819	20.4	18.1	393.1	231	372	15.0	1,624	277	(0)	1.88	.29	28.6	(0)
1888	Rice, shredded, added nutrients	0	1,778	23.6	1.4	402.8	64	431	8.2	3,837	—	(0)	1.76	—	32.0	(0)
	Rice with protein concentrate, mainly—															
1889	Casein, other added nutrients	0	1,733	181.4	.9	248.6	721	1,442	79.8	2,722	—	(0)	7.71	9.53	79.8	240
1890	Wheat gluten, other added nutrients	0	1,751	90.7	1.4	337.5	240	848	56.2	3,629	—	(0)	6.35	7.71	77.1	159
1892	**Rockfish**, including black, canary, yellowtail, rasphead, and bocaccio, flesh only, raw	0	440	85.7	8.2	0	—	—	—	272	1,760	—	.28	.54	—	—
	Roe:															
	Raw:															
1894	Including carp, cod, haddock, herring, pike, and shad	0	590	110.7	10.4	6.8	—	—	2.7	—	—		.45	3.45	6.2	64
1896	Including salmon, sturgeon, and turbot	0	939	114.3	47.2	6.4	—	—	—	—	—	—	1.71	3.28	10.4	82
1897	Canned, including cod, haddock, and herring, solids and liquid	0	535	97.5	12.7	1.4	68	1,569	5.4	—	—	—	—	—	—	10
	Rolls and buns: [26]															
	Ready-to-serve:															
1899	Danish pastry	0	1,914	33.6	106.6	205.8	227	494	4.1	1,660	508	1,410	.30	.67	3.4	Trace
	Hard rolls:															
1900	Enriched	0	1,415	44.5	14.5	259.9	213	417	10.4	2,835	440	Trace	1.17	1.06	12.2	Trace
1901	Unenriched	0	1,415	44.5	14.5	259.9	213	417	3.6	2,835	440	Trace	.23	.39	3.9	Trace
	Plain (pan rolls):															
1902	Enriched	0	1,352	37.2	25.4	240.4	336	386	8.6	2,295	431	Trace	1.26	.82	10.1	Trace
1903	Unenriched	0	1,352	37.2	25.4	240.4	336	386	3.2	2,295	431	Trace	.26	.41	3.4	Trace
1904	Raisin rolls or buns	0	1,247	31.3	13.2	255.8	340	413	6.4	1,742	1,111	Trace	.26	.44	3.1	Trace
1905	Sweet rolls	0	1,483	38.6	41.3	223.6	386	485	3.6	1,765	562	320	.31	.67	3.8	Trace
1906	Whole-wheat rolls	0	1,166	45.4	12.7	237.2	481	1,275	10.9	2,558	1,325	Trace	1.54	.60	13.4	Trace

		Partially baked (brown-and-serve)															
1907		Enriched	0	1,356	35.8	30.8	229.5	213	372	8.2	2,327	413	Trace	1.08	.93	9.5	Trace
1909		Unenriched	0	1,356	35.8	30.8	229.5	213	372	3.2	2,327	413	Trace	.29	.42	3.7	Trace
		Roll dough, unraised, frozen.															
1911		Enriched	0	1,216	34.0	22.7	215.0	150	345	7.7	2,186	372	Trace	1.22	.90	9.9	Trace
1913		Unenriched	0	1,216	34.0	22.7	215.0	150	345	4.1	2,186	372	Trace	.38	.41	4.4	Trace
1915		**Roll mix**	0	1,783	50.8	26.8	328.0	336	581	[119]3.6	1,869	735	Trace	[112].38	[112].74	[112]4.9	Trace
		Root beer. See Beverages, item 408															
1917		**Roseapples,** raw (refuse caps, seeds)	33	170	1.8	.9	43.2	88	49	3.6	—	—	400	.07	.10	2.4	67
		Rum. See Beverages, items 395–399.															
1918		**Rusk**	0	1,901	62.6	39.5	322.1	91	540	5.9	1,116	730	1,040	.39	1.00	4.9	Trace
1919		**Rutabagas,** without tops, raw (refuse, parings)	15	177	4.2	.4	42.4	254	150	1.5	19	922	2,240	.27	.26	4.3	166
		Rye:															
1921		Whole-grain	0	1,515	54.9	7.7	332.9	(172)	1,706	16.8	(5)	2,118	(0)	1.94	1.02	7.1	(0)
		Flours															
1922		Light	0	1,619	42.6	4.5	353.4	100	839	5.0	(5)	708	(0)	.67	.31	2.9	(0)
1923		Medium	0	1,588	51.7	7.7	339.3	(122)	1,188	11.8	(5)	921	(0)	1.35	.54	11.2	(0)
1924		Dark	0	1,483	73.9	11.8	308.9	245	(2,431)	20.4	5	3,901	(0)	2.76	.98	12.2	(0)
1925		**Rye wafers,** whole-grain	0	1,560	59.0	5.4	346.1	240	1,760	17.7	4,001	2,722	(0)	1.44	1.12	5.4	(0)
1926		**Sablefish,** raw															
	a	Whole (refuse head, tail, fins, entrails, bones, and skin)	58	362	24.8	28.4	0	—	—	—	107	682	—	.21	.17	—	—
	b	Flesh only	0	862	59.0	67.6	0	—	—	—	254	1,624	—	.51	.40	—	—
1927		**Safflower seed kernels,** dry:															
	a	In hull (refuse hulls)	49	1,423	44.2	137.6	28.7	—	—	—	—	—	—	—	—	—	—
	b	Hulled	0	2,790	86.6	269.9	56.2	—	—	—	—	—	—	—	—	—	—
1928		**Safflower seed meal,** partially defatted	0	1,610	179.6	37.2	165.6	340	2,812	—	—	—	—	5.08	1.81	10.0	0
		Salad dressings commercial: [113]															
		Blue and Roquefort cheese:															
1929		Regular	0	2,286	21.8	237.2	33.6	367	336	.9	4,962	168	950	.02	.43	.4	7
		Special dietary (low-calorie):															
1930		Low-fat (approx. 5 Cal. per tsp.)	0	345	13.6	26.8	18.6	290	213	.5	5,026	154	770	Trace	.34	.3	7
1931		Low-fat (approx. 1 Cal. per tsp.)	0	86	6.4	5.0	6.4	159	109	.5	5,144	132	360	Trace	.16	Trace	8
		French															
1932		Regular	0	1,860	2.7	176.5	79.4	50	64	1.8	6,214	358	—	—	—	—	—
		Special dietary (low-calorie)															
1933		Low-fat (approx. 5 Cal. per tsp.)	0	435	1.8	19.5	70.8	50	64	1.8	3,570	358	—	—	—	—	—
1934		Low-fat with artificial sweetener (approx. 1 Cal. per tsp.)	0	45	1.8	.9	8.2	50	64	1.8	3,570	358	—	—	—	—	—
1935		Medium-fat with artificial sweetener (approx. 10 Cal. per tsp.).	0	708	3.2	76.7	5.4	50	64	1.8	3,570	358	—	—	—	—	—
		Italian															
1936		Regular	0	2,504	.9	272.2	31.3	45	18	.9	9,489	68	Trace	Trace	Trace	Trace	—
1937		Special dietary (low-calorie, approx. 2 Cal. per tsp.)	0	227	.9	21.3	11.8	9	23	.9	3,570	68	Trace	Trace	Trace	Trace	—
1938		Mayonnaise	0	3,257	5.0	362.4	10.0	82	127	2.3	2,708	154	1,270	.08	.16	Trace	—
1939		Russian	0	2,241	7.3	230.4	47.2	86	168	2.7	3,937	712	3,130	.20	.21	2.7	26
		Salad dressing (mayonnaise type)															
1940		Regular	0	1,973	4.5	191.9	65.3	64	118	.9	2,658	41	1,000	.07	.13	Trace	—
1941		Special dietary (low-calorie, approx. 8 Cal. per tsp.).	0	617	5.0	57.6	21.8	82	127	.9	535	41	1,000	.07	.13	Trace	—
		Thousand island															
1942		Regular	0	2,277	3.6	227.7	69.9	50	77	2.7	3,175	513	1,450	.09	.15	.7	13
1943		Special dietary (low-calorie, approx. 10 Cal. per tsp.)	0	816	4.1	62.1	70.8	50	77	2.7	3,175	513	1,450	.09	.15	.7	13
		Salad oil. See Oils, item 1401															
		Salami. See Sausage, cold cuts, and luncheon meats items 2017–2018.															
		Salmon:															
		Atlantic:															
1946		Raw:															
	a	Whole (refuse: head, tail, fins, bones, skin, and entrails)	35	640	66.3	39.5	0	233	548	2.7	—	—	—	—	.24	21.2	27
	b	Flesh only	0	984	102.1	60.8	0	358	844	4.1	—	—	—	—	.36	32.6	41
1947		Canned, solids and liquid, including bones	0	921	98.4	55.3	0	—	—	—	—	—	—	—	—	—	—
		Chinook (king):															
1948		Raw:															
	a	Steak (refuse: bones)	12	886	76.2	62.3	0	—	1,201	—	180	1,593	1,240	.40	.92	—	—
	b	Flesh only	0	1,007	86.6	70.8	0	—	1,365	—	204	1,810	1,410	.46	1.05	—	—

[79] For additional data and information, see discussion of bread and rolls in Notes on Foods, p. 172

[110] Raspberry- and strawberry-flavored mixes contain about 771 mg. calcium and a trace of phosphorus per pound.

[111] Values for iron, thiamine, and niacin are based on the minimum levels of enrichment specified in standards of identity. See Notes on Foods, p. 171 for appropriate value for riboflavin.

[112] Based on mix containing unenriched flour. If mix is made with enriched flour, approximate values in milligrams per pound are as follows: Iron, 11.8 mg.; thiamine, 1.81 mg.; riboflavin, 1.54 mg.; niacin, 15.0 mg.

[113] Values apply to products containing salt. For those without salt, sodium content is low, ranging from less than 45 mg. to 227 mg. per pound; the amount usually is indicated on the label.

TABLE 2.—NUTRIENTS IN THE EDIBLE PORTION OF 1 POUND OF FOOD AS PURCHASED—Continued

[Numbers in parentheses denote values imputed—usually from another form of the food or from a similar food. Zero in parentheses indicates that the amount of a constituent probably is none or is too small to measure. Dashes denote lack of reliable data for a constituent believed to be present in measurable amount. Calculated values, as those based on a recipe, are not in parentheses]

Item No.	Food and description	Refuse	Food energy	Protein	Fat	Carbohydrate total	Calcium	Phosphorus	Iron	Sodium	Potassium	Vitamin A value	Thiamine	Riboflavin	Niacin	Ascorbic Acid
(A)	(B)	(C)	(D)	(E)	(F)	(G)	(H)	(I)	(J)	(K)	(L)	(M)	(N)	(O)	(P)	(Q)
	Salmon—Continued	Percent	Calories	Grams	Grams	Grams	Milligrams	Milligrams	Milligrams	Milligrams	Milligrams	International units	Milligrams	Milligrams	Milligrams	Milligrams
	Chinook (king)—Continued															
1949	Canned, solids and liquid, including bones	0	953	88.9	63.5	0	[114] 699	1,311	4.1	[85] —	1,660	1,040	0.12	0.64	33.1	—
	Chum:															
1950	Raw:															
a	Steak (refuse: bones)	12	—	—	—	—	—	—	—	212	1,713	—	.41	.24	—	—
b	Flesh only	0	—	—	—	—	—	—	—	240	1,946	—	.46	.27	—	—
1951	Canned, solids and liquid, including bones	0	631	97.5	23.6	0	[114] 1,129	1,597	3.2	[85] —	1,524	270	.11	.70	32.2	—
	Coho (silver):															
1952	Raw:															
a	Steak (refuse: bones)	12	—	—	—	—	693	922	—	[86] 192	1,681	—	.35	.44	—	5
b	Flesh only	0	—	—	—	—	794	1,048	—	[86] 218	1,910	—	.39	.49	—	6
1953	Canned, solids and liquid, including bones	0	694	94.3	32.2	0	[114] 1,107	1,306	4.1	[85] 1,592	1,528	360	.12	.79	33.7	—
	Pink (humpback):															
1954	Raw:															
a	Steak (refuse: bones)	12	475	79.8	14.8	0	—	—	—	[88] 255	[87] 1,222	—	.57	.18	—	—
b	Flesh only	0	540	90.7	16.8	0	—	—	—	[88] 290	[88] 1,358	—	.65	.21	—	—
1955	Canned, solids and liquid, including bones	0	640	93.0	26.8	0	[114] 889	1,297	3.6	[85] 1,755	1,637	320	.15	.83	36.2	—
	Sockeye (red):															
1956	Raw:															
a	Steak (refuse: bones)	12	—	—	—	—	—	—	—	192	1,561	600	.57	.29	—	—
b	Flesh only	0	—	—	—	—	—	—	—	218	1,774	680	.64	.33	—	—
1957	Canned, solids and liquid, including bones	0	776	92.1	42.2	0	[114] 1,175	1,560	5.4	[85] 2,368	1,560	1,040	.19	.74	33.2	—
1960	**Salmon, smoked**	0	798	98.0	42.2	0	64	1,111	—	—	—	—	—	—	—	—
1961	**Salsify,** raw:															
a	With tops (refuse: tops, scrapings, rootlets)	53	([illegible])	6.2	1.3	[8] 38.4	100	141	3.2	—	810	20	.07	.09	.6	23
b	Without tops (refuse: scrapings, rootlets)	13	([illegible])	11.4	2.4	[8] 71.0	185	260	5.9	—	1,499	30	.14	.17	1.0	42
1963	**Salt,** table	0	0	0	0	0	1,148	—	.5	175,896	18	0	0	0	0	0
1964	**Salt pork,** raw, with skin	4	3,410	17.0	370.	0	Trace	Trace	2.6	5,278	183	(0)	(.78)	(.17)	(3.9)	—
	Salt sticks:															
1965	Regular type	0	1,742	54.4	13.2	341.6	127	449	4.1	7,593	417	Trace	.25	.30	4.4	Trace
1966	Vienna bread type	0	1,379	43.1	14.1	263.1	204	404	3.6	7,099	426	Trace	.22	.39	3.8	Trace
	Sanddab. See Flatfishes, item 1018.															
	Sandwich spread (with chopped pickle):															
1967	Regular	0	1,719	3.2	164.2	72.1	68	91	3.2	2,840	417	1,270	.05	.13	Trace	28
1968	Special dietary (low-calorie, approx. 5 Cal. per tsp.)	0	508	4.5	40.8	36.3	68	91	3.2	2,840	417	1,270	.05	.13	Trace	28
1969	**Sapodilla,** raw (refuse: skin, seeds)	20	323	1.8	4.0	79.1	76	44	2.9	44	700	220	Trace	.05	.7	52
1970	**Sapotes** (marmalade plums), raw (refuse: skin, seeds)	24	431	6.2	2.1	108.9	134	97	3.4	—	—	1,410	.03	.07	6.3	70
	Sardines, Atlantic, canned in oil:															
	Portion used:															
1971	Solids and liquid	0	1,411	93.4	110.7	2.7	1,606	1,969	15.9	2,313	2,540	820	.10	.74	20.1	—
1972	Drained solids (refuse: liquid)	18	755	89.3	41.3	—	[89] 1,626	[89] 1,856	10.8	3,062	2,195	820	.10	.74	20.1	—
	Sardines, Pacific:															
1973	Raw	0	726	87.1	39.0	0	150	975	8.2	—	—	—	—	—	—	—
	Canned:															
1974	In brine or mustard, solids and liquid	0	889	85.3	54.4	7.7	1,374	1,606	23.6	3,447	1,179	120	—	—	—	—
1975	In oil (refuse: oil)	(18)	—	—	—	—	—	—	—	—	—	—	.03	1.13	27.5	—
1976	In tomato sauce, solids and liquid	0	894	84.8	55.3	7.7	2,037	2,168	18.6	1,814	1,452	120	.05	1.22	24.1	—
1977	**Sauerkraut,** canned, solids and liquid	0	82	4.5	.9	18.1	163	82	2.3	[92] 3,388	635	240	.14	.17	.8	64
1978	**Sauerkraut juice,** canned	0	45	3.2	Trace	10.4	168	64	5.0	[92] 3,570	—	—	.13	.18	.8	80
1979	**Sauger,** raw:															
a	Whole (refuse: head, tail, fins, entrails, scales, bones, and skin)	65	135	28.4	1.3	0	—	—	—	—	—	—	—	—	—	—
b	Flesh only	0	381	81.2	3.6	0	—	—	—	—	—	—	—	—	—	—
	Sausage, cold cuts, and luncheon meats:															
1980	Blood sausage or blood pudding	0	1,787	64.0	167.4	1.4	—	—	—	—	—	—	—	—	—	—
1981	Bockwurst	0	1,198	51.3	197.5	2.7	—	—	—	—	—	—	—	—	—	—
	Bologna:															
1982	All samples	0	1,379	54.9	124.7	5.0	32	581	8.2	5,897	1,043	—	.72	.98	12.0	—
1983	All meat	0	1,256	60.3	103.4	16.8	—	—	—	—	—	—	—	—	—	—
1984	With nonfat dry milk	0	—	60.8	—	—	—	—	—	—	—	—	—	—	—	—
1985	With cereal	0	1,188	64.4	93.4	17.7	—	—	—	—	—	—	—	—	—	—
1986	Braunschweiger	0	1,447	67.1	124.3	10.4	45	1,111	26.8	—	—	29,620	.78	6.55	37.0	—
1987	Brown-and-serve sausage, before browning	0	1,783	61.2	163.3	12.2	—	—	—	—	—	—	—	—	—	—
1989	Capicola or Capacola	0	2,263	91.6	207.7	0	—	—	—	—	—	—	—	—	—	—

		Cervelat														
1990		Dry	0	2, 046	111. 6	170. 6	7. 7	64	1, 334	12 2	—	—	(0)	1. 22	1. 04	24 9	—
1991		Soft	0	1, 393	84. 4	111. 1	7. 3	50	971	12. 7	—	—	—	. 51	1 17	19. 2	—
1992		Country-style sausage	0	1, 565	68. 5	141. 1	0	41	762	10. 4	—	—	—	1 00	. 87	14. 0	—
1993		Deviled ham, canned	0	1, 592	63 1	146. 5	0	36	417	9. 5	—	—	(0)	. 64	. 45	7. 3	—
		Frankfurters:														
		Raw:														
1994		All samples	0	1, 402	56. 7	125. 2	8. 2	32	603	8. 6	4, 990	998	—	. 71	. 90	12. 2	—
1995		All meat	0	1, 343	59. 4	115. 7	11 3	—	—	—	—	—	—	—	—	—	—
1996		With nonfat dry milk	0	1, 361	59. 4	116. 1	15. 4	—	—	—	—	—	—	—	—	—	—
1997		With cereal	0	1, 125	65. 3	93. 4	. 9	—	—	—	—	—	—	—	—	—	—
1998		With nonfat dry milk and cereal	0	—	64. 4	98 4	—	—	—	—	—	—	—	—	—	—	—
2000		Canned	0	1, 002	60. 8	82 1	9	41	658	10. 0	—	—	—	. 15	. 56	10. 7	—
2001		Headcheese	0	1, 216	70. 3	99. 8	4. 5	41	785	10. 4	—	—	(0)	. 18	. 45	4. 0	—
2002		Knockwurst	0	1, 261	64 0	105. 2	10 0	36	699	9 5	—	—	—	(. 77)	(. 95)	(11. 8)	—
		Liverwurst														
2003		Fresh	0	1, 393	73. 5	116. 1	8. 2	41	1, 080	24 5	—	—	28, 800	. 91	5 90	25. 9	—
2004		Smoked	0	1, 447	67 1	124 3	10. 4	45	1, 111	26. 8	—	—	29, 620	. 78	6. 55	37 0	—
		Luncheon meat:														
2005		Boiled ham	0	1, 061	86. 2	77 1	0	50	753	12 7	—	—	(0)	2 00	. 68	11 8	—
2006		Pork, cured ham or shoulder, chopped, spiced or unspiced, canned.	0	1, 334	68 0	112. 9	5. 9	41	490	10. 0	5, 597	1, 007	(0)	1 41	. 95	13 6	—
2007		Meat loaf	0	907	72 1	59. 9	15. 0	41	807	8. 2	—	—	—	. 59	1. 00	11 3	—
2008		Meat, potted (includes potted beef, chicken, and turkey).	0	1, 125	79 4	87. 1	0	—	—	—	—	—	—	. 12	1. 02	5. 5	—
2009		Minced ham	0	1, 034	62. 1	76 7	20 0	36	404	9. 5	—	—	(0)	1 68	1. 00	15. 4	—
2010		Mortadella	0	1, 429	92. 5	113. 4	2. 7	54	1, 080	14 1	—	—	—	—	—	—	—
2011		Polish-style sausage	0	1, 379	71 2	117. 0	5. 4	41	798	10 9	—	—	(0)	1 54	. 86	14 1	—
2012		Pork and beef (chopped together)	0	1, 524	70 8	135. 6	0	41	789	10 4	—	—	—	—	—	—	—
2013		Pork sausage, links or bulk, raw	0	2, 259	42. 6	230 4	Trace	23	417	6. 4	3, 357	635	(0)	1. 95	. 76	10. 4	—
		Pork sausage, canned:														
2015		Solids and liquid	0	1, 882	62. 6	174. 2	10. 9	36	680	9. 5	—	—	(0)	. 85	86	15 0	—
		Pork sausage, link, smoked. See Sausage, country-style: item 1992.														
		Salami.														
2017		Dry	0	2, 041	108. 0	172 8	5 4	64	1, 284	16. 3	—	—	—	1. 68	1. 13	24 0	—
2018		Cooked	0	1, 411	79. 4	116 1	6 4	45	907	11 8	—	—	—	1 13	1 09	18 6	—
2019		Scrapple	0	975	39. 9	61. 7	66 2	23	290	5. 4	—	—	—	. 86	. 41	8 2	—
2020		Souse	0	821	59 0	60. 8	5 4	—	—	—	—	—	(0)	—	—	—	—
2021		Thuringer	0	1, 393	84 4	111. 1	7. 3	50	971	12. 7	—	—	—	. 51	1 17	19. 2	—
2022		Vienna sausage, canned	0	1, 089	63 5	89 8	1 4	36	694	9 5	—	—	—	. 39	. 58	11 9	—
2023		Scallops, bay and sea, muscle only, raw	0	367	69. 4	9	15 0	118	943	8 2	[123] 1, 157	[123] 1, 796	—	—	. 29	5. 8	—
		Scrapple. See Sausage, cold cuts, and luncheon meats: item 2019														
		Scup. See Porgy, item 1658.														
2026		Seabass, white, flesh only, raw	0	435	97. 1	2. 3	0	—	—	—	—	—	—	—	—	—	—
		Seaweeds, raw.														
2027		Agar	0	—	—	1. 4	—	2, 572	100	28. 6	—	—	—	—	—	—	—
2028		Dulse	0	—	—	14. 5	—	1, 343	1, 211	—	9, 458	36, 560	—	—	—	—	—
2029		Irishmoss	0	—	—	8. 2	—	4, 014	712	40 4	13, 118	12, 900	—	—	—	—	—
2030		Kelp	0	—	—	5. 0	—	4, 958	1, 089	—	13, 640	23, 918	—	—	—	—	—
2031		Laver	0	—	—	2. 7	—	—	—	—	—	—	—	—	—	—	—
		Sesame seeds, dry:														
2032		Whole	0	2, 554	84 4	222. 7	98 0	5, 262	2, 794	47. 6	272	3, 289	140	4. 43	1 08	24. 3	0
2033		Decorticated	0	2, 640	82. 6	242. 2	79 8	499	2, 685	10. 9	—	—	—	. 80	. 59	24. 5	0
		Shad or American shad:														
2034		Raw:														
	a	Whole (refuse: head, tail, fins, bones, skin, and entrails).	52	370	40. 5	21. 8	0	44	566	1. 1	118	718	—	. 33	. 52	18. 3	—
	b	Flesh only	0	771	84 4	45 4	0	91	1, 179	2 3	245	1, 497	—	. 68	1 09	38. 1	—
2037		Canned, solids and liquid	0	689	76. 7	39 9	0	—	—	3. 2	—	—	—	—	. 72	—	—
2038		Shad, gizzard (gizzard shad), raw:														
	a	Whole (refuse: head, tail, fins, skin, bones, and entrails).	67	299	25 7	21. 0	0	—	—	—	—	—	—	—	—	—	—
	b	Flesh only	0	907	78 0	63. 5	0	—	—	—	—	—	—	—	—	—	—
2039		Shallot bulbs, raw (refuse: skins)	(12)	287	10 0	. 4	67 1	148	240	4. 8	48	1, 333	Trace	22	. 08	. 7	31
		Sheefish. See Inconnu, item 1145.														

* A large proportion of the carbohydrate in the unstored product may be inulin, which is of doubtful availability. During storage, inulin is converted to sugars

[114] Based on total contents of can. If bones are discarded, value will be greatly reduced.

[115] For product canned without added salt, value is approximately the same as for raw salmon.

[116] Sample dipped in brine contained 858 mg sodium per pound of steak and 975 mg., flesh only.

[117] Values for salmon dipped in brine averaged 1,888 mg of sodium and 503 mg. of potassium per pound.

[118] Values for salmon dipped in brine averaged 2,146 mg of sodium and 572 mg of potassium per pound.

[119] Values range from 28 Calories per pound for freshly harvested salsify to 175 Calories for the product after storage.

[120] Values range from 51 Calories per pound for freshly harvested salsify to 324 Calories for the product after storage.

[121] Values for sardines without skin and bones canned in oil are: Calcium, 201 mg per pound, phosphorus, 1,187 mg.

[122] Values for sauerkraut and sauerkraut juice are based on salt contents of 1 9 and 2.0 percent respectively in the finished products. The amounts in some samples may vary significantly from this estimate.

[123] Based on frozen scallops, possibly brined.

284-853 O - 79 - 8

TABLE 2.—NUTRIENTS IN THE EDIBLE PORTION OF 1 POUND OF FOOD AS PURCHASED—Continued

[Numbers in parentheses denote values imputed—usually from another form of the food or from a similar food. Zero in parentheses indicates that the amount of a constituent probably is none or is too small to measure. Dashes denote lack of reliable data for a constituent believed to be present in measurable amount. Calculated values, as those based on a recipe, are not in parentheses]

Item No. (A)	Food and description (B)	Refuse (C)	Food energy (D)	Protein (E)	Fat (F)	Carbohydrate total (G)	Calcium (H)	Phosphorus (I)	Iron (J)	Sodium (K)	Potassium (L)	Vitamin A value (M)	Thiamine (N)	Riboflavin (O)	Niacin (P)	Ascorbic Acid (Q)
		Percent	Calories	Grams	Grams	Grams	Milligrams	Milligrams	Milligrams	Milligrams	Milligrams	International units	Milligrams	Milligrams	Milligrams	Milligrams
2040	**Sheepshead, Atlantic,** raw:															
a	Whole (refuse: head, tail, fins, skin, bones, and entrails)	62	159	29.0	3.9	0	—	277	—	142	329	—	—	—	—	—
b	Flesh only	0	513	93.4	12.7	0	—	894	—	458	1,061	—	—	—	—	—
	Sheepshead, fresh water. See Drum, item 959.															
2041	**Sherbet,** orange	0	608	4.1	5.4	139.7	73	59	Trace	45	100	270	0.05	0.14	Trace	9
	Shortbread. See Cookies, item 830.															
	Shrimp:															
2042	Raw:															
a	In shell (refuse: shell)	31	285	56.7	2.5	4.7	197	520	5.0	458	589	—	.06	.09	10.0	—
b	Flesh only	0	413	82.1	3.6	6.8	286	753	7.3	635	998	—	.09	.14	14.5	—
	Canned:															
2044	Solids and liquid, wet pack	0	363	73.5	3.6	3.6	268	680	8.2	—	—	220	.03	.12	6.6	—
2045	Solids only:															
a	Wet pack (refuse: liquid)	36	337	70.3	3.2	2.0	334	762	9.0	—	354	170	.02	.09	5.2	—
b	Dry pack (use also for drained solids)	0	526	109.8	5.0	3.2	522	1,193	14.1	—	553	270	.04	.15	8.2	—
2046	Frozen, breaded, raw; not more than 50% breading	0	631	55.8	3.2	90.3	172	503	4.5	—	—	—	.12	.13	9.0	—
2047	**Shrimp or lobster paste,** canned	0	816	94.3	42.6	6.8	—	—	—	—	—	—	—	1.18	—	—
	Sirups:															
2048	Cane	0	1,193	0	0	308	272	132	16.3	—	1,928	0	.59	.27	.5	0
2049	Maple	0	1,143	—	—	295	472	36	5.4	45	798	—	—	—	—	0
2050	Sorghum	0	1,166	—	—	308	780	113	56.7	—	—	—	—	.45	.5	—
	Table blends:															
2051	Chiefly corn, light and dark	0	1,315	0	0	340	209	73	18.6	308	18	0	0	0	0	0
2052	Cane and maple	0	1,143	0	0	295	73	5	Trace	9	118	0	0	0	0	0
	Siscowet. See Lake trout, items 1170–1171.															
2053	**Skate** (raja fish), flesh only, raw	0	445	97.5	3.2	0	—	—	—	—	—	—	.11	—	—	—
	Smelt, Atlantic, jack, and bay:															
2054	Raw:															
a	Whole (refuse: head, tail, fins, bones, skin, and entrails)	45	244	46.4	5.2	0	—	679	1.0	—	—	—	.02	.31	3.4	—
b	Flesh only	0	445	84.4	9.5	0	—	1,234	1.8	—	—	—	.04	.56	6.1	—
2055	Canned, solids and liquid	0	907	83.5	61.2	0	1,624	1,678	7.7	—	—	—	—	—	—	—
	Smelt, eulachon. See Eulachon, item 990.															
2056	**Snail,** raw	0	408	73.0	6.4	9.1	—	—	15.9	—	—	—	—	—	—	—
2057	**Snail, Giant African,** raw	0	331	44.9	6.4	20.0	—	—	—	—	—	—	—	—	—	—
	Snapper, red. See Red and gray snapper, item 1853.															
	Soft drinks. See Beverages, items 402–409.															
	Sole. See Flatfishes, item 1018.															
2058	**Sorghum grain,** all types	0	1,506	49.9	15.0	331.1	127	1,302	20.0	—	1,588	(0)	1.72	.68	17.7	(0)
	Sorrel. See Dock, item 953.															
	Soups, commercial:															
	Canned, condensed:															
2059	Asparagus, cream of	0	245	9.1	6.4	38.1	100	141	2.7	3,720	454	1,130	.14	.32	2.7	—
2062	Bean with pork	0	608	29.0	20.9	78.5	227	458	8.2	3,656	1,442	2,360	.45	.26	3.4	9
2064	Beef broth, bouillon, and consomme	0	118	19.1	0	10.0	Trace	118	1.8	2,957	490	Trace	Trace	.09	4.5	—
2066	Beef noodle	0	259	14.5	10.0	26.3	27	181	3.2	3,466	290	230	.18	.23	4.0	5
2068	Celery, cream of	0	327	6.4	19.1	33.6	181	136	2.3	3,611	408	770	.05	.26	2.0	5
2071	Chicken consomme	0	82	12.7	.5	6.8	45	268	4.5	2,731	—	—	—	—	—	—
2073	Chicken, cream of	0	358	10.9	21.8	30.4	86	132	1.8	3,670	299	1,590	.05	.26	2.1	Trace
2076	Chicken gumbo	0	209	11.8	5.9	27.7	73	95	2.3	3,593	404	820	.09	.14	4.8	18
2078	Chicken noodle	0	240	12.7	7.3	29.9	32	136	1.8	3,701	209	140	.05	.09	3.0	Trace
2080	Chicken with rice	0	177	11.8	4.5	21.3	32	95	1.4	3,466	372	590	Trace	.09	2.7	—
2082	Chicken vegetable	0	281	15.4	9.1	34.9	68	150	2.3	3,833	363	8,160	.09	.14	4.1	—
2084	Clam chowder, Manhattan type (with tomatoes, without milk)	0	299	8.2	9.5	45.4	132	172	4.1	3,475	680	3,220	.09	.09	4.1	—
2086	Minestrone	0	395	18.1	12.7	52.6	136	222	3.2	3,688	1,157	8,620	.27	.23	4.1	—
2088	Mushroom, cream of	0	503	8.6	36.3	38.1	154	195	1.4	3,606	372	270	.05	.45	2.8	Trace
2091	Onion	0	245	20.0	9.5	19.5	104	104	1.8	3,969	390	Trace	Trace	.09	Trace	—
2093	Pea, green	0	481	20.9	8.2	83.5	163	413	3.2	3,320	726	1,270	.17	.23	4.1	27
2096	Pea, split	0	535	31.8	11.8	77.1	113	553	5.0	3,479	898	1,630	.90	.34	5.0	4
2098	Tomato	0	327	7.3	9.5	57.6	50	122	2.7	3,593	853	3,670	.23	.14	4.2	15
2101	Turkey noodle	0	295	16.3	10.9	31.8	54	163	2.3	3,774	290	730	.19	.19	4.5	Trace
2103	Vegetable beef	0	295	19.1	8.2	35.8	45	177	2.7	3,574	594	9,980	.44	.18	3.6	—

No.		Food															
2105		Vegetable with beef broth	0	290	10.0	6.4	49.9	73	145	3.2	3,130	889	11,340	.14	.09	4.5	—
2107		Vegetarian vegetable	0	290	8.2	7.7	48.1	73	145	3.6	3,103	635	10,430	.14	.14	3.2	—
		Dehydrated mix:															
2109		Beef noodle	0	1,755	61.7	33.6	296.2	218	671	9.1	10,746	1,043	540	2.40	1.25	18.4	18
2111		Chicken noodle	0	1,737	65.8	45.4	263.5	268	649	10.9	19,405	662	1,500	2.35	1.24	19.1	23
2113		Chicken rice	0	1,601	40.8	30.8	284.9	204	313	2.7	19,786	322	Trace	.19	.10	5.1	—
2115		Onion	0	1,583	63.1	48.1	244.5	430	513	6.4	30,282	2,508	270	.50	.34	3.3	68
2117		Pea, green	0	1,642	101.6	18.6	279.4	272	1,420	24.5	10,705	3,964	540	1.98	2.09	18.8	5
2119		Tomato vegetable with noodles	0	1,579	39.5	36.3	284.4	209	508	9.1	27,837	785	10,890	1.37	.84	11.7	118
		Frozen, condensed:															
2121		Clam chowder, New England type (with milk, without tomatoes).	0	485	16.8	29.0	39.0	530	308	3.6	3,946	839	230	.14	.32	1.8	—
		Oyster stew. See item 1448															
2124		Pea, green, with ham	0	512	34.5	10.4	72.6	113	463	7.3	3,402	912	820	.68	.27	4.5	—
2126		Potato, cream of	0	395	12.2	19.5	45.4	218	231	3.2	4,445	839	1,540	.18	.23	1.8	—
2129		Shrimp, cream of	0	603	18.1	44.9	32.7	145	181	1.8	3,901	218	410	.14	.23	1.4	—
2132		Vegetable with beef	0	318	24.5	10.4	31.8	109	286	3.6	3,593	658	9,980	.18	.32	6.8	—
2134		**Soursop,** raw (refuse: skin, seeds)	32	200	3.1	.9	50.3	43	83	1.9	43	817	20	.22	.14	2.6	60
		Souse. See Sausage, cold cuts, and luncheon meats: item 2020															
		Soybeans:															
		Immature seeds.															
2135		Raw:															
	a	In pods (refuse: pods)	47	322	26.2	12.3	31.7	161	541	6.7	—	—	1,660	1.06	.38	3.3	69
	b	Shelled	0	608	49.4	23.1	59.9	304	1,021	12.7	—	—	3,130	2.00	.72	6.2	130
2137		Canned, solids and liquid	0	340	29.5	14.5	28.6	249	454	13.2	[10] 1,070	—	—	.40	.40	—	39
2139		Mature seeds, dry, raw	0	1,828	154.7	80.3	152.0	1,025	2,513	38.1	23	7,607	360	4.99	1.43	10.1	—
		Fermented products:															
2141		Natto (soybeans)	0	758	76.7	33.6	52.2	467	826	16.8	—	1,129	0	.32	2.27	5.0	0
2142		Miso (cereal and soybeans)	0	776	47.6	20.9	106.6	308	1,402	7.7	13,381	1,515	180	.29	.44	1.3	0
2143		Sprouted seeds, raw	0	209	28.1	6.4	24.0	218	304	4.5	—	—	360	1.03	.88	3.9	58
2145		**Soybean curd** (tofu)	0	327	35.4	19.1	10.9	581	572	8.6	32	191	0	.26	.14	.7	0
		Soybean flours:															
2146		Full-fat	0	1,910	166.5	92.1	137.9	903	2,531	38.1	5	7,530	500	3.85	1.41	9.6	0
2147		High-fat	0	1,724	186.9	54.9	151.0	1,089	2,948	40.8	5	8,051	—	4.06	1.61	10.3	0
2148		Low-fat	0	1,615	196.9	30.4	166.0	1,193	2,876	41.3	5	8,432	360	3.76	1.63	12.0	0
2149		Defatted	0	1,479	213.2	4.1	172.8	1,202	2,971	50.3	5	8,256	180	4.97	1.56	11.8	0
		Soybean milk:															
2150		Fluid	0	150	15.4	6.8	10.0	95	218	3.6	—	—	180	.36	.13	1.0	0
2151		Powder	0	1,946	189.6	92.1	127.0	1,247	—	—	—	—	—	—	—	—	—
		Soybean milk products, sweetened: [30]															
2152		Liquid concentrate	0	572	21.8	33.1	55.8	136	268	3.6	195	1,075	Trace	.27	.15	1.0	0
2153		Powder	0	2,050	92.5	105.2	219.5	592	1,293	22.7	5	4,150	90	1.36	1.11	6.6	0
2154		**Soybean protein**	0	1,461	339.7	.5	68.5	544	3,057	—	953	816	—	—	—	—	0
2155		**Soybean proteinate**	0	1,415	365.6	.5	34.9	—	—	—	5,443	—	—	—	—	—	0
2156		**Soy sauce**	0	308	25.4	5.9	43.1	372	472	21.8	33,226	1,660	0	.10	1.13	1.8	0
		Spaghetti:															
2157		Enriched	0	1,674	56.7	5.4	341.1	122	735	[31] 13.0	9	894	(0)	[31] 4.0	[31] 1.7	[31] 27.0	(0)
2160		Unenriched	0	1,674	56.7	5.4	341.1	122	735	5.9	9	894	(0)	.42	.29	7.7	(0)
2164		**Spaghetti in tomato sauce with cheese,** canned	0	345	10.0	2.7	69.9	73	159	5.0	1,733	549	1,680	.64	.50	8.2	20
2166		**Spaghetti with meat balls in tomato** sauce, canned	0	467	22.2	18.6	51.7	95	204	5.9	2,214	445	1,810	.28	.30	4.2	11
2167		**Spanish mackerel,** raw:															
	a	Whole (refuse: head, tail, fins, skin, bones, and entrails).	39	490	54.0	28.8	0	198	689	2.8	188	730	—	.35	.39	13.3	—
	b	Flesh only	0	803	88.5	47.2	0	322	1,129	4.5	308	1,198	—	.58	.64	21.8	—
		Spinach:															
2169		Raw															
		Trimmed (packaged).															
	a	Good quality	0	118	14.5	1.4	19.5	422	231	14.1	322	2,132	36,740	.44	.91	2.8	231
	b	Fair quality (refuse damaged leaves, trimmings)	8	109	13.4	1.3	17.9	388	213	12.9	296	1,961	33,800	.40	.83	2.5	213
		Untrimmed (in bulk).															
	c	Good quality (refuse large stems, roots)	28	85	10.5	1.0	14.0	304	167	10.1	232	1,535	26,450	.32	.65	2.0	167
	d	Fair quality (refuse: stems, damaged leaves, roots)	39	72	8.9	.8	11.9	257	141	8.6	196	1,300	22,410	.27	.55	1.7	141
		Canned:															
2171		Regular pack, solids and liquid	0	86	9.1	1.8	13.6	388	118	9.5	[10] 1,070	1,134	24,950	.09	.45	1.5	62
2174		Special dietary pack (low-sodium), solids and liquid	0	95	11.3	1.8	15.0	388	118	9.5	154	1,134	24,950	.09	.45	1.5	62
		Frozen:															
2177		Chopped	0	109	14.1	1.4	17.2	513	204	9.5	259	1,606	35,830	.41	.73	2.2	133
2179		Leaf	0	112	13.6	1.4	19.1	476	204	11.3	240	1,746	36,740	.45	.73	2.3	159
		Spinach, New Zealand. See New Zealand spinach, item 1375															

[10] Estimated average based on addition of salt in the amount of 0.6 percent of the finished product

[30] Values apply to products without added vitamins and minerals

[31] Based on product with minimum level of enrichment. See also Notes on Foods, p. 171

TABLE 2.—NUTRIENTS IN THE EDIBLE PORTION OF 1 POUND OF FOOD AS PURCHASED—Continued

[Numbers in parentheses denote values imputed—usually from another form of the food or from a similar food. Zero in parentheses indicates that the amount of a constituent probably is none or is too small to measure. Dashes denote lack of reliable data for a constituent believed to be present in measurable amount. Calculated values, as those based on a recipe, are not in parentheses]

Item No.		Food and description	Refuse	Food energy	Protein	Fat	Carbohydrate total	Calcium	Phosphorus	Iron	Sodium	Potassium	Vitamin A value	Thiamine	Riboflavin	Niacin	Ascorbic Acid
(A)		(B)	(C)	(D)	(E)	(F)	(G)	(H)	(I)	(J)	(K)	(L)	(M)	(N)	(O)	(P)	(Q)
		Spiny lobster. See Crayfish, item 927.	Percent	Calories	Grams	Grams	Grams	Milligrams	Milligrams	Milligrams	Milligrams	Milligrams	International units	Milligrams	Milligrams	Milligrams	Milligrams
		Spleen, raw:															
2181		Beef and calf	0	472	82.1	13.6	0	----	1,234	48.1	----	----	----	----	1.67	37.2	----
2182		Hog	0	485	77.6	17.2	0	----	1,352	133.4	----	----	----	----	1.79	----	----
2183		Lamb	0	522	85.3	17.7	0	----	----	----	----	----	----	----	----	----	----
2184		**Spot,** fillets, raw [86]	0	993	79.8	72.1	0	----	----	----	277	----	----	0.73	1.00	----	----
		Squab (pigeon), raw:															
2186		Total edible:															
	a	Live (refuse: blood, feathers, head, feet, inedible viscera, and bones).	63	468	31.2	37.1	0	29	690	----	----	----	----	----	----	----	----
	b	Dressed, head removed (refuse: feet, inedible viscera and bones).	55	569	38.0	45.1	0	35	839	----	----	----	----	----	----	----	----
		Squash, raw:															
		Summer:															
2191		All varieties:															
	a	Good quality (refuse: stem ends)	3	84	4.8	.4	18.5	123	128	1.8	4	889	1,800	.23	.38	4.5	95
	b	Fair quality (refuse: stem ends, blemishes)	13	75	4.3	.4	16.6	110	114	1.6	4	797	1,620	.21	.34	4.1	86
2193		Crookneck and Straightneck, Yellow:															
	a	Good quality (refuse: stem ends)	2	89	5.3	.9	19.1	124	129	1.8	4	898	2,040	.24	.38	4.6	111
	b	Fair quality (refuse: stem ends, blemishes)	12	80	4.8	.8	17.2	112	116	1.6	4	806	1,840	.21	.34	4.1	100
2195		Scallop varieties, white and pale green:															
	a	Good quality (refuse: stem ends)	(2)	93	4.0	.4	22.7	124	129	1.8	4	898	840	.24	.38	4.6	82
	b	Fair quality (refuse: stem ends, blemishes)	(12)	84	3.6	.4	20.4	112	116	1.6	4	806	760	.21	.34	4.1	73
2197		Zucchini and Cocozelle (Italian marrow type), green:															
	a	Good quality (refuse: stem ends)	5	73	5.2	.4	15.5	121	125	1.7	4	870	[105] 1,380	.23	.37	4.4	82
	b	Fair quality (refuse: stem ends, trimmings)	18	63	4.5	.4	13.4	104	108	1.5	4	751	[105] 1,190	.20	.32	3.8	71
		Winter:															
2199		All varieties (refuse: cavity contents, rind, stem ends).	29	161	4.5	1.0	39.9	71	122	1.9	3	1,189	[106] 11,920	.14	.35	1.8	43
2202		Acorn (refuse: cavity contents, rind)	24	152	5.2	.3	38.6	107	79	3.1	3	1,324	[106] 4,140	.16	.38	2.0	49
2205		Butternut (refuse: cavity contents, rind, stem ends).	30	171	4.4	.3	44.4	102	184	2.5	3	1,546	[106] 18,100	.14	.55	1.8	29
2208		Hubbard (refuse: cavity contents, rind, stem ends).	34	117	4.2	.9	28.1	57	93	1.8	3	650	[106] 12,870	.13	.33	1.7	32
		Squash, frozen:															
2211		Summer, Yellow Crookneck	6	95	6.4	.5	21.3	64	145	3.2	14	758	680	.32	.18	2.0	43
2213		Winter	0	172	5.4	1.4	41.7	113	145	4.5	5	939	17,600	.14	.32	2.2	44
2215		**Squid,** raw, flesh only	0	381	74.4	4.1	6.8	54	540	2.3	----	----	----	.09	.54	----	----
		Starch. See Cornstarch, item 894															
		St. Johnsbread. See Carob flour, item 617.															
2216		**Stomach,** pork, scalded	0	689	74.8	40.8	0	----	535	----	----	----	----	----	----	----	----
		Strawberries:															
2217		Raw:															
	a	Good quality (refuse: caps, stems)	4	161	3.0	2.2	36.6	91	93	4.4	4	714	260	.12	.29	2.6	257
	b	Fair quality (refuse: caps, stems, green and damaged berries).	13	146	2.8	2.0	33.1	83	83	3.9	4	647	240	.11	.26	2.4	233
		Canned, solids and liquid:															
2218		Water pack, with or without artificial sweetener	0	100	1.8	.5	25.4	64	64	3.2	5	503	180	.05	.15	1.8	90
		Frozen, sweetened:															
2219		Sliced	0	494	2.3	.9	126.1	64	77	3.2	5	508	150	.09	.27	2.4	240
2220		Whole	0	417	1.8	.9	106.6	59	73	2.7	5	472	150	.09	.27	2.3	249
		Sturgeon:															
2221		Raw:															
	a	Sections (refuse: bones and skin)	15	362	69.8	7.3	0	----	----	----	----	----	----	----	----	----	----
	b	Flesh only	0	426	82.1	8.6	0	----	----	----	----	----	----	----	----	----	----
2223		Smoked	0	676	141.5	8.2	0	----	----	----	----	----	----	----	----	----	----
2224		**Succotash** (corn and lima beans), frozen	0	440	19.5	1.8	97.5	64	404	5.0	[7] 204	1,238	(1,360)	.50	.27	6.7	42
2226		**Suckers, including white and mullet suckers,** raw:															
	a	Whole (refuse: entrails, heads, fins, scales, and bones).	57	203	40.2	3.5	0	----	429	----	109	655	----	Trace	----	2.3	----
	b	Fillets	0	472	93.4	8.2	0	----	998	----	254	1,524	----	Trace	----	5.4	----
2227		**Sucker, carp,** raw:															
	a	Whole (refuse: head, tail, fins, entrails, bones, and skin).	61	196	34.0	5.7	0	----	----	----	----	----	----	----	----	----	----

b	Flesh only	0	503	87.1	14.5	0	—	—	—	—	—	—	—	—	—	—
2228	**Suet** (beef kidney fat), raw	0	3,874	6.8	426.	0	—	—	—	—	—	—	—	—	—	—
	Sugars:															
	Beet or cane															
2229	Brown	0	1,692	0	0	437.3	386	86	15.4	136	1,560	0	05	.15	8	0
2230	Granulated	0	1,746	0	0	451.3	0	0	.5	5	14	0	0	0	0	0
2231	Powdered	0	1,746	0	0	451.3	0	0	5	5	14	0	0	0	0	0
	Dextrose:															
2232	Anhydrous	0	1,660	0	0	451.3	—	—	—	—	—	0	0	0	0	0
2233	Crystallized	0	1,520	0	0	413	—	—	Trace	—	—	0	0	0	0	0
2234	Maple	0	1,579	—	—	408.	649	50	6.4	64	1,098	—	—	—	—	0
2235	**Sugarapples** (sweetsop), raw (refuse: skin, seeds)	55	192	3.7	.6	48.4	45	84	1.2	22	561	20	.21	.29	2.0	69
2236	**Sunflower seed kernels,** dry.															
a	In hull (refuse: hulls)	46	1,372	58.8	115.8	48.7	294	2,050	17.4	73	2,253	120	4.80	.57	13.3	—
b	Hulled	0	2,540	108.9	214.6	90.3	544	3,797	32.2	136	4,173	230	8.90	1.05	24.7	—
2237	**Sunflower seed flour,** partially defatted	0	1,538	205.0	15.4	171.0	1,579	4,073	59.9	254	4,899	—	16.33	2.11	124.0	—
	Surinam-cherry. See Pitanga, item 1627.															
2238	**Swamp cabbage,** raw (refuse: inedible stems, trimmings).	19	107	11.0	1.1	19.8	268	187	9.2	—	551	23,150	.25	.44	2.6	118
	Sweetbreads (thymus), raw:															
2240	Beef (yearlings)	0	939	66.2	72.6	0	—	1,783	—	435	1,633	—	—	—	—	—
2242	Calf	0	426	80.7	9.1	0	—	—	—	—	—	—	37	.76	11.7	—
2244	Lamb	0	426	64.0	17.2	0	—	998	—	—	—	—	—	—	—	—
	Sweetbread, hog. See Pancreas, hog: item 1469															
	Sweetpotatoes															
	Raw															
2246	All (refuse: parings, trimmings, damaged spots)	19	419	6.2	1.5	96.6	118	173	2.6	37	893	32,330	36	.22	2.2	77
2247	Firm-fleshed,[127] Jersey types (refuse: parings, trimmings, damaged spots)	19	375	6.6	2.6	82.7	118	173	2.6	37	893	[128] 33,800	36	.22	2.2	85
2248	Soft-fleshed,[127] mainly Porto Rico variety (refuse: parings, trimmings, damaged spots)	19	430	6.2	1.1	100.3	118	173	2.6	37	893	[129] 31,960	.36	22	2.2	73
	Canned.															
	Liquid pack, solids and liquid															
2252	*Regular pack in sirup*	0	517	4.5	.9	124.7	59	132	3.2	218	(544)	22,680	.15	.14	2.5	36
2253	Special dietary pack, without added sugar and salt.	0	209	3.2	5	49.0	59	132	3.2	54	544	22,680	.15	.14	2.5	36
2254	Vacuum or solid pack	0	490	9.1	.9	112.9	113	186	3.6	[130] 218	907	35,380	.21	.20	2.9	62
2255	Dehydrated flakes	0	1,719	19.1	2.7	408.2	272	363	10.0	821	2,549	[131] 213,190	29	.59	5.9	204
	Sweetsop. See Sugarapples, item 2235															
	Swisschard. See Chard, Swiss: item 639.															
	Swordfish, flesh only.															
2257	Raw	0	535	87.1	18.1	0	86	885	4.1	—	—	7,170	24	.23	36.4	—
2259	Canned, solids and liquid	0	463	79.4	13.6	0	—	—	—	—	—	7,170	06	22	51.7	—
2260	**Tamarinds,** raw (refuse: pods, seeds)	52	520	6.1	1.3	136.1	161	246	6.1	111	1,700	70	73	.31	2.7	3
	Tangelos, raw, portion used—															
2261	Juice (refuse: peel, membranes, seeds)	44	104	1.3	(.3)	24.6	—	—	—	—	—	—	—	—	—	69
2262	**Tangerines** (Dancy variety), raw (refuse: rind, seeds)	26	154	2.7	.7	38.9	134	60	1.3	7	423	1,410	.20	.05	.4	105
	Tangerine juice:															
2263	Raw (Dancy variety)	0	195	2.3	9	45.8	82	64	.9	5	807	1,910	.27	.07	.6	142
	Canned															
2264	Unsweetened	0	195	2.3	.9	46.3	82	64	.9	5	807	1,910	(.25)	(.07)	(.6)	102
2265	Sweetened	0	227	2.3	9	54.4	82	64	9	5	807	1,910	(.25)	(.07)	(.6)	102
2266	Frozen concentrate, unsweetened	0	735	7.7	(3.2)	173.7	281	218	3.2	9	2,781	6,620	.92	.25	2.0	435
2268	**Tapioca,** *dry*	0	1,597	2.7	.9	391.9	45	82	1.8	14	82	(0)	(0)	(0)	(0)	(0)
	Taros, raw															
2271	Corms and tubers (refuse: skins)	16	373	7.2	.8	90.3	107	232	3.8	27	1,958	80	.51	.14	4.0	14
2272	Leaves and stems	0	181	13.6	3.6	33.6	345	268	4.5	—	—	—	—	—	—	141
	Tartar sauce:															
2273	Regular	0	2,409	6.4	262.2	19.1	82	145	4.1	3,207	354	1,000	06	.14	Trace	4
2274	Special dietary (low-calorie, approx. 10 Cal. per tsp.)	0	1,016	2.7	101.6	30.4	82	145	4.1	3,207	354	1,000	06	.14	Trace	4
2275	**Tautog** (blackfish), raw															
a	Whole (refuse: head, tail, fins, entrails, bones, and skin).	63	149	31.2	1.8	0	—	381	—	—	—	—	—	—	—	—
b	Flesh only	0	404	84.4	5.0	0	—	1,030	—	—	—	—	—	—	—	—
2276	**Tea,** instant (water-soluble solids), carbohydrate added, dry powder.	0	1,334	—	Trace	362.9	50	—	7.3	—	20,548	—	—	4.31	40.3	—
	Tendergreen. See Mustard spinach, item 1370															

[117] Average weighted in accordance with commercial practices in freezing vegetables. See also Notes on Foods, p. 177.

[124] Values are based on samples caught in October. Content of fat may vary greatly from this average at other seasons of the year.

[125] Applies to squash including skin, flesh has no appreciable vitamin A value.

[126] Value for freshly harvested squash. The carotenoid content increases during storage, the amount of increase varying according to variety and conditions of storage. More information is needed on the relative contents of the individual carotenoids and their rates of increase under usual storage conditions before a suitable vitamin A value can be derived for the stored product.

[127] *Term refers to the flesh of the cooked product.*

[128] Values for commercial varieties having deep-orange flesh average about 37,000 I.U. per pound, light-yellow, about 2,000 I.U.

[129] Values for commercial varieties range from 29,000 to more than 73,000 I.U. per pound. Porto Rico, the main variety, has a value around 29,000 I.U.

[130] Applies to regular pack. For special dietary pack (low-sodium), value is 54 mg. per pound.

[131] Value varies widely; it is related to variety of sweetpotato. Range is 95,000 to 327,000 I.U. per pound.

TABLE 2.—NUTRIENTS IN THE EDIBLE PORTION OF 1 POUND OF FOOD AS PURCHASED—Continued

[Numbers in parentheses denote values imputed—usually from another form of the food or from a similar food. Zero in parentheses indicates that the amount of a constituent probably is none or is too small to measure. Dashes denote lack of reliable data for a constituent believed to be present in measurable amount. Calculated values, as those based on a recipe, are not in parentheses]

Item No.	Food and description	Refuse	Food energy	Protein	Fat	Carbohydrate total	Calcium	Phosphorus	Iron	Sodium	Potassium	Vitamin A value	Thiamine	Riboflavin	Niacin	Ascorbic Acid
(A)	(B)	(C)	(D)	(E)	(F)	(G)	(H)	(I)	(J)	(K)	(L)	(M)	(N)	(O)	(P)	(Q)
		Percent	Calories	Grams	Grams	Grams	Milligrams	Milligrams	Milligrams	Milligrams	Milligrams	International units	Milligrams	Milligrams	Milligrams	Milligrams
2278	**Terrapin** (diamond back), raw:															
a	In shell (refuse: shell)	79	106	17.7	3.3	0	—	—	2.6	—	—	—	—	—	—	—
b	Muscle only	0	503	84.4	15.9	0	—	—	14.5	—	—	—	—	—	—	—
	Thuringer. See Sausage, cold cuts, and luncheon meats: item 2021.															
2279	**Tilefish,** raw:															
a	Whole (refuse: head, tail, fins, entrails, bones, and skin).	49	183	40.5	1.2	0	—	—	—	—	—	—	—	—	—	—
b	Flesh only	0	359	79.4	2.3	0	—	—	—	—	—	—	—	—	—	—
2281	**Tomatoes, green,** raw (refuse: cores, stem ends)	9	99	5.0	.8	21.1	54	111	2.1	12	1,007	1,110	0.26	0.15	2.0	83
	Tomatoes, ripe:															
2282	Raw, portion used:															
a	Whole fruit	0	100	5.0	.9	21.3	59	122	2.3	14	1,107	4,080	.29	.18	3.0	[13] 102
b	Peeled fruit (refuse: skins, hard cores, stem ends, trimmings).	12	88	4.4	.8	18.8	52	108	2.0	12	974	3,590	.26	.16	2.6	[13] 90
	Canned, solids and liquid:															
2284	Regular pack	0	95	4.5	.9	19.5	[9] 27	86	2.3	590	984	4,080	.24	.13	3.1	76
2285	Special dietary pack (low-sodium)	0	91	4.5	.9	19.1	[9] 27	86	2.3	14	984	4,080	.24	.13	3.1	76
2286	**Tomato catsup,** bottled	0	481	9.1	1.8	115.2	100	227	3.6	[13] 4,727	1,647	6,350	.41	.29	7.3	70
2287	**Tomato chili sauce,** bottled	0	472	11.3	1.4	112.5	91	236	(3.6)	[13] 6,069	(1,678)	(6,350)	(.42)	(.30)	(7.4)	(71)
	Tomato juice:															
	Canned or bottled:															
2288	Regular pack	0	86	4.1	.5	19.5	32	82	4.1	907	1,036	3,630	.24	.13	3.4	73
2289	Special dietary pack (low-sodium)	0	86	3.6	.5	19.5	32	82	4.1	14	1,020	3,630	.21	.11	3.1	73
2290	Canned concentrate	0	345	15.4	1.8	77.6	122	318	15.9	3,583	4,028	14,970	.88	.54	14.2	223
2292	Dehydrated (crystals, 1.0% moisture)	0	1,374	52.6	10.0	309.4	386	1,266	35.4	(17,845)	15,958	59,400	2.36	1.81	61.2	1,084
2294	**Tomato juice cocktail,** canned or bottled	0	95	3.2	.5	22.7	45	82	4.1	907	1,002	3,630	.23	.09	2.7	73
2295	**Tomato paste,** canned	0	372	15.4	1.8	84.4	122	318	15.9	[14] 172	4,028	14,970	.88	.54	14.2	221
	Tomato puree, canned:															
2296	Regular pack	0	177	7.7	.9	40.4	59	154	7.7	1,810	1,932	7,260	.39	.24	6.3	148
2297	Special dietary pack (low-sodium)	0	177	7.7	.9	40.4	59	154	7.7	27	1,932	7,260	.39	.24	6.3	148
2298	**Tomcod, Atlantic,** raw:															
a	Whole (refuse: head, tail, fins, entrails, bones, and skin).	61	136	30.4	.7	0	—	—	—	—	—	—	—	.30	—	—
b	Flesh only	0	349	78.0	1.8	0	—	—	—	—	—	—	—	.77	—	—
	Tongue, raw:															
	Beef:															
2299	Very fat (refuse: skin and trimmings)	(24)	934	49.6	79.0	1.4	—	—	—	—	—	—	—	—	—	—
2300	Fat (refuse: skin and trimmings)	(24)	795	54.1	62.0	1.4	—	—	—	—	—	—	—	—	—	—
2301	Medium (refuse: skin and trimmings)	24	714	56.5	52.0	1.4	28	627	7.2	252	679	—	.42	.99	17.2	—
2303	Thin (very thin), raw (refuse: skin and trimmings)	(24)	603	60.0	38.0	1.4	—	—	—	—	—	—	—	—	—	—
2304	Smoked (refuse: skin and trimmings)	26	—	57.7	96.7	—	—	—	—	—	—	—	—	—	—	—
2305	Calf (refuse: skin and trimmings)	23	454	64.6	18.5	3.1	—	—	—	—	—	—	.44	.71	10.1	—
2307	Hog (refuse: skin and trimmings)	24	741	57.9	53.8	1.7	100	641	4.8	—	—	—	.59	(.99)	(17.2)	—
2309	Lamb (refuse: skin and trimmings)	27	659	46.0	50.7	1.7	—	487	—	—	—	—	—	—	—	—
2311	Sheep (refuse: skin and trimmings)	(27)	877	45.4	72.2	7.9	—	—	—	—	—	—	—	—	—	—
	Tongue, canned or cured (beef, lamb, etc.):															
2313	Whole, canned or pickled	0	1,211	87.5	92.1	1.4	—	—	—	—	—	—	—	—	—	—
2314	Potted or deviled	0	1,315	84.4	104.3	3.2	—	—	—	—	—	—	.16	.30	5.9	—
2315	**Towelgourd,** raw (refuse: parings)	15	69	3.1	.8	15.8	73	127	3.5	—	—	1,470	.12	.15	1.5	32
	Tripe, beef:															
2316	Commercial	0	454	86.6	9.1	0	576	390	7.3	327	41	—	—	.68	7.3	—
2317	Pickled	0	281	53.5	5.9	0	—	—	—	209	86	—	—	—	—	—
	Trout. See Lake trout, items 1170–1171.															
2318	**Trout, brook,** raw:															
a	Whole (refuse: head, tail, fins, entrails, bones, and skin).	51	224	42.7	4.7	0	—	591	—	—	—	—	—	.36	—	—
b	Flesh only	0	458	87.1	9.5	0	—	1,207	—	—	—	—	—	.33	—	—
	Trout, rainbow or steelhead:															
2319	Raw, flesh with skin	0	885	97.5	51.7	0	—	—	—	—	—	—	.34	.92	38.0	—

2320		Canned	0	948	93.4	60.8	0	—	—	—	—	—	—	—	—	—	—
		Tuna:															
		Raw:															
2321		Bluefin, flesh only	0	658	114.3	18.6	0	—	—	5.9	—	—	—	—	—	—	—
2322		Yellowfin, flesh only	0	603	112.0	13.6	0	—	—	—	[134] 168	—	—	—	—	—	—
		Canned															
		In oil:															
		Portion used															
2323		Solids and liquid	0	1,306	109.8	93.0	0	27	1,334	5.0	3,629	1,365	410	.18	.39	46.0	—
2324		Drained solids (refuse: liquid)	15	760	111.1	31.6	0	(31)	902	7.3	—	—	310	.19	.45	46.0	—
2325		In water, solids and liquid	0	576	127.0	3.6	0	73	862	7.3	[135] 186	[136] 1,266	—	—	.45	60.3	—
		Turkey, raw:															
		All classes															
2327		Total edible															
	a	Live (refuse: blood, feathers, head, feet, inedible viscera, and bones).	45	544	50.1	36.7	0	—	—	—	—	—	—	—	—	—	—
	b	Dressed (refuse: head, feet, inedible viscera, and bones).	39	603	55.6	40.7	0	—	—	—	—	—	—	—	—	—	—
	c	Ready-to-cook (refuse: bones)	27	722	66.6	48.7	0	—	—	—	—	—	—	—	—	—	—
		Young birds (24 weeks and under)															
2340		Total edible															
	a	Live (refuse: blood, feathers, head, feet, inedible viscera, and bones)	46	355	52.4	14.7	0	—	—	—	—	—	—	—	—	—	—
	b	Dressed (refuse: head, feet, inedible viscera, and bones).	39	401	59.2	16.6	0	—	—	—	—	—	—	—	—	—	—
	c	Ready-to-cook (refuse: bones)	27	480	70.9	19.9	0	—	—	—	—	—	—	—	—	—	—
		Medium-fat birds (26–32 weeks)															
2344		Total edible															
	a	Live (refuse: blood, feathers, head, feet, inedible viscera, and bones)	44	577	50.5	40.1	0	—	—	—	—	—	—	—	—	—	—
	b	Dressed (refuse: head, feet, inedible viscera, and bones)	38	638	56.0	44.4	0	—	—	—	—	—	—	—	—	—	—
	c	Ready-to-cook (refuse: bones)	27	752	65.9	52.3	0	—	—	—	—	—	—	—	—	—	—
		Fat mature birds (more than 32 weeks)															
2348		Total edible															
	a	Live (refuse: blood, feathers, head, feet, inedible viscera, and bones).	44	871	46.7	74.4	0	—	—	—	—	—	—	—	—	—	—
	b	Dressed (refuse: head, feet, inedible viscera, and bones).	38	965	51.7	82.4	0	—	—	—	—	—	—	—	—	—	—
	c	Ready-to-cook (refuse: bones)	27	1,136	60.9	97.0	0	—	—	—	—	—	—	—	—	—	—
2349		**Turkey, canned,** meat only, boned	0	916	94.8	56.7	0	45	—	6.4	—	—	590	10	63	21.4	—
		Turkey, potted. See Sausage, cold cuts, and luncheon meats item 2008.															
2351		**Turkey potpie,** frozen	0	894	26.3	47.2	91.2	54	254	4.1	1,674	517	4,040	39	35	7.2	10
2352		**Turnips,** raw															
		With tops.															
	a	Good quality (refuse: tops, rootlets, parings, trimmings).	35	88	2.9	.6	19.5	115	88	1.5	144	790	Trace	.12	19	1.7	106
	b	Fair quality (refuse: tops, rootlets, parings, trimmings).	45	75	2.5	.5	16.5	97	75	1.2	122	669	Trace	.10	.16	1.4	90
		Without tops															
	c	Good quality (refuse: parings, rootlets, trimmings).	14	117	3.9	.8	25.7	152	117	2.0	191	1,045	Trace	16	.26	2.2	140
	d	Fair quality (refuse: parings, rootlets, trimmings).	27	99	3.3	.7	21.9	129	99	1.7	162	887	Trace	14	22	1.9	119
		Turnip greens, leaves including stems:															
2354		Raw:															
	a	Trimmed	0	127	13.6	1.4	22.7	1,118	263	8.2	—	—	34,470	(.94)	(1.78)	(3.4)	628
	b	Untrimmed (refuse: discarded leaves)	16	107	11.4	1.1	19.0	937	221	6.9	—	—	28,960	(.79)	(1.49)	(2.9)	530
2357		Canned, solids and liquid	0	82	6.8	1.4	14.5	454	136	7.3	[10] 1,070	1,102	21,320	08	.41	2.8	87
2358		Frozen	0	104	11.8	1.4	18.1	594	186	7.7	104	853	31,300	.27	.50	2.4	153
		Turtle, green:															
2360		Raw:															
	a	In shell (refuse: shell)	76	97	21.6	.5	0	—	—	—	—	—	—	—	—	—	—
	b	Muscle only	0	404	89.8	2.3	0	—	—	—	—	—	—	—	—	—	—
2361		Canned	0	481	106.1	3.2	0	—	—	—	—	—	—	—	—	—	—

[10] Estimated average based on addition of salt in the amount of 0.6 percent of the finished product

[96] Federal standards provide for addition of certain calcium salts as firming agents, if used, these salts may add calcium not to exceed 118 mg. per pound of finished product

[132] Year-round average. Samples marketed from November through May average around 45 mg per pound for whole fruit, and 40 mg for peeled fruit, from June to October, around 118 mg per pound for whole fruit, and 104 mg for peeled fruit.

[133] Applies to regular pack. For special dietary pack (low-sodium), values range from 23 to 159 mg per pound

[134] Applies to the more usual product with no salt added. If salt is added, the sodium content is about 3,580 mg per pound

[135] Brined sample contained 1,991 mg. of sodium per pound

[136] One sample with salt added contained 3,969 mg of sodium per pound and 1,247 mg of potassium

TABLE 2.—NUTRIENTS IN THE EDIBLE PORTION OF 1 POUND OF FOOD AS PURCHASED—Continued

[Numbers in parentheses denote values imputed—usually from another form of the food or from a similar food. Zero in parentheses indicates that the amount of a constituent probably is none or is too small to measure. Dashes denote lack of reliable data for a constituent believed to be present in measurable amount. Calculated values, as those based on a recipe, are not in parentheses]

Item No.	Food and description	Refuse	Food energy	Protein	Fat	Carbohydrate total	Calcium	Phosphorus	Iron	Sodium	Potassium	Vitamin A value	Thiamine	Riboflavin	Niacin	Ascorbic Acid
(A)	(B)	(C)	(D)	(E)	(F)	(G)	(H)	(I)	(J)	(K)	(L)	(M)	(N)	(O)	(P)	(Q)
		Percent	*Calories*	*Grams*	*Grams*	*Grams*	*Milligrams*	*Milligrams*	*Milligrams*	*Milligrams*	*Milligrams*	*International units*	*Milligrams*	*Milligrams*	*Milligrams*	*Milligrams*
	Veal: [1]															
	Carcass with bone, raw:															
	Including kidney and kidney fat:															
2362	Fat class, 62% lean, 19% fat	19	911	66.1	70.	0	37	654	9.9			—	0.48	0.88	22.2	----
2363	Medium-fat class, 64% lean, 15% fat	21	742	67.4	50.	0	39	681	10.0			—	.49	.90	22.6	----
2364	Thin class, 67% lean, 11% fat	22	612	68.6	35.	0	39	704	10.3			—	.50	.91	23.0	----
	Excluding kidney and kidney fat:															
2365	Fat class, 64% lean, 17% fat	19	816	68.0	59.	0	40	680	10.3			—	.50	.90	22.8	----
2366	Medium-fat class, 66% lean, 13% fat	21	681	68.4	43.	0	39	692	10.4			—	.50	.91	22.9	----
2367	Thin class, 68% lean, 9% fat	23	545	68.8	28.	0	38	702	10.5			—	.50	.92	23.1	----
	Retail cuts, untrimmed, raw:															
	Chuck:															
	Fat class:															
2368	Total edible:															
a	With bone, 68% lean, 14% fat	18	736	70.7	48.	0	41	711	10.4			—	.52	.94	23.7	----
b	Without bone, 83% lean, 17% fat	0	898	86.2	59	0	50	866	12.7			—	.63	1.15	28.8	----
	Medium-fat class:															
2369	Total edible:															
a	With bone, 69% lean, 11% fat	20	628	70.4	36.	0	40	722	10.5			—	.52	.94	23.6	----
b	Without bone, 86% lean, 14% fat	0	785	88.0	45	0	50	903	13.2			—	.64	1.17	29.5	----
	Thin class:															
2371	Total edible:															
a	With bone, 70% lean, 8% fat	22	492	70.4	21.	0	42	729	10.6			—	.51	.94	23.6	----
b	Without bone, 90% lean, 10% fat	0	631	90.3	27.	0	54	934	13.6			—	.66	1.20	30.3	----
	Flank:															
	Fat class:															
2372	Total edible:															
a	With bone, 49% lean, 50% fat	1	1,738	65.1	162.	0	36	566	9.9			—	.48	.87	21.8	----
b	Without bone, 49% lean, 51% fat	0	1,755	65.8	163.	0	36	572	10.0			—	.48	.88	22.0	----
	Medium-fat class:															
2373	Total edible:															
a	With bone, 60% lean, 39% fat	1	1,410	74.1	121.	0	45	696	11.2	([37])	([38])	—	.54	.98	24.8	----
b	Without bone, 61% lean, 39% fat	0	1,424	74.8	122.	0	45	703	11.3			—	.54	.99	25.1	----
	Thin class:															
2375	Total edible:															
a	With bone, 72% lean, 27% fat	1	1,078	81.3	81.	0	45	804	12.1			—	.59	1.08	27.2	----
b	Without bone, 73% lean, 27% fat	0	1,089	82.1	82.	0	45	812	12.2			—	.60	1.09	27.5	----
	Foreshank:															
	Fat class:															
2376	Total edible:															
a	With bone, 45% lean, 8% fat	47	416	46.6	24.	0	26	478	7.0			—	.34	.62	15.6	----
b	Without bone, 84% lean, 16% fat	0	785	88.0	45.	0	50	903	13.2			—	.64	1.17	29.5	----
	Medium-fat class:															
2377	Total edible:															
a	With bone, 45% lean, 7% fat	48	368	46.5	19.	0	26	479	7.1			—	.34	.62	15.6	----
b	Without bone, 87% lean, 13% fat	0	708	89.4	36.	0	50	921	13.6			—	.65	1.19	29.9	----
	Thin class:															
2379	Total edible:															
a	With bone, 46% lean, 5% fat	49	303	46.5	12.	0	28	483	6.9			—	.34	.62	15.6	----
b	Without bone, 91% lean, 9% fat	0	594	91.2	23.	0	54	948	13.6			—	.67	1.21	30.5	----
	Loin:															
	Fat class:															
2380	Total edible:															
a	With bone, 67% lean, 17% fat	16	819	70.9	57.	0	42	712	10.7			—	.52	.94	23.7	----
b	Without bone, 80% lean, 20% fat	0	975	84.4	68	0	50	848	12.7			—	.62	1.12	28.3	----
	Medium-fat class:															
2381	Total edible:															
a	With bone, 71% lean, 12% fat	17	681	72.3	41.	0	41	734	10.9			—	.53	.96	24.2	----
b	Without bone, 85% lean, 15% fat	0	821	87.1	50	0	50	885	13.2			—	.64	1.16	29.2	----
	Thin class:															
2383	Total edible:															
a	With bone, 72% lean, 9% fat	19	573	72.4	29.	0	40	746	11.0			—	.53	.96	24.2	----
b	Without bone, 89% lean, 11% fat	0	708	89.4	36.	0	50	921	13.6			—	.65	1.19	29.9	----

		Plate:															
		Fat class:															
2384		Total edible:															
	a	With bone, 53% lean, 28% fat	19	1,032	63 6	85.	0	37	617	9.6			—	.46	.85	21.3	—
	b	Without bone, 66% lean, 34% fat	0	1,275	78.5	104.	0	45	762	11.8			—	.57	1.04	26.3	—
		Medium-fat class:															
2385		Total edible:															
	a	With bone, 58% lean, 21% fat	21	828	65 6	61	0	39	652	9 7			—	.48	.87	22 0	—
	b	Without bone, 74% lean, 26% fat	0	1,048	83.0	77.	0	50	826	12.2			—	.61	1.10	27 8	—
		Thin class:															
2387		Total edible:															
	a	With bone, 63% lean, 14% fat	23	664	66.7	42.	0	38	674	10 1			—	.49	.89	22.4	—
	b	Without bone, 82% lean, 18% fat	0	862	86 6	54	0	50	875	13 2			—	.63	1.15	29 0	—
		Rib:															
		Fat class:															
2388		Total edible:															
	a	With bone, 59% lean, 19% fat	22	877	63.7	67.	0	35	630	9.6	([137])	([138])	—	.46	.85	21 3	—
	b	Without bone, 76% lean, 24% fat	0	1,125	81.6	86.	0	45	807	12.2			—	.59	1.08	27.4	—
		Medium-fat class:															
2389		Total edible:															
	a	With bone, 63% lean, 14% fat	23	723	65 7	49.	0	38	664	9 8			—	.48	.87	22.0	—
	b	Without bone, 82% lean, 18% fat	0	939	85.3	64.	0	50	862	12.7			—	.62	1.13	28 6	—
		Thin class:															
2391		Total edible:															
	a	With bone, 65% lean, 10% fat	25	558	66.3	31.	0	37	680	9.9			—	.48	.88	22 2	—
	b	Without bone, 87% lean, 13% fat	0	744	88 5	41	0	50	907	13.2			—	.64	1.17	29.6	—
		Round with rump:															
		Fat class:															
2392		Total edible:															
	a	With bone, 66% lean, 12% fat	22	672	67.6	42.	0	39	683	10 3			—	.49	.90	22 6	—
	b	Without bone, 84% lean, 16% fat	0	862	86.6	54.	0	50	875	13.2			—	.63	1.15	29.0	—
		Medium-fat class:															
2393		Total edible:															
	a	With bone, 67% lean, 10% fat	23	573	68.1	31.	0	38	699	10.1			—	.50	.90	22.8	—
	b	Without bone, 87% lean, 13% fat	0	744	88.5	41.	0	50	907	13 2			—	.64	1 17	29 6	—
		Thin class:															
2395		Total edible:															
	a	With bone, 68% lean, 7% fat	25	473	67.7	20	0	41	701	10.2			—	.49	.90	22.7	—
	b	Without bone, 91% lean, 9% fat	0	631	90.3	27.	0	54	934	13.6			—	.66	1.20	30 3	—
2396		**Vegetable juice cocktail**, canned	0	77	4 1	.5	16 3	54	100	2.3	(907)	(1,002)	3,180	.23	.14	3.6	39
		Vegetable main dishes, canned:															
		Principal ingredients:															
2397		Peanuts and soya	0	1,075	53.1	76 7	60 8	—	—	—	—	—	—	—	—	—	—
2398		Wheat protein	0	494	73.9	3 6	39 9	—	—	—	—	—	—	—	—	—	—
2399		Wheat protein, nuts or peanuts	0	962	92 1	32 2	80 3	—	—	—	—	—	—	—	—	—	—
2400		Wheat protein, vegetable oil	0	857	86.6	47 2	23.6	—	—	—	—	—	—	—	—	—	—
2401		Wheat and soy protein	0	472	73.0	5 4	34 5	—	—	—	—	—	—	—	—	—	—
2402		Wheat and soy protein, soy or other vegetable oil	0	680	73 0	25.4	43 1	—	—	—	—	—	—	—	—	—	—
2403		**Vegetables, mixed** (carrots, corn, peas, green snap beans, lima beans), frozen	0	295	15.0	1 4	62.1	118	299	6 4	[17] 268	943	22,680	.59	32	5.3	42
		Vegetable-oyster. See Salsify, item 1961.															
2405		**Venison**, lean meat only, raw	0	572	95.	18.	0	45	1,129	—	—	—	—	1.03	2.19	28 6	—
		Vienna sausage. See Sausage, cold cuts, and luncheon meats: item 2022.															
		Vinegar:															
2406		Cider	0	64	Trace	(0)	26 8	(27)	(41)	(2.7)	5	454	—	—	—	—	—
2407		Distilled	0	54	—	—	22.7	—	—	—	5	68	—	—	—	—	—
2408		**Vinespinach** (basella), raw	0	86	8.2	1.4	15.4	494	236	5.4	—	—	36,290	23	—	2 3	463
		Vodka. See Beverages, items 395–399.															
2411		**Waffles**, frozen, made with enriched flour	0	1,148	32.2	28 1	190 5	553	943	[139] 8.2	2,921	717	590	[139] 76	[139] .72	[139] 5.6	Trace
		Waffle mixes:															
		Mix with—															
2412		Enriched flour	0	2,077	29 0	87 1	296.7	535	889	7 3	4,658	386	540	1.02	.81	7.6	Trace
2414		Unenriched flour	0	2,077	29 0	87.1	296 7	535	889	2 7	4,658	386	540	.20	.35	2 0	Trace
		Mix (pancake and waffle) with:															
2416		Enriched flour	0	1,615	39.0	8 2	343.4	2,041	2,676	14 1	6,500	735	0	2.00	1.53	13 0	0
2418		Unenriched flour	0	1,615	39 0	8.2	343 4	2,041	2,676	6.4	6,500	735	0	.54	.36	5 0	0

[4] See Notes on Foods, p. 180.

[17] Average weighted in accordance with commercial practices in freezing vegetables. See also Notes on Foods, p. 177.

[137] Average value for 1 pound, all cuts without bone or with a small proportion of bone is 410 mg For cuts with average bone content (21 percent), the value is 320 mg.; for those with high bone content (as foreshanks), 210 mg. See also Notes on Foods, p. 180.

[138] Average value for 1 pound, all cuts without bone or with a small proportion of bone is 1,450 mg. For cuts with average bone content (21 percent), the value is 1,150 mg, for those with high bone content (as foreshanks), 755 mg See also Notes on Foods, p. 180.

[139] With unenriched flour, approximate values per pound are: Iron, 5.0 mg; thiamine, 0.27 mg.; riboflavin, 0 41 mg; niacin, 1.8 mg.

TABLE 2.—NUTRIENTS IN THE EDIBLE PORTION OF 1 POUND OF FOOD AS PURCHASED—Continued

[Numbers in parentheses denote values imputed—usually from another form of the food or from a similar food. Zero in parentheses indicates that the amount of a constituent probably is none or is too small to measure. Dashes denote lack of reliable data for a constituent believed to be present in measurable amount. Calculated values, as those based on a recipe, are not in parentheses]

Item No.		Food and description	Refuse	Food energy	Protein	Fat	Carbohydrate total	Calcium	Phosphorus	Iron	Sodium	Potassium	Vitamin A value	Thiamine	Riboflavin	Niacin	Ascorbic Acid
(A)		(B)	(C)	(D)	(E)	(F)	(G)	(H)	(I)	(J)	(K)	(L)	(M)	(N)	(O)	(P)	(Q)
			Percent	Calories	Grams	Grams	Grams	Milligrams	Milligrams	Milligrams	Milligrams	Milligrams	International units	Milligrams	Milligrams	Milligrams	Milligrams
		Walnuts:															
2420		Black:															
	a	In shell (refuse: shells)	78	627	20.5	59.2	14.8	Trace	569	6.0	3	459	300	0.22	0.11	0.7	—
	b	Shelled	0	2,849	93.0	269.0	67.1	Trace	2,580	27.2	14	2,087	1,360	.99	.49	3.3	—
2421		Persian or English:															
	a	In shell (refuse: shells)	55	1,329	30.2	130.6	32.2	202	776	6.3	4	918	60	.67	.26	1.9	4
	b	Shelled	0	2,953	67.1	290.3	71.7	449	1,724	14.1	9	2,041	140	1.49	.58	4.2	9
2422		**Waterchestnut,** Chinese (matai, waternut), raw (refuse: skin).	23	272	4.9	.7	66.4	14	227	2.1	70	1,746	0	.49	.70	3.5	14
2423		**Watercress** leaves including stems, raw (refuse: stem ends).	8	79	9.2	1.3	12.5	630	225	7.1	217	1,177	20,450	.35	.68	3.6	330
		Water ice. See Ices, water: item 1144.															
2424		**Watermelon,** raw (refuse: rind, seeds, cutting loss)	54	54	1.0	.4	13.4	15	21	1.0	2	209	1,230	.06	.06	.3	15
2425		**Waxgourd** (Chinese preserving melon), raw (refuse: tough skin, cavity contents).	31	41	1.3	.6	9.4	59	59	1.3	19	347	0	.13	.34	1.3	40
2426		**Weakfish,** raw:															
	a	Whole (refuse: head, tail, fins, entrails, bones, and skin).	52	263	35.9	12.2	0	—	—	—	163	690	—	.20	.13	5.9	—
	b	Flesh only	0	549	74.8	25.4	0	—	—	—	340	1,438	—	.41	.27	12.4	—
		West Indian cherry. See Acerola, item 3.															
2429		**Whale meat,** raw	0	708	93.4	34.0	0	54	653	—	354	100	8,440	.39	.35	—	29
		Wheat, whole-grain: [139]															
2430		Hard red spring	0	1,497	63.5	10.0	313.4	163	1,737	14.1	(14)	1,678	(0)	2.59	.54	19.5	(0)
2431		Hard red winter	0	1,497	55.8	8.2	325.2	209	1,606	15.4	(14)	1,676	(0)	2.35	.53	19.5	(0)
2432		Soft red winter	0	1,479	46.3	9.1	327.0	191	1,814	15.9	(14)	1,706	(0)	1.95	.50	(16.3)	(0)
2433		White	0	1,520	42.6	9.1	342.0	163	1,787	13.6	(14)	1,769	(0)	2.41	.54	24.1	(0)
2434		Durum	0	1,506	57.6	11.3	318.0	168	1,751	19.5	(14)	1,973	(0)	3.00	.54	(20.0)	(0)
		Wheat flours:															
2435		Whole (from hard wheats)	0	1,510	60.3	9.1	322.1	186	1,687	15.0	14	1,678	(0)	2.49	.54	19.7	(0)
2436		80% extraction (from hard wheats)	0	1,656	54.4	5.9	336.1	109	866	5.9	9	431	(0)	1.16	.33	9.3	(0)
2437		Straight, hard wheat	0	1,656	53.5	5.4	337.9	91	440	6.4	9	431	(0)	.53	.32	6.5	(0)
2438		Straight, soft wheat	0	1,651	44.0	4.5	348.8	91	440	5.0	9	431	(0)	.36	.23	5.5	(0)
		Patent:															
		All-purpose or family flour:															
2439		Enriched	0	1,651	47.6	4.5	345.2	73	395	[33] 13.0	9	431	(0)	[33] 2.0	[33] 1.2	[33] 16.0	(0)
2440		Unenriched	0	1,651	47.6	4.5	345.2	73	395	3.6	9	431	(0)	.28	.21	4.1	(0)
		Bread flour:															
2441		Enriched	0	1,656	53.5	5.0	338.8	73	431	[33] 13.0	9	431	(0)	[33] 2.0	[33] 1.2	[33] 16.0	(0)
2442		Unenriched	0	1,656	53.5	5.0	338.8	73	431	4.1	9	431	(0)	.35	.25	4.4	(0)
2443		Cake or pastry flour	0	1,651	34.0	3.6	360.2	77	331	2.3	9	431	(0)	.14	.14	3.0	(0)
2444		Gluten flour (45% gluten, 55% patent flour)	0	1,715	187.8	8.6	214.1	181	635	—	9	272	(0)	—	—	—	(0)
2445		Self-rising flour, enriched (anhydrous monocalcium phosphate used as a baking acid) [141]	0	1,597	42.2	4.5	336.6	1,202	2,114	[33] 13.0	4,894	[142] —	(0)	[33] 2.0	[33] 1.2	[33] 16.0	(0)
2446		**Wheat bran,** crude, commercially milled	0	966	72.6	20.9	280.8	540	5,788	67.6	41	5,085	(0)	3.25	1.59	95.3	(0)
2447		**Wheat germ,** crude, commercially milled	0	1,647	120.7	49.4	211.8	327	5,071	42.6	14	3,751	(0)	9.10	3.09	19.2	(0)
		Wheat, parboiled. See Bulgur, items 497–501.															
		Wheat products used mainly as hot breakfast cereals:															
2448		Wheat, rolled	0	1,542	44.9	9.1	345.6	163	1,551	14.5	9	1,724	(0)	1.65	.55	18.6	(0)
2450		Wheat, whole-meal	0	1,533	61.2	9.1	328.0	204	1,805	16.8	9	1,678	(0)	2.30	.61	21.2	(0)
		Wheat and malted barley cereal, toasted:															
2452		Quick-cooking	0	1,737	54.4	7.3	356.1	227	1,568	11.8	5	—	(0)	1.54	.29	—	(0)
2454		Instant-cooking	0	1,733	63.5	7.3	345.6	181	1,769	18.6	5	—	(0)	1.54	.39	—	(0)
		Also see Farina, items 991–997.															
		Wheat products used mainly as ready-to-eat breakfast cereals:															
		Wheat bran. See Bran, items 439–442.															
2456		Wheat flakes, added nutrients	0	1,606	46.3	7.3	365.1	186	1,402	20.0	4,681	—	(0)	2.92	.62	22.4	(0)
2457		Wheat germ, toasted	0	1,774	136.1	52.2	224.5	213	4,917	40.4	9	4,296	500	7.48	4.45	23.9	45
		Wheat, puffed:															
2458		Added nutrients, without salt	0	1,647	68.0	6.8	356.1	127	1,461	19.1	18	1,542	(0)	2.49	1.04	35.4	(0)
2459		Added nutrients, [143] with sugar and honey	0	1,706	27.2	9.5	400.5	118	680	15.0	730	449	(0)	2.20	.82	29.3	(0)

		Wheat, shredded:															
2460		Without salt or other added nutrients	0	1,606	44.9	9.1	362.4	195	1,760	15.9	14	1,579	(0)	1.00	.51	20.0	(0)
2461		With malt, salt, and sugar added	0	1,660	41.3	13.2	370.6	177	1,678	15.4	3,162	—	(0)	.40	.67	21.5	(0)
2462		Wheat and malted barley flakes, nutrients added	0	1,778	39.9	5.0	382.4	222	1,134	11.8	3,538	----	(0)	2.09	.48	17.7	(0)
2463		Wheat and malted barley granules, nutrients added	0	1,774	45.4	2.7	382.8	240	798	12.7	3,221	1,043	(0)	2.09	.32	24.0	(0)
		Whey:															
2464		Fluid	0	118	4.1	1.4	23.1	231	240	.5	----	----	50	.15	.65	.3	----
2465		Dried	0	1,583	58.5	5.0	333.4	2,930	2,672	6.4	----	----	230	2.26	11.39	3.6	----
		Whisky. See Beverages, items 395–399.															
		Whitefish, lake:															
2466		Raw:															
	a	Whole (refuse: head, tail, fins, entrails, bones, and skin).	53	330	40.3	17.5	0	----	576	.9	111	637	4,820	.30	.26	6.4	----
	b	Flesh only	0	703	85.7	37.2	0	---	1,225	1.8	236	1,356	10,250	.64	.54	13.6	----
2468		Smoked	0	703	94.8	33.1	0	100	1,243	----	----	----	----	----	----	----	----
		Whiting. See Kingfish, item 1164.															
2472		Wildrice, raw	0	1,601	64.0	3.2	341.6	86	1,538	19.1	32	998	(0)	2.02	2.87	27.9	(0)
		Wine. See Beverages, items 400–401.															
2473		Wreckfish, fillet, raw	0	517	83.5	17.7	0	213	776	14.5	----	1,279	----	----	----	----	----
2474		Yam, tuber, raw (refuse: skin)	14	394	8.2	.8	90.5	78	269	2.3	----	2,341	Trace	.39	.16	2.0	36
2475		Yambean, tuber, raw (refuse: parings)	10	225	5.7	.8	52.2	61	73	2.4	----	----	Trace	.17	.12	1.2	81
		Yeast: [45]															
		Baker's:															
2476		Compressed [144]	0	390	(54.9)	1.8	49.9	59	1,787	22.2	73	2,767	Trace	3.22	7.48	50.8	Trace
2477		Dry (active)	0	1,279	(167.4)	7.3	176.5	(200)	(5,856)	(73.0)	(236)	(9,063)	Trace	10.57	24.54	166.5	Trace
2478		Brewer's, debittered	0	1,284	(176.0)	4.3	174.2	[145]953	7,952	78.5	549	8,591	Trace	70.81	19.41	171.9	Trace
2479		Torula	0	1,256	(175.1)	4.5	167.8	[146]1,923	7,770	87.5	68	9,261	Trace	63.55	22.95	201.4	Trace
2480		Yellowtail (Pacific coast), fillet, raw	0	626	95.3	24.5	0	----	----	----	----	----	----	----	----	----	----
		Yoghurt:															
2481		Made from partially skimmed milk	0	227	15.4	7.7	23.6	544	426	.2	231	649	320	.16	.79	.3	5
2482		Made from whole milk	0	281	13.6	15.4	22.2	504	396	.2	213	599	640	.14	.73	.3	5
		Youngberries. See Blackberries, item 417.															
2483		Zwieback	0	1,919	48.5	39.9	337.6	59	313	2.7	1,134	680	170	.22	.34	4.3	(0)

[45] See Appendix A, section on Protein, p. 162, and see Appendix B, section on foods containing considerable nonprotein nitrogen, p. 182

[52] Based on product with minimum level of enrichment. See also Notes on Foods, p. 171.

[140] Values for proximate constituents adjusted to 12 percent—the moisture content of wheat as it reaches the mill prior to tempering

[141] The acid ingredient most commonly used in self-rising flour. When sodium acid pyrophosphate in combination with either anhydrous monocalcium phosphate or calcium carbonate is used, the value for calcium is approximately 540 mg. per pound; for phosphorus, 2,470 mg.; for sodium, 6,170 mg

[142] 410 mg of potassium per pound contributed by flour. Small quantities of additional potassium may be provided by other ingredients.

[143] Values are based on the addition of iron, sodium (as salt), thiamine, riboflavin, and niacin, however, not all of these nutrients are added in every brand If the label does not indicate the addition of a specified nutrient, values per pound are: Iron, 10 0 mg , sodium, 45 mg.; thiamine, 0.14 mg ; riboflavin, 0.18 mg ; niacin, 15.9 mg.

[144] Product is sometimes fortified. For fortified compressed yeast, value for thiamine ranges from 11 8 to 113.9 mg per pound, for niacin, from 503 to 798 mg.

[145] Values range from 320 to 3,450 mg per pound.

[146] Values range from 270 to 4,530 mg. per pound.

TABLE 3.—SELECTED FATTY ACIDS IN FOODS

[Item numbers correspond to those of table 1. Letters a through g in column A designate items that have the same chemical composition for the edible portion in table 1 but differ in the amount of refuse, and also designate items made with different specified fats. Data in columns D through G apply to 100 grams of edible portion of the item, although it may be purchased with the refuse indicated in column L and described or implied in column B. For information on the nature of the refuse listed in column L, refer to the comparable item in table 2]

Item No.	Item	Principal sources of fat	Amount in 100 grams, edible portion: Total fat	Amount in 100 grams, edible portion: Total saturated fatty acids	Amount in 100 grams, edible portion: Unsaturated fatty acids: Oleic $C_{18}(-2H)$	Amount in 100 grams, edible portion: Unsaturated fatty acids: Linoleic $C_{18}(-4H)$	Amount in edible portion of 1 pound as purchased: Total fat	Amount in edible portion of 1 pound as purchased: Total saturated fatty acids	Amount in edible portion of 1 pound as purchased: Unsaturated fatty acids: Oleic $C_{18}(-2H)$	Amount in edible portion of 1 pound as purchased: Unsaturated fatty acids: Linoleic $C_{18}(-4H)$	Refuse from item as purchased
(A)	(B)	(C)	(D)	(E)	(F)	(G)	(H)	(I)	(J)	(K)	(L)
			Grams	*Grams*	*Grams*	*Grams*	*Grams*	*Grams*	*Grams*	*Grams*	*Percent*
5	Albacore, raw		7.6	3	1	Trace	34.5	14	6	Trace	0
	Almonds:										
8	Dried:										
a	In shell		54.2	4	36	11	125.4	10	84	25	49
b	Shelled		54.2	4	36	11	245.9	20	165	49	0
9	Roasted and salted		57.7	5	39	12	261.7	21	175	52	0
10	Almond meal, partially defatted		18.3	1	12	4	83.0	7	56	17	0
25	Apple brown betty	Butter, bread crumbs.	3.5	1	1	Trace					
	Avocados, raw:										
64	All commercial varieties		16.4	3	7	2	55.8	11	25	7	25
65	California, mainly Fuerte		17.0	3	8	2	58.6	12	26	8	24
66	Florida		11.0	2	5	1	33.4	7	15	4	33
	Bacon, cured:										
125	Raw:										
a	Sliced. (Use also for item 127.)		69.3	22	33	6	314.3	101	151	28	0
b	Slab		69.3	22	33	6	295.5	95	142	27	6
126	Cooked, broiled or fried, drained		52.0	17	25	5					
	Bacon, Canadian:										
128	Unheated. (Use also for item 129.)		14.4	5	6	1	65.3	23	27	6	0
144	Barbecue sauce	Corn oil	6.9	1	2	4	31.3	3	9	17	0
	Beans, common, mature seeds:										
	Canned, solids and liquid:										
156	With pork and tomato sauce	Pork	2.6	1	1	Trace	11.8	4	5	1	0
157	With pork and sweet sauce	do	4.7	2	2	Trace	21.3	8	9	2	0
207	Beechnuts:										
a	In shell		50.0	4	27	16	138.4	11	75	43	39
b	Shelled		50.0	4	27	16	226.8	18	122	70	0
	Beef:										
	Carcass, trimmed to retail level, raw:										
214	Choice grade		25.1	12	11	1	97.1	47	43	2	15
215	Good grade		20.4	10	9	Trace	78.3	38	34	2	15
216	Standard grade		15.8	8	7	Trace	59.5	29	26	1	17

No.		Food	Fat source									
		Retail cuts, trimmed to retail level:[1]										
		Entire chuck, 1st–5th ribs, arm, and neck, choice grade:										
218		Total edible, raw:										
	a	With bone		19. 6	9	9	Trace	75. 0	36	33	1	16
	b	Without bone		19. 6	9	9	Trace	88. 9	43	39	2	0
220		Separable lean, raw		7. 4	4	3	Trace	33. 6	16	15	1	0
222		Separable fat, raw		76. 3	37	34	2	346. 1	166	152	7	0
		Chuck rib, 5th, choice grade:										
223		Total edible, raw:										
	a	With bone		31. 4	15	14	1	120. 4	58	53	2	16
	b	Without bone		31. 4	15	14	1	142. 4	68	63	3	0
225		Separable lean, raw		11. 0	5	5	Trace	49. 9	24	22	1	0
227		Separable fat, raw		80. 0	38	35	2	362. 9	174	160	7	0
		Porterhouse steak, choice grade:										
257		Total edible, raw		36. 2	17	16	1	148. 8	71	65	3	9
297		Double-bone sirloin steak, choice grade, raw.		29. 1	14	13	1	108. 4	52	48	2	18
		Rib, entire, 6th–12th ribs, choice grade:										
327		Total edible, raw:										
	a	With bone		37. 4	18	16	1	156. 1	75	69	3	8
	b	Without bone		37. 4	18	16	1	169. 6	81	75	3	0
329		Separable lean, raw		11. 6	6	5	Trace	52. 6	25	23	1	0
331		Separable fat, raw		82. 2	39	36	2	372. 9	179	164	7	0
		Round, entire, choice grade:										
352		Total edible, raw:										
	a	With bone		12. 3	6	5	Trace	53. 9	26	24	1	3
	b	Without bone		12. 3	6	5	Trace	55. 8	27	25	1	0
354		Separable lean, raw		4. 7	2	2	Trace	21. 3	10	9	Trace	0
356		Separable fat, raw		73. 6	35	32	1	333. 8	160	147	7	0
		Rump, choice grade:										
357		Total edible, raw:										
	a	With bone		25. 3	12	11	1	97. 4	47	43	2	15
	b	Without bone		25. 3	12	11	1	114. 8	55	50	2	0
		Hamburger (ground beef):										
367		Lean, raw		10. 0	5	4	Trace	45. 4	22	20	1	0
369		Regular ground, raw		21. 2	10	9	Trace	96. 2	48	42	2	0
		Beef and vegetable stew:										
371		Cooked (home recipe with lean beef chuck).	Beef	4. 3	2	2	Trace					
373		Beef, canned, roast beef		13. 0	6	6	Trace	59. 0	28	26	1	0
		Beef, corned, boneless, medium-fat:										
374		Uncooked		25. 0	12	11	Trace	113 4	54	50	2	0
375		Cooked		30. 4	15	13	1					
377		Canned		12.	6	5	Trace	54.	26	24	1	0
379		Beef, corned-beef hash, canned	Beef	11. 3	5	5	Trace	51. 3	25	23	1	0
		Beef, dried, chipped.										
380		Uncooked		6. 3	3	3	Trace	28. 6	14	13	1	0
381		Cooked, creamed	Milk, butter, beef	10. 3	6	3	Trace					
		Beef potpie:										
382		Home-prepared, baked	Vegetable shortening, beef.	14. 5	4	9	1					
383		Commercial, frozen, unheated	do	9. 9	3	6	1	44. 9	14	25	3	0

[1] If fatty acid values are required for cuts listed in tables 1 and 2 but omitted here, select from column D or column H a value for total fat similar to that in the cut for which data are wanted and apply the indicated fatty acid values.

TABLE 3.—*Selected fatty acids in foods*—Continued

[Item numbers correspond to those of table 1. Letters a through g in column A designate items that have the same chemical composition for the edible portion in table 1 but differ in the amount of refuse, and also designate items made with different specified fats. Data in columns D through G apply to 100 grams of edible portion of the item, although it may be purchased with the refuse indicated in column L and described or implied in column B. For information on the nature of the refuse listed in column L, refer to the comparable item in table 2]

Item No.	Item	Principal sources of fat	Amount in 100 grams, edible portion: Total fat	Total saturated fatty acids	Unsaturated fatty acids: Oleic $C_{18}(-2H)$	Linoleic $C_{18}(-4H)$	Amount in edible portion of 1 pound as purchased: Total fat	Total saturated fatty acids	Unsaturated fatty acids: Oleic $C_{18}(-2H)$	Linoleic $C_{18}(-4H)$	Refuse from item as purchased
(A)	(B)	(C)	(D)	(E)	(F)	(G)	(H)	(I)	(J)	(K)	(L)
			Grams	*Grams*	*Grams*	*Grams*	*Grams*	*Grams*	*Grams*	*Grams*	*Percent*
410	Biscuits, baking powder, baked from home recipe, made with:										
a	Lard	Lard	17. 0	6	8	2	77. 1	29	35	8	0
b	Vegetable shortening. (Use also for items 411 and 412.)	Vegetable shortening.	17. 0	4	11	1	77. 1	18	49	6	0
	Biscuit dough, commercial:										
413	Chilled in cans	do	6. 4	1	4	1	29. 0	6	18	3	0
414	Frozen	do	11. 9	3	8	1	54. 0	12	34	5	0
	Biscuit mix and biscuits baked from mix:										
415	Mix, dry form	do	12. 6	3	8	1	57. 2	13	36	5	0
416	Biscuits, made with milk	do	9. 3	2	6	1	42. 2	9	26	4	0
443	Brazilnuts:										
a	In shell		66. 9	13	32	17	145. 6	29	70	38	52
b	Shelled		66. 9	13	32	17	303. 5	61	146	79	0
461	Breads, white, made with 3%–4% nonfat dry milk. (Use for all breads except Italian.)	Vegetable shortening.	3. 2	1	2	Trace	14. 5	3	8	2	0
475	Breadcrumbs, dry, grated	do	4. 6	1	3	1	20. 9	4	12	3	0
476	Bread pudding with raisins	Milk, butter, eggs, breadcrumbs.	6 1	3	2	Trace					
	Bread stuffing mix and stuffings prepared from mix:										
477	Mix, dry form	Vegetable shortening.	3. 8	1	2	1	17. 2	4	10	2	0
	Stuffing:										
478	Dry, crumbly: prepared with water, fat.	Vegetable shortening, butter.	21. 8	11	8	1					
479	Moist: prepared with water, egg, fat.	Butter, vegetable shortening, egg.	12. 8	7	5	1					
505	Butter		81.	46	27	2	367. 4	202	121	11	0
506	Butter oil or dehydrated butter		99. 5	55	33	3	451. 3	248	149	14	0
510	Buttermilk, dried		5. 3	3	2	Trace	24. 0	13	8	1	0

Item		Food	Fat sources									
		Cakes:										
		Baked from home recipes:										
532		Fruitcake, light:										
	a	Made with vegetable shortening.	Vegetable shortening, almonds, cream.	16.5	4	10	2	74.8	16	46	9	0
	b	Made with butter	Butter, almonds, cream.	15.7	6	7	2	71.2	26	33	7	0
534		Plain cake or cupcake without icing:										
	a	Made with vegetable shortening. (Use for other cakes made with vegetable shortening listed in tables 1 and 2 but omitted here.)	Vegetable shortening, egg, milk.	13.9	4	8	1	63.1	17	38	5	0
	b	Made with butter. (Use for other cakes made with butter listed in tables 1 and 2 but omitted here.)	Butter, egg, milk	12.7	7	4	1	57.6	30	20	2	0
		Pound:										
538		Old-fashioned (equal weights of flour, sugar, fat, eggs):										
	a	Made with vegetable shortening.	Egg, vegetable shortening.	29.5	7	18	2	133.8	32	83	10	0
	b	Made with butter	Egg, butter	26.4	14	9	1	119.8	62	41	5	0
539		Modified.										
	a	Made with vegetable shortening.	Vegetable shortening, egg, milk.	18.7	5	11	1	84.8	21	51	6	0
	b	Made with butter	Butter, egg, milk	16.0	8	6	1	72.6	36	26	3	0
540		Sponge	Egg	5.7	2	2	Trace	25.9	8	11	2	0
		Frozen, commercial, devil's food:										
547		With chocolate icing	Butter, vegetable shortening, chocolate, egg, milk.	17.6	9	7	1	79.8	41	30	3	0
548		With whipped-cream filling, chocolate icing.	Vegetable shortening, cream, chocolate, milk, egg.	21.9	7	12	1	99.3	32	54	6	0
		Cake mixes and cakes baked from mixes:										
		Cupcake:										
555		Mix, dry form. (Use for all commercial cake mixes.)	Vegetable shortening.	13.6	3	9	1	61.7	14	39	5	0
556		Cake, made with eggs, milk, without icing. (Use for all uniced cakes made from commercial cake mixes.)	Vegetable shortening, egg, milk.	12.0	3	7	1	54.4	14	32	4	0
557		Cake, made with eggs, milk, chocolate icing. (Use for all iced cakes made from commercial cake mixes.)	Vegetable shortening, chocolate, egg, milk.	12.6	5	6	1	57.2	23	28	3	0
		Cake icings:										
570		Caramel. (Use also for item 573.)	Butter, milk	6.7	4	2	Trace					
571		Chocolate	Chocolate, butter, milk.	13.9	8	5	Trace					
572		Coconut	Coconut	7.7	7	1	Trace					

TABLE 3.—*Selected fatty acids in foods*—Continued

[Item numbers correspond to those of table 1. Letters a through g in column A designate items that have the same chemical composition for the edible portion in table 1 but differ in the amount of refuse, and also designate items made with different specified fats. Data in columns D through G apply to 100 grams of edible portion of the item, although it may be purchased with the refuse indicated in column L and described or implied in column B. For information on the nature of the refuse listed in column L, refer to the comparable item in table 2]

Item No.	Item	Principal sources of fat	Amount in 100 grams, edible portion				Amount in edible portion of 1 pound as purchased				Refuse from item as purchased
			Total fat	Total saturated fatty acids	Unsaturated fatty acids		Total fat	Total saturated fatty acids	Unsaturated fatty acids		
					Oleic $C_{18}(-2H)$	Linoleic $C_{18}(-4H)$			Oleic $C_{18}(-2H)$	Linoleic $C_{18}(-4H)$	
(A)	(B)	(C)	(D)	(E)	(F)	(G)	(H)	(I)	(J)	(K)	(L)
			Grams	*Grams*	*Grams*	*Grams*	*Grams*	*Grams*	*Grams*	*Grams*	*Percent*
	Cake-icing mixes and icings made from mixes:										
	Chocolate fudge:										
575	Mix, dry form	Vegetable shortening, cocoa.	9.8	3	6	1	44.5	12	27	3	0
576	Icing, made with water, fat	Vegetable shortening, butter, cocoa.	14.4	6	7	1					
	Creamy fudge (contains nonfat dry milk):										
577	Mix, dry form. (Use also for item 578.)	Vegetable shortening, cocoa.	7.4	2	4	Trace	33.6	10	20	2	0
579	Icing, made with water, fat	Vegetable shortening, butter, cocoa.	15.2	7	7	1					
	Candy:										
580	Butterscotch. (Use also for item 602.)	Butter	3.4	2	1	Trace	15.4	8	5	Trace	0
586	Chocolate, sweet. (Use also for items 584, 585, 587.)	Chocolate, cacao butter.	35.1	20	13	1	159.2	89	59	3	0
	Chocolate-coated:										
590	Almonds	Almonds, chocolate, vegetable shortening.	43.7	7	29	6	198.2	34	132	25	0
591	Chocolate fudge. (Use also for items 582, 592, 601.)	Chocolate, vegetable shortening.	16.0	6	8	1	72.6	29	38	3	0
597	Honeycombed hard candy, with peanut butter. (Use also for items 595, 596.)	Vegetable shortening, chocolate, peanut butter.	19.5	6	11	2	88.5	26	50	10	0
599	Peanuts	Peanuts, chocolate, vegetable shortening.	41.3	11	22	7	187.3	49	98	33	0
600	Raisins. (Use also for items 593, 614.)	Chocolate, milk, cacao butter.	17.1	10	6	Trace	77.6	43	28	2	0

Item No.	Food	Fat source									
	Fudge:										
604	Chocolate, with nuts	Chocolate, animal and vegetable shortening, English walnuts.	17.4	6	5	6	78.9	26	24	27	0
605	Vanilla. (Use also for items 581, 583, 594, 598, 603, 606.)	Animal and vegetable shortening.	11.1	5	5	1	50.3	22	21	5	0
611	Peanut bars	Peanuts	32.2	7	14	9	146.1	32	63	42	0
612	Peanut brittle	do	10.4	2	4	3	47.2	10	20	14	0
	Sugar-coated:										
613	Almonds	Almonds	18.6	1	12	4	84.4	7	57	17	0
628	Cashew nuts		45.7	8	32	3	207.3	35	145	15	0
641	Charlotte russe, with ladyfingers, whipped-cream filling.	Cream, egg	14.6	7	5	1	66.2	33	23	3	0
	Cheeses, natural and processed, cheese foods, cheese spreads:										
	Natural cheeses:										
646	Cheddar (domestic type, commonly called American). (Use also for items 643, 644.)		32.2	18	11	1	146.1	80	48	4	0
647	Cottage (large or small curd), creamed.		4.2	2	1	Trace	19.1	10	6	1	0
649	Cream		37.7	21	12	1	171.0	94	56	5	0
652	Swiss (domestic). (Use also for all other cheeses and cheese foods.)		28.0	15	9	1	127.0	70	42	4	0
658	Cheese fondue, from home recipe	Cheese, egg, milk, butter.	18.3	9	7	2					
659	Cheese souffle, from home recipe	Butter, cheese, egg, milk.	17.1	9	6	1					
660	Cheese straws:										
a	Made with vegetable shortening	Vegetable shortening, milk, lard.	29.9	10	16	2	135.6	46	72	8	0
b	Made with lard	Lard, milk	29.9	13	12	2	135.6	59	56	11	0
	Chicken:[1]										
	Fryers:										
	Flesh, skin, and giblets:										
686	Raw		4.9	2	2	1	15.1	5	6	3	32
687	Cooked, fried	Vegetable shortening.	11.8	3	6	2					
	Skin only:										
692	Raw		17.1	5	6	3					
693	Cooked, fried	Vegetable shortening.	28.9	9	12	5					
	Dark meat with skin:										
698	Raw		6.3	2	2	1					
699	Cooked, fried	Vegetable shortening.	13.6	4	6	2					
	Dark meat without skin:										
702	Raw		3.8	1	1	1					
703	Cooked, fried	Vegetable shortening.	9.3	3	4	1					

[1] If fatty acid values are required for parts listed in tables 1 and 2 but omitted here, select from column D or column H a value for total fat similar to that in the part for which data are wanted and apply the indicated fatty acid values.

284-853 O - 79 - 9

TABLE 3.—*Selected fatty acids in foods*—Continued

[Item numbers correspond to those of table 1. Letters a through g in column A designate items that have the same chemical composition for the edible portion in table 1 but differ in the amount of refuse, and also designate items made with different specified fats. Data in columns D through G apply to 100 grams of edible portion of the item, although it may be purchased with the refuse indicated in column L and described or implied in column B. For information on the nature of the refuse listed in column L, refer to the comparable item in table 2]

Item No.	Item	Principal sources of fat	Amount in 100 grams, edible portion				Amount in edible portion of 1 pound as purchased				Refuse from item as purchased
			Total fat	Total saturated fatty acids	Unsaturated fatty acids		Total fat	Total saturated fatty acids	Unsaturated fatty acids		
					Oleic $C_{18}(-2H)$	Linoleic $C_{18}(-4H)$			Oleic $C_{18}(-2H)$	Linoleic $C_{18}(-4H)$	
(A)	(B)	(C)	(D)	(E)	(F)	(G)	(H)	(I)	(J)	(K)	(L)
			Grams	*Grams*	*Grams*	*Grams*	*Grams*	*Grams*	*Grams*	*Grams*	*Percent*
	Chicken—Continued										
	Hens and cocks:										
	Total edible:										
731	Raw		24.8	8	9	5	82.1	26	31	16	27
732	Cooked, stewed		29.5	9	11	6					
	Flesh and skin:										
735	Raw		18.8	6	7	4					
736	Cooked, stewed		22.8	7	9	5					
747	Chicken, canned, meat only, boned		11.7	4	4	2	53.1	17	20	11	0
748	Chicken a la king, cooked, from home recipe.	Chicken, vegetable shortening, cream, egg, milk.	14.0	5	7	1					
749	Chicken fricassee, cooked, from home recipe.	Chicken	9.3	3	4	2					
	Chicken potpie										
750	Home-prepared, baked	Vegetable shortening, cream, chicken, butter.	13.5	5	7	1					
751	Commercial, frozen, unheated	Vegetable shortening, chicken, cream, corn oil.	11.5	3	6	1	52.2	13	29	6	0
752	Chicken and noodles, cooked, from home recipe.	Chicken, egg	7.7	2	3	1					
753	Chickpeas or garbanzos, mature seeds, dry, raw.		4.8	Trace	2	2	21.8	2	11	8	0
	Chili con carne, canned:										
756	With beans	Beef	6.1	3	3	Trace	27.7	13	12	1	0
757	Without beans	do	14.8	7	7	Trace	67.2	32	30	1	0
759	Chocolate, bitter or baking		53.0	30	20	1	240.4	135	89	5	0
	Chocolate sirup:										
760	Thin type		2.0	1	1	Trace	9.1	5	3	Trace	0
761	Fudge type	Chocolate, animal and vegetable shortening, milk	13.7	7	5	Trace	62.1	31	20	2	0

		Chop suey, with meat:										
762		Cooked, from home recipe	Butter, beef, pork	6.8	3	2	Trace					
763		Canned	Pork, beef, corn oil.	3.2	1	1	Trace	14.5	5	6	1	0
764		Chow mein, chicken (without noodles), cooked, from home recipe.	Chicken, corn oil, soybeans.	4.0	1	1	1					
		Cocoa- and chocolate-flavored beverage powders:										
778		Cocoa powder with nonfat dry milk.	Cocoa, milk	2.9	2	1	Trace	13.2	7	4	Trace	0
779		Cocoa powder without milk	Cocoa	2.0	1	1	Trace	9.1	5	3	Trace	0
780		Mix for hot chocolate	Chocolate, milk	10.6	6	4	Trace	48.1	27	18	1	0
		Cocoa, dry powder:										
		High-fat or breakfast:										
781–782		Plain and processed with alkali		23.7	13	9	Trace	107.5	60	40	2	0
		Medium-fat:										
		High-medium fat:										
783–784		Plain and processed with alkali.		19.0	11	7	Trace	86.2	48	32	2	0
		Low-medium fat:										
785–786		Plain and processed with alkali.		12.7	7	5	Trace	57.6	32	21	1	0
787		Low-fat		7.9	4	3	Trace	35.8	20	13	1	0
788		Coconut cream (liquid expressed from grated coconut meat).		32.2	28	2	Trace					
		Coconut meat:										
789		Fresh:										
	a	In shell		35.3	30	2	Trace	83.3	72	6	Trace	48
	b	Shelled		35.3	30	2	Trace	160.1	138	11	Trace	0
		Dried:										
790		Unsweetened		64.9	56	5	Trace	294.4	253	21	Trace	0
791		Sweetened, shredded		39.1	34	3	Trace	177.4	153	12	Trace	0
792		Coconut milk (liquid expressed from mixture of grated coconut meat and water).		24.9	22	2	Trace					
		Coleslaw, made with:										
801		French dressing (homemade):										
	a	Made with corn oil	Corn oil	12.3	1	3	6					
	b	Made with cottonseed oil	Cottonseed oil	12.3	3	3	6					
802		French dressing (commercial). (Use also for item 804.)	Soybean oil, cottonseed oil, corn oil.	7.3	1	2	4					
803		Mayonnaise	do	14.0	2	3	7					
		Cookies:										
		Brownies with nuts:										
813		Baked from home recipe:										
	a	Made with vegetable shortening.	Pecans, vegetable shortening, chocolate, egg.	31.3	7	18	4	142.0	32	83	17	0
	b	Made with butter. (Use also for item 819.)	Pecans, butter, chocolate, egg.	29.9	10	14	3	135.6	45	64	14	0
		Chocolate chip:										
817		Baked from home recipe:										
	a	Made with vegetable shortening.	Vegetable shortening, chocolate, walnuts, egg.	30.1	8	16	4	136.5	37	72	19	0
	b	Made with butter	Butter, chocolate, walnuts, egg.	28.1	13	9	3	127.5	60	40	15	0

TABLE 3.—*Selected fatty acids in foods*—Continued

[Item numbers correspond to those of table 1. Letters a through g in column A designate items that have the same chemical composition for the edible portion in table 1 but differ in the amount of refuse, and also designate items made with different specified fats. Data in columns D through G apply to 100 grams of edible portion of the item, although it may be purchased with the refuse indicated in column L and described or implied in column B. For information on the nature of the refuse listed in column L, refer to the comparable item in table 2]

Item No.	Item	Principal sources of fat	Amount in 100 grams, edible portion				Amount in edible portion of 1 pound as purchased				Refuse from item as purchased
			Total fat	Total saturated fatty acids	Unsaturated fatty acids		Total fat	Total saturated fatty acids	Unsaturated fatty acids		
					Oleic $C_{18}(-2H)$	Linoleic $C_{18}(-4H)$			Oleic $C_{18}(-2H)$	Linoleic $C_{18}(-4H)$	
(A)	(B)	(C)	(D)	(E)	(F)	(G)	(H)	(I)	(J)	(K)	(L)
			Grams	*Grams*	*Grams*	*Grams*	*Grams*	*Grams*	*Grams*	*Grams*	*Percent*
	Cookies—Continued										
820	Fig bars. (Use also for items 821, 822, 825, 828.)	Vegetable shortening, egg, milk.	5.6	1	3	Trace	25.4	6	15	2	0
823	Macaroons	Coconut, almonds	23.2	16	5	1	105.2	71	22	5	0
831	Sugar, soft, thick:										
	Baked from home recipe:										
a	Made with vegetable shortening. (Use also for items 814, 816, 818, 826, 827, 829, 830, 832, 833.)	Vegetable shortening, egg, milk.	16.8	4	10	1	76.2	19	47	6	0
b	Made with butter. (Use also for items 815, 824.)	Butter, egg, milk	15.2	8	5	1	69.0	36	23	3	0
	Cooky mixes and cookies baked from mixes:										
	Brownie:										
	Complete mix:										
834	Dry form	Vegetable shortening, cocoa, egg.	12.0	3	7	1	54.4	14	33	4	0
835	Brownies, made with water and nuts.	Walnuts, vegetable shortening, cocoa, egg.	18.7	3	7	7	84.8	13	30	31	0
	Incomplete mix:										
836	Dry form	Vegetable shortening, cocoa.	16.4	4	10	1	74.4	19	47	5	0
837	Brownies made with egg, water, nuts.	Vegetable shortening, walnuts, cocoa, egg.	20.1	4	9	5	91.2	18	43	22	0
838	Plain mix, dry form. (Use also for items 839, 840.)	Vegetable shortening.	24.2	6	16	2	109.8	25	71	8	0
841	Cooky dough, plain, chilled in roll, unbaked. (Use also for item 842.)	Vegetable shortening, egg.	22.6	5	14	2	102.5	24	66	8	0
843	Corn, field, whole-grain, raw		3.9	Trace	1	2	17.7	2	6	8	0
860	Corn flour		2.6	Trace	1	1	11.8	1	4	5	0

861	Corn fritters	Vegetable shortening, egg, milk, butter.	21.5	5	13	2					
875	Corn pudding	Milk, vegetable shortening, egg.	4.7	2	2	Trace					
	Cornbread, baked from home recipe:										
876	Cornbread, southern style, made with whole-ground cornmeal. (Use also for items 877, 878, 879.)	Lard, egg	7.2	2	3	1					
880	Spoonbread, made with white whole-ground cornmeal.	Lard, egg, milk	11.4	4	5	1					
	Cornbread mix and cornbread baked from mix:										
881	Mix, dry form	Vegetable shortening, egg.	12.8	3	8	1	58.1	14	35	5	0
882	Cornbread, made with egg, milk	Vegetable shortening, milk, egg.	8.4	3	4	1					
	Cornmeal, white or yellow:										
883	Whole-ground, unbolted. (Use also for item 884.)		3.9	Trace	1	2	17.7	2	6	8	0
889	Self-rising, whole-ground, with soft wheat flour added. (Use also for item 890.)		2.9	Trace	1	1	13.2	1	4	6	0
895	Cottonseed flour		9.8	2	2	5	44.5	11	9	22	0
	Crackers:										
912	Cheese. (Use also for item 911.)	Vegetable shortening, butter, cheese.	21.3	8	10	1	96.6	36	47	6	0
913	Graham, chocolate-coated	Vegetable shortening, chocolate.	23.5	7	15	1	106.6	31	69	3	0
916	Saltines. (Use also for other crackers not itemized here.)	Vegetable shortening.	12.0	3	7	1	54.4	12	34	6	0
917	Sandwich type, peanut-cheese	Vegetable shortening, cheese, peanut butter.	23.9	6	13	4	108.4	28	57	18	0
	Cream, fluid:										
928	Half-and-half (cream and milk)		11.7	6	4	Trace	53.1	29	18	2	0
929	Light, coffee, or table		20.6	11	7	1	93.4	51	31	3	0
930	Light whipping		31.3	17	10	1	142.0	78	47	4	0
931	Heavy whipping		37.6	21	12	1	170.6	94	56	5	0
932	Cream substitutes; e g, dried, containing cream, skim milk (calcium reduced) and lactose. (Use also for item 933.)		26.7	15	9	1	121.1	67	40	4	0
934	Cream puffs with custard filling	Vegetable shortening, egg, milk.	13.9	4	8	1	63.1	19	35	4	0
948	Custard, baked	Milk, egg	5.5	3	2	Trace					
	Doughnuts:										
957	Cake type	Vegetable shortening, egg.	18.6	4	12	1	84.4	20	52	6	0
958	Yeast-leavened	Vegetable shortening, egg.	26.7	6	17	2	121.1	28	78	9	0
965	Eclairs with custard filling and chocolate icing.	Vegetable shortening, egg, milk, chocolate, butter.	13.6	4	7	1	61.7	19	33	4	0

Table 3.—*Selected fatty acids in foods*—Continued

[Item numbers correspond to those of table 1. Letters a through g in column A designate items that have the same chemical composition for the edible portion in table 1 but differ in the amount of refuse, and also designate items made with different specified fats. Data in columns D through G apply to 100 grams of edible portion of the item, although it may be purchased with the refuse indicated in column L and described or implied in column B. For information on the nature of the refuse listed in column L, refer to the comparable item in table 2]

Item No.		Item	Principal sources of fat	Amount in 100 grams, edible portion: Total fat	Amount in 100 grams, edible portion: Total saturated fatty acids	Amount in 100 grams, edible portion: Unsaturated fatty acids: Oleic $C_{18}(-2H)$	Amount in 100 grams, edible portion: Unsaturated fatty acids: Linoleic $C_{18}(-4H)$	Amount in edible portion of 1 pound as purchased: Total fat	Amount in edible portion of 1 pound as purchased: Total saturated fatty acids	Amount in edible portion of 1 pound as purchased: Unsaturated fatty acids: Oleic $C_{18}(-2H)$	Amount in edible portion of 1 pound as purchased: Unsaturated fatty acids: Linoleic $C_{18}(-4H)$	Refuse from item as purchased
(A)		(B)	(C)	(D)	(E)	(F)	(G)	(H)	(I)	(J)	(K)	(L)
				Grams	*Grams*	*Grams*	*Grams*	*Grams*	*Grams*	*Grams*	*Grams*	*Percent*
966		Eel, American, raw:										
	a	With bones		18.3	4	7		63.1	15	23		24
	b	Without bones		18.3	4	7		83.0	19	30		0
967		Eel, smoked		27.8	6	10		126.1	29	45		0
		Eggs, chicken:										
		Raw:										
968		Whole										
	a	Fresh		11.5	4	5	1	45.9	15	20	3	11
	b	Frozen		11.5	4	3	1	52.2	17	23	4	0
		Yolks:										
970		Fresh		30.6	10	13	2	138.8	44	61	10	0
971		Frozen		26.9	9	12	2	122.0	39	54	9	0
972		Frozen, sugared		24.0	8	11	2	108.9	35	48	8	0
		Cooked:										
973		Fried	Egg, butter	17.2	6	7	1					
974		Hard-cooked. (Use also for items 975, 976, 977.)		11.5	4	5	1					
		Dried:										
978		Whole. (Use also for item 979.)		41.2	13	18	3	186.9	60	82	13	0
982		Yolk		56.6	18	25	4	256.7	82	113	18	0
999		Fats, cooking:										
	a	Vegetable fat		100.0	23	65	7	453.6	104	295	32	0
	b	Animal and vegetable fat		100.0	43	41	11	453.6	195	186	50	0
1008		Filberts (hazelnuts):										
	a	In shell		62.4	3	34	10	130.2	7	70	21	54
	b	Shelled		62.4	3	34	10	283.0	14	153	45	0
1108		Ham croquette	Butter, ham, vegetable shortening.	15.1	6	7	1					
		Herring, raw:										
1124		Atlantic:										
	a	Whole		11.3	2		2	26.1	5		5	49
	b	Flesh only. (Use also for items 1126–1132.)		11.3	2		2	51.3	10		10	0
1125		Pacific, flesh only		2.6	Trace		Trace	11.8	2		2	0

1133		Hickorynuts:										
	a	In shell		68.7	6	47	12	109.1	9	74	20	65
	b	Shelled		68.7	6	47	12	311.6	25	212	56	0
1140		Ice cream and frozen custard, regular, approximately 12% fat. (Use also for items 1139, 1141.)		12.5	7	4	Trace	56.7	31	19	2	0
1142		Ice cream cones	Vegetable shortening.	2.4	1	1	Trace	10.9	2	6	2	0
1143		Ice milk		5.1	3	2	Trace	23.1	13	8	1	0
		Lamb: [1]										
1176		Composite of cuts (leg, loin, rib, and shoulder, trimmed to retail level): Choice grade.		21.3	12	8	1	81.3	46	29	2	16
1178		Separable fat, cooked		75.6	42	27	2	---	---	---	---	---
		Retail cuts, trimmed to retail level:										
		Leg, choice grade:										
1184		Total edible, raw:										
	a	With bone		16.2	9	6	Trace	61.7	35	22	2	16
	b	Without bone		16.2	9	6	Trace	73.5	41	26	2	0
1186		Separable lean, raw		5.0	3	2	Trace	22.7	13	8	1	0
1188		Separable fat, raw		72.2	40	26	2	327.5	183	118	10	0
		Rib, choice grade:										
1214		Total edible, raw:										
	a	With bone		30.4	17	11	1	110.2	62	40	3	20
	b	Without bone		30.4	17	11	1	137.9	77	50	4	0
1216		Separable lean, raw		8.4	5	3	Trace	38.1	21	14	1	0
1218		Separable fat, raw		77.1	43	28	2	349.7	196	126	10	0
		Shoulder, choice grade:										
1229		Total edible, raw:										
	a	With bone		23.9	13	9	1	92.0	52	33	3	15
	b	Without bone		23.9	13	9	1	108.4	60	39	3	0
1231		Separable lean, raw		7.7	4	3	Trace	34.9	20	13	1	0
1233		Separable fat, raw		70.1	39	25	2	318.0	178	114	10	0
1241		Lard		100.0	38	46	10	453.6	172	209	45	0
		Liver, hog:										
1273		Raw		3.7	1	1	Trace	16.8	6	5	1	0
1274		Cooked, fried	Vegetable shortening.	11.5	3	5	1	---	---	---	---	---
		Macaroni and cheese:										
1304		Baked, made from home recipe	Cheese, margarine, milk, butter.	11.1	5	5	1	---	---	---	---	---
1305		Canned	Cheese, corn oil, milk.	4.0	2	1	1	18.1	8	6	3	0
1317		Margarine, first ingredient named on label:										
	a	Hydrogenated or hardened fat		81.	18	47	14	367.4	82	215	65	0
	b	Liquid oil		81.	19	31	29	367.4	86	141	132	0
		Milk, cow:										
		Fluid (pasteurized and raw):										
1321		Whole, 3.7% fat. (Use also for item 1320.)		3.7	2	1	Trace	16.8	9	6	1	0
1323		Partially skimmed, with 2% nonfat milk solids added.		2.0	1	1	Trace	9.1	5	3	Trace	0
1324		Canned, evaporated, unsweetened. (Use also for item 1325.)		7.9	4	3	Trace	35.8	20	12	1	0
1326		Dry, whole		27.5	15	9	1	124.7	69	41	4	0

[1] If fatty acid values are required for cuts listed in tables 1 and 2 but omitted here, select from column D or column H a value for total fat similar to that in the cut for which data are wanted and apply the indicated fatty acid values.

TABLE 3.—*Selected fatty acids in foods*—Continued

[Item numbers correspond to those of table 1. Letters a through g in column A designate items that have the same chemical composition for the edible portion in table 1 but differ in the amount of refuse, and also designate items made with different specified fats. Data in columns D through G apply to 100 grams of edible portion of the item, although it may be purchased with the refuse indicated in column L and described or implied in column B. For information on the nature of the refuse listed in column L, refer to the comparable item in table 2]

Item No.	Item	Principal sources of fat	Amount in 100 grams, edible portion				Amount in edible portion of 1 pound as purchased				Refuse from item as purchased
			Total fat	Total saturated fatty acids	Unsaturated fatty acids		Total fat	Total saturated fatty acids	Unsaturated fatty acids		
					Oleic $C_{18}(-2H)$	Linoleic $C_{18}(-4H)$			Oleic $C_{18}(-2H)$	Linoleic $C_{18}(-4H)$	
(A)	(B)	(C)	(D)	(E)	(F)	(G)	(H)	(I)	(J)	(K)	(L)
			Grams	*Grams*	*Grams*	*Grams*	*Grams*	*Grams*	*Grams*	*Grams*	*Percent*
	Milk, cow—Continued										
1331	Chocolate drink, fluid, commercial, made with skim milk. (Use also for item 1332.)	Cocoa	2.3	1	1	Trace	10.4	6	3	Trace	0
1333	Chocolate beverages, homemade, hot chocolate. (Use also for item 1334.)	Chocolate, milk	5.0	3	2	Trace					-
1335	Milk, goat, fluid		4.0	2	1	Trace	18.1	11	5	1	0
1336	Milk, human, U.S. samples		4.0	2	1	Trace	18.1	8	6	1	0
1338	Millet, proso (broomcorn, hogmillet), whole-grain.		2.9	1	1	1	13.2	4	3	5	0
	Muffins, baked from home recipes:										
1343	Plain. (Use also for item 1344.)	Vegetable shortening, egg.	10.1	2	6	1	45.8	11	28	4	0
	Other:										
1345	Blueberry	Vegetable shortening, egg, milk.	9.3	3	5	1	42.2	12	23	3	0
1346	Bran	Butter, egg, milk	9.8	5	3	1	44.5	21	16	3	0
1347	Corn. (Use also for item 1348.)	Lard, milk, egg	10.1	4	4	1	45.8	18	20	5	0
	Muffin mixes, corn; and muffins baked from mixes:										
1349	Mix, dry form. (Use also for item 1351.)	Vegetable shortening.	11.5	3	7	1	52.2	12	33	5	0
1350	Muffins, made with egg, milk. (Use also for item 1352.)	Vegetable shortening, milk, egg	10.6	3	6	1	48.1	13	28	4	0
1377	Noodles, egg, dry form. (Use also for item 1379.)	Egg	4.6	1	2	Trace	20.9	7	9	1	0
	Oat products used mainly as hot breakfast cereals:										
1382	Oat cereal with toasted wheat germ and soy grits, dry form.		9.0	2	2	4	40.8	7	11	18	0
1388	Oat and wheat cereal, dry form. (Use also for items 1384, 1386, 1390, 1392.)		5.0	1	2	2	22.7	5	7	9	0

1401		Oils, salad or cooking:										
	a	Corn		100. 0	10	28	53	453. 6	45	127	240	0
	b	Cottonseed		100. 0	25	21	50	453. 6	113	95	227	0
	c	Olive		100. 0	11	76	7	453. 6	50	345	32	0
	d	Peanut		100. 0	18	47	29	453. 6	82	213	132	0
	e	Safflower		100. 0	8	15	72	453. 6	36	68	327	0
	f	Sesame		100. 0	14	38	42	453. 6	64	172	191	0
	g	Soybean		100. 0	15	20	52	453. 6	68	91	236	0
		Olives, pickled; canned or bottled:										
		Ripe:										
1407		Ascolano (extra large, mammoth, giant, jumbo), (use also for items 1406, 1408):										
	a	With pits and liquid		13. 8	2	10	1	28. 2	3	21	2	55
	b	With liquid		13. 8	2	10	1	29. 4	3	22	2	53
1409		Mission (small, medium, large, extra large):										
	a	With pits and liquid		20. 1	2	15	1	41. 0	5	31	3	55
	b	With liquid		20. 1	2	15	1	42. 9	5	33	3	53
1410		Sevillano (giant, jumbo, colossal, supercolossal):										
	a	With pits and liquid		9. 5	1	7	1	19. 4	2	15	1	55
	b	With liquid		9. 5	1	7	1	20. 3	2	15	1	53
1411		Ripe, salt-cured, oil-coated, Greek style.		35. 8	4	27	3	103. 9	11	79	7	20
1453		Pancakes, baked from home recipe. (Use also for item 1454.)		7. 0	2	4	1					
		Pancakes, baked from mixes, plain and buttermilk:										
1456		Made with milk. (Use also for item 1459.)	Vegetable shortening, milk.	5. 6	2	3	Trace					
1457		Made with egg, milk. (Use also for item 1460.)	Vegetable shortening, milk, egg.	7. 3	3	4	1					
1475		Pastinas, egg, enriched, dry form	Egg	4. 1	1	2	Trace	18. 6	6	8	1	0
		Peanuts:										
1492		Raw, with skins (use also for item 1493):										
	a	In shell		47. 5	10	20	14	157. 3	35	68	46	27
	b	Shelled		47. 5	10	20	14	215. 5	47	93	63	0
1494		Boiled		31. 5	7	14	9					
1495		Roasted with skins (use also for item 1496):										
	a	In shell		48. 7	11	21	14	148. 0	33	64	43	33
	b	Shelled		48. 7	11	21	14	220. 9	49	95	64	0
1499		Peanut butters made with moderate amounts of added fat, sweetener, salt. (Use also for items 1497, 1498, 1500.)	Peanuts, vegetable shortening.	50. 6	9	25	14	229. 5	42	112	62	0
1501		Peanut flour, defatted		9. 2	2	4	3	41. 7	9	18	12	0
1536		Pecans:										
	a	In shell		71. 2	5	45	14	171. 2	12	108	34	47
	b	Shelled		71. 2	5	45	14	323. 0	23	203	65	0
1547		Peppers, sweet, garden varieties, immature green, cooked, stuffed with beef and crumbs.	Beef, butter, bread, milk.	5. 5	3	2	Trace					

TABLE 3.—*Selected fatty acids in foods*—Continued

[Item numbers correspond to those of table 1. Letters a through g in column A designate items that have the same chemical composition for the edible portion in table 1 but differ in the amount of refuse, and also designate items made with different specified fats. Data in columns D through G apply to 100 grams of edible portion of the item, although it may be purchased with the refuse indicated in column L and described or implied in column B. For information on the nature of the refuse listed in column L, refer to the comparable item in table 2]

Item No.		Item	Principal sources of fat	Amount in 100 grams, edible portion: Total fat	Total saturated fatty acids	Unsaturated fatty acids: Oleic $C_{18}(-2H)$	Linoleic $C_{18}(-4H)$	Amount in edible portion of 1 pound as purchased: Total fat	Total saturated fatty acids	Unsaturated fatty acids: Oleic $C_{18}(-2H)$	Linoleic $C_{18}(-4H)$	Refuse from item as purchased
(A)		(B)	(C)	(D)	(E)	(F)	(G)	(H)	(I)	(J)	(K)	(L)
				Grams	*Grams*	*Grams*	*Grams*	*Grams*	*Grams*	*Grams*	*Grams*	*Percent*
		Pies, baked:										
1566		Apple (use for all pies but pecan):										
	a	Made with vegetable shortening	Vegetable shortening, butter.	11.1	3	7	1	50.3	12	32	4	0
	b	Made with lard	Lard, butter	11.1	4	5	1	50.3	19	23	5	0
1580		Pecan:										
	a	Made with vegetable shortening	Pecans, vegetable shortening, egg.	22.9	3	14	4	103.9	14	65	16	0
	b	Made with lard	Pecans, lard, egg	22.9	4	13	4	103.9	18	59	17	0
1589		Pies, frozen, in unbaked form, apple. (Use also for other frozen pies, baked or unbaked.)	Vegetable shortening.	8.3	2	5	1	37.6	9	24	3	0
		Pie mix, coconut custard, and pie baked from mix:										
1595		Mix, filling and piecrust, dry form	Vegetable shortening, coconut.	20.0	8	10	1	90.7	36	45	5	0
1596		Pie prepared with egg yolk and milk, baked.	Vegetable shortening, coconut, milk, egg.	7.9	3	4	Trace					
1597		Piecrust or plain pastry, unbaked (use also for items 1598, 1599, 1600):										
	a	Made with vegetable shortening	Vegetable shortening.	31.0	7	19	2					
	b	Made with lard	Lard	31.0	12	14	3					
1601		Piecrust mix (including stick form, dry). (Use also for item 1602.)	Vegetable shortening.	32.7	7	21	3	148.3	34	95	12	0
1605		Pigs' feet, pickled		14.8	5	6	1	67.1	24	28	6	0
1626		Pistachio nuts:										
	a	In shell		53.7	5	35	10	121.8	12	79	23	50
	b	Shelled		53.7	5	35	10	243.6	24	158	46	0
		Pizza, with cheese:										
1628		From home recipe, baked with cheese topping. (Use also for item 1629.)	Cheese, vegetable shortening, olive oil.	8.3	3	4	1	37.6	15	17	2	0
1630		Chilled, partially baked. (Use also for item 1631.)	do	5.8	2	3	1	26.3	9	13	2	0

1632		Frozen, partially baked. (Use also for item 1633.)	do	6.6	2	3	Trace	29.9	11	15	2	0
		Plate dinners, frozen, commercial, unheated:										
1635		Beef pot roast, whole oven-browned potatoes, peas, and corn.	Beef, butter	3.2	2	1	Trace	14.5	7	6	Trace	0
1636		Chicken, fried; mashed potatoes; and mixed vegetables (carrots, peas, corn, beans).	Vegetable shortening, chicken, butter.	8.5	3	3	1	36.2	13	13	6	6
1638		Turkey, sliced; mashed potatoes; and peas.	Turkey, butter	3.0	1	1	Trace	13.6	6	5	1	0
		Popcorn, popped:										
1654		Plain. (Use also for item 1653.)		5.0	1	1	3	22.7	2	6	12	0
1655		Oil and salt added:										
	a	Coconut oil added	Coconut oil	21.8	15	2	2	98.9	72	11	9	0
	b	Butter added	Butter	21.8	10	7	3	99.3	47	32	12	0
1656		Sugar-coated	Coconut oil	3.5	1	1	1	15.9	5	3	6	0
1657		Popovers, baked (from home recipe)	Vegetable shortening, egg, milk.	9.2	3	4	1	------	------	------	------	------
		Pork, fresh, medium-fat class: [1]										
		Carcass, raw:										
1662		Total edible		52.0	19	22	5	185.2	67	78	17	21
1663		Separable lean		10.5	4	4	1	47.6	17	20	4	0
1664		Separable fat		83.7	30	35	8	379.7	137	159	34	0
		Composite of trimmed lean cuts, ham, loin, shoulder, and spareribs:										
1682		Total edible, raw:										
	a	With bone and skin		26.7	10	11	2	99.8	36	42	9	18
	b	Without bone and skin		26.7	10	11	2	121.1	44	51	11	0
1684		Separable lean, raw		10.2	4	4	1	46.3	17	19	4	0
1686		Separable fat, raw		81.3	29	34	7	368.8	133	155	33	0
		Retail cuts, trimmed to retail level:										
		Ham:										
1698		Total edible, raw:										
	a	With bone and skin		26.6	10	11	2	102.6	37	43	9	15
	b	Without bone and skin		26.6	10	11	2	120.7	43	51	11	0
1700		Separable lean, raw		7.5	3	3	1	34.0	12	14	3	0
1702		Separable fat, raw		80.7	29	34	7	366.1	132	154	33	0
		Loin:										
1715		Total edible, raw:										
	a	With bone		24.9	9	10	2	89.0	32	37	8	21
	b	Without bone		24.9	9	10	2	112.9	41	47	10	0
1718		Separable lean, raw		11.4	4	5	1	51.7	19	22	5	0
1721		Separable fat, raw		77.7	28	33	7	352.4	127	148	32	0
		Boston butt:										
1734		Total edible, raw:										
	a	With bone and skin		24.5	9	10	2	104.1	37	44	9	6
	b	Without bone and skin		24.5	9	10	2	111.1	40	47	10	0
1736		Separable lean, raw		11.3	4	5	1	51.3	18	22	5	0
1738		Separable fat, raw		74.6	27	31	7	338.4	122	142	30	0
		Picnic:										
1749		Total edible, raw:										
	a	With bone and skin		24.7	9	10	2	92.2	33	39	8	18
	b	Without bone and skin		24.7	9	10	2	112.0	40	47	10	0

[1] If fatty acid values are required for cuts listed in tables 1 and 2 but omitted here, select from column D or column H a value for total fat similar to that in the cut for which data are wanted and apply the indicated fatty acid values

TABLE 3.—*Selected fatty acids in foods*—Continued

[Item numbers correspond to those of table 1. Letters a through g in column A designate items that have the same chemical composition for the edible portion in table 1 but differ in the amount of refuse, and also designate items made with different specified fats. Data in columns D through G apply to 100 grams of edible portion of the item, although it may be purchased with the refuse indicated in column L and described or implied in column B. For information on the nature of the refuse listed in column L, refer to the comparable item in table 2]

Item No.		Item	Principal sources of fat	Amount in 100 grams, edible portion				Amount in edible portion of 1 pound as purchased				Refuse from item as purchased
				Total fat	Total saturated fatty acids	Unsaturated fatty acids		Total fat	Total saturated fatty acids	Unsaturated fatty acids		
						Oleic $C_{18}(-2H)$	Linoleic $C_{18}(-4H)$			Oleic $C_{18}(-2H)$	Linoleic $C_{18}(-4H)$	
(A)		(B)	(C)	(D)	(E)	(F)	(G)	(H)	(I)	(J)	(K)	(L)
				Grams	*Grams*	*Grams*	*Grams*	*Grams*	*Grams*	*Grams*	*Grams*	*Percent*
		Pork, fresh, medium-fat class[1]—Con.										
		Retail cuts, trimmed to retail level—Con.										
		Picnic—Continued										
1751		Separable lean, raw		7.4	3	3	1	33.6	12	14	3	0
1753		Separable fat, raw		73.2	26	31	7	332.0	120	139	30	0
		Spareribs:										
1761		Total edible, raw:										
	a	With bone		33.2	12	14	3	89.7	32	38	8	40
	b	Without bone		33.2	12	14	3	150.6	54	63	14	0
		Pork, cured, medium-fat class:										
		Dry, long-cure, country-style:										
1766		Ham:										
	a	With bone		35	13	15	3	138	50	58	12	13
	b	Without bone		35	13	15	3	159	57	67	14	0
		Light-cure, commercial:										
		Ham:										
1768		Total edible, raw:										
	a	With bone and skin		23.0	8	10	2	89.7	32	38	8	14
	b	Without bone and skin		23.0	8	10	2	104.3	38	44	9	0
1770		Separable lean, raw		8.5	3	4	1	38.6	14	16	3	0
1772		Separable fat, raw		68.1	25	29	6	308.9	111	130	28	0
		Boston butt:										
1773		Total edible, raw:										
	a	With bone and skin		24.1	9	10	2	101.7	37	43	9	7
	b	Without bone and skin		24.1	9	10	2	109.3	39	46	10	0
1775		Separable lean, raw		12.3	4	5	1	55.8	20	23	5	0
1777		Separable fat, raw		60.2	22	25	5	273.1	98	115	25	0
		Picnic:										
1778		Total edible, raw:										
	a	With bone and skin		23.6	8	10	2	87.8	32	37	8	18
	b	Without bone and skin		23.6	8	10	2	107.0	39	45	10	0
1780		Separable lean, raw		8.4	3	4	1	38.1	14	16	3	0
1782		Separable fat, raw		58.3	21	24	5	264.4	95	111	24	0
1783		Pork, cured, canned, ham		12.3	4	5	1	55.8	20	23	5	0
1784		Pork and gravy, canned		17.8	6	7	2	80.7	29	34	7	0

	Potatoes:										
	Cooked:										
1789	French-fried	Cottonseed oil	13. 2	3	3	7					
1790	Fried from raw	Vegetable shortening.	14. 2	3	9	1					
1791	Hash-browned after holding overnight.	do	11. 7	3	8	1					
1793	Mashed, milk and butter added. (Use also for item 1795.)	Butter, milk	4. 3	2	1	Trace					
1794	Scalloped and au gratin, with cheese.	Cheese, butter, milk.	7. 9	4	3	Trace					
	Dehydrated, mashed, prepared from—										
1798	Flakes without milk. Water, milk, butter added.	Butter, milk	3. 2	2	1	Trace					
1800	Granules without milk. Water, milk, butter added.	do	3. 6	2	1	Trace					
1802	Granules with milk. Water, butter added.	Butter	2. 2	1	1	Trace					
	Frozen:										
1804	Diced, cooked, hash-browned	Cottonseed oil	11. 5	3	2	6					
1805	French-fried, not thawed. (Use also for item 1806.)	do	6. 5	2	1	3	29. 5	7	6	15	0
1808	Mashed, heated	Butter, milk	2. 8	2	1	Trace					
1809	Potato chips	Cottonseed oil	39. 8	10	8	20	180. 5	45	38	90	0
	Potato salad, from home recipe, made with—										
1811	Cooked salad dressing, seasonings	Butter, milk, egg	2. 8	1	1	Trace					
1812	Mayonnaise and French dressing, hard-cooked eggs, seasonings.	Soybean oil, cottonseed oil, corn oil, eggs.	9. 2	2	2	4					
1813	Potato sticks	Cottonseed oil	36. 4	9	8	18	165. 1	41	35	83	0
	Puddings with starch base, prepared from home recipes:										
1823	Chocolate	Milk, chocolate	4. 7	3	2	Trace					
1824	Vanilla (blanc mange)	Milk	3. 9	2	1	Trace					
	Pudding mixes and puddings made from mixes:										
	With starch base:										
1825	Mix, chocolate, dry form	Chocolate	2. 1	1	1	Trace	9. 5	5	4	Trace	0
1826	Pudding made with milk, cooked	Chocolate, milk	3. 0	2	1	Trace					
1828	Pudding made with milk, without cooking.	Milk, chocolate	2. 5	1	1	Trace					
	With vegetable gum base:										
1830	Pudding made with milk, cooked	Milk	3. 5	2	1	Trace					
1833	Pumpkin and squash seed kernels, dry:										
a	In hull		46. 7	8	17	20	156 8	28	56	66	26
b	Hulled		46 7	8	17	20	211 8	38	76	89	0
1840	Rabbit, domesticated, flesh only, raw		8.	3	3	1	28 7	11	10	3	21
1860	Rennin dessert, home-prepared with tablet. (Use also for items 1861, 1862, 1864.)	Milk	3. 5	2	1	Trace					
1891	Rice pudding with raisins	do	3. 1	2	1	Trace					
	Rolls and buns:										
1898	Baked from home recipe with milk. (Use also for item 1905.)	Vegetable shortening, milk, egg.	8. 7	2	5	1					

[1] If fatty acid values are required for cuts listed in tables 1 and 2 but omitted here, select from column D or column H a value for total fat similar to that in the cut for which data are wanted and apply the indicated fatty acid values

TABLE 3.—*Selected fatty acids in foods*—Continued

[Item numbers correspond to those of table 1. Letters a through g in column A designate items that have the same chemical composition for the edible portion in table 1 but differ in the amount of refuse, and also designate items made with different specified fats. Data in columns D through G apply to 100 grams of edible portion of the item, although it may be purchased with the refuse indicated in column L and described or implied in column B. For information on the nature of the refuse listed in column L, refer to the comparable item in table 2]

Item No.		Item	Principal sources of fat	Amount in 100 grams, edible portion: Total fat	Total saturated fatty acids	Unsaturated fatty acids: Oleic $C_{18}(-2H)$	Linoleic $C_{18}(-4H)$	Amount in edible portion of 1 pound as purchased: Total fat	Total saturated fatty acids	Unsaturated fatty acids: Oleic $C_{18}(-2H)$	Linoleic $C_{18}(-4H)$	Refuse from item as purchased
(A)		(B)	(C)	(D)	(E)	(F)	(G)	(H)	(I)	(J)	(K)	(L)
				Grams	*Grams*	*Grams*	*Grams*	*Grams*	*Grams*	*Grams*	*Grams*	*Percent*
		Rolls and buns—Continued										
		Commercial, ready-to-serve:										
1899		Danish pastry	Vegetable shortening, butter, egg.	23.5	7	14	2	106.6	30	62	8	0
1902		Plain (pan rolls). (Use also for items 1900, 1901, 1903, 1904, 1906–1916 incl.)	Vegetable shortening.	5.6	1	3	1	25.4	6	15	3	0
1918		Rusk	Vegetable shortening, egg, milk.	8.7	2	5	1	39.5	11	22	3	0
1927		Safflower seed kernels, dry:										
	a	In hull		59.5	5	9	43	137.6	11	21	99	49
	b	Hulled		59.5	5	9	43	270.0	22	41	194	0
1928		Safflower seed meal, partially defatted		8.2	1	1	6	37.2	3	6	27	0
		Salad dressings, commercial:										
		Blue and Roquefort cheese:										
1929		Regular	Soybean oil, cottonseed oil, corn oil, cheese.	52.3	11	11	25	237.2	48	52	114	0
1930		Special dietary (low-calorie) low-fat (approx. 5 Cal. per tsp.).	Cheese	5.9	3	2	Trace	26.8	15	9	1	0
		French:										
1932		Regular	Soybean oil, cottonseed oil, corn oil.	38.9	7	8	20	176.5	31	37	92	0
		Special dietary (low-calorie):										
1933		Low-fat (approx. 5 Cal. per tsp.).	do	4.3	1	1	2	19.5	3	4	10	0
1935		Medium-fat with artificial sweetener (approx. 10 Cal. per tsp.).	do	16.9	3	4	9	76.7	13	16	40	0
		Italian:										
1936		Regular	do	60.0	10	13	31	272.2	47	57	142	0
1937		Special dietary (low-calorie, approx. 2 Cal. per tsp.).	do	4.7	1	1	2	21.3	4	4	11	0

1938		Mayonnaise	Soybean oil, cottonseed oil, corn oil, egg.	79.9	14	17	40	362.4	64	79	183	0
1939		Russian	do	50.8	9	11	26	230.4	41	50	116	0
		Salad dressing (mayonnaise type):										
1940		Regular	do	42.3	8	9	21	191.9	35	42	95	0
1941		Special dietary (low-calorie, approx. 8 Cal. per tsp.).	do	12.7	2	3	6	57.6	10	13	29	0
		Thousand Island:										
1942		Regular	do	50.2	9	11	25	227.7	40	49	114	0
1943		Special dietary (low-calorie, approx. 10 Cal. per tsp.).	do	13.7	2	3	7	62.1	11	13	31	0
		Salad dressings, made from home recipe:										
1944		French:										
	a	Made with corn oil	Corn oil	70.1	7	20	37					
	b	Made with cottonseed oil	Cottonseed oil	70.1	18	15	35					
1945		Cooked	Butter, milk, egg	9.9	5	3	Trace					
		Salmon:										
		Chinook (king):										
1948		Raw:										
	a	With bones		15.6	5	5	Trace	62.3	19	18	1	12
	b	Without bones		15.6	5	5	Trace	70.8	22	21	1	0
1949		Canned, solids and liquid		14.0	4	4	Trace	63.5	20	19	1	0
		Pink (humpback):										
1954		Raw:										
	a	With bones		3.7	1	1	Trace	14.8	4	3	Trace	12
	b	Without bones		3.7	1	1	Trace	16.8	4	4	Trace	0
1955		Canned, solids and liquid		5.9	2	1	Trace	26.8	7	6	Trace	0
1964		Salt pork, raw		85.	32	39	5	371.	141	170	22	4
1965		Salt sticks, regular type. (Use also for item 1966.)	Vegetable shortening.	2.9	1	2	Trace	13.2	3	7	2	0
		Sausage, cold cuts, and luncheon meats:										
1986		Braunschweiger	Pork	27.4	10	12	2	124.3	45	52	11	0
1989		Capicola or Capacola	do	45.8	16	19	4	207.7	75	87	19	0
1992		Country-style sausage	do.[1]	31.1	11	13	3	141.1	51	59	13	0
1993		Deviled ham, canned	do	32.3	12	14	3	146.5	53	62	13	0
2001		Head cheese	do	22.0	8	9	2	99.8	36	42	9	0
		Luncheon meat:										
2005		Boiled ham	do	17.0	6	7	2	77.1	28	32	7	0
2006		Pork, cured ham or shoulder, chopped, spiced or unspiced, canned.	do	24.9	9	11	2	112.9	41	51	8	0
2009		Minced ham	do	16.9	6	7	2	76.7	28	32	7	0
		Pork sausage, links or bulk:										
2013		Raw	do	50.8	18	21	5	230.4	83	97	21	0
2014		Cooked	do	44.2	16	19	4					
2015		Pork sausage, canned, solids and liquid. (Use also for item 2016.)	do	38.4	14	16	3	174.2	63	73	16	0
2020		Souse	do	13.4	5	6	1	60.8	22	26	5	0
		Sesame seeds, dry:										
2032		Whole		49.1	7	19	21	222.7	31	85	94	0
2033		Decorticated		53.4	7	20	22	242.2	34	92	102	0
2058		Sorghum grain, all types		3.3	Trace	1	1	15.0	2	6	7	0

[1] Country-style sausage may at times contain some beef. For such products, these fatty acid values do not apply.

Table 3.—*Selected fatty acids in foods*—Continued

[Item numbers correspond to those of table 1. Letters a through g in column A designate items that have the same chemical composition for the edible portion in table 1 but differ in the amount of refuse, and also designate items made with different specified fats. Data in columns D through G apply to 100 grams of edible portion of the item, although it may be purchased with the refuse indicated in column L and described or implied in column B. For information on the nature of the refuse listed in column L, refer to the comparable item in table 2]

Item No.	Item	Principal sources of fat	Amount in 100 grams, edible portion				Amount in edible portion of 1 pound as purchased				Refuse from item as purchased
			Total fat	Total saturated fatty acids	Unsaturated fatty acids		Total fat	Total saturated fatty acids	Unsaturated fatty acids		
					Oleic $C_{18}(-2H)$	Linoleic $C_{18}(-4H)$			Oleic $C_{18}(-2H)$	Linoleic $C_{18}(-4H)$	
(A)	(B)	(C)	(D)	(E)	(F)	(G)	(H)	(I)	(J)	(K)	(L)
			Grams	*Grams*	*Grams*	*Grams*	*Grams*	*Grams*	*Grams*	*Grams*	*Percent*
	Soups, commercial:										
	Canned:										
	Chicken, cream of:										
2073	Condensed	Chicken, corn oil, milk.	4.8	1	1	2	21.8	3	6	10	0
2074	Prepared with equal volume of water.	do	2.4	Trace	1	1					
2075	Prepared with equal volume of milk. (Use for all soups with more than 2% total fat except mushroom.)	do	4.2	1	1	1					
	Mushroom, cream of:										
2088	Condensed	Corn oil, cream	8.0	1	2	4	36.3	5	10	18	0
2089	Prepared with equal volume of water.	do	4.0	1	1	2					
2090	Prepared with equal volume of milk.	Corn oil, milk, cream.	5.8	2	2	2					
	Dehydrated:										
2109	Beef noodle mix, dry form. (Use also for all other dehydrated soup mixes.)	Vegetable shortening, egg.	7.4	2	4	1	33.6	9	19	2	0
	Frozen:										
	Potato, cream of:										
2126	Condensed	Cream	4.3	2	1	Trace	19.5	11	6	1	0
2127	Prepared with equal volume of water.	do	2.2	1	1	Trace					
2128	Prepared with equal volume of milk.	Cream, milk	3.9	2	1	Trace					
	Soybeans:										
2135	Immature seeds, raw:										
a	In pods		5.1	1	1	3	12.3	2	2	6	47
b	Shelled. (Use also for items 2136, 2137, 2138.)		5.1	1	1	3	23.1	5	4	12	0
	Mature seeds, dry:										
2139	Raw		17.7	3	4	9	80.3	12	16	42	0
2140	Cooked		5.7	1	1	3					

Item No.	Food	Source of fat									
	Fermented products:										
2141	Natto (soybeans)		7. 4	1	1	4	33. 6	5	7	17	0
2142	Miso (cereal and soybeans)	Rice, soybean	4. 6	1	1	2	20. 9	3	4	11	0
2145	Soybean curd (tofu)		4. 2	1	1	2	19. 1	3	4	10	0
	Soybean flours:										
2146	Full-fat		20. 3	3	4	11	92. 1	14	18	48	0
2147	High-fat		12. 1	2	2	6	54. 9	8	11	29	0
2148	Low-fat		6. 7	1	1	3	30. 4	5		16	0
2151	Soybean milk, powder		20. 3	3	4	11	92. 1	14	18	48	0
	Soybean milk products, sweetened:										
2152	Liquid concentrate	Soybean	7. 3	1	1	4	33. 1	5	7	17	0
2153	Powder	Soybean, coconut oil, olive oil.	23. 2	10	4	6	105. 2	48	18	29	0
2163	Spaghetti in tomato sauce with cheese, cooked from home recipe.	Olive oil, cheese	3. 5	1	2	Trace					
2165	Spaghetti with meat balls in tomato sauce, cooked from home recipe. (Use also for item 2166.)	Olive oil, pork, beef, cheese, egg, bread-crumbs, milk.	4. 7	2	3	Trace					
2236	Sunflower seed kernels, dry:										
a	In hull		47. 3	6	9	30	115. 8	14	23	73	46
b	Hulled		47. 3	6	9	30	214. 6	26	43	135	0
2237	Sunflower seed flour, partially defatted		3. 4	Trace	1	2	15. 4	2	3	10	0
2251	Sweetpotatoes, cooked, candied	Butter	3. 3	2	1	Trace					
2270	Tapioca dessert, cream pudding	Milk, egg	5. 1	2	2	Trace					
2319	Trout, rainbow or steelhead, raw. (Use also for item 2320.)		11. 4	3	2	Trace	51. 7	11	11	2	0
	Tuna:										
	Raw:										
2321	Bluefin		4. 1	1	1	Trace	18. 6	6	4	Trace	0
2322	Yellowfin		3. 0	1	1	Trace	13. 6	5	2	Trace	0
	Canned in oil:										
2323	Solids and liquid	Cottonseed oil, tuna.	20. 5	5	4	8	93. 0	25	20	38	0
2324	Drained solids	Tuna, cottonseed oil.	8. 2	3	2	2	31. 6	10	7	6	15
2326	Tuna salad	Cottonseed oil, soybean oil, corn oil, tuna, egg.	10. 5	3	3	3					
	Turkey: [1]										
	All classes:										
2327	Total edible, raw		14. 7	4	6	3	48. 7	14	21	10	27
2330	Flesh only, raw		6. 6	2	3	1	29. 9	9	13	6	0
2332	Skin only, raw		39. 2	11	17	8	177. 8	52	76	37	0
2349	Turkey, canned, meat only		12. 5	4	5	3	56. 7	16	24	12	0
2350	Turkey potpie, home-prepared, baked. (Use also for item 2351.)	Vegetable shortening, cream, turkey, butter.	13. 5	4	7	1					

[1] If fatty acid values are required for parts listed in tables 1 and 2 but omitted here, select from column D or column H a value for total fat similar to that in the part for which data are wanted and apply the indicated fatty acid values.

TABLE 3.—*Selected fatty acids in foods*—Continued

[Item numbers correspond to those of table 1. Letters a through g in column A designate items that have the same chemical composition for the edible portion in table 1 but differ in the amount of refuse, and also designate items made with different specified fats. Data in columns D through G apply to 100 grams of edible portion of the item, although it may be purchased with the refuse indicated in column L and described or implied in column B. For information on the nature of the refuse listed in column L, refer to the comparable item in table 2]

Item No.		Item	Principal sources of fat	Amount in 100 grams, edible portion				Amount in edible portion of 1 pound as purchased				Refuse from item as purchased
				Total fat	Total saturated fatty acids	Unsaturated fatty acids		Total fat	Total saturated fatty acids	Unsaturated fatty acids		
						Oleic $C_{18}(-2H)$	Linoleic $C_{18}(-4H)$			Oleic $C_{18}(-2H)$	Linoleic $C_{18}(-4H)$	
(A)		(B)	(C)	(D)	(E)	(F)	(G)	(H)	(I)	(J)	(K)	(L)
				Grams	*Grams*	*Grams*	*Grams*	*Grams*	*Grams*	*Grams*	*Grams*	*Percent*
		Veal:[1]										
		Carcass, raw:										
2366		Excluding kidney and kidney fat, medium-fat class.		12.	6	5	Trace	43.	21	19	1	21
		Retail cuts, untrimmed:										
2369		Chuck, medium-fat class: Total edible, raw.		10.	5	4	Trace	36.	17	16	1	20
2389		Rib, medium-fat class: Total edible, raw.		14.	7	6	Trace	49.	23	22	1	23
2405		Venison, lean meat only, raw		4.	3	1	Trace	18.	11	4	1	0
		Waffles:										
2409		Baked from home recipe. (Use also for item 2410.)	Vegetable shortening, egg, milk.	9.8	3	5	1					
2411		Frozen	Vegetable shortening, egg.	6.2	2	4	1	28.1	7	16	3	0
		Waffle mixes and waffles baked from mixes:										
2412		Mix, dry form. (Use also for item 2414.)	Vegetable shortening, egg.	19.2	4	12	2	87.1	20	55	7	0
2413		Waffles, from waffle mix, made with water. (Use also for item 2415.)	do	14.0	3	9	1					
2417		Waffles, from pancake and waffle mix, made with egg, milk.	Vegetable shortening, milk, egg.	10.6	4	5	1					
		Walnuts:										
2420		Black:										
	a	In shell		59.3	4	21	28	59.2	4	21	28	78
	b	Shelled		59.3	4	21	28	269.0	16	94	129	0
2421		Persian or English:										
	a	In shell		64.0	4	10	40	130.6	9	20	81	55
	b	Shelled		64.0	4	10	40	290.3	20	44	180	0
2423		Welsh rarebit	Cheese, butter, milk.	13.6	7	4	Trace					

2429	Whale meat, raw		7.5	1	2		34.0	5	7		0
2447	Wheat germ, crude, commercially milled.		10.9	2	3	5	49.4	7	11	24	0
2457	Wheat germ, added nutrients, toasted; used mainly as ready-to-eat breakfast cereal.		11.5	2	3	6	52.2	8	12	25	0
2470	White sauce, medium	Butter, milk	12.5	7	4	Trace					
2482	Yoghurt, made from whole milk		3.4	2	1	Trace	15.4	8	5	Trace	0
2483	Zwieback	Vegetable shortening, egg.	8.8	2	5	1	39.9	9	25	4	0

[1] If fatty acid values are required for cuts listed in tables 1 and 2 but omitted here, select from column D or column H a value for total fat similar to that in the cut for which data are wanted and apply the indicated fatty acid values.

TABLE 4.—CHOLESTEROL CONTENT OF FOODS

[Letters a and b designate items that have the same chemical composition for the edible portion but differ in the amount of refuse. The data in column C apply to 100 grams of edible portion of the item, although it may be purchased with the refuse indicated in column E and described or implied in column B. For information on the nature of the refuse, see comparable items in table 2]

Item No.		Item	Amount of cholesterol in—		Refuse from item as purchased
			100 grams, edible portion	Edible portion of 1 pound as purchased	
(A)		(B)	(C)	(D)	(E)
			Milligrams	*Milligrams*	*Percent*
1		Beef, raw:			
	a	With bone	70	270	15
	b	Without bone	70	320	0
2		Brains, raw	>2, 000	>9, 000	0
3		Butter	250	1, 135	0
4		Caviar or fish roe	>300	>1, 300	0
		Cheese:			
5		Cheddar	100	455	0
6		Cottage, creamed	15	70	0
7		Cream	120	545	0
8		Other (25% to 30% fat)	85	385	0
9		Cheese spread	65	295	0
10		Chicken, flesh only, raw	60		0
11		Crab:			
	a	In shell	125	270	52
	b	Meat only	125	565	0
12		Egg, whole	550	2, 200	12
13		Egg white	0	0	0
		Egg yolk:			
14		Fresh	1, 500	6, 800	0
15		Frozen	1, 280	5, 800	0
16		Dried	2, 950	13, 380	0
17		Fish:			
	a	Steak	70	265	16
	b	Fillet	70	320	0
18		Heart, raw	150	680	0
19		Ice cream	45	205	0
20		Kidney, raw	375	1, 700	0
21		Lamb, raw:			
	a	With bone	70	265	16
	b	Without bone	70	320	0
22		Lard and other animal fat	95	430	0
23		Liver, raw	300	1, 360	0
24		Lobster:			
	a	Whole	200	235	74
	b	Meat only	200	900	0
		Margarine:			
25		All vegetable fat	0	0	0
26		Two-thirds animal fat, one-third vegetable fat	65	295	0
		Milk:			
27		Fluid, whole	11	50	0
28		Dried, whole	85	385	0
29		Fluid, skim	3	15	0
30		Mutton:			
	a	With bone	65	250	16
	b	Without bone	65	295	0
31		Oysters:			
	a	In shell	>200	>90	90
	b	Meat only	>200	>900	0
32		Pork:			
	a	With bone	70	260	18
	b	Without bone	70	320	0
33		Shrimp:			
	a	In shell	125	390	31
	b	Flesh only	125	565	0
34		Sweetbreads (thymus)	250	1, 135	0
35		Veal:			
	a	With bone	90	320	21
	b	Without bone	90	410	0

TABLE 5.—MAGNESIUM CONTENT OF FOODS

[Letters a and b designate items that have the same chemical composition for the edible portion but differ in the amount of refuse. The data in column C apply to 100 grams of edible portion of the item, although it may be purchased with the refuse indicated in column E and described or implied in column B. For information on the nature of the refuse, see comparable items in table 2]

Item No.	Item	Amount of magnesium in— 100 grams, edible portion	Edible portion of 1 pound as purchased	Refuse from item as purchased
(A)	(B)	(C)	(D)	(E)
		Milligrams	*Milligrams*	*Percent*
1	Almonds, dried:			
a	In shell	270	625	49
b	Shelled	270	1, 225	0
	Apples:			
	Raw:			
2	Not pared	8	33	8
3	Pared	5	20	14
	Dried (24% moisture):			
4	Uncooked	22	100	0
5	Cooked, without added sugar	6		
6	Frozen slices, sweetened	4	18	0
7	Apple juice or cider, canned or bottled	4	18	0
8	Applesauce, canned, sweetened	5	23	0
	Apricots:			
9	Raw	12	51	6
10	Canned, solids and liquid	7	32	0
	Dried (25% moisture):			
11	Uncooked	62	281	0
12	Cooked, fruit and liquid, without added sugar	20		
13	Frozen, sweetened	9	41	0
	Asparagus:			
14	Raw	20	51	44
15	Frozen	14	64	0
16	Avocados, all commercial varieties, raw	45	153	25
	Bacon, cured:			
17	Raw:			
a	Sliced	12	54	0
b	Slab	12	51	6
18	Cooked, broiled or fried, drained	25		
	Bacon, Canadian:			
19	Unheated	20	91	0
20	Cooked, broiled or fried, drained	24		
	Bananas:			
21	Raw	33	102	32
22	Dehydrated, or banana powder (3% moisture)	132	599	0
	Barley:			
23	Pearled, light	37	168	0
24	Whole-grain	124	562	0
	Beans, common, mature seeds, dry:			
	White:			
25	Raw	170	771	0
26	Canned, baked	37	168	0
27	Red, raw	163	739	0
	Beans, lima:			
	Immature seeds:			
28	Raw	67	304	0
29	Frozen	48	218	0
30	Mature seeds, dry, raw	180	816	0
	Beans, snap:			
31	Raw	32	128	12
32	Canned, drained solids	14		
33	Frozen	21	95	0

TABLE 5.—*Magnesium content of foods*—Continued

[Letters a and b designate items that have the same chemical composition for the edible portion but differ in the amount of refuse. The data in column C apply to 100 grams of edible portion of the item, although it may be purchased with the refuse indicated in column E and described or implied in column B. For information on the nature of the refuse, see comparable items in table 2]

Item No.		Item	Amount of magnesium in— 100 grams, edible portion	Amount of magnesium in— Edible portion of 1 pound as purchased	Refuse from item as purchased
(A)		(B)	(C)	(D)	(E)
		Beef cuts trimmed to retail basis:	*Milligrams*	*Milligrams*	*Percent*
34		Composite of cuts from carcass, raw	18	69	15
		Cuts for braising, simmering, or pot-roasting, as chuck:			
		Total edible, lean and fat:			
35		Raw:			
	a	With bone	21	80	16
	b	Without bone	21	95	0
36		Cooked	15		
		Lean only:			
37		Raw	24	109	0
38		Cooked	18		
		Hamburger (ground beef):			
		Lean:			
39		Raw	21	95	0
40		Cooked, broiled	25		
		Regular ground:			
41		Raw	17	77	0
42		Cooked, broiled	21		
		Roast, oven-cooked, no liquid added:			
		Relatively fat, such as rib:			
		Total edible, lean and fat:			
43		Raw:			
	a	With bone	17	71	8
	b	Without bone	17	77	0
44		Cooked	20		
		Lean only:			
45		Raw	23	104	0
46		Cooked	28		
		Relatively lean, such as round:			
		Total edible, lean and fat:			
47		Raw	22	97	3
48		Cooked	28		
		Lean only:			
49		Raw	24	109	0
50		Cooked	29		
		Steak for broiling:			
		Relatively fat, such as sirloin:			
		Total edible, lean and fat:			
51		Raw:			
	a	With bone	17	71	7
	b	Without bone	17	77	0
52		Cooked	21		
		Lean only:			
53		Raw	22	100	0
54		Cooked	29		
		Relatively lean, such as round:			
		Total edible, lean and fat:			
55		Raw	22	97	3
56		Cooked	28		
		Lean only:			
57		Raw	24	109	0
58		Cooked	29		
		Beets, common, red:			
59		Raw:			
	a	With tops	25	45	60
	b	With part tops	25	56	51
60		Canned, drained solids	15		

TABLE 5.—*Magnesium content of foods*—Continued

[Letters a and b designate items that have the same chemical composition for the edible portion but differ in the amount of refuse. The data in column C apply to 100 grams of edible portion of the item, although it may be purchased with the refuse indicated in column E and described or implied in column B. For information on the nature of the refuse, see comparable items in table 2]

Item No.	Item	Amount of magnesium in—		Refuse from item as purchased
		100 grams, edible portion	Edible portion of 1 pound as purchased	
(A)	(B)	(C)	(D)	(E)
		Milligrams	*Milligrams*	*Percent*
61	Beet greens, common, raw	106	269	44
62	Blackberries, raw	30	129	5
63	Blackberry juice, raw	21	----	----
	Blueberries:			
64	Raw	6	25	8
65	Canned, solids and liquid	4	18	0
	Frozen:			
66	Unsweetened	6	27	0
67	Sweetened	4	18	0
	Boysenberries, frozen:			
68	Unsweetened	18	82	0
69	Sweetened	12	54	0
70	Brazilnuts:			
a	In shell	225	490	52
b	Shelled	225	1,021	0
	Breads:			
71	Cracked-wheat	35	159	0
72	French or vienna	22	100	0
73	Raisin	24	109	0
	Rye:			
74	American, light (⅓ rye, ⅔ clear flour)	42	191	0
75	Pumpernickel, dark	71	322	0
76	White, made with 3% to 4% nonfat dry milk	22	100	0
77	Whole-wheat	78	354	0
	Broccoli:			
78	Raw spears	24	85	22
79	Frozen	21	95	0
	Brussels sprouts:			
80	Raw	29	121	8
81	Frozen	21	95	0
	Buckwheat:			
82	Whole-grain	229	1,039	0
83	Flour, light	48	218	0
84	Butter	2	9	0
85	Buttermilk, fluid, cultured	14	64	0
86	Cabbage, common varieties, raw	13	53	10
87	Cabbage, Chinese, also called celery cabbage, raw	14	56	12
88	Candy, hard	Trace	Trace	0
	Carrots:			
89	Raw:			
a	With full tops	23	62	41
b	Without tops	23	86	18
90	Dehydrated (4% moisture)	73	331	0
91	Cashew nuts	267	1,211	0
	Cauliflower:			
92	Raw	24	109	0
93	Frozen	13	59	0
94	Celery, raw	22	75	25
95	Chard, Swiss, raw	65	271	8
	Cheeses:			
96	Cheddar, domestic type	45	204	0
97	Parmesan	48	218	0

TABLE 5.—*Magnesium content of foods*—Continued

[Letters a and b designate items that have the same chemical composition for the edible portion but differ in the amount of refuse. The data in column C apply to 100 grams of edible portion of the item, although it may be purchased with the refuse indicated in column E and described or implied in column B. For information on the nature of the refuse, see comparable items in table 2]

Item No.	Item	Amount of magnesium in—		Refuse from item as purchased
		100 grams, edible portion	Edible portion of 1 pound as purchased	
(A)	(B)	(C)	(D)	(E)
	Cherries:	*Milligrams*	*Milligrams*	*Percent*
	Sour, red:			
98	Raw	14	58	8
	Frozen:			
99	Unsweetened	10	45	0
100	Sweetened	8	36	0
101	Sweet, Royal Anne, canned, solids and liquid	9	41	0
102	Chestnuts, fresh	41	151	19
	Chicken, white meat:			
103	Raw	23	82	21
104	Cooked, stewed	19		
105	Chicory, Witloof, bleached head, raw	13	52	11
106	Chives, raw	32	145	0
	Chocolate:			
107	Bitter or baking	292	1, 325	0
108	Milk	58	263	0
109	Sweet	107	485	0
110	Chocolate sirup, thin type	63	286	0
111	Cinnamon	59	268	0
112	Cocoa, dry powder	420	1, 905	0
	Coconut meat:			
113	Fresh, in shell	46	109	48
	Dried:			
114	Unsweetened	90	408	0
115	Sweetened, shredded	77	349	0
116	Coconut water (liquid from coconut)	28		
117	Cod, fillet, without bone and skin, raw	28	127	0
118	Coffee, instant, dry powder	456	2, 068	0
	Collards:			
119	Raw, leaves without stems	57	176	32
120	Frozen	35	159	0
121	Cookies: vanilla wafers, shortbread	15	68	0
122	Corn, field, whole-grain, raw	147	667	0
	Corn, sweet:			
123	Raw	48	78	64
124	Canned, drained solids	19		
	Frozen:			
125	Kernels, cut off cob	22	100	0
126	Kernels, on cob	34	85	45
127	Corn flakes (breakfast cereal)	16	73	0
	Corn grits:			
128	Dry form	20	91	0
129	Cooked	3		
	Cornmeal:			
130	Whole-ground, bolted, dry form	106	481	0
	Degermed:			
131	Dry form	47	213	0
132	Cooked	7		
133	Cornsalad, raw	13	57	4
134	Cornstarch	2	9	0
135	Cottonseed flour	650	2, 948	0
	Cowpeas, including blackeye peas:			
136	Immature seeds (blackeye peas only), frozen	55	249	0
137	Mature seeds, dry	230	1, 043	0
138	Crab, blue, cooked, steamed:			
a	In shell	34	74	52
b	Meat only	34	154	0

TABLE 5.—*Magnesium content of foods*—Continued

[Letters a and b designate items that have the same chemical composition for the edible portion but differ in the amount of refuse. The data in column C apply to 100 grams of edible portion of the item, although it may be purchased with the refuse indicated in column E and described or implied in column B. For information on the nature of the refuse, see comparable items in table 2]

Item No.		Item	Amount of magnesium in—		Refuse from item as purchased
			100 grams, edible portion	Edible portion of 1 pound as purchased	
(A)		(B)	(C)	(D)	(E)
		Crackers:	*Milligrams*	*Milligrams*	*Percent*
139		Graham	51	231	0
140		Soda	29	132	0
141		Cranberries, raw	8	35	4
142		Cranberry sauce, sweetened, canned, strained	2	9	0
		Cream:			
143		Light, coffee or table	11	50	0
144		Light whipping	9	41	0
145		Heavy whipping	8	36	0
146		Cucumbers, raw	11	36	27
147		Currants, red and white, raw	15	66	3
148		Currants, dried (seedless)	34	154	0
149		Curry powder	284	1,288	0
150		Dandelion greens	36	163	0
151		Dates, domestic, natural and dry:			
	a	With pits	58	229	13
	b	Without pits	58	263	0
152		Eggplant, raw	16	59	19
		Eggs:			
		Raw:			
153		Whole	11	44	12
154		Whites	9		
155		Yolks	16		
156		Dried, whole	41	186	0
157		Endive, raw	10	40	12
		Farina:			
		Regular:			
158		Dry form	25	113	0
159		Cooked	3		
160		Quick-cooking, cooked	3		
161		Instant, cooked	4		
		Figs:			
162		Raw	20	91	0
163		Dried (23% moisture)	71	322	0
164		Filberts (hazelnuts):			
	a	In shell	184	384	54
	b	Shelled	184	835	0
165		Flounder, fillet, without bone and skin, raw	30	136	0
166		Fruit cocktail, canned, solids and liquid	7	32	0
167		Garlic cloves, raw	36	144	12
168		Garlic salt	20	91	0
169		Gelatin, dry	33	150	0
170		Gooseberries, raw	9	41	0
171		Granadilla, purple (passionfruit), pulp and seeds, raw	29	68	48
		Grapefruit:			
172		Raw	12	27	51
173		Canned segments, solids and liquid	11	50	0
174		Grapefruit juice (chilled juice), raw	12	54	0
		Grapefruit juice, frozen concentrate, unsweetened:			
175		Undiluted	33	150	0
176		Diluted with 3 parts water by volume	9		
		Grapefruit juice and orange juice blended, frozen concentrate, unsweetened:			
177		Undiluted	32	145	0
178		Diluted with 3 parts water by volume	9		
		Grapes, raw:			
179		American type, slip skin	13	37	37
180		European type, adherent skin	6	24	11

TABLE 5.—*Magnesium content of foods*—Continued

[Letters a and b designate items that have the same chemical composition for the edible portion but differ in the amount of refuse. The data in column C apply to 100 grams of edible portion of the item, although it may be purchased with the refuse indicated in column E and described or implied in column B. For information on the nature of the refuse, see comparable items in table 2]

Item No. (A)		Item (B)	Amount of magnesium in— 100 grams, edible portion (C)	Edible portion of 1 pound as purchased (D)	Refuse from item as purchased (E)
			Milligrams	*Milligrams*	*Percent*
		Grape juice:			
181		Raw	13		
182		Canned or bottled	12	54	0
		Frozen concentrate, sweetened:			
183		Undiluted	12	54	0
184		Diluted with 3 parts water by volume	4		
185		Grape jelly	4	18	0
186		Guavas, common, raw	13	57	3
187		Haddock, fillet, without bone and skin, raw	24	109	0
188		Heart, beef, lean, raw	18	82	0
189		Hickorynuts:			
	a	In shell	160	254	65
	b	Shelled	160	726	0
190		Honey, strained	3	14	0
191		Horseradish, raw	34	113	27
192		Ice cream, approximately 12% fat	14	64	0
193		Jerusalem-artichoke, raw	11	34	31
		Kale:			
194		Raw, leaves without midribs	37	107	36
195		Frozen	31	141	0
196		Kohlrabi, raw	37	123	27
197		Lake herring, fillet, without bone and skin, raw	17	77	0
		Lamb cuts trimmed to retail basis:			
198		Composite of cuts from carcass, raw	15	57	16
		Chop, loin:			
		Total edible, lean and fat:			
199		Raw:			
	a	With bone	14	55	14
	b	Without bone	14	64	0
200		Cooked, broiled	17		
		Lean only:			
201		Raw	18	82	0
202		Cooked, broiled	22		
		Leg:			
		Total edible, lean and fat:			
203		Raw:			
	a	With bone	16	61	16
	b	Without bone	16	73	0
204		Cooked, roasted	21		
		Lean only:			
205		Raw	18	82	0
206		Cooked, roasted	18		
		Shoulder:			
		Total edible, lean and fat:			
207		Raw:			
	a	With bone	13	50	15
	b	Without bone	13	59	0
208		Cooked, roasted	17		
		Lean only:			
209		Raw	17	77	0
210		Cooked, roasted	22		
211		Leeks, raw	23	54	48
		Lemon juice:			
212		Raw	8		
213		Frozen, single-strength	7	32	0

TABLE 5.—*Magnesium content of foods*—Continued

[Letters a and b designate items that have the same chemical composition for the edible portion but differ in the amount of refuse. The data in column C apply to 100 grams of edible portion of the item, although it may be purchased with the refuse indicated in column E and described or implied in column B. For information on the nature of the refuse, see comparable items in table 2]

Item No.	Item	Amount of magnesium in—		Refuse from item as purchased
		100 grams, edible portion	Edible portion of 1 pound as purchased	
(A)	(B)	(C)	(D)	(E)
		Milligrams	*Milligrams*	*Percent*
	Lemonade concentrate, frozen:			
214	Undiluted	5	23	0
215	Diluted with 4⅓ parts water by volume	1		
216	Lentils, mature seeds, dry	80	363	0
217	Lettuce, crisphead varieties, raw	11	47	5
	Liver:			
	Beef:			
218	Raw	13	59	0
219	Cooked, fried	18		
	Calf:			
220	Raw	16	73	0
221	Cooked, fried	26		
	Hog:			
222	Raw	16	73	0
223	Cooked, fried	24		
	Lamb:			
224	Raw	14	64	0
225	Cooked, fried	23		
226	Lobster, whole, raw	22	26	74
227	Loganberries, raw	25	108	5
	Macaroni:			
228	Dry form	48	218	0
229	Cooked, firm stage (8–10 min.)	20		
230	Cooked, tender stage (14–20 min.)	18		
231	Mackerel, Atlantic, fillet, without bone and skin, raw	28	127	0
232	Malt extract, dried	140	635	0
233	Mangos, raw	18	55	33
234	Marmalade, citrus	4	18	0
	Milk, cow:			
	Fluid (pasteurized and raw):			
235	Whole	13	59	0
236	Skim	14	64	0
	Canned:			
237	Evaporated, unsweetened	25	113	0
238	Condensed, sweetened	25	113	0
	Dry:			
239	Whole	98	445	0
	Skim (nonfat solids):			
240	Regular	143	649	0
241	Instant	142	644	0
242	Milk, goat, fluid	17	77	0
243	Milk, human	4	18	0
244	Millet, proso, whole-grain	162	735	0
	Molasses, cane:			
245	First extraction or light	46	209	0
246	Second extraction or medium	81	367	0
247	Third extraction or blackstrap	258	1,170	0
248	Mullet, striped, fillet, without bone and skin, raw	32	145	0
	Mushrooms, *Agaricus campestris*:			
249	Raw	13	57	3
250	Canned	8	36	0
251	Muskmelons (cantaloups), raw	16	36	50
	Mussels:			
252	Raw, in shell	23	30	71
253	Cooked, boiled	25		
	Mustard greens:			
254	Raw	27	86	30
255	Frozen	23	104	0

TABLE 5.—*Magnesium content of foods*—Continued

[Letters a and b designate items that have the same chemical composition for the edible portion but differ in the amount of refuse. The data in column C apply to 100 grams of edible portion of the item, although it may be purchased with the refuse indicated in column E and described or implied in column B. For information on the nature of the refuse, see comparable items in table 2]

Item No. (A)		Item (B)	Amount of magnesium in— 100 grams, edible portion (C)	Edible portion of 1 pound as purchased (D)	Refuse from item as purchased (E)
			Milligrams	*Milligrams*	*Percent*
		Mustard:			
256		Dried	206	1, 343	0
257		Prepared	48	218	0
258		Nectarines, raw	13	54	8
259		New Zealand spinach, raw	40	181	0
260		Oats, whole-grain	169	767	0
261		Oat flour	110	499	0
262		Oat products (breakfast cereals): Oats, puffed	112	508	0
		Oatmeal or rolled oats:			
263		Dry form	144	653	0
264		Cooked	21		
		Okra:			
265		Raw	41	145	22
266		Frozen	53	240	0
267		Olives, green, pickled	22	53	47
		Onions, mature (dry):			
268		Raw	12	50	9
269		Dehydrated, flaked (4% moisture)	106	481	0
270		Oranges, raw	11	36	27
		Orange juice:			
271		Raw	11	50	0
		Canned concentrate, unsweetened:			
272		Undiluted	57	259	0
273		Diluted with 5 parts water by volume	12		
		Frozen concentrate, unsweetened:			
274		Undiluted	37	168	0
275		Diluted with 3 parts water by volume	10		
		Oysters, raw:			
276		Eastern:			
	a	In shell	32	15	90
	b	Meat only	32	145	0
277		Pacific, meat only	24	109	0
278		Japanese, meat only	48	218	0
		Parsley:			
279		Raw	41	186	0
280		Dried	283	1, 284	0
281		Parsnips, raw	32	123	15
		Peaches:			
282		Raw	10	34	24
283		Canned, sirup pack, solids and liquid	6	27	0
		Dried (25% moisture):			
284		Uncooked	48	218	0
285		Cooked, fruit and liquid, without added sugar	15		
286		Frozen, sliced, sweetened	6	27	0
		Peanuts:			
287		Raw:			
	a	In shell	206	682	27
	b	Shelled	206	934	0
288		Roasted:			
	a	In shell	175	532	33
	b	Shelled	175	794	0
289		Peanut butter	173	785	0
290		Peanut flour, defatted	360	1, 633	0
		Pears:			
291		Raw	7	29	9
292		Canned, solids and liquid	5	23	0
		Dried (26% moisture):			
293		Uncooked	31	141	0
294		Cooked, fruit and liquid, without added sugar	15		

TABLE 5.—*Magnesium content of foods*—Continued

[Letters a and b designate items that have the same chemical composition for the edible portion but differ in the amount of refuse. The data in column C apply to 100 grams of edible portion of the item, although it may be purchased with the refuse indicated in column E and described or implied in column B. For information on the nature of the refuse, see comparable items in table 2]

Item No.		Item	Amount of magnesium in—		
			100 grams, edible portion	Edible portion of 1 pound as purchased	Refuse from item as purchased
(A)		(B)	(C)	(D)	(E)
		Peas, green, immature:	*Milligrams*	*Milligrams*	*Percent*
295		Raw	35	60	62
		Canned, drained solids:			
296		Regular process	20		
297		Blair process	38		
298		Frozen	24	109	0
299		Peas, mature seeds, dry	180	816	0
300		Peas and carrots, frozen	19	86	0
301		Pecans:			
	a	In shell	142	341	47
	b	Shelled	142	644	0
302		Pepper (condiment)	45	204	0
303		Peppers, hot, red, dried chili powder	169	766	0
304		Peppers, sweet, immature, green, raw	18	67	18
305		Persimmons, Japanese or kaki, raw	8	30	18
		Pickles, cucumber:			
306		Dill	12	54	0
307		Sweet	1	5	0
308		Pigeonpeas, mature seeds, dry	121	549	0
		Pineapple:			
309		Raw	13	31	48
310		Canned, solids and liquid	8	36	0
311		Frozen chunks, sweetened	10	45	0
		Pineapple juice:			
312		Canned, unsweetened	12	51	0
		Frozen concentrate, unsweetened:			
313		Undiluted	35	159	0
314		Diluted with 3 parts water by volume	9		
315		Pistachionuts:			
	a	In shell	158	358	50
	b	Shelled	158	717	0
		Plums:			
316		Raw	9	38	6
317		Canned, purple (Italian prunes) sirup pack, solids and liquid	5	22	4
		Pork cuts, fresh, trimmed to retail basis:			
		Composite of cuts for roasting:			
		Total edible, lean and fat:			
318		Raw:			
	a	With bone	18	67	18
	b	Without bone	18	82	0
319		Cooked, roasted	23		
		Lean only:			
320		Raw	22	100	0
321		Cooked, roasted	29		
		Cuts for chops, such as loin:			
		Total edible, lean and fat:			
322		Raw:			
	a	With bone	19	68	21
	b	Without bone	19	86	0
323		Cooked, broiled	27		
		Lean only:			
324		Raw	23	104	0
325		Cooked, broiled	32		
		Cuts for simmering, such as picnic:			
		Total edible, lean and fat:			
326		Raw:			
	a	With bone	18	67	18
	b	Without bone	18	82	0
327		Cooked, simmered	14		

TABLE 5.—*Magnesium content of foods*—Continued

[Letters a and b designate items that have the same chemical composition for the edible portion but differ in the amount of refuse. The data in column C apply to 100 grams of edible portion of the item, although it may be purchased with the refuse indicated in column E and described or implied in column B. For information on the nature of the refuse, see comparable items in table 2]

Item No.		Item	Amount of magnesium in— 100 grams, edible portion	Amount of magnesium in— Edible portion of 1 pound as purchased	Refuse from item as purchased
(A)		(B)	(C)	(D)	(E)
		Pork cuts, fresh, trimmed to retail basis—Continued	*Milligrams*	*Milligrams*	*Percent*
		Cuts for simmering, such as picnic—Continued			
		Lean only:			
328		Raw	22	100	0
329		Cooked, simmered	18		
		Pork, light-cure ham:			
		Total edible, lean and fat:			
330		Raw:			
	a	With bone	16	62	14
	b	Without bone	16	73	0
331		Cooked, roasted	17		
		Lean only:			
332		Raw	19	86	0
333		Cooked, roasted	20		
		Pork sausage, links and bulk:			
334		Raw	9	41	0
335		Cooked, broiled	16		
		Potatoes:			
		Raw:			
336		Not peeled	34	154	0
337		Peeled	22	81	19
338		Dehydrated mashed, without milk, dry form	100	454	0
		Frozen:			
339		Diced for hash-browning	18	82	0
340		French-fried	25	113	0
341		Mashed	12	54	0
		Prunes, dried (28% moisture):			
342		Uncooked	40	154	15
343		Cooked fruit and liquid, without added sugar	20		
344		Prune juice, canned or bottled, unsweetened	10	45	0
345		Pumpkin, raw	12	38	30
346		Radishes, common, raw:			
	a	With tops	15	43	37
	b	Without tops	15	61	10
		Raisins, seedless (18% moisture):			
347		Uncooked	35	159	0
348		Cooked, fruit and liquid, added sugar	16		
349		Rape, raw	15	68	0
		Raspberries:			
		Raw:			
350		Black	30	132	3
351		Red	20	88	3
352		Canned, red, solids and liquid	13	59	0
353		Frozen, red, sweetened	11	50	0
354		Red snapper, fillet, without bone and skin, raw	28	127	0
		Rhubarb:			
355		Raw	16	33	55
356		Cooked, added sugar	13		
357		Frozen, sweetened	12	54	0
		Rice:			
		Brown:			
358		Raw	88	399	0
359		Cooked	29		
		White, fully milled or polished:			
360		Raw	28	127	0
361		Cooked	8		
362		Rutabagas, raw	15	58	15
363		Rye, whole-grain	115	522	0

TABLE 5.—*Magnesium content of foods*—Continued

[Letters a and b designate items that have the same chemical composition for the edible portion but differ in the amount of refuse. The data in column C apply to 100 grams of edible portion of the item, although it may be purchased with the refuse indicated in column E and described or implied in column B. For information on the nature of the refuse, see comparable items in table 2]

Item No.		Item	Amount of magnesium in—		Refuse from item as purchased
			100 grams, edible portion	Edible portion of 1 pound as purchased	
(A)		(B)	(C)	(D)	(E)
			Milligrams	*Milligrams*	*Percent*
364		Rye flour, light	73	331	0
		Salad dressings, commercial:			
365		French	10	45	0
366		Mayonnaise	2	9	0
		Salmon, canned, solids and liquid:			
367		Chinook (king)	27	122	0
368		Chum	30	136	0
369		Coho (silver)	30	136	0
370		Pink (humpback)	30	136	0
371		Sockeye (red)	29	132	0
372		Salt	119	540	0
373		Sardines, Pacific, whole, raw	24	109	0
374		Sesame seeds, whole, raw	181	821	0
		Shrimp:			
375		Raw	42	131	31
376		Cooked, boiled	51		
377		Soybeans, mature seeds, dry	265	1,202	0
378		Soybean curd (tofu)	111	503	0
		Soybean flours:			
379		Full-fat	247	1,120	0
380		High-fat	272	1,234	0
381		Low-fat	289	1,311	0
382		Defatted	310	1,406	0
		Spinach:			
383		Raw	88	399	0
384		Canned	63	286	0
385		Dehydrated	954	4,327	0
386		Frozen	65	295	0
387		Squash, summer, Yellow Crookneck, frozen	16	73	0
		Squash, winter:			
388		Raw	17	55	29
389		Frozen	17	77	0
		Strawberries:			
390		Raw	12	52	4
391		Frozen, sliced, sweetened	9	41	0
392		Strawberry jam	5	23	0
393		Sugar, granulated	Trace	Trace	0
394		Sunflower seed kernels:			
	a	In hull	38	93	46
	b	Hulled	38	172	0
		Sweetpotatoes:			
395		Raw	31	114	19
396		Dehydrated flakes	100	454	0
397		Tapioca, dry	3	14	0
398		Tea, instant, dry powder	395	1,792	0
		Tomatoes:			
399		Raw	14	64	0
400		Canned	12	54	0
		Dehydrated crystals (1% moisture):			
401		Dry form	155	703	0
402		Prepared with water (1 lb. yields approx. 1¾ gal.)	38		
403		Tomato catsup, bottled	21	95	0
404		Tomato juice, canned or bottled	10	45	0
405		Tomato puree, canned	20	91	0
406		Tomato soup, canned, condensed, diluted for serving	9	41	0
407		Tongue, beef, raw	16	55	24
408		Turkey, cooked, roasted	28		

TABLE 5.—*Magnesium content of foods*—Continued

[Letters a and b designate items that have the same chemical composition for the edible portion but differ in the amount of refuse. The data in column C apply to 100 grams of edible portion of the item, although it may be purchased with the refuse indicated in column E and described or implied in column B. For information on the nature of the refuse, see comparable items in table 2]

Item No.	Item	Amount of magnesium in—		Refuse from item as purchased
		100 grams, edible portion	Edible portion of 1 pound as purchased	
(A)	(B)	(C)	(D)	(E)
		Milligrams	*Milligrams*	*Percent*
409	Turnips, raw:			
a	With tops	20	59	35
b	Without tops	20	78	14
	Turnip greens:			
410	Raw	58	221	16
411	Frozen	26	118	0
	Veal, retail cuts:			
412	Composite of cuts from carcass, raw	15	54	21
	Cutlet, without bone:			
413	Raw	16	73	0
414	Cooked, broiled	18	----------	----------
	Roast, such as rib:			
415	Raw:			
a	With bone	15	52	23
b	Without bone	15	68	0
416	Cooked, roasted	20	----------	----------
417	Vegetable soup, canned, condensed, diluted for serving	10	45	0
418	Venison, roasted	33	----------	----------
419	Vinegar, distilled	1	5	0
	Walnuts:			
420	Black:			
a	In shell	190	190	78
b	Shelled	190	862	0
421	Persian or English:			
a	In shell	131	267	55
b	Shelled	131	594	0
422	Waterchestnut, Chinese (matai, waternut), raw	12	42	23
423	Watercress, raw	20	83	8
424	Watermelon, raw	8	17	54
425	Wheat, whole-grain	160	726	0
	Wheat flours:			
426	Whole-wheat	113	513	0
427	Patent, all-purpose	25	113	0
	Wheat bran:			
428	Crude	490	2, 223	0
429	Added sugar and malt extract (breakfast cereal)	420	1, 905	0
430	Wheat germ	336	1, 524	0
	Wheat products (breakfast cereals):			
	Wheat and malted barley cereal, toasted, instant-cooking:			
431	Dry form	168	762	0
432	Cooked	31	----------	----------
433	Wheat, shredded	133	603	0
434	Whey, dried	130	590	0
	Wildrice:			
435	Raw	129	585	0
436	Parched	112	508	0
	Wines:			
437	Apple	5	23	0
438	Blackberry	10	45	0
439	Currant	5	23	0
440	Loganberry	9	41	0
441	Vermouth	10	45	0
	Yeast:			
442	Baker's, compressed	59	268	0
443	Brewer's, debittered	231	1, 048	0
444	Torula	165	748	0

APPENDIX A.—NOTES ON ENERGY VALUES AND NUTRIENTS

Energy Value

The energy values of foods listed in this publication represent the energy available after deductions have been made for losses in digestion and metabolism. The values are in terms of the large or kilogram calorie,[1] the unit customarily used by nutritionists for measuring the energy needs and expenditures of man and the energy value of foods.

The system for determining these energy values was developed through the classic investigations of W. O. Atwater and his associates at the Storrs (Connecticut) Agricultural Experiment Station. A detailed report of this work was published in 1900 (*4*). Working with human subjects, he determined the available energy values of a wide range of different types of foods.

The Atwater system of arriving at the available energy value of foods was carefully reviewed in 1947 by a committee of experts of the Food and Agriculture Organization of the United Nations, and the factors were found to be satisfactory when correctly used (*8*). This system is the one used as the basis of the calorie values in the tables of food composition published by that organization.

The data in table 7 illustrate the excellent agreement between calories determined from bomb calorimetry measurements on food and excreta and those calculated by applying calorie factors from table 6 to data on chemical composition. The widest discrepancy among the cases here is found for the diet consisting solely of bananas. The use of the calorie factors with data on the composition of bananas underestimated the calorie value found by direct determination but by only 5 percent.

The Atwater procedure, in brief, is to adjust the heats of combustion (gross calories) of the fat, protein, and carbohydrate in a food to allow for the losses in digestion and metabolism found for human subjects, and to apply the adjusted calorie factors to the amounts of protein, fat, and carbohydrate in the food. The contents of protein and fat are determined by chemical analysis, and the percentage of carbohydrate is obtained by difference; that is, it is taken as the remainder after the sum of the fat, protein, ash, and moisture has been deducted from 100. This so-called total carbohydrate, therefore, includes fiber as well as any noncarbohydrate residue present.

The energy factors that Atwater derived from his digestibility experiments have been expanded and modified to take into account additional experiments conducted with human subjects since his time. The current factors are shown here in table 6. Most of these factors had been developed before 1950 and were applied in calculating the calories listed in the 1950 publication of Agriculture Handbook No. 8. The details on derivation of the calorie factors have been published (*20*).

Protein

The values for protein shown in tables 1 and 2 of this publication were calculated from determinations of the content of nitrogen in the food. Some of the first proteins to be analyzed by the early chemists were found to have close to 16 percent nitrogen. This led to the practice, established many years ago, of determining the content of nitrogen for a food and calculating the content of protein by multiplying the total nitrogen by 6.25 (100÷16=6.25). The same general procedure is still used to obtain figures for protein in most foods. However, the content of nitrogen has been found to differ in the proteins of different types of foods. Instead of the conversion factor 6.25 based on an average content of 16 percent nitrogen, the conversion factors recommended by Jones in 1931 (*16*) for specific kinds of foods and later supplemented by him (*22*, p. 47) are now used. They are shown here in table 8.

[1] The large or kilogram calorie is the amount of heat required to raise the temperature of 1 kilogram of water 1 degree Centigrade. With a few exceptions, which are to be found mainly in the reports of early investigations, nutritionists have used the large or kilogram calorie. The small calorie is one-thousandth of the large calorie.

TABLE 6.—DATA USED FOR CALCULATING ENERGY VALUES OF FOODS OR FOOD GROUPS BY THE ATWATER SYSTEM

Food or food group	Protein			Fat			Carbohydrate		
	Coefficient of digestibility	Heat of combustion less 1.25 [1]	Factor to be applied to ingested nutrients	Coefficient of digestibility	Heat of combustion	Factor to be applied to ingested nutrients	Coefficient of digestibility	Heat of combustion	Factor to be applied to ingested nutrients
(A)	(B)	(C)	(D)	(E)	(F)	(G)	(H)	(I)	(J)
Eggs, Meat products, Milk products:	*Pct*	*Cal./gm.*	*Cal./gm.*	*Pct.*	*Cal./gm.*	*Cal./gm.*	*Pct*	*Cal./gm.*	*Cal./gm.*
Eggs	97	4.50	4.36	95	9.50	9.02	98	3.75	3.68
Gelatin	97	4.02	3.90	95	9.50	9.02			
Glycogen							98	4.19	4.11
Meat, fish	97	4.40	4.27	95	9.50	9.02			(2)
Milk, milk products	97	4.40	4.27	95	9.25	8.79	98	3.95	3.87
Fats, separated:									
Butter	97	4.40	4.27	95	9.25	8.79	98	3.95	3.87
Other animal fats				95	9.50	9.02			
Margarine, vegetable	97	4.40	4.27	95	9.30	8.84	98	3.95	3.87
Other vegetable fats and oils				95	9.30	8.84			
Fruits:									
All (except lemons, limes)	85	3.95	3.36	90	9.30	8.37	90	4.00	3.60
All fruit juice (except lemon, lime) unsweetened	85	3.95	3.36	90	9.30	8.37	[3] 98	4.00	[3] 3.92
Lemons, limes	85	3.95	3.36	90	9.30	8.37	[3] 90	2.75	[3] 2.48
Lemon juice, lime juice, unsweetened	85	3.95	3.36	90	9.30	8.37	98	2.75	2.70
Grain products:									
Barley, pearled	78	4.55	3.55	90	9.30	8.37	94	4.20	3.95
Buckwheat flour, dark	74	4.55	3.37	90	9.30	8.37	90	4.20	3.78
Buckwheat flour, light	78	4.55	3.55	90	9.30	8.37	94	4.20	3.95
Cornmeal, whole-ground	60	4.55	2.73	90	9.30	8.37	96	4.20	4.03
Cornmeal, degermed	76	4.55	3.46	90	9.30	8.37	99	4.20	4.16
Dextrin							98	4.11	4.03
Macaroni, spaghetti	86	4.55	3.91	90	9.30	8.37	98	4.20	4.12
Oatmeal, rolled oats	76	4.55	3.46	90	9.30	8.37	98	4.20	4.12
Rice, brown	75	4.55	3.41	90	9.30	8.37	98	4.20	4.12
Rice, white or polished	84	4.55	3.82	90	9.30	8.37	99	4.20	4.16
Rye flour, dark	65	4.55	2.96	90	9.30	8.37	90	4.20	3.78
Rye flour, whole-grain	67	4.55	3.05	90	9.30	8.37	92	4.20	3.86
Rye flour, medium	71	4.55	3.23	90	9.30	8.37	95	4.20	3.99
Rye flour, light	75	4.55	3.41	90	9.30	8.37	97	4.20	4.07
Sorghum (*kaoliang*), whole or nearly whole meal	20	4.55	.91	90	9.30	8.37	96	4.20	4.03
Wheat, 97–100 percent extraction	79	4.55	3.59	90	9.30	8.37	90	4.20	3.78
Wheat, 85–93 percent extraction	83	4.55	3.78	90	9.30	8.37	94	4.20	3.95
Wheat, 70–74 percent extraction	89	4.55	4.05	90	9.30	8.37	98	4.20	4.12
Wheat, flaked, puffed, rolled, shredded, whole meal	79	4.55	3.59	90	9.30	8.37	90	4.20	3.78
Wheat bran (100 percent)	40	4.55	1.82	90	9.30	8.37	56	4.20	2.35
Other cereals, refined	85	4.55	3.87	90	9.30	8.37	98	4.20	4.12
Wildrice	78	4.55	3.55	90	9.30	8.37	94	4.20	3.95
Legumes, Nuts:									
Mature dry beans, cowpeas, peas, other legumes; nuts	78	4.45	3.47	90	9.30	8.37	97	4.20	4.07
Immature lima beans, cowpeas, peas, other legumes	78	4.45	3.47	90	9.30	8.37	97	4.20	4.07
Soybeans, dry; soy flour, flakes, grits	78	4.45	3.47	90	9.30	8.37	97	4.20	4.07
Sugars:									
Cane or beet sugar (sucrose)							98	3.95	3.87
Glucose							98	3.75	3.68
Vegetables:									
Mushrooms	70	3.75	2.62	90	9.30	8.37	85	4.10	3.48
Potatoes and starchy roots	74	3.75	2.78	90	9.30	8.37	96	4.20	4.03
Other underground crops [4]	74	3.75	2.78	90	9.30	8.37	96	4.00	3.84
Other vegetables	65	3.75	2.44	90	9.30	8.37	85	4.20	3.57
Miscellaneous foods:									
Alcohol [5]									
Chocolate, cocoa	42	4.35	1.83	90	9.30	8.37	32	4.16	1.33
Vinegar							98	2.45	2.40
Yeast	80	3.75	3.00	90	9.30	8.37	80	4.20	3.35

[1] The correction, 1.25 Calories, has been subtracted from the heat of combustion. This gives values applicable to grams of digested protein and identical with Atwater's factors per gram of available protein.

[2] Carbohydrate factor, 3.87 for brain, heart, kidney, liver; 4.11 for tongue and shellfish.

[3] Unpublished revision made since 1955.

[4] Vegetables such as beets, carrots, onions, parsnips, radishes.

[5] Coefficient of digestibility, 98 percent; heat of combustion, 7.07 Calories per gram; factor to apply to ingested alcohol, 6.93 Calories per gram.

TABLE 7.—AVAILABLE ENERGY FROM DIFFERENT TYPES OF DIETS: COMPARISON OF CALORIE VALUES BASED ON DIRECT DETERMINATION AND ON CALCULATIONS MADE ACCORDING TO THE ATWATER SYSTEM

Type of diet	Gross energy value of diet (from bomb calorimetry)	Metabolic and digestive loss (from bomb calorimetry)	Available energy value of diet—		
			Direct from bomb calorimetry	Calculated from factors	Deviation of calculated from direct determination
Mixed diets:					
With large amounts of—					
Fruits and nuts or peanuts:	*Calories*	*Calories*	*Calories*	*Calories*	*Percent*
A	1, 227	180	1, 047	1, 070	+2
B	2, 010	260	1, 750	1, 741	−1
C	2, 832	433	2, 399	2, 406	0
Legumes:					
A	2, 555	349	2, 206	2, 268	+3
B	3, 324	388	2, 936	2, 913	−1
C	3, 606	521	3, 085	3, 121	+1
D	3, 283	409	2, 874	2, 938	+2
Cereals and dairy products:					
A	3, 953	412	3, 541	3, 587	−2
B	4, 384	498	3, 886	3, 815	−2
C	2, 651	271	2, 380	2, 348	−1
Vegetables:					
A	2, 225	202	2, 023	2, 019	0
B	2, 363	241	2, 122	2, 149	+1
C	2, 679	200	2, 479	2, 481	0
Other mixed diets:					
A	3, 862	358	3, 504	3, 578	+2
B	2, 683	272	2, 411	2, 408	0
Diets of a single food:					
Bananas	1, 280	120	1, 160	1, 098	−5
Bread (wheat flour, patent)	2, 320	172	2, 148	2, 183	+2

TABLE 8.—FACTORS FOR CALCULATING PROTEIN FROM NITROGEN CONTENT OF FOOD[1]

Food	Factor	Food	Factor
Animal origin		*Plant origin*—Continued	
Eggs	6. 25	Legumes—Continued	
Gelatin	5. 55	Beans—Continued	
Meat	6. 25	Soybeans	5. 71
Milk	6. 38	Velvetbeans	6. 25
Plant origin		Peanuts	5. 46
Grains and cereals:		Nuts:	
Barley	5. 83	Almonds	5. 18
Corn (maize)	6. 25	Brazil	5. 46
Millets	5. 83	Butternuts	5. 30
Oats	5. 83	Cashew	5. 30
Rice	5. 95	Chestnuts	5. 30
Rye	5. 83	Coconuts	5. 30
Sorghums	6. 25	Hazelnuts	5. 30
Wheat:		Hickory	5. 30
Whole-kernel	5. 83	Pecans	5. 30
Bran	6. 31	Pinenuts	5. 30
Embryo	5. 80	Pistachio	5. 30
Endosperm	5. 70	Walnuts	5. 30
Legumes:		Seeds:	
Beans:		Cantaloup	5. 30
Adzuki	6. 25	Cottonseed	5. 30
Castor	5. 30	Flaxseed	5. 30
Jack	6. 25	Hempseed	5. 30
Lima	6. 25	Pumpkin	5. 30
Mung	6. 25	Sesame	5. 30
Navy	6. 25	Sunflower	5. 30

[1] Adapted from Jones, 1941 (*16*, p. 14, table 5) and from unpublished data obtained from him.

Values for protein calculated by the use of these factors and data on the total nitrogen content of foods are satisfactory for tables of composition to be used in the calculation of nutritive values, since a high proportion of the nitrogen in most foods is present as protein, protein derivative, or free amino acids. Often the term "crude protein" has been used in recognition of the fact that small amounts of nonprotein nitrogenous compounds may be present. In a few foods these compounds that are unrelated to protein make up a fairly large proportion of the total nitrogenous matter. Allowance for this portion of a nonprotein character was made in calculating the content of protein shown for cocoa, chocolate, coffee, yeast, and mushrooms in tables 1 and 2.

Fat

Fat is the term used most often for those components in food that are insoluble in water and soluble in ethyl ether and other fat solvents employed to extract them. The term "fat" is a loose one, since it may embrace several different types of compounds that are removed by the extraction—as neutral fat, fatty acids, nonsaponifiable fractions, and other matter. Other solvents used alone or as mixtures in the determination of fat or lipid content of foods include petroleum ether, chloroform, acetone, and chloroform-methanol mixtures.

"Crude fat," "total fat," "oil," "ether extract," and "total lipids" are other terms sometimes used in tables and reports on the composition of food and in texts on chemistry to call attention to the heterogeneous character of the "fat" extracted from plant and animal products. The interpretation of the data for fat reported for foods is somewhat confused, because the extraction of the lipid portion may be incomplete, resulting in some underestimation, and on the other hand, some nonlipid matter may be included in the extract.

A portion of the lipid in some foods may be bound with protein or carbohydrate and resist extraction unless released prior to extraction. Also the lipid in some prepared foods may be so coated or enmeshed with carbohydrate that the solvent cannot be entirely effective. Much has already been done to develop procedures for determining fat that are adapted specifically to problems peculiar to different kinds of foods—cereals, chocolate, yeast, eggs, and other. Data for fat obtained by these procedures are accumulating, but as yet the values shown in this publication include a majority of determinations made by simple extraction with organic solvent. Solvent extraction may be the most efficient for many foods, especially those containing chemical constituents adversely affected by acids or strong alkalies, whereas other foods require acid hydrolysis or saponification to effect complete extraction of lipids. Sometimes sufficient information about the method of analysis employed is not reported to reveal what steps may have been taken to determine fat.

Fatty Acids

The fatty acids are important components of the total lipid fraction and usually are present as neutral fats; that is, they are in combination with glycerol, a trihydroxy alcohol. These fats are saponifiable and the fatty acids are released from glycerol on saponification.

The data on fatty acids in table 3 were adapted principally from a published compilation, "Fatty Acids in Food Fats," Home Economics Research Report No. 7 (*9*). Information on the individual data used in preparing this compilation has also been published (*10*) but in a limited edition which is much less generally available. The compilation was based on determinations of the fatty acid content of fats made before 1955, as the urgency for the information did not allow waiting for results of the more highly refined techniques and newer methods in process of development.

For the saturated fatty acids, data in table 3 include the total of short-chain fatty acids such as butyric acid [$CH_3(CH_2)_2COOH$], which is one of several fatty acids making up the fat of butter, and those of longer chain length such as palmitic acid [$CH_3(CH_2)_{14}COOH$], found in vegetable fats and to a lesser extent in animal fats, and stearic acid [$CH_3(CH_2)_{16}COOH$], present in animal fats and to some extent in fats of plant origin. Fats with short-chain saturated fatty acids are liquid or soft at room temperature. As chain lengths increase, the fats become harder.

Unsaturated fatty acids (liquid at room temperature) also are present in foods. Data for two kinds have been included in table 3, those of the C_{18} series with one double bond as oleic acid, and those in this series with two double bonds as linoleic acid. Values for other unsaturated fatty acids have not been included inasmuch as they occur in only small amounts in most foods.

Methods by which the data shown for these fatty acids were obtained are being superseded by newer, more specific methods. The gas-liquid-chromatographic procedure appears to be sufficiently specific and reasonably quantitative, and is being applied to foods as well as to separated fats. Work now in progress is expected to provide a better basis for data on fatty acids in future editions of these tables.

Foods having only a small amount of total lipids, 2 percent or less, were not listed in table 3. Unfortunately, many other items from table 1 which are probably important sources of fatty acids had to be omitted because of lack of data. The dearth of analyses for common kinds of fish was particularly marked, and unpublished work made available for rainbow trout, two kinds of salmon, and four kinds of tuna was used to supplement values in Home Economics Research Report No. 7 (*9*).

Present information indicates that the unsaturated fatty acids in fish and shellfish tend to have longer carbon chains and a higher degree of unsaturation than the fatty acids in most other foods. Inasmuch as the highly unsaturated, long-chain fatty acids were not included in table 3, this accounts for part of the relatively large difference between the figure for total lipid and the sum of the values listed for the fatty acids in a fish or shellfish item and in a few other foods. Glycerol and nonsaponifiable matter also contribute to differences between the values in the column for total lipids and the sum of the data for fatty acids. However, as the data have been rounded to the nearest whole number, calculation of lipid fractions not listed should not be made from figures in table 3.

Recently published studies were used as the basis for the average values for margarine in table 3 because changes in the manufacture of margarine within the past few years have markedly altered the fatty acid content of this product. Present indications are that products such as margarine and cooking fats will continue to change markedly with the increasing use of oils and changing practices as to kinds of fat used in manufacturing processes.

Cholesterol and Other Nonsaponifiable Matter

Cholesterol and other sterols (alcohols of high molecular weight) and some other nonsaponifiable matter often comprise a small but important part of the total lipid in food. Vitamin A and the carotenoid pigments are in this category. Other nonsaponifiable matter of particular significance to food technologists and nutritionists include the tocopherols and ergosterols.

Tocopherols are useful as antioxidants for fats in foods and are added to some manufactured foods to delay the development of rancidity. Some of the tocopherols, particularly alpha-tocopherol, are active as vitamin E.

Vitamin E is widely distributed in common foods. It is found in considerable quantities in vegetable and seed oils and in green leafy vegetables. It is present also in meat, egg yolk, and dairy products. Wheat-germ oil is probably the richest natural source of the vitamin. At present there is insufficient quantitative information on the mixtures of tocopherols and their relative biological potencies to include a column for vitamin E in the tables.

Cholesterol, a sterol, derives its name from the Greek "chole" for bile and "steros" for solid. It occurs only in products of animal origin—blood, muscle, bone marrow, the liver, and other organs. It is present in especially large amounts in nerve tissues, so that such foods as brains from calf, beef, lamb, or hog would be exceptionally concentrated sources.

As cholesterol does not occur in plants, none would be present in cereals, fruits, nuts, vegetables, or in the oils and various products prepared from them and used for food.

Cholesterol supplied by the diet is sometimes referred to as exogenous cholesterol, to distinguish it from that which is synthesized within the body in normal metabolic processes.

Data on the content of cholesterol in foods are shown in table 4. They were based largely on determinations made according to the Liebermann-Burchard colorimetric method or by the procedure of Windaus, involving precipitation of cholesterol with digitonin with or without modifications of Schonheimer and Sperry. As yet no data are available on cholesterol determined by using tomatine, a more recently discovered precipitant, and one considered more specific than digitonin.

Except for milk and eggs, values listed in table 4 for the content of cholesterol were based on limited samplings of foods. The values in this table are offered as suggested figures for making dietary calculations when samples of the specific foods eaten are not analyzed.

Several kinds of fish have been analyzed and for most kinds the content of cholesterol reported by various investigators fell within a fairly narrow range, 60 to 75 milligrams per 100 grams. The data available indicate that oil, liver, and skin of fish have a higher content of cholesterol than the muscle has, but unfortunately many samples were not clearly described. As there was insufficient basis to relate the content of cholesterol to the content of fat in fish or to provide separate values for the different kinds of fish, only a single average figure for fish has been shown in this summary. A few kinds of shellfish have been analyzed.

Little information is available on the cholesterol content of meats and poultry. The meat from the young animal of each species appears to have a somewhat greater concentration of cholesterol than that from the mature animal—that is, veal has more than beef; lamb, more than mutton.

Carbohydrate

Carbohydrates of many kinds occur in foods—starches, dextrins, sugars, celluloses, pentosans, pectins, gums, and others. The cell walls and the structural framework of seeds, leaves, and stems are composed largely of fibrous forms of carbohydrate—cellulose and hemicellulose. Cereal grains deposit starch in their seeds for the young plant to use as it develops. Kernels of corn in the "milk stage" contain sugar, which is transformed to starch as the kernel matures. Starches and sugars are present in seeds of leguminous plants and in roots and tubers. Immature fruits contain starch which is converted into sugar as the fruit ripens.

Sugars of several kinds are present in foods. The commonly used household sugar is sucrose, a disaccharide. It may be either cane sugar or beet sugar, as these are identical in chemical composition. It is present in different degrees in numerous fruits and vegetables. The predominating sugars in most fruits are sucrose and the monosaccharides, fructose (levulose) and glucose (dextrose). When glucose and fructose are present in equal amounts, the mixture is often referred to as invert sugar. Most of the solid matter of honey consists of these two monosaccharides. A few foods, notably Jerusalem-artichoke, globe or French artichoke, and salsify contain inulin, a polysaccharide, which may not be directly available to man. In some circumstances, fairly large proportions are apparently converted to a readily available sugar—fructose. Other forms of carbohydrate also found in edible parts of plants include various gums, pectins, and pentosans.

Only a few foods of animal origin contain carbohydrate. Eggs and shellfish have small amounts. Glycogen, a complex carbohydrate, present in liver in the live animal, is rapidly broken down to glucose when the animal is slaughtered. Blood contains glucose at low, narrowly regulated levels. Milk is exceptional in that over one-third of the solid matter is lactose, a disaccharide commonly called milk sugar.

Most of the values shown in tables 1 and 2 are for "total carbohydrate" or "carbohydrate by difference." They are not obtained by direct analysis but are calculated—that is, the values are the difference between 100 and the sum of the percentages of crude protein, crude fat, ash, and water. Figures shown for total carbohydrate are composed largely of sugars, starches, fiber, and some other complex forms, but as with crude protein and crude fat fractions, this "total carbohydrate" fraction includes some compounds that, strictly speaking, are not carbohydrate from a chemical standpoint. For example, the small amounts of organic acids that occur in some foods would also be included.

Starches, dextrins, and the sugars that are disaccharides are converted by the body into simple sugars, mostly glucose, and fructose, and are well utilized as sources of energy. Less is known about digestion and use of cellulose and the other complex forms of carbohydrate. As the calorie factors for carbohydrate shown in table 6 were based on experiments with human subjects, they take into account differences in utilization of the "total carbohydrate" fractions present in different kinds of food.

For purposes other than the calculation of physiologic energy values, information on specific kinds of carbohydrates is desirable. For calculating carbohydrate in diets for diabetic patients, usually a figure for the total of the starches, dextrins, and sugars is wanted. Unfortunately, satisfactory methods of routine determination of individual carbohydrates in foods have not been found. Various procedures have been reported in the literature, based on measurements of the reducing action of the hydrolyzed products of these carbohydrates on copper reagents. None of these procedures, however, is entirely satisfactory when applied to foods containing mixtures of carbohydrates. Not only do the various sugars differ in their capacity to reduce the copper reagent, but the measurements are further complicated if other reducing substances are present in food. Satisfactory data may in the future be obtained by entirely different techniques, possibly by chromatographic procedures, to provide values for each of the separate kinds of carbohydrates.

Another approach to a figure for the carbohydrate fraction that is readily converted to sugars has been to subtract the content of fiber determined by a routine procedure from the figure for "total carbohydrate." The remainder, which is called nitrogen-free-extract, has been considered a reasonably good estimate of the carbohydrate present in most foods which the body can convert to simple sugars. This nitrogen-free-extract has been used as the basis for classifying carbohydrates in fruits and vegetables for diabetic diets (*1*).

Nearly all of the values for fiber shown in table 1 were obtained by the Weende procedure. These values may be too low; values obtained by more recent procedures for fiber in some foods are three to four times higher.

Mineral Elements (Ca, P, Fe, Na, K, Mg)

Data on the content of six mineral elements—calcium, phosphorus, iron, sodium, potassium, and magnesium—are presented in this publication; magnesium, separately in table 5.

Calcium, phosphorus, and iron have been listed in tables of food composition in this series beginning with the tables published in 1945. Since then the array of data on file for the content of each of these three mineral elements has been augmented by additional values located in the literature and by other values from unpublished sources. Even now, however, relatively few data for these three elements are available for a great many food items.

Sodium and potassium are included as a part of tables 1 and 2 in this edition. Growing recognition over the past 15 to 20 years of their importance and the development of more expeditious methods, especially the flame photometric methods, stimulated more work on the determination of the content of sodium and potassium in foods.

The data assembled show wide ranges in contents of both sodium and potassium, particularly in foods of plant origin. One of the reasons for the differences for sodium appears to be the analytical method used. Values reported for the content of sodium in the early literature were relatively high. They were based largely on gravimetric methods and probably included some potassium.

Values for sodium have been determined also by the magnesium uranyl acetate method, a gravimetric method which is considered satisfactory even for foods containing small amounts of sodium. Still other data on sodium were based on colorimetric and flame photometric methods. The values obtained by these three types of methods were usually lower than those reported for sodium in the early literature.

Data on the content of potassium in these tables are, in a large measure, based on relatively recent analyses in which flame photometric procedures were used. Results obtained by the older gravimetric and colorimetric procedures were on file for some foods and were similar to the newer values where items could be considered comparable. As potassium occurs in highly soluble forms, a significant proportion of the amount originally present can be lost from vegetables or other foods that are blanched or cooked in water and drained. Presumably this is partial explanation for values reported for frozen vegetables and for drained solids from canned vegetables when lower than the data for the comparable raw item.

Magnesium values have been introduced in this publication as a separate table because of the preliminary nature of the figures. Although magnesium has been recognized as an essential element for some 30 years, comparatively few studies have included data on the amounts present in individual foods. The tentative values on the content of magnesium shown in table 5 have been assembled to meet an anticipated growing demand for information on magnesium in foods. In numerous instances the figures are based on only single determinations; for a very few items the values are averages based on many samples.

Many of the data for magnesium in table 5 were based on the long-established gravimetric or volumetric methods of analyses. The results were reported to the nearest whole milligram per 100 grams of food analyzed, and as such were considered accurate for expressing the content of this element.

The values listed for each of the six mineral elements for most foods in this publication are based on chemical and physical methods which measure the total amount of each present in the food. Included in the figure for the content of each mineral are amounts, if any, added to the product in its preparation for the retail market. For example, small amounts of sodium or phosphorus added in the manufacture of some of the quick-cooking breakfast cereals, or of calcium compounds added to pickles, canned tomatoes, or other products as firming agents, would be included. Minerals may be contributed also by water used in processing. Calcium, iron, magnesium, and sodium, for example, may be picked up in this way. Inasmuch as the data for frozen and canned vegetables were based on direct analyses of commercially prepared products, the values include the amounts of the mineral retained by the vegetable and any that might come from brine or water used at various steps in the production line. However, the values shown for sodium in the regular packs of canned vegetables were based on an estimate of the usual amount of salt added in canning. Data for sodium and potassium in canned fruit were calculated from average values for the raw fruit, and do not include amounts picked up at various steps in preparation.

This practice of listing the total amount of a mineral was followed in the previous tables of composition in this series. It remains the most feasible basis for reporting data for individual foods although, ideally, amounts available to the body might be preferred and are at times requested. In view of the many factors and multiplicity of conditions that influence utilization of the elements, there is at present no clear-cut basis for reporting the available portion. In addition to the chemical combination in which an element occurs in foods, other important factors affecting utilization include dietary and physiological conditions under which the food containing the element is ingested by the individual. Also, the presence in the food or the diet of other chemical constituents would have to be considered, such as the type of carbohydrate and the presence of fiber, fat, oxalic acid, and phytic acid.

Calcium and magnesium, for example, may combine with oxalic acid to form highly insoluble compounds. If these elements occur in the food already bound in this way or if the combination takes place following ingestion of the meal, part of the calcium and magnesium may be excreted as the insoluble oxalates. However, the actual extent to which oxalic acid may be expected to limit the utilization of these elements has not been established.

Relatively few foods have sufficient oxalic acid to bind a nutritionally significant amount of calcium and magnesium from either the same food or some other source. Baking or bitter chocolate, peanuts, pecans, and wheat germ contain moderate amounts of oxalic acid, 200 to 400 milligrams per 100 grams. Carrots, collards, kale, leeks, okra, parsnips, potatoes, and sweetpotatoes contain smaller quantities of oxalic acid. The total amount of calcium and magnesium present in these foods is probably more than enough to combine with all the oxalic acid. Samples of beet greens, New Zealand spinach, rhubarb, spinach, and swiss chard, on the other hand, have been found to have more oxalic acid than would combine with the calcium and magnesium usually present in these foods. The upper portion of the stalk of rhubarb has a higher concentration of the acid than has the lower portion. For many oxalate-containing foods such as beets, rice, and especially the foods with high content (500 to 1,000 milligrams and more, such as dock, lambsquarters, poke, and purslane), analyses are needed for oxalic acid, calcium, and magnesium on the same samples to determine whether the food can be expected to contribute any calcium and magnesium.

Much of the phosphorus present in nuts, legumes, and the outer layers of cereal grains occurs as phytic acid. This is a phosphoric acid ester of inositol which may combine with part of the calcium, magnesium, and iron in insoluble forms and pass through the body without being absorbed.

Vitamins

Data for the five vitamins—vitamin A value, thiamine, riboflavin, niacin, and ascorbic acid—shown in tables 1 and 2, are based on a much larger volume of analyses than was used in the preparation of the figures published in the 1950 publication of this Handbook. Information on a sixth vitamin, folic acid, another of the B vitamins, was published in a separate bulletin (*25*) issued in 1951. Very little additional work has been reported since that time, either on the content of this vitamin in foods or on the improvement of the methodology for determining folic acid. Information on the content in foods for two other B vitamins, pantothenic acid and cobalamin (vitamin B_{12}), is becoming available from a number of sources. For information on these two vitamins the reader is referred especially to original data for fairly extensive lists of foods published as Agriculture Handbook No. 97, "Pantothenic Acid in Foods" (*35*) and Home Economics Research Report No. 13, "Vitamin B_{12}" (*19*).

Vitamin A Value

The figures for vitamin A value in this publication are expressed in international units and include the preformed vitamin A which is found in liver and other foods of animal origin and the carotenoids which are precursors of vitamin A and are found in foods of plant origin. Some foods of animal origin, such as butter and yolk of egg, have both vitamin A per se and beta-carotene or other precursors.

Originally the plan for presenting data on vitamin A value in these tables was to include, in addition to a column for total vitamin A value, separate columns for beta-carotene, other precursors, and the preformed vitamin A. However, the data available from the various original sources did not permit summarizing the data on this basis so only the one column of values has been presented in this publication.

Yellow-pigmented foods of plant origin presented special problems in the derivation of vitamin A values. Cryptoxanthin, a biologically active pigment, makes up a significant portion of the total carotenoid pigments in some foods, such as oranges and yellow corn. When only carotene is measured in the chromatographic procedure, the other biologically active pigments are underestimated considerably.

Many of the yellow- and also red-pigmented foods contain a large fraction of carotenoids that are not physiologically available. If this fraction has not been separated completely or if total carotenoids have been measured without any fractionation, the resultant value may overestimate the biologically active portion as much as several hundred percent.

An appropriate estimate of the vitamin A value is complicated further in some cases by the large increases in total carotenoid pigments that occur with advancing maturity or during storage of the food. These data are particularly difficult to interpret, as little or no information is available on the relative rates of increase of the various carotenoids under these conditions.

The present status of the data on carotenoids as a basis for estimating vitamin A values points to the need of greater specificity in carotenoid analyses and greater emphasis on studies of behavior of the individual carotenoids during maturing and storing, and under other conditions that may affect concentration either favorably or adversely. This is true particularly for the yellow- and red-pigmented foods.

Whereas in the 1950 issue of this Handbook many of the vitamin A values were based on biological methods, most of the values in the current publication are based on physical-chemical determinations of total carotenoids or of individual carotenes and cryptoxanthin. Results reported by an investigator in terms of carotene were converted to international units of vitamin A on the basis that 0.6 micrograms of beta-carotene and 1.2 micrograms of other commonly occurring carotenes having vitamin A activity or of cryptoxanthin were equivalent to 1 international unit of vitamin A value. Data expressed in terms of vitamin A alcohol were converted on the basis that 0.3 microgram vitamin A (alcohol) is equivalent to 1 international unit and 0.34 microgram vitamin A acetate is equivalent to 1 international unit. No allowance has been made for the differences in physiological equivalence of vitamin A to the various precursors or for differences in availability of the precursors as sources of vitamin A value from different types of food.

Thiamine

Vitamin B_1, more technically termed "thiamine," is also known as the antineuritic vitamin and as aneurin. The early biological tests with various animals have been superseded by methods using lower forms of life, such as bacteria, molds, yeasts, and protozoa; methods based on bacterial growth have been widely accepted. Most determinations of the thiamine content of foods, however, have been made by a chemical procedure in which thiamine is oxidized to thiochrome and measurement made of the fluorescence of this product. For the assay of foodstuffs by the thiochrome method, interfering substances have to be separated from the vitamin by use of an appropriate adsorbent and solvent. Collaborative studies on a few foods have shown good agreement between the microbiological and thiochrome methods.

Thiamine is present in most foods, although it is abundant in only a few foods, such as pork, nuts, and cereal germs. Yeast powder is a very rich source of this nutrient.

Thiamine is soluble in water and easily destroyed by heat. These two properties are responsible for appreciable losses of thiamine from processed and stored foods. An acid medium favors the retention of thiamine, whereas an alkaline medium such as could be produced by the use of soda is detrimental to the retention of thiamine.

Riboflavin

Early names for riboflavin included vitamin B_2, lactoflavin, and vitamin G. This vitamin is present in a wide variety of foods. Yeast, milk, egg white, liver, heart, kidney, and leafy vegetables are good sources.

As with thiamine, the early cumbersome and expensive biologic assays with laboratory animals have given way to a variety of rapid procedures. These include fluorometric, colorimetric, polarigraphic, enzymatic, and microbiological methods.

Fluorometric and microbiological methods are generally preferred for determining riboflavin in foods. With either procedure it is necessary to use a preliminary acid or enzymatic digestion to release riboflavin from its combined forms. Over the years many modifications have been made in the digestion procedures to obtain more complete release of bound riboflavin. The problem is not entirely solved, as some foods continue to show an increase in the content of this vitamin after cooking.

Niacin and Niacin Equivalent

Niacin is the official term for the vitamin, nicotinic acid, which is widely distributed in foods in the acid, amide, and other related forms. Niacin is stable to heat and light, also to acid and alkali. It is soluble in water, however, so is subject to considerable loss if the water used in cooking and the drippings from meat are discarded.

Values for niacin in tables 1 and 2 are based on chemical and microbiological assay methods which measure the free acid following its release by enzyme, acid, or alkali treatment of the sample. Various modifications have been introduced over the years to obtain complete conversion to free nicotinic acid and to remove interfering substances.

Trigonelline, a biologically inactive derivative of niacin, is present in large quantities in seeds of a few plants. It is particularly interesting that in coffee, the ordinary roasting procedures convert trigonelline to the vitamin, which is readily dissolved into the beverage by the usual brewing procedures.

In addition to niacin, nearly all foods contain tryptophan, an essential amino acid, which has been found to function as a precursor of niacin. The term "niacin equivalent" is used to apply to the potential niacin value—that is, to the sum of the preformed niacin and the amount of niacin that could be derived from tryptophan.

Both Goldsmith (*11*, *12*) and Horwitt (*13*) found from studies with adults on niacin-deficient diets that from 33 to 86 milligrams of tryptophan were needed to have the effect of 1 milligram of preformed niacin. The average conversion ratio was 60 milligrams tryptophan to 1 milligram niacin, and this ratio has become the basis of calculating niacin equivalents (*21*, p. 18).

The inclusion of values for niacin equivalents in this publication was considered. However, there is a need for tryptophan over and above its use as a precursor of niacin, and this need has not been established. At the present time, therefore, a listing of calculated values that include the potential niacin from tryptophan was deemed inappropriate—particularly as the tables may be used for estimating nutritive values of dietaries for individuals under many different conditions and for various age and activity groups which may differ in their basic requirements for tryptophan.

As an estimate of the maximum potential contribution of tryptophan to niacin, niacin equivalents have been calculated for food groups in the national food supply and are shown in table 9. If a deduction is made of 500 milligrams of tryptophan per day, an amount suggested by Rose (*24*) as a safe allowance to meet the needs of tryptophan in young men and considerably more than amounts indicated in Leverton's work with young women (*18*), the niacin equivalent value of the food supply would be about 50 percent higher than the figure for the content of preformed niacin.

TABLE 9.—PREFORMED NIACIN AND POTENTIAL NIACIN EQUIVALENT VALUE OF NATIONAL PER CAPITA FOOD CONSUMPTION PER DAY, 1960

Food group	Tryptophan	Niacin[1] from tryptophan	Preformed niacin	Niacin equivalent
	Mg.	*Mg.*	*Mg.*	*Mg.*
Dairy products	320	5.3	0.6	5.9
Eggs	99	1.6	.0	1.6
Meat, poultry, fish	417	7.0	10.2	17.2
Dry beans, peas, nuts	56	.9	1.3	2.2
Vegetables and fruits	76	1.3	3.4	4.7
Grain products	220	3.7	4.5	8.2
Miscellaneous			.1	.1
Total	1,188	19.8	20.1	39.9
Allowance for tryptophan	-500			
Adjusted total	688	11.5	20.1	31.6

[1] Assumes 60 mg. tryptophan converted to 1 mg. niacin.

Ascorbic Acid

A wide variety of fruits and vegetables contain ascorbic acid, or vitamin C. Very little occurs in most foods of animal origin.

The literature providing data is voluminous and shows that the content of ascorbic acid in foods is related to many factors and, further, that the importance of any one factor differs for different kinds of food.

The derivation of representative values is complicated often by lack of pertinent information about the sample analyzed and also by the presence in some foods of dehydroascorbic acid, an oxidized form which has practically the same physiological activity as reduced ascorbic acid but is not always included in the determinations. The dehydro form is even less stable than the reduced form and readily undergoes further oxidation to diketogulonic acid, which is without activity as vitamin C, but has at times been included in the determination and reported as ascorbic acid.

Most of the data in the literature on well-described products are results of analyses for reduced ascorbic acid. A number of investigators, however, have determined and reported both the reduced and dehydro forms in the samples which they analyzed; a few have reported the sum of the two active forms without indicating how much of each was present; and still others have included the oxidized, inactive form as part of the total ascorbic acid.

The vitamin occurs predominantly if not entirely as reduced ascorbic acid in freshly harvested products, but some oxidation to dehydroascorbic acid occurs during storage, especially if the tissue is cut or macerated. Data for reduced ascorbic acid formed the basis of the values shown in tables 1 and 2 for raw, canned, and dehydrated fruits and vegetables, because data available on the total ascorbic acid content were much too limited and too erratic. Although considered reasonably satisfactory for these foods, the values shown are probably conservative. Data for several fresh products exhibit variable and frequently large proportions of the vitamin in the dehydro form.

To the extent that dehydroascorbic acid in canned products is formed and not oxidized further to diketogulonic acid, these values may be too low. No suitable basis was found for estimating the content of total ascorbic acid; that is, the sum of the reduced and dehydro forms for fresh, canned, and dehydrated foods.

Total ascorbic acid was determined for a large representative sampling of frozen foods that had been held frozen under conditions found experimentally to permit practically complete retention of ascorbic acid. These values have been used in tables 1 and 2 but may be somewhat higher than would be found in products held under less ideal conditions. They were used because there was no generally suitable basis for estimating the extent of oxidation when the frozen foods are handled under less ideal conditions in ordinary commercial channels and in homes, or for estimating losses during thawing of frozen fruits prior to serving. Furthermore, in recent years special study has been made of ways of improving commercial handling of frozen foods to prevent quality changes and also to reduce the nutrient loss.

All research that could be located was studied and many factors were considered before data were selected and used as the basis for deriving the values in the column under ascorbic acid. Although the figures listed are not on a completely uniform basis, they are believed to be as representative for the product described as current information permits.

APPENDIX B.—NOTES ON FOODS

This section provides information that could not be handled readily in footnotes and supplementary data believed useful to better understanding of values in this publication.

Cereals and Grain Products

Enriched foods and standards of enrichment.—Items described as "enriched" are items for which Federal standards for enrichment have been promulgated. To be labeled "enriched" these products must contain amounts of certain nutrients within the limits specified in the standard for the particular product. The quantities specified for the nutrients required have been summarized for convenience in table 10.

Federal standards for enriched rice became effective February 27, 1958, for all the nutrients except riboflavin, as is indicated in table 10. The requirement for riboflavin was stayed pending further hearings. If the regulation becomes effective, the figure for riboflavin in table 10 should be used. The corresponding figures per 100 grams would be 0.26 milligram for enriched rice in the dry form (items 1871, 1873, and 1875) and 0.07 milligram for the cooked forms (items 1872, 1874, and 1876). Meanwhile, or until further action is taken by the Food and Drug Administration, data for riboflavin in comparable forms of unenriched rice should be used.

The minimum levels stated for the nutrients apply to packaged rice bearing on the label the statement, "To retain vitamins do not rinse before or drain after cooking." The standards require, furthermore, that the label must not contain directions for cooking that call for washing and draining. If the label does not carry such a statement, or if cooking directions call for washing and draining, these nutrients must be present in such quantity or form that the enriched rice, after washing, contains not less than 85 percent of the minimums specified.

The standards provide for enrichment of wholeground and bolted cornmeals as well as for degermed meals and for self-rising cornmeals. Values in tables 1 and 2 for calcium in self-rising

TABLE 10.—STANDARDS FOR ENRICHMENT: MINIMUM AND MAXIMUM AMOUNTS OF REQUIRED NUTRIENTS SPECIFIED FOR FOODS LABELED "ENRICHED" [1] [2]

[Milligrams per pound of product]

Item	Thiamine		Riboflavin		Niacin		Iron		Calcium	
	Min.	Max.	Min.	Max.	Min.	Max.	Min.	Max.	Min.	Max.
	Mg.	*Mg.*	*Mg.*	*Mg.*	*Mg.*	*Mg.*	*Mg.*	*Mg.*	*Mg.*	*Mg.*
Bread, rolls, and buns, white	1.1	1.8	0.7	1.6	10.0	15.0	8.0	12.5		
Cornmeal; corn grits	2.0	3.0	1.2	1.8	16.0	24.0	13.0	26.0		
Cornmeal, self-rising	2.0	3.0	1.2	1.8	16.0	24.0	13.0	26.0	500	1,750
Farina	2.0	2.5	1.2	1.5	16.0	20.0	13.0	(3)		
Flour, white	2.0	2.5	1.2	1.5	16.0	20.0	13.0	16.5		
Flour, self-rising	2.0	2.5	1.2	1.5	16.0	20.0	13.0	16.5	500	1,500
Macaroni products; noodle products	4.0	5.0	1.7	2.2	27.0	34.0	13.0	16.5		
Rice, milled	2.0	4.0	[4] 1.2	[4] 2.4	16.0	32.0	13.0	26.0		

[1] The information in this table, with the exception of that for rice and self-rising cornmeal, was taken from the Federal Register of December 20, 1955 (*28*). Information for rice and for self-rising cornmeal was from the Federal Register for August 27, 1957, and August 10, 1961, respectively (*29*, *30*).

[2] The standards for enrichment provide also for the inclusion of calcium and vitamin D within stated limits as optional ingredients for the products listed in this table, except self-rising cornmeal and self-rising flour. For these items calcium is required as indicated.

[3] No maximum level has been established.

[4] Requirement for riboflavin stayed pending further hearings.

cornmeal are based on a formula which includes anhydrous monocalcium phosphate at a level of 1¾ pounds per 100 pounds of cornmeal or cornmeal and wheat flour. The values for calcium are considered applicable to both the enriched and the unenriched forms. An amendment to the original standards which provided for raising the maximal level of calcium to 1,750 milligrams per pound for enriched self-rising cornmeal became effective on January 27, 1962 (*31*).

Pastinas are included among the items that may be enriched. Those prepared with vegetables are vegetable-macaroni products and those with egg are noodle products. They are used primarily by young children and by individuals using bland foods. Data for pastinas have been entered under this name in the main tables.

Cereal products with added nutrients.—Many breakfast-food cereals on the market, particularly those in ready-to-serve form, have added nutrients, usually one or more of the following: Iron, thiamine, riboflavin, and niacin. However, a few products contain added amounts of one or more other nutrients, such as calcium, ascorbic acid, and special protein concentrate. At present, there are no Federal standards regarding the addition of nutrients in the manufacture of these products.

The values for the breakfast-food products with added nutrients shown in the tables are averages of the compositional data reported for commercial products that have the same generic classification and have approximately the same levels of added nutrients. The composition of these products changes frequently; therefore, before applying these data in any particular calculation, as in dietary studies, it would be well to check the data with the information on the packages of several kinds in the current market, to see whether values in these tables continue to be applicable.

Salt is usually an ingredient in the manufactured cereal products that are ready to serve as purchased. On the other hand, salt is not ordinarily an ingredient of the dry cereals that require cooking. Usually directions call for adding salt to the water or milk used in preparation of the cereal for serving.

Unless otherwise noted, it may be assumed that the data for sodium content of dry forms of cereals that require cooking before they are served apply to products manufactured without added salt. The data for sodium in most cereals purchased ready-to-serve and for sodium in cooked cereals apply to products to which salt has been added.

Alimentary pastes.—Macaroni, noodles, pastinas, and spaghetti are ordinarily manufactured without added salt, and the values in the tables for the dry forms of these products are without salt. Directions for cooking usually specify boiling in salted water. Inasmuch as a representative amount of salt in the drained, cooked products could not be estimated, the data in table 1 for the plain cooked forms apply to the products cooked in the unsalted water. However, the data for mixed dishes such as macaroni and cheese apply to products in which salt has been added in accordance with a typical recipe for the product.

Bread and rolls.—Nutritive values for commercial white breads in tables 1 and 2 are based on several hundred samples obtained from retail outlets throughout the country. Values for other kinds of bread and rolls are based on far fewer samples, but are considered representative of the item described inasmuch as they agree well with compositional values calcaluated for each item from formulas typical in recent commercial practice.

Federal definitions and standards of identity have been promulgated for the most commonly used bakery products: White bread and rolls, enriched and unenriched; milk bread and rolls; raisin bread and rolls; whole-wheat bread and rolls. These standards, originally published in the Federal Register for May 15, 1952 (*27*), specify the ingredients required, the optional ingredients permitted, and limitations in quantities of certain ingredients for these bakery products if they are shipped across State lines. States also may have standards, and in some instances the State standards apply to more kinds of bread and roll items than do the Federal standards. Also, in some States laws require that the white bread distributed be enriched and labeled to show that it is enriched bread.

For many of the specialty breads and rolls on the market there are no standards.

Nonfat dry milk is permitted under Federal regulations as an optional ingredient in commercial breads. It is customary to express the amount used as percentage of the weight of flour in the formula. Relatively little bread has over

6 percent nonfat dry milk (6 pounds of nonfat dry milk per 100 pounds of flour).

White breads made with nonfat dry milk at different specified levels within the range most commonly used in the baking industry have been included in the tables. The level is stated as part of the description of the bread item. For the past several years, bread having 3 to 4 percent nonfat dry milk has been considered the most usual kind on the market, and it is suggested that the values for this bread continue to be used for calculations when the level is unknown.

Compounds to retard spoilage caused by molds and compounds to improve handling characteristics of the dough are permitted under Federal specifications that limit kind and quantity. Such compounds are usually included by bakers in commercial breads. The amounts permitted are small but if the mold inhibitor and the dough conditioner selected by the baker contain calcium, these compounds, together with the nonfat dry milk, account for significant amounts of calcium in bread. For example, when bread is made with 3 to 4 pounds of nonfat dry milk per 100 pounds of flour and with 0.25 pound of a calcium-containing dough conditioner and 0.2 pound of calcium propionate (a mold inhibitor widely used), a 1-pound loaf would have about 145 milligrams of calcium from the milk, about 50 milligrams from the dough conditioner, and about 110 milligrams from the mold inhibitor.

If sodium propionate or another compound that does not contain calcium is used as the mold inhibitor in breadmaking, figures for calcium could be considerably lower than shown in tables 1 and 2, as those figures reflect the widespread use of calcium propionate. Likewise, higher figures for sodium would be expected if the formula had included sodium propionate. Values for the content of calcium and of sodium calculated for bread and roll items made with sodium propionate are shown in table 11.

Cakes.—Values for cakes made from home-type recipes were calculated from ingredients. The shortening used as the basis for calculation of the values listed in tables 1 and 2 was cooking fat, item 999. Some homemakers use butter or fortified margarine, and the resultant cakes would have higher vitamin A values as indicated by the values in table 12.

Computation was made also of the sodium content of cakes made without salt and with a low-sodium baking-powder preparation, item 135, substituted for the sodium aluminum sulfate

TABLE 11.—CALCIUM AND SODIUM CONTENT OF BREAD AND ROLL ITEMS MADE WITH SODIUM PROPIONATE

Item Nos. from tables 1 and 2	Item	Sodium propionate per 100 pounds of flour	Calcium in—		Sodium in—	
			100 grams	1 pound	100 grams	1 pound
	Breads:	*Pounds*	*Milligrams*	*Milligrams*	*Milligrams*	*Milligrams*
444	Cracked-wheat	0.31	48	218	577	2,617
452	Raisin	.20	55	249	393	1,782
	Rye:					
454	American (light)	.31	33	150	608	2,758
456	Pumpernickel	.31	41	186	622	2,821
	White; made with—					
459, 465	1%–2% nonfat dry milk	.20	42	191	537	2,436
461, 467	3%–4% nonfat dry milk	.20	57	259	536	2,431
463, 469	5%–6% nonfat dry milk	.20	71	322	523	2,372
	Whole-wheat; made with—					
471	2% nonfat dry milk	.31	60	272	575	2,608
473	Water	.31	44	200	579	2,626
	Rolls or buns:					
	Ready-to-serve:					
1904	Raisin	.20	57	259	406	1,842
	White:					
1902, 1903	Pan or plain	.20	50	227	536	2,431
1905	Sweet	.20	65	295	414	1,878
1906	Whole-wheat	.31	64	290	615	2,790
1908, 1910	Brown-and-serve, browned	.20	51	231	562	2,549
1912, 1914	Frozen, baked	.20	39	177	560	2,540

TABLE 12.—VITAMIN A VALUES OF CAKES MADE WITH UNFORTIFIED FATS AND OF CAKES MADE WITH BUTTER OR WITH MARGARINE HAVING VITAMIN A ADDED

Item Nos. from tables 1 and 2	Type of cake	Vitamin A value			
		100 grams of cake made with—		1 pound of cake made with—	
		Unfortified fat	Butter, or with margarine having vitamin A added	Unfortified fat	Butter, or with margarine having vitamin A added
		International units	*International units*	*International units*	*International units*
522	Boston cream pie	210	390	950	1,770
	Caramel cake:				
523	Without icing	180	660	820	2,990
524	With caramel icing	200	570	910	2,590
	Chocolate devil's food cake:				
525	Without icing	150	480	680	2,180
526	With chocolate icing	160	410	730	1,860
527	With uncooked white icing	180	430	820	1,950
	Cottage pudding:				
528	Without sauce	140	390	640	1,770
529	With chocolate sauce	100	290	450	1,320
530	With fruit sauce (strawberry)	120	310	540	1,410
	Plain cake or cupcake:				
534	Without icing	170	540	770	2,450
535	With chocolate icing	180	440	820	2,000
536	With boiled white icing	130	410	590	1,860
537	With uncooked white icing	200	460	910	2,090
538	Pound cake, old-fashioned	280	1,010	1,270	4,580
539	Pound cake, modified	290	710	1,320	3,220
	White cake:				
541	Without icing	30	520	120	2,360
542	With coconut icing	20	350	80	1,590
543	With uncooked white icing	110	440	500	2,000
	Yellow cake:				
544	Without icing	150	480	680	2,180
545	With caramel icing	170	450	770	2,040
546	With chocolate icing	160	410	730	1,860

baking powder used in the recipes for obtaining the values in tables 1 and 2. The sodium values for the cake items listed in table 12 (except for old-fashioned pound cake which does not contain baking powder) were calculated to have 20 to 40 milligrams per 100 grams if made without salt and with the low-sodium baking-powder preparation, but from 186 to 323 milligrams per 100 grams if prepared from the ordinary recipe.

The potassium content of the cakes made with the low-sodium baking-powder preparation would average about 210 milligrams per 100 grams, and range from about 140 to 290 milligrams. This is about one and a half to three and a half times higher than if the sodium aluminum sulfate baking powder was used.

Fruits and Vegetables

The nutrient or nutrients of greatest importance and known to be variable in concentration received special consideration in developing representative values for each fruit and vegetable. For most of these foods this meant finding and applying information on the particular factors such as variety, maturity, storage, and processing that are related to the content of ascorbic acid or vitamin A value. These are the nutrients of greatest importance in most fruits and vegetables, and the content of each generally varies over a wide range from sample to sample.

Apples.—The values for ascorbic acid in apples are weighted by the more important commercial varieties. It is not considered feasible to show separate data for different varieties of apples at this time.

The leading variety of summer apples is Gravenstein; other varieties include Early Harvest and Yellow Transparent. The average ascorbic acid value for freshly harvested summer apples eaten with the skin is 11 milligrams per 100 grams. The important varieties of fall apples are Jonathan, Wealthy, and Grimes Golden; they provide about 7 milligrams of ascorbic acid per 100 grams. Winter apples make up the major part of the total production, and of these the four leading varieties are Delicious, McIntosh, Winesap, and Rome Beauty. Other commercially important winter apples are Stayman, York Imperial, Golden Delicious, Yellow Newtown, Cortland, Baldwin, Northern Spy, Rhode Island Greening, Ben Davis, Gano, and Black Twig. Winter apples eaten with skin also provide about 7 milligrams of ascorbic acid per 100 grams when freshly harvested.

A few varieties of winter apples have ascorbic acid values considerably higher than the average value for the group or than the average shown in table 1 for all apples. For example, Willowtwig, Northern Spy, and Yellow Newtown contain 19, 16, and 14 milligrams respectively per 100 grams of freshly harvested or recently harvested apple with skin. On the other hand, freshly harvested Delicious, McIntosh, Winesap, and Rome Beauty, which account for about half of the total commercial apple crop for the year, contain about 6, 5, 8, and 5 milligrams of ascorbic acid respectively per 100 grams. After several months' storage the ascorbic acid value of apples drops to one-half or less of the original content.

Cabbage, chopped or shredded; cantaloups, freshly cut; squashes, freshly cut; strawberries, capped.—The ascorbic acid in these foods is exceptionally unstable, and a large proportion becomes oxidized readily. The values in the tables do not allow for any losses that might occur from cutting or capping in preparation for serving, and therefore overestimate the content of ascorbic acid to the extent that dehydroascorbic acid is oxidized further to diketogulonic acid, the inactive oxidized form.

Carrots.—Variety and stage of maturity account for much of the wide range in the vitamin A values reported for fresh carrots—1,300 to over 28,000 micrograms of carotene per 100 grams, equivalent to about 2,200 to 47,000 international units of vitamin A per 100 grams—and contribute also to the differences among the average values for the fresh, canned, and dehydrated forms of carrots.

Imperator is the predominant variety marketed as the fresh vegetable. When harvested at prime maturity for the market, the vitamin A value is approximately 11,000 international units per 100 grams. At later stages the value would be nearly doubled.

Chantenays and Danvers are the principal varieties used for the processed products. Vitamin A values of Chantenays and Danvers are respectively about 7,000 and 12,000 international units per 100 grams at prime maturity for use as fresh vegetables, and the values increase to 17,000 and 38,000 international units respectively at the maximum stage of maturity considered acceptable. The comparatively high vitamin A values found by analyses of canned and dehydrated carrots, and shown in this publication, indicate that these two forms are prepared from carrots more mature than those harvested for market as fresh vegetables.

Corn-on-the-cob.—The carbohydrate content of corn is variable; two of the more important determining factors are maturity and variety. As the kernels develop from the early to later milk stages on to the dough stage, the moisture decreases and the content of carbohydrate increases. This increase in carbohydrate from the beginning to the end of the edible stages could increase the energy value as much as 40 Calories per 100 grams of kernel.

Different varieties of sweet corn show differences in composition at comparable stages of use. The carbohydrate in kernels of one variety may be greater at the beginning of the period of good eating quality than that of another variety toward the end of the period. At present, there is insufficient information for separating data according to variety and maturity. The values shown in the tables for the proximate composition and for energy value are averages that have taken into account such information as was available on maturity and on varieties of commercial importance.

Oranges.—The ascorbic acid content of oranges is related to area of origin, variety, and time of harvest—the content decreasing as the season progresses. All these factors were taken into account in deriving the single figure for ascorbic acid listed for item 1420, Oranges, all commercial varieties. Oranges to be marketed as fresh fruit are supplied mainly by the California-Arizona area and by Florida—in approximately equal quantities. Information on relative quantities of oranges of important varieties shipped each month for use as fresh fruit was applied in arriving at this figure, which may be used therefore as a year-round, countrywide value. Many older data on vitamin C were discarded in deriving this value because the fruit sampled earlier did not meet the current quality standards for maturity.

As the general figure for ascorbic acid content of oranges is not sufficient for some purposes, data have been provided also for California-Arizona Navels and Valencias and for Florida early and midseason varieties including Temple, and for Florida late-season Valencias.

Frozen orange juice concentrate and canned orange juice on the retail market are prepared mainly from Florida oranges and reflect the nutritive value of these oranges. Approximately two-thirds of a canned concentrate which is packed largely for institutional use is prepared from California Valencias; the remainder, from Florida oranges.

Potatoes.—Literally thousands of analyses of the ascorbic acid content of potatoes have been reported, the values ranging from 50 milligrams in 100 grams of freshly dug, immature potatoes to less than 10 milligrams for potatoes stored for periods of many months.

Variety and storage are the important factors to consider in deriving a suitable average figure for ascorbic acid in potatoes. The value in this publication reflects the relative quantities of different commercial varieties of potatoes in the market each month of the year, as well as the usual lengths of storage periods, and represents the year-round average amount of ascorbic acid in potatoes in the market.

Sweetpotatoes.—Vitamin A values differ widely with variety. Many new varieties having flesh of deep-orange color have been developed in recent years and have been replacing varieties with light-colored flesh. As a result, the average vitamin A value for sweetpotatoes in commercial production has increased more than 11 percent—from the value 7,700 international units per 100 grams, shown in the 1950 edition of this Handbook, to the present value of 8,800 international units per 100 grams.

Cooked vegetables.—The values shown in table 1 for boiled vegetables apply in most instances to products that are cooked in small or moderate amounts of water until tender and then drained. Because significant amounts of the soluble nutrients dissolve into the cooking water, the values listed for them are somewhat lower than those obtained when the vegetables are cooked by steaming, pressure cooking, and other methods in which the volume of cooking water is held to a minimum.

The values for the vitamins in boiled vegetables were calculated by applying average percentage retention figures to the values for raw vegetables in table 1. The percentage retentions for the vitamins were based on published reports of carefully conducted studies of losses—solubility and/or destruction—expressed in terms of the original weights of the raw vegetables.

Similar studies of losses of proximate constituents and minerals were too scant to provide suitable bases for deriving retention factors. The retention factors used for these several constituents were based mainly on the percentage distribution of soluble nutrients between the drained solids and drained liquid in canned vegetables. Estimated in this way, the content of the nutrients shown in the table for cooked vegetables is probably too low for vegetables cooked by methods recommended for conserving nutrients.

Although values derived in this way are not completely satisfactory, they are considered more representative and more reliable than those obtained by averaging all the data on cooked vegetables noted in the literature. The calculated values were compared with the actual values found in the literature for boiled vegetables and were considered reasonable insofar as data on suitable well-described products were available for properly evaluating the two kinds of data. Many of the values reported in the literature were on products not well described in regard to either the original raw vegetable or the details of the cooking method.

The figures for sodium in table 1 are for unsalted drained vegetables. These values may be an underestimation if the cooking water has a high natural sodium content. The values on the content of sodium in the cooked dry vegetables, such as dry beans, lima beans, cowpeas, split peas, and soybeans, are also for the unsalted products.

There is no satisfactory basis for estimating a representative figure for the content of sodium in vegetables cooked with salt or salted at time of serving. A typical content of salt (NaCl) in canned vegetables, 0.6 percent in the finished product, might be used as a guide for moderately salted items. On this basis the amounts of sodium listed in table 1 for drained, cooked vegetables would have to be increased by 236 milligrams per 100 grams.

Canned fruits and vegetables.—Commercially canned fruits are available in a number of forms. For any one kind of fruit there may be whole style, halves, slices, chunks, crushed pieces, or puree. The packing medium designated on the can label may vary from water or fruit juice, either plain or slightly sweetened, to extra heavy sirup, or fruit-juice sirup. The proportions of drained solids and liquid in the can vary with the style, the size of can, and the packing medium. The nutritive values for canned fruits shown in the table take into account the proportions of drained solids and liquid and the packing medium used.

For this publication several representative packs were selected; namely, water pack, juice pack, and three sirup packs—light, heavy, and extra heavy.

Nutritive values are shown for approximately 20 different canned fruits but not in every instance for all five packing mediums. Some fruits are not canned in all packs. In other instances a fruit may be canned in these various packs, but information on chemical composition was inadequate for deriving nutritive values.

Heavy sirup is the predominant kind of sirup pack, and probably the values for this pack should be used in calculating diets when the concentration of the sirup is not known.

In addition to the regular packs, many fruits and vegetables are packed for *special dietary use.* A number of fruits are canned in water without added sugar for use in low-calorie diets or in diets for patients with diabetes. These products are described in this publication as "water pack, with or without artificial sweetener."

If artificial sweeteners are added, the usual ones are calcium cyclamate and calcium or sodium saccharinate. These sweeteners add insignificant amounts of calcium and sodium to the canned fruit. Calcium cyclamate adds about 2 milligrams of calcium per 100 grams of canned fruit. Saccharin salt (calcium or sodium) is added in an amount about one-tenth that of calcium cyclamate, or about 0.002 percent, and contributes negligible amounts of calcium or sodium to the product.

Several vegetables are canned for use in sodium-restricted diets. Data for vegetables canned without salt and with special precautions to avoid other sources of sodium are designated in this publication as special dietary pack (low-sodium).

Sources of sodium in processed fruits and vegetables in addition to water of high sodium content used either as the packing medium or for blanching, include lye used for peeling, brine used for quality separation, and dilute salt solutions used to prevent discoloration of the product. The content of sodium in foods subjected to these treatments is variable and may be well above the figures listed in this publication. This variation in content of sodium was noted in several of the strained and junior fruits included in the group of canned baby foods in tables 1 and 2. For example, a mixture of applesauce and apricots had values that ranged from 3 to 45 milligrams per 100 grams of product, whereas the values for peaches and for mixed pear and pineapple ranged from 4 milligrams or less to as high as 75 milligrams.

A number of canned foods, particularly fruit products, have added nutrients; for example, ascorbic acid is added to some of the nectars. For ingredients, note the information on the label.

Frozen fruits and vegetables.—Approximately 50 frozen fruit and vegetable items are included in this publication. Several of these foods had an extremely wide range in values for either ascorbic acid or sodium.

Some packs of apricots and of peaches contain added ascorbic acid. Because of this difference in commercial practices, ascorbic acid values per 100 grams of fruit can range from 6 to 100 milligrams in frozen apricots and from 11 to 76 milligrams in frozen peaches. For other fruit products that may contain added ascorbic acid, note the information on the label.

Several frozen-food items have a wide range in sodium content, although they normally contain only small amounts. The amounts in frozen apples range from 2 to 200 milligrams in 100 grams. Values in the upper part of the range represent packs to which preservatives containing sodium have been added to prevent darkening of the apple slices. Wide ranges in sodium content occur in several of the frozen vegetables; namely, large or Fordhook lima beans, baby limas, blackeye peas, green peas, mixed peas and carrots, mixed vegetables, and succotash. A large amount of sodium may be picked up by a vegetable when sodium chloride brine is used in quality grading before freezing or when salt is added as seasoning. The maximum sodium content in milligrams per 100-gram portions of these vegetables was: large or Fordhook limas, 345; baby limas, 390; blackeye peas, 200; green peas, 305; mixed peas and carrots, 144; mixed vegetables, 108; and succotash, 155.

Problems of classification.—Many problems of classification were encountered for foods of plant origin. In the following paragraphs, attention is called to foods for which the usual nomenclature is particularly confusing.

Garden cress, *Lepidium sativum*, is a cultivated plant brought originally to this country from Europe. However, it can easily get out of bounds and grow wild, and because of this characteristic is called field cress in some areas. Other species of *Lepidium*, such as *L. virginicum*, are native wild species in this country. They are eaten sometimes but are not available on the market.

Endive and chicory have often been confused with each other. Varieties of endive grown in the United States have the species name *Cichorium endivia*, and are quite different in structural appearance from Witloof chicory (*Cichorium intybus*), which is sometimes called French or Belgian endive.

Endive (*Cichorium endivia*) is always marketed in the headed form, the larger heads weighing more than a pound. The heads are low, spreading, and loose-leaved. The leaves vary from deeply cut and deeply curled in some varieties, to the broad, slightly cut and curled leaf of escarole. The outer leaves are green, and the center leaves or heart and the midribs are pale green to creamy white.

Chicory can be marketed as blanched heads, greens, or roots. The three main varieties of chicory are Witloof, Cicoria di catalogna (Radichetta or asparagus), and large rooted (Magdeburg). Witloof chicory is the variety commonly forced, and can be identified by its very small, elongated, compact, well-blanched head, which resembles a small shoot and weighs approximately 2 ounces.

Witloof chicory also is grown for greens, as are the Radichetta and Magdeburg varieties. The leaves are dark green in color. Some varietal differences occur in the shape and form of the leaves, but all are nonheading and grow tall and upright as compared with the small, compact heads of headed Witloof chicory, or the low-spreading heads of endive.

The roots of Witloof and Magdeburg are dried and used as a substitute for coffee.

The Temple orange is botanically a tangor, which is a hybrid of the sweet orange and the tangerine (a mandarin orange); it has the scientific name *Citrus sinensis* × *Citrus reticulata*. For practical purposes, since it is marketed as an orange, it has been classified with the sweet oranges (*Citrus sinensis*) in the nomenclature of the tables and included in the average for all Florida oranges.

The tangelo is a hybrid of the grapefruit and tangerine with the scientific name *Citrus paradisi* × *Citrus reticulata*. This fruit is relatively a newcomer on the citrus market.

Acerola, Barbados-cherry, West Indian cherry are common names for a small fruit of the genus *Malpighia*, resembling the cherry in appearance, found in tropical and subtropical America. This genus has been variously reported to have from 15 to 40 known species.

The species *Malpighia punicifolia* has received most attention in recent years and has been growing in economic importance in the United States. Interest in it was stimulated by its extremely high content of ascorbic acid, ranging from 1,000 to more than 2,000 milligrams per 100 grams in the ripe fruit and even higher in the unripe fruit.

The ascorbic acid content reported for other species of the genus *Malpighia* is far lower; for example, values reported for samples of *M. glabra* grown in Central America averaged around 20 milligrams per 100 grams. Because of the magnitude of the difference in the ascorbic acid content of the different species, they have been treated as separate fruits.

The values in this publication apply only to *M. punicifolia*, as they are based on data for samples identified as *punicifolia* in the literature.

Acerola is the common name arbitrarily selected for use here. The two common names which include the word "cherry" are misnomers, as the fruit is not a cherry.

Acerola should not be confused with the Surinam-cherry (or pitanga) *Eugenia uniflora*. The two fruits are similar in size and general appearance, both having a thin skin varying in color from light to dark crimson, with juicy, aromatic flesh. The main distinguishing feature is the number of lobes or ridges, the acerola fruit having three and the Surinam-cherry eight or nine.

Meat

Data for the principal kinds of meat—beef, lamb, pork, and veal—are provided on several bases. The description of each item includes data on its physical composition; that is, the relative proportions of separable fat, separable lean, and where applicable in table 2, the proportion of bone and other parts that cannot be eaten.

The first items listed for each kind of meat are for the carcass. The data on the chemical composition are for the total of the lean and fat present in the carcass. These meat items have been included for purposes that require data on the composition of meats on the wholesale basis, and for establishing the average composition for each grade or class of meat as it comes to the market.

The values for meats have been developed step by step from the total carcass basis, through retail cutting and trimming, and finally to the cooked meat. Thus the final values for meat as eaten are directly related to the average composition of each grade at the carcass level, and different cuts are related to each other as they would be in the same carcass.

Separable lean and separable fat are shown in table 2 for beef, lamb, and pork, although they are not often available in the stores completely separated. They have been listed in this way so that calculations can be made of cuts of meat that vary markedly from the composition of "total edible" as shown. Comparable data for veal were not available.

Beef.—For beef, average values for carcasses of six U.S. Government grades have been listed. When the carcass or side is subdivided into major divisions or wholesale cuts, there is a small amount of trimming, mainly of fat and bone. Wholesale cuts may be further divided into smaller units; that is, the retail cuts, with additional trimming of fat, some bone, and unavoidably at times, of some lean.

Data for the composite of the trimmed retail cuts from the carcass have been included in this publication for beef of three grades—Choice, Good, and Standard. The composite of the trimmed retail cuts from each of the major wholesale cuts except the loin and short loin is shown for Choice grade. In addition, data are shown for numerous individual retail cuts inasmuch as there is considerable difference in composition among the retail cuts obtained from a single wholesale cut. For example, item 218 applies to the composite of the trimmed retail cuts obtained from the chuck—first five ribs, arm, and neck—and items 223 and 233 to two individual retail cuts, fifth rib and arm respectively. Cuts from the short loin and loin end are shown as individual cuts and not as composites because of the wide variation in composition in different portions of these parts.

The retail cuts, whether composites or individual, represent meat that has been trimmed to one-half inch or less of surface fat. Data were available for this amount of trim and it was considered reasonably applicable to market practice. Between the muscles in many cuts of meat are deposits of fat that are not removed at the retail level. The proportions of lean and fat remaining in the cuts after trimming are shown in the column of description on "total edible." The data for "total edible" relate to the total nutrients in both lean and fat in the proportion indicated for each item. Since additional trimming may be made in the kitchen or at the table, the proportions of lean and fat in the "total edible" may not be suitable for a particular situation. Adjustments can then be made in the nutritive values by calculations from data on the lean and the fat which are listed separately for each cut.

Such adjustment may be calculated in two ways. For example, a cut, 5th chuck rib, of average composition may be used for illustration. Assume that fat amounting to 10 percent of the weight of the cut is trimmed off in the kitchen. The nutrients in 10 grams of fat could be subtracted from the amounts in 100 grams of total edible listed in table 1 as follows:

	Weight	Separable fat	Water	Protein	Fat	Ash
	Grams	*Grams*	*Grams*	*Grams*	*Grams*	*Grams*
Entire cut	100	30	51. 7	16. 2	31. 4	0. 7
Fat trim	10	10	1. 4	. 5	8. 0	. 02
Trimmed cut	90	20	50. 3	15. 7	23. 4	0. 68
		Percent	*Percent*	*Percent*	*Percent*	*Percent*
Composition	100	22	55. 9	17. 4	26. 0	0. 8

The values labeled "percent" are those to be applied to the cut after fat amounting to 10 percent of its weight has been removed.

The calculations may be made also by a second method using data on the separable lean and separable fat from table 1. If a cut has 78 percent lean and 22 percent fat or if ground beef is prepared with 78 percent lean and 22 percent fat, the calculations are as follows:

	Weight	Water	Protein	Fat	Ash
	Grams	*Grams*	*Grams*	*Grams*	*Gram*
Lean	78	52. 6	16. 1	8. 6	0. 7
Fat	22	3. 1	1. 2	17. 6	. 04
Cut or ground beef	100	55. 7	17. 3	26. 2	0. 74
	Percent	*Percent*	*Percent*	*Percent*	*Percent*
Composition	100	55. 7	17. 3	26. 2	0. 74

Values are included for cooked meat on the basis of total edible and of separable lean. These values were calculated from the raw cuts immediately preceding them in the tables. For cooked separable fat, composite data were prepared by combining fat from all cuts.

Calcium and iron values were calculated as 58 and 15 milligrams respectively for each 100 grams of protein. Phosphorus was calculated by regression analysis based on a number of studies for all muscle meats relating the element to protein. For sodium and potassium, average values for beef based on a number of recent studies are shown, inasmuch as no satisfactory basis for relating these nutrients to composition by cut, grade, or proportion of lean and fat is apparent at this time.

The following factors were used for estimating vitamin content of raw beef:

Vitamin A	2.0 international units per gram of fat.
Thiamine	.0043 milligram per gram of protein.
Riboflavin	.0089 milligram per gram of protein.
Niacin	.240 milligram per gram of protein.

The data for lean hamburger are based on heel of round. The averages for regular ground hamburger are based on several hundred samples selected nationwide. They represented a wide range in composition, but a great preponderance of samples clustered close to the average.

Pork.—As pork is not usually sold by grade, data on carcasses and the cuts made from them have been classified by fat content into three groups, described as thin, medium-fat, and fat. In addition to the values for the untrimmed carcasses as they appear on the market, data have been included for three wholesale cuts, also untrimmed—bacon or belly, backfat, and entire shoulder.

The term "lean cuts" as used in item 1677 refers to a composite of the total edible meat (lean and fat) of ham, loin, shoulder, and spareribs. The composite applies to these cuts trimmed to the relative proportion of lean and fat indicated in the description of the individual items listed in the tables.

Data for the retail cuts—ham, loin, picnic, Boston butt, and spareribs—are shown individually after trimming. Loin is trimmed to about one-half inch or less of surface fat. Values for spareribs are listed as they are stripped from the sides. About one-fourth of the fat on ham, picnic, and Boston butt has been removed.

Mineral content was calculated as described under beef. The factors used for determining vitamin content follow:

Vitamin A	(0) imputed.
Thiamine	0.0486 milligram per gram of protein.
Riboflavin	.0117 milligram per gram of protein.
Niacin	.260 milligram per gram of protein.

Data on cooked cuts were calculated from the raw cuts immediately preceding each one.

Lamb.—Three grades of lamb are shown—Prime, Choice, and Good. Lamb grades are those that were in effect until March 1, 1960. At that time, grades were changed in such a way that the fat content may now be somewhat lower than the values shown. No suitable studies related to current standards have been located to provide a basis for changing the data on composition.

Calcium, sodium, and potassium were calculated as described under beef. Phosphorus and iron were calculated by regression analysis based on extensive unpublished data on lamb.

The factors used for estimating vitamin content were:

Thiamine	0.0089 milligram per gram of protein.
Riboflavin	.0124 milligram per gram of protein.
Niacin	.289 milligram per gram of protein.

Veal.—No comprehensive studies have been made of chemical composition of veal by current grades. The data in this publication are for carcasses, and their cuts classified as fat, medium fat, and thin. Data on the chemical composition of separable fat and separable lean of veal are not available.

Mineral content and vitamin values for cooked meat have been calculated in the same way as described under beef.

The factors used for estimating vitamin content were:

Thiamine	0.0073 milligram per gram of protein.
Riboflavin	.0133 milligram per gram of protein.
Niacin	.335 milligram per gram of protein.

Poultry

Chickens are shown by current market classes except that broiled flesh of the lighter weight birds (under 1¾-pound ready-to-cook weight with neck and giblets) is shown separately from the "fryer" group. They are usually very low in fat content and are often cooked by broiling rather than by frying.

Recent studies indicate that the newer strains of chickens raised on modern rations are, in general, considerably lower in fat content than were the types of birds previously raised on the old rations. A study performed under contract for this Department provided data on fryers of the modern type over 1¾-pound ready-to-cook weight. However, no comprehensive studies on the smaller birds of this class are available at this time, so the only data shown for the lightweight broilers are for broiled flesh.

Values shown for roasters and stewers are based on studies made quite a number of years ago, but it is believed at this time that the differences between earlier and modern types of birds of these classes are not so wide as for the younger birds.

Fish

Many studies on the proximate composition of fish, both raw and cooked, have been made in recent years, and the number of items included in the tables has increased greatly. Data on minerals, vitamins, and fatty acids are still grossly inadequate. The averages shown for these nutrients are based, for the most part, on very few studies. Some of the values shown for calcium are notably high; possibly many of the samples contained small amounts of bone. However, until many more analyses of fish flesh carefully separated from all traces of bone are made, it will be impossible to set the limits of credibility for this nutrient. Probably the values greatly in excess of those for muscle meats are not based on flesh alone.

The classification of fish by content of fat in some of the previous publications from this Department has been dropped. More comprehensive studies made during recent years have indicated that most kinds of fish may vary widely in fat content during different seasons of the year, in different localities, and at various stages of maturity.

Milk and Milk Products

Many partially skimmed milks are appearing in different sections of the country. They are skimmed to various levels of fat content, and many of them have added nonfat milk solids in differing amounts. Estimated values have been included for one product, skimmed to 2 percent fat and having 2 percent added nonfat milk solids. When values are needed for milks of other fat and solids levels, estimates of their composition can be made by combining appropriate quantities of the milk products shown in the table; that is, whole milk, skim milk, and cream.

Nonfat milk solids are being added also to an increasing number of other milk products, including whole milk. Adjustments should be made in the nutritive values shown in these tables wherever local practices indicate the need; added nonfat milk solids may appreciably increase the nutrient content of any product to which they are added.

Miscellaneous Food Items

Alcoholic beverages.—Food energy was calculated for alcoholic beverages as the total potential calories from any nutrients present (protein, fat, carbohydrate) plus those from alcohol. The factor 6.93 was applied to the alcoholic content by weight. For protein and carbohydrate in wines, the factors used were those for "All fruit juice (except lemon, lime)." For protein and carbohydrate in beer, the factors for "Other cereals, refined" were used. These factors are listed in table 6.

Dessert wines as classified in these tables include those containing more than 15 percent alcohol (by volume), such as apple, muscatel, sherries, port, and tokay. Aperitif wines and vermouths will also fall in this classification.

Table wines to which the data in these tables apply include those containing less than 15 percent alcohol (by volume), such as barbera, burgundy, cabernet, chablis, champagnes, chianti, claret, Rhine wines, rosé, and sauternes. Cherry, peach, berry, and varietal wines usually fall in this class, though some may be high enough in alcohol content to be classified with dessert wines.

Within each group there is a rather wide range in total carbohydrate content; the carbohydrate is less in dry wines than in sweet wines.

Foods containing considerable nonprotein nitrogen.—The figures for protein listed in this publication for chocolate and cocoa products, coffee, mushrooms, and yeasts do not include the nitrogenous matter of nonprotein character that is present in fairly sizable proportions in these foods. However, to avoid overestimating the content of carbohydrate, total nitrogenous matter and not protein was used as the basis for calculating the carbohydrate by difference for these foods. Total nitrogenous matter was used also for obtaining the energy values. The derivation of the factor 5.63, used for calculating the content of total nitrogenous matter in chocolate and cocoa products from nitrogen, and the basis for estimating the energy values have been presented in detail elsewhere (*20*, pp. 40–42). The protein in these foods makes up nearly 85 percent of the nitrogenous matter. Approximately one-third of the total carbohydrate in chocolate and cocoa is starch and sugar. The remaining portion is made up of materials thought to be utilized only poorly if at all, and the values shown for calories have been reduced accordingly. The data for protein shown for chocolate and cocoa in these tables were the ones used for calculating values for recipes having chocolate or cocoa as ingredients.

To the extent that data were available, the same general procedures for arriving at values for protein, carbohydrate, and calories for chocolate and cocoa products were followed in arriving at the figures for mushrooms, yeast, and coffee. The basis of the data for mushrooms and yeasts has been reported also (*20*, pp. 39–40, 42). Approximately two-thirds of the nitrogen in mushrooms was counted as protein nitrogen, and four-fifths of the nitrogen in yeasts.

The nitrogenous compounds in instant coffee include caffeine, which constitutes about 3 to 4 percent of the powdered coffee, and very much smaller amounts of amino nitrogen compounds, choline, trigonelline, and niacin. Much of the carbohydrate in coffee is unavailable.

Mellorine-type frozen desserts.—These are similar to ice creams and ice milks except that fats other than milk fat are used in their preparation. They have not been included in this publication inasmuch as they are made and sold in only a few States, and the minimum standards for fat established by law vary considerably. Some States require the addition of vitamin A to the products. Except for fatty acids, nutritive values for ice cream and ice milk may be used for mellorine where standards for fat are similar. If vitamin A is not added to mellorine, this nutrient should be considered negligible; otherwise, it will be similar to ice cream.

APPENDIX C.—IDENTIFICATION OF FOODS

Identification of foods from their common names is often confused because in many instances these names are not applied to the same food in different localities. To aid in identifying individual foods listed in table 1, the scientific names are presented in table 13. Although there is not complete agreement on nomenclature among scientists, the scientific and common names as listed in table 13 are the ones recommended by experts in the various fields who were asked to review them. Some cross references have been included in table 1 for common names previously in common use, but not all alternative common names have been so listed.

The names for foods of plant origin—cereals, fruits, vegetables, nuts—were reviewed by staff of the Crops Research Division, Agricultural Research Service, which is represented on the Department's Committee on Plant Nomenclature. Their recommendations were based on the International Code of Botanical Nomenclature (*14*) and the International Code of Nomenclature for Cultivated Plants (*15*).

For foods of animal origin except fish and other aquatic animals, the common and technical names were reviewed by staff of the Animal Husbandry Research Division, Agricultural Research Service.

The publication, "A List of Common and Scientific Names of Fishes from the United States and Canada," (*2*) was used as the basis of the nomenclature for fishes in table 1. The names were then submitted to Dr. Reeve M. Bailey, Curator of Fishes at the University of Michigan, who reviewed and edited the list.

Staff of the Fish and Wildlife Service of the U.S. Department of the Interior and staff of the Smithsonian Institution reviewed the terminology for shellfish and other aquatic animals.

TABLE 13.—COMMON AND SCIENTIFIC NAMES OF ANIMALS AND PLANTS USED FOR FOODS LISTED IN THIS PUBLICATION

[Item Nos. are from table 1 and often refer not only to the individual food but also to products made with it as the principal ingredient. Common and scientific names apply to only the individual food. Letters in parentheses following the common names of fish refer to area of occurrence: (A), Atlantic Ocean; (P), Pacific Ocean; (F), Fresh water]

Item No. from table 1	Common name	Scientific name
1–2	Abalone	*Haliotis* species.
3–4	Acerola	*Malpighia punicifolia.*
5	Albacore (A, P)	*Thunnus alalunga*
6–7	Alewife (A, F)	*Alosa pseudoharengus.*
8–10	Almond	*Prunus amygdalus.*
11	Amaranth	*Amaranthus* species.
12	Anchovy (A, P)	Engraulidae.
13–29	Apple	*Malus sylvestris.*
30–43	Apricot	*Prunus armeniaca.*
44–45	Artichoke, globe or French	*Cynara scolymus.*
46–63	Asparagus	*Asparagus officinalis.*
64–66	Avocado	*Persea* species.
140	Bamboo	*Bambusa* species and *Phyllostachys* species.
141	Banana, common	*Musa* × *paradisiaca.*
142	Banana, red	*Musa* × *paradisiaca.*
145–146	Barley	*Hordeum vulgare.*
147	Barracuda, Pacific (P)	*Sphyraena argentea.*
148–149	Bass, black sea (A)	*Centropristes striatus.*
150	Bass, smallmouth and largemouth (F)	*Micropterus dolomieui* and *M. salmoides.*
151–152	Bass, striped (A, F, P)	*Roccus saxatilis.*
153	Bass, white (F)	*Roccus chrysops.*
154–163	Bean, common	*Phaseolus vulgaris.*
164–178	Bean, lima	*Phaseolus limensis.*
179–181	Bean, mung	*Phaseolus aureus.*
182–204	Bean, snap	*Phaseolus vulgaris.*
206	Beaver	*Castor canadensis.*

TABLE 13.—*Common and scientific names of animals and plants used for foods listed in this publication*—Continued

[Item Nos. are from table 1 and often refer not only to the individual food but also to products made with it as the principal ingredient. Common and scientific names apply to only the individual food. Letters in parentheses following the common names of fish refer to area of occurrence: (A), Atlantic Ocean; (P), Pacific Ocean; (F), Fresh water]

Item No. from table 1	Common name	Scientific name
207	Beechnut	*Fagus* species.
208–381	Beef	*Bos taurus.*
384–393	Beet, common red	*Beta vulgaris.*
417–423	Blackberry (including dewberry, boysenberry, and youngberry).	*Rubus* species
424–428	Blueberry	*Vaccinium* species.
429–431	Bluefish (A)	*Pomatomus saltatrix.*
432	Bonito (including Atlantic, Pacific, and striped) (A, P).	*Sarda sarda, S. chiliensis,* and *S. orientalis.*
435–437	Boysenberry	*Rubus ursinus* var. *loganobaccus.*
443	Brazilnut	*Bertholletia excelsa.*
480	Breadfruit	*Artocarpus altilis.*
481–482	Broadbean	*Vicia faba.*
483–488	Broccoli	*Brassica oleracea* var. *botrytis.*
489–492	Brussels sprout	*Brassica oleracea* var. *gemmifera.*
493–495	Buckwheat	*Fagopyrum esculentum.*
496	Buffalofish (F)	*Ictiobus* species
502	Bullhead, black (F)	*Ictalurus melas.*
503–504	Burbot (F)	*Lota lota.*
507–508	Butterfish (A)	*Poronotus triacanthus.*
511	Butternut	*Juglans cinerea.*
512–517	Cabbage, common, red and savoy	*Brassica oleracea* var. *capitata.*
518	Cabbage, celery or Chinese	*Brassica pekinensis.*
519–520	Cabbage, spoon or pakchoy (white mustard cabbage).	*Brassica chinensis.*
615	Carambola	*Averrhoa carambola*
616	Carissa, or natalplum	*Carissa grandiflora.*
617	Carob	*Ceratonia siliqua.*
618	Carp (F)	*Cyprinus carpio.*
619–627	Carrot	*Daucus carota* var. *sativa.*
628	Cashew	*Anacardium occidentale.*
629	Catfish (F)	*Ictalurus* species.
630–633	Cauliflower	*Brassica oleracea* var. *botrytis.*
636	Celeriac	*Apium graveolens* var. *rapaceum.*
637–638	Celery	*Apium graveolens.*
639–640	Chard	*Beta vulgaris* var. *cicla.*
642	Chayote	*Sechium edule.*
661	Cherimoya	*Annona cherimola.*
662–675	Cherry	*Prunus* species.
676	Chervil	*Anthriscus cerefolium.*
677–679	Chestnut	*Castanea* species.
681–747	Chicken	*Gallus domesticus.*
753	Chickpea	*Cicer arietinum.*
754–755	Chicory	*Cichorium intybus.*
758	Chive	*Allium schoenoprasum.*
759	Chocolate	*Theobroma cacao.*
766	Chub (F)	*Coregonus* species.
767	Citron	*Citrus medica.*
768–769, 772–776	Clam, soft (A, P)	*Mya arenaria.*
770–776	Clam, hard or round (quahog) (A, P)	*Mercenaria mercenaria.*
774–776	Clam, razor (P)	*Siliqua patula.*
788–793	Coconut	*Cocos nucifera.*
794–798	Cod (A, P)	*Gadus morhua* and *G. macrocephalus.*
799–800	Coffee	*Coffea* species.
805–811	Collard	*Brassica oleracea* var. *acephala.*
843–892	Corn	*Zea mays.*
893	Cornsalad	*Valerianella olitoria.*
895	Cottonseed	*Gossypium* species.
896–904	Cowpea (including blackeye pea)	*Vigna sinensis.*
905–906	Crab (including blue, Dungeness, rock, and king) (A, P).	*Callinectes sapidus, Cancer* species, and *Paralithodes camschatica.*
909	Crabapple	*Malus* species.
920–924	Cranberry	*Vaccinium macrocarpon.*
926	Crappie, white (F)	*Pomoxis annularis.*
927	Crayfish, freshwater (F) and spiny lobster (A, P).	*Cambarus* species, *Astacus* species, and *Panulirus* species.

TABLE 13.—*Common and scientific names of animals and plants used for foods listed in this publication*—Continued

[Item Nos. are from table 1 and often refer not only to the individual food but also to products made with it as the principal ingredient. Common and scientific names apply to only the individual food. Letters in parentheses following the common names of fish refer to area of occurrence: (A), Atlantic Ocean; (P), Pacific Ocean; (F), Fresh water]

Item No. from table 1	Common name	Scientific name
935–937	Cress, garden (peppergrass)	*Lepidium sativum.*
938–939	Croaker, Atlantic (A)	*Micropogon undulatus.*
940	Croaker, white (P)	*Genyonemus lineatus.*
941	Croaker, yellowfin (P)	*Umbrina roncador.*
942–943	Cucumber	*Cucumis sativus.*
944–945	Currant (black, European, red, white)	*Ribes* species.
946–947	Cusk (A)	*Brosme brosme.*
949	Custardapple, bullocksheart	*Annona reticulata.*
950–951	Dandelion	*Taraxacum officinale.*
952	Date	*Phoenix dactylifera.*
953–954	Dock, curly or narrowleaf, broadleaf, and sheep sorrel.	*Rumex* species.
955	Dogfish, spiny (grayfish) (A, P)	*Squalus acanthias.*
956	Dolly Varden (P, F)	*Salvelinus malma.*
959	Drum, freshwater (F)	*Aplodinotus grunniens.*
960	Drum, red (redfish) (A)	*Sciaenops ocellata.*
961–962	Duck, domesticated	*Anas platyrhynchos.*
963–964	Duck, wild	*Anas boschas.*
966–967	Eel, American (A, F)	*Anguilla rostrata.*
986–987	Eggplant	*Solanum melongena.*
988	Elderberry	*Sambucus* species.
989	Endive (curly endive and escarole)	*Cichorium endivia.*
990	Eulachon (smelt) (P, F)	*Thaleichthys pacificus.*
1000	Fennel, common	*Foeniculum vulgare.*
1001–1007	Fig	*Ficus carica.*
1008	Filbert or hazelnut	*Corylus* species.
1009	Finnan haddie (smoked haddock) (A)	*Melanogrammus aeglefinus.*
1018–1019	Flatfish (flounder, sole, and sanddab) (A, P)	*Pseudopleuronectes americanus, Paralichthys dentatus, P lethostigma, Platichthys stellatus, Limanda ferruginea, Atheresthes stomias, Parophrys vetulus, Microstomus pacificus, Eopsetta jordani, Hippoglossoides elassodon, Glyptocephalus zachirus, Lepidopsetta bilineata, Citharichthys sordidus, Psettichthys melanostictus.*
1020	Frog (F)	*Rana* species.
1020	Garlic	*Allium sativum.*
1034–1035	Ginger, common	*Zingiber officinale.*
1041–1047	Goose, domesticated	*Anser anser.*
1048–1051	Gooseberry	*Ribes* species.
1052	Granadilla, purple (passionfruit)	*Passiflora edulis.*
1053–1078	Grapefruit	*Citrus paradisi.*
1084–1091	Grape (American and European types)	*Vitis* species.
1092	Groundcherry	*Physalis* species.
1093	Grouper (including red, black, and speckled hind) (A).	*Epinephelus morio, Mycteroperca bonaci* and *Epinephelus drummondhayi.*
1094	Guava, common	*Psidium guajava.*
1095	Guava, strawberry	*Psidium littorale.*
1096–1098	Guinea	*Numida meleagris.*
1099–1101	Haddock (A)	*Melanogrammus aeglefinus.*
1102	Hake (including Pacific hake, squirrel hake, and silver hake or whiting) (A, P).	*Merluccius productus, Urophycis chuss,* and *Merluccius bilinearis.*
1103–1105	Halibut, Atlantic and Pacific (A, P)	*Hippoglossus hippoglossus* and *H. stenolepis.*
1106	Halibut, California (P)	*Paralichthys californicus.*
1107	Halibut, Greenland (A)	*Reinhardtius hippoglossoides.*
1109	Haw (hawthorn), scarlet	*Crataegus* species.
1124	Herring, Atlantic (A)	*Clupea harengus harengus.*
1125	Herring, Pacific (P)	*Clupea harengus pallasi.*
1133	Hickorynut	*Carya* species.
1135–1136	Horseradish	*Armoracia rusticana.*
1137–1138	Hyacinth-bean	*Dolichos lablab.*
1145	Inconnu (or sheefish) (F)	*Stenodus leucichthys.*
1146	Jackfruit	*Artocarpus integra.*
1147	Jack mackerel (P)	*Trachurus symmetricus.*
1150	Jerusalem-artichoke	*Helianthus tuberosus.*
1151–1152	Jujube, common (Chinese date)	*Ziziphus jujuba.*
1153–1158	Kale	*Brassica oleracea* var. *acephala.*
1164	Kingfish; southern, gulf, and northern (whiting) (A).	*Menticirrhus americanus, M. littoralis,* and *M. saxatilis.*

TABLE 13.—*Common and scientific names of animals and plants used for foods listed in this publication*—Continued

[Item Nos. are from table 1 and often refer not only to the individual food but also to products made with it as the principal ingredient. Common and scientific names apply to only the individual food. Letters in parentheses following the common names of fish refer to area of occurrence: (A), Atlantic Ocean; (P), Pacific Ocean; (F), Fresh water]

Item No. from table 1	Common name	Scientific name
1165–1166	Kohlrabi	*Brassica oleracea* var. *gongylodes.*
1167	Kumquat	*Fortunella* species.
1168	Lake herring or cisco (F)	*Coregonus artedii.*
1169	Lake trout (F)	*Salvelinus namaycush.*
1170–1171	Lake trout (siscowet) (F)	*Salvelinus namaycush.*
1172–1238	Lamb	*Ovis aries.*
1239–1240	Lambsquarters	*Chenopodium album.*
1242	Leek	*Allium porrum.*
1243–1252	Lemon	*Citrus limon.*
1253–1255	Lentil	*Lens culinaris.*
1256–1259	Lettuce	*Lactuca sativa.*
1260–1264	Lime	*Citrus aurantifolia.*
1265	Lingcod (P)	*Ophiodon elongatus.*
1279–1280	Lobster, northern (A)	*Homarus americanus.*
1283–1288	Loganberry	*Rubus ursinus* var. *loganobaccus.*
1289–1290	Longan	*Euphoria longan.*
1291	Loquat	*Eriobotrya japonica.*
1295–1296	Lychee	*Litchi chinensis.*
1297	Macadamia nut	*Macadamia ternifolia.*
1306–1308	Mackerel, Atlantic (A)	*Scomber scombrus.*
1309–1310	Mackerel, Pacific (P)	*Scomber japonicus.*
1315	Mamey or mammeeapple	*Mammea americana.*
1316	Mango	*Mangifera indica.*
1319	Menhaden, Atlantic (A)	*Brevoortia tyrannus.*
1338	Millet, proso	*Panicum miliaceum.*
1353	Mullet, striped (A, F, P)	*Mugil cephalus.*
1354–1355	Mushroom, cultivated	*Agaricus campestris.*
1357	Muskellunge (F)	*Esox masquinongy.*
1358	Muskmelon, cantaloup	*Cucumis melo* var. *cantalupensis.*
1358	Muskmelon, other netted varieties	*Cucumis melo* var. *reticulatus.*
1359	Muskmelon, casaba (Golden Beauty)	*Cucumis melo* var. *inodorus.*
1360	Muskmelon, Honeydew	*Cucumis melo.*
1362	Muskrat	*Ondatra zibethica.*
1363–1365	Mussel, Atlantic and Pacific (A, P)	*Mytilus edulis* and *M. californianus.*
1366–1369	Mustard	*Brassica juncea.*
1370–1371	Mustard spinach	*Brassica perviridis.*
1374	Nectarine	*Prunus persica* var. *nectarina.*
1375–1376	New Zealand spinach	*Tetragonia expansa.*
1382–1395	Oat	*Avena sativa.*
1396–1398	Ocean perch, Atlantic (or redfish) (A)	*Sebastes marinus.*
1399	Ocean perch, Pacific (P)	*Sebastodes alutus.*
1400	Octopus (P)	*Octopus bimaculatus.*
1402–1405	Okra	*Hibiscus esculentus.*
1406–1411	Olive	*Olea europaea.*
1412–1417	Onion	*Allium cepa.*
1418	Onion, Welsh	*Allium fistulosum.*
1419	Opossum	*Didelphis virginiana.*
1420–1439 (except 1431)	Orange, sweet (except Temple)	*Citrus sinensis.*
1431	Orange, Temple (hybrid-tangor)	*Citrus sinensis* × *C. reticulata.*
1443, 1446–1447	Oyster, Eastern (A, P)	*Crassostrea virginica.*
1444, 1446–1447	Oyster, Pacific and Western (Olympia) (P)	*Crassostrea gigas* and *Ostrea lurida.*
1470	Papaw	*Asimina triloba.*
1471	Papaya	*Carica papaya.*
1472	Parsley, common garden and curly	*Petroselinum crispum* and *P. crispum* var. *latifolium*
1473–1474	Parsnip	*Pastinaca sativa.*
1479–1491	Peach	*Prunus persica.*
1492–1501	Peanut	*Arachis hypogaea.*
1502–1512	Pear	*Pyrus communis.*
1513–1514	Pea, edible-podded	*Pisum sativum* var. *macrocarpum.*
1515–1533	Pea, green immature and mature seeds	*Pisum sativum.*
1536	Pecan	*Carya illinoensis.*

TABLE 13.—*Common and scientific names of animals and plants used for foods listed in this publication*—Continued

[Item Nos. are from table 1 and often refer not only to the individual food but also to products made with it as the principal ingredient. Common and scientific names apply to only the individual food. Letters in parentheses following the common names of fish refer to area of occurrence: (A), Atlantic Ocean; (P), Pacific Ocean; (F), Fresh water]

Item No. from table 1	Common name	Scientific name
1537–1544	Pepper, hot, chili	*Capsicum annuum.*
1545–1548	Pepper, sweet, garden varieties	*Capsicum annuum.*
1549	Perch, white (A, F)	*Roccus americanus.*
1550	Perch, yellow (F)	*Perca flavescens.*
1551	Persimmon, Japanese or kaki	*Diospyros kaki.*
1552	Persimmon, native	*Diospyros virginiana.*
1553–1556	Pheasant	*Phasianus colchicus.*
1557	Pickerel, chain (F)	*Esox niger.*
1603–1604	Pigeonpea	*Cajanus cajan.*
1606	Pike, blue (F)	*Stizostedion vitreum glaucum.*
1607	Pike, northern (F)	*Esox lucius.*
1608	Pike, walleye (F)	*Stizostedion vitreum vitreum.*
1609	Pilinut	*Canarium ovatum.*
1610	Pimiento	*Capsicum annuum.*
1611–1621	Pineapple	*Ananas comosus.*
1624	Pinenut, pignolia	*Pinus pinea.*
1625	Pinenut, piñon	*Pinus cembroides* var. *edulis.*
1626	Pistachionut	*Pistacia vera.*
1627	Pitanga (Surinam-cherry)	*Eugenia uniflora.*
1634	Plantain, or baking banana	*Musa × paradisiaca*
1639–1646	Plum (including damsons, Japanese and hybrids, prune type, and greengage).	*Prunus* species.
1647–1648	Pokeberry or poke	*Phytolacca americana.*
1649–1650	Pollock (A)	*Pollachius virens.*
1651	Pomegranate	*Punica granatum.*
1652	Pompano (A)	*Trachinotus carolinus.*
1653–1656	Popcorn	*Zea mays* var. *everta.*
1658	Porgy and scup (A)	*Calamus* sp., *Stenotomus caprinus* and *S. chrysops.*
1659–1784	Pork	*Sus scrofa.*
1785–1813	Potato	*Solanum tuberosum.*
1815	Pricklypear	*Opuntia* species.
1816–1821	Prune	*Prunus* species.
1831	Pumpkin	*Cucurbita pepo.*
1834–1835	Purslane	*Portulaca* species.
1836–1838	Quail	*Bonasa umbellus* and *Colinus virginianus.*
1839	Quince	*Cydonia oblonga.*
1840–1841	Rabbit, domesticated	*Oryctolagus cuniculus.*
1842	Rabbit, wild	*Sylvilagus floridanus.*
1843	Raccoon	*Procyon lotor.*
1844	Radish	*Raphanus sativus.*
1845	Radish, oriental (including daikon or Japanese and Chinese).	*Raphanus sativus* var. *longipinnatus.*
1846–1847	Raisin	*Vitis* species.
1848–1852	Raspberry (black and red)	*Rubus* species.
1853	Red and gray snapper (A)	*Lutjanus blackfordi* and *L. griseus.*
1854	Redhorse, silver (F)	*Moxostoma anisurum.*
1855–1858	Reindeer	*Rangifer* species.
1865–1868	Rhubarb	*Rheum rhaponticum.*
1869–1890 (except 1879)	Rice	*Oryza sativa.*
1879	Rice, glutinous	*Oryza glutinosa.*
1892–1893	Rockfish (including black, canary, yellowtail, raspheart, and bocaccio) (P).	*Sebastodes pinniger, S. melanops, S. flavidus, S. ruberrimus,* and *Sebastodes* species.
1917	Roseapple	*Eugenia jambos.*
1919–1920	Rutabaga	*Brassica napobrassica.*
1921–1924	Rye	*Secale cereale.*
1926	Sablefish (P)	*Anoplopoma fimbria.*
1927–1928	Safflower	*Carthamus tinctorius.*
1946–1947	Salmon, Atlantic (A, F)	*Salmo salar.*
1948–1949	Salmon, chinook (or king) (P, F)	*Oncorhynchus tshawytscha.*
1950–1951	Salmon, chum (P, F)	*Oncorhynchus keta.*
1952–1953	Salmon, coho (or silver) (A, F, P)	*Oncorhynchus kisutch.*
1954–1955	Salmon, pink (or humpback) (A, F, P)	*Oncorhynchus gorbuscha.*
1956–1957	Salmon, sockeye (or red) (P, F)	*Oncorhynchus nerka.*

TABLE 13.—*Common and scientific names of animals and plants used for foods listed in this publication*—Continued

[Item Nos. are from table 1 and often refer not only to the individual food but also to products made with it as the principal ingredient. Common and scientific names apply to only the individual food. Letters in parentheses following the common names of fish refer to area of occurrence: (A), Atlantic Ocean; (P), Pacific Ocean; (F), Fresh water]

Item No. from table 1	Common name	Scientific name
1961–1962	Salsify or vegetable-oyster	*Tragopogon porrifolius.*
1969	Sapodilla or sapota	*Achras zapota.*
1970	Sapote, or marmalade plum	*Calocarpum sapota.*
1971–1972	Sardine, Atlantic (A)	Clupeidae.
1973–1976	Sardine, Pacific (P)	*Sardinops sagax.*
1979	Sauger (F)	*Stizostedion canadense.*
2023–2025	Scallop, bay and sea (A)	*Pecten* species and *Placopectens magellanicus.*
2026	Seabass, white (P)	*Cynoscion nobilis.*
2027	Seaweed, agar	*Gelidium* species.
2028	Seaweed, dulse	*Dilsea edulis.*
2029	Seaweed, Irishmoss	*Chondrus crispus.*
2030	Seaweed, kelp	*Laminaria* species.
2031	Seaweed, laver	*Porphyra laciniata.*
2032–2033	Sesame	*Sesamum indicum.*
2034–2037	Shad or American shad (A, F, P)	*Alosa sapidissima.*
2038	Shad, gizzard (A, F)	*Dorosoma cepedianum.*
2039	Shallot	*Allium ascalonicum.*
2040	Sheepshead, Atlantic (A)	*Archosargus probatocephalus.*
2042–2046	Shrimp (A, P)	*Penaeus* and *Pandalus* species, and others.
2053	Skate (or raja fish) (A, P)	*Raja* species.
2054–2055	Smelt, Atlantic, jack, and bay (A, F, P)	*Osmerus mordax, Atherinopsis californiensis,* and *Atherinops affinis.*
2056	Snail	*Helix pomatia.*
2057	Snail, Giant African	*Achatina fulica.*
2058	Sorghum	*Sorghum vulgare.*
2134	Soursop	*Annona muricata.*
2135–2155	Soybean	*Glycine max.*
2167	Spanish mackerel (A)	*Scomberomorus maculatus.*
2169–2180	Spinach	*Spinacia oleracea.*
2184–2185	Spot (A)	*Leiostomus xanthurus.*
2186–2190	Squab (pigeon)	*Columba livia.*
2191–2196, 2211–2212	Squash, summer; Crookneck, Straightneck, and Scallop varieties.	*Cucurbita pepo* var. *melopepo.*
2197–2198	Squash, summer; Italian marrow group (including Zucchini and Cocozelle).	*Cucurbita pepo* var. *medullosa.*
2199–2210, 2213–2214	Squash, winter; Acorn, Butternut, and Hubbard.	*Cucurbita maxima.*
2215	Squid (A, P)	*Ommastrephes* species and *Loligo* species.
2217–2220	Strawberry	*Fragaria* species.
2221–2223	Sturgeon (A, F)	*Acipenser oxyrhynchus.*
2226	Sucker (including white sucker and mullet sucker) (F).	*Catostomus commersoni* and *Catostomidae* species.
2227	Sucker, carp (F)	*Carpiodes forbesi* and *C. cyprinus.*
2235	Sugarapple (sweetsop)	*Annona squamosa.*
2236–2237	Sunflower	*Helianthus annuus.*
2238–2239	Swamp cabbage	*Ipomoea reptans.*
2246–2256	Sweetpotato	*Ipomoea batatas.*
2257–2259	Swordfish (A, P)	*Xiphias gladius.*
2260	Tamarind	*Tamarindus indica.*
2261	Tangelo	*Citrus paradisi* × *C. reticulata.*
2262–2267	Tangerine	*Citrus reticulata.*
2268	Tapioca	*Manihot esculenta.*
2271–2272	Taro	*Colocasia* species.
2275	Tautog or blackfish (A)	*Tautoga onitis.*
2276–2277	Tea	*Camellia sinensis.*
2278	Terrapin (diamond back)	*Malaclemys* species.
2279–2280	Tilefish (A)	*Lopholatilus chamaeleonticeps.*
2281–2297	Tomato	*Lycopersicon esculentum.*
2298	Tomcod, Atlantic (A)	*Microgadus tomcod.*
2315	Towelgourd	*Luffa acutangula.*
2318	Trout, brook (A, F)	*Salvelinus fontinalis.*
2319–2320	Trout, rainbow or steelhead (A, F, P)	*Salmo gairdneri.*
2321	Tuna, Bluefin (A, P)	*Thunnus thynnus.*
2322	Tuna, Yellowfin (A, P)	*Thunnus albacares.*
2327–2349	Turkey	*Meleagris gallopavo.*
2352–2359	Turnip	*Brassica rapa.*

TABLE 13.—*Common and scientific names of animals and plants used for foods listed in this publication*—Continued

[Item Nos. are from table 1 and often refer not only to the individual food but also to products made with it as the principal ingredient. Common and scientific names apply to only the individual food. Letters in parentheses following the common names of fish refer to area of occurrence: (A), Atlantic Ocean; (P), Pacific Ocean; (F), Fresh water]

Item No. from table 1	Common name	Scientific name
2360–2361	Turtle, green	*Chelonia mydas.*
2362–2395	Veal	*Bos taurus.*
2405	Venison (deer)	*Odocoileus* species.
2408	Vinespinach	*Basella* species.
2420	Walnut, black	*Juglans nigra.*
2421	Walnut, Persian, English	*Juglans regia.*
2422	Waterchestnut, Chinese (matai, waternut)	*Eleocharis dulcis.*
2423	Watercress	*Nasturtium officinale.*
2424	Watermelon	*Citrullus vulgaris.*
2425	Waxgourd or Chinese preserving melon	*Benincasa hispida.*
2426–2427	Weakfish (A)	*Cynoscion regalis.*
2429	Whale (A, P)	*Balaena glacialis, Balaenoptera borealis, B. physalus, B. musculus,* and *Physeter catadon.*
2430–2463 (except 2434)	Wheat	*Triticum aestivum.*
2434	Wheat, Durum	*Triticum durum.*
2466–2468	Whitefish, lake (A, F)	*Coregonus clupeaformis.*
2472	Wildrice	*Zizania aquatica.*
2473	Wreckfish (A)	*Polyprion americanus.*
2474	Yam (true yam of tropical areas)	*Dioscorea* species.
2475	Yambean	*Pachyrrhizus* species.
2476–2477	Yeast, baker's	*Saccharomyces cerevisiae.*
2478	Yeast, brewer's	*Saccharomyces cerevisiae.*
2479	Yeast, torula	*Torulopsis utilis.*
2480	Yellowtail (Pacific coast) (P)	*Seriola dorsalis.*

LITERATURE CITED

(1) ADAMS, G., and CHATFIELD, C.
1935. CLASSIFICATION OF FRUITS AND VEGETABLES ACCORDING TO THEIR CARBOHYDRATE CONTENT. Amer. Dietet. Assoc. Jour. 10: 383-390.

(2) AMERICAN FISHERIES SOCIETY.
1960. A LIST OF COMMON AND SCIENTIFIC NAMES OF FISHES FROM THE UNITED STATES AND CANADA. Spec. Pub. 2, Ed. 2, 102 pp. Ann Arbor, Mich.

(3) ATWATER, W. O., and BRYANT, A. P.
1899. THE CHEMICAL COMPOSITION OF AMERICAN FOOD MATERIALS. U.S. Off. Expt. Stas., Expt. Sta. Bul 28 (rev. ed.), 87 pp.

(4) ——— and BRYANT, A. P.
1900. THE AVAILABILITY AND FUEL VALUE OF FOOD MATERIALS. Conn. (Storrs) Agr. Expt. Sta. 12th Ann. Rpt. (1899), pp. 73-110.

(5) ——— and BRYANT, A. P.
1906. THE CHEMICAL COMPOSITION OF AMERICAN FOOD MATERIALS. U.S. Off. Expt. Stas., Expt. Sta. Bul. 28 (rev. ed.), 87 pp.

(6) ——— and WOODS, C. D.
1896. THE CHEMICAL COMPOSITION OF AMERICAN FOOD MATERIALS. U.S. Off. Expt. Stas., Expt. Sta. Bul. 28, 47 pp.

(7) CHATFIELD, C., and ADAMS, G.
1940. PROXIMATE COMPOSITION OF AMERICAN FOOD MATERIALS. U.S. Dept. Agr. Cir. 549, 91 pp.

(8) FOOD AND AGRICULTURE ORGANIZATION OF THE UNITED NATIONS.
1947. ENERGY-YIELDING COMPONENTS OF FOOD AND COMPUTATION OF CALORIE VALUES. 23 pp. Washington, D.C.

(9) GODDARD, V. R., and GOODALL, L.
1959. FATTY ACIDS IN FOOD FATS. U.S. Dept. Agr. Home Econ. Res. Rpt. 7, 4 pp.

(10) ——— and GOODALL, L.
1959. FATTY ACIDS IN ANIMAL AND PLANT PRODUCTS. U.S. Dept. Agr. (processed, unnumbered), 65 pp.

(11) GOLDSMITH, G. A., MILLER, O. N, and UNGLAUB, W. G.
1961. EFFICIENCY OF TRYPTOPHAN AS A NIACIN PRECURSOR IN MAN. Jour. Nutr. 73: 172-176.

(12) ——— SARRETT, H. P., REGISTER, U. D, and GIBBONS, J.
1952. STUDIES OF NIACIN REQUIREMENT OF MAN. I. EXPERIMENTAL PELLAGRA IN SUBJECTS ON CORN DIETS LOW IN NIACIN AND TRYPTOPHAN. Jour. Clin. Invest 31: 533.

(13) HORWITT, M. K., HARVEY, C. C., ROTHWELL, W. S., and others.
1956. TRYPTOPHAN-NIACIN RELATIONSHIPS IN MAN. Jour. Nutr. 60, suppl. 1, 43 pp.

(14) INTERNATIONAL ASSOCIATION FOR PLANT TAXONOMY, INTERNATIONAL BUREAU FOR PLANT TAXONOMY AND NOMENCLATURE.
1961. INTERNATIONAL CODE OF BOTANICAL NOMENCLATURE. (Adopted by the Ninth International Botanical Congress, Montreal, August 1959.) 372 pp. Utrecht, Netherlands.

(15) INTERNATIONAL UNION OF BIOLOGICAL SCIENCES, INTERNATIONAL COMMISSION FOR THE NOMENCLATURE OF CULTIVATED PLANTS.
1961. INTERNATIONAL CODE OF NOMENCLATURE FOR CULTIVATED PLANTS 1961. Regnum Vegetabile 22, 30 pp. Utrecht, Netherlands.

(16) JONES, D. B.
1931. FACTORS FOR CONVERTING PERCENTAGES OF NITROGEN IN FOODS AND FEEDS INTO PERCENTAGES OF PROTEIN. U.S. Dept. Agr. Cir. 183, 22 pp. Sl. rev. 1941, 22 pp.

(17) LEUNG, W-T. WU, PECOT, R. K., and WATT, B. K.
1952. COMPOSITION OF FOODS USED IN FAR EASTERN COUNTRIES. U.S. Dept. Agr. Handb. 34, 62 pp.

(18) LEVERTON, R. M., JOHNSON, N., PAZUR, J., and ELLISON, J.
1956. THE QUANTITATIVE AMINO ACID REQUIREMENTS OF YOUNG WOMEN. III. TRYPTOPHAN. Jour. Nutr. 58: 219-229.

(19) LICHTENSTEIN, H., BELOIAN, A., and MURPHY, E. W.
1961. VITAMIN B_{12}—MICROBIOLOGICAL ASSAY METHODS AND DISTRIBUTION IN SELECTED FOODS. U.S. Dept. Agr. Home Econ. Res. Rpt. 13, 15 pp.

(20) MERRILL, A. L., and WATT, B. K.
1955. ENERGY VALUE OF FOODS—BASIS AND DERIVATION. U.S. Dept. Agr. Handb. 74, 105 pp.

(21) NATIONAL ACADEMY OF SCIENCES—NATIONAL RESEARCH COUNCIL.
1958. RECOMMENDED DIETARY ALLOWANCES. (A report of the Food and Nutrition Board.) Natl. Acad. Sci.—Natl. Res. Council Pub. 589 (rev. 1958), 36 pp., illus. Washington, D.C.

(22) ORR, M. L., and WATT, B. K.
1957. AMINO ACID CONTENT OF FOODS. U.S. Dept. Agr. Home Econ. Res. Rpt. 4, 82 pp.

(23) PECOT, R. K., and WATT, B. K.
1956. FOOD YIELDS SUMMARIZED BY DIFFERENT STAGES OF PREPARATION. U.S. Dept. Agr. Handb. 102, 93 pp.

(24) ROSE, W. C., WIXOM, R. L., LOCKHART, H. B., and LAMBERT, G. F.
1955. THE AMINO ACID REQUIREMENTS OF MAN. XV. THE VALINE REQUIREMENT; SUMMARY AND FINAL OBSERVATIONS. Jour. Biol. Chem. 217: 987-995.

(25) TOEPFER, E. W., ZOOK, E. G., ORR, M. L., and RICHARDSON, L. R.
1951. FOLIC ACID CONTENT OF FOODS—MICROBIOLOGICAL ASSAY BY STANDARDIZED METHODS AND COMPILATION OF DATA FROM THE LITERATURE. U.S. Dept. Agr. Handb. 29, 116 pp.

(26) UNITED STATES BUREAU OF HUMAN NUTRITION AND HOME ECONOMICS.
1945. TABLES OF FOOD COMPOSITION IN TERMS OF ELEVEN NUTRIENTS. U.S. Dept. Agr. Misc. Pub. 572, 30 pp.

(27) UNITED STATES FOOD AND DRUG ADMINISTRATION.
1952. DEFINITIONS AND STANDARDS OF IDENTITY: BAKERY PRODUCTS; BREAD AND ROLLS. [U.S.] Natl. Arch. Fed. Register 17: 4453-4464. Also in Code of Fed. Regulat., title 21, pt. 17.

(28) ———
1955. DEFINITIONS AND STANDARDS OF IDENTITY: CEREAL FLOURS AND RELATED PRODUCTS; ALIMENTARY PASTES; BAKERY PRODUCTS. [U.S.] Natl. Arch. Fed. Register 20: 9570-9580. Also in Code of Fed. Regulat., title 21, pt. 16.

(29) ———
1957. CEREAL FLOURS AND RELATED PRODUCTS; RICE AND RELATED PRODUCTS. [U.S.] Natl. Arch. Fed. Register 22: 6887-6888. Also in Code of Fed. Regulat., title 21, pt. 15.

(30) ———
1961. DEFINITIONS AND STANDARDS OF IDENTITY: CEREAL FLOURS AND RELATED PRODUCTS; ENRICHED CORN MEALS; CALCIUM. [U.S.] Natl. Arch. Fed. Register 26: 7223. Also in Code of Fed. Regulat., title 21, pt. 15, sec. 15.513.

(31) ———
1962. DEFINITIONS AND STANDARDS OF IDENTITY: CEREAL PRODUCTS AND RELATED PRODUCTS; ENRICHED CORN MEALS. [U.S.] Natl. Arch. Fed. Register 27: 618. Also in Code of Fed. Regulat., title 21, pt. 15, sec. 15.513.

(32) UNITED STATES INSTITUTE OF HOME ECONOMICS.
1960. NUTRITIVE VALUE OF FOODS. U.S. Dept. Agr. Home and Garden Bul. 72, 30 pp.

(33) WATT, B. K.
1962. CONCEPTS IN DEVELOPING A FOOD COMPOSITION TABLE. Amer. Dietet. Assoc. Jour. 40: 297-300.

(34) ——— and MERRILL, A. L.
1950. COMPOSITION OF FOODS—RAW, PROCESSED, PREPARED. U.S. Dept. Agr. Handb. 8, 147 pp.

(35) ZOOK, E. G., MACARTHUR, M. J., and TOEPFER, E. W.
1956. PANTOTHENIC ACID IN FOODS. U.S. Dept. Agr. Handb. 97, 23 pp.

U. S. GOVERNMENT PRINTING OFFICE · 1979 O - 284-853

www.ingramcontent.com/pod-product-compliance
Lightning Source LLC
LaVergne TN
LVHW020225210425
809164LV00034B/789

* 9 7 8 1 0 1 3 8 8 1 2 8 2 *